MONEY, BANKING,
AND ECONOMIC WELFARE

MONEY, BANKING,
AND ECONOMIC WELFARE

second edition

PAUL B. TRESCOTT

Professor of Economics, Kenyon College

McGraw-Hill Book Company

New York   St. Louis   San Francisco
Toronto   London   Sydney

To Ruth, Jeffrey, Jill, and Andrew

PREFACE

This book, which is intended as a text for undergraduate courses in money and banking, stresses analysis, appraisal, and public policy. It does not attempt to deal with banking and finance from a managerial point of view, but financial practices relating to the composition of bank assets, bank supervision, speculation, insurance, and other matters are described where they appear to have significant implications for the public welfare.

The basic objective of the book is to analyze the relations between money and finance and economic welfare to promote better guidance of monetary and financial policies. Description is subordinated to analysis of how things occur and evaluation of their significance for welfare and policy. The sequence of topics was chosen for this purpose. First the student is presented with the analytical instruments required to understand how things work. Then he is shown how they have worked in the past. Only after this foundation of theory and history has been laid can a wholly adequate discussion of policy be conducted. For this reason, discussion of contemporary monetary policy comes at the end, where it is extensively treated.

Throughout the book the stress is on breadth of treatment. I have tried to spell out fully the relations between the central topics and various complementary areas of study. My own course, in which this material was developed, is essentially a broad course in intermediate economics that stresses money and finance rather than merely one specialized area of advanced economics. I believe this approach will be valuable for the economics major in helping him fit the subject matter into its place relative to his other courses. This method should also make the book more valuable and palatable to majors in fields other than economics, who will not take extensive work in the complementary areas.

It seems foolish to expect students to take a critical and scholarly attitude toward economic "science" if it is presented to them as a series of scholastic exercises in abstract reasoning, devoid of evidence. I have tried throughout to give a maximum empirical foundation to theory and assertion.

Although the general conception and organization have not substantially changed from the first edition, I have made extensive revision in the detailed exposition. Many of the theoretical sections in Parts Two and Three have been reformulated for increased clarity. Much revision has also been devoted to bringing the book up to date. This process has embraced not only the direct statistical and empirical foundation, but also the enormous volume of scholarly work which has been published on these subjects since 1960. The revision embodies extensive new data on the historical relations among spending, output, unemployment, and the price level (in Chapter 7) and incorporates at many points conclusions of the research studies sponsored by the Commission on Money and Credit.

In addition, I have attempted to update the book analytically, with particular reference to the "new quantity theory." Whether one actually accepts the degree of monetary causality claimed by partisans of the theory, one can hardly deny the usefulness of many of its elements as vehicles for concise and orderly treatment of monetary theory. Consequently, in this revision I have given extensive attention to the possible causal linkages running from the "monetary base" to the money supply to the expenditure flow to employment, output, and prices, with considerable discussion devoted to the rates of change of these factors. By stressing these elements in a consistent manner, the book achieves a higher degree of unity and coherence in Parts Two, Three, Four, and Seven. At the same time, the exposition of monetary theory in Part Three still retains an organizational structure consistent with the "neotraditional" view which many monetary economists still hold.

In revising the book, I have also changed the amount of space devoted to individual topics. An additional chapter has been included on the determination of the money supply as a whole. The section on financial institutions now incorporates more institutional material, as well as an exposition of the relations among debt, spending, and wealth. The concluding chapters on monetary policy have been enlarged as well as extensively rewritten. To make room for these expansions, two chapters on American financial history prior to 1914 have been eliminated, save for a brief reprise in Chapter 2.

In revision, as in writing the first edition, I have received great assistance from reviewers chosen by the publisher—Professors Arnold W. Sametz and John M. Culbertson. In addition, I have benefited greatly from the opportunity, afforded by a previous book, for discussions with top staff members of the American Bankers Association, particularly Charls Walker, Harold Cheadle, Carter Golembe, and Leslie Peacock. Furthermore, the ABA conferences on money and banking have given me the benefit of discussion with many leading monetary economists, among whom I cite with particular appreciation Donald Hodgman, Karl Brunner, Allan Meltzer, and my former teachers Henry Wallich and Lester V. Chandler.

Finally, it would be presumptuous not to include a word of gratitude to the people who made this revised edition possible by buying the first edition, giving me the opportunity to eliminate old errors and infelicities, and, I suppose, commit new ones.

PAUL B. TRESCOTT

CONTENTS

part three

monetary theory

part four

the world

of finance

part five

international

financial relations

part six

history of money

and monetary policy

in the United States

since 1914

part seven
current problems
of monetary policy

part one

INTRODUCTORY

chapter one

THE NATURE AND
FUNCTIONS OF MONEY

WHAT MONEY IS AND DOES

Introductory   If money is not the heart of our economic system, it can certainly be considered its bloodstream. Through payments of money, the products and services which are the real end result of the economic process move from their producers to ultimate users, and those who contribute their labor or property to the productive process receive a share of the fruits. Further, the desire to acquire money incomes and monetary wealth furnishes (to change the metaphor) both a steering wheel and an engine for the economic machine. The monetary motive provides an incentive for workers or property owners to put their resources to work. The money prices or incomes established by the system provide a set of guides indicating which products should be produced, by what methods, and where each person's labor or property can be used in the most productive manner.

Money has two vital functions to perform in economic life. First, it serves as the unit of account, or measure of value, in which prices are quoted. In a price system such as our own, the monetary unit (dollar, franc, pound) becomes a common denominator of economic value. Second, money serves as a medium of payment and exchange. Sellers of goods and services

3

receive money in payment for them, which they in turn spend to buy the goods and services they desire. In a money economy like our own, money becomes an intermediary in the process through which individuals exchange their labor or property services for consumer goods and services. For most of us, "real" economic life consists of performing productive efforts and receiving in exchange real goods and services. Money may be compared to a chemical catalyst, which makes a reaction take place efficiently but is not contained in the final compound.

One may distinguish between the monetary unit and the actual money of exchange. Our monetary unit is the dollar, while our money of exchange consists of coins, paper currency, and bank deposits transferable by check. The money of exchange has its value fixed in terms of the unit of account.

The ultimate test of whether a thing is money is whether it is used as a medium of payment. Whatever serves as money *is* money, whether it be a metal coin, a cigarette, or a string of shells. The variety of things which have served as money is impressive evidence of human ingenuity, as we shall see in the following chapter.

The "Mystique" of Money Money has two faces, figuratively as well as literally. To the economist, it is a social device which serves in many ways to increase economic productivity. Traditional economics visualizes money as a mere convenience, sought by individuals merely as the means of acquiring the goods and services which are the real object of their desires. Economists of the nineteenth century spoke of "the veil of money," indicating their feeling that whatever its convenience, money did not alter the fundamental processes of production and distribution, which could conceivably be carried on without it.

Such an attitude contrasts with the emotional intensity which many people feel toward money. This emotional attitude arises from the intensity of desire for the things money will buy and from the fact that money incomes and wealth are pervasively regarded as indexes of prestige, social status, and achievement. Raymond Moley once remarked, "The earned dollar is still a measure of the value that others put upon our efforts and as such it is a measure of personal achievement and personal satisfaction." Because money is the focal point in the emotionally intense quest for security, status, and self-regard, it has acquired for many individuals a *mystique* which contrasts greatly with the purely utilitarian status accorded it in traditional economics. This dualism between mystical and practical appears throughout monetary history.

The *mystique* of money is compounded with terminological confusion between money itself and broader conceptions of income and wealth. We say that a man "has a lot of money" when we really mean he has a large income or great wealth, although money may constitute only a small proportion of his assets.[1] Some people desire to accumulate money itself, a desire which appears pathological in the miser, more reasonable in the numismatist. Psychologists observe that some people express frustration by dreams of finding money and also that in experiments coins appear larger to children of poor families than to more prosperous youngsters. Thousands of people each year visit the Bureau of Engraving and Printing to watch currency being created—people who would never think of going to see the Government Printing Office. And if we took a poll, asking people what single improvement in their lives they would choose first, no doubt many of them would reply, "More money." [2] In these and other ways our society expresses its mystical veneration for money.

Such matters are principally the concern of the psychologist or the moralist; but the economist cannot ignore them, for the way people feel about money may have important implications for the way they permit it to perform its utilitarian functions. During the heyday of gold and silver money (sixteenth to nineteenth centuries), monetary policies were strongly influenced by semimystical attitudes toward money. The doctrines of bullionism led whole nations to subordinate their national economic policies to the accumulation of gold and silver. Later, the doctrines of *laissez faire* and "sound money" were shaped around the faith that a money system based on precious metals would function beneficially without government intervention.

The reader must be on guard for terminological confusions latent in his own conception of money. In general, the term "money" is used in this book to refer to "stuff that gets spent" and specifically, in the modern American economy, to coins, paper currency, and bank checking deposits.

MONEY AND ECONOMIC WELFARE

Nature of Economic Welfare We are concerned with money not as a source of pleasure in itself but as an influence on the functioning of the

[1] Consider the following (tongue-in-cheek) passage from a children's storybook: "Now the City was a place where Mr. Banks went every day—except Sundays, of course, and Bank Holidays—and while he was there he sat in a large chair in front of a large desk and made money. All day long he worked, cutting out pennies and shillings and half-crowns and threepenny-bits." P. L. Travers, *Mary Poppins*, Reynal & Hitchcock, Inc., New York, 1934, pp. 3–4.

[2] A news service release describing the findings of a study entitled *Americans View Their Mental Health* (Basic Books, Inc., New York, 1960) began as follows:

"Children and sufficient money are the major sources of happiness for Americans.

"Debts and insufficient housing—not enough money, in other words—are the major reasons for unhappiness."

productive economy. To analyze the effects of money on economic welfare we shall look first at the significance of the existence of money as an institution, and second at the consequences of changes in the quantity of money and the flow of money expenditures.

But what are the important measures of economic welfare? First and foremost, the economic welfare of a group of people can be identified with their "real income"—with the quantity of economic goods and services which they have at their disposal. Whether rising real incomes make people "better off" in some moral or psychological sense need not be debated here. Rising real incomes have certainly brought great improvements in physical well-being to the majority of people in the industrial nations—better levels of health and nutrition, more comfortable shelter and clothing, less back-breaking drudgery. Furthermore, rising real incomes bring with them enlarged opportunities for education and leisure time, which greatly extend the range of opportunities for self-development open to people.

For one individual, real income depends on his money income and on the prices of things he wants to buy. But for society as a whole, real income consists primarily of the *current production* of goods and services. High productivity—the ability to turn out a lot of the desired goods and services per person—is the principal measure of how well an economy promotes economic welfare.

In addition, the economic welfare of particular individuals in the society depends on how the goods and services produced are divided among them—upon the *distribution* of real income.

Most people would agree that distribution should meet some standard of fairness, though they might not agree on what the standard should be. However, it is likely they would grant the desirability of a broad distribution of economic benefits, rather than extreme concentration of income and wealth. And whether or not distribution seems fair to an outside observer, it is important that income recipients should not feel themselves victims of grossly unfair treatment.

In recent years, economists have placed increased emphasis upon the importance of *employment* as a separate factor in economic welfare. High employment is important as a means to high production and wide distribution, but it also has a social and psychological significance of its own. An individual's status in the eyes of others and himself depends in our society partly on his ability to get and keep a suitable job.

Achieving high production and employment and wide distribution of benefits at any one time, however, is not sufficient indication of economic welfare. In a society where individuals attach great psychological significance to the economic aspects of their lives, they are likely to develop an intense dislike for violent and radical changes in economic conditions, changes of the sort which have arisen in the past out of depressions or wars.

Furthermore, individuals in our society have been strongly conditioned to expect a steady improvement in their status as a confirmation of their merit and worth. Fulfilling such expectations with a minimum of social friction is easiest in an economy where total output per person is rising. Thus *growth* and *stability* tend to become separate goals in their own right.

Productivity and Its Foundations In the long run, economic welfare depends on and is limited by the nation's capacity to produce. This capacity is in turn determined largely by the amount of *productive resources* available and by the efficiency with which they are combined. Among productive resources are land and natural resources (including climate and topography), capital goods such as machinery and buildings, and most important, human effort of many kinds. The *quality* of these resources is also a critical factor. It is desirable that workers be educated and skillful, healthy, and able to work effectively together, accept responsibility, and adapt to change. The quality of the managerial and entrepreneurial personnel is particularly important.

The efficiency with which resources are used depends importantly on *technology*. Advanced technology requires knowledge, but it also requires suitable manpower and equipment to put this knowledge into application.

Even with the fund of modern technological knowledge at his disposal, an individual in isolation could not produce very much. High productivity in our world has been the consequence of social endeavor, the result of organization and cooperative effort by many individuals. This group effort has permitted us to enjoy the benefits of *specialization* in the use of resources. Instead of trying to be self-sufficient or even to produce a single product singlehandedly, most workers in our economy limit themselves to a specialized function. Specialization permits each worker to develop a high degree of skill and efficiency within the limited range of operations. Specialized job opportunities can take advantage of differences in aptitudes and interests among workers. And of great importance in our technically advanced society, capital equipment can achieve extraordinary efficiency when limited to highly specialized operations.

However, specialization brings its problems as well as its advantages. One is the problem of organization—what jobs are to be done, and who is to do each one? Another is the necessity for exchange. Each individual specializes as a producer, but as a consumer he still wants a wide variety of goods and services. The economic system must provide a means whereby the specialized activity of each individual enables him to enjoy the fruits of the specialization of others.

Where does money fit into this pattern? Clearly it is not in itself a productive resource. You can't dig a ditch with it, or plow a field. The institution of money makes its contribution to the organization of economic activity by guiding specialization and facilitating exchange. Through the use of money, efficient economic organization can be established without resort to centralized authoritarian controls or coercion. Competitive capitalism seeks efficiency through individual initiative and enterprise subject to financial rewards and penalties.

HOW THE PRICE SYSTEM GUIDES ECONOMIC ACTIVITY

Scarcity and Choice   Economic resources are scarce relative to our desires for goods and services and for leisure. Thus we can't have everything we might want. Choices must be made among the different products and services which might be consumed, for the more resources we devote to one product, the less remain for other uses. Choices must also be made between the enjoyment of current consumption and the more ample provision for the future which can arise from saving and investment, from research, and from education. Other necessary choices concern which methods of production to use and where and how individual workers and material resources are to be employed. Finally, some method is required for sharing output among consumers, since there will not be enough to satisfy all the competing desires for it.

Every society solves these problems in some manner, but if the solutions are to yield a high level of economic welfare, as we have identified it, they should display the following attributes:

1. The types and quantities of products and services produced should reflect the strength of consumers' desires. For most things, these preferences are best expressed through individual purchase decisions.

2. Methods of production should be economically efficient in order to minimize the "real cost" of each product—that is, the amount of scarce resources required to make it. Efficiency in production promotes economic welfare by enabling the society to obtain more goods and services from a given endowment of productive resources.

3. As a corollary, each resource should be used where it is most productive. This means, first, it should be used in producing the products most desired by consumers, and second, it should be assigned to the function in which its productivity is highest.

4. Individual products should go to people who value them highly.

5. Distribution of total output among individuals should meet two standards. First, it should be fair and equitable. Second, it should support and be consistent with the productivity of the system and provide opportunity and incentive for people to work, save, invest, and engage in other productive actions.

Since the time of Adam Smith, economists have argued that under appropriate circumstances, the interplay of supply and demand in free markets can bring about a good pattern of economic organization. To achieve this result, buyers and sellers must be willing and able to shop around in order to improve their positions, and must have sufficient knowledge of market conditions to shop wisely. Markets must be "free" both from improper government interference and also from excesses of monopoly power. Some minimum standards of honesty and fair dealing must prevail. Of particular importance, there must be a sufficient number of persons willing to assume the risks and responsibilities of entrepreneurship and management. The range of choices available to workers and consumers in a market economy is in large measure determined by what the entrepreneurs offer them.

The existence of these conditions does not guarantee a high degree of economic welfare, but their absence makes it difficult to achieve. The extent to which these conditions are achieved depends on the entire culture pattern of a given society—the customs, habits, attitudes, and values of the people.

The Interplay of Buying and Selling The functions of the money economy in guiding specialization and carrying out exchange both emerge from the continuous interplay of buying and selling. This interaction of the basic economic units can be described as a circular flow of incomes and expenditures among households and business firms as shown in Figure 1-1. House-

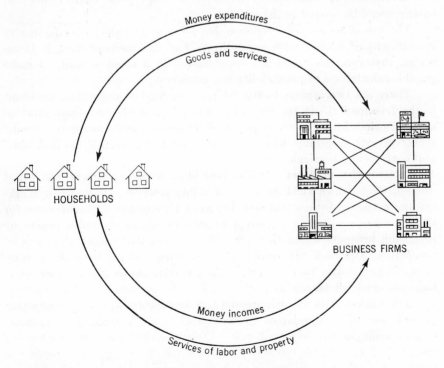

Figure 1-1. The circular flow of income and expenditures.

holds obtain money incomes by selling services (personal or property) to business and use their money incomes to buy consumer goods from business. Business firms spend money to employ labor and other resources to produce goods and services for sale at a profit. There is considerable buying and selling among firms, but the ultimate goal is production for the consumer market.

Each firm and household enters the market as both buyer and seller, and each is strongly influenced in its purchase and sale decisions by the prices of things it can buy or sell. Each buyer is shopping around to find relatively inexpensive means of meeting his desires; each seller is shopping around to find the most remunerative markets for his products or services. Comparison of alternative opportunities is essential for this process of shopping around. And the existence of prices expressed in terms of the common denominator of money is almost indispensable for such comparisons. If goods had to be exchanged directly for goods, the number of separate exchange ratios could easily become overwhelming. Among 10 products, for instance, there are 45 possible bilateral ratios of exchange relating each product to each of the others. If the number of products were 1,000, the number of separate ratios would rise to 499,500! Few individuals could choose intelligently under such circumstances, and a great deal of time and energy would be wasted in the effort.

The use of money as a common denominator of values also facilitates comparisons of income with expenditure. For the business firm, it is essential that revenues and costs be expressed in a common unit, to make possible calculations of profitability and efficiency.

There are two aspects to the interplay of buying and selling decisions in the free market. At the individual level, households and firms react to existing prices in a manner conditioned by tastes and technology. Socially, such reactions determine what the prices are to be, even if no individual unit controls any particular price.

Determination of Prices At the individual level, consumers will select those products which yield the greatest utility relative to their price. Workers and property owners will seek the most remunerative employments for their services or property. Entrepreneurs will try to maximize profits by producing products which they can sell at prices that exceed the costs of production. And each will employ those resources which have the highest productivity relative to their price. Each participant is alike in trying to buy cheap and sell dear.

The market price of each product will be determined by the interaction of purchase and sale decisions—demand and supply. Demand by consumers —their willingness to buy—will reflect the strength of their preferences for one product relative to another. Producers' willingness to offer goods and services for sale will depend on their unit costs, which are ultimately dependent on the amount of resources required for production. Through trial and error, market prices and quantities will settle at levels which balance desires to buy against willingness to produce and sell.

Supply and demand will also be at work in markets for productive resources. Supplies of natural resources and capital goods may be largely fixed in the short run, while the supply of labor will depend on the size of the population and on people's willingness to take productive jobs. The demand for any productive resource by business firms depends on the *productivity* of the resource, most particularly on how much its employment can add to the revenues of a firm. The pulling and hauling of supply and demand will produce equilibrium prices here also, drawing the available resources toward productive uses.

Of course, these two segments of the market are mutually interacting. Consumer demands for particular products will affect the business demand for specialized resources. The price which prevails for a particular resource, such as labor, will affect production costs of individual products and thus the quantities supplied. If a general equilibrium position can be reached, however, the price structure will show two significant characteristics. First, the price of each resource will be equal to the value of its contribution to production in its various uses. Each firm which buys a given resource will have to pay for it a price which reflects the value of other things that resource could have produced. Second, the selling price of each product will equal its cost of production (including a "normal" return to capital and enterprise). This cost represents the payments for resources used in each unit of the product, and since the price of each resource reflects its productivity in other sectors of the economy, the cost of each product equals the value of other products which could have been produced with the same resources.

If the price structure approximates these characteristics, it will provide a set of guideposts which direct the self-interested conduct of buyers and sellers in directions which promote economic efficiency. Self-interest will lead workers to prefer higher-paying jobs; the higher pay is a reflection of higher productivity, perhaps because the product being produced is in stronger demand, perhaps because the individual worker possesses some particular fitness for the job. To be sure, workers are influenced by other dimensions of a job besides pay. Nevertheless, pay differentials provide a strong incentive for workers to enter areas where their productivity is high, and also to try to increase their productivity through such means as further education. Paying wages in proportion to productivity is not only functional but fair—at least, most Americans seem to think so.

The competitive price structure also provides guidance to consumers as they shop around for best values. A high price tag on any product is a sign that it requires a relatively large sacrifice of productive resources and, by implication, of other products those resources could have produced. Each consumer has an incentive to seek out products which meet his needs without imposing heavy sacrifices of this sort.

For the business firm, the profit motive leads to shopping around both as a buyer and as a seller. In choosing the types and quantities of products to sell, each firm is drawn toward those which will yield a selling price in excess of cost. Socially, these are products which consumers strongly desire (in preference to other products which the same amount of resources could have produced). As a buyer, each firm attempts to minimize costs by making use of productive resources which are most productive relative to the expense they entail. Socially, this tends to pull each resource into those uses where its productivity is highest. Ideally, the pursuit of profits will also lead firms to employ the most efficient technology and to seek further improvements in methods of production and in the types and quality of products.

Thus prices induce producers to provide the things people want and induce buyers to economize on the scarce resources of the community. Through the price system, the decisions of millions of individuals are reconciled with each other. Specialization and exchange are efficiently organized without central direction or coercion. Furthermore, the system provides a continuous sensitive mechanism to adjust to changes in desires, technology, or resource supplies. Just as our sensory organs receive impressions from the outside world and transmit them to the brain, where they become meaningful sense perceptions, the price system registers economic changes and converts them into price variations.

For example, increased preference for hats relative to shoes would tend to raise the price of hats and lower the price of shoes. Then, just as our sensory data form the basis for behavior reactions, so the changes registered by the price system lead to behavior responses in the economy. The increase in the price of hats encourages more production of hats and exerts a demand pull on resources to draw them into hat production. The lower price of shoes leads to production cutbacks, releasing productive resources into the economy.

Such economic efficiency is possible only if firms can determine profits by expressing revenues and costs in a single unit and if consumers, businesses, and resource owners can compare the alternative purchase and sale opportunities in terms of a common denominator of money.

Qualifications It is fairly obvious that in reality free economic interplay does not function as well as this description suggests. It is difficult to prevent monopoly and private restraint of economic freedom. Incomes may be unfairly distributed, to the point where they reflect differences in genetic or economic inheritance, unequal environmental backgrounds, and variation in opportunity. Such products and services as national defense, education, public health, police and fire protection, and highways, which might be very desirable, would not be profitable to produce in optimum quantities by private firms. It also appears that markets for productive resources—land, labor, and capital—contain inherent characteristics which make free-market adjustments work less well than they do on product markets. Resource-market transactions often involve a degree of long-run commitment which produces a high level of uncertainty and makes trial-and-error adjustments more difficult. However, these deficiencies would not easily be remedied by abolishing money as the common denominator of value.

Finally—and this may historically have been the greatest shortcoming of all—the free-market money economy is subject to instability in the flow of total expenditure. Traditional price-system theories assumed that all the incomes created in the productive process would be smoothly respent on current production, so that neither depression nor inflation would occur. In actuality, however, there are numerous ways in which total spending may diverge from the ideal amount. We shall have a great deal more to say about this.

Our economy is far from *laissez faire,* but the major part of our economic life follows the kind of price-system directives we have described. Many of the activities our governments do perform are necessary supplements to the market or serve actually to improve the environment for market forces by controlling monopolies, promoting fair dealing, and particularly, helping to keep fluctuations in the flow of aggregate expenditures within reasonable bounds. One method of influencing aggregate expenditures is by the control of money and credit.

MONEY AS A MEDIUM OF PAYMENT AND DEBT

Money and Exchange Just as money prices help guide specialization, so money as a medium of payment makes possible the exchanges which are necessary if specialization is to succeed. The pattern of specialization in modern society is incredibly complex. Each consumer normally buys hundreds of products and services during a year. There are tens of thousands of different specialized occupations and employments. The exchanges necessary to permit such specialization have two important characteristics which render money indispensable:

1. The necessary exchanges are *multilateral.* Normally, the individual specializes in the performance of a few functions in connection with a few products produced by one firm. But the products he wants come from the specialized activities of thousands of other individuals working for dozens of other firms. Often the individual will not consume any of the products or services which his employer produces. Money incomes provide a means

whereby each person's services are put into a common pool, so to speak, in exchange for claims against all the things in the pool. Without money, individuals and firms would be reduced to bartering, which usually can operate only on a bilateral basis, where each individual A needs to find another who has what A wants and wants what A has—a very restrictive condition. The use of money is particularly important to a satisfactory wage relationship, as comparison with the infamous "truck system" of paying wages in goods well illustrates.[3]

2. Economic activity takes place under conditions of *uncertainty and change*. Changes in consumer tastes, in resource availability, and in technology are continually disrupting the pattern of specialization and exchange. Money provides a means for flexible adaptation. Individuals can change jobs without having to alter consumption patterns, and vice versa.

Money is advantageous in exchange because it is a "bearer of options" —it provides general purchasing power in the exercise of which the holder enjoys wide freedom of choice. First, he is free to work in the production of any product or to supply a service whether or not he himself wants to consume it. Second, he is free to subdivide his purchases among many different sellers. Third, he can change his spending pattern from what it has been in the past. Fourth, he has the freedom to spend all his money or to hold onto it until later.

Like most freedoms, those conferred by money entail risks. Individuals may use their freedom of choice over commodity purchases in ways which disappoint some producers and resource owners. Demand for certain products may fall, inflicting losses on those prepared to produce them. Individuals may exercise their option to postpone spending, so that the total demand for goods and services falls short of what existing resources might produce.

In the modern world, the actual purchase of goods does not always involve the simultaneous exchange of money. An important alternative is the

[3] A workingman testifying before a government commission in Britain in 1845 described his problems under the truck system as follows: "When Saturday night came I had to turn out with a certain quantity of meat and candles or tobacco or ale or whatever I had drawn in wages to dispose of at a serious loss. I used to take a can of ale to the barber to get shaved with, and a can to the sweep to sweep my chimney. . . . I was obliged to take a pound of candles at sevenpence and leave it for the newspaper, the price of which was fourpence halfpenny. I used to take my beef at sevenpence a pound and sell it to the coal woman . . . for fivepence, and any bit of sugar or tea or anything of the kind that my employer did not sell, I used to get from the grocer by swapping soap or starch. . . ." Quoted in L. C. A. Knowles, *The Industrial and Commercial Revolutions in Great Britain during the Nineteenth Century*, E. P. Dutton & Co., Inc., New York, 1933, p. 88.

use of "book credit," as exemplified by the charge account. The buyer agrees to pay later for goods received now, and the seller records the transaction and subsequently bills the buyer. Book-credit transactions differ from other credit transactions in that there is no actual loan of money. Since book-credit liabilities must ordinarily be settled in cash at some time, the use of book credit does not actually eliminate cash expenditures. Access to such credit may, however, reduce the amount of cash balances which people need to keep.

While charge accounts, credit cards, and the like are not money, it does not require a very large further step to arrive at a form of book credit which can be freely transferred from one person to another as a means of payment. Such are the checking deposits of commercial banks, which furnish the medium for most of our payments and are therefore considered to be money.

Money, Credit, and Capital Money has also contributed to economic productivity by serving as the medium in which debt claims are expressed, incurred, and discharged. Because money facilitates such transactions, individuals become more willing to borrow and to lend. Ease of borrowing contributes to ease of capital investment. Capital goods such as machinery and buildings can greatly enhance economic productivity, but they must be produced and acquired before increased productivity occurs and before the added revenues from it are received. Facility of borrowing increases the amount of capital which individual firms can acquire. Out of the resulting higher productivity they can pay interest to the lenders, reap a profit for themselves, and still possibly benefit consumers and workers through cheaper and better products, better job opportunities, and higher wages. Ability to acquire claims payable in a fixed sum of money also encourages a higher degree of saving. In the process, specialization is served by permitting capital to accumulate under the direction of specialized managers while the saving is done by those who can afford it. Saving-investment transactions are very complex exchanges, and it is hard to conceive of them in a world of barter.

In our economy, this specialization is carried one step further by the extensive development of financial intermediaries such as banks and insurance companies. These institutions obtain funds by incurring debts in forms which are directly useful to the public—bank deposits, insurance policies. These funds they invest in "primary securities" issued by ultimate borrowers.

While the existence of money as an institution makes possible money debts, in the modern economy most money has come to consist of debts! Paper currency is composed of government promissory notes, and bank checking deposits are debts owed by banks to their depositors.

MONEY AND ECONOMIC IDEOLOGY

Money as a Symbol of Capitalism   For as long as the institution of money has been known to Western society, money has been regarded as a symbol of acquisitiveness and avarice. We all know St. Paul's observation that "the love of money is the root of all evil." In medieval times the Christian church labeled acquisitiveness as the sin of usury and denounced particularly the lending of money at interest. Following Aristotle, the church held money to be barren and unproductive and argued that interest was really a payment for time, which was God's to dispose of, not man's.

The institution of money made possible the emergence of capitalism, and it was inevitable that critics of capitalism should denounce money itself, as well as the love of money, as a root of evil. Karl Marx tried to show that the existence of money made possible the accumulation of capital, which in turn led to the exploitation of labor through "surplus value." In painting his view of the world to come, he argued that ultimately under communism money would be abolished and goods exchanged directly—a situation made possible by the great abundance of all products which he anticipated.

The defenders of money have not been silent either. Accepting the association of money with capitalism, they have argued not only that money is essential to the economic abundance which capitalism has brought, but that it is ethically good because it enhances personal freedom and responsibility.[4]

Most people today would not question the morality of the institution of money itself. They recognize it as a means to facilitate human actions. If the actions are motivated toward worthy ends and produce beneficial consequences, the means are commendable. On their face, economic productivity and freedom seem desirable. If the existence of money brought a debasement of human personality, its morality as an institution might well be impugned; but greed and avarice existed long before money and cannot be

[4] Consider the following, spoken by a character in a novel:

"To trade by means of money is the code of the men of good will. Money rests on the axiom that every man is the owner of his mind and his effort. Money allows no power to prescribe the value of your effort except the voluntary choice of the man who is willing to trade you his effort in return. . . . Money permits no deals except those to mutual benefit by the unforced judgement of the traders. . . .

"So long as men live together on earth and need means to deal with one another—their only substitute, if they abandon money, is the muzzle of a gun. . . .

"To the glory of mankind, there was, for the first and only time in history, a *country of money*—and I have no higher, more reverent tribute to pay to America, for this means: a country of reason, justice, freedom, production, achievement." Ayn Rand, *Atlas Shrugged*, Random House, Inc., New York, 1958, pp. 388–391. The use of the dollar sign as a symbol by a "capitalist underground" movement in this book is an interesting example of monetary mysticism.

proved to be more extensive since its appearance. More serious exception may be taken to the economic disadvantages attending the use of money—chiefly economic instability. Experience indicates, however, that these can be controlled without impairing the beneficial functions of money.

Money under Communism—Soviet Russia Despite the hostility toward money displayed by Marx, Lenin, and other Communist leaders, the actual experience of the Soviet Union indicates that money is indispensable to an advanced industrial economy. When the Bolsheviks seized power in 1917, the Russian economy was in a chaotic state. Inflation was already under way, and the revolutionary regime soon accelerated this into hyperinflation by issuing vast quantities of currency to finance government expenditures. Prices were doubling on the average of every three or four months in 1918–1921. At the same time extensive direct requisition and free distribution of goods were conducted by the government, which "hoped to effect a transition to a 'natural' economy in which purchase and sale, and the medium with which they were carried out—i.e., money—would have no place." [5]

The New Economic Policy adopted in 1921 retreated from many favored Communist dogmas, including the abolition of money, in order to restore the economy to productive health. When extensive central planning and collectivization were undertaken in the late 1920s, a system of money and banking was accorded an important economic role, which it still performs. Soviet leaders still pay lip service to the idea that sometime money will be abolished and all transactions carried on in terms of goods, but nothing is being done toward that goal.

The monetary system of the Soviet Union is subordinated to the centralized planning and control of economic life, but it still performs many of the same functions as in a free-market economy. To be sure, Soviet production goals are set by government authorities and carried out chiefly in state-controlled enterprises. Decisions about what to produce are made by the authorities without direct reference to money costs and prices. These decisions reflect political choices about priorities of need, rather than free consumer choice. Supplies of resources are estimated directly, and methods of production are prescribed chiefly on the basis of engineering criteria of efficiency. Officially, then, the price system does not furnish directives about what to produce and how to produce it.

Money does play a major official role as a medium of exchange. Wages and salaries are paid chiefly in currency, which consumers are free to spend on whatever products are available. Some products and services are distributed free or at a nominal cost, but most food, clothing, and durable goods reach their ultimate consumers through voluntary purchase in the marketplace. Consumer demand does not directly guide production, al-

[5] Arthur Z. Arnold, *Banks, Credit, and Money in Soviet Russia*, Columbia University Press, New York, 1937, p. 54.

though the planning authorities do not ignore it. Instead, the regime uses consumer prices as a rationing device. Prices are set to induce consumers to take whatever supplies the authorities have decided to provide them with. Use of money incomes and prices allows individual products to flow to particular individuals in a manner which gives some scope to differences in preferences and needs.

The Soviet authorities do rely extensively on the price mechanism to allocate labor among jobs and to keep work incentives at a high intensity. They have found that coercion not only is objectionable to the workers, but is also inefficient. In recent years, with minor exceptions, recruitment of workers into high-priority occupations, product lines, or regions has been based on high wages and fringe benefits. And the wage structure provides strong incentives for high productivity and advancement along either technical or managerial lines. Still, wage rates are those set by the authorities, not by the free market.

Within the limits set by the plans, the management of individual production units in the Soviet economy is based to a surprising degree on a variant of the profit motive. Each enterprise must maintain accounts of revenue and costs, and success in achieving or surpassing some target for "planned profit" means extra benefit for the management and for the employees. Profit considerations are supposed to give the firm maximum incentive to produce the planned outputs with maximum efficiency. However, the plans contain enough loopholes that managers can frequently substitute high-profit outputs for low-profit ones. And they can and do alter production methods, within limits, to make greater use of cheap inputs. This input substitution, which leads to efficiency in a free-market economy, does not always do so in the Soviet Union, because individual inputs are not priced on the basis of scarcity and productivity. In particular, interest rates charged on loans to buy capital goods have been low or nonexistent, despite the great shortage and high productivity of capital. This has led enterprises to be unduly wasteful in "empire-building" very capital-intensive plants, notably in hydroelectric power facilities. By the early 1960s Soviet authorities were plainly aware of these sources of inefficiency and were seeking ways to improve the rationality of the pricing process, even if they had to use some "bourgeois" economic concepts in doing so.

In sum, the Russian economy relies on money as a standard of value and as a medium of payment, but the price system does not provide the kind of guidance to production and distribution that it does in a free-market economy.[6] Soviet authorities have overcome their ideological antipathy to

---

[6] On the foregoing aspects of the Soviet economy, see Nicholas Spulber, *The Soviet Economy: Structure, Principles, Problems*, W. W. Norton & Company, Inc., New York, 1962, and Morris Bornstein, "The Soviet Price System," *American Economic Review*, March, 1962.

money because of its efficiency in helping them achieve many goals. In relying on price-directed free choice to match workers with jobs and to match consumers with products, the authorities have also yielded a small but precious area of personal freedom to the Russian people.

THE PROBLEM OF AGGREGATE MONEY EXPENDITURES

Spending and Welfare *In the long run, economic welfare depends on* the resources available and the efficiency with which they are organized. The economy's capacity to produce always sets limits beyond which its productivity cannot rise. But in the short run, economic welfare may fall seriously short of its maximum potential. Economic welfare requires that there be an adequate (but not excessive) level of money *demand* (expenditure) for currently produced goods and services.

Production and employment in a market economy depend on the prospect that entrepreneurs can gain profits by selling their output at prices which exceed the cost of ingoing resources. Whether they will be able to do so will depend on the amount of money people are willing and able to spend on their products. If the total demand for goods and services is too low, firms will reduce production and resources will be unemployed. Total output and real income will fall below their potential, and maximum economic welfare will not be achieved.

During the 1930s this problem afflicted the United States and much of the rest of the industrial world. Because expenditures to buy current production fell off sharply, business firms were obliged to cut back on production. Millions of workers lost their jobs; prices fell; bankruptcies and property foreclosures were widespread. The economic hardships and misery arising from the Depression led in turn to enhanced social tensions and political upheavals, to totalitarianism and war in Europe and Asia.

On the other hand, the flow of expenditures may also be too large—the characteristic problem of the 1940s. As the economy strains at the limits of productive capacity, costs and prices tend to rise rapidly. Between 1942 and 1952 prices in the United States doubled, causing unhappiness and injustice in the distribution of real income and wealth. The pinch was felt by retired persons, teachers, ministers, and others whose money incomes lagged behind the price trend. And the inflation sharply reduced the real value of savings held in such fixed-dollar forms as life insurance, bank deposits, or savings bonds.

As we shall demonstrate later, the economic system always creates enough current income going to consumers, businesses, and government to purchase the current output at current prices. If each economic unit spent all its income as it was received, the flow of spending would be just adequate to keep the economy stable. In practice, however, some units spend more, and some less, than their incomes. This creates the basis for a flow of loans from savers to borrowers. However, no automatic mechanism equates the surpluses of the savers with the deficits of dissavers. If the surpluses predominate, total expenditure will decline. If the deficits predominate, total expenditure will rise. If total expenditure is to grow from year to year, to keep pace with the growth in productive capacity, there must be a predominance of deficits—the economy as a whole must "live beyond its income."

Money and the Expenditure Flow The quantity of money is one of the factors influencing the flow of expenditures. Indeed, there have been times when economists drifted into the habit of expecting that the expenditure flow would maintain relatively constant proportionality to the quantity of money. Strict proportionality has not been maintained, for there have also been changes in the rate at which existing money is spent—in its "velocity of circulation." Nevertheless, variations in the quantity of money definitely affect the expenditure flow and can be judged according to whether they contribute to desirable patterns of total spending.

Every money economy faces the problems of determining what the quantity of money shall be and how it shall change. Historically, the behavior of the money supply has often been determined by the choice of the type of money to be used. A monetary system using gold and silver coins, for instance, would normally produce variations in the money supply in proportion to variations in the nation's stock of monetary metals. If bank notes and bank deposits constituted the bulk of the money supply, variations in the quantity of money would result from variations in the volume of bank loans.

However, another influence on the quantity of money has been present throughout monetary history, irrespective of the type of money in use. This has been the habitual reliance of needy or impecunious governments on increases in the money supply as a sure-fire method of financing expenditures. In early times, monarchs achieved this by reducing the precious metal content of the monetary units. More recently, governments have issued paper money to cover expenditures—the expedient of our Revolutionary and Civil Wars. Nowadays they do it by the more roundabout process of "borrowing" newly created deposits from banks.

Precious metals, bank lending, and the exigencies of government finance have been the factors which long determined our money supply, and they still exercise a substantial influence. But each has at times caused inappropriate variations in the supply of money. Gold exports and reduction of bank lending have often come during periods when spending was already declining, thus aggravating the tendencies toward depression and unemployment. Large increases in the money supply through government spending have caused serious inflations—every major war in our history has been financed partly through new money and has produced a substantial inflation.

Consequently, few contemporary students of money believe that its quantity should be left to the uncontrolled variations of precious metals, bank lending, and government finance. Most agree with the noted nineteenth-century financial writer, Walter Bagehot, that "money will not manage itself," and that the government should attempt to control and vary the quantity of money with a view to producing the best possible pattern of total spending. This means, first of all, that the government should prevent the money supply from being an active cause of undesirable changes in spending. Second, the government should try to manipulate the money supply so as to reduce or eliminate undesired fluctuations in total spending arising from private spending decisions. We shall investigate in detail how these results may be sought, and see to what extent they have been achieved.

The Pathology of Money—The German Inflation of 1919–1923   One of the most frightening illustrations of what can happen when money gets out of control is the example of Germany in the years following World War I. The peace settlement imposed on Germany a heavy burden of reparations, payable in gold. And the new government of the Weimar Republic was weak in political support and deficient in such vital powers as taxation.

Government expenditures for reparations and reconstruction increased much faster than taxes could be levied. The resulting deficits were financed by loans from the Reichsbank (the German central bank)—loans made in the form of newly created deposits and bank notes. Deficit spending and newly created money pushed up prices in an economy where resources were fully employed. As prices rose, business firms became more eager to borrow money to speculate or to expand productive facilities. Loans were readily expanded by the Reichsbank and private commercial banks, further increasing the volume of bank notes and deposits.

By 1921, prices had risen 16-fold over those of 1918. The quantity of paper marks in circulation had risen from less than 7 billion in 1914 to 140 billion in 1921. A vicious circle developed: Rising prices obliged the government to spend more and more to obtain the same goods and services, while revenues from a clumsy tax system failed to keep pace. During 1922, prices rose 30-fold. The climax came in 1923, when the French moved an army of occupation into German territory to force payment of reparations. The German government subsidized industrial shutdowns in resistance to the French, and bank credit remained easy to get. The consequence was a monetary explosion. The supply of paper currency increased during 1923 some 250-million-fold. Prices skyrocketed—10-fold in August, 25-fold in September, 300-fold in October, 100-fold in November.

With the dizzying decline in the value of money, people rushed to spend it as rapidly as they could. Wages were paid as often as twice a day, and workers rushed to the factory gates to hand the money to family members to be spent. People bought anything they could find, whether they wanted the goods or not, realizing that almost any goods were a better store of value than money. Thus the increase in the rate of expenditure (velocity) of money helped spur inflation, as did the increase in the money supply itself which resulted from the government deficits and bank credit expansion.

By 1923 the inflation led to the disorganization and demoralization of the German economy. The price system was totally incapable of serving as an adequate guide to production and distribution. Efficiency of production was greatly reduced, since costs of resources bore no relation to their relative scarcity and productivity. Distribution became chaotic. Although industrial wages kept up fairly well with prices, other salaries, notably those of government employees, fell far behind. The worst injustices befell holders of fixed-value assets, notably the bonds issued by the German government during and after the war. Business firms and farmers were sometimes able to make great gains, although many found their costs as well as their revenues rising.

At the end of 1923, officials in the German and Allied governments finally united to stem the tide of catastrophe. The troops were withdrawn from the Ruhr, reparations payments scaled down, and foreign loans extended to Germany. The German government cut its expenditures, raised taxes, and halted the runaway expansion of private bank credit. The old mark currency was removed from circulation and a new currency issued in exchange, in the ratio of one mark of the new for one trillion of the old. Curbing deficits and credit expansion prevented further increases in the quantity of money, while the currency exchange helped restore public confidence and reduce the volume of spending to more normal levels. The inflation stopped.[7]

The German inflation was socially disastrous in many ways. It destroyed incomes and property in such forms as bonds and insurance policies held by the thrifty middle class. It stirred up hatred for the business classes—"profiteers"—among the workers. Many of the discontented were alienated from the democratic parties of the Weimar government and were ripe for the temptations of extremists.

The last echo of the inflation was the most devastating. The German economy had recovered by 1929, when the world economic depression struck Germany with particular force. The government might have been able to reduce the shock by such policies as exchange-rate depreciation and government deficit spending, but it shunned these devices because of their association with the hyperinflation. Instead, a disastrous policy of deflation

---

[7] Edwin W. Kemmerer, *Money*, The Macmillan Company, New York, 1938, pp. 271–317; Frank D. Graham, *Exchange, Prices and Production in Hyper-inflation: Germany, 1920–1923*, Princeton University Press, Princeton, N.J., 1930.

was tried in an attempt to squeeze down wages and prices. The effects on production, employment, and morale were intolerable. More than half the electorate became supporters of either the Nazis or the Communists, both of whom favored destruction of parliamentary democracy. In 1933 Adolf Hitler became Chancellor, and a chain of events was set in motion which led to World War II.

Germany's experience with inflation was not unique. Similar episodes occurred in Poland, Russia, Hungary, Austria, and other countries after World War I. Hungary, Greece, and others went through similar nightmares during and after World War II. China endured a hyperinflation in the 1940s which contributed to the triumph of the Communists there.

In other countries, a different process of steady erosion of the currency has gone on, never quite achieving the runaway status of hyperinflation but lasting much longer. The French franc began to deteriorate during World War I, and the process has continued intermittently. In 1959 the De Gaulle regime announced the creation of a new "heavy franc" equal to 100 old francs and equivalent in dollar value to the pre-1914 franc. A similar erosion of value has been at work in several South American countries. In Brazil prices rose tenfold from 1954 to 1963. Such inflation has resulted mainly from protracted government deficits and rapid expansion of the money supply. Although the social consequences are by no means as severe as in Germany, such a process makes great changes in the whole nature of money, credit, debt, and economic life.

MONEY AS A STORE OF VALUE

Its status as generalized purchasing power confers on money a considerable attraction as a store of value. Just as the holder of money can choose among a wide range of currently available goods and services, so he can choose between present and future expenditure.

There are, however, many forms of wealth available which can serve as repositories of value. At one extreme, these include real assets, such as houses or factories, which can yield direct consumption or production services to the owner. However, such assets may be subject to wide variations in market value, affecting their status as stores of general purchasing power. Money occupies the opposite pole. Its "price" is fixed, and it can easily be spent or used to repay debts. Between the extremes fall various other financial assets, combining in various degrees fixity and security of monetary value with income and other sources of utility.

Assets may be classified by their "liquidity"—that is, the ease with which they can be exchanged for money on stable and predictable terms. Money itself possesses complete liquidity, but other assets, such as savings deposits and United States savings bonds, come very close to it. Consequently, there are close substitutes for money as a store of value.

Money is, by definition, a perfect store of *nominal* value. But its virtues as a store of *real* value depend on what happens to its purchasing power. Substantial inflation of price levels reduces the value of money and impairs its attraction as a store of real value. If price changes are anticipated, buyers and sellers begin to speculate on the future, and current prices cease to function well as directives to economic activity.

The use of money as a standard for debt contracts and as a store of value also presupposes relatively stable value. With unstable money, debtors or creditors may be subjected to unexpected losses. Price changes may cause arbitrary shifts in the distribution of income and wealth which are much resented by the victims. Yet if people come to expect monetary instability, they may cease to rely on fixed-money-value debts or to hold money as a store of value. If so, neither function is likely to be performed as well as it would be by stable money.

SUMMARY

Money as an institution is valuable because it facilitates economic productivity. As a unit of account, in which prices are stated, money makes possible the price-profit-cost comparisons needed to permit the price system to allocate resources efficiently. Price directives guide specialization into complex patterns without central control or coercion. Money as a medium of payment facilitates the patterns of exchange needed to make specialization workable. Money as the unit of debt and credit promotes saving and investment and thereby makes possible the benefits of capital formation on productivity and permits specialization in the use of capital. Although money and capitalism evolved together historically and although Marx and other critics of capitalism denounced money, the experience of Soviet Russia shows that money as a unit of account and medium of payment is indispensable to an advanced industrial economy, even when production decisions are not based on price-profit considerations.

The quantity of money affects economic welfare through its relation to total expenditures. If total spending is too low, resources will be unemployed and the economy will be depressed, as in the United States and Europe in the 1930s. If spending is too high, price inflation may create its own detriments to economic welfare, as in Germany in the 1920s. In the past, variations in the money supply were often left to market forces, but in the modern world, governments have accepted the responsibility of managing the quantity of money in the public interest.

PLAN OF THE BOOK

In the following chapters, the topics touched on here are developed more fully. In the next chapter, we deal with the evolution of money and the various forms it has taken. Then in Part Two we examine in detail the monetary system of the contemporary United States, with emphasis on the manner in which changes in the money supply take place and are controlled by the government.

Part Three proceeds to the analysis of total spending. Here we analyze the influence of spending on production, employment, and prices and examine the causes of variations in spending. Part Four takes a broader look at the nation's financial system as a whole, with particular reference to its relation to saving and investment.

In Part Five international monetary and financial matters are discussed. Some of the historical threads are picked up from Chapter 2 and end in a more detailed analysis of monetary and financial developments in the twentieth century. The historical emphasis continues in Part Six, which describes the recent monetary and financial history of the United States. This order was chosen with the belief that the theoretical analysis of the earlier parts is useful in understanding evolution of institutions and policies.

Since a basic use of theory and of historical information is as a guide to subsequent action, the book concludes with a discussion of contemporary problems in monetary policy. This subject is placed last because it is what everything else is leading up to.

In much of the book (notably Part Three) emphasis is on the relation between money and the volume of spending. Such an emphasis should never divert attention from the fact that money is important because of its relation to the productive economy in which real resources of the community are transformed into economic goods and services. Financial values are never the ultimate measures of welfare.

QUESTIONS FOR STUDY

1. According to E. A. Goldenweiser, money is "the universal solvent" of economic life.[8] Karl Marx attacked this principle in the Communist Manifesto. "The bourgeoisie . . . has put an end to all feudal, patriarchal, idyllic relations. It has pitilessly torn asunder the motley feudal ties that bound man to his 'natural superiors,' and has left no other nexus between man and

[8] *American Monetary Policy*, McGraw-Hill Book Company, New York, 1951, p. 8.

man than naked self-interest, than callous 'cash payment.' It has drowned the most heavenly ecstasies of religious fervor, of chivalrous enthusiasm, of Philistine sentimentalism, in the icy water of egotistical calculation. It has resolved personal worth into exchange value. . . . The bourgeoisie has stripped of its halo every occupation hitherto honored and looked up to with reverent awe. It has converted the physician, the lawyer, the priest, the poet, the man of science, into its paid wage laborers."

Is it desirable for human relations to be so extensively conducted in money terms? Evaluate the alternatives.

2. "The cost of any product is the alternatives which must be foregone to obtain it." Explain this from the standpoint of an individual and from the standpoint of the economy as a whole.

3. According to John Stuart Mill, "There cannot . . . be intrinsically a more insignificant thing, in the economy of society, than money; except in the character of a contrivance for sparing time and labor. It is a machine for doing quickly and commodiously, what would be done, though less quickly and commodiously, without it. . . . " *Principles of Political Economy* (1848).

In what sense is this a useful observation, and in what sense is it very misleading?

4. A proposal popular among Socialists in the past was to create a money system based on labor. Each unit of money would represent a certain number of hours worked, and each worker would receive an amount commensurate with his efforts. How do you think this would work?

SUGGESTED READINGS

Burstein, Meyer: *Money,* Schenkman Publishing Company, Cambridge, Mass., 1963.

Bye, Raymond T.: *Social Economy and the Price System,* The Macmillan Company, New York, 1950.

Cagan, Phillip: "The Monetary Dynamics of Hyperinflation," in Milton Friedman (ed.), *Studies in the Quantity Theory of Money,* The University of Chicago Press, Chicago, 1956.

Heilbroner, Robert: *The Quest for Wealth,* Simon and Schuster, Inc., New York, 1956.

Kemmerer, Edwin W.: *Money,* The Macmillan Company, New York, 1938.

Patinkin, Don: *Money, Interest, and Prices,* 2d ed., Harper & Row, Publishers, Incorporated, New York, 1965.

chapter two

TYPES AND
EVOLUTION OF MONEY

TYPES OF MONEY

Commodity Money and Abstract Money   We have defined money as being anything which is used as a general medium of payment and which is denominated in terms of the monetary unit of account. A vast variety of things have achieved the status of money in different societies, and in the Western world, there has been an evolutionary process in which money has undergone great changes.

Although there are many ways of classifying kinds of money, for our purposes they can usefully be divided into two main categories. The first we shall call "commodity money." Money of this description consists of commodities which can be put to nonmonetary use and have some value aside from their monetary status. Commodity money may consist of purely utilitarian commodities, such as nails, tobacco, or cigarettes. Or the commodities may be items whose nonmonetary uses are religious or artistic—gold and silver, jewels, beads, shells. Commodity money may be "full-bodied," in which case the commodity value is approximately equal to the monetary value; or the money may have a commodity value well below its monetary value. (The monetary value cannot be less than the commodity value, or the commodity will cease to serve as money.) In our monetary system, the only commodity money consists of metal coins. Although the coin object itself is not a commodity, the metal it contains can be converted to non-monetary uses.

The second kind of money we shall call "abstract money." This refers to money which has no significant value or use other than as money. Paper currency is abstract money, for even though it is made from a commodity and has tangible existence, in its finished form its commodity value is of no significance. The most extreme form of abstract money is a bank deposit. Bank deposits are regarded as money because with the proper arrangements they can be spent directly, that is, by writing checks. As we shall see, such bank deposits make up the bulk of our money supply and provide the medium for most of the payments in our economy.

Origins of "Moneyness" In an important sense, money is a social *institution*. The status of money is conferred on things by their social acceptability. Nothing possesses "moneyness" intrinsically; it must be earned. Of course, the individual treats money as money because other people so regard it and will accept it in payments. For society as a whole, the monetary status of commodities has generally evolved from spontaneous social usage, and this has been true of such abstract forms as checking deposits as well. There must be consistency between the money a society uses and its broader pattern of institutions and ideas. Just as a currency of shells or beads would be inappropriate for a modern industrial economy, so would efforts to use bank deposits have been badly out of place in a less developed society lacking the framework of law and custom required.

Some economists have argued that money is a creation of the state. As a historical generalization, this is questionable. However, the modern money supply is either issued directly by government or greatly influenced by programs of banking control and protection. The government may influence the acceptability of particular types of money by agreeing to convert one into another or accept them in taxes. It may bestow legal-tender status on types of money, thus obliging creditors to accept them in payment of debts and forbidding sellers to demand payment in some other medium if legal-tender money is offered.

Nevertheless, public attitudes toward money do set limits beyond which government monetary policies cannot go. In particular, the government cannot, in a free economy, set the purchasing power of money over commodities by decree. History abounds with instances where government-created money was rejected by the public and lost its value. The Continental currency of the Revolution and the Confederate paper of the Civil War met this fate. And consider the unwillingness of the American public to use silver dollars, two-dollar bills, or the zinc-coated "white" cents of World War II. Government has great power over the monetary system, but its control is not unlimited.

EVOLUTION OF MONEY

How It Started The history of money demonstrates a remarkable capacity of human society spontaneously to generate useful and functional social patterns. We have seen that money as a standard and a medium is virtually indispensable to an economic system characterized by specialization and multilateral exchange and by uncertainty and change. History furnishes repeated examples of parallel social evolution of extensive commerce and trade along with a system of money which has at first arisen out of commercial usage and in turn reacted upon it. The use of money in the world cannot be traced back to a single "germ," or source. It was not invented once and for all in one time and place. On the contrary, not only the institution of money but important specific types of money can be traced to numerous independent origins.

In Western economic society, money passed through two major phases. In the first phase, things which had value as commodities came to be used as money also. The second phase has involved the progressive substitution of abstract forms of money for commodity money—a process which is now almost complete. Although we regard the second phase as a recent development, it had its inception far back in the past. Evolution of Western money resulted from the interplay between spontaneous private actions of businessmen and policies imposed by governments.

Because we cannot speak of "the" origin of money as a historically unique event, it is useful to examine the process by which so many different societies independently conferred monetary status on things which initially had value as commodities. The development of money in any society has reflected the existence of some social need plus some articles suitable to meet that need. To be suitable as money, a commodity would already have had to possess a high degree of acceptability among the members of the society. In addition, it should be durable, portable, and divisible. General acceptability might reflect the fact that the commodity was a useful article of virtually universal consumption. In pastoral societies, domestic animals often achieved this status. The use of cattle as a medium of exchange and store of value is commemorated in our vocabulary in such words as "pecuniary" and "capital." Tobacco in bulk achieved monetary status in colonial America and, in the form of cigarettes, enjoyed it again in Europe during and after World War II. General acceptability as money also often stemmed from the fact that the commodity was a symbol of wealth and prestige for the owner, perhaps because it was esteemed for religious or esthetic reasons. Such articles often had an advantage over utilitarian products, since they were usually durable and their enjoyment did not entail physical destruction. Gold and silver probably derived their monetary status from previous mystical and esthetic esteem. It is certain that they were regarded as precious metals in many societies independently—among the Incas and Aztecs, for instance, as well as the peoples of the ancient empires of the eastern Mediterranean.

Granted the existence of some commodity which enjoyed wide acceptance and which possessed other suitable characteristics, what social needs might induce people to use it as money? In some cases, people engaged in specialized occupations discovered the inconvenience of barter and turned therefore to an intermediary commodity. Such cases are illustrated by the commodity money of colonial America. Recognizable money systems have also been found in many primitive societies in which the pattern of specialization and exchange was determined by custom and status rather than by deliberate and conscious individual choice. Such societies have had little need for money to facilitate their economic operations—yet it has developed. Often a commodity of mystical or esthetic veneration became a commonly accepted and desired symbol of wealth and was transferred in social ceremonies attending marriage or as compensation for injuries. Ultimately, some members of the society engaged in specialized production and exchanged their product for the money needed for ceremonial use. In the end, the money may come to be used chiefly in market transactions rather than in ceremonies—but many primitive cultures do not get that far.[1]

Money in Primitive Societies   A few examples from anthropological studies will illustrate the pervasiveness of the evolution of nonutilitarian commodities into money even where the economic organization of the society does not seem to require its use.

1. Among many American Indian tribes, wampum of beads or shells was widely used. Because of its durable, portable, and divisible nature, this was well suited for monetary use. For the Indians, accumulation of wampum was an end in itself, since it was worn for decorative or religious purposes and its possession was regarded as conferring prestige on the owner. Although most of the economic activities of the tribes were performed on a collective basis through patterns based on tradition and status, individual trading to obtain wampum did occur. In the seventeenth-century American colonies, white settlers used wampum not only in trading with the Indians but to some extent in trading among themselves. Ultimately the whites developed cheap techniques for reproducing the beads, and the wampum lost most of its exchange value.

2. The Yurok Indians of northern California used as money dentalium shells, woodpecker scalps, and obsidian blades. These were highly charged

---

[1] See A. Hingston Quiggin, *A Survey of Primitive Money*, Methuen & Co., Ltd., London, 1949, especially pp. 3–12, 321.

with mystical and religious significance. Yurok mythology gave an important place to "the land where money makes its home." According to one anthropologist, "The persistence with which the Yurok desire wealth is extraordinary. They are firmly convinced that persistent thinking of money will bring it." [2] Money was used in market transactions, but its chief use was in ceremonies. When a person died, he was buried with money, which was expected to make his afterlife safe and happy. Injury by one person or clan to another might be compensated by payments in money, and a man was expected to pay money to his bride's family when he married.

3. Natives of the island of Yap in the South Pacific have a monetary system based on enormous round chunks of stone, resembling millstones in size and shape. These are prized for their appearance and serve as a visible index of the owner's wealth. They are used as a medium of payment for such specialized activities as fishing and carpentry, although most economic production is self-sufficient agriculture. Many stones are so large that transactions are carried on by exchanging the ownership of the stone rather than its physical possession. Although Western ways and moneys have influenced the life of the natives, they still value and use their stone money.

Money in the Societies of Antiquity The mainstream of the history of Western culture begins with the ancient societies of the Near East— Assyria, Babylonia, Persia, Egypt—which flourished in the period following 4000 B.C. Each of these achieved a high stage of development in economic productivity as well as in culture. They were fundamentally agricultural and drew their prosperity initially from the great fertility of the valleys of the Nile, Tigris, and Euphrates. At their peak, however, they possessed a high degree of urbanization, commerce, and manufacturing. In their early phases, these societies developed the principles of simple metallurgy, which not only brought a great advance in productive technology but also opened the way for widespread use of gold and silver. These metals appear as objects of esthetic and religious veneration early in the history of this area.

These great empires were not organized chiefly on the basis of free enterprise and market relationships but rested mostly on relations of a feudal or servile sort. Nevertheless, each contained a mercantile element and did rely to some extent on money. In particular, Babylonia had developed by 2000 B.C. a money system based on silver. No coins were used, and metal passed by weight. "Shekels" and "talents" were used as units of account; they were actually measures of weight which originated with grain. It is possible that standard ingots, stamped to attest their fineness, were used. Such use of metal was also practiced in Egypt, Greece, and among the He-

---

[2] A. L. Kroeber, *Handbook of the Indians of California*, Smithsonian Institution, Bureau of American Ethnology, Bulletin 78, 1925, p. 40; quoted by Quiggin, *ibid.*, p. 294.

brew tribes of the Old Testament. Much later, units of weight survived in such monetary units as the pound, livre, lira, penny, and mark. And in Babylonia, instruments resembling modern bills of exchange and drafts were in use, possibly for payments as well as credit.[3]

Coinage originated spontaneously in many places. Coins have been discovered which are over 5,000 years old. The earliest ones were irregular lumps of metal with some identifying mark impressed on them, which may have guaranteed fineness but not weight. The kingdom of Lydia in Asia Minor (land of fabled Croesus) produced such coins about 700 B.C. to promote the export of precious metals which it produced in abundance.

By that time there was under way a flourishing development of commerce and civilization in the territory touching the eastern Mediterranean. At first the dominant role was played by Phoenician and Syrian traders, but soon the predominance shifted to Greece. The merchants of that age were the direct predecessors of the modern businessman. Their commerce was profit-seeking and relatively unrestrained. These societies were not capitalistic, but a mixture in which feudal and traditional elements still figured prominently. Nevertheless, their production and commerce represented specialization and exchange of the sort for which money is extremely convenient, and it was from this point that money became firmly established in Western culture.

The Greek city-states generally adopted coinage systems in the sixth century B.C. which were well managed and produced an artistic product. Their coins, mostly of silver, were intended to be of uniform weight as well as fineness and were undoubtedly used in domestic transactions without the necessity for weighing at every exchange. However, Sparta for a time used a system of iron coins whose metal value was much below their money value. Greek merchants also used transferable book credits and promissory notes which may have passed as money.

Although some coinage was carried on by merchant groups for their own benefit, in most cases coinage gravitated into the hands of the political sovereigns. In part this was to protect the public interest, but chiefly it reflected the fact that coinage could be used as a source of revenue. The common practice of levying a charge for coinage is still referred to as "seigniorage." [4]

There were chronic difficulties in the way of achieving a circulation of uniform full-bodied coins which could pass without the need to weigh

[3] Paul Einzig, *Primitive Money in Its Ethnological, Historical, and Economic Aspects*, Eyre & Spottiswoode (Publishers), Ltd., London, 1949, pp. 211–215.

[4] In both Greece and Rome, there was a close affinity between coinage and religion. Images of gods were often used on coins, and coinage was sometimes controlled by priests. In fact, the word "money" derives from the fact that the Roman mint was located in the temple of Juno Moneta.

or assay them repeatedly. Private persons had extensive temptations and opportunities to counterfeit coins or to remove some of the precious metal from genuine coins by clipping, sweating, abrasion, hollowing, or other devices. During the ascendancy of Rome, debasement of the coinage became a common means for the political sovereign to meet large expenditures or to pay debts. Thus a given revenue collected in full-bodied coins could support a larger expenditure in debased coins if the latter could be passed at the former value. In the Roman Republic, plated coins were occasionally issued as a wartime expedient. Under the Empire, debasements became common in the second and third centuries. Fineness of coins was reduced until the "silver" coins contained only about 2 per cent silver.[5] When practiced surreptitiously, such debasement was nothing better than counterfeiting. During the later years of the Roman Empire, the coinage prerogative was held by many petty territorial rulers, and the coinage was continually debased until the economy became virtually reduced to a nonmoney basis.

Money in the Age of Feudalism, A.D. 500–1100 The decay of coinage and of the use of money was soon accompanied by the decay of commerce and of activity in which money was much needed. In the pattern of feudal society into which Western Europe evolved, the basic economic unit was the manor. Each manor was largely self-sufficient, and its internal relations of production and distribution were determined by status and custom. Trade and commerce declined with the collapse of the Roman Empire and received a *coup de grâce* when the spread of Islam cut off most of the trading communities around the Mediterranean. As Europe became predominantly moneyless and marketless, it also came under the church doctrine that any activity undertaken for the sake of profit was usurious and sinful.

The use of money continued to a small extent in transactions outside the manor—the commerce in silks and spices, the transactions of governments and church. Control of coinage was decentralized among feudal lords and widely abused.[6] Significantly, in the Byzantine empire of the East and in the lands under Islam, both commerce and the use of money were much more widespread. Both of these areas continued to rely on gold coins suitable for the large transactions of flourishing commerce, while Europe came to use silver coins almost exclusively.

Money in the Renaissance, A.D. 1100–1600 The revival of commerce and the rise of national states which proceeded after the twelfth century revived

[5] Arthur R. Burns, *Money and Monetary Policy in Early Times*, Alfred A. Knopf, Inc., New York, 1927, p. 424.

[6] Henri Pirenne notes one German prince who debased his coinage an average of three times a year during a reign of thirty-two years. *Economic and Social History of Medieval Europe*, Harcourt, Brace and Company, Inc., New York, 1937, p. 112.

the use of money. Gold coinage rose from its desuetude in Europe just as it was declining in the territories of Byzantium and Islam. The emergence of the absolute monarchs in Europe brought a gradual trend toward centralization of coinage authority, but it was only toward the end of this period that order began to emerge from the chaos of multiple denominations and issues and varying degrees of public and private debasement. A notable step was the effort of Elizabeth I in England to restore the value of the coinage in the sixteenth century.

The commercial revival which began in Italy also brought important developments in credit and abstract money. There the first recognizable banks were founded about the twelfth century. Their function was initially the traditional one of money changer. In almost all commercial centers, the circulation of coins included a diverse collection of issues in various states of decrepitude. The money changer made it possible for individuals to exchange one type of money for another. The earliest banks extended this principle by accepting deposits of coin or bullion and giving the depositor a credit in their books which he could transfer to another person. Such transfers conferred upon these early bank deposits the status of money, although as long as the banker retained all the coin and bullion deposited, his operation would have no significant effect on the quantity of money. Banking on this principle was highly convenient for a center of international commerce and was later embodied in institutions in such northern centers as Amsterdam and Hamburg. Such banks had no necessary relation to the operation of lending.

However, in Italy, Spain, and other southern commercial centers, the lending function developed along with that of money changing. Once the bank deposit became in itself an acceptable means of payment, the depositor did not need to withdraw his coin or bullion to make payments. Thus the bankers found it possible to make loans with a portion of their holdings of precious metal. Such loans brought an increase in the total supply of money, for the depositor retained a deposit credit, which he could spend by transferring it, and the borrower had metal money which he could readily spend.

Since the deposit credit was so acceptable as a means of payment, it soon occurred to the bankers that they need not lend out their gold and silver holdings at all! They could make loans at interest merely by creating deposit credits on their books in favor of the borrowers.

According to Professor Usher, banking in the Mediterranean countries had reached the latter sophisticated stage as early as the thirteenth century. However, early deposit banking was primitive in certain respects, for deposit transfer usually could be made only by oral order in person. It was not until about the sixteenth century that notes which could easily pass from hand to hand came into use. These developed in two important forms—the check, by which deposit credits could be transferred, and the demand note payable to bearer, which the banker might issue to depositors or borrowers.[7] With these developments, banking achieved substantially its modern character—a character which evolved through spontaneous commercial usage.

The early sixteenth century witnessed a great monetary revolution attending the discovery of the treasures of the New World. As precious metals poured in from Peru and Mexico, prices rose, the availability of money greatly increased, and commerce and industry were greatly stimulated. A great social change came about as many feudal obligations, originally expressed in terms of goods and services, were commuted into money terms. This hastened the decay of remaining feudal relations in Western Europe and accelerated the trend toward a market economy. The spread of money and monetary relationships contributed to the parallel development of personal liberty and of capitalism.

With the influx of treasure, the sixteenth century became an age of considerable monetary mysticism. Under the doctrines of bullionism and mercantilism, the major nations tried to manipulate their foreign relations so as to attract gold and silver and retain them. This objective was in part a rational attempt to avoid the depressing effects of deflation and keep business booming, but with many people it represented an irrational conviction that treasure constituted the ultimate wealth and intrinsically guaranteed their welfare. This obsession with precious metals manifested itself also in the great interest in alchemy—the attempt to transform base metals into gold.

The sixteenth century also witnessed the birth of the dollar as a monetary unit. The term was apparently an Anglicized version of a German name applied to a Spanish coin![8]

Money in the Seventeenth and Eighteenth Centuries By the seventeenth century the commercial center of gravity had shifted to the north of

---

[7] Abbott P. Usher, *The Early History of Deposit Banking in Mediterranean Europe*, Harvard University Press, Cambridge, Mass., 1943.

[8] The flood of treasure from America brought a strong infusion of Spanish coins into world commerce. As Professor Nussbaum puts it, "The most popular pieces, valued at eight reals . . . were termed 'pesos.' In English-speaking countries the pesos came to be called 'pieces of eight' or 'dollars.' Dollar is an anglicization of the German 'Thaler.' Thaler, again, is an abbreviation of 'Joachimsthaler,' Joachimsthal being a Bohemian county whose counts in 1517 produced the silver coin which gained wide reputation as the Joachimsthaler. Its pattern was adopted by the Reich, whence the 'Reichsthaler,' or in English, 'rix-dollar.' The rix-dollar, which developed into a standard type of European mintage, was of approximately the same size and silver content as the peso. The London dealers in foreign exchange extended the name 'dollar' to the peso, which became thereby the 'Spanish dollar.' " Arthur Nussbaum, *A History of the Dollar*, Columbia University Press, New York, 1957, p. 10.

Europe and brought with it the techniques of banking and finance prevalent earlier in the south. In England, banking evolved from the activities of the goldsmiths. They developed the practice of accepting deposits of coin or bullion for safekeeping and giving in exchange either deposit credits or redeemable paper receipts. Both the deposits and the receipts became acceptable media for hand-to-hand payments. Ultimately the goldsmiths discovered the possibilities of lending out the metal they had received, thus increasing the quantity of money. This development in turn yielded to the stage in which the loans were made directly in the form of deposit credit or paper notes. Banking development in seventeenth-century England was climaxed by the establishment of the Bank of England in 1694. However, coin remained the chief medium of circulation.

The seventeenth century was a period of currency disorders, but changes in values were unlike the debasements of earlier times. They were undertaken more commonly to ward off deflation when scarcity of money resulted from low production of metals or from trade imbalance. In coinage practices, systematic attention was now given to the ratio between gold and silver. Frequent changes in the relative market values of the metals gave rise to frequent changes in mint values, usually achieved by devaluing the monetary unit.[9] Use of debasement as a revenue source largely disappeared, partly because of the development of new ways of achieving the same results.

The seventeenth century witnessed the first direct issues of paper currency to finance government deficits. The British government issued a modest amount of Exchequer orders, which were government promissory notes and which were used by merchants for payments. In 1690 the colonial government of Massachusetts issued paper currency, and in the eighteenth century such paper furnished a major medium of payment in the American colonies.

More important for Britain, however, was the discovery that bank credit could easily be tapped to aid the government. The Bank of England was chartered in the first place so that the government could obtain a loan, and it continued to be a source of financial aid. Of course, when the government borrowed from the Bank, the latter would create deposits or notes to lend, and the money supply would be increased.

By the eighteenth century, the transition toward abstract money was well under way. Among merchants, the paper promissory notes of banks or merchants or deposit credits on the books of a bank or merchant, transferable by check or draft, had become major methods of conducting transactions. Since such money was easily created, it is not surprising that abuse occurred. The most notable example was found in the banking and commercial ventures of John Law, a Scottish adventurer, in France in 1718–

[9] B. E. Supple, "Currency and Commerce in the Early Seventeenth Century," *Economic History Review*, December, 1957.

1720. A runaway speculation developed in shares of Law's commercial ventures, to which he contributed by rapid expansion of deposits and currency through his bank. Ultimately this "Mississippi Bubble" collapsed amid great public outrage.

Money in the Age of Revolution and War, 1775–1815   The successive events of the American and French Revolutions and the Napoleonic Wars brought vast monetary upheavals and financial unsettlement in the United States, France, and Great Britain. The revolutionary governments in both France and America issued large amounts of paper money. In the United States, the large volume of issues caused prices to rise, and the money depreciated ultimately to the point of worthlessness. However, paper money had served to finance the transfer of needed resources to the government's disposal. After the war, economic depression led some states again to issue paper money; but influential public opinion was so hostile to the idea that the Constitution adopted in 1787 banned such state issues. Most people thought that Federal paper issues were also prohibited by implication.

In France, the revolutionary government issued paper "assignats," which were nominally claims against the vast lands and other property seized from the church and the aristocrats. After 1793, foreign wars and domestic upheavals caused excessive issues, and a rapid inflation of prices soon reduced the value of the assignats virtually to zero. Further issues ceased in 1797. Napoleon, who came to power in 1799, achieved the remarkable record of financing his foreign adventures while keeping the franc on a gold basis. He was aided in this by the credit facilities of the newly founded Bank of France.

During their worst moments of inflation, both France and the United States tried to curb depreciation by price fixing and by making the paper legal tender, with heavy penalties for refusal to accept it. These efforts were unsuccessful. Both countries emerged from the period with one notable achievement, however—both established decimal coinage systems which were vastly simpler for calculations than the involved relationships typified by pounds, shillings, and pence.

The British government also incurred heavy deficits in its wars with France in the period 1794–1815, but financed these by borrowing from the Bank of England. These loans resulted in the creation of bank notes and bank deposits, and before long the Bank was unable to continue to redeem these liabilities in gold and silver. By 1815, inflation carried British prices to a level double that of 1790. Even this, however, was mild by French or American standards. Britain was passing through the most rapid phase of the Industrial Revolution, and the increase in the quantity of money was met by an increase in the production of things to spend it on. All three countries demonstrated how variations in the quantity of money could be brought about through government deficit spending.

The Age of Sound Money, the Nineteenth Century   After Waterloo, Europe enjoyed a century free from major wars. Capitalism became the dominant pattern of economic life, and enterprise was liberated from feudal and mercantilistic restraints. The political trend was toward representative government and protection of individual liberties.

Although governments in Europe and America differed considerably in their economic roles, their monetary policies were based on some widely accepted principles. One principle was that the determination of the quantity of money was not an appropriate responsibility for government. Instead, each government was expected to establish a monetary unit to be defined in terms of gold and/or silver.

Full-bodied coins of precious metal were the foundation of the system. These were kept at par by free coinage, free movement in international trade, and freedom of melting. In this way each nation would find itself on a monetary "standard" which would fix its currency's value in terms of all others and thus provide a uniform international unit of pricing and means of payment. In each country, the quantity of money would be determined by the quantity of gold and would supposedly vary appropriately with changing economic circumstances. The world's money supply would be protected from rapid change. Governments should not, of course, issue paper currency. The experiences of the American and French Revolutions were endlessly cited as proof of this principle.

However, the economy might rely on the bank notes and deposits of private commercial banks (which became in fact the dominant media of business transactions in Britain and the United States). To guard against excessive creation of these types of money, the banks should be required to redeem their liabilities in coin upon demand and to confine their lending to short-term loans secured by goods already produced and moving from producer to consumer. Under these conditions, it was expected that variations in the money supply would be appropriate to the state of the economy.

There were varying attitudes toward the metallic standard itself. France and the United States experimented at length with bimetallism, in which the monetary unit was defined independently in gold and in silver. Gold and silver coins would circulate in a country simultaneously only if the prices of the two metals remained at a constant ratio to each other in the open market, and this they never did in the nineteenth century. Shifts in market price ratios often led to the disappearance of one metal or the other from circulation. England avoided this by maintaining the pound on a gold basis and by using silver coins which were worth less as metal than as money. Eventually the other countries followed suit, and by 1900 the gold standard was the accepted norm.

The nineteenth-century attitude toward money was paradoxical. It implied a fairly rigid restraint on the growth of the money supply just when the world's output was growing by leaps and bounds. In practice, the implied restraint was avoided by erecting an ever-growing superstructure of bank notes and deposits on the gold reserve. The notes and deposits were reconciled with the dogma of sound money by their convertibility into coin on demand, but the actual volume of coin in circulation was relatively small.

Not only did commercial banks provide the sort of growth in the money supply needed to keep pace with rising output, but they did this through the expansion of credit. The newly created bank notes and deposits went chiefly to entrepreneurs to finance expenditures on capital goods. As a result, the rate of economic growth was probably accelerated. However, slow growth in the money supply contributed to painful price deflation in the last half of the nineteenth century, and the peculiarities of fractional reserve banking and currency issue produced several severe monetary panics.

The Twentieth Century The composition of the money supply has not changed much in the United States and other industrial countries since 1900, but monetary systems have undergone vast transformation, from relatively automatic adjuncts of private commercial decisions to instruments of government economic control. The transformation was started by World War I and carried to conclusion by the world Depression of the 1930s.

World War I forced most of the belligerent countries to suspend temporarily the convertibility of paper currency and bank deposits into gold. Widespread experience with wartime inflation and postwar hyperinflation made most Europeans eager to return to the stability and discipline they associated with the gold standard. The return to gold was not easy to achieve—in Great Britain it imposed heavy deflationary pressures, leading to unemployment and social unrest after 1925. Britain and some other countries withdrew gold coins from circulation, but allowed the public to convert deposits and paper currency into gold bullion if they wished. Even so, countries' gold reserves were pitifully small in relation to their potential liabilities.

When depression struck in 1929, country after country was hit by panic demands to obtain gold in exchange for currency and deposits. Since there was nowhere enough gold, the major countries eventually had to abolish convertibility. But their struggles to stay on the gold standard as long as possible produced great economic harm. Countries tried to protect their gold reserves by tightening credit and reducing the quantity of money, thus worsening the economic downswing. And even after the downward movement had halted, gold-standard principles often blocked the adoption of expansionary measures to expand credit and create money through central-bank actions or government deficits.

As a result, the sound-money dogma was repudiated, and gold standards of the traditional type, allowing private citizens access to gold coins or gold bullion, were generally abolished. Control over the quantity of money became a matter for deliberate government action, designed to achieve a level of total expenditures appropriate for full employment. Further experience with inflation during and after World War II has altered the objectives of this policy somewhat but has not occasioned any marked retreat from managed money.

AMERICAN MONETARY EVOLUTION

Origins   There were no commercial banks in the American colonies, and government paper currency went into disrepute because of the inflation accompanying the Revolutionary War. The Constitution forbade state governments to issue paper currency or to make anything but gold and silver legal tender, while it authorized the Federal government to coin money and regulate its value. The Mint was established in 1792 and began turning out gold, silver, and copper coins. A contemporary observer might have been justified in believing that the country had been firmly committed to a regime of metallic money.

This was not the outlook of Alexander Hamilton, whose influence, as first Secretary of the Treasury, was predominant in the determination of financial policy. Hamilton was convinced of the advantages of commercial banks, and at his urging Congress in 1791 authorized the establishment of a "national" bank—the first Bank of the United States. Modeled after the Bank of England, this institution was expected to perform beneficial services through increasing the money supply, extending credit, and assisting the Treasury's financial operations.

State governments chartered other commercial banks, and soon the banking system was growing at a rapid rate. Crude as the early banks were by modern standards, they performed the functions which still constitute the essence of commercial banking—the extension of *credit* through the creation of *money*. Credit was eagerly sought by farmers and businessmen to make capital improvements which appeared so advantageous in an underdeveloped frontier economy. The money which banks created was at first generally in the form of paper bank notes, printed to the specifications of each bank, without standardization of size, design, or denomination, and issued to borrowers as the medium in which loans were made. Checking deposits became increasingly popular for business transactions, however, and banks began to make some loans by merely crediting borrowed sums to the deposit account of the borrower. By 1800 bank notes and deposits constituted a larger proportion of the money supply than did coin. Of course, the banks promised to redeem their notes and deposits in coin on demand, and they maintained cash reserves for this purpose.

War of 1812 The economy went through a series of violent financial disorders associated with the War of 1812. The charter of the Bank of the United States had expired in 1811, and Jeffersonian opposition forced it to close. State-chartered banks sprang up in great numbers. During the war, the government borrowed heavily from the banks, whose bank-note and deposit liabilities were so extended that many of them were forced to suspend the convertibility of their liabilities into coin. Suspension opened the way to further credit expansion, much of it coming from unchartered banks in frontier areas. The economy suffered from inflation of prices and from the disappearance of a satisfactory medium of payments.

Once the war was over, Congress attempted to clean up the monetary muddle by chartering a new, and larger, Bank of the United States in 1816. Instead of bringing matters under control, the Bank permitted credit to expand further, until international financial influences precipitated a serious financial panic at the end of 1818. Bank failures were widespread, agricultural prices fell heavily, and many borrowers—farmers and merchants—were forced into bankruptcy and foreclosure. The second Bank of the United States, which played a strongly deflationary role once the panic had begun, aroused bitter hostility in many quarters.

Jackson versus Biddle Once the most serious period of economic crisis was past, the second Bank took on a more constructive role. Under the leadership of Nicholas Biddle, it helped to uphold the quality of the bank-note circulation and to use credit creation to counteract disturbances arising both at home and abroad. This promising development did not last long. Andrew Jackson, who became President in 1829, brought with him a strong hostility to banks and especially the "national" bank. He vetoed an attempt to extend its charter, and the Bank became a major issue in the election of 1832. Jackson denounced the Bank as a tool of the rich and of foreigners and argued that it represented an excessive concentration of irresponsible power. Whether true or not, these arguments were politically persuasive. Jackson was triumphantly reelected, and the Bank was obliged to obtain a state charter in Pennsylvania to keep its commercial operations going.

Although Jackson's attack on the Bank was motivated by antagonism to banks in general, his policies had the effect of giving state-chartered banks greater freedom of operation. For the two Banks of the United States had helped to restrain note issue by the state-chartered banks. As custodians of Treasury funds, the "national" banks received notes of other banks, and by demanding prompt settlement in coin for these they were continually holding the banks to strict accountability.

Bank credit was expanding rapidly in the 1830s, because investment funds were pouring into the country from foreign investors attracted by canal projects and by the opening of new lands. The upsurge culminated in a serious financial panic beginning in 1837 and giving way to economic depression lasting well into the 1840s. The Bank of the United States finally failed in 1841, leaving a controversial heritage which still has historians arguing about its relative merits. The political verdict was unequivocal, however—central banking as an institution was thoroughly discredited. The United States went through the remainder of the nineteenth century without a central bank, and when one was ultimately created in 1913, it was very different from its predecessors.

State Banking   The demise of the Bank of the United States left the United States committed to a decentralized system of a multitude of local "unit" banks. By 1860 there were some 1,500 state-chartered banks, and nearly every one of these issued its own notes. In addition, more than 500 "private" banks operated without charters, secure in a common-law right to engage in deposit business as long as they did not issue notes.

This system had its advantages. It expanded the money supply rapidly enough to keep pace fairly well with the expansion of output and with the spread of a market economy. And the credit created by the banks helped to finance capital developments in industry, transportation, commerce, and agriculture which contributed to the growth of productivity.

However, decentralized banking had substantial disadvantages as well. Bank credit and money fluctuated too much over the business cycle, expanding unduly during booms and contracting excessively in recessions. Turnover among banks was too high, especially in the interior. In normal times it was easy to start a bank, but failure rates were often high. A currency composed of the unstandardized notes of hundreds of banks was unsatisfactory in many ways, especially in vulnerability to counterfeiting and fraud.

State governments experimented with a variety of banking policies in an effort to minimize these deficiencies. Some prohibited chartered banking entirely; others established banks owned and controlled by the state government. Between these extremes, many regulatory devices were used. Banks were threatened with heavy penalties for refusing to redeem their liabilities on demand. Some states imposed reserve requirements. Bank examinations were increasingly imposed to check on the honesty and solvency of bank operations.

One of the most provocative experiments, begun in the 1830s, was "free banking." This provided that charters would be issued almost automatically to any group of people who met certain minimum requirements. These usually involved some minimum initial cash capital and a requirement that bank notes could be issued only if the bank deposited with the banking authorities an equal (or greater) sum in Federal or state government securities. In this manner, it was hoped, easy entry into banking would enable bank credit facilities to expand, while the securities-reserve provision would ensure that holders of bank notes would be protected against loss.

Easy Credit versus Sound Money State regulatory policies were, how-ever, attempting to deal with an unusually difficult problem inherent in the nature of banking. On the one hand, the state governments wanted abundant credit to promote capital expenditures and economic improvement. On the other hand, they wanted sound money—convertible into coin, stable in value, widely acceptable—and sound banks, safe and honest. If the banks were given free rein to expand credit, they would also be creating money at a rapid pace, and danger of monetary disturbance would increase. If regula-tory policy stressed sound money at all cost, it might well result in drastic reduction in the supply of credit available.

The conflict between sound money and easy credit showed up most strongly in the persistent problem of bank *liquidity*. How much cash should banks maintain on hand to meet demands for payment? If they kept large cash reserves, their ability to expand loans would be correspondingly re-duced. If they kept small reserves, they would run the risk of being unable to meet demands for payment.

Unfortunately for the banks, the public's demands upon the banking system were far from stable. During periods of calm, banks might have little call for cash and could allow their reserves to fall to rather slender proportions. Then a period of disturbance might ensue, in which banks would be engulfed by unforeseen demands for cash. Prior to the establish-ment of the Federal Reserve System, there was no source from which the banking system as a whole could obtain more cash to meet the upsurge of demand. Instead, the country was periodically ravaged by financial panics, like those we have noted in 1818–1819 and 1837–1839.

The Civil War The financial upheavals associated with the Civil War brought far-reaching changes to the American system of money and bank-ing. To finance the vast increase in Federal spending, Congress authorized the issue of Federal paper currency—greenbacks. These could not be kept at par with gold, but were made legal tender. In 1863, to help promote the sale of bonds and to reduce the disorder of the monetary system, Congress also created the national banking system. The Federal government was author-ized to grant charters to individual commercial banks, provided they met certain minimum standards with respect to capital, reserve requirements, and loans. National banks were authorized to issue a new kind of bank-note currency, uniform for all banks and backed by the goodwill of the govern-ment. However, for every dollar of these national bank notes issued, the banks had to deposit $1.11 of Treasury bonds with the banking authorities.

No bank was forced to join the national system. But a heavy tax was imposed on bank-note issues by nonnational banks, and most of the former state-chartered banks did obtain national charters in the mid-1860s.

Postwar Currency Controversies The financial policies of the Civil War caused a substantial rise in prices. When the war ended in 1865, the prin-

cipal forms of money—greenbacks, national bank notes, and bank deposits—
were no longer at par in gold. For the next thirty years, the country experienced a series of bitter national controversies over the composition of
the money supply and over the relative roles of gold and silver. At first, the
chief dispute concerned a return to the gold standard on the prewar basis.
This was opposed by farmers and businessmen who feared it would involve
a contraction of money and credit and thus would cause economic distress.
Eventually the dollar was restored to gold convertibility on prewar terms
(in 1879).

By that time, attention had shifted to dispute over the role of silver
money in the system. Coinage of silver dollars had virtually ceased during
the war and was not resumed afterwards. Silver production had increased
greatly, and silver producers sought the restoration of the guaranteed
market which coinage had formerly offered. They were joined by many
people, especially farmers, who were being adversely affected by declining
prices and who conceived of expanded silver coinage as a means for increasing the supply of money and, they hoped, giving them improved selling
prices and higher money incomes.

These monetary controversies waxed and waned with the state of the
business cycle. During periods of depression, they came to the fore, to re-
cede into the background when more prosperous conditions returned. The
silver dispute reached its climax as a result of the financial upheavals and
depression of 1893–1896. In 1896, William Jennings Bryan and the Democratic party based their principal electoral appeal on expansion of the silver
money circulation. Bryan lost by a narrow margin, in part because business
conditions had begun to improve even before the election. The alleged shortage of money began to disappear in the face of increased output of South
African gold. A long period of price deflation which had been under way
since 1865 reversed itself. The currency controversies largely evaporated
under the golden sunshine from the "Rand."

Banking Developments　The establishment of the national banking system did wonders for improving the quality of the nation's bank-note circulation. It also raised standards of bank examination and contributed to a
lowering of rates of bank failure. But it had two major deficiencies. First,
it placed the national banks under very rigid restrictions with respect to
their ability to extend credit—most notably, national banks could not make
mortgage loans. Second, the national banking system did not provide any
"lender of last resort"—any source from which the banking system as a
whole could obtain additional cash in a crisis.

The restrictions imposed on national banks soon led to renewed growth
of banks outside the national system—state-chartered banks and, in impressive numbers, private banks operating without charters. Nonnational

banks could no longer issue notes, but found it possible to operate on the basis of deposit business alone. By meeting the credit needs which national banks could not serve, nonnational banks expanded in number until they outnumbered national banks two to one by 1900. In the process, they helped carry bank deposits to the predominant position in the money supply which they hold today.

The failure to provide a source of additional cash for the banking system as a whole was reflected in the repeated experience with financial panics. A financial crisis in 1907 finally aroused public opinion sufficiently to bring congressional action, culminating in the Federal Reserve Act of 1913. After nearly eighty years, the country once again had a central bank.

We shall describe the evolution of the Federal Reserve System more fully in subsequent chapters. Here it will suffice to say that the new central bank was authorized to issue its own paper currency—Federal Reserve notes —and to make loans to commercial banks in a manner which would, it was hoped, enable them to obtain currency in a crisis.

The Great Depression It would be nice to be able to stop here and say "they lived happily ever after," but they didn't. The newly created Federal Reserve System exerted influences on monetary and banking conditions which were little foreseen by its creators and often not well understood by its managers. Most seriously of all, it failed to cope with the financial crisis of 1929–1933. Thousands of banks failed, and monetary and credit conditions aggravated the economic calamity instead of alleviating distress.

As a consequence, the structure and powers of the Federal Reserve System were extensively revised. A program for Federal insurance of bank deposits was established. The spirit of free banking, which had been sustained for nearly a century in such forms as easy entry into the banking business, freedom to operate banks without charters, and lax regulation of chartered banks, was now decisively brought to a halt. Banking in particular and financial business in general became subject to extensive government controls.

The structure of the American monetary, banking, and financial system remains very much in the pattern into which it was cast by the Depression experience. Little structural change has occurred in the Federal Reserve System since the 1930s. However, its function has become principally to maintain continuous control of the supply of money and credit to keep the flow of aggregate spending at an appropriate level.

Our commercial banking system is composed mainly of banks which survived the Depression—three-fourths of present-day banks were established prior to 1930. We still have a "dual" banking system consisting partly of national and partly of state-chartered banks, but the differences in their powers and responsibilities, which were so pronounced in the late nineteenth century, have been greatly reduced. In addition, virtually all commercial banks have come under Federal authority through the influence of the Federal Reserve and the Federal Deposit Insurance Corporation.

Gold   The Depression also brought about the present-day arrangements with respect to the monetary role of gold. Gold coins were withdrawn from circulation, and convertibility of currency and deposits into gold was terminated. Indeed, domestic private ownership of gold, except for jewelry and other manufacturing or artistic uses, was made illegal, and gold transactions were subjected to licensing restriction by government. Transactions in monetary gold became in practice an affair between the Treasury and foreign governments and central banks. Gold lost virtually all significance as an element in the domestic monetary situation, but remained an important medium for international financial transactions.

American Experience in Review   It is useful to note the recurrent influences which have shaped American monetary experience. One of the foremost has been war. The Revolutionary War brought the flood of paper-money issues; the War of 1812 led directly to the establishment of the second Bank of the United States; the Civil War produced the greenbacks and the national banking system. As we shall see later, the wars in which the United States has been involved in the twentieth century have greatly influenced the functioning of the monetary system, if not its structure.

A second important influence has been the business cycle, and particularly business depressions. Popular discontent has frequently led to changes in the monetary and banking system, either to remedy depression or to prevent its recurrence. Hostility aroused by the depression of 1819–1822 had much to do with the ultimate overthrow of the second Bank of the United States, while the depression of 1907–1908 resulted in the restoration of central banking in 1913. The far-reaching impact of the Depression of the 1930s has already been noted.

Finally, one cannot overemphasize the importance of the prominent monetary role of commercial banking, characterized by the uneasy coexistence between credit extension and money creation. By accepting the principle that money creation was an appropriate source of credit for capital expenditures, Americans probably gained a more rapid rate of economic growth, but suffered a greater degree of economic instability than might have occurred under a "hard-money" system. Much effort was expended in trying to reconcile easy credit with monetary stability, and there was a tendency to swing from undue emphasis on one to excessive stress on the other. Since the reforms of the 1930s, a better reconciliation of the two has emerged, though it is still not completely satisfactory.

Contemporary Money   At present, the money of the United States consists of coins and paper currency issued by the Treasury and the Federal

Reserve banks, plus the checking deposits of over 13,000 commercial banks. The metal coins represent the smallest denominations and are the only portion of the money supply which has any commodity value. For a long time, none of our circulating coins were full-bodied, but in the early 1960s, a pronounced rise in the market price of silver brought it up nearly to its monetary value, and American silver dollars thereby became approximately full-bodied. The proportionately smaller silver content of lesser silver coins thereby rose to about 90 per cent of their monetary value. The use of coins has increased substantially with the spread of parking meters and vending machines—the latter reporting $3 billion in sales transactions in 1963. Despite expanded production by the mints, periodic shortages of small coin were reported in the early 1960s.

Coin and currency are used chiefly in payments of wages and in retail transactions. They possess the advantage of universal acceptability and are subject to minimal risk from forgery or counterfeiting. However, use of coin and currency does entail risks of loss or theft, particularly when mailed. The use of checking deposits possesses advantages and disadvantages complementary to those of coin and currency. Checks are not legal tender, and there are many occasions on which a person may be unable to cash or make payment with a check. Risks of forgery or fraud are somewhat higher. In compensation, however, the risks from loss or theft are minimal for checking-deposit funds. Checks can be conveniently used for payments of large sums and of odd sums. Checks are well suited for payment by mail. Moreover, the canceled checks which are returned to the depositor provide him with receipts for payments made and with a record of his transactions.

The public is free to decide what proportion of its money it wishes to hold in coin and currency and in checking deposits. In reflection of the advantages just noted, the public has elected to hold about four-fifths of its money in checking deposits. It is estimated that about 90 per cent of the dollar volume of money transactions in the economy consists of check payments. In 1962 Americans wrote about 14 billion checks to make payments totaling $3,700 billion. Since we rely so extensively on bank deposits as money, variations in bank lending are an important influence on the money supply. However, the Federal Reserve now possesses means to control the volume of bank lending.

Importance of the Quantity of Money In the nineteenth century and in earlier times, money was highly visible. When its quantity changed substantially, people were aware of the fact. It was not difficult to connect the great increases in the quantity of money attending the Revolutionary and Civil Wars with the price inflations experienced in those times. Similarly, the large contractions of bank credit and bank notes were obviously contributors to business depressions. Not surprisingly, informed opinion in the nineteenth century stressed the causal role of money in economic instability.

As time passed, however, a number of circumstances tended to blur this perception. Visible money, in coin or paper currency, became a proportionately smaller element in total money. And the corresponding rise of bank deposits to monetary predominance was accompanied by increasing stress on bank credit, stress placed in ways which directed attention away from the quantity of money. Various qualitative standards arose, designed initially to provide appropriate variations in the quantity of money, but tending ultimately to divert attention from it. One element stressed that "sound" money must be convertible into gold on demand, while another stressed the desirability that bank loans be channeled into short-term "productive" uses as opposed to "investment" and "speculation."

These qualitative standards developed in the search for an automatic monetary system in which deliberate government management of the quantity of money would be avoided. The qualitative standards and the general principle of automatic monetary operation were discredited by the Depression of the 1930s. Yet paradoxically, the Depression gave rise to new attitudes which also tended to attribute a less than major role to the quantity of money. One contributing feature was the alleged failure of monetary ease and low interest rates to stimulate private investment spending and bring prosperity in the 1930s. Another was the spread of concepts of economic analysis popularized by John Maynard Keynes and his followers. Emphasis shifted away from the quantity of money as a prime source of economic instability and tended to concentrate instead on variations in business profit expectations. In the policy sphere, stress shifted from control of the quantity of money to fiscal policy—deliberate management of government revenues and expenditures—as a means of influencing the money flow.

By the mid-1960s, however, a substantial shift was evident in economic analysis, bringing a reassertion of the great importance of the quantity of money. Advocates of the "new quantity theory" did not claim that the expenditure flow was simply proportional to the quantity of money. They pointed out that variations in the *rate of change* of the quantity of money have been followed by similar variations in the rate of change of expenditures in a great variety of times and places. They challenged the view that the 1930s proved monetary policy to be ineffective against depression, criticized the tendency for Keynesian analysis to misplace emphasis, and maintained a skeptical attitude toward fiscal policy.

Despite their differences of opinion concerning the quantity of money, most economists would agree about the general manner in which the money supply changes and by what linkages these changes are connected with the expenditure flow. The next group of chapters explains the manner in which changes in the money supply occur. Then in Part Three we analyze the determinants of the expenditure flow and the manner in which the money supply affects it.

SUMMARY

In any society, money is an institution which must be consistent with other social usages and which may arise spontaneously from such usages. The evolution of money has included the following stages:

1. Primitive money, often items of religious or esthetic value, used first perhaps in ceremonial exchanges in a society where commercial specialization and exchange did not exist.

2. Precious metal by weight, probably developing from primitive esteem for ornament and ceremony, but requiring some techniques of assay and measurement. This stage was reached by the ancient empires of the Near East before 1000 B.C.

3. Full-bodied coins, representing metal marked to attest its weight and fineness. These became common in Greece and other Mediterranean commercial centers after 700 B.C.

4. A mixed system including coins and abstract money in the form of transferable private debts. This order existed to some degree in antiquity, but its modern significance dates largely from the Renaissance.

5. Abstract money in the form of paper currency and bank deposits, together with some coins of less than full weight. This is the modern system, brought into existence largely during the Depression of the 1930s.

Equally important have been the evolutionary changes in the manner in which the quantity of money might vary. In the eighteenth and nineteenth centuries, for instance, the money supply of Western countries was subject to determination by free-market forces affecting the supply of precious metals and the volume of bank credit, with occasional crosscurrents (usually of a disturbing sort) arising from government measures of war finance. Since the Depression of the 1930s, however, governments have assumed control of the quantity of money as a means for avoiding economic disturbance.

The monetary history of the United States has been strikingly affected by the predominant role of commercial banks. The effort to reconcile sound money with easy credit, however, created many problems, which were particularly evident in periodic panics and crises relating to bank liquidity. The Federal Reserve System was founded in 1913 to provide a source of funds for the banking system as a whole, and since the 1930s it has assumed a larger role as the chief agency by which the government regulates the money supply and the banking system. It is only recently, however, that emphasis among economists and policy makers has shifted to give increased prominence to the influence of money on expenditures. This influence tended to be downgraded by "qualitative" emphasis prior to 1929 and by the experience and intellectual innovations of the Depression of the 1930s.

QUESTIONS FOR STUDY

1. Why is a 50-cent piece worth 50 cents if it contains only 45 cents' worth of silver?

2. "Money can exist without commerce, but commerce tends to create its own money." Illustrate historically.

3. Suppose the alchemists had succeeded. What would the consequences have been?

4. Discuss the appropriateness of including each of the following in the measurement of the money supply:

  a. Travelers checks sold by banks or American Express
  b. Obsolete United States coin and currency (which the Treasury will redeem at par in current money)
  c. Subway tokens
  d. A United States savings bond, redeemable on demand
  e. A perfect counterfeit $10 bill

5. During much of American banking history, banks were under great pressure to maintain easy credit, needed for the development of the nation's economy. The banks extended credit by creating money in the form of bank deposits and, in earlier times, bank notes. Do you believe it was possible, merely by creating new money in this fashion, to cause an increase in the nation's stock of real capital goods? Why did maintenance of easy credit conditions tend to conflict with the ability of the banks to provide "sound money" of relatively stable quantity which was convertible into coin on demand?

SUGGESTED READINGS

Angell, Norman: *The Story of Money*, Garden City Books, New York, 1929.

Burns, Arthur R.: *Money and Monetary Policy in Early Times*, Alfred A. Knopf, Inc., New York, 1927.

Einzig, Paul: *Primitive Money in Its Ethnological, Historical, and Economic Aspects*, Eyre & Spottiswoode (Publishers), Ltd., London, 1949.

Jevons, W. Stanley: *Money and the Mechanism of Exchange*, Appleton-Century-Crofts, Inc., New York, 1883.

Nussbaum, Arthur: *A History of the Dollar,* Columbia University Press, New York, 1957.

Sutherland, C. H. V.: *Gold: Its Beauty, Power, and Allure,* McGraw-Hill Book Company, New York, 1960.

Trescott, Paul B.: *Financing American Enterprise: The Story of Commercial Banking,* Harper & Row, Publishers, Incorporated, New York, 1963.

part two

THE MONETARY SYSTEM
OF THE UNITED STATES

chapter three

COMMERCIAL BANKS AND
THE MONETARY SYSTEM

MEASURING THE MONEY SUPPLY AND ITS COMPONENTS

Issues We have defined money in terms of its functions—it is "that which" serves the functions of medium of payment and unit of account. In the contemporary United States, these functions are performed by coins, paper currency, and the checking deposits of commercial banks. Checking deposits are included because they can be spent directly, by writing checks on them, without the need to convert them into coin and currency. We do *not* include in the money supply such liquid financial assets as savings (time) deposits or government bonds. While these can be converted into cash readily, they cannot be spent directly. Further, in order to measure the quantity of money held by the public, it is customary to exclude currency and deposits held by the Federal Treasury. Coin and currency held by commercial banks are excluded, as are the deposits which some banks maintain with other banks.

After these adjustments, we are left with a money supply consisting of the coin, currency, and demand deposits of business firms, individuals, state and local governments, foreigners, and nonprofit institutions. We shall call this the public's money supply, or the privately held money supply. At times, however, we shall wish to use a more inclusive measure which contains Federal government cash and deposits also; it will always be specially identified when used. Table 3-1 shows the size and composition of the money supply in June, 1964.

Table 3-1   The public's money supply, June 30, 1964
(Billions of dollars)

	Amount	Per cent
Demand deposits	$123	79
Coin and currency	33	21
Total	$156	100

Detail of coin and currency outside Treasury and Federal Reserve:

	Treasury issue	Federal Reserve issue	Total
Coin	$3	—	$ 3
Currency			
$1–$10	2	9	11
$20–$50	—	15	15
$100–$10,000	—	8	8
Total	$5	$32	$37
Held by banks			$ 5
Held by public, as above			$33

Source: *Federal Reserve Bulletin*, August and December, 1964. Obsolete Treasury currency is excluded. Details may not add to totals because of rounding.

Checking deposits make up nearly four-fifths of the public's money supply. Their attractiveness is greatly enhanced by the deposit insurance program of the Federal government, which insures each account up to $10,000.

About $32 billion of the money supply consisted of paper currency, most of it in the form of Federal Reserve notes. The Treasury also issues currency in the smaller denominations, in the forms of silver certificates and United States notes. In 1963, however, Congress authorized the gradual withdrawal of silver certificates and their replacement by Federal Reserve notes.

Although the government has the power to determine the size of the total money supply, the preferences of the public determine the division between bank deposits on one hand and coin and currency on the other. In Chapter 4 we shall explain the mechanics of currency issue by the Federal Reserve and the Treasury.

Holders Most of the money supply was held in the cash balances of business firms and individuals, as shown by the data on cash holdings in Table 3-2.

Table 3-2 Holders of the money supply, December, 1963
(Billions of dollars)

	Amount	Per cent
Households	$ 75	50
Financial business	13	8
Nonfinancial corporations	29	19
Unincorporated businesses and farms	18	12
State and local governments	14	9
Foreign	2	2
Total	$151	100

Source: Federal Reserve Bulletin, October, 1964. The figures for households include a small amount for nonprofit institutions as well.

Consumer households held just about half of the public's money supply, with business firms and farms accounting for slightly under 40 per cent. Households held about two-thirds of the coin and currency, which are used chiefly in wage payments and retail transactions.

In Chapter 9, we shall analyze the motives for holding cash balances and the way in which the economy adjusts so that the sums people are willing to hold will equal the amount of money available to hold.

COMMERCIAL BANKS AND THE MONEY SUPPLY

Introductory Because checking deposits are the dominant element in our money supply, we shall begin our examination of the behavior of the money supply with the banks. The term "commercial bank" is applied to all banks which provide checking-deposit facilities for their patrons. We shall deal in detail with the structure and functioning of commercial banking in Chapter 12. Here we need summarize only a few basic facts about commercial banks in the United States, as follows:

1. Banks are business firms operating for the sake of profit.
2. There are a lot of banks in the United States—about 13,500 in 1963.
3. Many of these banks are relatively small, and each operates offices within a limited geographical region.
4. One-third of the banks are "national" banks, holding charters issued

by the Federal government, while two-thirds hold charters from individual states. However, even national banks are restricted to offices within one state.

5. Slightly fewer than half of the banks are "member banks" of the Federal Reserve System (about 6,100 in 1963), a classification which includes all national banks and such state banks as choose to join. Member banks account for five-sixths of bank resources, since nonmember banks are relatively small in size.

Bank Deposits   Commercial banks provide a useful service for the economy through the management of checking deposits, with their well-known advantages of safety and convenience. Deposit management puts the banks in the role of bookkeepers for the economy. Checks and bank statements serve business firms and individuals as valuable instruments in financial record keeping. Furnishing this service requires much bookkeeping by the banks themselves. Indeed, the management of checking deposits is essentially a process of bookkeeping operations by the banks.

To understand this, one must have a very clear understanding of what a bank deposit is. It is *not* a warehouse receipt showing that the bank has an equivalent amount of coin and currency in its vault ready for demands. Although the demand deposit is a promise to pay coin and currency on demand, it is a promise which banks make in the expectation that they will not be called on to fulfill it to any great extent at any one time. When this expectation has been disappointed, disastrous results have sometimes occurred.

The term "deposit" is unfortunate, for it implies a reference to "that which has been placed," whereas it is essential to distinguish between the deposit credit and the thing deposited. A deposit credit may come into existence through the depositing of coin and currency, but from then on credit and cash can go their separate ways. The original deposit credit may remain after the cash has been lent out, like "a grin without a cat."

The deposit itself is a claim against the bank by the depositor, a debt owed by bank to depositor. This claim is valuable to the depositor, not chiefly because it can be converted into cash, but because it can be transferred to others as a means of payment. Receiving and paying out coin and currency constitute only a small part of bank business compared with the transfers by check.

In a sense, the deposit is a state of mind—an expectation by the depositor, a readiness by the banker. The extent of the banker's readiness to honor the checks or withdrawal slips of a depositor will be determined by entries written in the books of the bank. In an important sense, Joe Doakes's checking account consists of the entries under his name.

Since the deposit credit is fundamentally a bookkeeping entity, the changes which occur in any deposit account when funds are added to it or checks drawn against it take place through changing figures in the books of the banks. The commonest changes are those in which a sum is subtracted from one account and added to another. This is easy to visualize when it all takes place in one bank. Suppose, for instance, that a business firm in a small town pays its employees by check, and most of them deposit their checks in the same bank where the firm has its account. The bank will deduct the amount of each check from the firm's account and add it to the account of the employee who deposited it. At the end of the month, all the checks written by the firm will be recorded on a statement, along with deposit credits. The canceled checks and statement will be sent back to the firm and will provide an accurate record of expenditures, as well as a set of receipts for the individual wage and salary payments.

Clearing and Collection of Checks Where several banks are involved, this process of adding and subtracting becomes somewhat more complex. Many check payments go to people who do not have accounts in the same banks on which the checks are drawn. What happens, for instance, when a check drawn on a New York bank is deposited in a bank in Chicago? Once deposited, the check becomes the property of the Chicago bank, which is entitled to collect the sum involved from the New York bank. One way of collecting would be to send a man to New York with a sack to cash the check and bring the proceeds home in currency. A century ago this was often the only means available for settling such accounts. Nowadays the problem is dealt with by means of a process of "clearing." The Federal Reserve operates a nationwide clearing system, but many banks also participate in local clearinghouses. Each bank presents to the clearinghouse the checks it has accumulated against the others. Most of the claims against each bank are offset by claims it has against the others. Ultimately a balance is struck by the clearinghouse, and some banks will end up as net debtors and must pay the amount of their deficiency into a common pool. This money is then divided among the banks which had a net surplus. Since every check is a net credit for one bank and an equal claim against another, total claims must equal total credits, and the whole process comes out even.

A large part of check clearing goes directly through the Federal Reserve banks, and they are likely to be involved even where local clearinghouses are used. Each member bank of the Federal Reserve System maintains a bank account with its regional Federal Reserve bank. These accounts are counted as legal reserves. They serve as a medium through which the Federal Reserve can influence the operations of commercial banks. An understanding of the relation of these accounts to the clearing process is a necessary preliminary to a discussion of Federal Reserve techniques.

When a bank receives checks drawn on other banks, it can collect these by sending them to the Federal Reserve, which will add the amount of the checks to the reserve account of the commercial bank. The Federal Reserve will in turn deduct the amounts of the checks from the reserve accounts of the banks against which they are drawn. Then it will send the checks to the latter banks. The actions of the Federal Reserve resemble the actions of the commercial bank in our payroll example above.

Since checks will be moving in both directions, the net change in any bank's reserve account will be the difference between the checks credited to its account (those against other banks) and those charged against its account (deposited by other banks). When checks are cleared through a local clearinghouse, the debtor banks are likely to settle their debts by paying with checks drawn against their reserve accounts with the Federal Reserve. The result is the same as if the clearing had gone through the Federal Reserve. The debtor banks' reserve accounts are reduced, and the corresponding amounts are added to the accounts of the creditor banks.

Checks drawn on nonmember banks can also be cleared through the Federal Reserve banks. A few nonmember banks (about 100 in 1963) maintained deposit accounts with the Federal Reserve banks for clearing purposes. Most commonly, however, nonmember banks keep funds on deposit with city banks which are members of the Federal Reserve System. Checks drawn on the nonmember bank are sent from the Federal Reserve bank to the city "correspondent" bank, which in turn charges them off against its country cousin's account. However, the Federal Reserve will not clear checks for "nonpar" banks—that is, for banks which make any sort of deduction from the face value before paying a check. In 1963 there were still some 1,600 banks which followed the practice of deducting "exchange" charges when paying checks (by contrast with the more customary practice of levying service charges against the depositors who write the checks). The nonpar banks are commonly small banks in small towns. Checks drawn on them must be returned through *ad hoc* arrangements among other commercial banks.

CREATION OF DEPOSITS

Relation of Deposits to Loans Managing existing checking deposits is an important economic function of banks, but it is not the most important of their activities, either from their own viewpoint or from that of the economy as a whole. A commercial bank is a business firm operating for profit. While banks do make service charges for handling checking accounts, these do not yield any great profits. Banks obtain the bulk of their profits by making loans at interest or by buying and holding interest-bearing securities.

The great economic significance of bank lending stems from the fact that banks can create deposits in the process of making loans or buying securities. This is quite at variance with the popular notion that banks expand their loans by lending out funds received through deposits. For the banking system as a whole, it is commonly the loans which give rise to the deposits, rather than the reverse.

Since all checking deposits consist of entries in the books of the banks, one might say that all deposits are "created" by the bank when it makes the appropriate entries. Of course, entries are not made capriciously. A depositor's balance will be increased when he has brought in coin, currency, or checks. In such cases a sum of deposit credit has been "created," but the aggregate money supply remains unchanged, since there is an equivalent decrease either in the coin and currency outside the bank or in some other deposit account.

The bank can also increase the amount of a depositor's account when it makes a loan to him or buys securities from him. In order to lend Joe Doakes $1,000, a bank needs only to credit his account with $1,000 in its books by a stroke of the pen. The bank will still receive something of value in exchange for the deposit credit—the customer's IOU, or an interest-bearing security. This kind of deposit creation increases the total money supply.

The process of creating deposits is obviously a simple and painless one for the banks. What is to stop them from expanding their deposits extensively in order to make more profits for themselves and to extend the blessings of credit to everyone?

The bank can be expected to exercise some restraint merely from motives of prudent self-interest. If it is to remain *solvent,* its total assets must exceed its liabilities. It will be reluctant to make loans unless repayment is reasonably certain. If a bank is to be sufficiently *liquid,* it must have a sufficiently large proportion of its assets in the form of cash or its equivalent in order to pay the claims of depositors. They may want currency or, more frequently, will write checks which are deposited in other banks and returned through the clearing process for payment. A banker will be reluctant to increase his deposit liabilities unless he is confident of having enough currency or reserve deposits to pay such claims.

However, at present, such voluntary restraints are eclipsed by the fact that banks are subject to legal *reserve requirements* imposed by the Federal Reserve authorities (for member banks) or by state governments (for nonmember banks). These requirements limit the amount of deposits to a certain multiple of reserves by requiring a certain amount of reserves for each dollar of deposits.

The Balance Sheet To understand the relation of bank reserves to loans and deposits, we must analyze the balance sheet of the banks. A balance sheet is simply an orderly listing of all the assets and liabilities of a business firm or individual. "Assets" consist of anything of value owned by the firm, including "real" assets such as machinery and buildings, or financial assets such as cash, securities, or debts owed *to* the firm. "Liabilities" consist of all the debts owed *by* the firm. Since bank deposits are debts owed by the banks, they appear as liabilities on bank balance sheets. (Of course they are assets to the depositors.)

If the firm under study is solvent, the value of its assets will exceed the liabilities against it. The excess of assets over liabilities is called the "net worth" of the firm and represents the ownership claim or *equity* in the firm. If the firm is a corporation, the net worth is the "book value" of the stockholders' property. The net worth is also referred to as "capital and surplus"; it includes the funds actually paid in by stockholders when the stock was issued, plus increases in the value of the firm resulting from the reinvestment of the firm's profits.

The balance sheet possesses a most important property: By definition,

Assets = liabilities + net worth

A change in the amount of one item in the balance sheet must be matched or offset by a change in one or more of the other items.

A consolidated balance sheet for all commercial banks in the United States as of June, 1964, is shown in Table 3-3.

Table 3-3   Assets and liabilities of United States commercial banks, June 30, 1964 (Billions of dollars)

Assets		Liabilities and capital	
Coin and currency	$ 5	Demand deposits (adjusted)*	$123
Reserve deposits with Federal Reserve banks	17	Time deposits	119
Deposits with other U.S. commercial banks	13	Deposits of other U.S. commercial banks	13
U.S. government securities	59	U.S. Treasury deposits	11
Other securities	36	Borrowings†	2
Loans	164	Miscellaneous	9
Miscellaneous	9	Net worth (capital and surplus)	27
Total	$303	Total	$303

* Demand deposits adjusted equals total demand deposits of $142 billion minus $19 billion of checks and other cash items in the process of collection.
   † Includes $0.1 billion debt to Federal Reserve banks.
   Source: Federal Reserve Bulletin, December, 1964. Details may not add up to totals because of rounding.

Before we proceed to examine the process of deposit creation in detail, a few general observations are in order about the data in Table 3-3.

1. Actual coin and currency in the vaults of commercial banks is only a microscopic fraction of banks' deposit liabilities. The liquidity of the bank-

ing system is protected primarily by the ability of the Federal Reserve System to create and issue additional currency as needed.

2. Banks' capital accounts are relatively small compared with assets and liabilities. Most bank assets are offset by deposit liabilities.

3. Most bank assets consist of *earning* assets—loans and securities account for about $259 billion, or about 85 per cent, of the $303 billion of listed assets. Coin, currency, and reserve deposits yield no income to banks.

4. The claims of depositors against the banks are "backed up" chiefly by the debt claims of the banks against their borrowers. Thus, the largest element of our money supply rests upon a structure of debts.

Time Deposits Strictly speaking, time deposits represent funds which depositors agree to leave on deposit for a certain length of time. These include negotiable time certificates of deposit, which can be bought and sold among private holders, but which the bank will redeem only after a specified period of time. More loosely, the category also includes savings deposits. Technically, banks have the right to insist on advance notice of withdrawal. In practice they do not ordinarily do this, so that savings deposits can generally be withdrawn on demand.

Despite their differences, these various kinds of time deposits are alike in that they bear interest (subject to maximum limits set by the Federal Reserve). They are not subject to transfer by check and are not included in the customary measures of the money supply. Banks are prohibited by law from paying interest on demand deposits.

Reserves and Reserve Requirements Commercial banks are required by law to hold reserves equal to some specified fraction of their deposit liabilities. Originally, reserve requirements were imposed to protect bank liquidity—their ability to pay depositors on demand—but the requirements have come to serve primarily as a means of controlling the supply of money and credit. Assets which are acceptable for meeting legal reserve requirements are sometimes called "primary reserves." Member banks of the Federal Reserve System must hold their required reserves in the form of coin and currency in vault or deposits with Federal Reserve banks. Requirements for nonmember banks vary from state to state; they generally permit required reserves to be held on deposit with other commercial banks. Because of the dominant position of member banks, our analysis will concentrate on them.

Reserve requirements for member banks are higher for banks in major cities (so-called reserve cities) than for country banks, and higher for demand deposits than for time deposits. Federal Reserve authorities are authorized to raise or lower the requirements within a limited range. The range of discretion and requirements in effect in 1964 are shown in Table 3-4.

Compliance with reserve requirements is determined on the basis of figures averaged over a week or two, not for each day taken separately. Thus a bank can offset an excess of reserves one day against a deficiency on another. A financial penalty is assessed for reserve deficiency. Individual

Table 3-4   Member bank reserve requirements, 1964

	"Reserve city" banks	Country banks
Demand deposits:		
Discretionary range	10–22%	7–14%
Requirement in effect June, 1964	16½%	12%
Time deposits:		
Discretionary range	3–6%	3–6%
Requirement in effect June, 1964	4%	4%
Number of banks in classification	209	5,970
Assets of banks in classification	$158 billion	$104 billion

Source: *Federal Reserve Bulletin*, August, 1964.

banks faced with potential reserve deficiency often resort to short-run borrowing to obtain additional reserves. They may borrow from the Federal Reserve banks or from other commercial banks which have more reserves than they need. There is an active market for loans of so-called Federal funds—deposits with the Federal Reserve banks.

A bank can treat its reserve deposit much as an individual can treat his demand deposit in a commercial bank. A bank's reserve deposit can be increased if the bank deposits coin and currency or checks drawn on other banks. The commercial bank can withdraw coin and currency from its account or write checks on it. However, the bank's reserve account can also be increased if the Federal Reserve makes a loan to the bank or buys securities from it. Since the reserve deposit consists essentially of entries in the books of the Federal Reserve, changes in reserves merely involve bookkeeping changes.

Excess Reserves and Credit Expansion   Let us examine a numerical example illustrating the calculations of required and excess reserves. Suppose the Mudville National Bank has the following balance sheet:

Assets		Liabilities and capital	
Reserves	$11,000	Demand deposits	$25,000
Loans and securities	39,000	Time deposits	20,000
		Net worth	5,000
Total	$50,000	Total	$50,000

If we assume that reserve requirements are 20 per cent for demand and 5 per cent for time deposits, we can ascertain the amount of reserves this bank must hold, as follows:

$25,000 demand deposits at 20%	$ 5,000
$20,000 time deposits at 5%	1,000
Total required reserve	$ 6,000
Actual reserves	$11,000
Less required reserves	6,000
Excess reserves	$ 5,000

The Mudville bank has more reserves than it needs. Its total reserve requirement is only $6,000, leaving it with $5,000 of excess reserves. The Mudville bank can therefore legally increase its deposit liabilities by making more loans or buying more securities. Furthermore, it will normally want to do so, in order to increase its profits. But how much can it expand? What limitations will it encounter?

Suppose it decides to make a loan of $5,000 to a local merchant and does so by adding $5,000 to his checking account. This raises total checking deposits to $30,000. To balance this, there must be an equal increase in the bank's assets, which occurs through the increase in loan assets. The balance sheet now looks like this:

Reserves	$11,000	Demand deposits	$30,000
Loans and securities	44,000	Time deposits	20,000
		Net worth	5,000
Total	$55,000	Total	$55,000

The bank has created demand deposits and thus increased the supply of money. What does this increase in deposits do to the reserve position of the bank? Since it has increased its deposit liabilities by $5,000, its required reserve increases by 20 per cent of this, or $1,000. This brings its total required reserve to $7,000, leaving $4,000 of excess reserves. So far, therefore, it appears that the bank is not in danger of running out of reserves, and it might feel free to expand loans still further.

Presumably, however, the borrower wanted the $5,000 to spend, not merely to hold. When he spends the money, one of three possibilities may occur: (1) He might make a payment to another depositor of the same bank, (2) he might make a payment to a depositor of another bank, or (3) he might withdraw coin and currency. The effect on the Mudville bank will depend on which of these occurs.

1. If the money is paid to other depositors of the same bank, its total deposit liabilities are not affected. The amount subtracted from the borrow-

er's account is added to others, and the bank's balance sheet remains unchanged. It still has $4,000 excess reserves and can expand its loans further.

How much further could the Mudville bank expand if it could be sure that all the newly created deposits would stay with it? It would be limited only by the reserve requirement. Of the total reserves of $11,000, the bank needs $1,000 as reserve for time deposits, leaving $10,000 to support demand deposits. On this base it could support $50,000 of demand deposits. To put it another way, the bank has excess reserves of $4,000, on which it could support $20,000 of additional deposits. Accordingly, under the assumption that deposits remain in the bank, it could expand its demand deposits and loans by a multiple of its excess reserves, the multiple depending on the percentage reserve requirement. However, the assumption is not very realistic.

2. It is more likely that the borrower will write checks which will be deposited in other banks. Suppose the merchant who borrowed $5,000 wrote a check for that amount which was deposited in a Chicago bank. That bank would send the check through the Federal Reserve for collection. The Federal Reserve would add $5,000 to the reserve account of the Chicago bank and deduct that amount from the reserve deposit of the Mudville bank. The check would then be returned to the Mudville bank, which would deduct $5,000 from the borrower's account and return the canceled check to him.

Consequently, the Mudville bank's reserves are reduced by $5,000 (leaving $6,000), while demand deposits are also reduced by $5,000 (leaving $25,000). We know from our original calculations that $6,000 is just enough reserve to support the remaining deposits—thus the Mudville bank is just in equilibrium. It expanded its loans and deposits by the amount of its excess reserves ($5,000) and lost both the new deposits and the excess reserves as a result. Hence the loss of new deposits to other banks drastically reduces the expansion potential for the Mudville bank looked at in isolation.

3. It is also possible, though unlikely, that the borrower will take the proceeds of the loan in coin and currency. If this flows back into the Mudville bank again, the effects are the same as in case 1. If the coin and currency remain outside the bank, the result is similar to case 2. Withdrawal of coin and currency reduces the Mudville bank's reserves. However, this third case differs from case 1 in its effects on other banks, as we shall explain more fully below.

Balance Sheet Equilibrium   It is useful to think of each bank as tending toward an equilibrium in the general structure of its balance sheet. The equilibrium pattern must conform, first of all, to requirements imposed by law and by regulatory authorities. Second, it will be influenced by the general state of the economic environment—by the willingness of the public to hold demand deposits, time deposits, or coin and currency, and by demand for loans by creditworthy borrowers. Within these limitations, each bank attempts to adjust its assets and liabilities in order to achieve its objectives of long-run survival and profitability.

We shall not attempt at this point to explore all the balance sheet relationships relevant to banks' pursuit of profits. Instead, we shall concentrate here on a general relation among three balance sheet elements: bank reserves, earning assets, and deposits.

Cash and reserve deposits yield no income to the banks, but they do provide liquidity. However, there are available other assets, particularly short-term government securities, which also provide liquidity (that is, they can be exchanged for cash on short notice with minimum risk of loss), but which in addition yield income. Such interest-bearing liquid assets are sometimes called "secondary reserve" assets. Under conditions prevailing since World War II, commercial banks have had very little incentive to keep more funds in primary reserves than are required by law. Even when they desire more liquidity than their primary reserves furnish, they have found it more advantageous to hold interest-bearing secondary reserve assets instead of excess primary reserves which earn no income.

We can use this information to state two useful propositions about the balance sheet equilibrium, as follows:

1. A bank will be in equilibrium when its excess reserves are equal to zero; it will not be in equilibrium if it has any substantial amount of excess reserves or deficiency of reserves.

2. A bank with excess reserves will, as a rule of thumb, add to its earning assets by extending loans or buying securities by an amount equal to its excess reserves.

The second proposition is implicit in our analysis of the Mudville bank above. It reflects the fact that a bank can afford to create new deposits equal to its excess reserves even if the new deposits are all withdrawn and take an equal amount of reserves with them. Sometimes, of course, not all the loan proceeds are withdrawn from the lending bank. Banks often require that borrowers keep a certain proportion of their loans on deposit with the lending banks (so-called compensating balances). In practice, this requires no change in the rule of thumb.

EXCESS RESERVES AND CREDIT EXPANSION BY THE BANKING SYSTEM

How Reserves Move Around For the individual bank, the most significant limitation on its ability to expand is usually the loss of reserves to other banks through check clearing. For the banking system as a whole, however, this is not a limitation. One bank's loss of reserves is another's gain. Transfer of reserves from bank to bank may slow down the expansion process and spread it over a wide area, but if all banks have the same reserve requirements, the shifting does not reduce the overall potential for expansion. Only the drain of coin and currency and the legal reserve requirements remain as external limitations on expansion. Thus the banking system as a whole can expand more on a given amount of excess reserves than can one bank. To illustrate how this can occur, let us pick up the narrative back at case 2. The Mudville bank, with $5,000 of excess reserves, expanded its loans and demand deposits by $5,000. The newly created deposits were then checked out and came to roost, let us say, in a Chicago bank. That bank would credit the deposit of the person bringing the check in and then send the check to the Federal Reserve for collection. As we noted, the Mudville bank emerges from the transaction shorn of its newly created deposits and its excess reserves. The Chicago bank, however, has gained the deposits and has the $5,000 of reserves credited to its account by the Federal Reserve. Its balance sheet is altered as follows:

Chicago bank	
Reserves +$5,000	Demand deposits +$5,000

The increase in demand deposit liabilities increases the required reserve which the Chicago bank must hold by $1,000. In addition, since its actual reserves have increased by $5,000, excess reserves are increased by $4,000. This provides it with the basis for expanding loans by the same amount. If it makes the additional loans, its balance sheet will be further altered thus:

Chicago bank	
Reserves +$5,000 (as above) Loans + 4,000 (new)	Demand deposits $\begin{cases}+\$5,000 \text{ (as above)}\\ + 4,000 \text{ (new)}\end{cases}$

Let us assume again that the borrower writes a check with the proceeds of his loan which is deposited in another bank, say, in Denver. The Denver bank will credit the depositor's account with $4,000 and send the check to the Federal Reserve for collection. The Federal Reserve will add $4,000 to the Denver bank's reserve account and subtract the same amount from the reserve account of the Chicago bank. Then the check is returned to the Chicago bank, which deducts the $4,000 from the borrower's account and returns the canceled check to him. When the process is completed, the balance sheets of the two banks will show the following changes:

Chicago bank	
Reserves +$1,000 ($5,000 − $4,000)	Demand deposits +$5,000 (original)
Loans + 4,000	

Denver bank	
Reserves +$4,000	Demand deposits +$4,000

The Chicago bank now retains just enough reserves to meet the requirement for $5,000 of deposits. So far as this series of transactions is concerned, it has no excess reserves (in other words, no more than it had to start with) and therefore cannot expand loans further.

The Denver bank finds itself with deposits and reserves increased equally by $4,000. Since its required reserve increases by only $800, the Denver bank acquires $3,200 of excess reserves and can expand its loans by that amount. If it does so and the proceeds are again checked out to another bank, say in Los Angeles, its final balance sheet will look like this:

Denver bank

Reserves +$ 800 ($4,000 − $3,200)	Demand deposits +$4,000
Loans + 3,200	

The Los Angeles bank would in turn receive $3,200 of additional deposits and reserves, which would give it excess reserves and lending power of $2,560. And so on, ad infinitum.

The student can now recognize that we have been describing a sequence of events which has the mathematical characteristics of an infinite geometric progression in which the successive increments grow ever smaller. Such a series approaches a finite limit. If we summarize the way it operates, this will be apparent. This is done in Table 3-5.

Table 3-5   Credit expansion by the banking system

Bank	Final increase in deposits		Final increase in reserves	
	One bank	Cumulative	One bank	Cumulative
Chicago	$ 5,000	$ 5,000	$1,000	$1,000
Denver	4,000	9,000	800	1,800
Los Angeles	3,200	12,200	640	2,440
Subsequent bank	2,560	14,760	512	2,952
Subsequent bank	2,048	16,808	410	3,362
Next five banks	5,500	22,307	1,100	4,461
Next five banks	1,805	24,112	361	4,822
Next five banks	603	24,715	121	4,943
Other banks	285	25,000	57	5,000
Total	$25,000		$5,000	

Note: Dropping fractions produces slight rounding discrepancies.

The cumulative totals show how the expansion of deposits starts out rapidly and then tapers off and approaches the limit. Although technically the limit is never reached, for all practical purposes the sequence is complete by the time twenty banks have been involved. The formula for the sum of a series of this type is $S = a/(1 - x)$, where a is the first term ($5,000) and x is the ratio of any term in the series to the one preceding—in this example, $\frac{4}{5}$. Thus the sum of the first column is $5,000 ÷ $\frac{1}{5}$, or $25,000.

For each bank the final increase in deposits is just five times the final increase in reserves. This is just sufficient to use up all the excess reserves and leave each bank in equilibrium, and the sum of the increases in reserves ultimately equals the amount of reserves which the Mudville bank lost to start the expansion process. Thus the successive expansions of the various banks have had the effect of dealing out the original excess reserves until they have all become the backing for deposits. When all the excess reserves have been used up in this way, the expansion halts. Finally, the ultimate increase in demand deposits made by the banking system as a whole is just equal to the increase which could have been made by the Mudville bank if all its deposits remained with it instead of being checked out. This shows how the loss of reserves through the clearing process limits the expansion of one bank but not the expansion of the banking system as a whole.

Expansion Coefficients   From the foregoing example one can derive a formula to measure the expansion potential of the banking system for a given amount of reserves. Letting A stand for the amount of excess reserves and R for the fractional reserve requirement, the total of additional demand deposits D which the system can support is given by

$$D = \frac{A}{R}$$

This could be applied to the foregoing example by substitution, so that $D = \$5,000/0.20 = \$25,000$.

The formula shows the permissible expansion of demand deposits provided the amount of reserves remains unchanged. In practice, an expansion of bank loans and demand deposits is likely to induce certain other changes which will affect the expansion. In particular, additional coin and currency will tend to be drawn into circulation, reducing bank reserves correspondingly. If we assume the public wants to hold a constant proportion between added demand deposits and added currency, currency outflow can easily be incorporated into the analysis of expansion coefficients.

For illustration, let us assume that the public holds currency equal to one-fourth its demand deposits and that the reserve requirement for demand deposits is 15 per cent. If the banks hold excess reserves and expand loans, what will happen to the excess reserves as lending expands? For every dollar of loan expansion, the public will hold 20 cents in currency and 80 cents in demand deposits. The 80 cents in demand deposits will require 12 cents in reserves. Thus each dollar of credit expansion by banks will eat up 32 cents of excess reserves—20 cents withdrawn in currency, and 12 cents tied up to back additional deposits. If we let R stand for the total absorption of reserves entailed for each dollar of money, we can use the same formula as above. That is, the expansion of the money supply possible with any given amount A of excess reserves is A/R. And the expansion coefficient to be applied to excess reserves is $1/R$. In our example, the coefficient is $1/0.32$, or 3.125. This is probably a realistic estimate for the United States monetary system in the mid-1960s.

We can illustrate the final outcome in balance sheet terms. We assume that the banks held $1,000 of excess reserves initially. Our coefficient indicates they should be able to expand their loans and securities by $3,125. Initially, of course, this expansion will be made by creating demand deposits. But the public wishes to hold one-fifth of its funds in currency and will thus draw out $625 in cash, reducing holdings of added demand deposits to $2,500 ($= 4 \times \$625$). The final balance sheet changes look like this:

Assets		Liabilities	
Reserves	−$ 625	Demand deposits	+$2,500
Loans and securities	+ 3,125		
Total	+$2,500	Total	+$2,500

Bear in mind that the total increase in the money supply consists of both the (net) increase in demand deposits and the additional currency in circulation. This total of $3,125 equals the increase in loans and securities.

What about Time Deposits? The analysis of expansion coefficients could be extended further by incorporating variations in time deposits. This would be useful if the public attempted to maintain a relatively stable proportionality among holdings of currency, demand deposits, and time deposits. Incorporating time deposits into the formula does not appreciably change the coefficient for expansion of the money supply. But it does cause a divergence between the absolute growth of money and the growth of bank loans and securities. Bank earning assets rise by more than the money supply, the difference reflecting growth of time deposits.[1]

There is no doubt that time deposits grow over time, but much doubt that this growth is determined by the rate of expansion of demand deposits, particularly in the short run. Rather, expansion of time deposits appears to depend on levels of income and saving and on interest rates on various types of savings assets.

There is another reason for not worrying too much about the formal

[1] Analysis of expansion coefficients can be carried much further along the lines we have suggested above. One can incorporate a range of financial institutions other than commercial banks as well as giving separate attention to different classes of commercial banks with different reserve requirements. For an example, see James M. Henderson, "Monetary Reserves and Credit Control," *American Economic Review*, June, 1960.

incorporation of time deposits. The size of the expansion coefficient may be less important than its stability over time. If we assume that reserve requirements and public asset preferences are constant, a very important result follows: Whatever the percentage rate of change in reserves, that same rate of change will appear in the money supply and in bank earning assets. The absolute changes in money and credit will, of course, be larger, but these differences in size tend to be played down by increasing stress placed on rates of change by the new quantity theory.

Even if we leave time deposits out of our formal analysis of expansion coefficients, we should not neglect the fact that changes in reserve requirements on time deposits, and variations in asset preference by the public, may affect the *amount* of banks' excess reserves and thus their expansion opportunities.

Shifts in Public's Asset Preference   Variations in the public's allocation of funds among currency, demand deposits, and time deposits can have substantial influence on bank reserve positions. Shifts between demand deposits and time deposits have occurred in response to variations in interest rates. For instance, in 1962 the Federal Reserve substantially raised the maximum interest rate permitted on commercial bank time deposits. Offers of higher rates soon resulted in a substantial rise in holdings of time deposits. A shift of funds from demand deposits to time deposits would increase banks' excess reserves by the difference in reserve requirements for the two deposit categories. For instance, a shift of $1,000 from demand deposits requiring 15 per cent reserves to time deposits requiring 5 per cent reserves would add $100 to excess reserves.

Bank reserve positions are also affected by shifts between deposits and currency. For instance, the relative desire for currency increased greatly during the financial panic of the early 1930s because of distrust of banks. Another increase accompanied World War II, arising in part from considerations of income tax evasion. Such drains of currency can cause substantial contraction of money and credit, as analyzed in the next section.

Credit Contraction   So far our discussion has dealt with credit expansion made possible by excess reserves. Much of the same analysis applies to credit contraction when reserves are deficient, but the situations are not wholly analogous. In particular, when they have excess reserves, the banks *may* expand credit. But when reserves are deficient, they *must* act, either to obtain more reserves or to reduce their deposit liabilities.

As an illustration, suppose the Mudville bank is in equilibrium, with reserves just sufficient for existing deposits, when it is subjected to an unexpected withdrawal of currency—say, $1,000. The net changes in its balance sheet look like this:

Mudville bank

Reserves —$1,000	Demand deposits —$1,000

This change reduces *excess* reserves by $800, since total reserves decline $1,000 and required reserves are lowered by $200 (assuming a 20 per cent reserve requirement).

There are a number of ways in which the Mudville bank can attempt to remedy the deficiency. If it has loans maturing—and most banks do try to keep maturities staggered—the bank can insist on repayment and refuse to relend the money. Suppose it receives repayment of $800 of loans. Will this remedy the deficiency? It all depends.

First, there is the possibility that local borrowers may repay by writing checks on their accounts in the Mudville bank itself. Demand-deposit liabilities go down by the amount of loans repaid in this manner, but the bank gains no additional reserve funds. If all the loans were repaid in this manner, the result would be as follows:

Mudville bank

Reserves —$1,000 (as above)	Demand deposits —$1,000 (initial)
Loans —800	—800 (loans repaid)

The Mudville bank will have to go a lot further if it is to remedy its difficulties by this route. Reducing demand-deposit liabilities cuts back its required reserves by $160, but this leaves a deficiency of $640. If the Mudville bank can collect only from its own depositors, it will have to collect on another $3,200 of loans before its deficiency is eliminated.

The Mudville bank will have a much easier time if it can succeed in having its loans repaid in currency or in checks on other banks. Perhaps it may attempt to achieve this result by selling securities to other banks or to their depositors. Every dollar obtained in this manner will increase the Mudville bank's reserves, so that it will need only $800 acquired in these forms to meet its initial reserve deficiency. Its final resting place would look like this:

Mudville bank

Reserves —$1,000 (initial change)	Demand deposits —$1,000 (initial)
+800 (from loan repayment)	
Loans —800	

Most commonly, this result would arise from repayment of loans with checks drawn on other banks. Suppose the Mudville bank receives a check for $800 drawn on a Chicago bank. Depositing the check with its Federal Reserve bank gives the Mudville bank a transfusion of $800 of reserves, and it is back in equilibrium.

However, this may mean only that the disequilibrium has been passed on to the Chicago bank, which loses $640 in *excess* reserves from the transfer of $800 in demand deposits and in total reserves to the Mudville bank.

If the Chicago bank is obliged to curtail loans, the process keeps on spreading.

If the banks have no excess reserves to start with and if each one attempts to remedy its deficiency of reserves by reducing loans and selling securities, it may take as much as a $4,000 curtailment of loans and demand deposits to meet a reserve deficiency which was initially only $800. The situation is now similar to the case where the Mudville bank received payment in its own checks. For the banking system as a whole, no increase in reserves takes place. Therefore demand deposits must be reduced by five times the deficiency. Since some banks will have excess reserves to start with, this may provide a cushion. Also, there may be some flow of coin and currency into the banks, providing additional reserves. However, there have been periods of panic when just the opposite occurred—coin and currency were withdrawn out of distrust for the banks just when they were under pressure to contract anyway.

Credit contraction on a wide scale can be an unpleasant affair, contributing to depression and unemployment. It was chiefly to avoid such possibilities that the Federal Reserve System was formed, and at present the facilities of the Federal Reserve provide means whereby banks can meet reserve deficiencies without disrupting the economy. The Federal Reserve banks can create additional reserves for banks by making loans to them or buying securities from them or their depositors, or they can relieve pressure by reducing the percentage reserve requirements. By such means the banks can obtain needed cash and still meet reserve requirements. The ability of the Federal Reserve to create cash and bank reserves is a vital safeguard against runaway panics and excessive contraction of credit.

Factors Affecting Reserve Positions The amount of reserves which banks have is subject to constant variation because of a number of forces. An inflow of currency from the public will increase bank reserves; an outflow will deplete them. Bank reserves may also be affected by the operations of the Federal Reserve and the Treasury. If the Federal Reserve makes a loan to a bank, it will add the sum to the bank's reserve account. When the Federal Reserve buys government securities from banks or other investors, bank reserves usually increase. When gold is imported or mined and sold to the Treasury, bank reserves normally increase. We shall analyze these transactions in detail when we discuss the role of the Federal Reserve and the Treasury in our monetary system. Such transactions place the dollar volume of bank reserves very much under the control of the government and provide ways in which reserves can be manipulated to produce the desired effects on the economy.

Changes in reserve requirements will also affect the expansion potential of the banks. We can illustrate this by returning to our original balance sheet for the Mudville bank.

Reserves	$11,000	Demand deposits	$25,000
Loans and securities	39,000	Time deposits	20,000
		Net worth	5,000
Total assets	$50,000	Total liabilities	$50,000

With reserve requirements of 20 per cent for demand deposits and 5 per cent for time deposits, the Mudville bank had a total required reserve of $6,000, leaving excess reserves of $5,000. For the banking system as a whole, these excess reserves could support up to $25,000 of additional demand deposits.

Suppose, however, that the Federal Reserve increased the reserve requirements for demand deposits to 25 per cent. Required reserves would thereby be increased by $1,250 ($25,000 × 0.05), so that excess reserves would fall to $3,750. Furthermore, the expansion potential would be reduced by the fact that each $1 of excess reserves can now support only $4 of demand deposits. Therefore the maximum expansion potential for the banking system as a whole would be only $15,000 instead of $25,000. Increasing the reserve requirement thus affects the banks in two ways: It reduces the amount of excess reserves they hold, and it reduces the expansion potential of each dollar of excess reserves remaining.

Reducing the reserve requirement would, of course, increase the excess reserves of the banks and at the same time increase the expansion potential of each dollar of excess reserves. Figure out for yourself what would happen if the reserve requirement for demand deposits were reduced to 10 per cent with the above amounts of deposits and total reserves. However, the magnitude of these effects is much less impressive if we use expansion coefficients which allow for currency withdrawals.

BANK ASSETS

Uses of Bank Credit So far we have treated only one aspect of bank assets—the relation between primary reserves and earning assets. Within the category of earning assets, however, the banks hold a great variety of types of loans and securities and furnish credit for a great variety of uses. A detailed listing of commercial bank loans and securities is given in Table 3-6.

Banks furnish substantial credit to all major nonfinancial sectors of the economy—consumers, business firms, farms, and governments—as well as financial businesses such as stockbrokers, mortgage companies, and finance companies. Banks' decisions about the composition of their assets may have substantial effects on the allocation of resources between consumption and investment. They can influence the allocation of capital funds among the industries of the country and can affect the kinds of capital which are acquired. Access to bank credit by new firms or small firms can intensify the degree of competition within an industry. For all these reasons, the operations of commercial banks have important implications for the growth and efficiency of the economy. These aspects of bank operations will be examined in more detail in Chapter 12.

Table 3-6   Commercial bank loans and securities, June, 1964
(Billions of dollars)

Loans:		
Commercial and industrial	$55	
Agricultural	8	
For purchasing or carrying securities	8	
To banks	3	
To other financial institutions	10	
Residential mortgages	28	
Other real estate loans	14	
Consumer installment loans	23	
Other loans to individuals	15	
Miscellaneous	4	
Total loans		$168
— Reserve against defaults		3
= Net loans as in Table 3-3		164
Securities:		
U.S. government		
3-month bills	$ 8	
Others due in less than 1 year	7	
Longer maturities	45	
State and local governments	31	
Other securities	5	
Total securities		$ 96
Total loans and securities		$260

Source: Federal Reserve Bulletin, December, 1964. Details may not add to totals because of rounding.

However, one aspect of the composition of bank earning assets is relevant at this point. We have already noted that banks protect their liquidity by holding a certain amount of secondary reserve assets—low-risk, short-term interest-bearing assets. In Table 3-6, the most prominent asset of this type is Treasury bills, of which the banks held about $8 billion. Almost as good are other United States government securities due to mature within a year. Besides these, banks consider as secondary reserves some of their business loans. "Commercial paper" and "acceptances" are technical names for two types of business IOUs which possess high liquidity. Like Treasury bills, they are virtually free from risk of default and have short maturities. Further, like Treasury bills they are bought and sold extensively, so that a holder who needs cash in a hurry can always sell such assets to another investor. Because of the short maturities, the prices of such assets fluctuate very little.

Assets such as Treasury bills, commercial paper, and acceptances are widely held by nonfinancial businesses and other investors who have need for liquidity but want to earn some income as well. The extensive buying and selling of such assets is often called "the money market," and they are considered money-market assets.

Why dwell on this phenomenon here? Because these money-market assets have a second sort of significance for the economy. They exist in a relatively large floating supply, most of which is held outside the banks. When banks acquire more money-market assets as secondary reserves, they usually buy them from other investors, directly or indirectly. Such acquisitions are frequently not associated with increased spending by the borrower on currently produced goods and services. By contrast, ordinary business and personal loans by banks do commonly go to finance purchases of current production.

It makes no difference in the size of the money supply whether banks lend to spenders or buy secondary reserve assets. But such asset choices may affect the *velocity* of money—the rate at which money circulates through the economy.

The banks may react to changes in reserves by changing the composition of their assets also. If banks receive additional reserves, their initial response is likely to be to reduce their debt to other banks or to the Federal Reserve. After that, remaining reserves are likely to be used to acquire additional secondary reserves. Then the banks will gradually expand their other loans and securities. Loans are the "bread and butter" of banks, and most bankers acknowledge a sense of community obligation to accommodate their borrowers. Nevertheless, loans expand slowly because it takes more time to process them and because the banks want to be sure the reserve increase is not just a transient phenomenon. This pattern means that there may be a delay before reserve increases cause an increase in active money.

Adjustment to contraction is likely to follow a parallel path. Initially, banks may adjust by borrowing from the Federal Reserve or from other banks. In a short time, the burden of adjustment will shift to secondary reserve assets, which may be sold or allowed to mature. In the long run, if necessary, other loans and securities will be reduced.

SUMMARY—COMMERCIAL BANKS AND THE MONEY SUPPLY

Commercial bank checking deposits are the largest element in our money supply. Banks can create deposits by bookkeeping entries when they make loans or buy securities. Individual banks are limited in their capacity to create deposits by the drain of funds into other banks or into circulating

cash. The banking system as a whole is limited by legal reserve requirements, which allow banks collectively to create demand deposits equal to a
multiple of their reserves. The ability of banks to expand loans and deposits
is thus limited by the reserve position of the banks, which depends partly
on the amount of reserves they have and partly on the amount of reserves
required to maintain existing deposits. The reserve position of the banking
system is determined partly by actions of the Federal Reserve and the
Treasury. These agencies influence the supply of reserves by their own acquisitions of assets; in addition, the Federal Reserve determines the member bank reserve requirements. Banks' reserve positions are also affected,
however, by the preferences of the public for currency, demand deposits,
and time deposits.

The commercial banks are the medium through which most changes in
the money supply take place. How close the connection is can be judged
from Figure 3-1, which compares the year-to-year absolute changes in the
money supply and in commercial bank loans and securities. The broad contours of the two show obvious similarities. However, no constant proportionality exists between the two, and at times they even move in opposite
directions.

Two broad problems for further investigation are suggested by the
relationship displayed by Figure 3-1. To the extent that changes in the

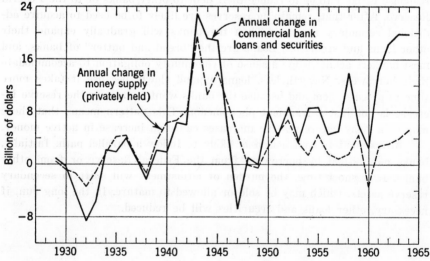

Figure 3-1. Year-to-year changes in the money supply and bank credit from June to
June, 1929–1964.

Sources: Milton Friedman and Anna Jacobson Schwartz, *A Monetary History of the United
States, 1867–1960; All-bank Statistics; Supplement to Banking and Monetary Statistics:
Banks and the Monetary System; Federal Reserve Bulletin,* June and August, 1964.

money supply result from variations in bank earning assets, how can those variations be explained? The immediate cause, of course, is variation in bank reserve positions. But what causes those? The answer includes some items already discussed—changes in the public's holdings of currency and changes in legal reserve requirements. But we still need to deal in detail with the important influence of the Federal Reserve and Treasury on the total amount of bank reserves.

Second, to the extent that variations in bank credit do *not* correspond to changes in the money supply, what factors account for divergence? Again, we have already noted some of these. Variations in bank credit may be absorbed by variations in time deposits—the chief source of discrepancy in the period 1954–1964. Treasury deposits may play a similar role, as in World War II and in 1950.

However, there are factors other than commercial bank credit which can affect the money supply directly, chiefly Federal Reserve dealings in securities and Treasury gold transactions. Thus a full explanation both of the money supply and of bank reserves requires us to explore the operations of the Treasury and the Federal Reserve. After that, we shall examine the interlocking workings of the monetary system as a whole.

QUESTIONS FOR STUDY

Assume that all banks are members of the Federal Reserve System and are subject to reserve requirements of 20 per cent for demand deposits and 5 per cent for time deposits.

1. The following items might appear in a consolidated balance sheet for all commercial banks. Arrange them in proper balance sheet form. Determine the size of the capital and surplus item. (Assume there are no items other than those listed.)

	Millions
Cash and reserves	$ 7,000
Demand deposits	20,000
Loans	9,000
Securities	10,000
Capital and surplus	?
Time deposits	5,000

Compute the amount of required reserves, excess reserves, and the amount by which the banks could expand their loans on the basis of existing reserves. Define each item in the account.

2. Compute the direct effects of each of the following on the dollar volume of bank reserves, the public's money supply, and the unused lending power of the banking system as a whole. Assume that all payments are made by check unless otherwise specified. Ignore borrowing by banks, and assume no effects on time deposits and currency unless specified.

 a. Banks lend $1 billion to business firms.

 b. Individuals repay $2 billion of bank loans.

 c. Individuals invest $1 million in the capital of a new bank.

 d. Individuals withdraw $2 billion coin and currency from

   (1) Demand deposits

   (2) Time deposits

 e. Individuals shift $1 billion from demand to time deposits.

 3. Using the figures in problem 1, compute the effect on excess reserves and lending power if the reserve requirement for demand deposits were increased to 25 per cent; if the requirement for time deposits were reduced to 4 per cent.

 4. Analyze the following statements:

 a. "Banks do not create money; they merely lend out money which is deposited with them."

 b. "Banks can always meet demands for cash by calling in loans of an equal amount, which will replenish their reserves."

 c. "But the banks will not have to call loans, because they can always use their deposits and capital to meet the demands of depositors."

 d. "It is unfair to require banks to keep reserves in a form which earns no interest. They should be allowed to count government securities as reserves, since they can always be turned into cash."

 5. A bank robber is undecided which of two banks in a given town he should rob. Both are equally vulnerable to robbery, and he wants to pick the one with the most cash on hand. The window of one bank says "Deposits: $3,000,000." The other says "Capital and surplus: $500,000." Assuming each bank is typical, which will probably have more cash on hand?

SUGGESTED READINGS

American Bankers Association: *The Commercial Banking Industry*, Prentice-Hall, Inc., Englewood Cliffs, N.J., 1962.

Brunner, Karl, and Allan H. Meltzer: "Some Further Investigations of Demand and Supply Functions for Money," *Journal of Finance*, May, 1964.

Kent, Raymond P.: *Money and Banking*, 4th ed., Holt, Rinehart and Winston, Inc., New York, 1961.

Reed, Edward W.: *Commercial Bank Management*, Harper & Row, Publishers, Incorporated, New York, 1963.

Shaw, Edward S.: *Money, Income, and Monetary Policy*, Richard D. Irwin, Inc., Homewood, Ill., 1950.

chapter four

THE FEDERAL RESERVE BANKS
AND THE TREASURY

The Federal Reserve banks and the Treasury exert influence on the monetary system in three principal ways. First, they issue our coin and paper currency. This proves to be the least important role of the three, however, since the supply of coin and currency is adapted to the demands of the public. Second, these agencies conduct transactions which directly affect the size of the money supply. Chief among these are Federal Reserve open-market transactions in government securities and Treasury purchases and sales of gold. Third, and probably most important, operations of these agencies can exert a major influence on commercial bank reserves. The third effect results chiefly from extension of Federal Reserve credit, from open-market operations or loans to banks, and from Treasury gold transactions. In this chapter, we examine the technical working of these influences and the manner in which they can be directed toward the objectives of economic stability.

THE FEDERAL RESERVE BANKS

Nature and Structure The Federal Reserve System, which has been in operation since 1914, is the principal means through which the Federal government regulates the supply of money and credit. There are twelve regional

Federal Reserve banks which carry on actual operations, but the Board of Governors in Washington is the major policy-making influence. Direct Federal Reserve jurisdiction extends only to such banks as choose to join the System (but a bank must join if it wishes to be a national bank); however, measured by money volume, most of the banking facilities of the country have come within the System. Although more than half the commercial banks by number remain outside, they hold only about 15 per cent of the country's demand deposits.

The Federal Reserve banks issue most of our paper currency. They hold the reserve deposits of member banks and can influence their amount by making loans or dealing in government securities. The Board controls the legal reserve requirement of banks within statutory limits. To examine the monetary implications of these operations in more detail, it is convenient to start with the balance sheet of the Federal Reserve banks, shown in Table 4-1.

The general structure of this balance sheet is similar to that of the commercial banks, but there are some unfamiliar items. Among the assets we find the familiar items of cash in vault, loans, and securities. Gold certificates, a form of quasi currency issued by the Treasury, serve as the legal reserves of the Federal Reserve. Each dollar of gold certificates is backed by a dollar of gold. The certificates are convertible into gold on demand but no longer circulate as money. The law requires the Federal Reserve to hold gold certificates equal to 25 per cent of Federal Reserve notes outstanding, but its reserve position has not exerted any influence on its policies for many years. Note that gold certificates and United States government securities together account for nine-tenths of Reserve bank assets.

Table 4-1   Balance sheet of Federal Reserve banks, June 30, 1964
(Billions of dollars)

Assets		Liabilities	
Gold certificates	$15.2	Federal Reserve notes	$32.4
Cash in vault	0.1	Member bank reserve deposits	17.0
Federal reserve credit:		Treasury deposits	0.9
United States securities	34.8	Other liabilities	0.5
Discounts and advances	0.1		
Float	1.6		
Other assets	0.6	Capital and surplus	1.6
Total	$52.4	Total	$52.4

Source: Federal Reserve Bulletin, July, 1964. Uncollected items other than float have been deducted from both sides.

The Federal Reserve holds a substantial volume of checks of commercial banks which are in the process of clearing. Some of these represent funds which have already been credited to the bank which deposited them but have not yet been charged to the bank against which they were drawn. These funds, which constitute a temporary loan to banks, are called "float."

Among the liabilities must be listed the Federal Reserve notes in circulation. As we have observed, these form the principal component of the country's supply of paper currency. The Federal Reserve also has deposit liabilities, consisting chiefly of the reserve accounts of the member banks, plus small balances for the Treasury, other government accounts, and foreign accounts. The Federal Reserve does not do a general banking business; it does not furnish ordinary demand deposits to business firms and individuals. It is a "bankers' bank."

Each member bank is required to purchase stock in the Federal Reserve. The Reserve capital account represents money thus paid in by member banks, plus reinvested earnings. Member banks receive a regular dividend of 6 per cent on their stock, but 90 per cent of net Reserve bank earnings are paid into the Treasury.

Federal Reserve "Chores" A large part of the activity of Federal Reserve employees consists of performing a number of highly useful service functions. These include the following:

1. Clearing and collecting checks.
2. Transferring funds by telegraph.
3. Managing Treasury funds and transactions.
4. Supplying banks with coin and currency and withdrawing worn-out pieces from circulation.
5. Supervising member banks and conducting on-the-spot examination of state member banks. (National banks are examined by the United States Comptroller of the Currency, the agency which issues charters to national banks.)

The money volume of the transactions involved in the foregoing is enormous. In 1963, the Federal Reserve banks handled coin and currency equal to the total amount in circulation, Treasury checks worth $130 billion, and United States securities worth $680 billion. The value of checks cleared was roughly $1.4 trillion, and telegraphic transfers of funds exceeded $3 trillion.[1]

The operations of the Federal Reserve banks and the Board of Governors are financed out of the interest received on loans and securities. In 1963, the System received just over $1 billion in interest, 99 per cent of it from United States government securities. The operating expenses of the System were just under $200 million, and dividends paid to member banks took $29 million. Ultimately nearly $900 million was paid back into the

[1] Board of Governors, Federal Reserve System, *Annual Report for 1963*, p. 226.

Treasury.[2] Two important observations can be made about these financial arrangements:

1. Government securities held by the Federal Reserve impose virtually no interest burden on the government and the taxpayers. Thus, acquisition of additional securities by the Federal Reserve System is similar to reduction of the size of the debt, as far as interest burden is concerned.

2. The Federal Reserve System is financially independent of the ordinary congressional control of appropriations and expenditures, a situation which greatly increases the freedom of action of Federal Reserve authorities.

FEDERAL RESERVE CONTROL OF MONEY AND CREDIT

Instruments of Control   The most important policies of the Federal Reserve System are those which affect the quantity of money and the cost and availability of credit. These consist chiefly of measures which operate on the reserve positions of the commercial banks. The Federal Reserve can affect the amount of bank reserves by making loans to banks or by buying and selling government securities. Member bank reserve positions are also affected by the reserve requirements set by the Board of Governors within statutory limits.

The Federal Reserve administers other policies which may affect credit conditions but which do not operate directly on commercial bank reserve positions. The Board of Governors has authority to set minimum "margin" requirements for stock market loans; these determine the maximum which can be borrowed on the basis of a given value of stock. The Board also sets the maximum interest rates which member banks are permitted to pay on time deposits.

In this chapter our emphasis will be on the former group of policy instruments—those which operate chiefly on commercial bank reserve positions—and we shall deal chiefly with the mechanical aspects of their operation. In later chapters of the book, we describe how these have been used historically and conclude with some evaluation of their effectiveness and desirability.

Reserve Requirements   As we noted in the previous chapter, the Board of Governors can raise or lower member bank reserve requirements within limits set by law. Those limits themselves provide for requirements which are higher for demand deposits than for time deposits—and higher for demand deposits of banks in so-called reserve cities than for other ("country") banks. This pattern of differentiation has been carried over from the distant past, when reserve requirements were imposed to protect bank liquidity.

[2] *Ibid.*, pp. 203–204.

They reflect supposed differences in liquidity needs for different banks and different classes of deposits. Today reserve requirements are an instrument of monetary control, and it is questionable whether the differential pattern retains much justification. It is true that reserve city banks hold substantial amounts of reserve deposits for nonmember banks. Higher reserve requirements for reserve city banks thus compensate to some extent for the fact that nonmember banks are treated more leniently with respect to reserve requirements.

Changing the reserve requirements does not alter the money supply directly but changes the ability of the banks to lend. Reducing the reserve requirement increases bank lending ability. If the banks are willing to make more loans or buy more securities, they can expand the money supply; the final choice is theirs. Raising reserve requirements can coerce the banks into contracting or prevent them from expanding—provided the Federal Reserve uses its other techniques to prevent the banks from obtaining more reserves.

Loans to Member Banks Member banks may borrow from the Federal Reserve banks to obtain reserves or currency. Originally it was expected that banks in need of funds would resell to Federal Reserve banks some of the IOUs of their customers. Since the 1930s, however, borrowing banks have more commonly obtained direct loans secured by collateral of government securities.[3]

When a bank borrows from the Federal Reserve, the proceeds of the loan are credited to its reserve account. Since the loan does not affect commercial bank deposit liabilities, the entire proceeds go to increase excess reserves or to reduce a reserve deficiency. With a 20 per cent reserve requirement, a loan of $1,000 provides enough reserves to avoid the need for a contraction of up to $5,000 in deposits and earning assets. When the commercial bank repays the loan, the sum will be deducted from its reserve account.

Federal Reserve authorities do not directly determine the volume of member bank borrowing. Instead, they influence borrowing by variations in the so-called discount rate—the interest rate which borrowing banks have to pay. Many banks do not borrow at all from the Federal Reserve, adhering to a tradition that it is bad banking to operate on borrowed reserves. Among those banks not averse to borrowing, the actual volume of borrowing is sensitive to the height of the discount rate, considered not in isolation, but in relation to other interest rates in the market, particularly those on short-term Treasury bills.

A bank confronted with a prospective reserve deficiency will look for

---

[3] Traditionally, many bank loans have been made by discounting a customer's IOU—deducting the interest in advance from the face value of the note. Sale of such paper to Federal Reserve banks was thus termed "rediscounting," and the interest charged was the rediscount rate.

the least disadvantageous method of adjustment. If the Federal Reserve discount rate is high in relation to market rates, the bank will be more likely to sell Treasury bills. If the discount rate is below the bill rate, however, the bank is more likely to borrow from the Federal Reserve. The cost and availability of loans from other banks will also affect the demand for Federal Reserve loans.

Loans from Federal Reserve banks are ordinarily extended to meet reserve deficiencies, and repayment is expected normally in about two weeks. Reserve bank officials expect a borrowing bank to adjust its portfolio to eliminate reserve deficiency, if necessary by reducing its assets. Because of this pressure, the authorities feel that borrowed reserves are not as expansionary as "free reserves" not encumbered by indebtedness. Not all economists are persuaded that the distinction is important for the banking system as a whole.

Federal Reserve policy generally has involved increasing the discount rate during periods of economic expansion and reducing it during recessions. However, this is not sufficient to cause a countercyclical pattern in member bank borrowing. Such a pattern could be produced only by consistently raising the discount rate by more than the normal rise in the bill rate during expansion, and lowering it by more than the bill rate during recessions. In practice, no consistent pattern in these terms has been followed.

OPEN-MARKET OPERATIONS

What They Are   The most important type of action which the Federal Reserve can take to influence the monetary and credit situation consists of open-market operations. In these the Federal Reserve buys and sells marketable United States government securities in transactions with other investors, rather than with the Treasury itself. The "open market" is not a physical trading location, but a network of trading connections held together mainly with telephone wire. At its center are about twenty major dealers in government securities (including a few commercial banks), who are continuously buying and selling securities in transactions with hundreds of other banks, brokerage firms, and other investors throughout the country.

Marketable government securities differ substantially from the savings bonds with which most people are familiar. Marketable securities are not redeemable on demand, but bear a maturity date established when they are issued. As their name implies, they can be bought and sold among private investors at any price which is mutually satisfactory (unlike savings bonds, which are not transferable). Market prices of marketable securities can and usually do differ from their maturity values; prices fluctuate with supply and demand.

Federal Reserve open-market operations are carried on through the Federal Reserve Bank of New York, where a "trading desk" maintains continuous communications with the major dealers. However, the directives controlling policy are handed down by the Federal Open Market Committee, which includes the seven members of the Board of Governors plus five Reserve bank presidents. When the Federal Reserve buys securities, it pays by handing over a check drawn on itself. When it sells, it acquires checks drawn on the buyers. Although the direct partner of Federal Reserve transactions is customarily one of the dealer firms, these ordinarily act merely as a conduit between the Federal Reserve and the vast number of banks and other investors throughout the country. In the following, we shall ignore the dealers and concentrate on the ultimate investors.

Effects The effects of Federal Reserve open-market operations depend to some extent on whether the other party involved is a commercial bank or some other investor. If the Federal Reserve buys securities from commercial banks, those banks receive checks drawn on the Federal Reserve Bank of New York (or their equivalent). By returning the checks to their regional Federal Reserve bank, the seller banks receive credit in their reserve accounts. Securities holdings of the commercial banks are reduced, while those of the Federal Reserve are increased. If the Federal Reserve were to buy $1,000 of securities from commercial banks, the changes in balance sheets would look like this:

Assets		*Liabilities*	
	Commercial banks		
Reserves	+$1,000	No change	
Securities	− 1,000		
	Federal Reserve		
Securities	+$1,000	Commercial bank reserve deposits	+$1,000

Since there is no increase in deposit liabilities of commercial banks, the required reserves are unchanged. Therefore, the entire $1,000 constitutes an increase in excess reserves, which for the banking system as a whole could support an expansion of loans and deposits of $5,000, assuming a 20 per cent reserve requirement and ignoring the withdrawal of coin and currency. Note, however, that the increase in demand deposits (and thus in the total money supply) only occurs if the commercial banks do in fact take advantage of their excess reserves to expand credit. The Federal Reserve's purchase of securities therefore permits an expansion of the money supply but does not bring it about directly.

Suppose, however, that the Federal Reserve purchased $1,000 of government securities from an individual investor or from any business firm other than a bank. The Federal Reserve will normally pay for the securities it buys by giving the seller a check drawn on itself. In most cases, the seller will deposit the check in his account with a commercial bank. That bank in turn will send the check back to the Federal Reserve, which will add the amount of the check to the reserve account of the commercial bank. The balance sheets would show the following changes:

Assets		Liabilities	
		Commercial banks	
Reserves	+$1,000	Demand deposits	+$1,000
		Federal Reserve	
Securities	+$1,000	Commercial bank reserve deposits	+$1,000

Note here that even though the commercial bank is not a direct party to the transaction, its situation is substantially affected by it. Even when the Federal Reserve conducts its open-market dealings with nonbank investors, the most important effects are those on the banks.

In this transaction, the demand-deposit liabilities of the commercial bank are increased directly, since the person who sold securities receives the increase in payment. Thus this transaction directly increases the total money supply. In addition, since commercial bank deposits and reserves are increased by the same amount, the commercial banks gain excess reserves. A $1,000 increase of deposits means that required reserves increase by only $200 (assuming 20 per cent requirement), leaving the banks with $800 more excess reserves, which would permit the banking system as a whole to expand credit by as much as $4,000.

Comparing these two variations will show that both cause commercial bank reserves to increase by the amount of the securities purchased. In the first case, when the Federal Reserve buys from banks, no direct increase in deposits occurs. It is up to the banks to use the reserves by expanding loans and securities. In the second case, however, deposits increase by the same amount as reserves, leaving the banks with only four-fifths as much potential for expansion.

When the Federal Reserve sells securities, the effects are just the reverse of those we have discussed. Bank reserves are reduced, and the money supply may be curtailed, directly or indirectly. The same two variations are relevant. If the Federal Reserve sells bonds to banks directly, it collects for them by deducting the amount of the sale from the reserve deposits of the commercial banks. The respective balance sheets then look like this:

Assets		*Liabilities*	
	Commercial banks		
Reserves	−$1,000	No change	
Securities	+ 1,000		
	Federal Reserve		
Securities	−$1,000	Commercial bank reserve deposits	−$1,000

Commercial bank demand-deposit liabilities, and thus the total money supply, are not affected directly by this transaction. However, because the entire $1,000 comes out of the excess reserves of the banks, there results at the least a curtailment in their expansion potential and perhaps an actual deficiency of reserves, requiring them to reduce their loans. The latter extreme may be regarded as unlikely, since the banks have voluntarily bought the securities from the Federal Reserve. They would probably not make such a purchase unless they had excess reserves which they were willing to part with.

When the Federal Reserve sells government securities to individuals, both the money supply and commercial bank reserves are reduced by the amount of the sale. The purchasers of the securities normally will pay for them with their checks on commercial bank deposits. The Federal Reserve will deduct the amount of the checks from the commercial banks' reserves and return the checks to them, where the same sum will be deducted from the accounts of the purchasers of securities.

A sale of $1,000 of securities by the Federal Reserve to nonbank buyers would change the balance sheets in the following manner:

Assets		*Liabilities*	
	Commercial banks		
Reserves	−$1,000	Demand deposits	−$1,000
	Federal Reserve		
Securities	−$1,000	Commercial bank reserve deposits	−$1,000

Since demand deposits are directly reduced, the total money supply is reduced by the same amount. Getting rid of $1,000 of demand deposits reduces the required reserve of the commercial banks by $200, but that still leaves $800 to come out of excess reserves. This withdrawal means at the least a curtailment in the expansion potential of the banks and may mean that they are actually made deficient in reserves, so that they must either reduce their loans or take some other action to replenish their reserves.

Differences between transactions with banks and with nonbank investors are not likely to be economically significant. If banks respond normally to changes in reserve positions, the ultimate effects on the money supply are the same in both cases. What is essential in each case is the influence of open-market transactions on commercial bank reserve positions. The conclusions should be memorized:

When the Federal Reserve banks buy securities, commercial banks gain reserves.

When the Federal Reserve banks sell securities, commercial banks lose reserves.

Effects on Interest Rates   Federal Reserve purchases and sales influence supply and demand conditions in the markets for government securities and thus tend to affect their market prices. Change in the price of a security affects its yield, or interest rate which it offers to a buyer. Consider a $1,000 Treasury bond which pays $40 a year interest. As long as it sells at par, it yields its holder 4 per cent. But if its price falls, the yield to a prospective purchaser goes up. He pays less for that $40 annual income, and he also stands to receive a capital gain when the bond matures. On the other hand, if the bond sells above $1,000, a purchaser would receive less than 4 per cent on his investment. He must pay more for the $40 income, and he also faces the prospect of a capital loss.

Federal Reserve open-market purchases tend to increase the demand for securities, to raise their prices, and thus to reduce their yields. Furthermore, efforts of investors to shift funds into higher-yielding assets will cause price increases in markets for privately issued securities. Thus market interest rates in general will tend to decline. Federal Reserve sales, by adding to the supply of securities, will tend to depress their prices and raise their yields. Market interest rates will thus tend to rise, not merely on government securities, but on private debt claims as well. Of course, these direct influences will be greatly reinforced by the reactions of commercial banks to variations in their reserve positions caused by open-market operations.

The possibility of variation in security prices also explains how the Federal Reserve officials can be sure of carrying out desired operations— how they can find buyers when they want to sell, for instance. Demand for government securities has a relatively high elasticity. When the Federal Reserve wants to sell, it can always find buyers if it is willing to lower the price slightly. And it can always find sellers by offering a slightly higher price.

Open-market policy is the most powerful and flexible instrument of Federal Reserve monetary policy. It possesses a degree of precision in timing and magnitude which other Reserve instruments lack. It can reach not only member banks, but nonmember banks and other institutions and investors as well. It can produce direct influences on the money supply and on market rates of interest. In fact, the Federal Reserve System could probably function quite well if it relied entirely on open-market operations to influence bank reserves and the money supply.

Federal Reserve Notes We have discussed three techniques by which the Federal Reserve can influence the monetary and credit situation—changing reserve requirements, rediscounting, and open-market dealings in government securities. The issue of Federal Reserve notes does *not* constitute a separate and independent policy technique of the Federal Reserve. Rather it is a passive instrument, subordinated to the others and to the desires of the public and the banks. The Federal Reserve does not force its notes into circulation but merely pays them out as the banks ask for them (provided, of course, that the commercial banks are willing and able to give up part of their reserve deposits in exchange). The commercial banks in turn are guided by the demands of the public for circulating currency. Since the public usually obtains the currency by drawing from its demand deposits, the total money supply is not directly affected.

The Federal Reserve does not use Federal Reserve notes to carry on its own major operations. When it purchases government securities, it pays by check, not with its own notes. If the seller of the securities wishes currency (an unlikely event), he obtains it from his bank. It is conceivable, of course, that a bank might obtain a loan from the Federal Reserve, or sell securities to it, and take the proceeds in notes rather than reserves. But this would be on the commercial bank's initiative.

On the whole, it is best for the student to treat the issue of Federal Reserve notes as one of the service functions of the Federal Reserve, comparable to the clearing of checks. Both functions are important and add significantly to the effectiveness of the three major techniques we have discussed, but they possess no independent policy significance of their own.

Federal Reserve Policy Technical differences among the three major instruments of Federal Reserve policy should not obscure the fact that all are principally means of influencing the reserve positions of the banks and through them the money supply. It probably makes some difference whether the excess reserves of the banking system are raised $200 million through reduction in reserve requirements, or through open-market purchases, or through bank response to a reduction in the discount rate. But such differences are not nearly so important as the difference between an increase in reserves of $200 million and an increase of $300 million.

Official statements from Federal Reserve authorities make clear their dedication to goals of economic stabilization to avoid both substantial unemployment and rapid increases in the price level. In their view, this objective is pursued by easier credit and lower interest rates in periods when the expenditure flow appears to be too low, and by tighter credit and higher interest rates when spending threatens to be excessive.

However, the concepts of credit "ease" and "tightness" are deplorably vague, and reliance on interest rates as a measure of what monetary policy is doing may fail to produce a very effective countercyclical policy. If Federal Reserve policy is judged solely on the rate at which bank reserve positions are enlarged (either by adding to the amount of reserves or by reducing reserve requirements), the Federal Reserve has not behaved in a consistent countercyclical manner.

The issues raised here require a much fuller development against a background of theoretical analysis and historical experience. Such development comes in Chapters 16 through 19.

THE TREASURY AND THE MONETARY SYSTEM

Kinds of Operations   The United States Treasury exerts a major influence on our monetary system. This influence arises in part from its issue of monetary liabilities. It issues coins and paper currency for general circulation and gold certificates which serve as reserves for the Federal Reserve banks. Other influences come through revenues, expenditures, and public-debt transactions. The general pattern of revenues and expenditures is determined by Congress and the administration, but Treasury officials possess substantial discretion in refunding the national debt and managing the Treasury cash balance. Treasury financial operations have often been a major monetary influence, sometimes supporting, but at times thwarting, the monetary policies of the Federal Reserve. This influence has been most in evidence during and after major wars.

Treasury Monetary Accounts   To facilitate discussion, we present in Table 4-2 a summary of those Treasury assets and liabilities which relate closely to the money supply.

One can hardly call this account a balance sheet, for it does not balance.

Table 4-2   Monetary assets and liabilities of the
United States Treasury, June 30, 1964
(Billions of dollars)

Assets		Liabilities	
Monetary gold stock	$15.5	Gold certificates	$15.2
Silver coin and bullion	1.9	Treasury currency issues:*	
Total monetary metal	$17.4	Silver certificates	1.8
Deposits with commercial banks	10.4	U.S. notes	0.3
Deposits with Federal Reserve†	1.0	Silver coin	2.5
		Minor coin	0.7
Total	$28.9	Total	$20.5

Source: Federal Reserve Bulletin, August and November, 1964. Details may not add up to totals because of rounding.
* Excludes small amount of obsolete currency still outstanding.
† Includes $0.1 billion Federal Reserve notes.

More fundamentally it is not a double-entry system, for the Treasury (unlike the commercial banks or Federal Reserve banks) does not always incur matching changes in assets and liabilities simultaneously. Its holdings of bank deposits rise and fall chiefly with the flow of current revenues and expenditures. Some of its monetary liabilities are fully backed by assets. Both gold certificates and silver certificates are "warehouse receipts," backed 100 per cent by coin and bullion.

Silver coin, although not "backed" by earmarked assets in the Treasury, contains metal worth almost its face value, so that the actual liability it represents to the Treasury is not as great as the $2.5 billion shown in the table. However, United States notes (ghosts of the Civil War "greenbacks" of a century ago) have only a 40 per cent gold reserve behind them. And pennies and nickels, with a metal value that is insignificant, are not matched by any specific assets at all. In the following chapter, we shall see that statisticians do make, by rather arbitrary adjustments, a Treasury "balance" sheet useful for analyzing the money supply as a whole. For present purposes, however, the somewhat untidy listing we have made will serve.

The Treasury Cash Balance   As Table 4-2 shows, the Treasury keeps a large amount of funds in its deposits with commercial and Federal Reserve banks. Most of these are kept in the form of "tax and loan accounts" with more than 10,000 commercial banks. Tax payments to the Treasury, which tend to be heavily bunched at certain calendar dates, are ordinarily paid into these tax and loan accounts initially. Often they remain in the bank on which taxpayers' checks are drawn. Similarly, proceeds of Treasury bond issues are paid into tax and loan accounts. When the Treasury wishes to use the funds in these accounts, it withdraws them on the basis of notification given in advance. The funds are transferred into the Treasury account in the Federal Reserve banks, and the actual expenditures are ordinarily made by checks on the Federal Reserve banks. The transfer and expenditures of funds are synchronized so that substantial fluctuations in the Treasury deposit with Federal Reserve banks are avoided.

These arrangements are intended to avoid possible disturbances to bank reserves and the money supply which would result from large shifts of funds between commercial banks and Federal Reserve banks. Suppose that all Treasury tax receipts (consisting of checks drawn on commercial banks) were deposited directly in the Federal Reserve banks. The sums added to the Treasury's deposit would be deducted from commercial bank reserves, as in the following illustration:

Federal Reserve banks

Treasury deposit	+$1,000
Member bank reserve deposits	− 1,000

Commercial banks

Reserves −$1,000	Demand deposits	−$1,000

The money supply would be decreased by $1,000 deducted from tax-payers' accounts, and bank reserves would be correspondingly reduced by the shift of funds into the Federal Reserve. Under such an arrangement, financial stringency might result any time the Treasury received a substantial cash inflow.

To avoid this danger, the present system provides for tax and other Treasury receipts to be kept on deposit with the commercial banks. An inflow of tax receipts under these arrangements merely produces this result:

Commercial banks
Treasury deposits   +$1,000
Demand deposits   − 1,000

No disturbance to bank reserves occurs. Withdrawals from these tax and loan accounts are synchronized with Treasury expenditures. Consequently reduction in Treasury deposits at commercial banks is generally offset by the simultaneous "reflation" of the demand deposits of business firms and individuals.

The Treasury's bank accounts are generally involved in those Treasury operations which affect the money supply. When the Treasury issues new currency or gold certificates, it usually receives an addition to its bank account. And when commercial banks buy new issues of Treasury securities, they can pay for them by creating additions to the Treasury deposits they hold. We now examine these monetary operations more fully.

The Treasury and Gold   Gold coins no longer circulate in the United States as money; yet technically the United States is still on a kind of gold standard, and gold serves in a nebulous way as the "base" of our monetary system. Our circulating coin, currency, and demand deposits are not convertible into gold on demand, and the law prohibits the hoarding of gold bullion by private individuals. However, gold may be used in manufacturing or in certain foreign-trade transactions, as licensed by the Treasury. The Treasury stands ready to sell gold for approved uses at the statutory price of $35 an ounce (plus a handling charge of about 9 cents). Similarly, the Treasury purchases newly mined or imported gold not destined for an approved private use, paying $35 an ounce (minus the handling charge).

The production of gold in the United States in recent years has been small in relation to our existing gold stock—about $60 million annually. The transactions which have the most important effects on our monetary situation are those involving gold imports and exports. Gold has traditionally served as a major medium of international payments, and that is still its most important function. Although gold itself is not a constituent of our circulating money, movements of gold into or out of the country may cause changes in the total money supply and in commercial bank reserves unless counteracted by other policies. Suppose, for example, that $1,000 of gold is imported and sold to the Treasury. The Treasury will pay the seller with a check on its account with the Federal Reserve. When the seller deposits the check, total demand deposits in commercial banks are increased by $1,000. When the bank returns the check to the Federal Reserve, commercial bank reserves are increased by $1,000. The balance sheet effects to this point are as follows:

Assets		Liabilities

Treasury

Assets		Liabilities
Gold bullion	+$1,000	
Deposit with Fed. Res.	− 1,000	

Federal Reserve

Assets		Liabilities	
		Commercial bank reserve deposits	+$1,000
		Treasury deposit	− 1,000

Commercial banks

Assets		Liabilities	
Reserves	+$1,000	Demand deposits	+$1,000

The important economic effects are those shown on the balance sheet for commercial banks. The money supply and bank reserves are both increased by $1,000. Excess reserves will thus be increased, and the lending power of the banks will rise by some multiple reflecting the percentage reserve requirement. The gold inflow is similar in monetary effect to Federal Reserve open-market purchases.

However, the balance sheets of Treasury and Federal Reserve may undergo further adjustment. With additional gold, the Treasury is now authorized to issue gold certificates. By doing so, it can replenish its depleted deposit with the Federal Reserve. By issuing $1,000 of gold certificates, the Treasury can bring the balance sheets to this final position.

Assets		Liabilities	

Treasury

Assets		Liabilities	
Gold bullion	+$1,000	Gold certificates	+$1,000
Deposit with Fed. Res.	−1,000 +1,000		

Federal Reserve

Assets		Liabilities	
Gold certificates	+$1,000	Commercial bank reserve deposits	+$1,000
		Treasury deposit	−1,000 +1,000

Gold Outflow   The opposite effect occurs if gold is purchased from the Treasury for export. The purchaser commonly will pay the Treasury with a check, which the Treasury will deposit with the Federal Reserve. The amount of the check—say, $1,000—will be added to the Treasury account and deducted from the reserve account of the commercial bank on which it is drawn. Then the check will return to that commercial bank, which will in turn deduct $1,000 from the demand-deposit account of the buyer of gold.

At that point, the balance sheet will show these changes:

Assets		Liabilities	
		Treasury	
Gold bullion	—$1,000		
Deposit with Fed. Res.	+ 1,000		
		Federal Reserve	
		Commercial bank reserve deposits	—$1,000
		Treasury deposit	+ 1,000
		Commercial banks	
Reserves	—$1,000	Demand deposits	—$1,000

Again, the important effects are those shown for commercial banks. The money supply is directly reduced by $1,000 as demand deposits are taken out of the system. Bank reserves are reduced by $1,000 also. Thus excess reserves are depleted, just as they would be by Federal Reserve sales of securities in the open market.

However, further balance sheet adjustments may arise because of gold certificates. With a reduction in the gold stock, the Treasury must withdraw $1,000 of gold certificates from the Federal Reserve, paying for them with a check on its deposit account. This wipes out the previous increase in that deposit. The further balance sheet adjustments produce this result:

Assets		Liabilities	
		Treasury	
Gold bullion	—$1,000	Gold certificates	—$1,000
Deposit with Fed. Res.	+1,000		
	—1,000		
		Federal Reserve	
Gold certificates	—$1,000	Commercial bank reserve deposits	—$1,000
		Treasury deposit	+1,000
			—1,000

Actual gold transactions are likely to be more complex than the examples we have used here, since the Treasury will usually be dealing directly with a foreign central bank or similar authority. For example, the British authorities might acquire dollar deposits in American banks in exchange for British pounds sold to Americans. The British could then purchase gold from the Treasury. The final effects on money and bank reserves in the United States would still be as we have described them.

Between 1957 and 1963, the monetary gold stock of the United States was reduced by $7 billion through exports. Explanation of this phenomenon must wait until Chapter 15 dealing with international finance. Here we must point out that this gold drain would have produced a drastic reduction in money and in bank reserves, had it not been counteracted by Federal Reserve policy. The Federal Reserve bought a sufficient amount of securities in the open market to prevent any deflationary effects. This had the effect of reducing the interest costs of the national debt, since the Federal Reserve paid back into the Treasury virtually all the interest it received on these extra securities.

The Treasury and Silver The monetary status of silver differs from that of gold in several respects. Silver coins and certificates actually circulate as money, but silver does not have the same acceptance as gold as a medium for settling international accounts. During most of the twentieth century, the metal value of silver was below its monetary value in United States coins; thus a silver dollar did not contain a dollar's worth of silver. The Treasury was able to make a seigniorage profit on its purchase of silver for coins.

Treasury purchases of silver were enlarged in order to subsidize silver producers. In the 1930s and 1940s, consequently, silver purchases greatly exceeded coinage needs, the excess providing the base for an expansion of the circulation of silver certificates, which were the only form of $1 bill.

By the late 1950s, a combination of low production and high industrial demand for silver gradually brought its market price up, until by 1963 it reached the monetary value of $1.29 an ounce. Thus for the first time since 1872, a silver dollar contained a dollar's worth of silver.

With industrial demand continuing to rise, the Treasury was confronted with the prospect that its stock of silver dollars and bullion would be withdrawn. This would in turn necessitate withdrawal of silver certificates from circulation. As a result, Congress voted in 1963 to authorize the issue of Federal Reserve notes in $1 denomination, with the expectation that silver certificates will be gradually withdrawn. This will leave the Treasury in a position to sell silver bullion, or to use it for small coins as needed, without any threat to the nation's paper currency.[4]

Withdrawal of silver certificates will leave the Treasury with little more monetary function than the supplying of coin. It was hard-pressed to keep up with demand for coin in the early 1960s, despite the fact that the value of coin in circulation was rising faster than the money supply as a whole. Rising demands were attributed to increased absorption in parking meters and vending machines and to the rapid spread of coin collecting.

[4] The rise in the price of silver also stimulated a flurry of speculative numismatic interest in silver dollars, culminating in a virtual "run" on the Treasury's supply in early 1964. As a result, the Treasury began using uncoined silver rather than coins to meet demands for redemption—which virtually ceased thereupon.

TREASURY RECEIPTS, EXPENDITURES, AND THE NATIONAL DEBT

Deficit Financing   An important influence of the Treasury on money may arise from the pattern of fiscal policy. The government's tax receipts and current expenditures are never precisely equal. When expenditures exceed revenues, the government has a deficit, which is usually financed by borrowing. When revenues exceed expenditures, the resulting current surplus is usually used to repay part of the national debt. Surpluses, deficits, and the management of the public debt can have substantial effects on the monetary situation.

Let us look first at the case of a government deficit. The Treasury might conceivably finance this by issuing new currency and spending it directly, as it did during the Civil War. That would obviously increase the money supply, and if the currency were deposited in banks, it would increase their reserves as well. As an alternative, the Treasury might spend its existing cash balance—its deposits with commercial banks and the Federal Reserve. This would increase the privately held money supply by shifting funds from Treasury to private deposits.

However, if the Treasury follows its customary procedure of financing a deficit by borrowing—issuing and selling securities—the money supply will not normally be affected. If the funds are borrowed from nonbank investors, existing money flows to the Treasury and back to the public as the Treasury spends it. If banks buy securities, they can do so only by displacing other loans and securities. No changes in the money supply occur that would not have come otherwise. This result is apparent if we follow the transaction through balance sheets. Initially, commercial banks pay for Treasury securities by creating deposits in favor of the Treasury. A purchase of $1,000 would initially appear as follows:

Commercial banks	
Securities +$1,000	Treasury deposits +$1,000

When the Treasury writes checks on these deposits, the funds are transferred into ordinary demand deposits, and the banks end up like this:

Commercial banks	
Securities +$1,000	Demand deposits +$1,000

In the process, the money supply increases. But the transaction is no different from any expansion of money and credit by the banks. It can only be carried out if they have some excess reserves which they would not have used for other lending. Normally, they would not have such reserves; thus lending to the government would come only at the expense of other lending, and no monetary expansion would occur that would not have come anyway.

However, two situations have occurred in which Treasury deficits led to monetary expansion. In the 1930s, banks held large excess reserves but were reluctant, considering the risks and returns available, to expand loans to private borrowers. However, they were willing to buy Treasury securities issued to finance Depression deficits. Deficit spending helped mobilize excess reserves.

During World War II, Treasury deficits also contributed to a large rise in the money supply. This resulted because the Federal Reserve purchased large amounts of securities in the open market, keeping the banks abundantly supplied with reserves. As the banks bought Treasury securities, they paid for them by crediting sums to the Treasury deposits on their books. When the Treasury spent the money, it passed into ordinary demand deposits and enlarged the money supply. The Treasury's operations would not have produced so expansionary a result without the assistance of the Federal Reserve. And the Federal Reserve's policy would not have been so expansionary had it not been directed toward facilitating Treasury borrowing. Similar highly expansionary results could occur if the Treasury borrowed directly from the Federal Reserve—something not customarily done.

Similar principles apply to the use of Treasury surpluses of revenue over expenditure. If used to repay securities held by the public, existing money is merely shuttled back and forth. If the securities redeemed are held by banks, the effect is like any loan repayment. The borrower's deposit is reduced, giving the banks enough excess reserves to reflate loans and deposits to the previous level. Thus under normal circumstances, using Treasury surpluses to retire debt has no monetary significance.

However, substantial monetary effects would result if Treasury surpluses were used to pay off securities held by Federal Reserve banks. When the Treasury transfers the surplus funds from commercial banks to the Federal Reserve, bank reserves are reduced by the full amount withdrawn. Paying the Federal Reserve has the effect of destroying Treasury deposits, which therefore do not find their way back into commercial banks again. The balance sheet effects would appear as follows:

Federal Reserve

Securities —$1,000	Commercial bank deposits —$1,000
	Treasury deposits + 1,000 (initial)
	— 1,000 (debt repayment)

Commercial banks

Reserves —$1,000	Demand deposits —$1,000

To be sure, if the Federal Reserve authorities did not like the result, they could counteract it by open-market purchases.

Indeed, the important conclusion is that the monetary effects of Treasury surpluses and deficits depend on the behavior of the Federal Reserve. If Federal Reserve policy is subservient to Treasury financing, then deficits and surpluses can have substantial monetary effects. If Federal Reserve policy is independent of the Treasury, then the latter's operations have little direct monetary significance.

Even if Treasury operations do not affect the money supply, however, they do affect the supply of government securities in existence. Treasury deficits tend to add to the supply of securities, lower their prices, and raise market interest rates. Short-term government securities are a fairly close substitute for cash, as a store of value for certain purposes. Increasing the supply of short-term securities may tend to reduce the amount of cash holdings people desire to maintain. Such changes may influence the expenditure flow by changing the velocity of the existing supply of money.

The National Debt and Monetary Policy   Even when the Treasury is not financing current deficits, it is continually confronted with the task of refunding large sums of the existing national debt—that is, issuing new securities to take the place of maturing issues which cannot be redeemed out of tax surpluses. In order to sell new securities at par, the Treasury must pay interest rates on them which are comparable to those prevailing in the economy. Naturally, the Treasury officials wish to keep the interest costs of the debt as low as possible. Consequently, they take a keen interest in interest rates generally and in Federal Reserve policies particularly. The Treasury viewpoint is likely to contain a certain predisposition toward easy credit and low interest rates.

If the Treasury view commands widespread political support, the Federal Reserve may find that its policy instruments are harnessed to a goal of low interest rates whether such a policy is economically desirable or not. Subservience to Treasury views led the Federal Reserve into excessively expansionary actions in 1950 when hostilities broke out in Korea. Since 1951, however, it has disclaimed responsibility for holding down interest rates on the national debt.

Debt management and Federal Reserve open-market operations share another common concern: Both can influence the composition of the public's holdings of Treasury securities, particularly the relative amounts of differing maturities. The composition of the debt in turn can affect the relative height of interest rates on long-term versus short-term obligations. A decision by the Treasury to refund maturing short-term bills by issuing long-term bonds would tend to raise long-term interest rates and lower short-terms. So would a decision by the Federal Reserve to buy bills and sell bonds.

Concern for the time structure of interest rates may arise when different rates seem to affect different things. In the early 1960s, for instance, the authorities were convinced that short-term interest rates had an influence on people's decisions whether to keep funds in the United States or abroad. In an effort to hold down the drain of funds abroad, Federal Reserve open-market purchases were managed to produce some upward influence on short rates relative to longs. The ultimate movement in the composition of the national debt depends on the combined policies of Federal Reserve and Treasury.

SUMMARY

There is much basic similarity between the monetary roles of the Federal Reserve and the Treasury. Each issues monetary liabilities of its own, but its chief monetary effects are on the quantity of demand deposits and bank reserves. Both deal in United States government securities—the Treasury as issuer and redeemer, the Federal Reserve in its open-market operations. Both can create demand deposits and bank reserves by buying assets from the public. Each enjoys an area of administrative discretion within a framework of law.

The Federal Reserve and the Treasury between them issue all the circulating coin and currency, but play a passive role in determining the amount, allowing the public to determine how much it desires. However, the Federal Reserve and the Treasury indirectly influence the volume of coin and currency in circulation by their influence on the total money supply.

Although it can change the money supply directly through open-market operations, the Federal Reserve operates chiefly on commercial bank reserve positions. The Federal Reserve can increase the amount of bank reserves by buying securities in the open market or by making loans to banks. It can decrease bank reserves by selling securities or reducing its volume of loans. Decreases in reserve requirements can add to bank excess reserves and also enlarge the potential expansion coefficients. Increases in reserve requirements reduce excess reserves and expansion coefficients.

The Treasury tends to increase the money supply and bank reserves when it buys gold or issues coin and currency. However, Treasury officials do not have much discretionary authority over such operations. It is also possible that Treasury deficits can increase the money supply (when securities are sold to commercial banks) and that Treasury surpluses can reduce the money supply (if used to retire bank-held debt). Whether these deficit-surplus arrangements have major monetary effects depends, however, on the state of commercial bank reserves and ultimately on the Federal Reserve. Treasury deficits enlarged the money supply so much during World War II because the Federal Reserve was willing to add funds to commercial bank reserves to enable them to support a vast increase in deposit liabilities. Looking solely at the financial mechanics, one would conclude that the

Federal Reserve can always prevail. Politically, however, circumstances have sometimes been such that the Federal Reserve has chosen to accept a secondary role.

In combination, the major monetary influence of the Federal Reserve and the Treasury since World War II has been exerted on the reserve positions of the commercial banks. And the chief media of this influence have been Federal Reserve open-market purchases, variations in reserve requirements, and Treasury gold transactions. Their role in monetary developments is more fully developed in the next chapter.

There is one important difference between some Treasury transactions and those of the Federal Reserve. When the Treasury collects a tax surplus, the money is withdrawn directly from the flow of private incomes and expenditures in a manner which the Federal Reserve cannot duplicate. Similarly, Treasury deficits channel funds directly into the stream of private incomes and expenditures, which Federal Reserve operations cannot do. Federal Reserve open-market transactions with the nonbank public can change the money supply directly, but they do so by altering the composition of investors' asset holdings without changing their incomes or total wealth. Thus, while Treasury and Federal Reserve actions can have similar effects on the money supply and bank reserves, Treasury surpluses and deficits will ordinarily have direct effects on incomes and expenditures which other monetary transactions do not have.

QUESTIONS FOR STUDY

Calculate and explain the effects of each of the following, taken separately, on the dollar volume of bank reserves, the volume of excess reserves, and the money supply. Assume all banks are subject to reserve requirements of 15 per cent for demand deposits.

1. Federal Reserve buys $1 billion government securities from banks.

2. Banks repay $1 million borrowed from Federal Reserve.

3. Federal Reserve sells $1 billion government securities to nonbank public.

4. Treasury borrows $1 billion from Federal Reserve and spends the money to buy goods and services from the public.

5. Same as case 4, except that Treasury borrows from
    a. Commercial banks
    b. Nonbank investors

6. Individuals buy $2 billion of gold from the Treasury for export.

7. The Treasury collects a tax surplus of $3 billion and uses it to repay securities held by
   a. Federal Reserve
   b. Commercial banks
   c. Nonbank investors
8. Treasury shifts $10 million of its cash balance from Federal Reserve to commercial banks.

SUGGESTED READINGS

Board of Governors, Federal Reserve System: *The Federal Reserve System: Purposes and Functions,* 5th ed., Washington, 1963.
————: *Annual Reports.*
Federal Reserve Bank of New York: *Bank Reserves: Some Major Factors Affecting Them,* 1951.
————: *The Treasury and the Money Market,* 1954.
U.S. Treasury Department: *Facts about United States Money,* 1958.
————: *Annual Reports of the Secretary of the Treasury on the State of the Finances.*

the Federal Reserve banks, and the Treasury 103

2. The Treasury collects a tax surplus of $3 billion and uses it to repay securities held by:
   a. Federal Reserve
   b. Commercial banks

3. Treasury shifts $10 million of its cash balance from Federal Reserve to commercial banks

SUGGESTED READINGS

Board of Governors, Federal Reserve System, *The Federal Reserve System: Purposes and Functions*, 4th ed., Washington, 1962.
──── *Annual Report.*
Federal Reserve Bank of New York, *Money: Master or Servant?*, New York, 1955.
──── *The Genesis and Use of Bank Reserves*, 1957.
────, *The Reserve Requirement Plan*
──── *A History of the Servicing of the Treasury ... Study of the Finances.*

chapter five

THE MONEY SUPPLY:
A CONSOLIDATED ANALYSIS

THE STATISTICAL UNDERPINNINGS

Direct Determinants of the Money Supply   In the previous two chapters we have dealt separately with the mechanical operations of the commercial banks, the Federal Reserve, and the Treasury. The emphasis has been on understanding how the operations which each carries on may affect the supplies of money and credit. Throughout the exposition, however, we have constantly been obliged to make cross-references, stressing the high degree of interlock among the three elements in the monetary situation.

In this chapter, the emphasis will be on the money-creating sector of the economy viewed as a whole. We shall begin by setting up a pair of statistical constructs which enable us to identify factors responsible for changes in the money supply and in bank reserves. Then we shall look briefly at the historical behavior of these factors in the years since 1929, with a view to identifying the most significant causal agents. Finally, we shall put together a formal equilibrium system in which both the money supply and bank reserves can be shown to be determined by four major causal influences: the monetary gold stock, Federal Reserve credit, the level of legal reserve requirements, and the asset preference of the public.

In recent years, economists have developed a set of accounts which deal systematically with the factors directly affecting the money supply and which can be used to determine the monetary effects of any transaction. This device is actually a consolidated balance sheet combining the accounts of the commercial banks, the Federal Reserve banks, and the Treasury. Items appearing on both sides of the consolidation are netted out, leaving a picture of relationships between the monetary sector as a whole and the rest of the economy. Table 5-1 presents such a consolidated account, one which has been derived directly from the data presented in Tables 3-3, 4-1, and 4-2.

However, a bit of fancy footwork is necessary to use Table 4-2, which did not balance in the original form. The principal adjustments are, first, to create a fictitious asset called "Treasury currency assets" equal in amount to Treasury coin and currency outstanding. This asset takes the place of silver coin and bullion and eliminates most of the imbalance between monetary assets and monetary liabilities. Second, the Treasury's holdings of bank deposits are not counted as assets in consolidating the balance sheets. They do appear, however, as liabilities of the Federal Reserve and commercial banks.

Table 5-1 Consolidated monetary balance sheet, June, 1964
(Billions of dollars)

Assets		Liabilities	
Monetary gold stock	$ 15	Money supply:	
United States securities		Demand deposits	$123
Held by Federal Reserve	35	Coin and currency (net)	33
Held by commercial banks	59	Total money	$156
Other commercial bank loans and		Nonmonetary liabilities and	
securities	199	capital:	
Treasury currency assets	5	Time deposits	119
		Treasury deposits and cash	12
		Capital and net miscellaneous	28
		Total nonmonetary	$159
Total assets	$314	Total liabilities	$314

Source: Tables 3-3, 4-1, and 4-2 consolidated and netted. Details do not add to totals because of rounding.

In consolidating the accounts, we omit entirely such items as commercial bank reserve deposits and gold certificates, which exist entirely within the monetary sector. In addition, coin and currency holdings of the Treasury, commercial banks, and the Federal Reserve are not shown. Interbank deposits are excluded, as are loans from Federal Reserve to commercial banks, or from one commercial bank to another.

The assets of the monetary system as a whole consist of gold, commercial bank loans and securities, Federal Reserve securities holdings, and that peculiar item called Treasury currency assets. The liabilities are divided into two categories—monetary and nonmonetary. The monetary liabilities constitute the money supply—demand deposits and coin and currency. Nonmonetary liabilities include Treasury deposits and cash, time deposits, and the capital accounts of banks and the Federal Reserve. Operating within a balance sheet framework, we can state the following necessary condition:

$$\text{Total assets of the} \atop \text{monetary system} = {\text{monetary liabilities} \atop \text{+ nonmonetary liabilities and capital}} \atop \text{accounts}$$

Or we can rearrange the items to isolate the monetary liabilities which constitute the money supply:

$$\text{Money supply} = \text{total assets of the monetary system} \\ - \text{nonmonetary liabilities and capital accounts}$$

Table 5-1 confirms the monetary importance of three factors—precious metals, bank lending, and government finance. Government finance is represented by the national debt, which provides one-third of the assets of the monetary system. Other commercial bank credit supplies about 60 per cent, and gold and silver the remaining 7 per cent.

Historical Behavior of the Money Supply Figure 5-1 shows the pattern of the money supply over major intervals since 1929, as well as its relation to total assets of the monetary system and nonmonetary liabilities. With the exception of the period 1945–1950, when certain abnormalities of World War II were being worked off, the money supply changed in the same direction as total assets did in each of the time-period subdivisions. Nonmonetary liabilities changed in the same direction as total assets in all the time periods. Shifts between money and nonmonetary liabilities have thus been less common than parallel changes in both.

However, the response of the money supply to a change in assets varied considerably. For the period 1929–1964 as a whole, the change in the money supply was almost exactly half the change in total assets. But for the period 1950–1964, the increase in the money supply was slightly less than 30 per cent of the increase in total assets. This is evident in the much flatter slope of the money-supply line in the right-hand portion of the chart.

These observed differences in the response of the money supply to changes in total assets chiefly reflect changing desires by the public to hold time deposits rather than demand deposits and currency. During the years 1933–1950, interest rates were generally low, and consequently people kept more funds in money and less in time deposits. With the higher interest rates of the 1950s and 1960s, the relative portion of funds held in time deposits increased substantially.

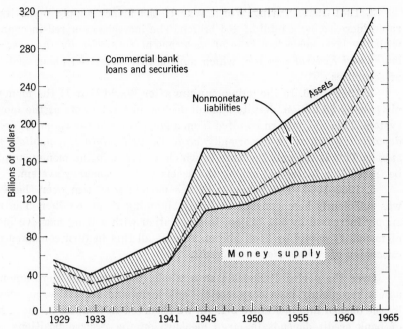

Figure 5-1. Direct determinants of the money supply, benchmark years, 1929–1964. 1941 and 1945 figures are for December; others are for June.

Sources: Federal Reserve Bulletin; Banking and Monetary Statistics and Supplements, All-bank Statistics.

Causes of Major Changes In each of the subdivisions of Figure 5-1, changes in the money supply can be associated with changes in one or two other factors in the consolidated balance sheet.

1. 1929–1933. During these years the economy was falling into deep depression. The money supply declined by $7 billion, a decline principally associated with a large *drop in commercial bank lending.* Bank credit was reduced because many banks were short of cash and reserves or were actually failing; also, demands for credit fell as the economy slumped.

2. 1933–1941. The economy gradually moved out of the depths of the Depression, and the money supply rose $31 billion. This increase was associated with a rise in two categories of monetary assets. There was a *rise in the monetary gold stock* of nearly $19 billion, partly resulting from the upward revaluation of existing gold reserves and partly from large gold shipments from Europe to the United States in the late 1930s as threats of social unrest and war spread. Second, there occurred a large *rise in commercial bank holdings of United States government securities,* issued to finance Treasury deficits.

3. 1941–1945. During World War II the money supply made its most rapid increase, by a total of $54 billion. The increase occurred in connection with the large-scale *purchase of government securities by the commercial banks and Federal Reserve,* which among them acquired about $90 billion of securities.

4. 1945–1950. In the quinquennium after World War II the money supply rose by $8 billion, despite a small decline in total assets of the monetary system. This odd pattern resulted from a *large shift in funds out of Treasury deposits* (which were abnormally large in 1945) *into the public's money supply.* This is the only instance in which a change in the money supply can be traced to a factor not among the assets of the monetary system.

5. 1950–1964. The behavior of the monetary system over these years was sufficiently homogeneous to justify lumping them together. The money supply increased by $41 billion, in association with a truly massive increase of monetary assets by $142 billion. Almost all this in turn consisted of the *expansion of commercial bank credit.*

Over the period 1929–1964 as a whole, the dominant item among the assets has plainly been commercial bank loans and securities, as identified by the dashed line in Figure 5-1. As we observed in Chapter 3, the behavior of bank credit depends in large measure on the reserve positions of the banks. This brings us to the next element in our consolidated analysis—a systematic treatment of the factors affecting the size of commercial bank reserves.

Factors Determining Bank Reserves   In the previous two chapters we have analyzed separately the major factors which change the amount of bank reserves. Bank reserves tend to be increased when there is an increase in the monetary gold stock held by the Treasury. Reserves may also be increased when there is an increase in Federal Reserve credit. This may come about through purchases of government securities, through loans to banks, or through increases in float—the amount of uncollected checks passing through the Federal Reserve. Finally, bank reserves may be increased by a net inflow of coin and currency from the public.

The relation of these factors (plus certain others of minor importance) to commercial bank reserves as of June 30, 1964, is shown in Table 5-2. The table is constructed on the assumption that coin and currency plus deposits at the Federal Reserve constitute the reserves for the commercial banking system as a whole. No separate consideration is given to nonmember bank reserves other than coin and currency.

The table actually embodies a balance sheet structure very much like that of the consolidated monetary accounts. The item labeled "sources" is sometimes known as the "monetary base," or the total stock of "high-powered money." It consists of the reserve assets of the monetary system. The claims against these assets fall into two main categories—currency in

Table 5-2   Determinants of commercial bank reserves, June 30, 1964
(Billions of dollars)

Sources:		
Monetary gold stock	$15	
Federal Reserve credit		
United States securities	35	
Loans and float	2	
Treasury currency issues	5	
Total sources		$57
Competing uses:		
Coin and currency in circulation	33	
Treasury cash and deposits with		
Federal Reserve	1	
Miscellaneous Federal Reserve		
accounts (net)	2	
Total (deduct)		$36
Commercial bank reserves:		
Deposits with Federal Reserve	17	
Coin and currency in banks	5	
Total reserves		$22

Source: Federal Reserve Bulletin, August and November, 1964. Details may not add up to totals shown because of rounding.

circulation, and commercial bank reserves. Bank reserves may thus be increased either by an increase in the monetary base or by a decrease in the public's holding of currency.

EQUILIBRIUM ANALYSIS OF MONEY AND RESERVES

Determinants of Money and Reserves   A comparison of the major items appearing in Tables 5-1 and 5-2 reveals a substantial overlap. The gold stock is a determinant of both money and reserves; so is the amount of government securities held by the Federal Reserve. Both accounts are also affected by the preference of the public for different types of financial assets. This preference affects the money supply through the choice between money and time deposits; it affects reserves through decisions to hold deposits or currency. Finally, the largest direct determinant of the money supply is commercial bank credit in the form of loans and securities. And this depends, of course, on the reserves available to the banks, on the reserve requirements, and on the asset preference of the public.

It does not require very much more construction work to erect on top of the theory of expansion coefficients (Chapter 3) an integrated equilibrium analysis of the money supply and bank reserves as a whole. For simplicity, we shall leave out of account Treasury currency and Treasury deposits, as well as certain other minor items. With these omissions, the basic balance sheet identities from Tables 5-1 and 5-2 can be reduced to the following:

1. Direct determinants of the money supply

Monetary gold stock (G) + Federal Reserve holdings of U.S. securities (FS) + commercial bank loans and securities (CB) = demand deposits (D) + currency in circulation (C) + time deposits (T) + capital and miscellaneous (CP)

2. Determinants of bank reserves

Monetary gold stock (G) + Federal Reserve holdings of U.S. securities (FS) + Federal Reserve loans and float (FL) = bank reserves (R) + currency in circulation (C)

Finally, an equilibrium equation is introduced in which it is assumed that the commercial banks have no excess reserves. All their reserves are absorbed as required reserves for existing deposit liabilities. For this equation, we need data on reserve requirements. Let d stand for the demand-deposit requirement and t for the requirement on time deposits. Our equilibrium equation can now be expressed as:

3. Sources and uses of required reserves

Bank reserves R = (amount of demand deposits D × reserve requirement d) + (amount of time deposits T × reserve requirement t)

Finally, the system rests on the pattern of asset preference of the public—its desire to allocate its funds among demand deposits, coin and currency, time deposits, and bank capital (in the form of bank stock). For simplicity, we assume the dollar amounts of time deposits and capital accounts are known and are (in the short run) independent of the other items in these equations. However, we assume that the public holds currency in some fixed proportion to its holdings of demand deposits.

Given the amounts of the gold stock G, the two components of Federal Reserve credit FS and FL, time deposits T, and capital CP, and given the size of reserve requirements and the asset preference of the public, one can determine the money supply and the other elements of the monetary situation.

As an illustration, let us take the following values as given:

Monetary gold stock G = \$16 billion.
Federal Reserve holdings of U.S. securities FS = \$32 billion.
Federal Reserve loans and float FL = \$2 billion.
Reserve requirements $d = 0.15$ and $t = 0.03$.

Time deposits $T = \$120$ billion.

Capital accounts $CP = \$28$ billion.

The public holds currency equal to $\frac{1}{4}$ its demand deposits. $D = 4C$

We solve this system by substituting in the respective equations as follows:

1. $G + FS + CB = D + C + T + CP$ and $D = 4C$

$\quad 16 + 32 + CB = 4C + C + 120 + 28$

$\qquad 48 + CB = 5C + 148$

$\qquad\quad CB = 5C + 100$

2. $G + FS + FL = R + C$

$\quad 16 + 32 + 2 = R + C$

$\qquad\quad 50 = R + C$

$\qquad\quad R = 50 - C$

3. $R = D(d) + T(t)$

$\quad = (4C)(0.15) + (120)(0.03)$

$\quad = 0.6C + 3.6$

Setting the solutions for equations 2 and 3 equal to each other, we get

$50 - C = 0.6C + 3.6$

$\quad 46.4 = 1.6C$

$\qquad C = 29$

Once we have obtained the value for C (currency), we can obtain the values for demand deposits and bank loans and securities, which are as follows:

$D = 4 \times 29 = 116$ (demand deposits)

$CB = 5C + 100 = 245$ (bank loans and securities)

The amount of bank reserves R is determined from equation 2, as follows:

$G + FS + FL = C + R$

$\quad 16 + 32 + 2 = 29 + R$

$\qquad\qquad R = 21$

This total for reserves should fulfill the conditions of equation 3, showing reserves required for deposits:

$R = D(d) + T(t)$

$\quad = (116)(0.15) + (120)(0.03)$

$\quad = 17.4 + 3.6$

$\quad = 21$

Thus our figure for actual reserves is equal to the figure for required reserves.

Finally, the results should fit together to produce a consistent consolidated monetary balance sheet, as follows:

Assets		Liabilities and capital		
Monetary gold stock	$ 16	Money supply		$145
Federal Reserve securities	32	Currency	$ 29	
Commercial bank loans		Demand deposits	116	
and securities	245	Time deposits		120
		Capital accounts		28
	$293			$293

Impacts of Changes in Data　One of the uses to which an equilibrium system of this sort can be put is to estimate the way in which changes in underlying assumptions will alter the equilibrium position. Since the assumptions were patterned after the actual monetary situation in the early 1960s, the estimates probably have some rough approximation to reality.

Table 5-3 shows what would happen to the equilibrium money supply (under the assumptions just described) in response to a number of changes in given conditions, each considered separately while the others are held constant.

Table 5-3　Effects on equilibrium money supply of changes in data (hypothetical)

	Billions
1. Increase of $1 billion in	
a. Monetary gold stock	+$3.13
b. Federal Reserve securities holdings	+ 3.13
c. Federal Reserve loans and float	+ 3.13
2. Increase of 0.01 in reserve requirements	
a. For demand deposits	− 3.55
b. For time deposits	− 3.75
c. For both	− 7.2
3. Public shifts $1 billion	
a. From currency to demand deposits	+ 2.66
b. From currency to time deposits	+ 2.03
c. From time deposits to demand deposits	+ 0.63

Each of these impacts can be derived from balance sheets of the sort we analyzed in the preceding chapters. Be sure you can make the derivation.

Table 5-3 consists of three parts, corresponding to the three major categories of factors bearing on the money supply. The first part contains the items which give rise to high-powered money, or the monetary base—the monetary gold stock and the components of Federal Reserve credit. A change in any of these items produces the same impact on the equilibrium size of the money supply—an increase measured by the expansion coefficient derived in Chapter 3. (This conclusion implies that banks behave the same with borrowed reserves as with owned reserves, which may not be precisely true.)

The second category of changes in Table 5-3 consists of changes in reserve requirements. The impact of such changes depends primarily on the amount of existing deposits affected. The table shows a larger impact from changing the time deposit requirement simply because the initial amount of time deposits was slightly larger than demand deposits.

The third category consists of changes in the asset preference of the public. A shift from currency to demand deposits is expansionary, though not so much as an equal increase in high-powered money from category 1. Expansion is slightly less for 3a because part of the reserves gained by currency inflow is needed to back the initial rise in demand deposits.

The shift from currency to time deposits has less of an expansionary impact on the money supply than the shift from currency to demand deposits. The reason is that initially 3b lowers the money supply by $1 billion, a decline which is later counteracted by expanding bank loans and demand deposits. The expansion of bank credit is greater in 3b than in 3a.

A shift from time deposits to demand deposits produces only a fractional rise in the money supply. True, demand deposits initially rise by $1 billion, but the shift creates a reserve deficiency and forces some reduction of bank credit.

Rates of Change over Time Equilibrium analysis is a useful analytical device for evaluating the relative magnitude of various changes in data, but it gives a somewhat misleading image of the monetary environment. To understand the influence of money on expenditures, one needs some understanding not merely of the size of the money supply, but of its rate of change over time. The focal point of the new quantity theory of money is the proposition that variations in the rate of change of the money supply tend to be transmitted to the rate of change of total expenditures.

Fortunately, the rate of growth of the money supply depends on the rate of change of the determinants analyzed in this and the preceding chapters. In particular, the rate of monetary change has historically been closely linked with the rate of change of commercial bank loans and securities, which has in turn responded to changes in reserve positions resulting from variations in high-powered money and in reserve requirements.

Figure 5-2 indicates the historical behavior of the rates of change over time of these central magnitudes: the money supply, commercial bank loans and securities, and a measure of the effective monetary base, consisting of the

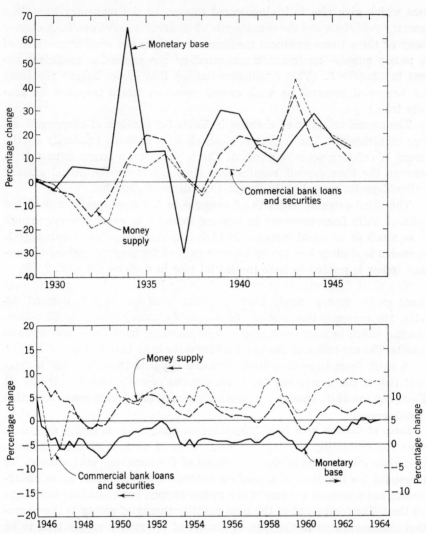

Figure 5-2. Year-to-year percentage changes in money supply, commercial bank loans and securities, and the monetary base, 1929–1964. Data for 1929–1946 are for June; subsequent figures are quarterly averages.

Sources: Milton Friedman and Anna Jacobson Schwartz, *A Monetary History of the United States, 1867–1960;* Supplements to *Banking and Monetary Statistics; Federal Reserve Bulletin,* June and August, 1964.

gold stock plus Federal Reserve credit adjusted for changes in reserve requirements. This reserve measure thus incorporates the elements from categories 1 and 2 of Table 5-3.

Considerable correspondence is apparent between the curves representing the rates of change of money and of bank credit. They diverged in 1946–1947, when a large shift of funds from Treasury to private deposits raised M in spite of a decline in bank credit, and in 1949–1950 when commercial banks bought securities from the Federal Reserve. Note, however, that since the early 1950s, the rate of increase of bank credit has been consistently higher than that of money. This reflects the proportionately more rapid growth of time deposits. The spread is particularly noteworthy in the early 1960s.

How closely have these variations in money and credit responded to changes in the monetary base? It is useful to look separately at different subperiods. During the 1930s and 1940s, fluctuations in the rate of change of the base (gold stock plus Federal Reserve credit adjusted for changes in reserve requirements) were wide. The increase in the price of gold in 1933 produced the huge increase in the value of the gold stock shown for 1934, while the ill-timed doubling of reserve requirements in 1936–1937 produced the sharp decrease in the monetary base shown for 1937.

During the panic period 1930–1933, bank credit and money decreased sharply, despite increases in the base. The divergence occurred because of heavy withdrawals of currency by the public in response to bank failures and depositor distrust. The increase in the supply of high-powered money was not sufficient to offset this drain, and bank reserves were sharply reduced.

In the decade following 1933, however, bank credit and the money supply followed the general contours of the movements in the monetary base, although with much less violent swings. Monetary growth speeded up in response to the reserve expansion of 1933–1934, then slowed down with reserve deceleration and decline in 1935–1937. A second sequence of acceleration and deceleration followed. During the decade as a whole, however, reserves expanded more rapidly than money. Much of the increase in reserves (resulting chiefly from gold inflow) went into excess reserves, particularly in 1938–1940.

This cushion of excess reserves was drawn on during the war itself and made it possible for the money supply to expand (as banks bought government securities) more rapidly than the monetary base, even though a substantial outflow of currency was occurring at the same time. By 1944 the excess reserves were largely worked off, and the movements of money and the base came into closer congruence.

Immediately after the war, the privately held money supply continued to expand despite the absence of growth in the monetary base. This occurred through transfer of funds from Treasury deposits. However, by 1948 the stagnation or decline in the monetary base produced a deceleration of growth and finally an actual decline in the money supply.

Since 1950, the movements of the reserve base and the money supply have been very close. Moreover, since 1953 variations in the rate of change of the base have tended to lead variations in monetary growth, suggesting a causal linkage. This close correspondence indicates that most variation in the rate of increase of money can be traced to changes in the gold stock, Federal Reserve credit, and reserve requirements.

MONEY AND EXPENDITURES

Our concern with the size and rate of change of the money supply arises chiefly because of our interest in the rate of expenditures for current production. The money supply is an important influence on the expenditure flow, which is in turn the principal short-run influence on production, employment, and prices.

The relation between money and expenditures is often discussed in terms of the velocity of money—that is, the average number of times each dollar gets spent per year. Measured velocity is simply the ratio between the total volume of expenditures and the money supply. If velocity were constant, the expenditure flow would be proportional to the money supply. But velocity is not constant, and the expenditure flow responds to influences other than changes in money.

However, the new quantity theory of money suggests that more impressive evidence of the influence of money on expenditures is found by comparing the rate of change of the money supply with the rate of change of total expenditures for production. Data on the respective rates of change are shown in Figure 5-3. Annual data for 1929–1947 indicate considerable conformity in the major swings of monetary and expenditure change, with somewhat more divergence during the war and immediate postwar years. Quarterly data for 1947–1964 also show conformity in major swings; however, the rate of growth of expenditures is substantially higher, on the average, and fluctuates over a much wider range.

The quarterly data provide evidence on one important proposition of the new quantity theory—that major cycle turning points in the rate of monetary growth tend to lead similar turning points in the rate of expenditure change, suggesting a causal link from money to expenditures. Such a lead is apparent for each major cyclical peak since 1954 and for the troughs in 1949–1950 and 1960–1961. In most other cases the monetary series turns in the same quarter. Evidence of monetary causation is least apparent in 1951–1953 and 1963–1964.

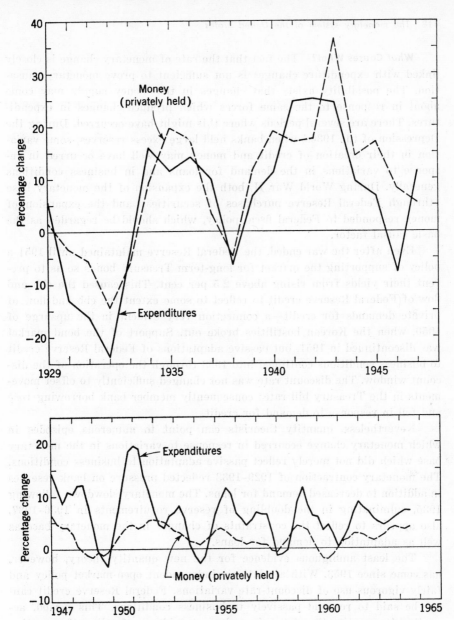

Figure 5-3. Year-to-year percentage changes in money supply and in expenditures for current output, 1929–1964.

Sources: Friedman and Schwartz, *A Monetary History of the United States, 1867–1960;* *Federal Reserve Bulletin; U.S. Income and Output; Survey of Current Business.* Change in expenditures calculated from annual data, 1929–1939, second quarter, 1940–1947. Money-supply changes are based on June figures, 1929–1947. Data for 1948–1964 were derived from quarterly averages.

What Causes What?   The fact that the rate of monetary change is closely linked with expenditure changes is not sufficient to prove monetary causation. The possibility exists that changes in the money supply may come about in response to the same forces which produce changes in expenditures. There are several periods where this might have occurred. During the Depression of the 1930s, when banks held large excess reserves, some variation in their creation of credit and money may well have occurred in response to variations in the demand for loans and in business conditions generally. During World War II, both the expansion of the monetary base (through Federal Reserve purchases of securities) and the expansion of money responded to Federal fiscal policy, which should be regarded as the basic causal factor.

Even after the war ended, the Federal Reserve maintained until 1951 a policy of supporting the market for long-term Treasury bonds so as to prevent their yields from rising above 2.5 per cent. This caused the ebb and flow of Federal Reserve credit to reflect to some extent the ebb and flow of private demands for credit—a connection very evident in the upsurge of 1950, when the Korean hostilities broke out. Support of the bond market was discontinued in 1951, but passive adaptations of Federal Reserve credit to business conditions continued into 1953 through the operation of the discount window. The discount rate was not changed sufficiently to offset movements in the Treasury bill rate; consequently member bank borrowing rose and fell in response to demand for credit.

Nevertheless, quantity theorists can point to numerous episodes in which monetary change occurred in response to variations in the monetary base which did not merely reflect passive adaptation to business conditions. The monetary contraction of 1929–1933 reflected pressure on bank reserves in addition to decreased demand for loans. The monetary slowdown following 1935, culminating in the doubling of reserve requirements in 1936–1937, also appears to reflect the constraints of changes in the monetary base as well as adaptation to demand for loans.

The least ambiguous evidence for the new quantity theory, however, has come since 1953. With a relatively independent open-market policy and fairly vigorous use of discount-rate variations, Federal Reserve credit cannot be said to respond passively to business conditions. This period, according to quantity theorists, gives clearest evidence of a line of causation running from changes in the monetary base to changes in money to changes in expenditures.

If this is true, then the rate of monetary expansion needs to be regarded as a major cause of economic fluctuations. Further, the monetary base emerges as a crucial instrument of economic policy. The Federal Reserve is clearly in a position to control the rate of growth of the base; this requires, of course, that they compensate for gold movements to produce a desired end result.

Agenda We can do no more at this point than present a prima-facie case for causal influence of money on expenditures. The sort of time-series correspondence we have described here leaves unanswered a multitude of questions, to which we shall turn in the subsequent chapters. First, we need to know more about the expenditure flow and its consequences. How is it defined and measured? What effects do expenditure variations produce on production, employment, and prices?

Second, we need to investigate more closely the linkage through which monetary changes affect expenditures. To be sure, we have already indicated something of the connection. Broadly speaking, monetary changes operate through interest rates, asset prices, and credit conditions. We need to look further at the sensitivity of various kinds of expenditures to interest rates and credit conditions, and also at the manner in which money influences them.

Third, we cannot identify the role of money without giving some attention to other factors which may influence the expenditure flow. The impact of Federal fiscal policy, especially during wartime, clearly needs consideration. So do variations in business investment incentives. Consideration of these elements may help us to understand why the amplitude of fluctuations in expenditure change is so much wider than those in the monetary rate of change. Even here the operation of the monetary system may be relevant, since the amplitude of expenditure variation is associated with swings in the composition of bank assets between loans and securities.

SUMMARY

By consolidating the accounts of the Federal Reserve banks, the commercial banks, and the Treasury, we can derive a system showing the direct determinants of the money supply. The money supply is equal to the assets of the monetary system (gold, Federal Reserve and commercial bank holdings of United States securities, commercial bank loans and other securities, Treasury currency assets) minus nonmonetary liabilities (time deposits, capital accounts, Treasury cash and deposits).

Historically, the behavior of the money supply has generally been associated with changes in monetary assets, of which the most important has been total commercial bank credit. The loans and securities of commercial banks are, however, determined in part by the amount of commercial bank reserves, which are the subject of a second consolidated analysis. Bank reserves are shown to depend on such sources as gold, Federal Reserve credit, and Treasury currency, minus coin and currency in circulation.

Finally, it is possible to amalgamate these consolidations to produce an analytical system in which bank reserves, the money supply, and bank credit are all determined by gold, Federal Reserve credit, reserve requirements, and the asset preference of the public.

The new quantity theory of money has shifted emphasis away from the size of the money supply at any moment of time to its rate of growth over time. This theory argues that one can identify historically a causal sequence in which important changes originate in the elements of the monetary base (chiefly the gold stock plus Federal Reserve credit adjusted for variations in reserve requirements). Through changes in bank reserves and in bank loans and securities, the variations in the monetary base are reflected in variations in the money supply. And variations in the rate of change of money are believed to exert a causal influence over the rate of change of expenditures for production. Historically, the evidence is somewhat ambiguous, although performance of the economy in 1954–1964 supports the theory. The chapters which follow provide a more detailed framework for analyzing the influence of monetary change on expenditures and on production, employment, and prices.

QUESTIONS FOR STUDY

1. Assume that the items included as direct determinants of the money supply have the following values. Arrange them in proper order and determine the size of the money supply. Some items in the list do not belong there. Explain which they are and why.

	Billions
Time deposits	$ 42
Monetary gold stock	25
Capital and miscellaneous liabilities	12
Commercial bank loans and securities	130
Treasury cash and deposits	5
Federal Reserve security holdings	20
Gold certificates	24
Treasury currency assets	4
Commercial bank reserves	16

2. Show how each of the following transactions would be entered in the consolidated account of direct determinants of the money supply and/or the determinants of bank reserves:

a. The Federal Reserve sells $1 billion of securities to banks.

b. The Treasury sells $500 million of gold for export.

  c. Commercial banks sell $100 million of securities to nonbank investors.

  d. Commercial banks borrow $10 million from the Federal Reserve.

  e. The Treasury borrows $1 billion from commercial banks and spends the money.

 3. Using the following assumptions, determine the equilibrium values for bank reserves, commercial bank loans and securities, demand deposits, and currency in circulation.

Monetary gold stock = $20 billion.

Federal Reserve holdings of government securities = $25 billion.

Federal Reserve loans and float = 0.

Time deposits = $80 billion.

Bank capital accounts = $20 billion.

The public desires to hold $1 of currency for every $5 of demand deposits.

Reserve requirements are 20 per cent for demand deposits and 4 per cent for time deposits.

 4. Using the equilibrium solution for question 3 as a starting point, calculate the change in the equilibrium money supply which would result from each of the following:

  a. The public shifts $1 billion from demand deposits to currency.

  b. There is a gold inflow of $2 billion.

  c. The Federal Reserve lowers reserve requirements on demand deposits from 20 per cent to 18 per cent.

SUGGESTED READINGS

Brunner, Karl, and Allan H. Meltzer: "Some Further Investigations of Demand and Supply Functions for Money," *Journal of Finance,* May, 1964.

Burstein, Meyer: *Money,* Schenkman Publishing Company, Cambridge, Mass., 1963.

Friedman, Milton, and Anna Jacobson Schwartz: *A Monetary History of the United States, 1867–1960,* Princeton University Press for National Bureau of Economic Research, Princeton, N.J., 1963.

part three

MONETARY THEORY

chapter six

THE MONEY ECONOMY:
A DESCRIPTIVE INTRODUCTION

INTRODUCTORY

Pattern of Money Flow   In Chapters 3 to 5 we dealt with the quantity of money in the economy and noted its composition and the factors directly determining its amount. The quantity of money is economically significant through its relation to the volume of expenditures and their influence on production, employment, and prices. In this chapter we shall describe the manner in which money expenditures flow through our economic system. In the following chapters we shall examine the causes of variations in the flow of expenditures and the consequences for economic welfare of such variations.

We noted in Chapter 1 that the basic money flow in the economy is the circular flow of spending from households to business firms and back again. In this simple pattern, each dollar's worth of goods sold to households gives rise to two dollars of payments—one in paying for the goods themselves, the other in paying income to the households whose resources produced the goods. Although the real world is much more complex, the principle remains valid that the production and sale of goods give rise to income of equal money value. However, not all the income goes to individuals. Part is retained within the firms for reinvestment, and a portion goes to the government in taxes. Correspondingly, we must make a place in our pattern for the flow of funds back from the government to producers and, of course, allow for a large volume of payments from one firm to another. For most products, there are several firms involved between the initial resource inputs and the final sale to the consumer.

All the transactions we have been describing are involved in the "main money circuit" of payments. They involve payments for currently produced goods and currently rendered services. It is main money circuit transactions which are most closely linked with economic welfare through their effects on production, employment, and prices. And it is with them that we shall be chiefly concerned.

Not all payments are in the main money circuit; many payments arise from the purchase and sale of financial assets. In this category are included borrowing and repayment, as well as transfers of existing stocks, bonds, and IOUs of all kinds. We shall call the area of these payments the "financial circulation." Transactions in this area fall roughly into three classifications. First, households, businesses, or government units obtain funds by bor-

Table 6-1   Money transactions in the United States, 1958
(Billions of dollars)

Main money circuit:		
1. Purchases of final output (gross national product)		
a. By consumers	$275	
b. By business, government, foreign	140	
2. Income payments to individuals	215	
3. Intermediate product transactions	665	
4. Tax payments and refunds	120	
Total (rounded estimate)		$1,400
Financial circulation:		
5. Acquisition and disposition of savings accounts	150	
6. Installment lending and repayment	80	
7. Home mortgage lending and repayment	70	
8. United States Treasury borrowing and repayment	210	
9. Other bank lending and repayment	360	
10. Transactions in newly issued securities	65	
11. Transactions in existing securities	680	
12. Commodity exchange transactions	50	
13. Other borrowing and repayment	70	
Total financial (rounded estimate)		$1,700
Miscellaneous:		
14. Second-hand goods and real estate	$ 80	
15. Grants and donations (nonpersonal)	25	
16. Gambling	40	
17. Other	60	
Total miscellaneous (rounded estimate)		200
Total transactions		$3,300

rowing or issuing securities or claims to spend for current production. Second, transactors acquire financial assets with funds received in current income. Third, a large volume of transactions consist of "financial turnover" transactions, in which existing claims are transferred from hand to hand or are refunded when the issuer redeems maturing obligations by issuing new ones.

Magnitudes of Money Flow   Table 6-1 shows some rough estimates of the volume of transactions in the economy in 1958. Our figure for total transactions, $3.3 trillion, is the estimate given by the Federal Reserve Board for total *debits* to private demand-deposit accounts (all checks drawn and withdrawals). Debits include some things which are not genuine payments—for example, conversion of demand deposits into currency, or transfers among deposits held by the same depositor in different banks. They also omit some things we want to include—government transactions, bank loans, and payments made with currency. However, the errors are roughly compensating, so that the total given by the debits series is a handy approximation to the volume of total money transactions in the economy.

Notes to Table 6-1

Total transactions were estimated to be approximately equal to the total debits to private demand-deposit accounts as estimated by the Federal Reserve Board of Governors in their mimeographed release No. 756.

Main circuit transactions and item 14 were initially estimated for 1953 and 1955 from Federal Reserve money-flow data in *Federal Reserve Bulletin*, October, 1957, p. 1191, and *Flow of Funds in the United States, 1939–1953*. Data for 1958 were estimated by raising earlier figures in proportion to the increase in gross national product.

Financial transactions were estimated as follows:

Item 5: Acquisition and disposition of savings deposits and savings and loan shares estimated chiefly from data in *Facts and Figures: Mutual Savings Banking*, May, 1963, p. 14.

Item 6: Installment lending and repayment data are given in the *Federal Reserve Bulletin*. Estimate is rounded, excludes transactions of nonfinancial credit sources, but adds $10 billion for estimated secondary transactions in installment paper.

Item 7: Mortgage lending and repayment data for some institutions are published in the *Federal Reserve Bulletin*. Estimate projects this relationship to total loans outstanding and adds $5 billion for estimated secondary transactions.

Item 8: Treasury public-debt transactions data appear in its *Annual Report*.

Item 9: Bank lending and repayment estimated on the assumption that loans turn over three times a year. Estimate excludes installment and mortgage loans and United States securities. Compare *Monthly Review*, Federal Reserve Bank of New York, January, 1962, p. 13.

Item 10: Transactions in newly issued securities estimated to equal three times the volume of new issues reported in the *Federal Reserve Bulletin*, excluding United States securities.

Item 11: Transactions in existing securities were estimated to include the following: (a) stock transactions, $155 billion; (b) open-market paper, $150 billion; (c) United States securities, $350 billion; and (d) other bonds, $25 billion.

a. Stock transactions equal total volume of trading on organized exchanges plus one-third for over-the-counter trading, total multiplied by 3 as the estimated number of payments involved per dollar of trading.

b. Open-market paper includes $100 billion for dealers and major finance companies estimated by New York Clearing House Association in *Member Bank Reserve Requirements, Hearings before the Committee on Banking and Currency*, United States Senate, March, 1959, p. 171. Estimate adds $50 billion for payments by investors.

c. United States securities are estimated approximately equal to the volume of purchases and sales by government securities dealers, as shown in *Treasury–Federal Reserve Study of the Government Securities Market*: part II, 1960, 140–141. It was assumed that transactions not involving dealers would be offset by the volume of new issues included in the official total.

d. Bond trading estimated to equal over-the-counter stock trading; transactions volume assumed to be twice trading volume. See 1949 data in Irwin Friend, *Activity on Over-the-counter Markets*, University of Pennsylvania Press, Philadelphia, 1951.

Item 12: Commodity exchange transactions estimated to equal twice the volume of trading, as estimated by U.S. Department of Agriculture.

Item 16: Gambling estimated from *Annals of the American Academy of Political and Social Science*, May, 1950, pp. viii, 32, 46, and 65.

Other items (13, 15, 17) are wild guesses.

Our data show total money transactions in the main circuit amounted to about $1.4 trillion. About $275 billion represented consumer spending for current output, and another $140 billion came from purchases of final goods and services by government and business. In combination, these items represent the transactions toward which the rest of the productive process is directed. Some of these expenditures put money directly into the hands of income recipients, such as government employees or owners of unincorporated businesses. In addition, some $215 billion of income payments to persons occurred through separate transactions. The largest category of main circuit payments was that of "intermediate" transactions between one business firm and another. These payments arise from purchases of current inputs at the various stages of production—raw materials to finished products, manufacturers to wholesalers to retailers.

Transactions in the financial circulation were slightly larger, totaling about $1.7 trillion. The greatest part of this total consisted of pure turnover transactions, of which the continual refunding of the national debt, private transactions in government securities, and trading on stock and commodity exchanges accounted for the largest portion. More closely linked with the main circuit were transactions involving borrowing or new securities issues. Even here, much of the gross volume represented turnover, as funds repaid by previous borrowers were lent out again to new ones. A substantial portion of the proceeds from gross borrowing went into expenditures for current output; however, if we consolidate the accounts of each major sector of the economy, the importance of credit as a source of expenditures is much reduced. Federal Reserve estimates show a net flow of about $15 billion from "saver" sectors—chiefly consumers—to "borrower" sectors—chiefly government and business.

Plan of Analysis   It is the volume of expenditures in the main money circuit with which we are chiefly concerned, and of these, most particularly the expenditures for currently produced goods and services. These expenditures have an important relation to economic welfare, for they determine, in the short run, the levels of output and employment which the economy will attain within the limits of existing resources, and they are a major factor in determining prices. In the succeeding sections of this chapter, we shall dissect the main money circuit to examine its structure as depicted by the national-income accounts. Material in this chapter will be largely descriptive, but in the chapters immediately following we shall attempt to answer two important questions about spending for current output: What causes its level to change, and how do such changes affect economic welfare?

However, we shall not ignore the financial circulation, either. Conditions in that area influence the behavior of main circuit transactions, particularly through interest rates, security prices, and the ease with which loans can be obtained. For this reason, we shall return our attention to the financial circulation in the last part of this chapter. In the subsequent treatment of monetary theory, factors originating in the financial circulation will be continually in view. When we have concluded our examination of monetary theory, we shall examine the structure and functioning of the financial circulation in relation to some other aspects of economic welfare.

GROSS NATIONAL PRODUCT

Output and Expenditure   In examining the main money circuit, our chief concern is with the volume of expenditures to buy currently produced goods and services. The best measure of this is the national-income concept of "gross national product" (GNP). Gross national product is defined as the money value (at market price) of goods and services produced in the economy during a specified period. Goods and services are included in GNP only when they reach the final purchaser; in this way we avoid double-counting the many intermediate transactions through which a product passes. We do not add the total value of steel and the total value of automobiles, for the latter includes a substantial part of the former. We shall illustrate this type of calculation in more detail later.

GNP is also a measure of the expenditures to buy current output, and it is in this sense that we shall examine it here.[1] We shall show how the GNP concepts and categories can be used to depict the basic circular flow of income and expenditure in the main money circuit. The descriptions and definitions involved then serve as the basis for more detailed explanations of the behavior of the flow.

GNP expenditures are classified according to the major spending sectors of the economy. While the largest portion of spending is done by consumers, we must also allow for purchases of final output by government, business firms, and foreign buyers. Let us examine each of these categories more carefully.

1. "Personal consumption expenditures" (or simply consumption) refers to purchases of current production by consumers for their own satisfaction or utility.

2. "Government purchases" of goods and services includes all the purchases of final output by Federal, state, and local governments. This category includes purchases from business firms of items like planes and typewriters. It also includes the purchases of services from the people who work for the government. It does *not* include "transfer payments"—income pay-

---

[1] Actually, about 5 per cent of total GNP consists of output not actually sold for money—food consumed by the producers, current rental value of owner-occupied homes, etc.; but no great inaccuracy arises if we assume all output flows through the money economy.

ments for which the government receives no currently produced goods or services in exchange. Pensions and interest payments on the public debt are considered transfer payments.

3. "Gross private domestic investment" refers to purchases of currently produced capital goods, for which business firms are regarded as final buyers. Most business expenditures go for intermediate products and services which are used up in making final products (the steel in automobiles) and are therefore not separately included in GNP. Capital goods consist of such items as equipment and buildings used in production and distribution. Also included are business inventories—stocks of goods or materials on hand. The distinction between consumer goods and capital goods may turn on the purpose for which they are acquired. A can of beans is a consumption good when purchased by someone who plans to eat the contents, but it is a capital good while owned by the grocer who holds it for resale.

The investment category of GNP includes all purchases of durable capital goods, such as machinery or buildings, whether acquired to replace worn-out items or to expand productive capacity. It also includes *net increases* in business inventories during a year. Inventory replacements are intermediate products and thus do not count separately; but the goods added to business inventories are items for which the firms are, for the year in question, the final buyers. Current production of residential housing is also included in investment rather than consumption. Houses are a kind of consumer capital yielding services in the future, and many houses are rented on a business basis. However, other types of consumer capital, such as automobiles, are classified as consumption goods.

The use of the term "investment" in this context is perhaps unfortunate, since it does not accord with the common use of the term to refer to any purchase of an asset for earnings or profit. Investment in the GNP sense does not include purely financial transactions such as purchases of stocks, bonds, or existing real estate. It is restricted to purchases of currently produced real capital goods.[2] The student should take special care to memorize this specialized use of the term "investment" and to be able to distinguish it from financial investment in general.

4. "Net exports" (the excess of exports over imports) are shown as a separate component of GNP. The three previous categories of consumption, government purchases, and investment include imports as well as home products acquired by the domestic purchasers. The figure for net exports measures the extent to which domestic production exceeds domestic acquisition of current output. If GNP is to equal the value of output, net exports must

---

[2] When firms produce their own capital goods instead of buying them from other firms, the "purchase" refers to the expenditures for the labor, materials, etc., to produce them.

be added to the acquisition of current production by domestic consumers, business, and government.[3]

For the United States, the amount of net exports is usually very small in relation to total GNP, and we will not devote much attention to it in this part of the book. However, the reader should bear in mind that the net export figure seriously understates the importance of foreign trade in our economy. The bulk of our exports is not shown separately in GNP because an equal amount of imports is included in the totals for consumption, investment, and government purchases. We shall deal with international transactions at length in Chapters 15 and 16.

Table 6-2 shows the volume of the components of GNP expenditure in 1963. Consumption expenditure accounted for about two-thirds of the total. Government furnished one-fifth and investment one-seventh. This manner of looking at GNP tells us who bought it and how much they spent. It focuses attention on the demand for goods and services. Much of our subsequent analysis will be devoted to trying to explain why these expenditures behave as they do.

Table 6-2   GNP expenditures, 1963
(Billions of dollars)

Type	Expenditure	Per cent
Consumption (C)	375	64
Gross private domestic investment (I)	82	14
Government purchases of goods and services (G)	123	21
Net exports:		
Exports 31	4	1
Imports 26		
Total expenditures	$584	100

Source: Survey of Current Business, July, 1964. Figures are rounded and may not add up to totals shown.

GNP as Total Values Added by Producers A second way of looking at GNP is from the standpoint of the producers. GNP data can be used to measure the net output of various sectors of the economy and their receipts from the sale of that output, for by definition the value of output sold must equal the receipts from its sale.

GNP does not, of course, include the gross output or sales receipts of all producers. Earlier, we eliminated double-counting in GNP by valuing

[3] In some versions of national-income accounting, net exports may be represented by the term "net foreign investment," since an export surplus is often a means of acquiring foreign assets. However, net foreign investment differs statistically from net exports by the amount of gifts and grants to foreigners.

all goods when they reached the final buyer and leaving out intermediate product transactions. We can achieve this result in another way—by summing up the value added by each firm in the economy to the productive process. Value added is a measure of the net contribution each firm makes to total output. It is measured by deducting from the gross receipts each firm gets from sales the total payments it makes to other firms for intermediate products and services used up in the productive process. Payments for capital goods are not deducted.

We can illustrate the calculation of value added by the following example. Suppose a loaf of bread sells at retail for 21 cents. The grocer buys it for 17 cents from the baker. The baker pays 5 cents for flour, out of which the miller pays 4 cents to the farmers for wheat, and the farmers pay 1 cent to other firms for seed, fertilizer, etc. If we merely added these figures together, we would overstate total production considerably. Instead, we can add up the value added at each stage, as follows:

Firm	Receipts	Paid other firms	Value added
Retailer	$0.21	$0.17	$0.04
Baker	0.17	0.05	0.12
Miller	0.05	0.04	0.01
Farmer	0.04	0.01	0.03
Others	0.01		0.01
Total	$0.48	$0.27	$0.21

Total transactions and gross receipts have amounted to 48 cents, but 27 cents of this represents intermediate transactions not counted separately in the value of output. By removing this sum we are left with values added totaling 21 cents, which is of course the same total we obtained by counting the loaf of bread at its retail price. By using this method, we have obtained an estimate of the contribution made by each sector of the economy in producing the loaf of bread.

Looking at GNP as value added tells us who produced it—the contribution to total output by each of the sectors of the economy. This approach also tells us how much of its gross revenue each sector had left after paying other firms for intermediate products and services.

GNP as Gross Incomes Received   Our next step is to see what each sector does with the revenue it receives. Besides the payments to its suppliers for intermediate products, which were deducted in calculating value added, each firm must meet three other categories of accounting costs: payments to individuals for wages, interest, and rent; payments to the government for taxes based on sales, production, and property; and depreciation and other capital consumption allowances representing the recovery of funds previously invested in capital assets. What remains after these costs is the profit accruing to the owners of the firm. For unincorporated businesses, this profit is all counted as personal income to the owners. For corporations, part of the profits goes to the government in profits taxes, part is reinvested in the firm, and part is distributed as dividends to the stockholders.

We shall call these cost and profit items "gross income shares." Since GNP equals total values added by all producers, GNP will also equal the total of gross income shares for the economy. The division of GNP into gross income shares for 1963 is shown in Table 6-3.

Table 6-3   Gross income shares, 1963
(Billions of dollars)

Type of income	Recipient			
	Persons	Business	Government	Total
Compensation of employees	$340			$340
Interest and rental income of persons	37			37
Income of unincorporated business	51			51
Indirect business taxes			$55	55
Capital consumption allowances		$51		51
Corporate profits taxes			25	25
Dividends paid to persons	18			18
Undistributed corporate profits		9		9
Total	$446	$60	$79	$584

Source: *Survey of Current Business*, July, 1964. Details may not add up to totals because of rounding; also, some small miscellaneous items have been omitted or consolidated.

GNP as Disposable Incomes and Net Government Revenue   Our next step is to link these gross income accruals to the expenditures of consumers, business, and government. To do this, we must determine the amount of disposable or spendable income received by each of the three sectors. These net income measures will be designated personal disposable income (PDI), business disposable income (BDI), and net government revenue (NGR).[4]

To determine personal disposable income (PDI), we start with the gross income earned by persons in production, totaling $446 billion in Table 6-3. To this must be added income from government transfer payments, such as pensions, veterans' benefits, and interest on government bonds. From this

[4] These income categories correspond to a tabulation which appears each year in the *Economic Report of the President* (*vide* 1964 edition, pp. 216–217) entitled "Receipts and expenditures by major economic groups." A small item for international transfer payments is omitted here. The official term "disposable personal income" has been altered to "personal disposable income" for reasons of emphasis.

total must be deducted personal taxes, chiefly income and social security levies. The calculation is as follows (totals in this tabulation and other similar ones rounded to the nearest billion) :

Gross personal income (Table 6-3)	$446
(+) Transfer payments	+43
(−) Personal taxes	−88
(=) Personal disposable income	$402

Business disposable income (BDI) is simply equal to the gross income retained in depreciation and undistributed profits, shown as $60 billion in Table 6-3.

The portion of gross income not accounted for by personal and business disposable incomes went to the government as net government revenue (NGR), which equals taxes minus transfer payments. Using data from the previous tables, we can calculate NGR as follows:

Business taxes (Table 6-3)	$ 79
Personal taxes	88
Total taxes	$168
(−) Transfer payments (including small amount to foreigners)	−45
(=) Net government revenue	$123

Finally, if we add up these three sector income categories, the total is equal to GNP:

Personal disposable income	$402
Business disposable income	60
Net government revenue	123
Gross national product	$584

We have now traced the circular flow of gross income back to its origins. We started with the expenditures of consumers, business, and government, and we end with the disposable incomes or net revenue flowing to each of these sectors. Our data demonstrate a very important principle—that expenditures for goods and services create an equal volume of spendable incomes. This equality arises from the definition of terms involved. In particular, income is measured when it accrues, rather than when it is actually paid. This eliminates disparities between expenditures and incomes which arise from the usual time lag between the receipt of funds by business and the payment of wages and other incomes. We shall return to this matter subsequently.

In equation form, our GNP relations look like this:

$$GNP = C + I + G = \text{value added by all producers}$$
$$= \text{gross incomes accruing} = PDI + BDI + NGR$$

Actually, the intermediate stages of this equation are not of direct concern. Our subsequent discussion will concentrate on the basic equality between expenditures for current output and the disposable incomes of persons, business, and government. Furthermore, it is useful to stress that, in the aggregate, it is the expenditures which determine the income. Thus,

$$C + I + G \rightleftarrows PDI + BDI + NGR$$

The arrow reminds us that we have a flow relationship, not merely an arithmetic equality.

Sector Behavior—Who Gets the Income? The preceding equation contains on both sides terms relating to the three major sectors of the economy—consumers, business, and government. To explain the behavior of their expenditures, it is useful to give attention to the factors which determine the division of income among them. Logically, the government takes its share of total income first, since its decisions over taxation and expenditure have an element of compulsion which the others lack. Of the remaining incomes, business firms have considerable latitude in deciding how much of their profits to retain within the firm. After government and business have taken their shares, the remainder goes to personal disposable income as a residual. Thus PDI depends on total GNP expenditure, on government tax policy, and on business decisions to retain income.

Business disposable income has been a stable proportion of gross income, largely because of the stability of depreciation allowances. Since 1950, BDI has consistently accounted for about 10 per cent of GNP. When tax rates are at a given level, the proportion of GNP going to the government is also relatively constant. If BDI and NGR take relatively constant proportions of GNP, then of course PDI will also take about the same fraction of GNP from year to year. For analytical purposes, we shall generally assume that the proportional division of income shares among the three sectors is stable over time, except when changes in tax rates occur.

Sector Behavior—Deficits and Surpluses Now we are ready to bring together our sector accounts and compare the disposable income of each sector with its expenditure.

Sector	Disposable income	Expenditure	Surplus or deficit
Consumers	$402	$375	+$28
Business	60	82	−23
Government	123	123	+1
Foreign	2	4	−2
Statistical discrepancy	−3		−3
Total	$584	$584	0

Figures may not add up to totals because of rounding.

After minor adjustments for the international account and statistical discrepancy, we arrive at a consistent set of accounts in which the total income and total expenditure are equal. By definition, then, the deficits and surpluses must balance out. In 1963, the consumer sector showed a substantial surplus and the business sector a substantial deficit. Surpluses in the consumer sector and deficits in the business sector have been characteristic of all the years since 1945.

These relationships are also expressed in terms of saving and investment. For the consumer and business sectors, saving is defined in national-income accounts as the difference between disposable income and consumption. Personal saving is equal to the sector surplus shown above, or $28 billion. Business firms do not spend for consumption, so business saving includes all BDI, or $60 billion in 1963. For completeness, we include a concept of government "saving," defined simply as the surplus or deficit of the government sector. (The figure is negative when the sector shows a deficit.)

After making minor allowances for the international account and statistical discrepancy, we arrive at a total for saving of $85 billion. This is equal to domestic investment of $82 billion, plus net foreign investment of $3 billion. For any given year, saving and investment are equal by definition. This equality is useful to the statistician, but it can be a source of great confusion when we attempt to explain the behavior of total expenditures. The term "saving" here means income not spent on consumption. Thus it includes direct purchases of capital goods and repayment of debts, as well as increased holdings of financial assets. Consequently, "saving" in this national-income sense is more inclusive than "financial saving."

The time relationship may also be confusing. The measure of saving used by national-income accounts is sometimes called "ex post saving," meaning that it is determined by looking back over a period of time which is completed and deducting the consumption of the period from the income of the same period. For purposes of explanation, however, it is sometimes more useful to use a different concept of saving, one that reflects the amount people intend or plan to save out of a given income. This is called saving "ex ante," since it is determined by looking ahead from income to subsequent saving and consumption. This may differ from saving ex post for several reasons. One is that the income measured by national-income data is income accruing, some of which may not actually have been paid out yet. A wage earner's wage is accruing every day he works, but he doesn't get it until the end of the pay period. It may be misleading to assume that his saving and spending this week represent his reaction to the income he will receive when the week is over. Furthermore, when people's incomes change, their reactions to the change may take a while to be completed, so that there is a time lag between the actual payment of income and the development of a desired saving-consumption pattern. We shall make use of this concept of ex ante saving when we attempt to explain spending behavior.

Income and Expenditure Discussion of surpluses and deficits for economic sectors implies that the "normal" state of affairs is for each transactor to spend an amount about equal to its income. There are certainly a large number of households, businesses, and government units for which this is true. Most of them are unable to spend very much more than their incomes and unwilling to spend much less.

For any individual transactor or sector, there are three possible sources of funds for spending. Spending can be financed out of income, out of borrowing or similar external financing, or by drawing on cash or other assets that were accumulated in the past. This can be expressed in the following equation:

Income + borrowing = spending + increased cash and other financial assets

Of course, where net repayment of debts or decreased holding of financial assets occurs, the relevant items would have minus signs.

From this equation, it is clear why most transactors cannot spend much more than their income. Their access to credit is limited, and they do not have a large amount of assets accumulated. On the other hand, most of them have incomes which are not excessive in relation to their desires to buy current output. Consequently they spend most of what they earn.

Expenditure behavior can usefully be considered to reflect the interplay of two forces—the desire to spend and the ability to do so. The latter in turn depends on income, existing assets, and the availability of credit. Or we can rearrange things slightly and say that the level of spending depends on the available amount of income and credit and on the relative strength of the desire to spend, the desire to accumulate cash and other financial assets, and the desire to avoid the costs of borrowing.

Here are the elements of a theory of expenditure behavior which we shall develop in the chapters which follow. Three factors emerging from our discussion so far will be stressed:

1. The tendency for changes in income to produce similar changes in expenditure, particularly for consumers

2. The way in which desires to save and to borrow influence and are influenced by interest rates and credit conditions

3. The relationship among the quantity of money in existence, the public's desire to hold cash balances, and the cost and terms of credit

GNP as a Flow over Time Although GNP data from the national-income accounts are accrual data in which expenditure and income receipt occur simultaneously, it is useful for analytical purposes to think of the process

as unfolding over time. This gives us a better understanding of how variations in GNP spending occur. We shall retain the notion that a given volume
of GNP expenditures creates an equal amount of income at the same time.
However, let us suppose that it takes a while for this income to be actually
paid and for people's spending to adjust to it. Expenditures in time period 1
become income in the same period, but that income is spent in period 2. The
process can be depicted in this flow chart:

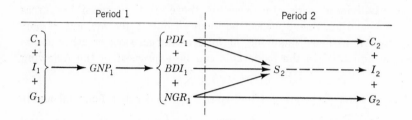

In this chart, the solid lines represent points of flow where equality
necessarily holds. Thus all GNP expenditures pass into disposable incomes
or NGR, all PDI goes into consumption or saving, all BDI goes into saving,
and all NGR goes into government purchases or saving (if we count a government surplus or deficit as positive or negative saving). But the saving
shown here is not the ex post saving we encountered before. It is saving ex
ante, representing the amount people want to save out of the income of
period 1, and is the difference between the income of period 1 and the expenditure of period 2. There is no necessity for it to be equal to investment.
That is why we have drawn only a broken line between S_2 and I_2. The
amount people decide to save out of the income of period 1 need not be equal
to the amount of investment which will be made in period 2.

This possibility of divergence is in accord with our commonsense notions of finance. Suppose people are struck with a great urge to save, cut
their expenditures accordingly, and hoard currency in their mattresses. As
sales fall off, businesses may well reduce their expenditures for capital
goods. Saving is up, investment down. Result: GNP spending in period 2
falls below that of period 1. Suppose in the next period everyone takes the
money out of his mattress and spends it. The delighted businessmen now
buy more capital goods. Saving is down, investment up, and GNP expenditures rise.

The surplus-deficit analysis is also useful as a means to analyze the flow
of GNP spending over time, provided we calculate surpluses and deficits ex
ante. If everyone were to spend in period 2 less than the income he received
in period 1, GNP expenditures would fall. In order for GNP to rise over
time, there must be sufficient deficit spending somewhere in the system so
that the expenditures of period 2 rise above the income of period 1. Tradi-

tionally, the business sector has spent sufficiently more than its income to offset the surplus of consumers and then some. But if private deficit spending falls short, government deficits may be a useful method of remedying the deficiency.

Whether one uses the terminology of saving and investment or surpluses and deficits is a matter of taste. Both focus attention on the same important area, which we might call the "gap" in the circular flow. Here funds pass out of the main circuit through financial saving, while borrowing brings money back into the main circuit. Clearly the gap is a point of linkage between the main money circuit and the financial circulation, and this is an appropriate place to turn our attention to the latter area.

THE FINANCIAL CIRCULATION

General Character The main money circuit derives its structure from the flow of resources from households to producers, and the flow of output from producers to households. The financial circulation, by contrast, derives its structure from the flow of funds from savers to borrowers. However, a large part of the financial circulation consists of turnover transactions which are related only marginally to saving or to spending on credit.

The financial circulation is the domain of financial institutions—commercial banks, savings banks, savings and loan associations, insurance companies, brokers, and many others. Most of the financial saving performed by households, business, and government pours funds into these institutions, and most of the spending on credit by the nonfinancial sectors draws funds from these institutions.

While the main money circuit involves payments for goods and services, the financial circulation involves payments for financial assets. A large volume of these consists of specialized claims against financial intermediaries —checking deposits, savings deposits and shares, insurance, and pension rights. With the exception of checking deposits, these assets are largely held by households and are not directly transferable. The other financial assets are the "primary securities" issued chiefly by nonfinancial deficit spenders (although some are issued by financial institutions).[5] Here are included corporate stocks and bonds, mortgages, government securities, and promissory notes of all descriptions. Most of the assets of financial intermediaries consist of primary securities, and they hold a large portion of the total amount in existence.

Primary securities of larger and better-known business firms or government units are actively bought and sold among investors. It is customary

[5] John G. Gurley and Edward S. Shaw, "Financial Intermediaries and the Saving-Investment Process," *Journal of Finance*, May, 1956.

to distinguish between transactions in the "money market" and those in the "capital market." Money-market transactions generally involve interest-bearing securities with low risk and short maturity. The chief forms are three-month Treasury bills, commercial paper, and negotiable certificates of deposit issued by commercial banks. Such assets are attractive to holders because they combine liquidity and income. Large nonfinancial corporations need such large holdings of liquid assets that it is worth their while to keep some of their funds in interest-bearing form. In the money market, they can buy short-term securities with perhaps only a few days to run. Some firms may engage in such operations almost every day, buying securities when cash piles up, selling them when cash needs rise. Commercial banks use the money market as a means of adjusting to variations in their reserves, by transactions in securities, commercial paper, or Federal funds.

The capital market involves mostly stocks and bonds—securities of long or indefinite maturity. Issuance of such securities is often initiated to finance purchases of current output. However, the bulk of capital-market transactions consists of transfers of existing securities—chiefly stocks. The importance of such transactions is that they influence the terms on which new security issues can be sold and thus may have an effect on GNP spending.

Because of the ease with which both borrowers and investors can substitute one class of financial claim for another, there is a considerable degree of interdependence between the money and capital markets. Of particular concern is the manner in which transactions in financial assets affect interest rates.

Interest Rates   Many categories of financial assets pay interest. One class consists of savings assets, such as savings accounts and United States savings bonds. Interest rates on such savings assets are commonly public knowledge, available to all comers, and change rather sluggishly over time. A second class of interest-bearing claims consists of promissory notes of business firms and individuals borrowing from banks and other lenders. Interest charges on such loans may differ among borrowers, depending on evaluations of risk, expenses of loan administration, and other variables.

Our concern here is primarily with a third class of interest-bearing claims: marketable debt securities such as bonds. A bond ordinarily carries a specific interest rate, which determines the dollar amount of interest it will pay. However, if an investor buys a bond at a price other than par, the rate of return he will receive will not be equal to the coupon rate specified on the bond. What he gets is called the "yield," the ratio between the expected money return (in interest and principal) and the actual cost of the bond. The yield is ordinarily calculated to the maturity date.

When a bond is newly issued or is selling at its redemption value, it is easy to calculate the yield. For instance, if a bond paying $40 a year interest and redeemable for $1,000 is now selling for $1,000, it will yield its purchaser 4 per cent. But suppose this bond is not selling at par. Let us assume that it can be purchased for $900 and matures in 10 years. The current purchaser will still receive $40 in interest but, in addition, at the end of 10 years will receive a capital gain of $100, which is the excess of redemption value over purchase price. This capital gain is equal to an average of $10 a year additional income, so that the average annual income is really about $50. This is the return on an investment of only $900 and comes to about 5.6 per cent. The decline in the market price of this bond raised its yield in two ways—by increasing the total money income and by reducing the original capital investment required to obtain it.

Accurate calculation of bond yields requires the use of a compound discount formula, in which the income of each time period is weighted inversely to its distance in the future. The general formula relating the yield r to the price P and income M of a bond is

$$P = \frac{M_1}{1 + r} + \frac{M_2}{(1 + r)^2} + \cdots + \frac{M_n}{(1 + r)^n}$$

In this, the subscripts to M represent the successive time periods. In our example above, M_1, M_2, . . . would represent the annual interest of $40 a year, while M_n ($n = 10$) would be $1,040, the interest and redemption value in the tenth year. Solving the equation indicates a true yield of about 5.4 per cent.

Let us see what happens when a bond sells above its maturity value. Suppose a bond which pays $50 a year and which will be redeemed in 5 years for $1,000 is selling for $1,100. What is its yield? Although the bond pays $50 interest each year, if held to maturity it will decline $100 in value, an average loss of $20 a year. Thus the average net return is only $30 a year on an investment of $1,100. The short-cut calculation suggests a yield of 2.73 per cent. Solving the discount formula indicates that the true value is 2.82 per cent. This difference shows how the short cut overweights the capital loss.

Our examples demonstrate an important conclusion: The yield of any given security issued in the past varies inversely with its current market price. Since the interest *payments* on existing bonds are fixed, it is through variations in their market prices that their yields can vary. The shorter the maturity of a bond, the more effect a given price change will have on its yield. With a 1-year bond, a 1 per cent increase in price will lower the prospective yield by about one percentage point. With a 10-year bond, however, a 1 per cent rise in price will cause the yield to fall only about one-eighth of a percentage point.

The Market Rate of Interest Given free operation of supply and demand, interest-bearing securities of similar risk and maturity will all tend to have about the same yield at any given time. The coupon rates of interest may differ, but the market prices will adjust to equalize the yields. The common rate of yield is called the "market rate of interest."

This equalization of yields comes about through the influence of *arbitrage,* which simply means buying something where it is cheap and selling it where it is expensive. Suppose an investor holds a government bond paying $30 interest, redeemable in 10 years for $1,000 and currently selling for $1,000. The investor discovers that he can buy for $1,000 another government bond of the same maturity and redemption value, but paying $40 interest a year. Obviously this situation cannot last. The investor will sell his $30 bond and use the proceeds to buy the $40 bond. And so will everyone else, until the market value of the $40 bond rises, that of the $30 bond falls, and eventually their prices reach a point where the percentage yields of the two are the same.

Changes in bond prices will affect all bonds of similar risk and maturity in similar fashion—arbitrage will tend to make them move up or down together. Such price changes will be equivalent to changes in the market rate of interest. A general rise in the prices of existing bonds is equivalent to a reduction in the market rate of interest, while a price reduction raises the interest rate. An increase in the market rate of interest implies a drop in the prices of bonds, and vice versa.

The Structure of Interest Rates   The yields of different kinds of bonds are not all the same at any one time. Yields differ in part because of differences in the credit standing of borrowers. The greater the risk that interest and/or principal may not be paid promptly, the higher the yield needed to get people to buy the bonds. This explains why United States government securities have lower yields than those of corporations. Other variations arise from peculiar features of individual bond issues. Interest on bonds of state and local governments is exempt from Federal income tax, with the result that such bonds can be sold to wealthy investors at low yields.

Interest-rate differentials also arise from differences in the length of time to maturity. The longer a bond has to go until it is redeemed, the wider the fluctuation to which its market price is subject, and consequently the greater the capital-value risk borne by an investor who may want his money before the maturity date. On the other hand, the *income* risk is greater if one invests in short-term securities. The term structure of rates is also affected by the willingness of borrowers to incur obligations of various durations. Attitudes of both borrowers and investors will be influenced by their expectations of the future course of interest rates and asset prices.

Although there is no such thing as "the" rate of interest, equal for all loans and bonds, the various yields on different securities do tend to move up and down together in response to the general currents of the economy. An increase in yields on government securities, for instance, will probably start a chain reaction which will tend to pull up yields on other types of securities as well. The constant shifting around by investors seeking high yields and by borrowers seeking low payments links together the various sectors of the capital market.

Causes and Consequences of Interest-rate Changes   These fluctuations in the general level of interest rates can be explained in terms of the forces of supply and demand. In one sense, they reflect changes in the supply of interest-bearing assets and in the demand for them. In another sense, they reflect the demand for loans and credit and the supply of loanable funds available. In Chapter 9 we shall develop a fuller explanation. Here we shall note that interest rates are influenced by many of the same decisions that influence the movements of GNP expenditures. Desires to save and invest affect the level of interest rates, and in turn interest rates may have an influence on the actual behavior of saving, investment, and GNP. More specifically, events in the main money circuit may be influenced in the following ways:

1. Interest rates and security prices affect people's willingness to acquire and hold earning financial assets instead of buying current output or holding idle cash.

2. Interest rates and security prices determine the cost of borrowing and influence willingness to borrow to buy current output.

3. Credit conditions determine the *amount* of funds prospective borrowers are *able* to obtain.

4. Interest rates influence the distribution of income between creditors and debtors. This is not very important economically, but its political repercussions are great.

SUMMARY

The focal point in analysis of the money economy is the volume of expenditures for currently produced goods and services, for this volume bears substantially on economic welfare through its influence on output, employment, and prices. This expenditure level and the resulting flow of income are measured by gross national product categories. *In toto*, these make up the main money circuit of incomes and expenditures. The important conclusions of GNP accounting are, first, that GNP expenditures (consumption, investment, and government purchases) are equal to (and help determine) the value of output; second, GNP expenditures give rise to an equal amount of disposable income for persons, business, and government.

Changes in GNP over time arise because saving (ex ante) diverges from investment. If saving is higher, GNP will fall. More funds pour out through the gap than are brought back in. If investment exceeds saving, GNP will rise.

However, a large portion of money payments occurs outside the main circuit, in the financial circulation. The two areas overlap in the area we have called the "gap" in the main circuit—the area between saving and investment. Saving, unless used directly for purchase of capital goods or held in idle cash, flows into financial assets or debt repayment. This flow pours funds into the financial circulation, from which they may be withdrawn to finance investment spending. The flow of funds in the financial circulation determines interest rates and credit conditions. Market rates of interest on outstanding fixed-income securities vary inversely with changes in the market prices of the securities.

Most transactions in the financial circulation are turnover transactions not directly involved in the saving-investment flow. However, these may affect saving and investment by influencing interest rates, security prices, and the availability of credit. The structure of the main circuit and financial circulation is impressionistically depicted by Figure 6-1.

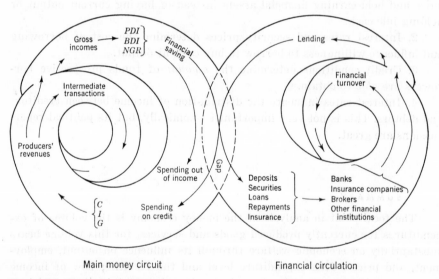

Figure 6-1. The money economy.

QUESTIONS FOR STUDY

1. "Since GNP is equal to private disposable incomes plus taxes minus government transfer payments, an increase in taxes will raise GNP." Discuss.

2. What is the difference between the money market and the capital market? What does the money market have to do with the operations of commercial banks?

3. How does saving ex post differ from saving ex ante? Why is the distinction important?

4. Suppose the flow of GNP into disposable incomes is rigidly constant, so that 70 per cent always goes to consumers, 20 per cent to net government revenue, and 10 per cent to business. Suppose in addition that each sector spends during any time period a rigidly constant percentage of the income received in the previous period. If consumers spend 90 per cent of their income, business firms 160 per cent, and government 120 per cent, what will happen to GNP over time? What financial arrangements may be necessary to make this result possible?

5. Define the following as used in GNP accounting:
  a. Consumption
  b. Investment
  c. Transfer payment
  d. Saving
  e. Disposable income
  f. Capital consumption allowances

6. In 1963, the United States exported more than $31 billion worth of output, but GNP, supposedly the value of output, showed only about $4 billion of "net" exports. Why?

7. Some financial transactions are closely related to the flow of GNP incomes and expenditures, and some are not. Explain the distinction.

8. Suppose a government bond paying $50 every December matures in December, 1968, for $2,500. How much will it sell for in January, 1966, if the market rate of interest is 4 per cent? If it sells for $2,200, what is the market rate of interest?

SUGGESTED READINGS

Board of Governors, Federal Reserve System: *Flow of Funds in the United States, 1939–1953,* Washington, 1955.
———: *Flow of Funds Accounts, 1945–1962,* Washington, 1963.
Copeland, Morris: *A Study of Moneyflows in the United States,* National Bureau of Economic Research, Inc., New York, 1952.
Lewis, John P.: *Business Conditions Analysis,* McGraw-Hill Book Company, New York, 1959.
U.S. Department of Commerce: *U.S. Income and Output,* Washington, 1958.
———: *Survey of Current Business* (issued monthly; July issue contains national-income data for previous year).

chapter seven

THE RELATION OF SPENDING
TO PRODUCTION, PRICES,
AND EMPLOYMENT

A GENERAL VIEW

The economic welfare of a society depends, as we have seen, on the level of its output, the way output is divided up, and the rapidity with which output grows. Economic welfare is also influenced by the extent of unemployment and by the stability of employment and prices.

In the long run, the significant determinants of productivity per capita operate on the side of supply, influencing the capacity to produce. Capacity depends on the quantity and quality of resources available for production and on the efficiency of the technology and management applied to them. Money and the financial system influence long-run productivity insofar as they contribute to the efficiency with which the economic system is organized.

In the short run, however, production, employment, and prices depend on the rate of money expenditures for goods and services. In a capitalistic economy, where economic activities are directed by the search for profits and high incomes, entrepreneurs' decisions about production are strongly influenced by the current and prospective demand for their products. If the total expenditure for goods and services is high, entrepreneurs will put to use the productive resources available in the country. Production and employment will be high. If expenditures are too high, price inflation may cause social tensions and disrupt distribution and even production. If expenditures are too low, firms will not employ all the productive resources available. People who want jobs will be unable to find them, even while output falls far short of meeting consumer desires.

Thus the volume of spending for current output (GNP) is the central concept for monetary theory. In the previous chapter, we examined the structure of the expenditure-transactions flow of the economy. Now we must move in both directions from this central concept. First, we must deal at greater length with the consequences of variations in GNP expenditures—their effects on output, employment, and prices, and the significance of these for economic welfare. Then we shall turn to the problem of explaining variations in GNP expenditures, with particular attention to the supply of money and people's desire to hold it or spend it. We take up the consequences of spending first to give perspective to the subsequent discussion of causes. Explaining variations in GNP becomes difficult at times, and it is desirable to know from the start just why the effort is important.

OUTPUT AND PRICES

Definitions and Measurements　One of the most important elements in gross national product accounting is the principle that *the flow of expenditures for current production is equal to the value of output currently produced.* The value of output has in turn two dimensions, one relating to the quantity of goods and services, and the other to their prices. Each of these dimensions bears significantly on economic welfare. Increases in the quantity of output are the method by which the real income and economic welfare of the population as a whole can increase. Changes in the price level may bring with them distorting effects on the distribution of real income and real wealth and thus appear as something we would prefer to minimize.

For any given year, the total value of GNP could be derived by multiplying the quantity of each item produced by its market price and then adding together the resulting dollar figures. When we attempt to compare GNP figures for different years, however, we find that prices never remain the same. To facilitate comparisons over time, the statisticians calculate a separate series for "gross national product in constant prices." The quantity of each item produced in each year is multiplied by the price it sold for in some base year (currently 1954). The result is a dollar aggregate showing how much the output of, say, 1960 would have sold for at prices prevailing in 1954. Changes in this dollar aggregate reflect the changes in the quantity of output over time.

The actual figure for GNP expenditures ("current prices") in 1960 was $503 billion, but the output of 1960, if valued at 1954 prices, would have sold for only $440 billion. The difference between the two values is a measure of the extent to which prices rose from 1954 to 1960. We can extract and quantify this price level change by dividing $440 billion into $503 billion. Such a calculation indicates that 1960 prices were 114 per cent of those of 1954. The price level indicators derived in this manner are called the "implicit price deflators" for GNP data.

In evaluating changes in the money value of GNP over time, these two statistical concepts are extremely useful. We shall use the data for GNP in constant prices as a measure of output and the figures for the implicit price deflator as a measure of prices. In this sense, GNP in each year is equal to output multiplied by price. Just how this works out quantitatively can be demonstrated by the following comparisons:

Year	GNP expenditures	=	Output in 1954 prices	×	Implicit price deflator (1954 = 100)
1950	$285 billion		$318 billion		90%
1954	363		363		100
1962	555		475		117

Between 1950 and 1962 GNP expenditures nearly doubled. However, prices increased by 30 per cent over this period. Consequently the increase in output was nearer to 50 per cent. Separate consideration of output and prices is clearly essential if one is to make a welfare evaluation of GNP changes over time.

We now have another fundamental equation for GNP to add to those of the preceding chapter. By definition,

$$GNP = O \times P$$

Changes in GNP expenditures must therefore produce changes in output and prices. Just what these changes are likely to be we shall explore later in this chapter. We conclude this section by noting that if one knows any two of the elements of this equation, one can determine the third. Output can be determined by dividing GNP by the price index, or the price index can be determined by dividing GNP by the figure for output.

Price Indexes   The implicit price deflator of GNP is merely one example of a price index. Another is the well-known consumer price index, and a third covers wholesale prices. Within all these are more detailed index numbers covering narrower groups of goods or services. A price index number expresses the average prices of one year as a percentage of those of another (base) year. If all the prices changed by the same proportion from year to year, it would be an easy task to construct price indexes. But they don't, and when we try to average changes of varying magnitudes in different prices, we encounter the problem of determining the relative importance of each price—the problem of weighting.

Not all prices are equally important. The most common method of making allowance for differences of importance is to weight more heavily the price changes of products on which people spend the most money.

Let us compute a simple price index to show how it is done. The following table shows some hypothetical price quotations for two separate dates and the quantities of the respective products purchased at each date.

| Commodity | First year | | | Second year | | |
	Price	Quan-tity	Expenditure	Price	Quan-tity	Expenditure
Steak	$1.00	500	$ 500 (30%)	$0.80	1,000	$ 800 (47%)
Shirts	3.50	200	700 (40%)	4.50	100	450 (26.5%)
Gasoline	0.25	2,000	500 (30%)	0.26	1,730	450 (26.5%)
Total expenditure			$1,700 (100%)			$1,700 (100%)

For each product, the price in the second year is expressed as a percentage of that in the first. Then each of the resulting "price relatives" is weighted by the percentage of expenditures devoted to each product. Using the expenditure pattern of the first year, the computation would be

Commodity	P_2/P_1 (%)		Weight (%)	
Steak	80	×	30	= 2,400
Shirts	129	×	40	= 5,160
Gasoline	104	×	30	= 3,120
Total			100	10,680

Dividing the total weights (100) into the aggregate of 10,680 gives us the price index of 106.8, which indicates a price increase of about 7 per cent from the first to the second year.

This is the way most indexes are calculated, but it is not the only possible way. For instance, we could, with ample justification, have calculated the index on the basis of the expenditure pattern of the second year. Try it. Comparing the results of the two methods illustrates very well how much the result depends on the weights given to individual products.

In interpreting changes in price indexes, it is also well to remember that individual consumption patterns differ widely. Consequently, the impact of price increases may be far from uniform. In the example just given, families who spend a large portion of their income on food may benefit from price changes on balance, while those who spend more on clothing and transportation will be adversely affected.

In constructing price indexes covering long periods of time, another difficulty arises. New products are introduced, and existing products change in quality. Often there is no "correct" way to work these changes into the price index. Since the trend has been for the nature and quality of products to improve, price indexes probably overstate the extent to which prices have risen during the last twenty-five years.

These factors should caution us against attributing to price indexes a degree of precision which, by their very nature, they cannot achieve.

Prices and the Value of Money   Much discussion in monetary theory has been devoted to the "value of money." This term is best interpreted to mean the amount of goods and services which can be purchased for a given sum. Thus the value of money will vary inversely with the prices of the things one wants to spend it on. The consumer price index is often used as a measure of such changes. A rise in the price index from 100 to 120 would indicate that the value of money had declined to $\frac{5}{6}$ of its previous level ($= 100/120$).

When using the consumer price index in this manner, one should keep in mind the limitations inherent in such price indexes. Even over short periods of time, they fail to reflect the variations in tastes among individual consumers. Over long periods they are unable to allow for improvements in product quality and for the introduction of new products. There are price indexes going back more than a hundred years which might be interpreted uncritically to imply that the value of the dollar has declined greatly since, say, 1860. Actually, a person from today's world returning to 1860 would find that his dollars would buy him lots of wheat, potatoes, common labor, and other elementary goods and services, but he would be unable to purchase most of the things which are integral parts of the modern standard of living. They simply did not exist. Even in a short-period analysis, price indexes are misleading unless goods are actually freely available at the indicated prices. During World War II, price controls held down the selling prices of many products, but the value of money was reduced by the fact that shortages and rationing rendered goods unavailable in the desired quantities at those prices.

Let us emphasize that the value of money is essentially a relationship between money and the things it will buy. It is not an intrinsic property of money itself. We cannot assert that the value of money has declined unless we can show that a dollar will buy less.

In this book, most references to "the price level" refer to the implicit price deflator—the price index for GNP. This index covers not only the prices of consumer goods and services, but also capital goods and government purchases of goods and services.

BEHAVIOR OF OUTPUT, EMPLOYMENT, AND PRICES

Historical Record   Historically, output, the price level, and the number of people employed have all varied directly with GNP expenditures. The extent of this influence can be inferred from Figures 7-1 and 7-2. Here are shown four scatter diagrams covering the years 1923–1963. On each, the vertical dimension measures the percentage change in GNP expenditures from year to year. Horizontally, three diagrams show the corresponding percentage changes in the price level of GNP, in total output, and in employment. The fourth shows the change in the percentage of workers unemployed from year to year.

In each case, the relationship can be reasonably well expressed by a straight line. The four regression lines, fitted by the method of least squares, are shown in the diagrams. All four fit fairly well; the coefficients of correlation range from .79 for prices through .86 for employment, .94 for unemployment, up to .99 for output.

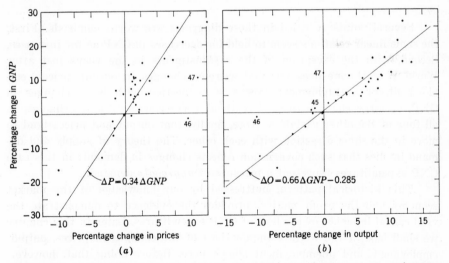

Figure 7-1. Year-to-year percentage changes in GNP expenditures, output, and prices, 1923–1963.

Source: Economic Report of the President. Output change is calculated from GNP in 1954 prices; price change is derived from GNP deflator, 1954 base.

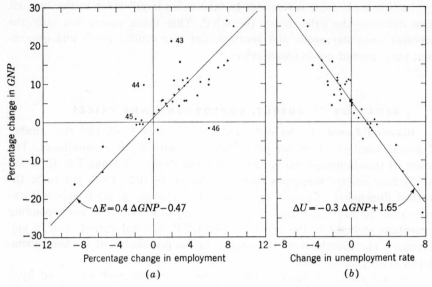

Figure 7-2. Year-to-year changes in GNP expenditures, employment, and unemployment, 1923–1963.

Source: Economic Report of the President. Changes in GNP and (civilian, nonfarm) employment are percentage changes in annual average levels. Change in unemployment is year-to-year change in percentage of labor force unemployed.

Several points revealed in these diagrams are worth emphasis. First, the same linear relations seem to hold for decreases in GNP as for increases. Second, with the exception of the readjustments in the years just after World War II, one does not find extreme changes in output, prices, employment, or unemployment except in connection with large changes in GNP, or large changes in GNP without correspondingly large changes in all four of the other variables. Note, finally, that output and prices tend to move in the same direction with each other. The theory of supply and demand implies that such covariation reflects changes in demand; in this case GNP expenditures represent a measure of *aggregate* demand.

This historical pattern, buttressed by our knowledge of the market economy and the profit motive, provides the evidence to demonstrate the vital causal influence of the flow of GNP expenditures. Later in this chapter we shall look at the welfare implications of the changes in prices, output, employment, and unemployment shown here. Before doing that, however, let us examine more closely some of the implications of the patterns shown in these diagrams.

The straight lines fitted to the data for output and prices have slopes of 0.66 and 0.34 respectively; since output and prices are the components of

GNP, the two coefficients should add up to unity. The coefficients indicate that variations in GNP expenditures have ordinarily gone about two-thirds into changes in output and about one-third into price changes. This record is not very encouraging to the prospects that we can achieve output growth without rising prices.

Employment and Unemployment   The data on employment and unemployment contain a number of interesting implications. The straight line derived for the employment data has this approximate value:

Percentage change in employment
$$= (0.4 \times \text{percentage change in GNP}) - 0.47$$

This implies that if GNP stays unchanged from one year to the next, employment falls. The reason for this is that the productivity of labor tends to rise over time. If output were to remain unchanged, it would take fewer men to produce it in the second year. In order to raise employment by 1 per cent, GNP expenditures would have to rise nearly 4 per cent.

The unemployment rate reflects changes in employment relative to changes in the number of people seeking work. As the population has grown, the American labor force has expanded steadily. In the period 1923–1963, the rate of growth was slightly in excess of 1 per cent per year. Thus if the number of jobs stayed constant, the unemployment rate would tend to rise by about 1 point. The equation for the straight line derived from the unemployment data is approximately this:

Change in per cent of labor force unemployed
$$= 1.65 - (0.3 \times \text{percentage change in GNP expenditures})$$

This implies that if GNP expenditures remained unchanged, the unemployment rate would tend to increase by 1.65 per cent of the labor force—reflecting a combination of the rise in the labor force and the rise in productivity we noted above.

On the average, it has been necessary for GNP expenditures to rise by 5 per cent per year to keep the unemployment rate from rising. And it has required a year-to-year rise of 8 per cent in GNP spending to reduce unemployment by 1 per cent of the labor force.

Ex Ante Relations   One should exercise extreme caution in using linear historical data of this sort for ex ante or forecasting purposes. There are complex interactions among output, prices, employment, and unemployment which condition their probable response to GNP change. Of particular importance is the influence of the existing level of unemployment.

The higher the existing level of unemployment, the more a given rise in GNP expenditures will tend to raise output and employment (and reduce unemployment) and the less it will tend to raise prices. In terms of the components of Figures 7-1 and 7-2, one might improve forecasting accuracy by shifting the regression lines to right or left on the basis of existing unemployment.

A second modification is necessary because the larger the rise in GNP expenditures, the more it will reduce the unemployment level, and thus the greater the probable proportionate influence on prices rather than output. Historically, the really large increases in GNP have mostly come when there was substantial unemployment. Thus the observations do not constitute a random sample. Ex ante, the lines relating GNP change to each of the other variables should probably bend.

A hypothetical illustration of these two possibilities is shown in Figure 7-3. Figure 7-3a shows the response of price change to GNP change. When initial unemployment is high, the response curve lies to the left and begins to bend to the right only at a relatively large GNP change. When initial unemployment is low, the price response curve lies farther to the right and begins to curve sooner.

Figure 7-3b shows the corresponding behavior for output, with the positions and curvature of the response schedules naturally being the reverse of those for prices. Curves drawn for employment would appear similar to those for output. We shall examine some of these response patterns in more detail later in this chapter.

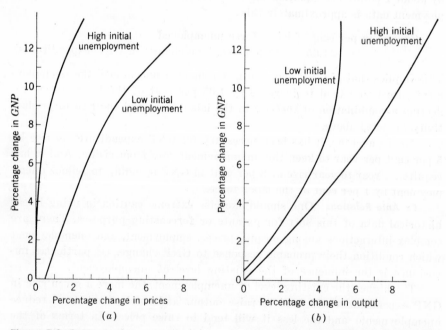

Figure 7-3. Response of output and prices to changes in GNP expenditures (hypothetical).

Other Influences Changes in GNP expenditures do not furnish a complete explanation for the behavior of output, prices, employment, and unemployment. The points in Figures 7-1 and 7-2 do not all lie on the regression line; there is substantial dispersion, particularly in the case of prices. Following are some of the possible reasons for these residual variations.

1. There may be significant trends over time in the response of the economy to variations in GNP expenditures, so that a relationship calculated for 1923–1963 as a whole does not measure very well what happens in shorter periods. This proves to be the case for prices in particular. As one approaches the present, price level changes become less and less responsive to year-to-year changes in GNP expenditures. For the years 1952–1963 inclusive, there is no significant relationship between year-to-year changes in GNP and in prices.

2. Output, prices, employment, and unemployment are clearly affected by factors other than aggregate demand. Important influences also arise from the side of aggregate supply. Changes in employment and unemployment are influenced by increases in the size and productivity of the labor force. Such increases also raise the productive capacity of the economy and thus make it possible for output to expand in response to the long-run growth of demand.

The response of output to changes in GNP expenditures would therefore tend to be greater, the greater the year-to-year increases in labor productivity. Even more significant, however, is the influence of unemployed manpower and productive capacity. A high rate of unemployment greatly increases the ease with which higher spending calls forth higher output—and correspondingly reduces the tendency for higher spending to push up prices.

3. Finally, we must remember that ultimately output, prices, employment, and unemployment are determined in individual product and service markets, and imperfections in the functioning of the market mechanism may be strong enough to affect the national totals in a manner which bears no close relation to aggregate demand. We note here two particular hypotheses which we shall explore subsequently. One is the hypothesis that our economy is subject to a systematic cost-push inflation, chiefly attributable to "administered" wage and price policies of powerful labor unions and giant business firms. The second is that our economy is troubled by "structural disequilibrium," arising from difficulties in transferring labor from areas of excess supply into areas where demand is strong.

We may properly observe, then, that the influence of aggregate demand on output, prices, employment, and unemployment is very strong and very important, but it is not the only influence on them, and its quantitative effects depend upon the behavior of supply factors and market imperfections. We shall explore these problems further in the paragraphs which follow. Since the unexplained variance was greatest for prices, our discussion will focus on price behavior and its implications.

The Behavior of Prices   From the consumer's standpoint, it often appears that business firms set their selling prices to suit themselves and that the customers can take them or leave them. Some would go as far as to say that most businessmen will charge the highest prices they can get. However, businessmen are chiefly interested in profits. The highest price is not always the most profitable price, for the quantity of things people will buy from a seller will usually vary inversely with the prices charged. If there are several independent sources of supply, the ability of any one seller to charge a high price may be very limited, since customers will quickly switch to his competitors. If monopoly or collusion exists, the customers may not have this option. Even then they may stop buying if the price gets too high, because they find some other product as a substitute or do without the product altogether.

Competition from other firms and other products thus helps to keep product prices down. The lower limits to prices are set by the costs of production. No firm can continue to operate very long if its selling prices consistently fall below average costs. Costs are incurred in buying productive resources or intermediate products and are also influenced by competition. Individual firms will be obliged to match or beat the going prices and wage rates if they are to obtain materials and labor. Producers' costs will depend on the prices determined in the markets for resources and for intermediate products. These prices will be determined by the quantity of resources which can be drawn upon and the demand for them. The demand for resources, however, is a derived demand which tends to move in response to the demand for finished products by consumers and other buyers.

Relation to Unemployment   In any market, a rise in demand can be absorbed without an increase in price if buyers can obtain increased quantities at the existing price. Such a situation exists in the market for labor and capital goods during a period of depression and unemployment, when men and machines are idle. If the demand for output rises, firms can hire more workers at the going wage rate and can put idle equipment into use. Costs of labor and capital goods are not likely to rise much, and consequently the additional output does not entail rising costs per unit produced. By contrast, if unemployment is low, rising demand for labor and other resources will be more likely to raise production costs.

The response of product prices to changes in demand depends very much on resource unemployment also. A business firm finding the demand for its products increased will be likely to raise its selling price if its efforts to increase output cause unit costs to rise and if the higher demand makes competition less effective. Both of these conditions occur when resources in the economy are nearly fully employed. If there is extensive resource unemployment, the firm faced with increased demand can expand output by drawing on unemployed resources, an action which will not exert much upward pressure on costs. What is more, competitors can do the same thing and may therefore be alert to take business away should the firm in question raise its price.

If our analysis is correct, it should be possible to derive from the statistics a formula for price changes using both GNP change and the level of unemployment as determining factors. Since the unemployment rate is influenced by changes in GNP, we cannot be sure that we are attributing precisely the proper weight to each factor. But the general behavior of the implicit price deflator for GNP for the years 1929–1962 can be very well estimated by this equation:

$$\text{Percentage change in price level} = (0.34 \times \text{per cent change in GNP}) + \frac{17.1}{\text{unemployment rate}} - 3.1$$

Two caveats are in order before one uses this equation for ex ante analysis. First, the unemployment rate is the average during the year in question. As we have seen, this itself is likely to be affected by the rate of change of GNP. For GNP changes within a "normal" range, the unemployment rate can probably be anticipated on the basis of a relationship similar to that implied by Figure 7-2. Second, the price level equation implies a linear relation between GNP change and price change. For large increases in GNP, this might better be replaced by a function similar to that shown in Figure 7-3.

Historical Behavior of Prices The degree to which our estimating equation describes price behavior since 1929 is indicated by Figure 7-4. This compares the actual level of the price deflator with that "predicted" by plugging in the estimates for price change to the actual price index for 1929. For comparison, the changes in GNP expenditures are also shown. Our equation does not fit the data perfectly, but it clearly matches the major movements and trend.

Let us look at the actual pattern of price changes a bit more closely.

1. Between 1929 and 1933 GNP expenditures dropped off sharply, and the price level fell in response to declining demand and increased unemployment. However, between 1932 and 1934 the actual price level rose more than it "should" have according to our equation. This suggests price-raising influences at work other than higher GNP and lower unemployment. Such influences can readily be identified in the form of some of the "recovery" measures of the New Deal, chiefly the NRA and the AAA, which had as a major goal raising price and wage levels.

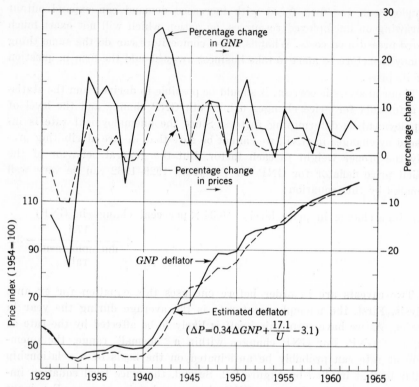

Figure 7-4. Behavior of the price level, 1929–1963, compared with behavior "predicted" by changes in GNP and level of unemployment.

Source: Calculated from data in *Economic Report of the President.*

2. From 1934 to 1943 our estimating line runs parallel to the actual price level, indicating that *changes* in prices followed the "normal" relation to changing GNP and the rate of unemployment. Note particularly that between 1934 and 1941, GNP expenditures went up by 94 per cent, but the price level rose by only 13 per cent. During this period the unemployment rate averaged nearly 17 per cent of the labor force.

3. With the coming of World War II, prices shot up in the face of rising expenditures and decreasing unemployment. However, the imposition of price controls kept actual prices from rising as much in 1944 and 1945 as our equation would have predicted. This relief was only temporary; once controls were lifted, prices rose more rapidly than our equation would warrant.

4. The outbreak of hostilities in Korea in 1950 brought another sharp rise in prices, although again not quite so great as our equation estimates. Since price controls were again in use, this may account for the divergence.

Over the period 1941–1952 inclusive, the price level nearly doubled. This resulted from a nearly threefold rise of GNP expenditures, a rise which exceeded the expansion potential of output. Unemployment was sharply reduced (it averaged under 4 per cent for 1941 through 1952), and the size and productivity of the labor force increased. But total output could increase only 72 per cent. The excess of demand over supply produced higher prices.

5. Since 1953, the price level has shown a gradual upward trend, corresponding closely with the trend estimated by our equation. Divergences appear in the year-to-year changes, but tend to balance out over time.

The following tabulation will help to summarize our historical analysis of the interaction of GNP expenditures, prices, output, and unemployment:

Period	Percentage increases in			Ratio of output change to price change	Rate of unemployment
	GNP	Prices	Output		
1934–1941	94	13	72	5.6	16.7
1941–1952	276	85	48	0.6	3.7
1952–1962	60	19	34	1.8	5.0

When unemployment is high, rising expenditures lead chiefly to increased output. Competition among workers and business firms tends to keep prices from rising very much. As full employment is more nearly reached, competition among buyers for scarce resources tends to pull prices up.

Demand Pull versus Cost Push It has been customary to distinguish between demand pull and cost push as upward influences on the price level, but the distinction is hard to sustain in practice. A strong upsurge of demand will tend to cause wage rates and other costs to rise as business firms bid for resources. If the business firms then increase prices in response to higher costs, the result may appear to be attributable to a cost push, whereas it originated in demand pull.

The conviction has been widely prevalent, however, that the American economy in recent years has been subject to an upward pressure on the level of wages and prices originating with sellers, rather than reflecting an excess of demand for goods and services. Emphasis is likely to fall upon the following areas:

1. *Wage-cost push.* Many people feel that labor unions have become sufficiently powerful in some sectors of the economy that they can force wages up more rapidly than the productivity of labor. To be sure, if the economy contains a lot of slack, employer resistance to wage increases may

be great, and the unions may exercise restraint for fear of causing unemployment. But if GNP expenditures are increasing and the demand for goods and labor is brisk, union policies will force up wage costs per unit and thus contribute to price increases.

2. *Administered prices.* Much attention has also been directed at some industries in which production is concentrated in a few firms, either nationally (automobiles) or locally (construction), among whom price competition may be relatively lacking. Through collusion, price leadership, or mental telepathy, firms in such markets may raise prices simply to gain a larger profit markup, whether or not costs have risen. Of course, firms will not want to do this if they sustain heavy losses of sales, so price restraint may be expected when demand is weak.

There is probably some truth in both cases, but their importance can easily be exaggerated. Wage and price increases which occur in markets with considerable monopoly power in labor or business might have occurred anyway. Granted that monopoly power may make a given wage or price higher than it would be otherwise, it does not follow that wages and prices will rise faster over time where monopoly power is strong.

Comparison of wage and price behavior prior to and subsequent to 1929 suggests that there has been an increase in the upward movement of wages and prices associated with a given state of demand and unemployment. The probable magnitude of the shift is 1 or 2 per cent per year. Furthermore, the spread of unionization and increased use of "personnel management" wage policies since the 1930s have reduced the tendency for wage rates to fall during a slump and have reduced the sensitivity of wage-rate changes to year-to-year variations in GNP.[1]

It seems more plausible to attribute the shift in wage-price behavior to wages than to profit margins. Union strength has risen greatly since 1929, whereas the degree of seller concentration in business has changed very little. There is some evidence that prices of more concentrated industries rose more than others during 1947–1958.[2] But some of this represented a "catch-up" phenomenon by industries whose prices had risen less during the earlier 1940s. And the steel and auto industries, which displayed the symptoms of sellers' inflation during the 1950s, were obliged to practice extreme restraint from 1958 on when the intensity of foreign competition increased.

Certainly an examination of the areas of consumer prices which continued to rise in 1958–1963 lends little support to theories which attribute

[1] Robert R. France, "Wages, Unemployment, and Prices in the United States: 1890–1932, 1947–1957," *Industrial and Labor Relations Review*, January, 1962, presents evidence that the upward tilt of wage rates has increased.

[2] Harold M. Levinson, "Postwar Movement of Prices and Wages in Manufacturing Industries," Study Paper 2, Joint Economic Committee, U.S. Congress, *Study of Employment, Growth, and Price Levels*, 1960, p. 6.

upward pressure to monopolistic union or business activity. Prices of consumer durable goods in 1963 were only 1 per cent above their 1957–1959 average, whereas rents were up 7 per cent and other services 12 per cent. The possibility remains, however, that monopoly elements in labor or business may have contributed indirectly to the upward movement in the general price level by making it more difficult for wages and prices to fall in areas of weak demand or rapid improvement in technology. This may appropriately be considered as a part of the next problem, that of structural disequilibrium.

Structural Disequilibrium The persistence of relatively high unemployment rates while the price level continued to inch upward in the years 1958–1963 brought attention to the problem of structural disequilibrium, a phenomenon capable of explaining both unemployment and rising prices as the result of inadequacies in the functioning of the market mechanism. The problem arises because of inability of supply to adjust to demand in individual sectors of the economy.

Structural disequilibrium may exist in the markets for individual products as a result of shifts in demand or technology. American agriculture is the most notable case: rapidly rising productivity in the face of inelastic demand has pushed down farm prices and incomes. Despite the steady decline in the number of persons engaged in farming, the amount of labor in that sector remains excessive in relation to the rest of the economy.

The steel industry has encountered similar problems, in part because of the increased pressure of foreign competition. Here industry concentration and union strength have prevented wages and prices from declining; instead, job opportunities on the production line have declined with the rise in labor productivity.

In other sectors, supply has been unable to keep pace with rapidly rising demand. Medical care and education since 1940 have been sectors where rising demand has encountered inelastic supply, sending prices steadily upward. Professor Charles Schultze has summarized the problem in these terms:

> In the modern American economy prices and wages are much more sensitive to increases in demand than to decreases. As a consequence, a rapid shift in the composition of demand will lead to a general rise in prices, even without an excessive growth in the overall level of demand or an autonomous upward push of wages. Prices rise in those sectors of the economy where demands are growing rapidly, and decline by smaller amounts, or not at all, in sectors where demands are falling.
>
> When the composition of demand changes rapidly, prices of semi-fabricated materials and components tend to rise, on the average, since price advances among materials in heavy demand are not balanced by price decreases for materials in excess supply. Wage rate gains in most industries tend to

equal or almost equal those granted in the rapidly expanding industries. As a consequence, even those industries faced by sagging demand for their products experience a rise in costs. This intensifies the general price rise, since at least some of the higher costs are passed on in prices.

The resulting inflation can be explained neither in terms of an overall excess of money demand nor an autonomous upward push of wages. Rather it originates in excess demands in particular sectors and is spread to the rest of the economy by the cost mechanism. It is characteristic of the resource allocation process in an economy with rigidities in its price structure.[3]

Labor-market Problems   Structural disequilibrium may also be a problem in markets for labor and other productive resources. Indeed, much of the recent concern for technological unemployment resulting from automation can be discussed in these terms. Even if the demand for labor as a whole is equal to the supply, there may be substantial discrepancies in demand and supply in particular industries, regions, or skill classifications. Ultimately the last classification is the most troublesome.

It may be unduly optimistic to expect labor to move from situations of labor surplus to those of labor shortage when, through lack of training or aptitude, many workers cannot qualify for the jobs currently seeking men. Attention has been directed especially at the displacement of workers by technological change. If automation reduces the number of people needed to produce a commodity, what will happen to those who aren't needed? Actually, the problem appears less sticky if we rephrase it something like this: If automation increases the amount each worker can produce, how can we provide incentives for business to expand output sufficiently to employ those who want to work?

Put in this form, the question points in two directions. First of all, we are brought back to the condition of aggregate demand. It is urgently necessary that aggregate demand expand rapidly enough to keep pace with the growth of productivity in the economy as a whole. This still leaves problems (typified by agriculture) when the rates of productivity change are not equal in different sectors. Here is where wage and price behavior becomes significant. Sectors where productivity is growing rapidly can market their added output by reducing prices. But this is not a pleasant solution for sellers to face, and they resist it if they can, either through administered pricing (steel) or through government intervention (agriculture, crude petroleum).

It is in connection with structural unemployment that union wage policies may most appropriately be criticized. Indeed, to the extent that there

[3] Charles L. Schultze, "Recent Inflation in the United States," Study Paper 1, Joint Economic Committee, U.S. Congress, *Study of Employment, Growth, and Price Levels,* 1959, pp. 1–2. Schultze attributes part of the increased rigidity of costs and prices to the increased importance of salary and other overhead expenses.

is a wage-cost push from union activity, it is much more likely to produce unemployment than serious inflation. Unions may be able to obtain a wage increase in the face of already existing unemployment and may cause job opportunities to shrink still further in the process. Rising wage costs increase the incentives for management to institute laborsaving methods of production; they may also cause loss of markets for the final product at home or abroad. Even if incumbent union members are not discharged, industries where wage rates are artificially high may not be able to offer employment to workers who are just entering the work force or are seeking to transfer from low-productivity segments of the economy.

Labor-market disequilibrium has been particularly acute for unskilled workers with low educational achievement, especially young persons just entering the labor force. In 1962, for instance, the unemployment rate for common laborers was over 12 per cent, while the rate for skilled craftsmen was about 5 per cent and the rates for professional and technical workers and for managers were less than 2 per cent. Unemployment among persons less than twenty years of age was 13 per cent.

In the early 1960s there was considerable disagreement about the extent to which existing unemployment could be attributed to deficiencies of aggregate demand or to structural disequilibrium arising from low mobility or mismatch of skill requirements. In truth, the two cannot be accurately separated. Rapidly rising aggregate demand is an effective solvent for structural unemployment and underemployment, as the period of the 1940s amply demonstrated. It is much easier for men to move out of farming and other declining industries, and out of depressed regions, when they are pulled by the near certainty of work in expanding sectors. When demand for goods is strong, employers are more flexible in their skill and experience requirements. They are more willing to upgrade workers through on-the-job training, or to readjust processes to make use of available skills. The allocation system for labor may thus function better when demand is strongly increasing.

However, this has its cost. Because the mobility of labor is low, and because prices and wages do not always adjust downward in the face of excess supply, the amount of demand sufficient to produce a satisfactory approximation to full employment is also likely to entail steady upward pressure on the price level. In the face of mild increases in GNP expenditures (3 or 4 per cent per year) structural imperfections are sufficient to cause some unemployment and some price increases. If aggregate demand grows rapidly, structural rigidities will induce price increases. If demand is less vigorous, they will produce unemployment.

The existence of structural problems is not new; one may question whether they have increased substantially since the 1920s. One can hardly doubt, however, that they have complicated the job of economic policy. Structural problems make it very difficult to achieve both full employment and price stability simultaneously. Before investigating this conflict further, we need to deal more explicitly with the relation of the factors we have been discussing—output, prices, employment, and unemployment—to economic welfare.

WELFARE ASPECTS OF PRICES, OUTPUT, AND UNEMPLOYMENT

Prices and Economic Welfare   The direct influence of prices on economic welfare comes mainly through their effects on the distribution of real incomes and wealth. Each household's real income depends heavily on its "terms of trade" with the rest of the economy—the prices it receives for what it sells in relation to the prices it pays for what it buys. (For one sector of the economy—agriculture—the movement of prices paid and received is carefully computed and publicized by the government in the so-called parity index.) Important effects on distribution result from changes in relative prices. During a period in which prices of consumer goods are rising, many people whose incomes are fixed in money terms will find their real incomes reduced. Incomes from such contractually fixed sources as interest, private pensions, and annuities are particularly vulnerable. Most incomes, of course, are not so literally fixed and will tend to rise in some measure—perhaps more than prices, perhaps less.

However, income distribution is not just a matter of prices received and prices paid. For workers, farmers, and businessmen it is also a question of quantities sold. The worker's actual income may vary with changes in hours worked, as well as with the hourly wage rate. Farm incomes change with farm output and productivity. For the economy as a whole, these changes in quantity sold are correlated with changes in total production and demand. Thus variations in income result in part from changes in relative prices but also from variations in production and demand. If a period of rising prices is also one of rising production, many workers will have rising real incomes even if their wage *rates* do not rise as much as the prices they pay. Since the movement of demand and prices affects production, it is hard to isolate those effects on real incomes which can be attributed to production from those resulting from price change.

Declining prices may also have somewhat complicated effects on income distribution. Recipients of contractually fixed incomes will find their real purchasing power increased—provided the incomes are paid as fixed in the contract and not defaulted. The real-income effects on the other sectors of the economy will depend on whether the price reductions reflect reduced demand or increased supply (perhaps reflecting improved technology). If demand has fallen, workers and businessmen may lose income, not so much because their "terms of trade" have deteriorated, but because the quantities they can sell have fallen. Workers may be laid off or go on short time, and changes in wage rates may have little to do with their final income changes. In agriculture, since output does not usually decline much, income changes will be closely linked to the movement of the parity index of prices received versus prices paid.

Price movements also affect the distribution of wealth, notably between debtors and creditors. Increases in prices of goods reduce the real value of assets and liabilities which have a fixed money value—bonds, insurance, and of course cash itself. Thus creditors tend to find their net worth deteriorating in real terms when commodity prices are rising, while debtors find theirs improving. However, the total effect on any household or firm will depend on the changes in real values of both assets and liabilities.

Aside from the "objective" effects of price changes on production and distribution, there may also be important subjective effects on the psychology of the public. Many people believe that "inflation lowers the value of our money and therefore makes us all worse off." If inflation entailed increases in prices without increases in money incomes, this attitude might be objectively justified; but inflation is likely to be accompanied—even caused—by increases in people's money incomes. For any household, the question is whether the increased number of dollars outweighs the decreased value of each one. For the economy as a whole, one should look at the volume of goods and services available. If a mild inflation stimulates greater production, people's real incomes may objectively be increased, not decreased, by the inflation. Subjectively, nevertheless, people may not feel this way about it. People have a way of regarding increases in their money incomes as being a long-overdue recognition of their inherent merit. They assume they would have received the higher incomes anyway, and of course the purchasing power of individual incomes would have been higher if prices had not risen. Such thinking creates an ambivalent public attitude toward inflation. On one hand, people want higher money incomes, and these may be possible only through inflation. On the other hand, they resent and oppose price increases. One of the dangers of inflation is that it may breed social tension and friction among people who feel cheated, even though their real incomes may actually have been raised by the inflation.

Burdens of Recent Inflation   Since American experience since the 1930s has been with a rising price level, much recent attention has been directed to identifying elements of the population whose real incomes and wealth have been adversely affected by the inflation. During the relatively rapid price rise of the 1940s, quite a few types of labor income failed to keep pace with rising living costs. Employees of government and nonprofit organizations such as schools and hospitals, and indeed, many white-collar workers in business, found their real incomes declining.

As public opinion has adjusted to the experience and expectation of rising prices, however, earned incomes have become "upward mobile" for most occupational groups. But within any group there are likely to be some wage and salary earners who lose by inflation—particularly those with low bargaining power and low mobility.

The adverse real-income effects of inflation have come to fall most systematically on the recipients of (relatively) fixed-dollar property incomes—interest, annuities, pensions, and to some degree, rents. One group in the population consists of people heavily dependent on incomes of this sort—old people.

Rising prices reduce the real value of assets held in fixed-dollar form—cash, liquid savings assets, bonds, insurance policies, and annuities. Most families hold some savings in these forms. However, higher-income households own substantial amounts of corporate stocks, which have risen in real value since 1950. Consequently, most of the burden of recent American inflation has fallen upon middle- and lower-income groups.[4] Of course, this adverse effect shows up particularly when a family desires to spend its accumulated savings for goods and services. This often occurs after retirement, and the accumulated erosion of savings, relatively imperceptible from year to year, may become painfully evident to the couple who have been looking forward for twenty years to the security promised by the insurance advertisements which used to read "Retire on $200 a Month!"

With a greater proportion of the population living past retirement age, the vulnerability of this group to inflation is no minor matter. To be sure, an increasing proportion of old people are covered by social security, and the benefits have been periodically increased at least sufficiently to match rising living costs. And private pension programs will benefit increasing numbers, although the proportion receiving substantial benefits from such sources in the early 1960s was not large.

However, in considering the impact of price increases on savings, one must note that interest rates moved to substantially higher levels after the mid-1950s. This meant also higher benefit payments under insurance company annuity programs. Surely the distribution effects of inflation are different when interest rates exceed 4 per cent and the price level rises less

---

[4] This is the conclusion reached by Oswald Brownlee and Alfred Conrad, "Effects upon the Distribution of Income of a Tight Money Policy," Commission on Money and Credit, *Stabilization Policies*, Prentice-Hall, Inc., Englewood Cliffs, N.J., 1963, p. 517. Using 1957 data, they estimated that losses would result for families with income of $6,000 or less.

than 2 per cent than was the case earlier when interest rates were closer to 2 per cent and prices were rising by 5 per cent a year.

Ultimately, of course, specific persons are harmed not by the rise of "the price level" in some abstract sense, but by the higher prices of those commodities which they particularly want or need. Medical services, which old people need more than the average, have increased in price more than the average in recent years. And older persons benefited less than younger families from declining prices of consumer durable goods.

To complicate matters still further, we must consider the possibility that the price indexes have an upward bias. Many economists have argued that improvements in the types and quality of goods are sufficient, over time, to offset an increase of 1 per cent or more per year in the measured index of consumer prices. It may, therefore, be misleading to claim that the value of money was declining at all during a period, such as 1958–1962, when the price index of GNP was rising an average of 1.4 per cent a year.[5]

Prices and Output   Since the prices of input and output clearly influence the quantity of production of individual items, it is sometimes argued that price level changes affect total output. Certainly the historical record since 1923 displays a tendency for higher prices and higher output to go together. But our analysis suggests that the real causal agent is the flow of expenditures. Movements of the price level are less a cause of higher output than they are a symptom of movements in demand. Increased demand can lead to higher output even if prices do not rise, while price increases are not likely to lead to higher production if demand is not increasing.

Output and Economic Welfare   Production is the foundation of the real income of the nation's population. Current production provides us with the bulk of the things which we currently consume, and also with additions to our productive capital which enable us to produce and consume more in the future. Increases in production over time are the basis for rising living standards, just as wide differences in production from country to country account for differences in their real income levels.

In using gross national product data as a measure of output, we have noted the necessity to deflate the figures on GNP expenditures by some measure of the price level. Further, if we are interested in making welfare evaluations of changing output levels, we should convert the national aggre-

---

[5] A study which related automobile prices to quantifiable elements such as size, weight, and horsepower concluded that prices of new cars had *declined* by 18 per cent from 1950 to 1959, during which period the consumer price index component for automobiles showed an *increase* of 31 per cent. Zvi Griliches, "Hedonic Price Indexes for Automobiles: An Econometric Analysis of Quality Change," *Government Price Statistics, Hearings before the Subcommittee on Economic Statistics, Joint Economic Committee*, 1961. Quality improvements also cast doubt on the degree to which costs of medical care have actually increased.

gates into per capita terms. Growth of our nation's output has generally been accompanied by growth in population, so that real output per person has not gone up so fast as total output.

The elements of gross national product do not all contribute equally to the economic welfare of consumers. A part of current output goes merely to replace durable goods which are wearing out. New capital goods do not raise consumer welfare directly, although they provide the basis for increasing it in the future. Goods and services directed toward war or national defense, necessary as they may be, do not contribute much to economic welfare directly.

Because not all output contributes equally to economic welfare, gross national product is probably inferior as a measure of welfare to other national-income concepts. *Net* national product, for example, provides a figure for total output excluding replacement investment. National income incorporates this adjustment and also subtracts from the sale price of net output the element of indirect business taxes, leaving a measure of net output valued in terms of the cost of the economic resources which go into it. Finally, as an extreme measure one can use personal disposable income, limiting the measurement of economic welfare to private consumption and saving. Using PDI as one's welfare measure would attribute no benefit to tax-financed government activity. This is an unfair judgment on such programs as schools, highways, and police and fire protection. However, none of the national-income concepts solves the problem of government contribution. Consequently we shall use PDI as a measure of consumer welfare, recognizing its limitations. For comparisons over time, adjustment should be made for changes in population and price levels.

Whatever measure of income and output we use, it will not directly reflect variations in the amount of effort required to obtain that output. Over the past half century, Americans have taken a part of their economic improvement in the form of shorter working hours and more holidays and vacation time. Working conditions have improved in many occupations. Thus increased output per person is only one aspect of the improvement of economic welfare.

A comparison of the behavior of GNP expenditures, total output, and real PDI per capita is presented in Figure 7-5. All the dollar figures have been converted to index numbers on a 1929 base to give them a common starting point. In the 1930s and 1940s the common cyclical influences—depression, recovery, and war—stand out in all series. During the downswing of the early 1930s, output and real income fell less than spending, the difference resulting from declining prices. Since the 1940s, however, GNP expenditures have risen more rapidly than output as the price level has moved upward.

The substantial drop in output at the end of the war is a reflection of supply factors rather than demand. During the war an abnormally high proportion of the population participated in the labor force. When the war ended, the proportion returned to normal. The bulge of real PDI per capita centering around 1944 is also somewhat misleading. The price indexes probably do not sufficiently reflect the decline in the value of the dollar during 1943–1945, when many commodities were available in reduced quantities and poorer qualities or not at all. Consequently the apparent decline in real incomes after the war is somewhat unrealistic also.

Since the late 1940s, each series has shown relatively stable growth along its own individual trend line. Furthermore, the trends since 1950 have followed very closely the path shown by drawing a straight line from 1929 to 1963 (a straight line on a semilogarithmic diagram reflects a constant percentage rate of increase). GNP expenditures have increased by about 5 per cent per year, while the output trend has been about 3 per cent. The divergence between the two reflects the rising price level. Real income per capita has grown by about 1.6 per cent per year, falling below the growth of total output because of the increasing size of the population. By 1963, GNP expenditures were more than 5 times their 1929 level. Output was 2½ times what it was in 1929. After allowing for higher prices and

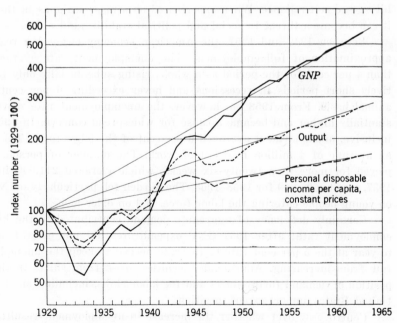

Figure 7-5. Index numbers of GNP expenditures, output, and per capita personal disposable income in constant prices, 1929–1963.

Source: Economic Report of the President.

larger population, the rise in real income per capita was about 70 per cent.

Unemployment and Economic Welfare Unemployment affects economic welfare adversely in three ways. First, unemployment means that total output is less than it might be. In the 1930s, failure to use our existing resources cost us heavily in lost production. Actual output fell short of potential by more than 20 per cent on the average in the years 1930 through 1941. Valued in 1954 prices, the loss exceeded $600 billion and represented about three years' output during the 1930s.

The second adverse effect of unemployment is, of course, the loss of income by the people who are out of work. To be sure, this adversity is mitigated by unemployment compensation. But compensation payments generally average only about one-third of previous wages—in 1962, benefits averaged $35 a week. Since the benefit period is limited in duration, financial burdens increase with the length of unemployment. In 1961, about two-fifths of the unemployed did not receive benefits.

Finally, unemployment has an adverse psychological effect on the people who are out of work. Our society places great emphasis on the moral goodness of work and on gainful employment as a measure of a man's worth and merit. Inability to find work diminishes a man's stature in the eyes of his neighbors and his family and, worst of all, himself. It can destroy ambition and self-reliance. When experienced on a mass scale, as in the 1930s, it can become a threat to social and political stability and order.

Between 1942 and 1957, the American economy enjoyed a reasonable approximation of full employment. The unemployment rate averaged less than 4 per cent for the period as a whole, rising substantially only for relatively short periods in recessions and never exceeding 6 per cent on an annual basis. From 1958 on, however, the unemployment rate moved substantially higher and became a cause for widespread concern. In 1958–1963 inclusive, unemployment averaged 6 per cent of the labor force. This meant an average of 4 million men out of work. The number of persons unemployed for more than twenty-six weeks, which averaged 211,000 in 1947–1957, rose to 606,000 for 1958–1963. The burden fell particularly on Negroes, on young people entering the labor force, and on older men.

Certainly deficiency of aggregate demand contributed to the high unemployment rate; after 1957 GNP expenditures did not grow from year to year at the 5 per cent rate historically needed to keep the unemployment rate from increasing. Additional difficulties arose from shifts in the composition of demand for products and for labor skills, including shifts in the United States import-export position.

Controversy over whether the increase in unemployment resulted from structural imbalance or from inadequate expansion of demand was not merely an academic issue, for each position implied a policy approach. Stress on structural factors tended to lead to policy proposals to operate on the supply side, through efforts to upgrade labor skills and improve mobility. In contrast, the deficient-demand view stressed the need to accelerate the expenditure flow through appropriate monetary and fiscal measures. Each policy outlook was conditioned somewhat by the fear that objectives of rising output, low unemployment, and stable prices would prove mutually inconsistent.

Full Employment versus Stable Prices The historical evidence of the period since 1923 suggests the existence of a conflict of objectives, with output growth and full employment tending to appear in opposition to stable prices. For instance, to reduce unemployment from 6 to 4 per cent over a two-year period would require, according to the historical pattern, increases in the flow of GNP expenditures of about 8 per cent per year. Our price level equation suggests that such increases in GNP at that level of unemployment have produced annual price increases of about 3 per cent. Once an unemployment rate of 4 per cent was achieved, maintaining it would require increases in GNP expenditures of about 5 per cent per year. This also implies annual price increases of about 3 per cent.

The problem can also be posed from the other end, by asking how much unemployment the economy would have to sustain in order to stabilize prices. Estimates range from 7 per cent upward.[6] Our price level equation implies a higher rate than this; if we assume GNP expenditures are rising by 4 per cent from year to year, it takes 10 per cent unemployment to keep the price level from rising.

Of course there is no magic necessity that the historical pattern be maintained. The historical record is heavily influenced by a very abnormal period of money-flow expansion from 1933 to 1953. Perhaps wage demands and expectations became heavily conditioned to such rates of expansion and will in turn become conditioned to the more moderate expansion of the money flow since 1953. Possibly government efforts to induce voluntary restraint in key wage and price decisions will have some effect.

From a welfare standpoint, one also remembers the probable upward bias of measured price indexes. Very possibly the average price rise of 1.5 per cent in 1958–1963 was matched by or even exceeded by improvements in product quality, so that the value of money did not decline. This assumption would greatly improve the outlook for reconciling full employment with stability in the value of money.

Some economists argue in favor of a more vigorously expansionary policy even if the price level does rise more. They feel the harm done to

[6] See the various estimates cited in Lawrence Klein and Ronald Bodkin, "Empirical Aspects of the Trade-offs among Three Goals: High Level Employment, Price Stability, and Economic Growth," Commission on Money and Credit, *Inflation, Growth, and Employment*, Prentice-Hall, Inc., Englewood Cliffs, N.J., 1964, pp. 391–394.

the unemployed by unemployment is at least as great as the harm done by inflation to those who actually lose by it. And they note that a more expansionary policy means more total output, benefiting many more people than those who might be unemployed.

There seems little doubt, however, that American public opinion tends to react strongly against price increases when they pass (roughly) the 3 per cent level. This was apparent in the political campaign of 1952, for example. Such an attitude may reflect an incomplete balancing of burdens and benefits, but it cannot be ignored.

SUMMARY

The flow of expenditures for gross national product has a strong positive influence on production and employment. Rising levels of GNP call forth increased production, within the limits of the nation's productive capacity, and higher production has led over time to higher real incomes for the American people generally. Rising levels of GNP expenditures and of production have enlarged job opportunities, a result which is necessary to keep pace with a growing labor force and higher productivity. Stagnation or decline in GNP expenditures has meant decreased production and increased unemployment. Thus within limits, the more rapid the rise of GNP expenditures, the greater the economic welfare of the public.

The limits have to be identified, however; they arise from the tendency for rising expenditures to push up the price level, perhaps producing unfair and unpleasant influences on the real incomes and wealth of certain groups, notably old people. If unemployment is high, the danger that higher spending will push up prices is reduced. But the lower the existing level of unemployment, the stronger the upward price pressures tend to be.

A rate of expenditure growth sufficient to maintain full employment appears likely to cause prices to rise, partly because of structural imperfections in the market mechanism and partly, perhaps, because of a wage push. Economists do not agree on the numerical magnitude of the conflict, but its probable existence creates problems for public policy. The hope is that there exists a range within which the rise of GNP is sufficient to produce good results for production and employment without serious harm in price increases. If not, then the values and preferences of the public will ultimately provide guidance for the policy makers in weighing a greater benefit in one dimension against a greater detriment in another.

The analysis in this chapter has not attempted to provide a complete explanation of the behavior of output, prices, and unemployment, but rather to identify the influence which the expenditure flow has on them. In particular, variations in prices and in unemployment may arise from factors unrelated to aggregate demand. But the evidence indicates that we are not likely to have a large increase in prices unless the expenditure flow rises at a rapid rate.

QUESTIONS FOR STUDY

1. The noted economist Milton Berle once commented that "Inflation is when your money won't buy as much as it would have during the Depression when you didn't have any." Comment on the implications this suggests for people's economic welfare.

2. "Between 1929 and 1962 GNP rose from $104 billion to $555 billion. Thus by 1962 Americans were more than five times as well off as in 1929." Discuss.

3. According to the equation accompanying Figure 7-1*b*, the year-to-year increase in output has averaged about two-thirds of the year-to-year change in GNP expenditures. Would our output grow by 10 per cent per year if we could keep GNP expenditures rising by 15 per cent per year? Discuss.

4. Structural disequilibrium provides a possible explanation for both price increases and unemployment. How? Why is it impossible to distinguish completely between structural unemployment and unemployment resulting from deficiency of aggregate demand?

5. Increases in the price level are less likely to occur when unemployment is high. Why should business firms be any less eager to raise prices just because of high unemployment?

6. Using the following information, compute an index of price change (*a*) using first-period weights and (*b*) using second-period weights. Explain

Product	1950		1955	
	Price	Quantity	Price	Quantity
Milk (qt)	$ 0.20	5,000	$ 0.24	5,000
Man's suit (ea.)	45.00	100	50.00	76
TV set (ea.)	200.00	10	175.00	14

the logic of weighting. Use the index based on first-period weights to compute (*c*) the change in the value of money from 1950 to 1955.

7. Comment on the issues raised by this statement by Robert Eisner to the Joint Economic Committee (*Hearings on Employment, Growth, and Price Levels*, 1959, p. 804) :

General price changes are essentially problems of distribution, in which some people may be better off and some people may be worse off but the economy as a whole is substantially unaffected. Thus if 70 million people are working, their total output will be pretty much the same regardless of whether prices have been stable or have been rising at a rate of 2 per cent or 5 per cent per year. But if employment is only 60 million, output will be very much less, no matter what the trend in prices. Thus economists are constrained to remind the people . . . that rather than cut employment to 60 million with its general loss of output [in order to prevent inflation], it should be possible to set up appropriate institutional arrangements so that those (perhaps fewer than we realize) who are really suffering from inflation can be reimbursed out of the extra output of the 10 million extra people working when demand is high enough to bring about rising prices. . . . It certainly is possible to have all of the people better off with the output of 70 million than the output of 60 million, regardless of the movement of prices.

SUGGESTED READINGS

Bronfenbrenner, Martin, and F. D. Holzman: "Survey of Inflation Theory," *American Economic Review,* September, 1963.

Commission on Money and Credit: *Stabilization Policies,* Prentice-Hall, Inc., Englewood Cliffs, N.J., 1963.

————: *Inflation, Growth, and Employment,* Prentice-Hall, Inc., Englewood Cliffs, N.J., 1964.

"Problem of Achieving and Maintaining a Stable Price Level" (papers and discussion by seven economists), *American Economic Review,* May, 1960.

U.S. Congress, Joint Economic Committee: *The Relationship of Prices to Economic Stability and Growth,* compendium of papers submitted by panelists, 1958.

————: *Staff Report on Employment, Growth and Price Levels,* 1959.

————: materials prepared in connection with the *Study of Employment, Growth, and Price Levels,* particularly:

Eckstein, Otto, and Gary Fromm: "Steel and the Postwar Inflation," Study Paper 2, 1959.

Harris, Seymour E.: "The Incidence of Inflation: Or Who Gets Hurt," Study Paper 7, 1959.

Levinson, Harold M.: "Postwar Movement of Prices and Wages in Manufacturing Industries," Study Paper 21, 1960.

Schultze, Charles L.: "Recent Inflation in the United States," Study Paper 1, 1959.

Hearings and *Final Report.*

chapter eight

DETERMINANTS OF EXPENDITURES AND INCOME

STRUCTURE OF THE ANALYSIS

Having indicated the importance of the expenditure flow as an influence on output, prices, and employment, we turn now to the problem of explaining the behavior of spending itself. We shall consider the economy as consisting of three major sectors—consumers, business, and government —and shall examine each of these sectors in turn. The analysis leans heavily on several basic propositions already put forth. They are:

1. The expenditures on current production by all sectors combined during any given period of time determine the amount of disposable income accruing to the sectors in the same time period.

2. The division of disposable income among the three sectors is relatively constant over time.

3. Each sector's expenditures take place within a framework of budgetary constraint. One useful form of this is as follows:

Income + borrowing = expenditures + increased cash holdings
+ increased holdings of other financial assets

Ultimately we are concerned not merely with the income-expenditure pattern of each sector, but with the behavior of financial assets and liabilities as well.

For each sector, the determinants of expenditure fall into three principal categories, as follows:

a. Amount of income. Each sector's expenditures tend to vary directly with its income, reflecting what we shall call the "propensity to spend."

b. Interest rates and credit conditions. Each sector finances a portion of its spending on credit and is thus influenced by the cost and availability of loans. The influence of the money supply operates chiefly through this channel.

c. Psychological tastes, preferences, and expectations. This may appear to be no better than a catchall category used to explain everything which the other two leave undetermined. In practice, however, it proves to have fairly definite (though different) dimensions for each sector.

In the chapter following, we shall examine the determinants of financial behavior with respect to assets and liabilities. We shall find that the same three broad categories of determinants explain these as well as expenditures.

Repercussions on Income and Credit Conditions   Analyzing sector spending-saving behavior is only half the task. The other half is to see how changes in sector behavior react upon the general state of incomes and credit conditions in the economy.

To illustrate how this works, it is convenient to rearrange the sector budget equation we have been using, so that it looks like this:

$$A \quad = \quad B \quad + \quad C$$

$$[\text{Income} - \text{expenditure}] = \begin{bmatrix} \text{increased holdings} \\ \text{of income-bearing} \\ \text{financial assets} \\ -\text{ borrowing} \end{bmatrix} + \begin{bmatrix} \text{increased} \\ \text{holdings} \\ \text{of cash} \end{bmatrix}$$

This arrangement enables us to see quickly the impact of spending-saving activities on the rest of the economy. The items in bracket A show the direct role of the sector in question in the behavior of the main money circuit. If the sector's expenditure rises more than its income, the effect on the main circuit is intrinsically expansionary. The flow of incomes to other transactors will therefore rise. But if spending declines in relation to income, the effect is to reduce the flow of income to others (or counteract an increase which might otherwise occur).

The items in bracket B represent the net amount of funds poured into or taken out of the financial circulation by this sector. The strength of these flows for all sectors combined determines interest rates and credit conditions. If households increase their willingness to acquire income-bearing financial assets or reduce their desire to borrow, this will tend to ease credit and lower interest rates. However, if consumers increase their borrowing demands and reduce their willingness to acquire income-bearing financial assets, credit will tighten and interest rates rise.

In many cases, income-expenditure and loanable-funds adjustments would occur simultaneously. Suppose there is an increase in consumer desire to hold interest-bearing assets in preference to current consumption. The direct effect on the main money circuit is contractionary. Consumers spend less; thus the flow of subsequent incomes is reduced. At the same time, consumers make funds available to the financial circulation. Consequently credit becomes easier. This may stimulate a higher level of spending on credit.

Thus each transactor stands, as it were, with one foot in the main money circuit and one foot in the financial circulation. His operations in one area are largely inverse to those in the other. Actions that decrease the flow of funds in one are likely to increase the flow in the other.

Cash-balance Variations Changes in the two areas are not necessarily offsetting. Possible disparity arises from variations in cash holdings, which do not directly constitute participation in either part of the flow of funds. If consumers decide to cut their spending and hold more cash, the decline in the flow of main circuit payments is not offset by a rise in the financial circulation. The flow of funds in both sectors can be raised simultaneously if people are willing to reduce their cash holdings in order to buy more goods and income-bearing assets.

However, changes in the cash holdings of the three sectors combined can only occur if the total *supply* of money changes. This focuses our attention upon a third area of interplay. For there may be disequilibrium between the quantity of cash which people want to hold and the actual amount in existence. If the quantity of money is kept constant, efforts to hold more cash can result only in lowered expenditures and/or higher interest rates. The interplay of monetary supply and demand will be explored further in the following chapter.

CONSUMPTION SPENDING

Income and Consumption Historically, consumer spending has tended to be a relatively constant proportion of income (PDI). This tendency appears in striking form if we plot a scatter diagram with PDI on one axis and consumption on the other, as shown in Figure 8-1. A straight line drawn through the origin to the value for 1963 describes the pattern reasonably well, indicating that the "normal" relationship of consumption to income has been about 93 per cent.

This relationship appears particularly normal for the years 1951–1963.

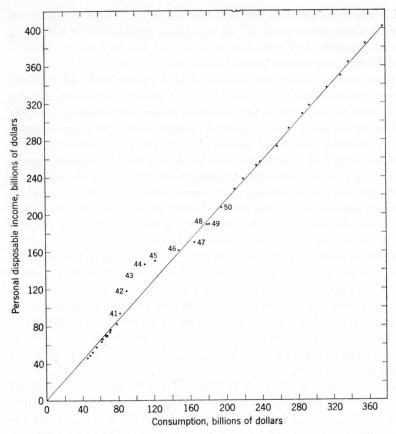

F:gure 8-1. Income and consumption, 1929–1963.

Source: Economic Report of the President.

Annual data show that consumption spending was consistently between 92.1 per cent and 93.8 per cent of PDI. The notion that consumption is a constant proportion of income is thus a reasonable approximation to the evidence, and in subsequent theoretical analysis we will commonly treat it as if it were.

The Propensity to Consume   The notion of a stable income-consumption relation was given prominence in economic thought by the British economist John Maynard Keynes. He labeled this relation the "propensity to consume" and made it one of the foundation stones of his *General Theory of Employment, Interest, and Money,* published in 1936.[1] Much of the analysis in this

---

[1] Keynes, who died in 1946, was one of the most influential and controversial economists of modern times. He effectively identified the behavior of aggregate demand as the key to depressions and refuted the notion that prosperity and full employment were a "normal" condition of the economy. He became wealthy by

chapter and the following is patterned after Keynes's approach, although it is not intended merely as an exposition of his ideas and diverges substantially at many points.

Keynes directed particular emphasis toward the *marginal* propensity to consume—the ratio between a change in income and a change in consumption. He used this to explain the process by which any disturbance to the expenditure flow would be transmitted and "multiplied" through its impact on consumer incomes and expenditures. We shall take up the theory of the "multiplier" effect later in this chapter.

The acceptance of Keynes's ideas was greatly facilitated when statistical estimates of income and consumption became available. Here appeared to be a sort of "magic constant," suitable for all sorts of prediction and control. However, sober second thoughts have revealed that the propensity to consume is not quite so simple as Figure 8-1 appears to suggest.

One reservation arises from the fact that both series are subject to a strong upward trend. Another is based on the high degree of feedback arising because consumption spending is a major determinant of PDI. And a third derives from the apparently systematic divergence of the actual data from the "normal" during the 1930s and 1940s. For these and other reasons, the assumption of a constant income-consumption ratio has not proved sufficiently reliable for short-run forecasting.

Past Income and Consumption   Some economists have attempted to remedy these deficiencies by postulating somewhat more complex relations between income and consumption. One hypothesis is that consumption is influenced by the highest levels achieved in the (recent) past. If incomes decline, consumers will be reluctant to reduce their accustomed living standards. Consumption may fall by less than income. Another hypothesis is that consumption is based on what consumers regard as their "permanent" income. Income changes which consumers regard as merely "transitory" would not be expected to produce changes in consumption.

Analysis along these lines helps to explain consumption behavior in the period 1929–1933 and during World War II. Consumption fell by less than income during the downswing of 1929–1933, perhaps because of reluctance to cut living standards or because the reduction was regarded as transitory. During the war, consumption rose less than income, perhaps because part of the increase in income was regarded as only temporary.

Despite differences in emphasis, theories of this sort are similar in suggesting that the response of consumption to changes in income may involve a lag. The assumption of a lag is a useful one analytically, and we shall em-

---

applying economic analysis to speculations and investments. Although he sometimes delighted to use the inflammatory language of a radical reformer, he argued fundamentally that acceptance of his financial proposals would help to conserve political and economic freedoms.

ploy it subsequently. It is proper to note, however, that the specific hypotheses about the influence of past or permanent income remain in dispute among economists.[2]

Expectations   Occasionally changes in consumer expectations about incomes and prices have been sufficiently great to produce variations in the income-consumption ratio. A notable example was the wave of "scare buying" in 1950–1951 accompanying the outbreak of the Korean conflict. There was widespread fear of price increases and return to wartime shortages and rationing. In the third quarter of 1950, the annual rate of consumption jumped $15 billion while PDI was rising only $9 billion.

Interest Rates and Credit Conditions   A substantial proportion of the funds spent for automobiles and other consumer durables comes from credit, and the gross extension of installment credit has been consistently close to the volume of consumer spending for durable goods.

Although consumers are often unaware of how much interest they are paying, interest charges affect the size of the monthly payments. Consequently, changes in the interest rate probably have some effect on purchases. An estimate for 1957 placed the probable interest elasticity of purchases of automobiles and other consumer durables near 0.2 and suggested that an increase of one point in interest rates would reduce such spending by about $1 billion.[3]

Interest rates charged on consumer loans are relatively sticky. Lenders are usually subject to rate ceilings and do not deviate very far from them. However, variations in credit conditions often affect the "choosiness" of lenders. When loanable funds are abundant, fewer loan applicants are rejected.

Finally, borrowers may be affected by terms other than the interest rate charged. Credit may be made to appear "easier" by reducing down payment requirements and by extending the number of months over which to repay. A quantitative investigation of the influence of credit terms concluded that the relative "easing" of down payment and maturity terms between 1951 and 1955 added about $5 billion to consumer spending in the latter year.[4]

Consumption and Income—Conclusions   If one is mainly interested in short-run forecasting, the notion of a stable proportionality of consumption to income is not sufficiently precise. Even a small change in the proportion

[2] Data on these points are presented in a comprehensive review of the literature on consumer behavior by Daniel B. Suits, "The Determinants of Consumer Expenditure: A Review of Present Knowledge," Commission on Money and Credit, *Impacts of Monetary Policy*, Prentice-Hall, Inc., Englewood Cliffs, N.J., 1963.

[3] Oswald Brownlee and Alfred Conrad, "Effects upon the Distribution of Income of a Tight Money Policy," Commission on Money and Credit, *Stabilization Policies*, Prentice-Hall, Inc., Englewood Cliffs, N.J., 1963, p. 509.

[4] Lawrence L. Werboff, "The Effects of Instalment Credit Term Variation," *Journal of Finance*, September, 1959.

may mean a variation of billions of dollars in actual expenditures. But as a long-run tendency, the constant ratio implied by Figure 8-1 is very impressive. In the perspective of the period 1929–1963 as a whole, deviations appear as temporary (and largely self-correcting) movements around the normal level. The principal amendment to the notion of a stable ratio of consumption to income is that it probably will not hold for declines in income (when consumption will fall less than income) or for large increases of income (which may be regarded as "transitory"). For the purposes of this book, we shall assume that aggregate consumption tends to be a constant proportion of PDI.

Consumption and GNP   The relation of consumption to GNP (viewed as the total income of the three sectors of the economy) will depend on the propensity to consume out of PDI and on the share of PDI in the total gross income. Historically, the proportion of income going to persons has been affected mainly by variations in tax rates. In 1929–1930, PDI absorbed about 80 per cent of GNP, but by the end of World War II the proportion was down to 70 per cent. Reduction of wartime tax rates raised it for a time, but the higher tax rates since 1950 have kept it close to the 70 per cent level.

If there exists relative constancy in C/PDI and PDI/GNP, then consumption spending will tend to be a constant proportion of GNP. Assuming normal values of 93 per cent and 70 per cent, respectively, one would expect consumption normally to amount to about 65 per cent of GNP.

Proportionality between GNP and consumption has not been maintained, however, during the recessions since World War II, for PDI and consumption have been relatively immune to recessions. The annual figures for GNP show declines in 1946, 1949, and 1954. In each case, PDI rose, and consumption rose even more, proportionately. In the recession of 1958, when the annual level of GNP rose only 0.4 per cent, both PDI and consumption increased nearly 3 per cent.

This (highly desirable) immunity resulted chiefly from shifts in government finance, either legislated or automatic. Recessions have meant reduced taxes and higher government transfer payments, particularly for unemployment compensation. So we would not be justified in assuming that proportionality between GNP and consumption would be maintained in case of an economic downswing.

IMPLICATIONS OF A STABLE PROPENSITY TO CONSUME

The Concept of Equilibrium   The impressive degree to which consumption changes reflect income changes helps greatly in explaining the behavior of GNP over time. Consumption spending appears as a passive factor that adapts itself to changes originating elsewhere. Variations in GNP are likely to originate with changes in investment or government purchases, even though large absolute variations in consumption may result.

The way in which such adjustments work themselves out can usefully be explored by using the notion of equilibrium in the level of GNP expenditures. Equilibrium is a condition of rest, where there are no inherent characteristics making for change in the state of affairs. If things are in equilibrium, they will tend to stay there. More important, if they are not in equilibrium, they will tend to move toward it. GNP is in equilibrium if it stays at the same level over time, instead of rising or falling.

We can illustrate this concept with a numerical example. If we assume that government transactions are so small that they can be ignored, GNP expenditures consist solely of consumption and investment. Gross income (GNP) consists of PDI and BDI. We need not concern ourselves with the proportionate division of gross income but assume that the proportion remains constant. Consumption is determined by income but lags behind it. We assume that consumption in any time period equals two-thirds of the gross income (GNP) of the preceding period. If we select a figure for investment, we can find an equilibrium value for GNP to correspond with it. Let us suppose investment is $60 billion.

We can find our equilibrium in the following manner. First, we express our data in equation form, as follows:

$$GNP_{t1} = C_{t1} + I_{t1}$$
$$C_{t2} = \tfrac{2}{3}\, GNP_{t1}$$
$$I = \$60 \text{ billion} \qquad (\text{same for } t1, t2, \text{ etc.})$$

The subscripts represent time periods $t1$, $t2$, etc. In order for equilibrium to exist, GNP must remain the same from one period to the next. We can set up our equations to show this, as follows:

$$GNP_{t1} = GNP_{t2}$$
$$GNP_{t1} = C_{t2} + I_{t2}$$
$$GNP_{t1} = \tfrac{2}{3}\, GNP_{t1} + \$60 \text{ billion}$$
$$\tfrac{1}{3} GNP_{t1} = \$60 \text{ billion}$$
$$GNP_{t1} = \$180 \text{ billion}$$

Equilibrium will exist if GNP equals $180 billion. If it does, the consumption of the following time period will be two-thirds as much, or $120 billion, and investment will be $60 billion; therefore total spending in the second period will again be $180 billion. So long as the level of investment and the propensity to consume remain the same, GNP will remain at the equilibrium level.

If GNP is not in equilibrium, it will tend to move toward the equilibrium level. Suppose it were for some reason at $150 billion, with the above data for investment and the propensity to consume. It would tend to rise, as the following figures illustrate:

Category	Time period						
	1	2	3	4	5	...	E
Consumption	—	100	107	111	114	...	120
Investment	—	60	60	60	60	...	60
Gross income (GNP)	150	160	167	171	174	...	180
Saving (ex ante)	50	53	56	57	58		60
Saving (ex post)	—	60	60	60	60	...	60

This kind of table, which we shall use frequently, follows the flow of expenditures and income over time. Read the events of each period from top to bottom, then move to the top of the next period. The reader is urged to work out the arithmetic of saving, consumption, and GNP, so that the logic of the figures is clear. Try calculating expenditures and saving for period 6.

In period 1, GNP is $150 billion. Since the propensity to consume is taken as two-thirds of this figure, consumption in period 2 will be $100 billion. The difference between C_{t2} and GNP_{t1} reflects the amount of disposable income which people want to save—ex ante saving. In our table, it comes immediately after GNP in order to show that by deducting it from GNP we determine the subsequent amount of consumer spending.

The figures show that it is consumption which pushes GNP up toward the equilibrium level. With gross income of $150 billion, consumers will spend $100 billion. Since investment is $60 billion, GNP rises to $160 billion. This means an equal rise in gross incomes, and consumption rises again in the next period. Income and consumption keep pushing each other up, but since the propensity to consume is less than 100 per cent, each successive increase is smaller than its predecessor. GNP increases at a progressively decreasing rate. Mathematically, the process describes an infinite series. The equilibrium level is the limit which the series approaches, but technically it never gets there.

If GNP were above the equilibrium level, it would decline. Consumption would not be enough, at the given level of investment, to keep total spending constant at any level above $180 billion. As consumption declined, it would drag down income and thereby lower consumption again. GNP would move in steps of decreasing magnitude toward the equilibrium level but would never quite get there.

Saving and Investment Equilibrium relations can usefully be analyzed in terms of saving and investment. Saving ex ante is the amount people wish to save out of any level of disposable income. Since saving equals income minus consumption, there is a propensity to save equal to 1 minus the propensity to consume. In our example, the propensity to save is equal to $1 - \frac{2}{3} = \frac{1}{3}$. Saving ex ante is equal to income times the propensity to save.

When GNP is in equilibrium, saving ex ante is equal to investment. The amount of money drawn out of the expenditure circuit through saving is just matched by the amount put back by investment; hence the flow remains constant. If investment does not equal saving ex ante, then GNP is out of equilibrium. For instance, when GNP was $150 billion in our example above, ex ante saving was $50 billion, while investment was $60 billion. The injection of spending through investment exceeded by $10 billion the withdrawal of funds through saving and GNP rose by $10 billion.

By contrast, the data for saving ex post do not tell us anything about equilibrium. Saving ex post is measured by subtracting the consumption of any period from the aggregate disposable income of the same period. Obviously the difference will always be equal to investment. Thus, when discussing equilibrium relations, we must be careful to use ex ante saving as the test.[5]

A Graphic Approach to GNP Determination The way in which GNP moves toward equilibrium at a given level of investment and propensity to consume can also be shown graphically. In Figure 8-2 we measure horizontally the gross incomes (GNP) received in any time period. Vertically we measure the amount of expenditures which are made out of these incomes in the next period. In order for equilibrium to exist, the expenditures must just equal the income of the previous period.

A line is drawn from the origin so that it makes an angle of 45° with the base. This line bisects the angle made by the horizontal and vertical coordinates. Each point on the 45° line is equally distant from the two axes. Thus the 45° line is the locus of all points which can meet the equilibrium conditions.

To show the determination of GNP, we draw on the diagram the amounts of consumption and investment which will take place at various levels of gross income (GNP). If we plot the numerical example we used above, consumption is two-thirds of GNP and can be shown by a straight

---

[5] In practice, it is sometimes useful to distinguish between ex post and ex ante investment. Business firms may at times engage in "involuntary" inventory investment or disinvestment. For instance, if sales fell off suddenly, a firm might find its inventories much larger than it wished, and some time might ensue before they could be disposed of. If equality with saving is achieved by such involuntary action, the result is not equilibrium. Technically, therefore, equilibrium requires that ex ante saving equal ex ante (intended) investment.

line that is drawn from the origin and makes an angle of 30° with the base. Investment we have treated as a constant that does not vary with GNP. It can be shown as a horizontal line, the height of which equals the given level of investment. In the diagram it is drawn equal to $60 billion.

The total amount of GNP expenditures equals the sum of C and I at the existing level of gross income. We can add C and I graphically by drawing a new line with a vertical distance equal to the combined vertical distances of C and I at that income. Since all equilibrium points must lie on the 45° line, we need merely find the place where the $C + I$ line crosses the 45° line. This occurs at a gross income of $180 billion, where C equals $120 billion and investment $60 billion, so that expenditures will equal income and GNP will remain the same.

We can also use the diagram to analyze the saving-investment relationship. Saving ex ante is equal to the amount by which consumption falls short of gross income, and thus is measured by the vertical distance between the C line and the 45° line. Investment is equal to the difference between the C line and the $C + I$ line (by definition). At the equilibrium point, these two vertical distances are equal; at other points they are not.

On first examination, the concept of equilibrium may appear to be of little use. In reality, conditions are always changing, and GNP is not likely to be given a chance to settle into a position of rest. However, the equilib-

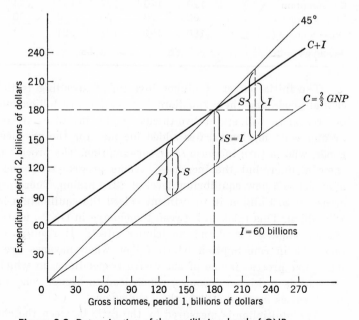

Figure 8-2. Determination of the equilibrium level of GNP.

rium concept is useful largely as an indication of tendency. When a change does occur in one of the underlying determinants, we can use equilibrium analysis to see what its effects are likely to be and how fast they may be brought about, even if we know that they will never be fully accomplished. The next section illustrates this approach to utilization of the equilibrum concept.

The Multiplier Effect   Because consumption spending is largely a passive factor that adjusts itself to income levels, changes in GNP will originate mainly from changes in investment and government finance. Because of the way in which income variations produce consumption variations, however, the ultimate effect on GNP of a given change in investment or government finance may be much larger than the initiating force. This magnification results from the multiplier effect, the operation of which we shall illustrate.

Let us start from our previous equilibrium, with GNP at $180 billion, investment at $60 billion, and consumers spending two-thirds of gross income. Then, for some reason investment rises to $70 billion and stays there. The effect on GNP is shown in the following figures:

Category	Time period						
	1	2	3	4	5	...	E
Consumption	120	120	127	131	134	...	140
Investment	60	70	70	70	70	...	70
Gross income (GNP)	180	190	197	201	204	...	210
Saving ex ante		60	63	66	67	...	70

The initial effect of higher investment spending is that producers of capital goods and their suppliers will receive $10 billion more income than before. They will spend two-thirds of the increase on consumption. The greater consumption creates added incomes for the producers of consumer goods, who in turn increase *their* consumption. The process continues in the same manner, but the increases become progressively smaller until GNP approaches a new equilibrium level of $210 billion. Therefore the initial increase of $10 billion in investment raised the equilibrium level of GNP by $30 billion. This relation between the change in GNP and the initial investment change is called the "multiplier effect." It results from the induced increases in consumption which follow when incomes are increased. The multiplier process is one of successive respendings, in which higher investment leads to higher incomes, which lead to higher consumption spending, which raises incomes still further, and so on.

The multiplier is measured by the ratio between the change in equilibrium level of GNP and the initiating change in investment. In our example, the multiplier would be 3. The size of the multiplier depends on the increases in consumption which result from increased GNP. The multiplier coefficient can be determined from the following formula:

$$\text{Multiplier coefficient} = \frac{1}{1 - (\Delta C/\Delta GNP)}$$

In our example, where consumption was two-thirds of GNP, the formula would work out as follows:

$$\text{Multiplier coefficient} = \frac{1}{1 - 0.67} = \frac{1}{0.33} = 3.0$$

In this formula, $\Delta C/\Delta GNP$ is the *marginal* propensity to consume—the change in consumption associated with a given change in gross income (GNP). When the ratio of consumption to GNP is constant, the marginal propensity is equal to that ratio. However, our formula is generalized to allow for cases in which the marginal propensity might differ from the average (as it did during the 1930s). The coefficient which emerges from this formula indicates that a change in investment will produce a change in the equilibrium level of GNP three times as large (and in the same direction, needless to add).

The larger the propensity to consume, the larger the multiplier. GNP goes up so much because people spend most of their increased incomes. The larger the proportion they spend, the larger the increase in GNP attending a given initial rise of investment.

The multiplier effect can also work in a downward direction. For example, suppose that from our equilibrium position of $180 billion, investment fell from $60 billion to $50 billion. A downward spiral would ensue, in which sellers of capital goods would suffer reduced incomes and would reduce their consumption; consequently, other producers would sustain reduced incomes and consumption. GNP would fall by successive stages toward a new equilibrium level of $150 billion.

Since the multiplier process involves successive respendings over time, it is useful to know how long the process takes. Data on the turnover of money in the economy indicate that it takes about three months for expenditures on current output to complete the circuit and be ready for expenditure again. Thus our time periods are about three months long.

For many purposes, it may be more useful to know approximately how much a given stimulus will raise GNP within a limited period, say, a year. The multiplier formula given above is of limited practical value, since it is unlikely that GNP will work its way to a new equilibrium position. If each time period is three months in length, if the initial stimulus occurs in the first period, and if consumption adjusts to income after a lag of one period, the equation for the one-year multiplier is:

$$\text{Multiplier} = 1 + \frac{\Delta C}{\Delta GNP} + \left(\frac{\Delta C}{\Delta GNP}\right)^2 + \left(\frac{\Delta C}{\Delta GNP}\right)^3$$

In the preceding example, where $\Delta C/\Delta GNP$ was 2/3 and the ultimate multiplier was 3, an increase of \$10 billion in investment raised GNP by \$24 billion at the end of one year. Thus the one-year multiplier was 2.4 ($=1 + 0.67 + 0.44 + 0.29$).

If the marginal propensity to consume is less than 100 per cent and if three months is the average period of income turnover, the one-year multiplier cannot be larger than 4. Variations in the propensity to consume will have much less effect on the size of the one-year multiplier than on the equilibrium multiplier. Large values for the equilibrium multiplier entail a large number of respendings, and thus a longer time is required for GNP to progress a given fraction of the way to its new equilibrium value.

Multiplier analysis implies that investment changes infrequently and stays constant for long periods despite large changes in consumption. This implication is unrealistic, and we shall remedy it subsequently. The purpose of multiplier analysis is to show the consequences for consumption from a given shift in investment.

The multiplier effect is shown graphically in Figure 8-3. The diagram shows GNP initially in equilibrium at \$180 billion. When investment increases to \$70 billion, the result is to raise the $C + I$ line throughout its length. This causes the point of intersection with the 45° line to shift to the right to a new equilibrium level of \$210 billion. The size of the multiplier is

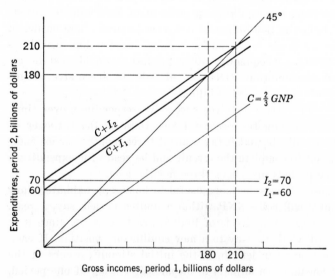

Figure 8-3. The multiplier effect.

represented graphically by the ratio between the vertical change in investment ($10 billion) and the horizontal movement of GNP to the equilibrium point. This ratio is determined by the slope of the C line, which represents the marginal ratio of consumption to GNP. The higher this ratio, the steeper the $C + I$ line and the greater the horizontal movement accompanying a given vertical change.

DETERMINANTS OF INVESTMENT

Some Classifications In the previous section, we have seen the consequences of change in investment when the propensity to consume is stable. Now it is time to inspect the causes of investment variation.

There are three main categories of investment spending—plant and equipment (business durable capital), net increases in business inventories, and residential construction. Our discussion will deal principally with business investment in inventories, plant, and equipment, but we shall deal briefly with residential construction before we finish.

Like other types of expenditures, business investment can be explained largely in terms of three factors: business income; interest rates and credit conditions; and psychological factors, chiefly expectations. The latter requires special emphasis. Business investment is undertaken only when it is expected to be profitable, and the amount of investment is strongly influenced by the state of profit expectations. To regard profit expectations as a psychological variable is perhaps misleading, for profit expectations are generally based upon past and present economic circumstances. Nevertheless, elements of risk and uncertainty are invariably present, and future-oriented business decisions are likely to involve elements of emotion and intuition.

The Marginal Efficiency of Investment Economists have found it convenient to analyze expected profitability in terms of the "marginal efficiency" of the proposed investment. Keynes, who coined the term, defined it as "that rate of discount which would make the present value of the series of annuities given by the returns expected from the capital-asset during its life just equal to its supply price." [6] Formally, then, determination of marginal efficiency is similar to the relationship we discussed in Chapter 6 between the present value of a financial asset and its expected income.

$$P = \frac{M_1}{1 + r} + \frac{M_2}{(1 + r)^2} + \cdots + \frac{M_n}{(1 + r)^n}$$

If $M_1, M_2, \ldots, M_n$ represent the expected additions to revenue attributable to the new capital in periods 1, 2, $\ldots$, n, and P represents the price

[6] John Maynard Keynes, *The General Theory of Employment, Interest, and Money*, Harcourt, Brace and Company, Inc., New York, 1936, p. 135.

of the capital asset, then the marginal efficiency would be given by r. However, the actual estimation of marginal efficiency differs from the analysis of financial yields in several important respects. First, the expected revenue from investment in capital goods is highly uncertain—indeed it is a residual from a calculation involving several uncertain magnitudes. Second, the expected income stream from an investment in capital goods is likely to be uneven, so that one cannot merely take one year's revenue as representative of the entire flow.

In making estimates of marginal efficiency, a firm would be obliged to take account of all the following considerations:

1. The technical productivity of the capital good. This would determine its physical life expectancy, the quantity and quality of output it could produce, and the amount of variable inputs (labor and materials) required in connection with it.

2. Expected demand for the finished products. This will influence the prices the firm can expect to receive and the volume it can expect to sell.

3. Expected costs of labor and materials. These must be deducted before the net revenue of the capital good can be determined. (However, interest costs of financing the investment are not deducted in calculating marginal efficiency.)

4. The initial cost of the capital good.

Of these, the fourth is known and the first can be estimated with reasonable accuracy. The second and third, however, require estimates of magnitudes that are subject to considerable variation over time—particularly the demand for the firm's products. Consequently marginal efficiency estimates involve considerable uncertainty and risk, and the actions a firm takes on the basis of marginal efficiency estimates will be conditioned by its attitude toward risk taking.

Calculating Expected Returns   The variety of elements which must be considered to obtain a marginal efficiency estimate can best be illustrated by a numerical example. The following table presents a set of hypothetical expectations relating to an investment in a machine which costs $10,000 initially and is expected to last five years.

Year	Output	Price	Variable cost per unit	Net revenue per unit	Total net revenue
1	1,100	$1.20	$0.20	$1.00	$1,100
2	2,327	1.25	0.21	1.04	2,420
3	3,697	1.30	0.22	1.08	3,993
4	3,079	1.30	0.23	1.07	3,294
5	2,659	1.30	0.24	1.06	2,819

Technological considerations underlie the figures for the quantity of output and the lifetime of the asset. Expected demand is reflected in the expected selling price and perhaps in the time shape of the expected output. Variable costs per unit are expected to rise steadily. Net revenue in each time period reflects the interaction of all these influences.

To estimate the marginal efficiency of this asset, the firm must solve this equation:

$$\$10,000 = \frac{\$1,100}{(1+r)} + \frac{\$2,420}{(1+r)^2} + \frac{\$3,993}{(1+r)^3} + \frac{\$3,294}{(1+r)^4} + \frac{\$2,819}{(1+r)^5}$$

Unfortunately there is no simple method of reaching a precise solution. However, this illustration has been cynically rigged to produce a simple solution, namely, a marginal efficiency of 0.10 (that is, 10 per cent).

The proof is as follows:

Total net revenue $\div$ $(1+r)^n$ = present value

Total net revenue	$(1+r)^n$	present value
$1,100	1.1	$ 1,000
2,420	1.21	2,000
3,993	1.331	3,000
3,294	1.464	2,250
2,819	1.611	1,750
		$10,000

Because of the mathematical complexities of this approach, firms may use other somewhat simpler methods of making an approximate estimate. For instance, they might estimate the annual net revenue minus depreciation and express this as a percentage of the initial cost. Another method is to use some standard rate of return (say, 8 per cent) as the discount factor r, calculate the present value with that discount factor, and see if the result exceeds the initial cost. This can be used as a short-cut screening device to isolate projects worth studying more precisely.

Whether their techniques are mathematically precise or not, major firms have come increasingly to employ relatively systematic estimates of expected rate of return as a guide to investment decisions.[7]

The Marginal Efficiency Schedule Let us now assume that an expected rate of return has been estimated for each prospective investment project in the economy, as well as the outlay involved for each investment. Assume further that these projects are now ranked in order of that expected rate of return, with the highest coming first, and so on. Such a ranking would

[7] See the interesting description of actual methods in William H. White, "The Changing Criteria in Investment Planning," Joint Economic Committee, U.S. Congress, *Variability of Private Investment in Plant and Equipment*, part II, 1962.

give us a *schedule* of marginal efficiency, a hypothetical illustration of which we have shown in Figure 8-4.

On the assumption that the most profitable investments will be undertaken first, the marginal efficiency schedule can be interpreted in two ways. First, it indicates the dollar volume of investments having a rate of return equal to or greater than any specific percentage. For instance, in Figure 8-4, there are $50 billion of projects offering a prospective return of 8 per cent or better. Second, for any given quantity of investment, the marginal efficiency schedule indicates the cutoff rate of return—that is, the return on the marginal project. In the diagram, if investment were $75 billion, this cutoff rate would be 4 per cent. Projects yielding more would be undertaken; those yielding less would not.

The downward slope of the schedule reflects the dispersion of expected yields on prospective investments. If one assumes that some projects are expected to yield between 4 and 8 per cent, then there will be more projects yielding 4 per cent or more than there are projects yielding 8 per cent or more. But it is difficult to be very precise about the shape of the schedule. We would expect it to flatten out at low rates of return, since there are probably a lot of investment projects with low but positive net returns.

Changes in conditions affecting the business profit outlook in general may cause the entire marginal efficiency schedule to shift. In particular, a rise in the aggregate demand for business products might well cause the entire schedule to increase. On the diagram, the curve would move up and to the right. When we speak of an increase in marginal efficiency, such a shift is what we refer to.

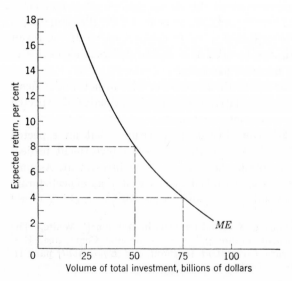

Figure 8-4. Hypothetical marginal efficiency schedule.

Cost and Availability of Funds The amount of investment undertaken depends on the amount of funds available from internal and external sources and on their cost. Only if the marginal efficiency of a project exceeds the costs of financing it will the firm actually make a net profit from it.

Much investment is financed out of business income—out of reinvested profits and depreciation allowances. Clearly the amount of internal funds available to a firm is limited, partly by the firm's flow of revenue, partly by the desire of owners for current income. The firm incurs no explicit cost in using internal funds for investment, but the rate of interest represents an "opportunity cost" of funds. The firm is not likely to undertake an investment which offers a return lower than current interest rates. Instead, it will use its money to pay its debts and perhaps to acquire financial assets. However, other limitations are likely to be in operation before the firm gets this far down the marginal efficiency schedule.

For many firms, attractive investment projects exceed the amount of income they can reinvest; therefore they must consider whether it is worthwhile to incur the costs of obtaining external funds. If the marginal efficiency of a prospective investment is higher than the interest costs of financing it, the firm will probably be willing to borrow to undertake it. In our example above, the project offered a return of 10 per cent. If the firm could borrow at 6 per cent to finance it, their profits would still be increased by $400 a year. On these terms, they would presumably undertake it. But if funds could only be obtained at 12 per cent, they would not.

The rate of interest which firms are prepared to pay will depend on the rate of return they expect from investment. Thus the marginal efficiency schedule becomes a sort of schedule of demand for loans. At low interest rates, firms will be willing to borrow more than at high rates, other things being equal. However, the demand for loans will be net of funds obtained from reinvested income.

Figure 8-5 illustrates the interaction of marginal efficiency, borrowing, and the interest rate, using some oversimplified assumptions. We take the quantity of internal funds as given at $25 billion and assume that firms can borrow all they want at the going interest rate of 6 per cent. Firms will borrow enough funds to make all the investments yielding more than 6 per cent. If ME_1 represents the marginal efficiency schedule, they will spend $60 billion for investment, borrowing $35 billion to do so. A decline in the interest rate to 4 per cent would raise investment to $75 billion. An increase in marginal efficiency to ME_2 would raise both borrowing and investment at any given interest rate. In reality, of course, the amount of internal funds used for capital expenditures might also depend on the interest rate.

Business financing and investment decisions are complicated by the influence of taxation. Corporate profits are subject to high rates of tax, and the income of unincorporated business is taxed as personal income for the owners. However, interest paid by business is a deductible expense, as is depreciation on capital. Taxation of corporate profits influences the amount of business income available for investment and also the *net* rate of return expected on capital after taxes.

Other things equal, the volume of borrowing and investment spending will tend to vary inversely with the rate of interest. However, it is not easy to identify empirically the size of this influence. Interest rates have their effect after a time lag, and it is difficult to disentangle their influence from the effects of many elements causing changes in marginal efficiency itself. Moreover, investment is affected by the quantitative availability of loans, as well as their cost.

Availability of Credit   It is simply not true that business firms can borrow all they want at current market rates of interest. Most firms are subject to quantitative limits on how much they can borrow. Banks and other institutional lenders usually limit the credit they will extend to any firm so that it bears some reasonable relation to the amount of capital which the owners of the firm have put into it. The precise dimensions of such "credit rationing" will differ according to differences in size of firms, risky nature of investments, character of management, and other factors.

Moreover, the availability of credit to borrowers generally tends to vary in response to changes in the relative ease or tightness of the general credit situation. When lenders have abundant funds seeking profitable use, they may relax their standards of creditworthiness. Some marginal borrowers who formerly could not obtain funds at all will now be accommodated. Existing firms may find their "line of credit" enlarged, so that they can bor-

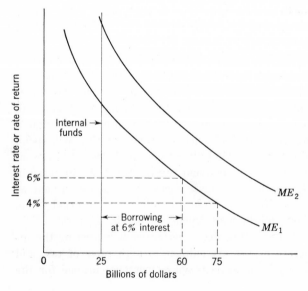

Figure 8-5. Marginal efficiency, internal finance, and borrowing.

row more than previously. When credit is scarce, however, lenders may reduce the availability of funds to individual borrowers.

The Acceleration Principle One of the major factors determining the marginal efficiency of investment is the need for new productive capacity to keep up with increases in the demand for finished products. One particular form of this relationship is called the "acceleration principle," which is based on the assumption that firms will attempt to maintain a constant ratio between the total amount of their capital goods and their output or sales. When output is rising rapidly, firms will be increasing their capital rapidly. But if demand stops growing, firms will have enough capital and will cut their rate of current investment sharply. If the demand for finished products is falling, firms may find that they have more capital than they need and may reduce their scale of operations by permitting some to be depleted without replacement. Thus the acceleration principle postulates that a portion of investment spending (called "induced investment") is determined by the *rate of change* in demand for final products.

If a large proportion of investment follows the pattern of the acceleration principle, there will be important consequences for the behavior of GNP. The accelerator will make even more unlikely the achievement of equilibrium and may produce cyclical fluctuations in GNP. Suppose that GNP is in equilibrium and that investment rises because of an increase in the marginal efficiency schedule. This will raise incomes and consumer spending through the multiplier effect and will also stimulate induced investment by producers of capital goods who wish to enlarge their capacity to meet the added demand. Thus GNP is raised by both higher consumption and higher investment, and this in turn stimulates still higher consumption and investment in the following period. As long as GNP rises at a progressively increasing rate, it produces a rising level of induced investment; but it is likely that an increasing rate cannot be maintained in face of the leakage of a portion of income into saving. When the rate of increase of GNP slows down, producers reduce their induced investment. This slows GNP growth even more and may finally cause GNP to level off. Once GNP stops growing, the need for induced investment comes to an end because producers have enough capital. The resulting drop in induced investment pushes GNP down and sets off a downward spiral. In the face of falling demand, producers have too much capital and therefore stop buying, even for replacement. This will aggravate the downswing. Ultimately the rate of decline will slacken, and conditions will start to improve.

There are several logical objections to the underlying assumption that the ratio between capital goods and output will remain constant. Business firms frequently have excess productive capacity during periods of slack demand, so that they do not need more capital goods when expansion begins. The theory implies that funds will always be available for investment. It takes no account of changing prices and implies a mechanical relation between current sales and current investment, whereas it is the demand expected in the future which may be more influential.

Modification of the Accelerator   Data on the behavior of business investment in plant and equipment do not provide much support for the existence of a "mechanical" relation between investment and the rate of change of output and demand. However, Prof. Robert Eisner has suggested a modification which is much more plausible. Investment, he reasons, should be expected to depend on "permanent" changes in output, in a manner analogous to the "permanent income" theory of consumption. Eisner believes that permanent changes in output can be inferred from recent and current output behavior and that the actual investment expenditures may occur after time lags involved in the execution of plans. The result is a theory in which "capital expenditures are a function of a number of past yearly sales changes." [8]

There can be no doubt that fixed-capital investment is strongly influenced by variations in the pressure of output on capacity arising from variations in sales and demand. Business plant and equipment investment is highly correlated with the general "operating rate" in industry—that is, the ratio of current output to capacity. Production levels above 90 per cent of capacity have generally led, after a time lag, to increased investment.

Modification of the accelerator gives theoretical plausibility to a very simple theory of fixed-capital investment—namely, that it tends to vary directly with the level of GNP expenditures. Statistically, this tendency is readily perceptible.[9] However, we know that part of the covariation arises from feedback; that is, variations in investment affect GNP through the multiplier process.

The Capital-stock Adjustment Principle   In recent discussions, the general theory of investment has been restated in a very useful form, called the "capital-stock adjustment principle." Briefly put, this states that investment in any given period will be proportional to the difference between the desired stock of capital goods and the actual stock of capital goods. This is broad enough to include the factors we have already analyzed. For instance, the desired stock of capital is determined by comparison of the marginal efficiency of capital and the interest rate; principal short-run variations in the desired stock are likely to arise from changes in business sales and output in the manner identified by the acceleration principle.

[8] Robert Eisner, "Investment: Fact and Fancy," *American Economic Review*, May, 1963, p. 242.

[9] For the period 1920–1960, the equation

Plant and equipment investment $= 0.095\ GNP - 1.237$

produces a remarkably high correlation. See *Variability of Private Investment in Plant and Equipment*, part I, p. 68.

Note the assumption that investment is merely proportional to, not necessarily equal to, the difference between desired and actual capital stock. Here one can allow for time lags in both the planning and execution of investment projects. Limitations on the availability of investment funds, either from reinvested income or from borrowing, will also influence the proportion.

In this formulation, decreases in the interest rate and increases in the quantitative availability of credit would both tend to increase investment spending, but for somewhat different reasons. Lower interest would raise the desired stock of capital, while greater availability of credit would increase the speed with which the desired stock of capital could be acquired.

One of the analytical virtues of the capital-stock adjustment principle is that it brings out the influence of the existing stock of capital goods on investment. In particular, it suggests that a high rate of investment in the recent past may reduce current investment incentives, since the existing stock of capital may have been brought fairly close to the desired stock.

Statistical Evidence on Financial Influences There have been numerous efforts to identify quantitatively the effects on investment of financial variables such as business income, interest rates, and the availability of credit. However, there are formidable difficulties in such an undertaking. First, it is virtually impossible to separate the influence of business income from that of the pressure of sales against capacity. Periods of business expansion generally raise both sales and business income, and there is no very precise method of disentangling the effects on investment of one and the other.

We may take comfort, however, in the fact that several recent investigations have yielded results of the same order of magnitude. These suggest a marginal propensity to spend on fixed capital ($\Delta I/\Delta BDI$) of about 30 per cent. This figure would mean that a $10 billion increase in business disposable income would produce about a $3 billion rise in investment spending for plant and equipment.[10] Part of this undoubtedly arises because movements of actual profits affect expectations of profits to come.

Determining the influence of interest rates and credit conditions has been even more difficult. Such influence undoubtedly operates after a time lag and may easily be swamped by effects of other influences. In addition it is extremely difficult to find quantitative measures of the availability, as distinct from the cost, of credit.

A fairly consistent pattern of influence does appear in a few recent studies. After allowing for time lags, these have concluded that the co-

---

[10] Arthur Okun suggests a value of 25 per cent in "The Predictive Value of Surveys of Business Intentions," *American Economic Review*, May, 1962, p. 224. Edwin Kuh arrives at a value of 10 to 15 per cent, but cites two other studies yielding values of 28 per cent and 20 to 40 per cent in "Theory and Institutions in the Study of Investment Behavior," *ibid.*, May, 1963, pp. 265–266.

efficient of elasticity for fixed-capital investment is about one-third in response to variation in interest on long-term bonds. (Elasticity is measured by dividing the percentage change in investment by the percentage change in interest rate.) Should interest rates rise by 10 per cent (e.g., from 6.0 to 6.6 per cent), fixed-capital expenditures would decline by slightly over 3 per cent after a lag of six months or more.[11]

Inventory Investment   Net increases in business inventories do not constitute a large component of GNP expenditures—they averaged less than 1 per cent of GNP in the decade ending in 1962. However, inventory investment is highly volatile, and its variations have at times furnished a substantial proportion of year-to-year *changes* in GNP expenditures.

Inventory investment conforms more nearly to the "mechanical" acceleration principle than any other type of investment. This is evident in the relatively stable ratio between inventories and sales in manufacturing and trade. Annual data for 1948–1962 show that inventories ranged from a low of 1.37 times monthly sales to a high of 1.61; however, in eleven out of fifteen years, the ratio was within the narrow range of 1.50 to 1.59, with an average ratio of 1.54. Examination of the month-by-month data for 1955–1962 indicates a range from a high of 1.72 to a low of 1.44, with two-thirds of the months falling in the range 1.50 to 1.59.[12] And some of the variations reflect lags in the actual adjustment of capital stock to its desired level, rather than variation in the desired ratio of inventories to sales.

If inventories behave according to the acceleration principle, we should find a correspondence between inventory investment and the rate of change of production and sales. Such a correspondence indeed exists; the major swings in inventory investment for 1948–1963 are well approximated by this equation:

$$In_{t2} = 0.244 \ (GNP_{t2} - GNP_{t1}) - \$2.04 \text{ billion}$$

We must bear in mind, however, that a high correlation between inventory investment and the change in GNP may reflect a feedback influence by which investment causes changes in GNP through the multiplier. The good fit of the estimating equation is consistent with the acceleration principle, but does not suffice to prove it. Our conviction of its validity is strengthened

[11] Dale Jorgenson arrives at a coefficient of 0.29 to 0.38 in "Capital Theory and Investment Behavior," *American Economic Review*, May, 1963, p. 258, while estimates for several subgroups of investment average out to 0.25 to 0.28 in Brownlee and Conrad, *op. cit.*, p. 509. An elasticity coefficient of 0.4 for nonelectrical machinery is the finding of Albert Ando, E. Cary Brown, Robert M. Solow, and John Kareken in "Lags in Fiscal and Monetary Policy," *Stabilization Policies*, p. 6.

[12] Annual data are from *Economic Report of the President, 1964*, p. 254; monthly data are from this and earlier editions of the *Economic Report*.

by the stable inventory/sales data and also by the findings of a number of other more sophisticated studies.[13]

It is possible that inventory investment may be influenced by other factors. Interest rates and credit conditions probably have some influence, and expectations of substantial price change may lead to inventory variations of a speculative nature. However, such influences appear to have been minor compared with variations in sales.

Residential Construction Expenditures for housing construction are large—they accounted for about 30 per cent of gross private domestic investment in the decade ending in 1962. Most housing construction is undertaken initially by business firms on a somewhat speculative basis, but their decisions are made with an eye on consumer demand.

Consumer desire for housing is conditioned by such long-run forces as the size and rate of growth of the population, its age distribution and geographic mobility, and rates of marriage and family formation. More variable in the short run are factors relating to the ability to pay—particularly disposable income. Cost and availability of credit and the existing liquid assets of households also influence ability to pay.

Business firms estimating the potential profits of new residential building for sale or for rent must (implicitly, at least) form a judgment as to the desired stock of housing. Following the logic of the capital-stock adjustment principle, we would expect new construction to be some proportion of the difference between the existing and desired stocks of housing. Because of delays in planning and executing construction, the capital-stock adjustment is here subject to substantial time lags.

Many observers have agreed that housing investment is quite sensitive to interest rates and credit conditions—perhaps more so than any other spending category. Credit variables may operate on individual home buyers; they also influence business firms engaged in construction. Purchases of homes by individuals generally involve a large proportion of credit—probably 75 per cent of the funds spent to buy new houses comes from borrowed money. Interest costs make up a large part of the monthly payment on a home mortgage. Borrowers may also be affected by variations in such terms as the down payment requirement and the number of years allowed to pay off the mortgage. Ability to obtain mortgage insurance or guarantee from the government is also important.

Firms engaged in the construction of housing and in the ownership of rental housing also operate with extensive use of borrowed funds. Cost and

[13] For a summary of statistical investigations of investment, both in fixed capital and in inventories, see Robert Eisner and Robert H. Strotz, "Determinants of Business Investment," *Impacts of Monetary Policy*; inventory studies are reviewed on pp. 193–227.

availability of credit may thus have their initial impact on housing invest-ment through builders rather than buyers.

Variations in credit costs and terms have apparently been strong enough to account for a substantial part of variation in housing investment. In particular, easing credit helped raise housing expenditures in recession periods in 1954 and 1958, while tighter credit reduced them in 1956–1957. Estimates of the interest elasticity of residential construction range from about 0.5 upward, usually allowing for a time lag of about one year.[14]

Summary of Investment Determinants If one is interested in short-run variations in investment spending, the most pervasive influence is the degree of pressure of production, sales, or demand on existing capacity. This pres-sure is the central concern of the acceleration principle, which implies that investment should be a function of the rate of change of production and sales. This explanation serves pretty well for inventory investment. For business fixed capital, modifications are needed to allow for the degree to which production and sales changes are expected to be "permanent" and for the lags in the execution of investment projects. Analogous principles apply to pressure of consumer demand on the existing stock of housing. Invest-ment in housing and in business plant and equipment is also sensitive to the cost and availability of funds from income and from credit.

Taking these factors in combination, we can conclude that both the *incentive* to invest and the *ability* to do so are directly affected by variations in the flow of GNP expenditures. Rising GNP means increased business sales and production and also higher business income. Firms have an incentive to increase their inventories. Consumer incomes are rising. If we ignore for the moment variations in interest rates and credit conditions, the simplest hypothesis we can advance concerning investment spending is that it tends to vary directly with the level of GNP expenditures.

In the long run, to be sure, investment incentives will be affected by all the elements entering into marginal efficiency analysis, particularly tech-nology, and by variations in the composition of demand for finished prod-ucts. Technical change keeps marginal efficiency increasing, so that invest-

---

[14] A study by Sherman Maisel obtains an unusually close fit to experience for 1950–1962 with an estimating equation for housing starts which utilizes for its credit term the average Treasury bill rate for the second, third, and fourth pre-ceding quarters. His equation implies an interest elasticity of about 0.5 ("A Theory of Fluctuations in Residential Construction Starts," *American Economic Review*, June, 1963). Brownlee and Conrad estimate elasticity at 0.56 (*op. cit.*, p. 509). A higher estimate is given by Richard Muth, "The Demand for Non-farm Housing," in Arnold Harberger (ed.), *The Demand for Durable Goods*, The Uni-versity of Chicago Press, Chicago, 1960. George F. Break finds that elasticity of a composite "terms of credit" variable ranges from 0.4 to 1.3 ("Federal Loan In-surance for Housing," Commission on Money and Credit, *Federal Credit Agencies*, Prentice-Hall, Inc., Englewood Cliffs, N.J., 1963, p. 23).

ment opportunities do not become saturated. On the whole, however, these elements do not vary enough in the short run to have much effect on year-to-year changes in investment.

GOVERNMENT FINANCE AND GNP

Determinants of Government Revenue and Expenditure More than any other sector, government has control over both its income and expenditures. By changing tax rates, it can alter its proportional share of gross income in a manner not available to the private sectors. In the long run, taxes and government expenditures are basically determined by the psychological tastes and preferences of the public, by their desire for public as opposed to private consumption and investment. These desires will be influenced by such objective factors as the international situation and will of course be asserted through the political process.

In the short run, however, tax rates are relatively stable. For state and local governments, expenditures may therefore depend on a level of income which is determined (in the political sense) and on willingness and ability to borrow or to repay existing debts. Since 1946, state and local governments have increased their indebtedness each year, chiefly through borrowing to finance capital expenditures for roads, schools, and other public facilities. However, the trend of their expenditures has kept pretty close to the trend of revenues, and the state and local government sector as a whole did not register a deficit as large as 10 per cent of revenue in any year over the period 1946–1963.[15]

The political pressures for high expenditures at the state and local level are very strong. Thus increases in tax revenues which result from rising levels of GNP expenditures are likely to be drawn into higher spending. Furthermore, the willingness and ability of many units of government to borrow depend on current tax revenue. Consequently borrowing and credit expenditures tend to rise with higher income also. The result for state and local governments may be a marginal propensity to spend out of income equal to or greater than unity.

Variations in interest rates exert some influence on borrowing and capital expenditures by state and local governments. A rise of rates between the initial planning and authorization of a bond-financed project and the sale of bonds may lead to postponement of borrowing and expenditure. The influence is chiefly on the timing of government activity, however, since the long-run levels of borrowing and capital expenditures appear relatively independent of interest-rate levels. Moreover, in the 1950s, the influence was

[15] *Economic Report of the President, 1964*, pp. 270, 276–277.

apparently concentrated on highway expenditures, while school construction showed no appreciable influence from interest-rate movements.[16]

The income-expenditure relation of the Federal government is somewhat different. It is true that Federal tax rates are changed only infrequently, so that Federal revenues tend to rise and fall with GNP. Over time, Federal expenditures rise with increasing revenues. However, in the short run there is a much less close relation between revenue and expenditure at the Federal level. The Federal government can engage in deficit spending on any desired scale, because of its ability (through the Federal Reserve System) to create any amount of money needed for expenditures.

This freedom also makes it possible for the Federal government to pursue a countercyclical fiscal policy, in which aggregate revenues and expenditures are determined in part to produce desired effects on total GNP. It also means that Federal financing is not affected by interest rates and credit conditions. Indeed, the influence may go the other way, as during and after World War II, when easy credit was deliberately maintained to keep down the interest paid on the large Federal debt incurred during the war.

Fiscal Policy and GNP   Fiscal policy is an important element in GNP behavior and can be manipulated deliberately to influence the behavior of total GNP. Its role can be illustrated here by a numerical example. Suppose tax rates equal 20 per cent of GNP, and business disposable income is 10 per cent of GNP. We shall omit government transfers, and the remaining 70 per cent of GNP will go into personal disposable income. Suppose 90 per cent of PDI is spent for consumption in the time period after the income is earned. Finally, suppose investment spending is constant at $60 billion and government purchases are constant at $80 billion. Let us first calculate the equilibrium level of GNP corresponding to these data.

$$C_{t2} = \tfrac{9}{10}\, PDI_{t1}$$
$$PDI_{t1} = \tfrac{7}{10}\, GNP_{t1}$$

Therefore

$$C_{t2} = 0.63\, GNP_{t1}$$
$$I = \$60 \text{ billion (all periods)}$$
$$G = \$80 \text{ billion (all periods)}$$

In equilibrium, the expenditures in period 2 must equal the GNP of period 1. Therefore,

[16] The data are surveyed by Charlotte DeMonte Phelps in "The Impact of Monetary Policy on State and Local Government Expenditures in the United States," *Impacts of Monetary Policy*. For two periods of credit tightening, 1956–1957 and 1958–1959, she finds an interest elasticity for municipal capital expenditures of slightly more than unity. For state governments the elasticity is probably lower.

$$GNP_{t1} = C_{t2} + I_{t2} + G_{t2}$$
$$GNP_{t1} = 0.63\ GNP_{t1} + \$140 \text{ billion}$$
$$0.37\ GNP_{t1} = \$140 \text{ billion}$$
$$GNP_{t1} = \$378 \text{ billion}$$

To prove this is an equilibrium, we should calculate its income and expenditure components, which are as follows:

Taxes	$ 76	Consumption	$238
BDI	38	Investment	60
PDI	264	Government purchases	80
GNP	$378	GNP	$378

If GNP is $378 billion, it would yield $264 billion of PDI (= 70 per cent of $378 billion). Out of this, consumers would spend $238 billion (= 90 per cent of $264 billion), which is just enough, with the existing $140 billion of investment and government purchases, to produce GNP of $378 billion again. Thus GNP is in equilibrium.

Taxes stand in about the same relation to the flow of income and expenditure as does saving. Both represent funds taken out of the flow. Furthermore, both tax revenues and saving tend to rise and fall in proportion to GNP. Most taxes are levied on incomes, profits, or sales. Thus changes in GNP are reflected in variations of the tax base, and collections fluctuate when rates remain constant. Government purchases are similar to investment in providing an injection of funds into the spending stream.

To apply the saving-investment criterion for equilibrium, it is necessary to define government saving as the excess of net government revenue over government purchases. In our example, the government deficit of $4 billion is deducted from the $64 billion saved by persons and business to equal the $60 billion of investment.

Surpluses and Deficits The principles involved in the saving-investment approach can also usefully be expressed in terms of sector surpluses and deficits. Each sector is said to have a deficit (ex ante) to the extent that its desired expenditures exceed its disposable income, and a surplus to the extent that income exceeds desired expenditures. The consumer sector ordinarily shows a surplus, equal to personal saving ex ante. The business sector ordinarily incurs a deficit, since investment spending commonly exceeds business disposable income.[17] If we assume a uniform time lag in the adjustment of expenditures to income, then a sector's surplus or deficit is simply the difference between its income in one period and its expenditures in the next.

[17] Note this does not imply that the business sector is running at a loss, in the accounting sense. Profits equal revenue minus accounting costs. The money-flow deficits for the business sector arise from capital expenditures, which are not included as costs when incurred, but only when capital is depreciated or sold.

We know that the income received by all sectors in any given period is determined by the expenditures by all sectors in that period. Changes in income from period to period can only occur, therefore, if the sum of sector expenditures differs from the sum of previous-period sector incomes. GNP expenditures can thus be in equilibrium only if the expenditures of all sectors combined equal the sum of previous-period incomes—that is, if the ex ante surpluses and deficits add up to zero.

In the numerical example given just above, the equilibrium pattern can be stated in this form:

	Income (period 1)	Expenditures (period 2)	Surplus (+) or deficit (−)
Consumers	$264	$238	+$26
Business	38	60	−22
Government	76	80	−4
	$378	$378	0

The surplus-deficit analysis throws some light on the virtues of living within one's income. Suppose the business and government sectors reduced their expenditures and eliminated their deficits, so that the surplus of the consumer sector stood alone. Expenditures in period 2 would thus fall $26 billion below incomes (and expenditures) in period 1. This would reduce period 2 incomes correspondingly. A predominance of ex ante surpluses in the money-flow sense means a contraction in the income-expenditure flow.

An economy in which population and productive capacity are growing functions best when the flow of expenditures for output is rising to match the increased capacity. Expenditures can rise from period to period, however, *only* if deficits predominate over surpluses. Traditionally business has provided the major deficit force, but business expenditures tend to be volatile. Government deficits may be economically beneficial if they take up the slack.

Surpluses and deficits in the money-flow sense have no moral significance in terms of thrift or extravagance. Moral evaluations can and should be directed at the objects of expenditure; these may be wasteful regardless of the sector involved. An economic system as a whole can only be thrifty, however, by using its productive resources to add to the quantity and quality of wealth in the broadest sense (including its human assets). Financial policies which produce expenditure deficiencies, leading to unemployment and unused capacity, are the antithesis of thrift.

Multiplier Effects of Fiscal Policy   Changes in government expenditures or tax rates will set off multiplier effects. An increase in government purchases operates much like an increase in investment. The increase raises GNP directly. In addition, higher incomes go to the sellers, who adjust their consumption upward, causing higher incomes for others, and so on. Increases in transfer payments do not raise GNP directly, but do increase private disposable incomes and expenditures. Similar effects follow from reductions in tax rates. These multiplier effects add to the potency of fiscal policy as a device for influencing the flow of GNP expenditures; they also increase the potential harm which can result from inappropriate fiscal actions.

International Trade Imports and exports interact with GNP. Exports are a category of demand for output and produce effects similar to investment or government purchases. An increase in foreign demand for American exports will raise GNP directly. In addition, producers of export products will have higher incomes and will increase their consumption. Thus variations in export sales produce multiplier effects.

Import purchases by Americans are similar to saving and taxes, for they represent a withdrawal of funds from the stream of domestic income and expenditure. Furthermore, imports resemble saving and taxes in that they rise and fall in response to changes in GNP. One can speak of a propensity to import, just as there is a propensity to consume.

By similar reasoning, American export sales are likely to fluctuate in response to variations in GNP in the importing countries. This relationship tends to transmit fluctuations from one country to another. For instance, rising GNP in the United States might lead to increased imports, which would raise GNP in the exporting countries, who might in turn buy more exports from the United States, and so on. Thus imports and exports affect each other through their influence on GNP. The ability of many countries to purchase imports also depends on the supply of foreign exchange which they receive from export sales or loans.

International transactions of the United States are not large in relation to GNP. In many other countries, they are much larger and may be the chief source of fluctuations in GNP. These countries are often significantly affected by the movement of GNP in the United States, which will affect their export sales, foreign-exchange earnings, and domestic incomes and employment.

SUMMARY AND GENERAL OBSERVATIONS

In this chapter we have examined the determinants of expenditures by the major sectors of the economy and some of the consequences of expenditure patterns. We have found that in each sector expenditures tend to vary directly with income, giving rise to a positive "marginal propensity to spend." [18] Dependence of expenditures on income is particularly stressed for the consumer sector, where it gives rise to the concept of the multiplier effect. Any disturbance to GNP expenditures will lead to a change in PDI which will produce induced movements in consumption in the same direction. These will in turn push GNP further, thus producing additional movements of disposable income and consumption. Ultimately the change in GNP may be several times as large as the initial stimulus, the relationship being described by the multiplier coefficient which varies directly with the marginal propensity to consume out of GNP.

Since government and business are also subject to a positive "propensity to spend," they will tend to display reactions similar to those involved in the multiplier analysis. All three sectors, not merely consumers, will tend to increase their spending in response to rising incomes, thus adding to the cumulative process. And business investment will be stimulated by the pressure of output and sales against capacity which is likely to occur during economic expansion. This pressure and reactions to it are described in a general way by the capital-stock adjustment principle, of which the mechanical theory of the acceleration effect is a special case.

Of particular interest for monetary policy is the sensitivity of expenditures to variations in interest rates and credit conditions. Our survey indicates relatively high sensitivity to short-run credit variations in expenditures for residential construction and for state and local government capital expenditures. Some influence, but lower sensitivity, appears to prevail for business plant and equipment investment and for consumer spending on durable goods. No appreciable influence is evident for Federal government expenditures, for consumer expenditures other than durables, and for state and local noncapital expenditures. The expenditures showing some sensitivity to credit conditions constituted about 23 per cent of total GNP expenditures in 1962.

Equilibrium analysis can be used to show the reciprocal interaction of income and expenditures when the sectors are brought together. Expenditures of all sectors determine the disposable incomes going to the sectors, and each sector adjusts its subsequent expenditures in response to changes in its income. GNP is in equilibrium—a state of rest—when saving and investment are equal (ex ante) and when the desired surpluses and deficits of the sectors just cancel out. If saving exceeds investment (and surpluses exceed deficits), GNP will fall; if investment exceeds saving (and deficits exceed surpluses), GNP will rise.

Our analysis in this chapter has been almost exclusively in terms of

[18] We thus give a qualified endorsement to Parkinson's second law: "Expenditure rises to meet income." C. Northcote Parkinson, *The Law and the Prophets*, Houghton Mifflin Company, Boston, 1960, p. 4. Though stated flippantly, the principle has much merit as a long-run tendency for all sectors.

money flows and money values, without specifying the extent to which changes in GNP expenditures give rise to changes in real output or the price level. If unemployment is high, rising GNP will lead primarily to higher real output; but the likelihood of price increases becomes greater as the unemployment level declines. Decreases in GNP expenditures (which have been small and infrequent since World War II) appear to lead mainly to reduced output rather than lower prices.

QUESTIONS FOR STUDY

1. Define the following terms:
   a. The propensity to consume
   b. The marginal propensity to consume
   c. The acceleration principle
   d. The multiplier
   e. Induced investment
   f. The schedule of marginal efficiency of investment
   g. The capital-stock adjustment principle

2. Omitting government transactions, calculate the equilibrium level of GNP if $C_{t2} = \frac{3}{4} \, GNP_{t1}$ and $I = \$50$ billion. Prove it is an equilibrium. Find the new equilibrium if I rises to 60 billion; if it falls to zero. If I remains at 50 billion and C_{t2} rises to $\frac{4}{5} \, GNP_{t1}$, what will the equilibrium level of GNP be?

3. What is meant by the equilibrium level of GNP? Of what use is the concept? Show how equilibrium can be expressed in terms of saving and investment, giving careful attention to the definition of saving.

4. Assume that $C_{t2} = \frac{4}{5} \, PDI_{t1}$, $I = \$30$ billion, government purchases $= \$20$ billion, and taxes $= \frac{1}{4} \, GNP$ ($BDI = 0$). Find the equilibrium level of GNP. What happens if I rises to 40 billion? What is the size of the multiplier? What determines its size?

5. Prove or illustrate the proposition that the larger the multiplier, the longer it takes to reach a given proportion of its final value.

6. Explain the process and the result that each of the following would produce in GNP:
   a. An increase in the schedule of the marginal efficiency of investment
   b. An increase in tax rates
   c. A shift from home products to imports by consumers
   d. Lowering of interest rates through Federal Reserve open-market purchases
   e. An increase in government transfer payments

SUGGESTED READINGS

Commission on Money and Credit: *Impacts of Monetary Policy,* Prentice-Hall, Inc., Englewood Cliffs, N.J., 1963.

————: *Stabilization Policies,* Prentice-Hall, Inc., Englewood Cliffs, N.J., 1963.

Duesenberry, James S.: *Business Cycles and Economic Growth,* McGraw-Hill Book Company, New York, 1958.

Eisner, Robert, Dale W. Jorgenson, and Edwin Kuh: papers dealing with investment determinants under general heading of "Topics in Economic Theory," *American Economic Review,* May, 1963.

Ferber, Robert: "Research on Household Behavior," *American Economic Review,* March, 1962.

Friedman, Milton: *A Theory of the Consumption Function,* National Bureau of Economic Research, Inc., New York, 1957.

Haberler, Gottfried (ed.): *Readings in Business Cycle Theory,* McGraw-Hill Book Company, New York, 1944.

Keynes, John Maynard: *The General Theory of Employment, Interest, and Money,* Harcourt, Brace and Company, Inc., New York, 1936.

Lewis, John P.: *Business Conditions Analysis,* McGraw-Hill Book Company, New York, 1959.

Maisel, Sherman J.: "A Theory of Fluctuations in Residential Construction Starts," *American Economic Review,* June, 1963.

chapter nine

CASH BALANCES,
LOANABLE FUNDS,
AND INTEREST RATES

INTRODUCTORY

So far in our discussion of monetary theory, we have concentrated our attention on the causes and consequences of variations in GNP expenditures. We have noted that activity in the main money circuit depends particularly on the relationship between saving and investment or between sector surpluses and deficits. Among the important determinants of the income-expenditure relationship we have included interest rates and credit conditions, which affect certain types of capital expenditures especially.

In this chapter, we reverse the emphasis. Here our emphasis will be on the financial circulation and on the manner in which interest rates and credit conditions are determined. We shall see that these are determined in part by the supply of saving coming from main circuit surpluses and by the demand for credit to finance main circuit deficits. In addition, however, interest rates and credit conditions depend on circumstances relating to money itself—to changes in its supply and in the desire of the public to hold cash balances.

But are we not begging the question if we use main circuit surpluses and deficits to help explain interest rates, when in the previous chapter we

used interest rates to help explain main circuit income-expenditure relations? In reality, the relationship is one of mutual determination. Once we
have sketched the behavior of the financial circulation in this chapter, we
shall bring the two parts together and demonstrate how this mutual determination operates, with the level of GNP and the interest rate being simultaneously determined by the underlying behavior patterns and propensities
in the economy.

Stocks and Flows   Our analysis of the main money circuit has run
chiefly in terms of *flow* concepts—income and expenditure, saving and investment. Flows involve a time dimension; they refer to a rate of activity
carried on over some specified period of time. Even in analyzing income and
expenditures, however, it is sometimes useful to shift to analysis in terms of
stocks—that is, quantities of items expressed in absolute terms, without any
reference to time. The capital-stock adjustment principle, in which investment activity is oriented toward attaining some desired total amount of real
capital, employs this outlook.

Stocks and flows are related to each other, in that the net *change* in the
stock of some items is itself a flow concept. The total quantity of business
inventories is a stock concept, but the net change in inventories during a
year is a flow.

Analysis in terms of stock concepts is handy because it lends itself
readily to supply-demand equilibrium considerations. We can first think of
each sector pursuing some sort of equilibrium balance sheet, in which the
volume and composition of assets and liabilities are determined on the basis
of costs and advantages. Indeed, we did this in some detail for the banking
system. Second, we can imagine that each type of asset is subject to a demand schedule (depending on the price of the asset, the income or utility
expected from it, and other considerations) and a supply schedule. The interplay of supply and demand will influence the prices and other characteristics
of assets in a manner which tends to equate supply and demand. Equilibrium would exist for the economy if each transactor had achieved its optimum balance sheet and if supply and demand were equal for each type of
asset and liability.

Analysis in terms of stock concepts is particularly appropriate for any
asset of which the total quantity is large in relation to the year-to-year
changes in it. This condition prevails for many types of financial assets. The
total quantity of "primary securities"—stocks and IOUs of nonfinancial sectors—is ten to twenty times as large as the normal year-to-year changes.
Indeed, money itself is such an asset, and our analysis in Part Two has provided us with the determinants of its supply, on the basis of a stock concept. One of our tasks in this chapter will be to complement this with an
analysis of the demand schedule for money as one type of financial asset.

One final consideration is very useful in discussing financial assets:

just as one man's expenditure is another's income, so one man's liability is another's asset. The supply schedule of debt claims of all sorts—bonds, mortgages, loans—depends on the willingness of transactors to go into debt. This provides a final link between the balance sheet adjustments of individuals and the supply-demand adjustments relating to types of financial assets.

Financial Net Worth One of the simplest ways of relating the financial circulation to the main money circuit is to use the concept of financial net worth. For any transactor, financial net worth is simply the total value of its financial assets minus its debts.[1] When a sector has a surplus of income over expenditure, its financial net worth increases by the amount of the surplus. When a transactor has a deficit, its financial net worth decreases by the amount that expenditures exceed income.

When a sector increases its financial net worth, three elements (or a combination) may be involved:

1. It may reduce its indebtedness.

2. It may acquire income-bearing financial assets.

3. It may increase its holdings of money (that is, currency and demand deposits).

Contrariwise, when a sector reduces its financial net worth, the operation is likely to involve some combination of increased indebtedness, decreased holdings of income-bearing assets, and decreased holdings of money.

If one is looking at specific business firms or individuals, all sorts of permutations and combinations may occur. But when we aggregate these units into major sectors, a fairly definite "normal" pattern of behavior emerges. Each major sector of the economy increases both its indebtedness and its holdings of financial assets (both money and other) over time. The surplus sectors (chiefly consumers) increase their holdings of financial assets more than their debts, while the deficit sectors (chiefly business) add to their debts more than to their financial assets.

Loanable Funds Flows Changes in financial assets issued and held can be reinterpreted in terms of the flow of loanable funds. When a sector acquires income-bearing financial assets, it supplies loanable funds. When a sector issues income-bearing claims against itself, it demands loanable funds. The conflicting pressures of supply and demand will bring about a structure of asset prices and yields which will tend toward equilibrium. In

---

[1] Financial net worth is not the same as net worth in general, which includes ownership of real assets. A business firm or individual might be very wealthy but have a negative financial net worth, offset by extensive ownership of real assets—land, buildings, machines. Note that changes in financial net worth may arise from changes in the capital value of financial assets, particularly stocks. Such capital-value changes are ignored in the text.

a flow sense, the supply of loanable funds will be equal to the demand. In a stock sense, the total supply of income-bearing financial assets will be equal to the demand.

Changes in money holdings represent a balancing item relating a transactor's behavior in the main circuit (surplus or deficit) and its position in the loanable funds market (supplier or demander). A transactor which made no change in its money holdings would supply loanable funds equal to its main circuit surplus, or demand loanable funds equal to its main circuit deficit. In some cases, however, a transactor might make a substantial shift between cash and other financial assets. Then there would be no simple relation between its position in the main circuit and its position in the financial circulation. Additions to money holdings by any transactor do not supply loanable funds, provided the division of holdings between currency and demand deposits remains constant. The net influence of any transactor in the loanable funds market is measured by the difference between its acquisition of income-bearing financial assets and its borrowing.

Analytically, we can treat each transactor's behavior as involving three flow elements—its position in the main circuit, its position in the loanable funds flow, and its adjustments in money holdings. These are held together by budgetary considerations, as expressed in the following:

$$\text{Income} - \text{expenditure} = (\text{acquisition of income-bearing financial assets} - \text{borrowing}) + \text{net increase in cash holdings}$$

Given any two of the elements, the third is determined residually. It might be more accurate to say, however, that all three are influenced to some extent by the same factors. In particular, decisions about holdings of money and income-bearing financial assets are related to each other. In the following sections, we shall deal explicitly with the demand for money balances, but the analysis will deal implicitly with demand for other financial assets as well.

THE DEMAND FOR CASH BALANCES

Meaning   All the money supply (except for funds in the mail) is part of the cash balance of some economic unit.[2] (By cash balance we mean simply the currency and demand deposits owned by anyone.) Most money is held by business firms and individuals. To the extent that people want to

---

[2] Or, as Gertrude Stein is said to have put it, "The money is always there, but the pockets change; it is not in the same pockets after a change, and that is all there is to say about money." It might be useful to transform Stein's law of pockets into a law of the conservation of money, to wit: "Money is neither created nor destroyed by ordinary acts of expenditure."

hold cash balances, we say that they have a "demand for money." This is a tricky concept. The mere fact that people would like to have more money does not constitute an economic demand for it, any more than an unfulfilled desire for any commodity would be a demand for it. With money, as with commodities, people must be willing to give up something in order to make their demand effective. Furthermore, when we speak of demand for money, we mean demand for money to hold, not to spend immediately.

Decisions to hold cash balances involve a weighing of costs and benefits. The costs of holding money arise from the sacrifice of alternatives. For consumers, one alternative is current consumption, and the "cost" is the psychological loss of utility. For business firms one alternative is investment in capital goods, and the cost would be measured by the marginal efficiency of the investment forgone. For any sector, another alternative is acquisition of income-bearing financial assets (or reduction of debt). Here the cost would be measured by the interest rate (or other income) on the financial assets or indebtedness.

Such a listing of the alternatives to holding cash also serves to remind us of the ways in which a transactor can increase its cash holdings. It can spend less relative to its income. It can sell assets, real or financial, or borrow. When we speak of an increase in the demand for cash balances, some process of acquiring the added cash must be involved.

Holding money yields neither the income of an investment nor the utility of consumption. Why are people willing to incur the costs implied by cash holdings? Because money performs functions which make it a useful asset. First, money is a medium of payment. People hold money balances as a convenience to carry on their transactions. Such cash holdings are often referred to as "transactions balances"; they involve active money, likely to be paid out soon after its receipt. Second, money is a store of value. People may choose to hold part of their wealth in the form of money. Cash balances held as a store of value may be termed "asset balances" or idle balances.

The desire to hold money as a medium of payment and as a store of value will be affected by the fact that substitutes are available for either purpose. The quantity of cash desired will thus be a function of the utility of money services on the one hand, qualified by concern for the costs of holding money and the availability of substitutes on the other.

Transactions Balances The need for cash to carry on transactions depends on the amount and timing of receipts and payments for individual transactors. Most consumers receive their incomes in lump sums at periodic intervals—every week, every month, or even less often for some property incomes. Consumers will wish to make expenditures at irregular dates in between such times. Many business firms find themselves in an opposite situation—sales receipts trickle in every business day, whereas payments for wages, interest, rents, etc., may occur infrequently. In either situation, a cash balance is convenient to bridge the discontinuity between receipts and payments.

Suppose Joe Doakes receives $70 a week in wages and spends $10 of it every day. The amount of transactions cash he keeps may range from $70 just after he gets paid down to zero just before. His average balance over the week would be about $35. (A prudent individual presumably would not permit his cash balance to fall to zero every week, but funds held in excess of current transactions needs may be regarded as asset balances, which are discussed below.)

The average amount of transactions cash Joe will need in relation to his income may change if the timing of his transactions changes. Suppose he is shifted to a monthly salary of $300 and continues to spend $10 a day. His annual income and expenditure are about the same, but he will need a larger cash balance. Over the 30-day interval, his balance may range from $300 to zero, but it would average about $150. Changing the timing of expenditures may also alter his need for cash. If he spent most of his income soon after payday, he would need a smaller cash balance, on the average, than when expenditures were spread evenly.

As long as the timing of receipts and expenditures is relatively unchanged, changes in the amount of transactions cash needed will chiefly reflect changes in the amount of income and expenditure. If Joe's monthly salary and expenditures rise to $400, his cash balance will tend to rise to $200 to finance an even flow of expenditures.

The cash-balance needs of business firms will also depend on the volume and timing of their sales and expenditures. The more closely payments follow receipts, the smaller the cash balance needed. The timing of business payments largely determines the timing of consumer income receipts, to which consumer cash balances are adjusted. Thus business payment practices are a basic determinant of the economy's need for cash balances. Since business payment practices do not vary much over short periods of time, the amount of transactions cash balances needed varies chiefly in response to variations in the amount of income and expenditures.

However, a cash balance is not the only medium available to permit expenditures and receipts to occur at divergent times. The ability to "charge it"—to buy goods by incurring book-credit liabilities to be discharged later—enables business firms and individuals to reduce the amount of cash holdings needed for transactions. Table 9-1 compares the cash holdings of business firms and households with their use of book credit.

For business firms and individuals combined, book-credit liabilities were about two-thirds as large as money holdings. However, for the business sector, book-credit liabilities substantially exceeded money holdings. Thus in large degree, business firms incurred debts to each other as a way of holding down their needs for cash.

The degree to which book credit is used instead of cash may vary in response to the level of interest rates. To illustrate, the nonfinancial business sector as a whole reduced its cash holdings by $4 billion and added about $5 billion to its trade credit liabilities between 1958 and 1962, a period of high interest rates.

Table 9-1   Money and its transactions substitutes, December 31, 1962
(Billions of dollars)

Book-credit liabilities	Households	Corporations	Noncorporate businesses*	Total
Charge accounts, credit cards, and service credit	$10	—	—	$10
Trade credit liabilities	—	$53	$13	66
Debit balances with stockbrokers	5	—	—	5
Total book-credit liabilities	$14	$53	$13	$80
Holdings of currency and demand deposits	$71	$32	$18	$121

* Noncorporate businesses include farms. Financial businesses are excluded.
Source: Federal Reserve Bulletin, August, 1963. Data are rounded and may not add up to totals.

Large firms also economize on transactions cash by the substitution of interest-bearing liquid assets. Only if the sums involved are large will the income be sufficient to compensate for the trouble and expense. Theoretically, we would expect business firms to shift between interest-bearing assets and cash as interest rates vary. However, in the period 1946–1962, they do not appear to have done so.[3]

On the whole, the amount of cash demanded for transactions purposes rises and falls in response to changes in the volume of transactions. With higher incomes, wage earners will keep more cash in their pockets and checking accounts. With higher sales and disbursements, business firms will keep more cash in the till and in the bank. Indeed, the simplest hypothesis about the demand for transactions balances is that people try to keep a constant ratio between their money holdings and GNP. However, since no data exist which literally measure transactions balances as such, we can only talk about the observed pattern for the money supply as a whole, after we have looked at the theory of asset balances.

Asset Balances   In addition to active cash balances, business firms and individuals are likely to keep additional money on hand as a liquid store of value. In discussing asset balances, our emphasis shifts to stock concepts—

[3] Data on corporate holdings of financial assets are derived from Board of Governors, Federal Reserve System, *Flow of Funds Accounts, 1945–1962*, Washington, 1963.

to the demand for a certain quantity of money in relation to the total desired stock of wealth of all kinds. Broadly speaking, we can treat the demand for asset balances as reflecting, first, the size of the total stock of wealth, and second, the proportion of wealth which people want to hold in the form of money.

In the short run, the size of the community's stock of wealth—of assets of all kinds—is relatively constant. The demand for assets will reflect expectations of psychological utility and income yield. But again we must ask— why hold money when other forms of wealth yield direct satisfaction (a house, a car) or money income (capital goods, stocks and bonds)? The simplest answer is liquidity. An asset possesses liquidity to the degree that its value is stable in terms of money and it can be converted into money with a minimum of cost and inconvenience. Money is the ultimate liquid asset because of its unique status as the means of payment, the embodiment of generalized purchasing power. In particular, the attractiveness of money arises from its ability to pay debts, which are a sort of "anti-money" bearing a fixed (negative) dollar value.

Since money alone can be spent directly, to buy things or to discharge debts, it is more liquid than other assets. Because of its greater liquidity, people are willing to hold it even though it yields no income. However, liquidity is a matter of degree. And there are assets which, while they cannot be spent directly, approach closely to the liquidity of currency and demand deposits. Chief among these are interest-bearing fixed-value claims which can be exchanged for money on demand: time and savings deposits, United States savings bonds, and related savings assets. Close to these come low-risk marketable assets such as short-term Treasury bills and commercial paper issued by large business firms.

We can now restate our approach to the demand for money as follows: The desired level of asset balances would reflect first, the desired holdings of liquid assets of all sorts, and second, the proportion of liquid assets which people want to hold in the form of money.

The Desire for Liquidity The principal attraction of liquid assets is simply that they are a good store of value—safe, immune to fluctuations in dollar value. The accumulation of liquid assets is particularly attractive in the face of uncertainty. One wishes to be prepared for unforeseeable financial emergencies (or opportunities).

Less liquid assets, real or financial, may offer greater income (explicit or implicit) but entail greater degrees of risk. Choice between assets will involve a balancing of these considerations, and desired asset holdings could shift if there were a substantial change in either the expected income or the risk associated with different types of assets. Liquid assets are particularly attractive when one's total wealth is not large enough to support the diversification and careful investment analysis required to absorb the risks of investment in nonliquid assets. Under such circumstances the income from one's wealth is a consideration distinctly subordinate to safety and stability of capital value, and the extra income to be gained by sacrifice of liquidity is not very great.

The attractiveness of liquid assets is evident from the fact that during much of the period since 1929, consumers have held liquid savings assets approximately equal to GNP. This relationship is examined in Chapter 11, and the evidence appears in Figure 11-2 (page 281). It suggests the existence of a demand for liquid assets proportional to income and wealth.

However, this proportional demand may be affected by two specific factors which would affect the desire for liquidity.

1. *Uncertainty*. Liquidity is advantageous chiefly because it does provide a hedge against uncertainty. The greater the public's sense of confusion, disturbance, and uncertainty, the greater one would expect to be their desire for liquidity.

2. *Price expectations*. Liquid assets are fixed in terms of dollar value. If prices of goods and services (and of nonliquid assets, for that matter) are rising, liquid assets lose much of their charm as a store of value. On the other hand, if prices fall, holding liquid assets can be very advantageous.

Bringing these considerations together, we would expect that the desire for liquidity would be strong (a) when the expected income from nonliquid assets is low relative to risks they entail, (b) when the general degree of uncertainty is high, and (c) when the price level is expected to fall. On the other hand, when nonliquid assets offer high income relative to risk, when uncertainty is low, and when the price level is expected to rise, liquid assets appear less desirable. These variations may represent deviations from a long-run trend in which total wealth and the desired amounts of liquid assets are both rising.

Given the demand for liquid assets as a whole, what proportion will be held in cash and what proportion in income-bearing forms? If there are no doubts about the safety of income-bearing liquid assets, the choice between them and cash will depend almost entirely on the rate of interest they pay. When interest rates are high, people will be more inclined to hold their assets in interest-bearing forms, such as bonds or savings deposits, and reduce their idle cash to a minimum. When interest rates are low, inertia or the positive advantages of liquidity may induce them to hold larger idle cash balances rather than to acquire earning assets with low rates of return.

If people do not expect drastic changes in incomes and prices, interest rates will be the chief determinant of the quantity of asset money demanded. This was the case in the 1950s. It takes considerable disturbance of expectations to affect the demand for money very much. Such a disturbance occurred during the serious economic downswing of 1929–1933, when declining incomes and prices, plus a great sense of risk and uncertainty, made people desire more cash. During periods of rapid inflation (as in Germany or Russia in the 1920s), the loss of real value drives people to reduce their holdings of cash and other liquid assets to a minimum.

Evidence on the Desired Level of Money Balances   The foregoing considerations on money as a medium of transactions and as a store of value suggest that the total quantity of money desired will tend to vary directly with the volume of transactions (for which we may use income as one measure) and also directly with the quantity of total wealth. However, interest rates have an inverse effect: The higher the interest rate, the lower the desired level of cash balances.

It is difficult to identify the relative influences of income (or transactions) versus wealth. Income and wealth are closely intercorrelated over time. In addition, statistical measurement of wealth is rendered difficult by problems of valuation and measurement. As a result, there has been room for disagreement among economists as to whether to treat the demand schedule for money as a function of current income, of "permanent" income, or of wealth.[4]

For our purposes, the following simple hypothesis is both convenient and consistent with the evidence: The desired quantity of money varies directly with disposable income (or GNP) and inversely with the level of interest rates. However, there is a different demand schedule for money for each of the major sectors of the economy.[5]

Figure 9-1 shows data on the cash holdings of business firms, households, and government for the years since 1929. For households, the diagram shows vertically the interest paid on commercial bank time deposits and horizontally the ratio of cash holdings to PDI. For government, the Treasury bill rate is shown vertically and the ratio of cash holdings to net government revenue horizontally. For business, GNP gives a better measure of transactions than BDI does, and thus the horizontal variable is the ratio of business cash holdings to total GNP. Vertically, the interest rate is the

[4] Milton Friedman argues that demand for cash balances depends on permanent income and that as income rises over time, the ratio of cash to income also tends to rise. See *Studies in the Quantity Theory of Money*, The University of Chicago Press, Chicago, 1956, and Milton Friedman and Anna J. Schwartz, *A Monetary History of the United States, 1867–1960*, Princeton University Press for National Bureau of Economic Research, Princeton, N.J., 1963, chap. 12. An alternative interpretation stressing wealth is presented by Allan Meltzer and Karl Brunner; see especially "The Demand for Money: The Evidence from the Time Series," *Journal of Political Economy*, June, 1963, and "Predicting Velocity: Implications for Theory and Policy," *Journal of Finance*, May, 1963.

[5] A detailed description and analysis of sector behavior appears in Richard Selden, "The Postwar Rise in the Velocity of Money: A Sectoral Analysis," *Journal of Finance*, December, 1961.

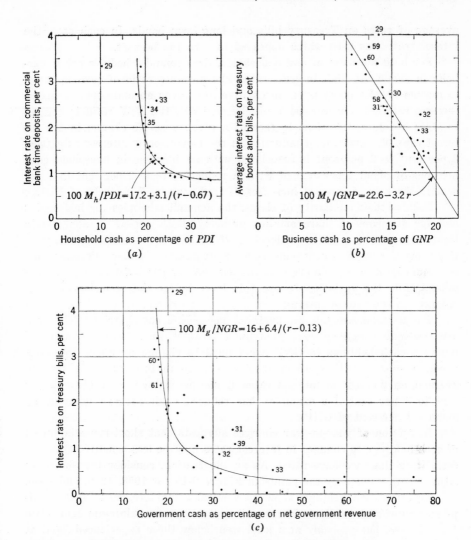

Figure 9-1. Cash balances, income, and interest rates, 1929–1963.

Sources: Cash balances 1929–1945: Author's estimates derived by combining data from Raymond Goldsmith, Robert Lipsey, and Morris Mendelson, *Studies in the National Balance Sheet of the United States*, Vol. II; Goldsmith, *A Study of Saving in the United States*, vol. I; *Federal Reserve Bulletin*, July, 1955. Cash balances 1946–1963: from *Flow of Funds Accounts, 1945–1962*, and *Federal Reserve Bulletin*, April, 1964. No estimates are given for households, 1930–1932. Sources for interest rates: Goldsmith, *Study of Saving; Annual Reports* of Federal Deposit Insurance Corporation; *Economic Report of the President; Banking and Monetary Statistics*.

average of rates on Treasury bills and long-term bonds. In each case, the interest rate was used which appeared to give the best fit.

For both government and households, the demand schedules are hyperbolic in shape. At high interest rates, the absolute ratio of cash holdings to income (M/Y) is relatively insensitive to a given absolute change in the interest rate. At low interest rates, by contrast, the M/Y ratio is subject to large absolute variations in face of a given absolute change in the interest rate. To illustrate, a reduction in the time-deposit interest rate from 3 per cent to 2 per cent is associated with an increase in household cash holdings of about 1 per cent of PDI. A reduction from 2 per cent to 1 per cent in the rate of interest increases desired cash by 7 per cent of PDI.

Besides their similarity of shape, the demand schedules for households and for government share another property. Both appear to approach a limit in terms of a minimum level of M/Y, and limits are approximately the same for both—about one-sixth of disposable income. Perhaps this minimum level of M/Y represents the desired quantity of transactions balances, while the variations above this level reflect the response of asset balances to the rate of interest.

The demand schedule for business has a different character. The data are reasonably well approximated by a straight line. Thus the ratio of business cash holdings to GNP has tended to change by about the same absolute amount with a given absolute change in interest rates. On the average, an increase in interest rates of one percentage point (from 2 per cent to 3 per cent, for example) has reduced business cash holdings by about 3.2 per cent of GNP.

Inspection of year-to-year changes suggests that short-run adaptation of cash holdings to changes in interest rates may be less sensitive than the estimating lines we have fitted. As an illustration, consider the short-run adjustments implied by the points in Figure 9-1*b* for 1958, 1959, and 1960.

Business cash holdings show no vertical asymptote, no implicit minimum level of cash holdings. There may well exist some minimum M/Y ratio for business, but probably at a level well below those experienced (and at an interest rate so high as to be almost purely hypothetical).

The interest sensitivity of cash holdings implied in Figure 9-1 is of the same order of magnitude as that shown by other studies.[6] However, some economists are skeptical as to whether statistical correlations of this sort really identify the functional dependence of cash holdings on the interest rate. They note that the evidence is heavily influenced by rather wide business cycle swings of the 1930s and 1940s. Milton Friedman argues that if one studies a really long time period, the influence of interest rates on desired cash holdings proves to be relatively slight.

[6] Besides the sources noted in footnote 4, one may call attention to estimates of the total demand schedule for cash by Carl Christ, which suggest interest

Shifts in Demand If these data reflect the functional dependence of cash holdings on interest rates and transactions, they also imply that variations in psychological desires, expectations, and the degree of uncertainty have not, since the mid-1930s, been great enough to cause shifts in the demand schedules.

By contrast, the figures for 1929–1933 show definite evidence of rightward shifts in the demand schedule as a whole. The onset of the Depression was uniquely suited to cause an increase in the desired ratio of cash to income: Prices were falling and were expected to fall further, uncertainty was greatly increased, and public confidence in assets other than money was severely shaken. In contrast, the inflationary experience of 1941–1952 does not appear to have caused a discernible leftward shift.

Aggregating the Sectors The differences in the observed demand patterns among the three sectors make it difficult to combine them into a single demand schedule for cash balances applicable to the entire economy. Even if the sector demand curves are stable, the aggregate demand for cash would change if there were a change in the division of incomes among the three sectors. Moreover, the sectors respond to different interest rates, and those interest rates do not maintain any simple, consistent relation to each other. The Treasury bill rate is highly volatile, while the rate on time deposits is very sluggish and tends to be unresponsive to short-run variations in the more volatile rates.

However, for illustrative purposes, Figure 9-2 shows a rough approximation (D) to a demand schedule for money balances based on the GNP level for 1963 ($584 billion), calculated on the assumption that the proportion between bond rate, bill rate, and time-deposit rate would be a constant. The curve is almost straight, with a slight curvature; it would flatten out drastically below a bond rate of 1.50. The curve does not hit the target exactly, as you can see from the dotted lines showing the actual money supply ($159 billion, including government) and the actual bond rate of 4.14.

Such a demand schedule is valid only for a given level of GNP. As incomes and transactions volume rise, the entire demand schedule shifts to the right. This is shown by the curve D_2, drawn for GNP of $700 billion, assuming a constant division of incomes among sectors.

Adjustments to Disequilibrium If the quantity of money demanded at the existing level of GNP and the effective interest rate is not equal to the available supply, a disequilibrium exists. Adjustments will be set in motion which will tend to equate supply and demand. Suppose the supply of money exceeds the demand. The transactors who have surplus cash may increase

---

elasticity of between 0.5 and 0.7 for the period 1892–1959. Cited in Joseph Asch-heim, "Financial Intermediaries and the Goals of Monetary Policy," *American Economic Review*, May, 1963, p. 369.

their expenditures for current output, which will raise GNP; or they may use the excess cash to acquire interest-bearing assets or repay debts, which will tend to reduce interest rates. Higher GNP and lower interest rates, separately or in combination, would raise the amount of cash balances people wanted to hold. Ultimately, even if the supply of money remained unchanged, people would become willing to hold the amount in existence. However, some of the excess supply might pass out of existence if people repaid bank debts and the banks did not make an equivalent amount of new loans.

Similar principles would hold if the demand exceeded the existing supply. People who desired to hold more cash might reduce their expenditures for current output, which would reduce GNP. Alternatively, they might borrow more heavily, reduce their acquisitions of interest-bearing assets, or even sell such assets, to acquire the cash. These actions would tend to raise interest rates. Lower GNP and higher interest rates, separately or in combination, would reduce the quantity of money people wanted to hold, until it became equal to the available supply. However, the excess demand for money

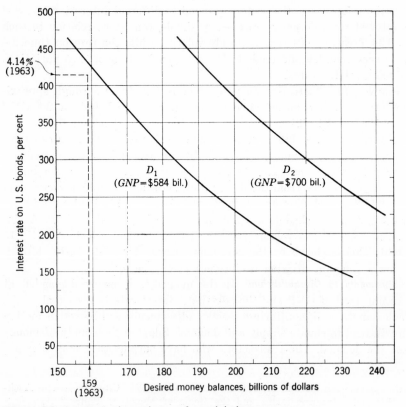

Figure 9-2. Aggregate demand curves for cash balances.

might be met by increased supply if demand for bank loans increased and the banks were willing and able to meet the higher demand.

We are most interested in the manner in which the quantity of cash balances demanded adjusts to the available supply. When supply exceeds demand, the efforts of some transactors to reduce their cash holdings merely pass these along to others, as in a game of "Old Maid," until, ultimately, economic conditions change sufficiently to induce people to hold the available supply. When demand exceeds supply, efforts of some transactors to hold more cash reduce the amount available for others. As in a game of musical chairs, all scramble for the insufficient supply until conditions change sufficiently to reconcile them to the limited amount available.

Variations in the demand schedule have not been a frequent source of disturbance. Thus the chief adjustment process has reflected the adaptation to variations in the money supply, through changes in income and interest rates. A fuller analysis of these adjustments is presented in Chapter 10.

Demand for Income-bearing Financial Assets   On the basis of the sort of sector budget equation we have referred to frequently, if we know the sector's income and expenditures in the main circuit and the net changes in its cash balance, we can obtain as a residual the net change in its income-bearing financial assets (or net indebtedness). Furthermore, our preceding analysis of the determinants of expenditures and cash holdings implies a definite pattern for holdings of income-bearing assets as well. The expenditures of each sector—business, households, and government—are affected somewhat by interest rates; each tends to spend more (relative to disposable income) when interest rates are low. Furthermore, each sector tends to hold more cash (relative to income) when interest rates are low. The conclusion follows that low interest rates push each sector toward a slower accumulation of income-bearing assets and/or a faster accumulation of debt.

Put another way, the interest rate not only helps to equate the demand for money with the supply but also performs a similar function for income-bearing financial assets. If the supply of such assets exceeds the demand, asset prices will tend to fall and their yields to rise, until people are willing to hold the existing supply. If demand for income-bearing financial assets exceeds the supply, their prices will tend to be bid up and their yields reduced until equilibrium is achieved. Of course, the supply of such assets is not insensitive to interest rates. If excess supply of bonds causes their interest rates to rise, some borrowers may refrain from borrowing, thus helping reduce supply.

We should point out that our analysis of the demand-supply relations for money itself and for other financial assets is part of a general theory of asset markets. Demand for most kinds of assets—money, other financial assets, houses, capital goods—varies directly with income and inversely with price (treating interest as the "price" of money). Supply consists mainly of the stock in existence, since year-to-year changes in the stock are small proportionally to the total. A discrepancy between the quantity in existence and the quantity people want to hold may be met by changes in supply, but much of the adjustment will occur in the price of the existing stock of assets.

An excess of demand will lead primarily to a higher price for the asset in question; the higher price may then in time draw forth an increase in the quantity supplied. An excess of supply will initially tend to reduce the price of the asset, but in time withdrawals may be made to reduce the actual stock. Short-run adjustments in asset markets involve mainly changes in asset prices, changes tending to bring a relatively flexible demand into equality with a relatively fixed supply. Such principles apply not only to money and other financial assets, but also to durable capital goods, housing, and particularly land, of which total supply is relatively constant.

This analysis is useful in helping us to understand the behavior of asset prices and yields. Indeed, it provides a basis for one approach to the theory of how interest rates are determined: Very generally, interest rates tend toward levels which equate the quantity demanded of each major type of asset with the supply. However, our chief concern is the way in which these asset-market adjustments, involving stocks, relate to the flows of income and expenditure in the main circuit. To this end, we shall now proceed to repeat many of the points made so far in this chapter, but in a frame of reference which stresses flows rather than stocks. Our focal point will be the flow of loanable funds.

DETERMINATION OF INTEREST RATES

Loanable Funds There are many different interest rates. These rates differ in their levels (reflecting differences in risks and maturities) and in their short-run sensitivity. Nevertheless, the various rates tend to rise and fall together in response to broad influences operating over substantial periods of time. These influences can be most simply described as the demand for and supply of loanable funds.

The demand for loanable funds includes applications for loans addressed to banks and other lenders and requests for credit from sellers of goods. It also includes sales of newly issued securities and, for that matter, sales of existing financial assets to raise funds. Roughly speaking, a sector acquires loanable funds to the extent that it increases its debt by more than it increases its income-bearing financial assets, or decreases its holdings of income-bearing financial assets by more than it decreases its debt. For the most part, demand for loanable funds arises from people who want to increase their expenditures in relation to their income.

Where do loanable funds come from? Borrowers obtain a considerable proportion of their funds from financial institutions such as insurance companies, banks, and savings institutions. These institutions in turn obtain their funds from the public in exchange for specialized financial obligations such as insurance coverage and savings deposits. The ultimate supply arises from people who are willing to increase their holdings of income-bearing financial assets by more than their debts, or to decrease their debts by more than their holdings of income-bearing financial assets. Debt repayment as well as asset acquisition supplies loanable funds. Finally, we must not overlook one source of special concern to us: The commercial banks can add to the supply of loanable funds by increasing the quantity of money. Let us turn now to the forces which determine the desires to supply and to demand loanable funds.

Loanable Funds Supply and Demand We can express the position of each sector in the loanable funds market in terms of a familiar budget equation:

Acquisition of income-bearing financial assets − borrowing
= income − expenditure − net increase in cash holdings

Each sector's net loanable funds position is indicated by the balance of the items to the left of the equals sign. The items to the right show that the sector's supply will be greater (or its demand less) the larger its income, the less its expenditures, and the smaller its demand for cash holdings.

When we look at loanable funds flows for the economy as a whole, a fairly simple relationship can be stated. The supply of loanable funds tends to vary directly with saving ex ante and with the supply of money. The demand for loanable funds tends to vary directly with investment and with the demand for cash balances. The interest rate will tend to adjust itself to a point at which the ex ante supply and demand are equal. At this point, the following equilibrium relationship will exist:

Saving + supply of money = investment + demand for cash balances

These relationships are muddled in practice by the fact that all four of the determinants may operate on either side of the market. However, their effects on the interest rate are unambiguous. Rather than dwell on the complexities of loanable funds measurement in itself, let us look directly at each of the four determinants in relation to the rate of interest.

1. *Saving.* Personal saving supplies loanable funds to the extent that the saving goes to acquire income-bearing financial assets—stocks, bonds, savings deposits—or to repay debts. However, personal saving includes direct purchases of capital goods such as housing and capital used in farming or other unincorporated business. Acts of saving directly associated with acts of investment in capital goods do not affect loanable funds flows

or the interest rate. The same is true when personal saving goes into increased holdings of cash.

Much the same analysis applies to business saving. Business saving provides loanable funds when firms add to their holdings of income-bearing financial assets or repay debts, but not when the acts of saving are directly connected with acquisition of capital goods or added cash holdings.

Government saving—that is, a government surplus—adds to the supply of loanable funds when the government uses its surplus to pay off part of the public debt, but not if the surplus is merely used to add to cash holdings. Suppose the government has a deficit; then its measured saving is negative. Its borrowing constitutes a demand for funds and tends to raise the interest rate.

Taking all sectors together, this conclusion is valid: An increase in saving either increases the supply of loanable funds or decreases the demand, except where the increase in saving is directly associated with increased investment or cash holdings. Other things equal, an increase in saving tends to lower interest rates.

2. *Investment.* The desire to spend for capital goods (including new housing) gives rise to a demand for loanable funds when the investment is to be financed by borrowing. However, a substantial amount of investment is financed directly out of saving, without recourse to external finance. And it is conceivable that investment expenditures could be financed by reducing cash holdings. Conclusion: Increased investment tends to increase interest rates, except to the extent that the acts of investment are directly associated with acts of saving or decreased cash holdings.

3. *Demand for cash balances.* An attempt to increase one's holdings of cash affects the availability of loan funds when it involves compensating changes in other assets and liabilities. One might sell income-bearing financial assets or borrow to obtain the added cash, or hold on to funds which otherwise would have gone to repay debts or to acquire income-bearing financial assets. In such cases, increases in the desired level of cash holdings mean decreases in the supply of (or increases in the demand for) loan funds, thus tending to raise interest rates.

However, changes in desired cash holdings may also be effected by changing one's income-expenditure position. Additions to cash holdings may be obtained by saving more and spending less. Such action would produce a measured rise in saving, if performed by households or government, and a measured decrease in investment if performed by business. Such variations in desired cash holdings do not directly affect loanable funds flows and interest rates.

Conclusion: An increase in the demand schedule for cash balances tends to decrease the supply of (or increase the demand for) loanable funds and thus to raise interest rates, except to the extent that the increase in desired cash holdings is directly associated with increased saving or decreased investment.

4. *The supply of money.* Most increases in the money supply come through the commercial banking system—through the expansion of bank loans and securities holdings. Consequently most increases in the money supply add to the supply of loanable funds.

However, there are occasions when increased money comes directly into the expenditure flow rather than into loanable funds. When the Treasury buys newly mined gold or silver, or when it issued greenbacks to finance Civil War deficits, the new money did not directly affect loanable funds or the interest rate. In such cases the increase in the supply of money is matched by a decrease in saving by government.

The money supply might also increase through an international gold inflow arising out of an export surplus of goods and services. Such a transaction is sometimes referred to as "net foreign investment" by the United States. Again, loanable funds and the interest rate are not affected, since the increase in the money supply is offset directly by increased investment.

Conclusion: Increases in the money supply tend to increase the supply of loanable funds and thus reduce interest rates, except to the extent that the increase in the quantity of money is directly associated with decreases in saving or increases in investment.

Supply and Demand Schedules   Bringing our four conclusions all together, things fall out very simply indeed: The interest rate tends to vary directly with the desire to invest and to hold cash balances, and inversely with the supply of money and the desire to save. Our next problem is to identify the determinants of the determinants.

The desired levels of saving, of investment, and of cash holdings can all be regarded as determined by the same set of influences—the level of income, interest rates, and psychological tastes and expectations. All three desired levels tend to rise and fall more or less proportionately with variations in income or GNP expenditures. For analysis of interest-rate determination, however, let us hold constant the level of income and the state of preferences and expectations. How do desired saving, investment, and money holdings vary in response to interest rates?

Saving is slightly influenced by interest rates. Consumer borrowing and spending for durable-goods purchases tend to be restrained by high interest costs, by increased severity of credit rationing, and by restrictive movements in down payment and maturity terms. Similar effects show up for state and local government borrowing and capital outlays. Thus at high interest rates, measured saving is greater at any given level of income, because these categories of dissaving are somewhat reduced. The relationship of investment to interest rates is embraced in the marginal efficiency

schedule. A reduction of interest rates will increase the amount of investment which firms can profitably undertake on the basis of a given marginal
efficiency schedule.

Desired cash holdings also tend to vary inversely with interest rates.
When interest rates are high, people reduce their holdings of idle cash and
hold more income-bearing financial assets instead. With low interest rates,
cash holdings tend to be greater in relation to income.

It is of considerable importance for monetary policy to know the relative sensitivity to interest rates of expenditures for current output (as
manifested in the interest sensitivity of saving and investment) as compared to the desired level of cash holdings. No very precise measurement
can be made, but the evidence suggests that cash holdings have a greater
quantitative sensitivity. Brownlee and Conrad prepared a set of estimates
for 1957 showing the total probable influence on expenditures of a 1 per
cent change in the interest rate (e.g., from its actual level of about 3.5 to
4.5 per cent). They concluded that saving would be affected by $1.14 billion
and investment by $4.54 billion, for a total of $5.68 billion.[7] If we treat this
as a constant percentage of GNP expenditures, its 1962 counterpart would
be about $7 billion. By contrast, our rough estimate for the demand schedule
for cash indicates that a 1 per cent change in interest rates would change
desired cash holdings by about $17 billion. However, we cannot be certain
that such estimates give an accurate picture of the causal impact of interest
rates.

What about our fourth determinant, the money supply? For this discussion, we shall assume it to be completely insensitive to market forces,
implying that it is determined by the monetary authorities.

Supply and Demand Curves   The process of interest-rate determination
is illustrated graphically by Figure 9-3. Each of the four determinants is
shown as a schedule dependent on the rate of interest. This implies that we
hold constant the level of income and the state of preferences and expectations. For simplicity, we treat as supply sources the quantity of money S_m
and the desired level of saving S_s. These two are combined to form the total
supply curve S at the right. We treat as demand elements the desired level
of investment D_i, which is equivalent to a marginal efficiency schedule, and
the demand for cash balances D_m. These two demand components are combined to form the demand curve D at the right.

Although the curves of total supply and demand do not literally measure
the flows of loanable funds, they do accurately reflect any gap between
them and do guide us to the equilibrium rate.

The interest rate will tend toward the level which equates the amount

[7] Oswald Brownlee and Alfred Conrad, "Effects upon the Distribution of Income of a Tight Money Policy," Commission on Money and Credit, *Stabilization
Policies*, Prentice-Hall, Inc., Englewood Cliffs, N.J., 1963, p. 509.

of loanable funds offered with the quantity demanded. In Figure 9-3 this equality is shown at a rate of 3 per cent. Suppose the rate were higher than 3 per cent. At the higher rate, saving would be greater and the desired levels of investment and cash holdings lower. The supply of funds would exceed the quantity demanded, and interest rates would be driven down. In a similar manner, a rate below 3 per cent would be forced up by an excess of demand over supply.

We must now enter two reservations about the analysis involved in Figure 9-3. First of all, it does not deal with credit rationing. In the real world, demand is brought into equality with supply partly through nonprice rationing of credit; in a sense, there is excess demand at the existing rate, but it is not accommodated. We evade this problem somewhat by assuming that the degree of credit rationing moves in step with the interest rate— for example, that tighter credit rationing will accompany rising interest rates. Credit rationing provides an untidy element in the analysis, but probably does not impair the qualitative validity of the conclusions.

A more substantial qualification is that, while the "equilibrium" interest rate in Figure 9-3 does equate total supply and demand for funds, it would not be an equilibrium rate with respect to the level of GNP expenditures. The reason is that saving and investment are not equal at the indicated interest rate. Nor, for that matter, are the supply and demand relating to cash balances equal. Saving exceeds investment, and the demand for cash balances exceeds the money supply. Both relationships tell us that GNP expenditures will fall. But three of our four components of supply and demand depend on the level of GNP. If GNP shifts, these curves will shift also. With lower GNP, the supply of saving will be lower, the quantity of cash balances demanded will decline, and the volume of investment spending will also fall. Only the supply of money can be expected to stay put. Because S_m

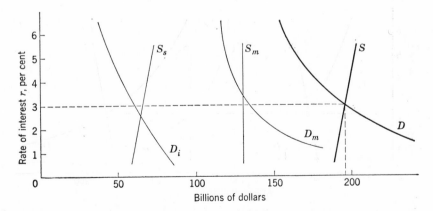

Figure 9-3. Loanable funds and the rate of interest.

does not fall, D will probably move further to the left than S. The rate of interest will be reduced. Ultimately the component curves may shift into a position of genuine equilibrium, as depicted in Figure 9-4. Here there is equality not only between aggregate demand and supply in the loanable funds market but also within the two components. Saving equals investment, and the demand for money equals the supply. By the nature of things, if two out of the three elements are in equilibrium, the third will be also; but all three must be in equilibrium, or all three will be shifted.

The diagram is useful for showing the conditions which are necessary for equilibrium. It is less useful for showing the process by which equilibrium is achieved, since shifts in the curves may be more important than movements along the existing curves. The trouble is that our schedules are related to more variables than we can conveniently represent in a two-dimensional diagram. A really adequate theory of interest rates must be a general equilibrium theory which shows how both GNP and the rate of interest are simultaneously determined by the basic desires of the public to spend, borrow, and hold assets. Such a theory is developed in Chapter 10.

Shifts in Components   A shift in any one of the four components would alter the equilibrium interest rate. Of particular interest is the influence of a change in the quantity of money. In Figure 9-5, we show an increase in the quantity of money, shifting the S_m curve to the right to S'_m. We assume this enters the loan market, coming from the Federal Reserve or from commercial banks. Consequently, the total supply S of loanable funds is also shifted to the right by the same amount. This lowers the point of intersection on the demand curve D, and the interest rate falls by an amount which depends on the slope of D. The steeper the demand curve D, the more the interest rate falls with a given increase in the quantity of money.

The lower interest rate produces shifts along the other three com-

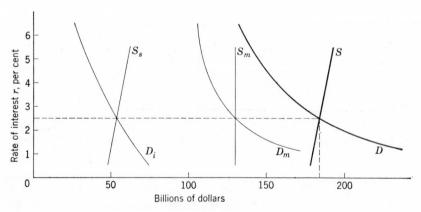

Figure 9-4. Loanable funds market in general equilibrium.

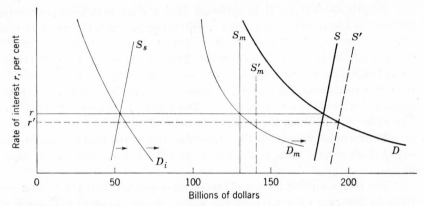

Figure 9-5. Response to increase in the money supply. Arrows show the tendency for schedules to shift as GNP rises in response to increase in quantity of money from S_m to S'_m.

ponent curves. It induces people to spend more (reflected in lower saving and higher investment), thus putting part of the new money into active circulation. However, the lower interest rate also increases holdings of idle cash. How much of the new money will be drawn into idle balances and how much will be spent depends on relative slopes of the curves. As drawn, the cash-balance curve D_m is flatter than the sum of the slopes of the saving S_s and investment D_i curves. Most of the new money goes into idle balances; less than half of it enters the spending stream.

However, these effects deal only with the initial impact of the new money. With the increase in expenditures for investment (shown explicitly) and for consumption and government purchases (implied by the decrease in saving), GNP is raised. The multiplier raises it still further. And as it rises, the curves representing saving, investment, and the demand for cash balances all shift to the right. Assuming no further change in the money supply, the interest rate cannot remain at the level to which it initially fell, but will be pulled back up to an extent determined by the secondary repercussions.

Rates of Change over Time It is useful to move beyond equilibrium analysis to consider the relationship among rates of change of the variables involved in interest-rate determination. Figure 9-6 provides the basis for some interesting observations. It shows the year-to-year percentage rates of change of the money supply and of GNP expenditures. Higher in the chart appears the arithmetic difference between these rates of change, compared with the year-to-year arithmetic change in the interest rate on long-term Treasury bonds. The level of this interest rate is shown at the top of the diagram.

Despite deviations, it is apparent that a close relation exists between changes in the interest rate and the difference between the rates of growth of money and of GNP expenditures. This pattern is consistent with our analysis of the loanable funds market. The rate at which GNP is rising reflects the excess of investment over saving and also the rate at which the transactions demand for money is increasing. Thus three of the four loanable funds components are accounted for. The fourth is the money supply itself. The difference between the rates of growth of money and of GNP can thus be interpreted as measuring the excess demand in the loanable funds market —and thereby indicating the extent to which interest rates can be expected to rise.

The new quantity theory of money stresses the hypothesis that variations in the rate of growth of the money supply tend to produce similar variations in the rate of growth of expenditures. Interest rates play a prominent role in transmitting the influence of money on expenditures. If the rate of monetary expansion is reduced during a phase of economic expansion, interest rates are forced up. This tendency is apparent during the

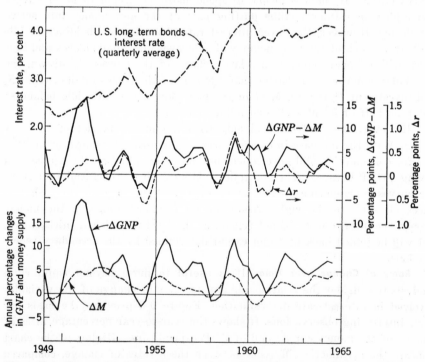

Figure 9-6. Changes in the interest rate compared with the year-to-year percentage changes in GNP and the money supply, quarterly, 1949–1964.

Sources: Federal Reserve Bulletin, U.S. Income and Output, Survey of Current Business.

monetary decelerations of 1952–1953, 1955–1957, and 1959. Quantity theorists feel these increases in interest rates have been sufficient to bring deceleration and decline in expenditures for production. Other economists attribute a somewhat smaller influence to money and interest rates, claiming that variations in fiscal policy and in private propensities to spend have played a larger part. Certainly the time-series data do not refute the quantity theory position.

Figure 9-6 also furnishes evidence on those situations, less frequently encountered, of monetary expansion during periods of slack in expenditures. As indicated most clearly by 1954 and 1958, monetary expansion in recessions brought sharp declines in interest rates. According to the quantity theory, this process has been sufficient to bring about recovery in the flow of expenditures. Other economists are skeptical.

Much of the uncertainty concerns the sensitivity of expenditures to variations in money, interest rates, asset prices, and credit conditions. Quantity theorists argue that it is relatively high and support their position with time-series data and economic analysis based on the logic of maximization. Skeptics point to the relatively low interest-elasticity figures which have usually emerged from econometric studies utilizing multiple correlation analysis. So far, neither side can prove the superiority of its data conclusively.

However, even if one is skeptical about some claims of the new quantity theory, there might be substantial merits in conducting monetary policy as if the theory were true. Such a policy might call for the authorities to accelerate or decelerate monetary expansion in proportion to the desired rate of GNP expansion. This would rule out drastic deceleration or actual monetary declines comparable to 1956–1957 and 1959. The apparent greater concern of the monetary authorities with the rate of monetary expansion since 1960 may provide a test for this aspect of the quantity theory.

THE STRUCTURE OF INTEREST RATES

Policy Aspects   Government policies may be concerned with the structure of interest rates as well as their level. Some people have argued that holdings of cash are adjusted principally to variations in the short-term (e.g., Treasury bill) rate, while expenditure decisions are affected chiefly by the long-term rate. Our evidence does not particularly confirm this view, but it may have some validity. If so, it has important implications for monetary policy. Policies which affect chiefly short-term rates should have little effect on expenditures for production, but would mainly operate on idle cash balances. Consequently, there would be a strong case for monetary policy aimed chiefly at long-term rates.

Is it possible for public policy to affect the rate structure, that is, the relative rates accompanying different maturities? Within limits, yes. The rates on assets of differing maturities are influenced by the relative supplies of those assets, and these can be influenced by the Federal Reserve banks and by the Treasury.

For example, suppose the Federal Reserve buys short-dated securities and sells long-terms. This will decrease the supply of short-term securities on the market, raising their prices and lowering their yields. The supply of long-term securities will be increased and their yields raised. Treasury debt management is continually obliged to refund issues approaching maturity. By choosing to stress long-term issues in refunding operations, the Treasury could increase supply and raise rates in the long-term segment of the market. Stress on short-terms would produce comparable effects at the other end of the spectrum.

There are definite limitations on this process, however. For one thing, government action may be partially offset by reactions of other issuers. Government action to raise long-term rates may simply send borrowers into shorter-term issues or loans from banks and other institutions. Second, investors are also likely to make substitutions along the maturity structure. If their expectations are such that they regard Treasury bills and Treasury bonds as fairly close substitutes, demand for both types will have high elasticity and substantial variations in relative supplies can be absorbed without substantial changes in yields.

Our view is that the structure of rates is distinctly secondary to the level of rates as a concern for public policy. It may well be true that long-term rates are more influential in determining expenditure decisions, but long-term rates also have substantial influence on cash holdings by households and business firms. Thus a stress on long-term rates would not assure a monetary policy operating chiefly on active money and expenditures. The only exception to this attitude toward rate structure concerns international finance, which requires further comment.

Interest Rates and International Finance We have limited our interest-rate and loanable funds analysis to domestic aspects for simplicity. However, the supply of loanable funds may be augmented by funds entering from abroad, and demand for loans may arise from foreign borrowers as well as domestic. Since World War II the United States has been, on balance, a lender abroad, and the net demand for loans by foreign users has tended to make American interest rates somewhat higher than they would have been if based on domestic supply and demand alone.

Moreover, American interest rates affect the international financial position of the United States in two important ways. First, if American long-term interest rates are low (relative to those in other countries), foreign borrowers are attracted to borrow in the United States, while American investors may tend to favor foreign assets (depending, of course, on their confidence in exchange rates and convertibility). Second, the relative level of short-term rates in the United States and in other countries will affect the willingness of foreigners to hold their liquid foreign-exchange assets in dollar forms such as time deposits in American banks and United States Treasury bills.

Thus the net international financial position of the United States can be affected by interest-rate movements. Higher interest rates tend to reduce the outflow of capital funds, while lower rates tend to increase it (assuming other countries' rates are relatively unchanged). The sensitivity appears to be particularly great with respect to short-term rates.[8]

In the years following 1957, as the United States sustained large outflows of payments in its international accounts generally, interest-rate policy was oriented to international objectives as well as domestic. Concern for external balance probably caused the Federal Reserve authorities to keep the level of interest rates higher than they otherwise would have. And international considerations definitely led them to operate on the structure of rates. An effort was made to keep short-term rates high in relation to long-term rates, to minimize the shifting of the liquid funds out of American assets.

SUMMARY AND CONCLUSIONS

Because expenditure decisions depend in part on interest rates and credit conditions, one cannot understand fully the flow of expenditures for production without some analysis of how interest rates and credit conditions are themselves determined.

Interest rates are determined by the interplay of loanable funds supply and demand. The supply of loanable funds arises from transactors who acquire income-bearing financial assets or repay debts. Demand for loanable funds arises from borrowers or from transactors who reduce their holdings of income-bearing financial assets.

Ultimately, loanable funds supply and demand depend on saving, investment, the demand for cash balances, and the supply of money. Increases in the money supply or in the desire to save tend to lower interest rates; increases in the desire to invest (as reflected by the marginal efficiency schedule) or in the desire to hold cash balances tend to raise interest rates. Interest rates will tend toward a level at which:

[8] See Robert F. Gemmill, "Interest Rates and Foreign Dollar Balances," *Journal of Finance*, September, 1961.

Saving + money supply = investment + demand for money

However, the economy will be out of equilibrium unless

Saving = investment   and   Supply of money = demand for money

The desired level of investment varies directly with the level of income and GNP and inversely with interest rates. Saving also varies directly with GNP but displays a positive relation to interest-rate levels, because some durable-goods spending by consumers and state and local governments is reduced by high interest rates.

For each sector there exists a demand schedule for cash balances arising from the need for money as a medium of exchange (transactions balances) and a store of value (asset balances). Each sector's desired cash holdings vary directly with its disposable income (or GNP) and inversely with interest rates.

For the economy as a whole, variations in GNP and interest rates tend to bring the demand for money into equilibrium with the supply. If demand for cash exceeds supply, GNP will tend to fall and interest rates to rise until the quantity demanded is reduced.

The impact of an increase in the money supply can be traced through these loanable funds concepts. If one starts from equilibrium, the increase in money will tend to raise the total supply of loanable funds and force down interest rates. With lower interest rates, there will be some increase in investment and in spending by consumers and state and local governments. There will also be an increase in holdings of idle cash. The effect of the increased money on spending, output, and prices will depend on the relative interest sensitivity of saving and investment, on one hand, and the demand for cash balances, on the other.

As an illustration, our rough estimates for 1962 imply that an increase of $10 billion in the money supply would have reduced interest rates from about 3.95 to 3.55 per cent, with about $3 billion of the new money going into increased spending and $7 billion into idle cash initially. However, as GNP was raised by the higher initial spending and its multiplier repercussions, interest rates would tend to rebound and idle cash to be somewhat reduced.

In the end, we find that interest rates and credit conditions are shaped in part by the saving and investment decisions which are also influential in the main money circuit. The behavior of GNP expenditures and of interest rates involves a process of reciprocal interaction among the income-expenditure conditions in the main circuit, loanable funds supply and demand, and the relation of the supply of money to the demand for cash balances. The manner in which these areas interact simultaneously in response to common underlying propensities is explored in the next chapter.

QUESTIONS FOR STUDY

1. Suppose that all business payments are made monthly and all consumers spend their entire incomes during the month. Each transactor holds cash solely to carry on its main money circuit transactions. There are no money substitutes. Look back to Table 6-1 and try to estimate demand for transactions balances as a proportion of GNP.

2. How would one recognize an increase in the demand for money balances if it took place? What might cause such an increase? What would be its probable effects on GNP and the level of interest rates?

3. Explain the contention that the effectiveness of monetary policy depends on the relative sensitivity to interest-rate changes of saving, investment, and the demand schedule for money.

4. Explain how each of the following would tend to affect the level of interest rates:

    a. Government increases tax rates in order to reduce the public debt.

    b. There is an increase in the marginal efficiency of capital.

    c. Consumers increase their saving in order to buy new housing.

    d. Consumers decide to hold more cash and less interest-bearing assets.

    e. Consumers increase their saving in order to hold more cash. (What would be the ultimate effect of this on interest rates?)

Try to illustrate each of these with a loanable funds diagram similar to Figure 9-4.

5. When the proposal to reduce Federal tax rates was being discussed in 1963, it was argued that the tax reduction (provided government expenditures remained unchanged) would tend to raise interest rates and that the higher interest rates would in turn tend to improve the international financial position of the United States. Explain the logic of this view.

SUGGESTED READINGS

Brunner, Karl, and Allan H. Meltzer: "Predicting Velocity: Implications for Theory and Policy" (and appended comments by Albert Ando and Martin J. Bailey), *Journal of Finance,* May, 1963.

————: "Some Further Investigations of Demand and Supply Functions for Money," *Journal of Finance,* May, 1964.

Burstein, Meyer: *Money,* Schenkman Publishing Company, Cambridge, Mass., 1963.

Commission on Money and Credit: *Stabilization Policies,* Prentice-Hall, Inc., Englewood Cliffs, N.J., 1963.

Conard, Joseph: *Introduction to the Theory of Interest Rates,* University of California Press, Los Angeles, 1959.

Meltzer, Allan: "The Demand for Money: The Evidence from the Time Series," *Journal of Political Economy,* June, 1963.

Selden, Richard: "The Postwar Rise in the Velocity of Money: A Sectoral Analysis," *Journal of Finance,* December, 1961.

Tsiang, S. C.: "Liquidity Preference and Loanable Funds Theories, Multiplier and Velocity Analyses: A Synthesis," *American Economic Review,* September, 1956.

chapter ten

MONEY, SPENDING,

AND WELFARE:

A SYNTHESIS

INTRODUCTORY

In explaining the behavior of expenditures for current output and their relation to money and credit, we have first examined the manner in which each transactor adjusts its expenditures, assets, and liabilities to "given" conditions of incomes, interest rates, and credit availability. In doing this, we have found useful the budget equation for each transactor, of which the following is one formulation:

Income + borrowing = expenditures + increased cash holdings
+ increased holdings of other financial assets

Access to incomes and credit may be beyond the control of individual consumers or business firms. Their problem is how to divide receipts among the categories on the right and how to rearrange the composition of their existing assets. Therefore the flow of income and the ease of credit will strongly influence the volume of expenditures and asset acquisition by each transactor. Interest rates will also affect the manner in which it divides its holdings of financial assets between cash and income-bearing assets. But the precise effects of income, interest rates, and credit conditions will depend on the psychological preferences and expectations of the transactors.

These decisions by individual transactors determine in turn the flow of income and loanable funds for the economy as a whole. Conditions which are "given" for individual transactors, in the sense that no individual transactor can alter them, become variable for the economy as a whole. Spending decisions react with incomes in the manner depicted by the multiplier and the acceleration principle. Decisions to borrow or hold income-bearing financial assets determine interest rates and credit conditions.

Income and expenditures, loanable funds supply and demand, and money supply and demand can be regarded as having a triangular relation to each other. Figure 10-1 shows this symbolically.

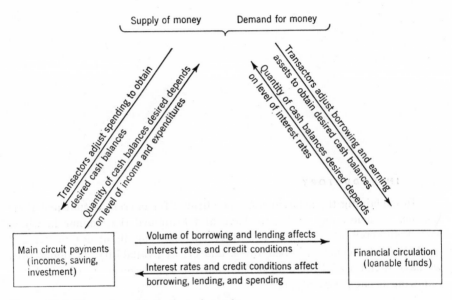

Figure 10-1. Money, loanable funds, and spending.

When income and interest rates become variables, the factors which remain as "ultimate" determinants of the economic process are the money supply and the various psychological tastes and expectations of individuals and business firms. However, even these may be influenced by the behavior of the economy. Expectations, particularly the estimates of the marginal efficiency of investment, are likely to be affected by changes in current economic conditions. Thus it is very likely that everything will depend on everything else.

GENERAL EQUILIBRIUM ANALYSIS

An Arithmetic Example The process by which these economic quantities are mutually determined can be illustrated numerically. The following example is roughly patterned after the economic situation of 1963 and uses numerical coefficients based on some of the materials cited in the previous chapters. We assume that six basic quantities or relationships are given: the division of disposable incomes among sectors, the propensity to consume, the marginal efficiency schedule, the government expenditures function, the demand schedule for money, and the supply of money. They are as follows:

1. The division of disposable incomes:

$$PDI_{t1} = 0.7 \ GNP_{t1}$$
$$BDI_{t1} = 0.1 \ GNP_{t1}$$
$$NGR_{t1} = 0.2 \ GNP_{t1}$$

2. The propensity to consume:

$$C_{t2} = 0.9 \ PDI_{t1} \qquad \text{(and therefore} = 0.63 \ GNP_{t1})$$

3. The marginal efficiency schedule (investment function):

$$I_{t2} = \$70 \ \text{billion} + BDI_{t1} - 10r_{t1}$$
$$= \$70 \ \text{billion} + 0.1 \ GNP_{t1} - 10r_{t1}$$

Investment spending is assumed to vary inversely with the rate of interest r and directly with business income, both operating after a time lag of one period. The relatively high marginal propensity to speed ($= 1$) out of income reflects a combination of two influences—greater availability of funds and higher sales in relation to capacity.

4. The government expenditures function:

$$G_{t2} = \$70 \ \text{billion} + 0.5 \ NGR_{t1}$$
$$= \$70 \ \text{billion} + 0.1 \ GNP_{t1}$$

5. The demand schedule for money:

$$D_{m\,t1} = 0.25 \ GNP_{t1} + \$100 \ \text{billion} - 22r_{t1}$$

Comparing the interest-rate term in equation 5 with that in equation 3 indicates that money holdings are slightly more than twice as sensitive to changes in the interest rate as investment spending is. For simplicity, the interest-rate terms in equations 3 and 5 are in linear form.

6. The supply of money (constant):

$$S_m = \$160 \ \text{billion}$$

In this model, acceleration effects are ignored; sensitivity of consumption or government expenditures to credit conditions is ignored; and it is assumed that variations in the availability of credit are adequately reflected in changes in interest rates.

For the economy to be in equilibrium, three conditions must be met. First, GNP must be in equilibrium, with saving ex ante equal to investment and with GNP_{t1} equal to GNP_{t2}. Second, the demand for money must be equal to the existing supply. Third, the demand for loanable funds ex ante must equal the supply ex ante. Each of these three equilibrium conditions can be expressed in an equation containing two unknowns, GNP and the interest rate r. However, any two of the equations determine the third. We can use any pair of them to find the equilibrium values, and the third equation will be consistent with the result.

The first equation states the equilibrium condition for GNP and is derived as follows:

$$GNP_{t1} = GNP_{t2}$$
$$GNP_{t1} = C_{t2} \qquad + I_{t2} \qquad\qquad\qquad + G_{t2}$$
$$GNP_{t1} = 0.63 \ GNP_{t1} + 70 + 0.1 \ GNP_{t1} - 10r_{t1} + 70 + 0.1 \ GNP_{t1}$$
$$GNP_{t1} = 0.83 \ GNP_{t1} + 140 - 10r_{t1}$$
$$0.17 \ GNP_{t1} = 140 - 10r_{t1}$$
$$GNP_{t1} = 824 - 58.8r_{t1}$$

This provides a formula showing all combinations of GNP and the interest rate at which saving equals investment.

The second equation is derived by setting the demand for money equal to the supply:

$$0.25 \ GNP_{t1} + 100 - 22r_{t1} = 160$$
$$0.25 \ GNP_{t1} = 60 + 22r_{t1}$$
$$GNP_{t1} = 240 + 88r_{t1}$$

Setting these two equations equal to each other, we can solve for r, as follows:

$$GNP_{t1} = 824 - 58.8r_{t1} = 240 + 88r_{t1}$$
$$146.8r_{t1} = 584$$
$$r_{t1} = 3.98$$

Substituting this value for r, we obtain the value for GNP:

$$GNP_{t1} = 824 - (58.8) \ (3.98) = 824 - 235 = 589$$

Thus our equilibrium values are GNP of $589 billion and an interest rate of 3.98 per cent. (Values given here are rounded; more precise figures are given in the first column of Table 10-1 below.) Next we calculate the income and expenditure coefficients of GNP to see if they really are in equilibrium.

$$PDI = 0.7 \times 589 = 412$$
$$BDI = 0.1 \times 589 = 59$$
$$NGR = 0.2 \times 589 = \underline{118}$$

Total 589

$$C = 0.9 \times 412 = 371$$
$$I = 70 + 59 - (10)\ (3.98)$$
$$ = 70 + 59 - 40 = 89$$
$$G = 70 + (0.5)\ (118) = \underline{129}$$

Total GNP 589

Thus our GNP components are in equilibrium, and GNP_{t2} will stay at the same level as GNP_{t1}.

We can also compare the demand for money with the supply:

$$(0.25)\ 590 + 100 - (22)\ (3.98) = 160$$
$$147.5 + 100 - 87.5 = 160$$

In equilibrium, the supply of saving ex ante must be equal to investment. Saving occurs in all three sectors, as follows:

Personal saving	$= 0.1\ PDI$	$= 0.07\ GNP$
Business saving	$= BDI$	$= 0.1\ GNP$
Government saving	$= NGR - G$	
	$= NGR - 0.5\ NGR - 70$	$= 0.1\ GNP - 70$
Total saving		$= \overline{0.27\ GNP - 70}$
		$= 0.27\ (590) - 70$
		$= 159 - 70 = 89$

It follows that the loanable funds market must also be in equilibrium, with saving plus the supply of money being equal to investment plus the desired level of cash holdings.

Graphic Analysis of Equilibrium The principles embodied in this numerical example can also be displayed geometrically, as shown by Figure 10-2. The two axes represent our two unknowns, GNP and the interest rate. Against these we graph two curves. The first shows all the combinations of GNP and the interest rate at which saving equals investment; thus we label it the $I = S$ curve. The solid part of the curve is simply a graph of the equation derived above, to wit:

$$GNP = 824 - 58.8r$$

However, it is unlikely that such a linear relation would hold for very high or very low interest rates; therefore we have substituted the dotted lines representing the probable curvature of the $I = S$ line at the extremes.

The $I = S$ line is derived by combining the propensities to spend of the three sectors of the economy. It reflects the facts that investment will vary directly with GNP but inversely with the interest rate and that saving will also vary directly with GNP. A shift in any sector's expenditure function would shift the $I = S$ curve.

The second curve reflects all the combinations of GNP and the interest rate at which the demand for money will be equal to the supply; thus we have labeled it $D_m = S_m$. The solid part graphs the equation we derived above, namely,

$$GNP = 240 + 88r$$

Again, this linear relation is unlikely to hold for very high or low interest rates, so we have added the dotted extension to show the probable curvature.

The location and shape of the $S_m = D_m$ curve depend on the demand schedule for money and on the size of the money supply. The curve shows that, to keep the demand for money equal to the (given) supply, higher levels of GNP (requiring higher transactions balances) have to be matched by higher levels of the interest rate (lowering asset balances). Changes in the money supply, or shifts in the demand schedule, will cause the $S_m = D_m$ curve to shift.

Equilibrium is reached when both conditions are satisfied simultaneously—saving equals investment, and the supply of money equals the quantity demanded. This will occur at the point where the two curves intersect, as they do where GNP is $589 billion and r is 3.98 per cent.

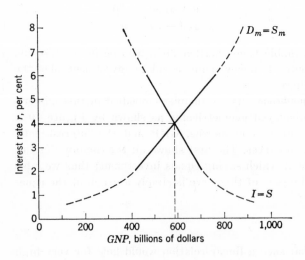

Figure 10-2. General equilibrium determination of GNP and the interest rate.

Adjustments to Changing Data The equilibrium situation depends on the values for all the underlying data—the propensity to consume, the marginal efficiency of investment, the division of income, the role of government, the demand for money, and the supply of money. Changing one or more of these underlying data would change both GNP and the rate of interest.

Since we are mainly interested in money, let us see what would be the effects of an increase in the supply of money. First we must note how the increase occurs. If it is introduced through monetary policy and enters the market for loanable funds, the effect will be different from the result if the new money enters the spending stream directly, as through a government deficit. We shall examine both cases to illustrate the difference.

Let us assume that the quantity of money is increased by $10 billion, to a total of $170 billion, through purchases of government securities in the open market by the Federal Reserve and commercial banks. This increase will tend to raise security prices and reduce interest rates. Higher security prices may encourage increased issues of new securities, while lower interest rates for loans will encourage increased borrowing for investment. However, the lower interest rates will also increase the quantity of cash demanded for asset balances. These are the initial effects.

Next, the higher investment will raise GNP and set off multiplier effects. In our example, consumption, investment, and government purchases are all determined partly by income, and all will therefore rise. This raises GNP further. With higher GNP, both the supply of savings and the demand for investment will increase. Higher GNP will also raise the demand for transactions cash balances. These secondary effects will alter supply and demand in the loanable funds market, and the rate of interest may change again. But changing the interest rate will bring about further repercussions on investment and the demand for money, and so on.

Table 10-1 shows the effects of the increased money supply. The data are arranged by time periods, so that they show the initial impact of the increase in M, the way in which the effects spread through the system, and the final equilibrium value where all the secondary effects have been reconciled.

Before we can work out the pattern of response, we need to know something more about how the interest rate is determined. Let us suppose that the interest rate r_{t1} is determined at the end of period $t1$ and in turn influences the quantity of cash balances held over into period $t2$ and the level of investment spending in $t2$. We shall treat r_{t1} as determined by loanable funds supply and demand as they exist at the end of period $t1$. The supply of funds arises out of income in period $t1$ but is used for spending in period $t2$.

The supply schedule of loanable funds is determined by the saving schedule and the money supply. Using the formula for saving derived above (with time subscripts omitted, being all the same), we have the following:

$$S = S_s + S_m$$
$$= 0.27 \ GNP - 70 + S_m$$

To obtain a demand schedule for loanable funds, we must add together the schedules for investment and the demand for money.

$$D = D_i + D_m$$
$$= 70 + 0.1 \ GNP - 10r + 0.25 \ GNP + 100 - 22r$$
$$= 170 + 0.35 \ GNP - 32r$$

We will be able to calculate the interest rate at the end of each time period on the basis of the GNP of that time period by setting demand and

Table 10-1   Adjustments to increased money supply: Part 1
(Billions of dollars)

	1	2	3	4	5		E
C	371.3	371.3	371.3	373.3	375.0	...	381.5
I	89.1	89.1	92.3	92.6	92.7	...	93.5
G	129.0	129.0	129.0	129.3	129.5	...	130.6
GNP	589.4	589.4	592.6	595.2	597.2	...	605.6
PDI	412.6	412.6	414.8	416.6	418.0	...	423.9
BDI	58.9	58.9	59.3	59.5	59.7	...	60.6
NGR	117.9	117.9	118.5	119.0	119.4	...	121.1
Saving ex ante:							
PS	41.3	41.3	41.5	41.7	41.8		42.4
BS	58.9	58.9	59.3	59.5	59.7	...	60.6
GS	−11.1	−11.1	−10.8	−10.5	−10.3	...	− 9.5
Total	89.1	89.1	90.0	90.7	91.2	...	93.5
Investment ex ante							
(previous *r*)	89.1	89.1	92.7	92.8	92.9	...	93.5
S_m	160.0	*170.0*	170.0	170.0	170.0	...	170.0
D_m (previous *r*)	160.0	160.0	167.7	168.1	168.3	...	170.0
Supply of loan funds ex ante	249.1	259.1	260.0	260.7	261.2	...	263.5
Demand for loan funds	249.1	249.1	260.4	260.9	261.2	...	263.5
Interest rate *r*, per cent	3.98	3.66	3.67	3.68	3.68	...	3.71

$$r = \frac{0.08 \ GNP + 240 - S_m}{32}$$

supply schedules equal and solving for r. This will give us the following formula:

$$0.27\ GNP - 70 + S_m = 170 + 0.35\ GNP - 32r$$
$$32r = 0.08\ GNP + 240 - S_m$$
$$r = \frac{0.08\ GNP + 240 - S_m}{32}$$

Given $S_m = 170$, this reduces to

$$r = \frac{0.08\ GNP + 70}{32}$$

To follow the sequence of events in Table 10-1, start at the top of period $t1$ and read down. In succession are shown expenditures, the incomes resulting from them, and the cash-balance and loanable-funds supplies and demands arising from the other conditions of the period. These determine the interest rate. Next, move to the top of period $t2$, where the events of the next period follow in the same sequence.

The process of change begins in period 2, when the money supply increases. This raises the supply of loanable funds above the demand and reduces the interest rate to 3.66 per cent. In period 3, the lower interest rate raises investment by about $3 billion, which raises GNP and all disposable incomes. Ex ante saving rises in response to the higher incomes but is still well below ex ante investment, which receives a secondary nudge from higher business income. Higher GNP and a lower interest rate increase the quantity of cash balances demanded to about $168 billion, but this does not absorb the entire money supply. The market for loanable funds is virtually in balance; demand exceeds supply very slightly, and the interest rate rises slightly.

In period 4, consumption increases in response to the higher income of the previous period. Investment and government purchases are similarly affected. Consequently, total GNP and disposable incomes rise by another $2.6 billion. Ex ante saving moves closer to investment and the demand for money closer to the supply.

From here on, it is merely a process of small additional changes of the type already described. Ultimately the economy approaches a new equilibrium with GNP of $606 billion and an interest rate of 3.71 per cent. Thus the increase of $10 billion in the money supply raised GNP by $16 billion, through higher investment and its multiplier consequences. Ultimately, of the $10 billion of new money, about $6 billion goes into increased holdings of idle cash at the lower interest rate, and about $4 billion is required for transactions balances to keep up with the rise in GNP.

Figure 10-3 shows how this increase in the money supply can be analyzed geometrically. With the rise in S_m, the entire $S_m = D_m$ curve shifts to the right. Since there is no change in the propensities to spend, the $I = S$ curve remains fixed. In effect, one slides down the $I = S$ curve to the new equilibrium point. The end result depends on how far the $S_m = D_m$ curve shifts initially and on its slope relative to the slope of the $I = S$ curve. These slopes reflect the different sensitivities of the demand schedule for money and the marginal efficiency schedule to the rate of interest.

Let us review the factors determining the effect of the monetary increase on GNP.

1. The degree to which the interest rate falls when S_m is increased depends on the interest sensitivity of the demand for and supply of loanable funds. If these curves are steep and inelastic, the interest rate will drop substantially. If the curves are flat, there will not be much decline. In our example, the critical relations are those of investment and the demand for money.

2. The degree to which investment is stimulated by the increase in S_m depends on the relative sensitivity to interest rates of investment and the demand for money. In our example, when S_m increased $10 billion and the interest rate declined to 3.66 per cent, the new money was divided between $7 billion of added idle cash balances and $3 billion of added investment. The more sensitive investment is to interest rates and credit conditions, relative to the demand for asset money, the bigger the effect of S_m on GNP.

3. The effect of higher investment on GNP depends chiefly on the size of the multiplier effect, which in turn depends on the marginal propensity to consume. GNP is also raised by the propensity to spend out of higher income by government and business. In our example, the marginal propensity to spend for all sectors combined is equal to 0.83 GNP. We could use this to calculate a sort of "supermultiplier," which would have a coefficient

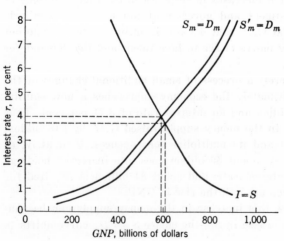

Figure 10-3. Response to increase in money supply.

of about 6. The larger the marginal propensity to spend by all sectors combined, the larger the ultimate impact on GNP of a given initial expenditure increase. Acceleration effects, ignored in the example, might add to the impact.

4. The effect of rising GNP on the interest rate depends on how sensitive loanable funds supply and demand are to changes in GNP. In our example, rising GNP caused the demand for loanable funds to rise more than the supply, which seems the way things happen in the real world as well. This means that some restraint will be imposed on rising GNP by tightening credit. The interest rate rises from 3.66 to 3.71, reducing investment by $0.5 billion, and causing GNP to rise by $3 billion less than if the interest rate had remained at 3.66.

Adjustment to Fiscal Policy In our previous example, the quantity of money was increased in the loanable funds market, and the level of GNP expenditures rose when easier credit stimulated spending. However, the new money could come into the GNP expenditures stream directly. One method would be for the government to engage in deficit spending financed by new money, perhaps borrowed from the banks or the Federal Reserve. Let us start from our initial equilibrium position, with the same data, and see what happens if S_m rises by $10 billion accompanied by a rise of $10 billion in government purchases. The results are shown in Table 10-2.

This time we get quite a different result. In period 2, the higher government expenditure raises GNP directly by $10 billion, and incomes rise correspondingly. Private saving ex ante rises, but the big increase in the government deficit causes total saving to fall markedly. The higher GNP absorbs some funds into transactions balances, but the total demand for money falls far short of the supply. The aggregate effect of these changes is to raise both the demand for and supply of loanable funds. The demand goes up slightly more, however, with the result that the interest rate begins to rise.

In period 3, all three sectors react to their higher incomes by spending more, and GNP and incomes rise by $8 billion. By the end of the period the quantity of cash balances demanded has risen again (despite the higher interest rate), and the supply of loanable funds is virtually equal to the demand.

The expenditure flow continues to move upward through the multiplier interaction of incomes and spending. Loanable funds supply and demand rise almost identically, so that at the end the interest rate is little changed from its initial value. Ultimate equilibrium is reached when GNP is $641 billion and interest 4.10 per cent.

The rise in GNP is $52 billion, arising from an initial stimulus of $10 billion. This falls slightly short of the supermultiplier, calculated from the

Table 10-2   Adjustments to increased money supply: Part 2
(Billions of dollars)

	1	2	3	4		E
C	371.3	371.3	377.6	382.7	...	403.8
I	89.1	89.1	89.9	90.8	...	93.1
G	129.0	139.0	140.0	140.8	...	144.1
GNP	589.4	599.4	607.5	614.3	...	641.0
PDI	412.6	419.6	425.2	430.0	...	448.7
BDI	58.9	59.9	60.8	61.4	...	64.1
NGR	117.9	119.9	121.5	122.9	...	128.2
Saving ex ante:						
PS	41.3	42.0	42.5	43.0	...	44.9
DS	58.9	59.9	60.8	61.4	...	64.1
GS	−11.1	−20.1	−19.3	−18.5	...	−15.9
Total	89.1	81.8	84.0	85.9	...	93.1
Investment ex ante (previous r)	89.1	90.1	91.0	91.4	...	93.1
S_m	160.0	170.0	170.0	170.0	...	170.0
D_m (previous r)	160.0	162.4	163.9	165.2	...	170.0
Supply of loans ex ante	249.1	251.8	254.0	255.0	...	263.1
Demand for loans ex ante	249.1	252.7	254.9	256.6	...	263.1
Interest rate r, per cent	3.98	4.00	4.02	4.04	...	4.10

$$r = \frac{0.08\ GNP + 250 - S_m}{32}$$

marginal propensities to spend, because of the slight tightening of credit which results as the economy expands.

To illustrate this case geometrically, we would show *both* schedules shifting to the right. This unequivocally raises GNP, without making much change in the interest rate. The actual movement in the interest rate depends on the precise size of the shifts and on the slopes of the two curves; it would not take much change in the underlying functions to cause this shift to reduce the interest rate slightly.

Increased Spending without Increased Money   To round out the analysis, let us see what the results would be if government expenditures were increased by $10 billion without any increase in the money supply. Here we assume that the government borrows the added funds from the public and spends the money. As Table 10-3 indicates, this operation tends to raise GNP by less and the interest rate considerably more than the case shown in Table 10-2. GNP rises only $36 billion to $625 billion, while the interest rate is driven up to 4.37 per cent.

Both impacts are shown as originating in period 2. The rise in government spending raises GNP directly. This raises private incomes and private saving, but the government's own saving falls so drastically that the total supply of loan funds is reduced, driving up the interest rate. The higher interest rate produces a sharp reduction of investment in period 3, which helps to offset the expansionary repercussions taking place through the multiplier process.

To describe the government's increased deficit as a decrease in loanable

Table 10-3   Adjustment to increased expenditures, money unchanged
(Billions of dollars)

	1	2	3	4		E
C	371.3	371.3	377.6	380.8	...	393.8
I	89.1	89.1	86.8	87.2	...	88.8
G	129.0	139.0	140.0	140.4	...	142.5
GNP	589.4	599.4	604.4	608.4	...	625.1
PDI	412.6	419.6	423.1	425.9	...	437.6
BDI	58.9	59.9	60.4	60.8	...	62.5
NGR	117.9	119.9	120.9	121.7	...	125.0
Saving ex ante:						
PS	41.3	42.0	42.3	42.6	...	43.8
BS	58.9	59.9	60.4	60.8	...	62.5
GS	−11.1	−20.1	−19.5	−19.1	...	−17.5
Total	89.1	81.1	83.2	84.3	...	88.8
Investment ex ante						
(previous r)	89.1	90.1	87.3	87.6	...	88.8
S_m	160.0	160.0	160.0	160.0	...	160.0
D_m (previous r)	160.0	162.4	156.3	157.1	...	160.0
Supply of loans ex ante	249.1	241.8	243.2	244.3	...	248.8
Demand for loans ex ante	249.1	252.5	243.6	244.7	...	248.8
Interest rate r, per cent	3.98	4.31	4.32	4.33	...	4.37

$$r = \frac{0.08\ GNP + 250 - S_m}{32}$$

funds supply is an unfortunate result of terminological conventions which have other merits. In reality, the government is a borrower and its actions increase the demand for loan funds. In part, the added demand is met by reduction in holdings of idle cash. The increased supply of government securities lowers their prices and raises their yields, leading investors to hold more securities and less cash. The cash they have relinquished is put in motion by the government expenditures and is ultimately absorbed by the extra transactions balances needed for the higher level of GNP expenditures.

Increases in government deficits (or anybody's deficits) tend to raise the GNP flow even when they are financed by borrowing from the public, without increases in the money supply. If the government is faced with war or other emergency requiring large deficits and wishes to avoid raising interest rates, it must increase the money supply. If it does so, however, the expansionary force of its expenditures becomes greater and the danger of inflation (given conditions of near-full employment) may be correspondingly increased. This conclusion does not take account, however, of the possible curtailment of private spending through direct economic controls.

The case of an increased propensity to spend, with no change in money supply or in the demand schedule for cash, is shown graphically in Figure 10-4. The higher spending propensity shifts the $I = S$ curve to the right, so that the system slides up the $S_m = D_m$ curve, ending with higher interest rate and higher GNP.

Shifts in Other Schedules The case we have just dealt with in Table 10-3 and Figure 10-4 also shows what would happen if there were an increase in the propensity to consume or the marginal efficiency of investment, assuming no change in the money supply or demand schedule for cash. Such increases in a sector's propensity to spend provide a clear illustration of how

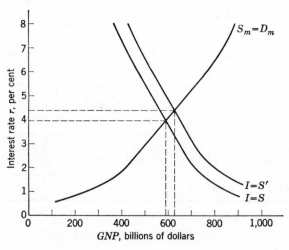

Figure 10-4. Response to increased propensity to spend.

its behavior affects both the main money circuit and the financial circulation. On the one hand, the increased spending sets off an expansionary movement in the income-expenditure flow, including a multiplier process. On the other hand, the increased investment or reduced saving means more borrowing or less acquisition of income-bearing assets. Interest rates are forced up, thus applying a dampening influence to the main circuit expansion process. However, the higher interest rates also activate idle cash, which in effect is used to finance the expansionary process.

So long as the demand schedule for money and the quantity of money remain fixed, GNP expenditures and the interest rate tend to rise and fall together. Both move in response to the same forces—saving and investment. Given the fixed monetary supply and demand, an excess of saving over investment lowers both GNP and the interest rate, while an excess of investment over saving raises both GNP and the interest rate. Ultimately, saving and investment tend toward equality, a tendency promoted by both GNP and the interest rate.

Shifts in the Demand Schedule for Money Shifts in the demand schedule for cash balances can be analyzed along lines analogous to our analysis of changes in the money supply. If the demand for money balances increases, something else must decrease. One possibility is that people will reduce their spending for current output in order to hold more cash. The consequences will be a substantial drop in GNP expenditures, with no direct effects in the loanable funds market. Ultimately, at lower GNP, interest rates will be reduced slightly. A decrease in the demand schedule for money, matched by a rise in spending, would strongly increase GNP in a manner similar to the example presented in Table 10-2.

More probably, a change in the demand for money will have its impact in the loanable funds market. An increased desire for cash will lead people to borrow more, to sell income-bearing financial assets, or to withhold their saving from the loan market. As a result, interest rates will rise and investment will be reduced, causing a decline in GNP directly and through the multiplier process. However, the higher interest rates will reduce somewhat the initially higher level of desired cash holdings. The decline in GNP would be considerably less than in the previous case, where the rise in D_m all came at the expense of current expenditures. If there were a decrease in the demand for cash, matched by a rise in desire to hold income-bearing financial assets, the interest rate would decline and investment and GNP would rise. The order of magnitude would be comparable to that of the example shown in Table 10-1. On the graph, this would be shown as a shift of the $S_m = D_m$ curve to the right.

We have assumed that shifts in the demand schedule for cash do not cause changes in the money supply. Thus the consequence of changes in the demand for cash is that economic conditions change until people are once again reconciled to holding the existing stock of money. These changes may not be very desirable; in particular, the increase in the demand for cash during the downswing of 1929–1933 greatly aggravated the Depression. Fortunately, it appears that substantial shifts in the demand schedule for cash do not occur frequently. However, if a shift should occur, it might well call for compensatory action by the Federal Reserve authorities.

Expansion of Bank Loans and Securities   Most of the increase in the money supply has come through the expansion of commercial bank loans and securities. Logically, these both involve a flow of cash into the loanable funds market. However, the consequences of monetary expansion may differ depending on whether banks are expanding loans, on one hand, or buying securities in the open market, on the other.

Bank loans go predominantly to people who will spend the money to buy current output. If banks create $10 billion and lend this sum to business firms and consumers, the effect may come very close to that described in Table 10-2, where money and initial expenditures rise by the same amounts.

But banks may also create new money in purchasing existing securities (chiefly Treasury securities) in the open market from nonbank investors. The latter will not turn around and spend the money for current output to any great extent; instead, they are likely to reinvest in other securities. The money permeates the loanable funds market; it raises securities prices and reduces yields. But it only affects spending if somebody is induced to borrow more and spend more on the basis of the lower interest rates. In any event, the reduction in open-market interest rates will lead people to increase their holdings of idle cash, and only a fraction of the new money will enter the spending stream.

Why should there be a difference between bank loans and bank securities purchases, if both involve the loanable funds market? Two factors may be noted. First, the expansion of bank loans may take place to a considerable degree through a relaxation in the standards of credit rationing. Thus it may not involve very much lowering of interest rates, and desired holdings of idle cash are not raised much. Second, even if the expansion of bank loans lowers interest charges on loans, these interest rates affect spending much more than they affect holdings of idle cash.

Thus the expansionary force of an increase in the money supply tends to be greater the larger the degree to which it arises from expansion of bank loans as distinct from open-market acquisitions of securities. (Newly issued securities can be just as expansionary as loans.) Just which assets the banks will stress depends on many things—on the banker's expectations and attitudes toward risk, on the demand for funds by prospective spenders, on the composition of existing bank portfolios, etc. There is a tendency for banks to expand chiefly through loans during periods of prosperity and to give more stress to securities during periods of slump, when the demand for loans may be weaker and the risks may appear somewhat greater.

Effects on Welfare   We have been analyzing the impact of various changes on GNP expenditures. The real consequences for economic welfare arise out of changes in production, employment, and prices. A rise in GNP is advantageous to the degree that it raises output and employment, an effect which depends on the existing extent of unemployment. If relatively full employment prevails, so that higher GNP raises prices, the adverse effects on distribution of incomes and wealth and on public psychology may outweigh the small additions to output and employment which might be achieved. However, even when the economy is near full employment, a gradual upward trend in GNP spending over time is desirable and furnishes a demand to match the rising productive capacity of the economy resulting from population growth, capital formation, and technological innovation.

Declining GNP, however, will almost invariably have a negative effect on economic welfare. Whether prices decline or not, output and employment are certain to fall. Indeed, in a growing economy, welfare may be adversely affected unless GNP increases. The recessions through which the American economy passed in the 1950s involved very slight reductions in GNP, but these were sufficient to increase unemployment and reduce per capita output appreciably.

Limitation of This Analysis   The approach followed in the preceding sections of this chapter is a compromise made in the interest of readers who share the author's lack of mathematical sophistication. A more advanced approach would have been to develop a set of algebraic response coefficients, equations showing how the reaction of GNP to any stimulus could be expressed as a mathematical function of the demand for money, the propensity to consume, the marginal efficiency of investment, etc. Or we could have tried to construct a precise econometric model, in which the values of all the data would be determined with great mathematical precision on the basis of past behavior. Our initial data are not precisely derived from past experience, but they are fairly realistic and much simpler than the alternatives just noted.

The purpose of the analysis is to stress the way in which the various elements interact, rather than to calculate precisely the actual mathematical outcome. With different data, different specific results are obtained. In particular, we could, without changing the initial data very much, derive a model in which the response of the loanable funds market to changes in GNP would be the opposite of the one depicted. The example we have used shows rising GNP raising the demand for funds more than supply, which is in accord with actual interest-rate behavior.

Our analysis omits entirely certain other possible responses. It does not allow for acceleration effects, although they certainly occur in the real world. Induced changes in expectations which might result from GNP variations could produce patterns different from those shown, although we have probably adjusted for this factor to some extent by linking investment to BDI. Our analysis here omits international repercussions, but these are developed in Chapter 14.

The purpose of the numerical method is to convey a sense of transactions flows over time, which can best be grasped by working out the arithmetic details of the tables and examples so that you can see how each figure is derived from the others. A useful exercise is to try to compute the data for the next period in the sequence of Tables 10-1 to 10-3.

THE QUANTITY AND VELOCITY OF MONEY

The Quantity Hypothesis For as long as money has existed, intellectuals and men of affairs have been fascinated by the behavior of money and its relation to economic activity. Aristotle, Plato, Thomas Aquinas, Copernicus, John Locke, and David Hume all devoted their attention to it, before the emergence of "economists" for whom it has always been a challenging subject.

In the eighteenth and nineteenth centuries, monetary theories tended to coalesce into a brief and unequivocal hypothesis, which we shall call the "quantity hypothesis." It stated that the value of money would vary inversely with changes in its quantity, because the price level would change in direct proportion to changes in the money supply. Thus if the money supply increased by one-fourth, the price level would also rise by one-fourth, which would mean a decline in the value of money of one-fifth.

This hypothesis has many merits. It is brief and to the point; it accords with common sense and can be tested by looking at the facts. This last characteristic is its downfall, however, for we can find numerous historical periods in which the facts do not support the theory. From an intellectual standpoint, the quantity hypothesis is also defective in that it does not provide an explanation of how changes in the quantity of money cause changes in the price level. Furthermore, it ignores the relation of money to production and employment.

The Fisher Equation In the twentieth century, considerable effort was devoted to developing an explicit and operational theory relating the quantity of money to the price level, and to output as well. One of the best known and most productive efforts was made by Irving Fisher.[1] Fisher's theory

---

[1] Fisher occupied a prominent place in American economic thinking for half a century prior to his death in 1947. In addition, he made a fortune from his invention of a visible-file system of card indexing. He was an ardent prohibitionist and

used the total volume of money expenditures and transactions as a link between the quantity of money and production and prices. He argued that the total volume of expenditures could be regarded as equal to the quantity of money multiplied by its *velocity* of circulation—the average number of times each dollar was spent during a given period of time. He noted that the total volume of expenditures was also equal to the total value of things sold for money, which consisted of the quantity of things multiplied by their respective prices. Putting the two parts together, he derived this equation:

$$MV = PT$$

where P represents the price level of things sold and T is the physical volume of trade or transactions.

The equation is an identity; it is true by definition. Like such identities as the balance sheet of assets and liabilities, it is useful because it sets a limiting framework around the behavior of its components. It is impossible for any single item in the equation to change unless at least one of the others changes also.

In Chapter 6 we estimated that the total volume of money expenditures and transactions in the economy in 1958 was about \$3.3 trillion. At first examination, the Fisher equation appears designed to apply to such a figure for total transactions and can, accordingly, be broken down into M and V. Since the average money supply was about \$144 billion, the average transactions velocity of each dollar was about 23. However, it is not so easy to break down total transactions into P and T, for many of the transactions consist of taxes, transfer payments, gifts, gambling transactions, and lending and repayment of debts. Prices cannot easily be assigned to these categories, and the quantitative concept of "things" sold for money does not exactly apply.

More important, the data on total transactions contain a large number of items one is not greatly interested in. Roughly half the transactions reflect financial turnover, and only 10 to 20 per cent are purchases of final output. Thus even if we could construct statistically meaningful indexes of P and T, they would be such composite aggregates as to be of little interest or significance. The price index would be weighted as heavily by stock and bond prices as by prices of goods and services, and the index of quantity of things sold for money would be as much affected by changes in the volume of shares of stock traded as by changes in current production.

---

thus believed that if people had a high liquidity preference, they should not be permitted to indulge their propensity to consume. During the stock market boom of the 1920s, he confidently asserted that prosperity would be permanent, because it rested on the increased productivity resulting from Prohibition. He lost heavily in the market crash and was thereafter highly critical of the banking system, which he argued should be required to maintain 100 per cent reserves.

Because of these difficulties, such a broad interpretation of the Fisher equation is not much used. Instead, the equation is commonly modified to focus attention on GNP transactions. It can then be written in this form:

$$MV_g = OP = GNP$$

Velocity now becomes V_g, the GNP or income velocity of circulation of money, defined as the average number of times each dollar is spent to buy currently produced final goods and services. Output and prices now simply correspond to the measures we have used in previous discussions of GNP. For some purposes, however, it may be useful to use measures of velocity based on total transactions. Statistically, V_g cannot be estimated independently of the other data in the equation. It is merely computed by dividing the money supply into GNP. There do exist independent direct data on transactions velocity as measured by the turnover of bank deposits. The behavior of the latter data is a useful check on computed values of V_g.

The following data illustrate the calculation of the modified Fisher equation in terms of GNP categories (dollar amounts in billions):

$M \times V_g$	=	GNP (current prices)	=	output (1954 prices)	$\times$	price index (1954 = 100)
1947: 115×2.04	=	$234	=	$282	$\times$	83%
1957: 141×3.13	=	$443	=	$410	$\times$	108%

Since government transactions are included in GNP, we include government deposits in the money supply when calculating velocity. Be sure you can determine from these data how one would compute velocity and how, given the price index, the figure for output is determined.

The Fisher equation brings together in a simple quantitative balance the factors we have been dealing with ever since Chapter 3. It explicitly relates the quantity of money, total expenditures, output, and prices. Since our chief problem has been to relate the quantity of money to output and prices, the concept of velocity seems made to order for the task.

The Nature and Behavior of Velocity   Since velocity of circulation is defined as the average number of times each dollar is spent, it depends on the average length of time people hold on to their money. "Normal" velocity is fairly well determined by the institutional pattern of payments in the economy—by the timing of business payments and the extent to which transactors use credit as a substitute for cash. These are the factors to which we attribute the level of demand for transactions cash balances. The velocity of money used in transactions is simply a reciprocal of the demand for such balances. If the demand for transactions balances is equal to one-fourth of GNP, the GNP velocity of these ("active") balances will be 4 per year.

Some users of the Fisher equation concentrated on these institutional determinants of velocity and concluded that, since they were not subject to large short-run variation, velocity itself was a relatively stable magnitude. If this were true, it would be of great importance, for variations in the quantity of money would be reflected in proportional variations in total spending.

Figure 10-5 illustrates the actual behavior of velocity since 1927, which has been far from constant. Over the period shown, GNP velocity has ranged between a high of 3.90 and a low of 1.71. V_g reached its peak in 1929 and then declined substantially as the Depression set in. This decline was chiefly a reflection of an increase in the demand schedule for money balances, resulting from pessimistic expectations and increased uncertainty. From 1934, V_g remained relatively stable, but took another downward swing during World War II.

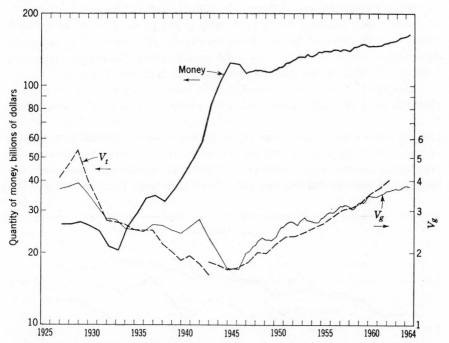

Figure 10-5. Money and velocity of circulation, 1927–1964. Money supply prior to 1947 is for June; in subsequent years it is the quarterly average of seasonally adjusted monthly figures. Treasury cash and deposits are included. V_g is computed by the author; V_t is the Federal Reserve estimate for turnover of demand deposits.

Sources: Friedman and Schwartz, *A Monetary History of the United States, 1867–1960; Supplement to Banking and Monetary Statistics: Banks and the Monetary System; Federal Reserve Bulletin;* Federal Reserve processed release 756–7; *U.S. Income and Output; Survey of Current Business.*

After 1947, V_g began to rise again and maintained the upward trend into 1964. By 1964 V_g had reached 3.80 and was approaching its previous peak levels of the late 1920s.

Transactions velocity, as measured by the turnover of demand deposits, maintained a level about ten times as large as V_g. This ratio reflects the large volume of transactions for intermediate products and services and of financial transactions relative to GNP, as shown by Table 6-1. The movement of V_t over the period shows the same broad pattern as that of V_g. However, V_t rose more than V_g in 1927–1929 and fell more in the years immediately following. This resulted from the great increase in financial turnover volume attending the stock market boom and from the great deflation in financial payments volume after the market crashed. Since 1950, the upward trend of V_t has been stronger than that of V_g, with financial transactions again the main factor.

Why Velocity Changes   Changes in velocity reflect changes in the ratio of people's cash holdings to GNP. A shift in the demand schedule for cash would thus be reflected in an (inverse) change in velocity. The increased demand for cash balances in 1930–1934 caused velocity to decline. However, substantial shifts in the demand schedule have not been frequent.

Measured velocity will also change in response to movements along a given demand schedule associated with changes in interest rates. Other things equal, people tend to hold larger quantities of cash balances at low interest rates than at high ones. Thus we would expect to find that periods of low interest rates are characterized by relatively large cash holdings in relation to income, and therefore, low velocity. Figure 10-6 compares the behavior of velocity and the interest rate on long-term Treasury bonds since

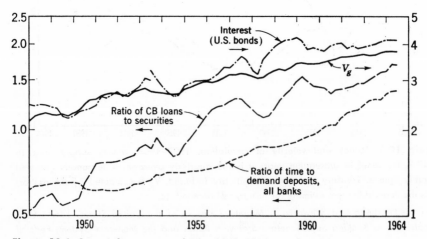

Figure 10-6. Some influences on velocity, 1948–1964.

Sources: Banking and Monetary Statistics and Supplements; Federal Reserve Bulletin.

1948. The two series display considerable similarity, both in trend and in cyclical variation, confirming our expectation.

However, it would be misleading to conclude that interest-rate variations *cause* changes in velocity in any significant sense. Rather, changes in interest rates and in velocity both occur in response to common causal influences, namely, disparities in the rate of expansion of the money supply and of GNP expenditures. We noted in Chapter 9 that in periods when the rate of monetary expansion is high relative to GNP expansion, interest rates have tended to fall. And when GNP expansion is high and monetary growth low, interest rates tend to rise. Now, by definition, changes in measured velocity also reflect disproportion between the rates of change of money and expenditures.

Approaching the matter in this way warns us against treating variations in velocity as a cause of change in GNP expenditures. It is more appropriate to regard measured velocity as a guide to the manner in which expenditure change has been financed. This can be illustrated by reference to Tables 10-2 and 10-3. Each describes the response of the economy to an increase in the propensity to spend by the government. In the first case, the money supply was increased; in the second, it was not. In the first case, velocity and the interest rate remained relatively unchanged. In the second, velocity and the interest rate rose substantially. Yet the rise in velocity was merely a symptom of the fact that someone's propensity to spend had risen without a corresponding degree of monetary expansion. (And remember that GNP rose less in the second case.)

The case illustrated by Table 10-3 helps to explain the behavior of interest rates and velocity in a period of slow monetary expansion, such as that between 1954 and 1960. An increase in the propensity to spend tends to put pressure on the loanable funds market. In our example, the government increased its borrowing to finance higher expenditures. The rise in interest rates helped the loan market to adjust to this rise in demand. To some extent, the higher interest rate reduced private borrowing and spending. But it also helped to draw funds out of idle cash holdings. This latter process, the mobilization of cash holdings, is the direct link between velocity changes and interest-rate changes.

Variations in measured velocity may also occur in response to variations in the quantity of money. Such a case is illustrated by Table 10-1. An increase in the money supply through open-market purchases lowers interest rates. This helps to stimulate higher expenditures, but also leads to larger holdings of idle cash. Thus variations in the money supply may actually produce inverse variations in velocity. The likelihood of such inverse variations depends, however, on just how sensitive expenditures are to changes in money and interest rates.

Adherents of the new quantity theory argue that such inverse variations will not be great and will tend to be only temporary. Indeed, they feel that rapid monetary growth can actually produce an opposite effect and cause velocity to rise, although this effect may appear after some delay. It can occur if interest-rate changes have a large direct effect on expenditures, and if there are large multiplier and accelerator repercussions from initial expenditure changes. Initially, monetary acceleration lowers interest rates. Investment then increases and drives GNP up so strongly, according to this view, that interest rates are pulled back up and may even go higher than they were to start with.

The notion that monetary change can induce velocity change in the same direction might be supported by the events of 1960–1964, as shown in Figure 10-5. As we have repeatedly observed, this was a period of rapid increase in the money supply. Yet after an initial decline in 1960, both interest rates and velocity trended upward. One's interpretation of the events depends, of course, on whether one regards the rapid monetary expansion as an important cause of the rapid rise of GNP. And on this, substantial disagreement remains.

Banks and Velocity In addition to their role as the major channel for change in the money supply, commercial banks are also involved in the process by which changes in velocity come about. The influence of changing interest rates on the public's cash holdings is partly channeled through effects on the composition of bank assets and liabilities.

The households of the economy keep most of their liquid assets either in money or in time deposits. When interest rates rise, they increase the proportion held in time deposits. When households shift funds from currency or demand deposits to time deposits, the initial effect is to reduce the money supply. Because the reduction comes largely out of idle balances, the velocity of remaining money increases. However, the shift gives the banks excess reserves. If coin and currency flow in, they have more total reserves. If the public shifts from demand to time deposits, some reserves formerly required are released. If the banks expand loans, the money supply may be restored to its previous level. Since the newly created money goes into active circulation, velocity remains higher than it was to start with.

The composition of bank assets also influences velocity. Banks are continually receiving a large inflow of loan repayments. If they use these funds to make new loans to business firms and consumers, the money will remain in active circulation. If the economy is prosperous, the banks will probably maintain or increase their loan volume; if a recession is under way, they may allow loan volume to contract and buy government securities in the open market instead. This action may reduce velocity, for securities will often be purchased from other investors, who are not likely to spend the money for current output. They may respend it for other financial investments, but this does not in itself produce a positive V_g. With low interest rates and high securities prices, investors may hold this money idle, await-ing more favorable investment conditions. This retention of the money will lower V_g.

Figure 10-6 shows two indicators of the composition of bank assets and liabilities. One is the ratio of time deposits in commercial and savings banks to demand deposits. The other is the ratio between commercial bank loans and securities holdings.

The deposit ratio helps to explain the upward trend of velocity. How-ever, the cyclical movements in the deposit ratio seem to lag sufficiently behind changes in interest rates and velocity so that, until 1961 at least, deposit shifts have tended in the short run to stabilize velocity. Since 1961, however, shifts in the deposit ratio may have had more short-run impact on velocity. Increases in 1962 and 1963 in the maximum interest rate per-mitted on time deposits, and the introduction of negotiable time certificates of deposits, produced some substantial deposit shifts. Velocity increases in early 1962 and late 1963 may reflect these shifts.

The ratio of loans to securities shows a much higher degree of con-formity to the short-run fluctuations in velocity; and the similarity of this ratio to the interest-rate series is particularly striking. It appears, however, that the connection between the loan ratio and velocity tends to be greater during a period of slow monetary growth, such as 1951–1960. When bank reserves are increasing only slowly, banks adjust to variations in demand for loans by shifting the composition of their assets. However, when their reserves are rising more rapidly, they can add to both loans and securities. Certainly the short-term correspondence between the loan ratio and velocity is less apparent for 1960–1964. In any event, the loan-security ratio is only an imperfect measure of the conceptual distinction we seek, between credit extended to spenders and acquisition by the banks of open-market assets from other financial investors. Loans for purchasing or carrying securities may have less connection with current expenditures than purchases of newly is-sued state and local government securities.

To say that banks are involved in these shifts does not mean that they cause them. In particular, the shifts in the loan ratio may arise chiefly from variations in the demand for loans, responding to changes in expendi-ture decisions. However, variations in the strictness of credit rationing by the banks may give them something of an active role in the behavior of the loan ratio. And even if the banks are passive, we cannot be sure that velocity movements of the same magnitude could occur without some institutional channel such as the banking system to handle the mobilization of idle bal-ances.

The New Quantity Theory Because of the weakness of velocity as an analytical tool, the Fisher approach lost ground in the 1930s, and the em-phasis in explaining the behavior of aggregate demand shifted to Keynesian concepts such as marginal efficiency and the propensity to consume. The quantity of money remained a formal element in the analytical system, as a determinant of interest rates, but the statistical evidence of expenditure behavior seemed to show that money and interest rates had only small influence on aggregate spending.

In recent years, however, attention has again been focused on the quantity of money, largely through the influence of Prof. Milton Friedman.[2] Although his own monetary analysis contains a number of elements which have not received wide support, it has made a major contribution in directing economists to examine the *rate of growth* of the money supply over time. Friedman offers abundant historical evidence to show that variations in the rate of monetary growth have tended to lead variations in the flow of aggregate expenditures, and in his view, to cause them.

A comparison between year-to-year changes in M and in GNP is presented in Figure 10-7. In general, the correspondence in their major swings supports the new quantity theory. Similar major swings appear in both series, and the monetary series either leads or coincides. To be sure, not all variations in GNP change can be attributed to monetary factors. Autonomous expenditure variation is evident in the period of the Korean crisis. However, examination of major turning points indicates that the monetary series commonly leads GNP or coincides with it. Apparent leads are marked with arrows in Figure 10-7.

In interpreting these rate of change data, it is important to know how the monetary changes come about. If they are merely induced by the same factors responsible for GNP variation, we would not be justified in attributing causation to the money supply. The response of the new quantity theory is that changes in M respond to changes in the monetary base, or the quantity of high-powered money, consisting chiefly of Federal Reserve credit, the monetary gold stock, and Treasury currency (as analyzed in Chapter 5). Some modification may be needed to allow for changes in commercial bank reserve requirements or in the desire of the public to hold currency, demand deposits, and time deposits. Since the monetary base is not automatically pulled about by changes in business conditions (at least, not since 1954), its importance tends to substantiate the view that monetary

---

[2] Friedman's ideas are set forth in relatively brief form in "The Supply of Money and Changes in Prices and Output," Joint Economic Committee, U.S. Congress, *The Relationship of Prices to Economic Stability and Growth*, Papers Submitted by Panelists, 1958; "The Relative Stability of Monetary Velocity and the Investment Multiplier in the United States, 1897–1958" (with David Meiselman), Commission on Money and Credit, *Stabilization Policies*, Prentice-Hall, Inc., Englewood Cliffs, N.J., 1963; and *The Federal Reserve System after Fifty Years, Hearings before the Subcommittee on Domestic Finance*, Committee on Banking and Currency, House of Representatives, 1964, pp. 1133–1175, 1220–1222.

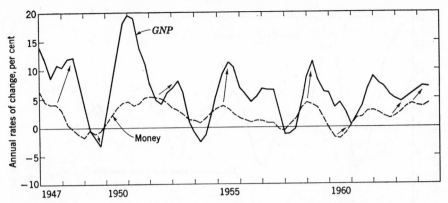

Figure 10-7. Year-to-year percentage changes in money supply and GNP expenditures, 1947–1964.

Sources: Supplement to Banking and Monetary Statistics: Banks and the Monetary System; Federal Reserve Bulletin; U.S. Income and Output; Survey of Current Business.

change is an important cause of GNP change, and not merely a symptom of it.

Figure 10-8 offers a comparison between the rates of change for the money supply and for a crude measure of the monetary base. The latter is approximated by the sum of Federal Reserve credit and the monetary gold stock, with adjustment for changes in reserve requirements. Simple as it is, this approximation to the monetary base clearly provides a close fit with monetary change.

Figure 10-8 also provides data on the manner in which monetary change is converted into expenditures change. The principal channel is commercial bank credit. Changes in the monetary base tend to produce corresponding changes in bank reserves, and these produce similar changes in the money supply and in bank earning assets. Changes in GNP growth appear shortly after, to be followed after another lag by variations in bank loans.

If we accept the data as indicating a causal sequence from monetary change to GNP change, the link would appear to be variations in interest rates. Variations in total bank credit lead movements in GNP, whereas variations in bank loans (since 1954 at least) have tended to lag behind GNP.

Interest rates play a major role in transmitting influence from money to expenditures. Variations in the rate of monetary expansion, even if concentrated initially in bank holdings of securities, have usually produced substantial interest-rate variations. These variations in turn have, according to quantity theorists, been sufficient to bring the expenditure flow into alignment with the rate of monetary expansion. No doubt variations in hous-

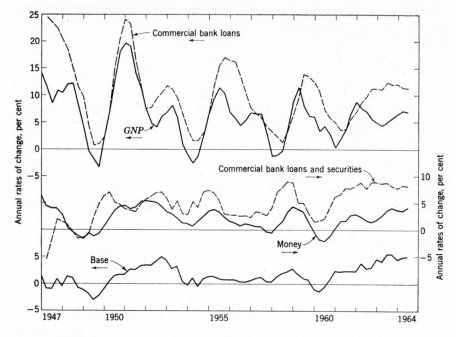

Figure 10-8. Year-to-year percentage changes in money, credit, and spending, 1947–1964.

Sources: Supplement to Banking and Monetary Statistics: Banks and the Monetary System; Federal Reserve Bulletin; U.S. Income and Output; Survey of Current Business.

ing expenditure play a prominent role in such adjustments. However, variations in a broad spectrum of asset prices and yields may be involved in the transmission of monetary influence.

While the rate of monetary expansion may help explain the turning points in expenditure change, variations in the expansion of bank loans help explain the amplitude of the expenditures cycles. Changes in bank loans appear to lag behind changes in GNP, suggesting that variation in the demand for loans may be a major cause of the variation. Whatever the cause, expansion of bank loans helps to contribute to the amplitude of GNP swings, as a vehicle either for further creation of money or for increase in velocity. However, variations in loan expansion certainly do not explain turning points in the rate of change of GNP.

Our theoretical apparatus has already led us to stress the difference between new money injected directly into the main money circuit and new money which enters through the financial circulation. Direct injection most commonly results from expansion of bank loans, but can also arise from bank purchase of government securities issued to finance current deficit expenditures. Historically, gold inflows to buy American exports have also caused direct injection. By contrast, new money created by open-market purchases of securities by the Federal Reserve and by commercial banks would enter the financial circulation. So would money created by a gold inflow arising from capital flight (as in the 1930s) or other transactions unrelated to current production.

When new money enters the main circuit directly, it retains a relatively high velocity and tends to raise GNP expenditures proportionately. But when it enters the financial circulation, the initial impact is on interest rates and security prices. Sellers of securities have more cash and less securities; their most likely reaction is to reinvest the funds in other financial assets. In the process, security prices are pushed up and yields fall. The decline in interest rates encourages increased borrowing and spending by credit-sensitive sectors of the economy such as construction. But it also encourages larger holdings of idle cash.

Controversy over the new quantity theory revolves in large part around the relative sensitivity to interest rates of expenditures and of cash holdings. A high sensitivity of expenditures and a low sensitivity of cash holdings would produce a result favorable to the quantity theory. Such a pattern of interest sensitivity reduces the importance of the method of money creation. Econometric studies relying on correlation techniques have generally found relatively low interest sensitivity of expenditures. But the techniques may be unsatisfactory if the influence of interest rates is subject to a time lag which is variable and distributed over several time periods. Even if the impact of interest-rate change is not large, the multiplier-accelerator repercussions may still produce a large ultimate response. The new quantity theorists rely on time-series correspondence between money and expenditures to support their contention that expenditures are more sensitive to monetary change and interest rates than the correlation studies indicate.

Our conclusion is that the interest sensitivity of expenditures is sufficient for monetary change to gain a foothold even when it operates entirely through the financial circulation. However, there is still an appreciable difference between the impact of money so created and money directly injected into the main circuit.

An increasing number of economists have come to accept the existence of an important causal link between the rates of growth of money and of total expenditures.[3] They draw the conclusion that monetary policy is much more potent than economists used to think it was. They are critical of the wide variations in monetary growth which have been permitted or caused

---

[3] Support for the new quantity theory is evident in many of the economists' contributions to the hearings on *The Federal Reserve System after Fifty Years.* See also J. M. Culbertson, *Full Employment or Stagnation?* McGraw-Hill Book Company, New York, 1964.

by Federal Reserve policy, and they urge that monetary policy be more closely oriented toward maintaining relatively steady growth in the money supply. While such a policy will not eliminate disturbances arising from variations in propensities to spend, it seems preferable to the degree of monetary instability which is shown in Figure 10-8.

Output and Prices The ultimate effects of monetary change on economic welfare occur through the influence of money on output, prices, and employment. This influence occurs through changes in spending. An increase in M which produces only a small rise in GNP expenditures will have little effect on output, prices, and employment.

Assuming that an increase in the money supply does raise GNP expenditures, the value of output will be increased in the same degree. The greater the existing level of unemployment, the greater will be the rise in output, employment, and welfare. If unemployment is low and rising expenditures act chiefly to push up prices, the welfare effect might be considered adverse. In the long run, growth in the labor force and productivity provide additional scope for expenditures to expand in a manner which raises welfare.

One must beware of analysis which attributes to money a unique causal influence over prices. Prices respond to variations in expenditures, whether those variations arise from changes in M or in V_g.

In terms of the Fisher equation, prices will rise over time in proportion to the money supply only if velocity changes in proportion to output. This proportionality did in fact result over the period 1950–1962. However, the result is a relatively unusual one. It is not found in the years 1933–1942, when output far outstripped velocity, or during the nineteenth century, when the money supply rose about 200-fold while prices trended slightly downward. Acceleration of monetary growth in the early 1960s did not cause a proportional acceleration in the rate of price increases. Instead, the monetary expansion caused output to expand more (absolutely and in relation to velocity) than would otherwise have been the case.

SUMMARY

The behavior of GNP expenditures can be explained in terms of the interaction of the propensities to spend of the major economic sectors, the division of income among the sectors, the demand schedule for cash balances, and the supply of money. If the demand schedule for cash and the supply of money are unchanged, increases in any sector's propensity to spend will raise GNP and interest rates.

The effect of an increase in the money supply depends on how the new money enters the economy. If injected directly into the main circuit (as through a rise in bank loans to spenders), the new money tends to raise GNP substantially and to leave interest rates relatively unchanged. If the new money enters by way of the financial circulation (as through open-market purchases of securities by the banking system), the immediate effects are to reduce interest rates and ease credit, which in turn stimulate a higher level of borrowing and spending by business firms, consumers, and some units of government. Since lower interest rates also tend to cause an increase in desired holdings of idle cash, the stimulating effect of such monetary expansion depends on the relative sensitivity to interest rates of expenditures and of cash holdings. The link between money and GNP spending will be relatively close if expenditures are directly sensitive to interest-rate variation, if interest-induced changes in spending are magnified by large multiplier-accelerator repercussions, and if cash holdings are relatively insensitive to interest-rate changes.

The expenditure flow does not maintain a strict proportionality to the quantity of money. Rather, there are variations in monetary velocity (defined as GNP/M). These have often been associated with variations in interest rates, which affect holdings of idle cash. Variations in the composition of bank assets between loans and securities also play a part in velocity changes.

Although velocity is not literally constant, there still appears to be a substantial causal relation historically between the rate of change of the money supply and the rate of change of GNP expenditures. Recognition of this fact has led to increased faith that control of the quantity of money

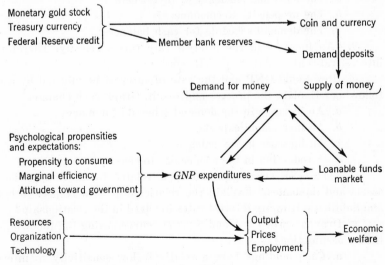

Figure 10-9. Money, spending, and welfare.

can be an important means of achieving desired levels of total spending.

The impact of expenditure behavior on economic welfare occurs chiefly through effects on output, prices, and employment. Decreases in GNP expenditures tend to decrease output and employment and thus diminish economic welfare. Increased expenditures tend to raise output and employment, but also to cause price increases. The higher the level of unemployment, the greater the likelihood that higher GNP expenditures will raise output, employment, and welfare. The probability of price inflation exists chiefly when the rate of increase of GNP is large and the unemployment level is very low.

The relationships we have been constructing since Chapter 3 are represented symbolically in Figure 10-9.

QUESTIONS FOR STUDY

1. The Federal government can bring about a general reduction in interest rates in either of two ways. It can reduce its expenditures relative to its revenue or increase the quantity of money (which might result from a reduction in the Treasury cash balance). Explain how each of these would tend to lower interest rates. What difference would it make for the behavior of GNP whether one or the other was chosen?

2. Explain how the magnitude and character of each of the following affect the way in which GNP would respond to an increase in the money supply through Federal Reserve open-market purchases:

    a. The marginal efficiency of investment

    b. The propensity to consume

    c. The demand schedule for cash balances

3. "An increase in the interest rate raises velocity. Therefore higher interest rates are inflationary." Discuss.

4. How would GNP and the rate of interest be affected by each of the following? Explain the process and result. Graph each change.

    a. An increase in the demand schedule for money

    b. An increase in exports

    c. An increase in tax rates

    d. A reduction in the propensity to consume

5. "The GNP velocity of money is related to the composition of bank assets and liabilities." Explain the relationship with respect to both assets and liabilities. How are interest rates involved in the relationship?

6. Draw a set of $I = S$ and $S_m = D_m$ curves using the following quantity theory assumptions:

    a. Cash holdings have a relatively low sensitivity to interest rates (but vary directly with income).

b. Investment spending is relatively sensitive to interest-rate variations.

Use the resulting diagram to analyze the impact of variations in the money supply.

7. What kind of $I = S$ curve would you get if you assume that the marginal propensity to spend for the three sectors combined is greater than 1? What effects result from changes in the money supply under such an assumption?

SUGGESTED READINGS

Ackley, Gardner: *Macroeconomic Theory,* The Macmillan Company, New York, 1961.

Baumol, William J.: *Economic Dynamics,* 2d ed., The Macmillan Company, New York, 1959.

Fisher, Irving: *The Purchasing Power of Money,* The Macmillan Company, New York, 1911.

Friedman, Milton (ed.): *Studies in the Quantity Theory of Money,* The University of Chicago Press, Chicago, 1956.

Garvy, George: *Debits and Clearings Statistics and Their Use,* 2d ed., Board of Governors, Federal Reserve System, Washington, 1959.

Lindahl, Erik: *Studies in the Theory of Money and Capital,* Holt, Rinehart and Winston, Inc., New York, 1939.

Lundberg, Erik: *Studies in the Theory of Economic Expansion,* Kelley and Millman, New York, 1954.

Lutz, Friedrich A., and Lloyd W. Mints (eds.): *Readings in Monetary Theory,* McGraw-Hill Book Company, New York, 1951.

part four

THE WORLD
OF FINANCE

chapter eleven

FINANCIAL ASPECTS
OF ECONOMIC GROWTH

INTRODUCTORY

In the preceding chapters we devoted considerable attention to the financial system as it relates to the supply of money, the level of interest rates and credit conditions, and the flow of expenditures in the main money circuit. With this chapter we begin a more detailed discussion of the structure and functioning of financial institutions in relation to other aspects of economic activity. Financial business is big business—it employs some 2 million Americans—and its magnitude warrants the question, "What good is it?"

Financial institutions affect economic welfare in many ways, aside from their influence on the flow of aggregate spending. Commercial banks, by providing an efficient medium for payments, help the market system itself to function more efficiently. Consumer welfare and business efficiency are both directly served by insurance and related services, such as pension rights. Access to credit from financial institutions affects the intensity of competition in markets for goods and services generally, as well as the opportunities open to new firms and small firms. The financial system has a great deal to do with the forms in which the majority of people keep their savings and with the incomes and risks attending those savings. Finally, the financial system has an influence on the allocation of productive resources to various uses, and particularly their allocation between consumption and investment. It is the latter influence which we shall stress, for the extent to which resources are invested in ways which add to the nation's real wealth is significantly related to the rate of economic growth.

FACTORS UNDERLYING ECONOMIC GROWTH

The dimension of economic growth which is significant for economic welfare is the rise in real output per capita, which is the foundation of rising levels of economic welfare for the population. The process of economic growth in a market economy involves both supply and demand. Growth must entail an increase in the nation's capacity to produce (supply). Productive capacity in turn depends on the quantity and quality of productive resources and the efficiency with which they are organized and combined. Capital goods are one important category of productive resources, and the process by which capital is increased through saving and investment is thus one important element in the growth process.

However, the demand for goods and services—GNP expenditures— plays a part in the process also. From a short-run standpoint, unless the expenditure flow is adequate, the economy may fail to make full use of its resources. Furthermore, if demand is weak, the growth of supply may be impaired also. Weak demand may impair the profit outlook and thus undermine business profit incentives. As a result, investment spending and capital accumulation may fall short of their potential.

The growth process can thus be facilitated if there is a balanced expansion between rising aggregate demand on one hand and the total productivity capacity of the economy on the other.

Quantitative estimates of the relative role of various supply factors in twentieth-century American economic growth have been presented in an influential study by Edward Denison. His conclusions are summarized in Table 11-1. Denison's estimates cover the period 1909–1957, during which time the total output of the American economy quadrupled and output per capita doubled.

The increased labor force resulting from population growth was, of course, a substantial element adding to the nation's capacity to produce. Hours of work were substantially shortened, but Denison feels that shorter hours raised output per hour sufficiently to offset much of the loss of work hours. In addition, labor quality was increased by increased educational attainment, a form of "investment in human capital" vital both to productivity and to personal welfare.

Increase in the quantity of capital goods is credited by Denison for about 20 per cent of growth in the period as a whole. In addition, much of the improvement credited to "advance of knowledge" represents technological innovation, which generally pays off only when it is embodied in capital goods.

Denison limits his concern to capital in the national-income sense—that is, plant and equipment, business inventories, and housing. Other in-

Table 11-1   Sources of American economic growth, 1909–1957

Elements contributing to growth	Percentage of total growth rate attributed to each element	
	1909–1929	1929–1957
1. Labor input	(54)	(54)
a. Change in number employed	+39	+34
b. Change in hours worked	−8	−18
c. Effect of shorter hours on quality	+8	+11
d. Increased education	+12	+23
e. Other	+3	+3
2. Increase in quantity of capital	+26	+15
3. Elements leading to higher output per unit of input	(+20)	(+32)
a. Economies of scale resulting from growth of market	(+10+)	+12
b. Advance of knowledge	(+10−)	+20
Total	+100	+100
Average annual rate of growth	2.82	2.93

Note: Figures are rounded and do not always add up to totals shown.
Source: Edward Denison, *The Sources of Economic Growth in the United States,* Committee for Economic Development, New York, 1962, p. 266.

vestigators have noted the importance to economic growth and economic welfare of national wealth in the broad sense—the nation's stock of useful assets of all kinds. Economic growth entails a buildup not only of business capital but also of social capital, in such forms as highways, schools, and parks. Finally, American economic growth has involved extensive accumulation of real assets other than housing by consumers for their own use and enjoyment—automobiles, furniture, clothing, appliances.

Financial institutions and operations have a great deal to do with the process by which productive capital, in the narrow sense, and real wealth, in the broad sense, are increased. Much of the remainder of this chapter will be concerned with the financial aspects of the growth of real wealth.

Real assets are not the only kind of assets which people want to accumulate as the economy grows, however. An expanding stock of financial assets has also been a significant element in the American growth process. Growth in the supply of money has been important to facilitate an efficient market economy and to enable the expenditure flow to rise commensurately with the rise in productive capacity. Growth in liquid assets has supplemented money as a store of value and has provided an attractive outlet for personal saving.

THE ROLE OF DEBT

Debt and Economic Growth   Many of the foregoing considerations come to focus on a much maligned institution—debt. An analysis of some aspects of debt provides a handy introduction to a number of important factors relating to economic growth, as well as an introduction to the study of financial institutions.

By debts we mean promises or obligations to pay which bear fixed values in terms of money. Debts include the promissory notes of individuals and business firms and their book-credit liabilities. Debts also include bonds and related securities issued by government units or by business firms. Finally, a very different category of debts consists of the obligations of financial institutions—bank deposits, insurance and pension rights, etc.

The debts of the nonfinancial sectors of the economy are commonly summarized under the heading "net public and private debt." Its magnitude and composition in 1962 are shown by Table 11-2.

Table 11-2   Net public and private debt in the United States, 1962
(Billions of dollars)

Corporate debt	$ 346
Individual and noncorporate:	
Mortgage	211
Commercial and financial	37
Consumer	64
Farm	31
Government:*	
Federal	256
State and local	74
Total	$1,017

* Federal government debt excludes holdings of government agencies and trust funds. State and local government figures are for June 30, others for end of year.

Source: Economic Report of the President, 1964, p. 270. Figures are rounded and do not add up precisely to total shown.

The word "debt" clearly carries the connotation of money being owed by someone. It is vital to remember, however, that debt also involves money owed *to* someone. One man's debt is another's asset, just as one man's expenditure is another's income. More than half the indebtedness of the nonfinancial sectors is owed to financial institutions—banks, insurance companies, savings institutions. These holdings of debt constitute the chief assets of those institutions and thus constitute the "backing" for the debts owed by those institutions to the public. The debts of financial institutions, in such forms as bank deposits and insurance policies, constitute a large proportion of the financial assets held by business firms and individuals.

There are three ways in which debt bears an important relationship to economic growth and economic welfare. They are as follows:

1. Increases in debt (public or private) appear to be essential to finance the deficits (public or private) needed for rising GNP expenditures over time.

2. Increases in debt are needed if the supply of financial assets—and particularly money and liquid savings assets—is to grow over time.

3. Because the purchase of durable real assets is financed in substantial degree by borrowing, the growth of debt is intimately related to the increase in the productive capital and real wealth of the economy.

Debt and Expenditures If GNP is to rise from year to year, there must be deficit spending somewhere in the economy—that is, some transactors must spend more than their incomes. Generally, deficit spending is financed by borrowing, by increases in debt. Consequently, changes in debt are related to changes in the flow of GNP expenditures.

Figure 11-1 shows how changes in debt and spending have been related in the United States since 1929. On the vertical axis is measured the year-to-year percentage change in net public and private debt. Horizontally the corresponding percentage change in GNP expenditures is shown.

If we consider all the points together, there is a definite positive relation between the two variables, a relation perhaps better represented by a curve than a straight line. However, if we date the points, they form themselves into three definite groupings, each of which can be approximated by a straight line. Such lines are shown for the periods 1929–1941, 1942–1945, and 1947–1963.

Comparing the prewar and postwar groupings, one discerns differences in slope and intercept which reflect differences in the degree to which expenditures were debt-propelled in the two periods. During the Depression, changes in GNP tended to be proportional to changes in debt at a ratio of about 3 to 1. In the postwar period, it has required an annual increase in debt of about 3 per cent to keep GNP constant. This minimum debt increase reflects offsetting surpluses and deficits by the various sectors of the economy. On the average during 1947–1963, an added 1 per cent increase in debt was associated with an added 2 per cent increase in GNP.

Aside from the Depression period, large increases in GNP have occurred only in connection with large increases in debt. And whatever the time period, reductions in debt have been associated with declines in GNP.

Debt and Financial Assets   Economic growth produces a rising demand for many types of financial assets, particularly those issued by financial institutions. Increasing transactions volume requires more money, chiefly bank checking deposits. Increasing personal incomes give rise to increased personal saving. For many savers, safety, liquidity, and protection against financial risks are important motives for saving. These objectives are well served by liquid savings assets, such as savings deposits with commercial banks or mutual savings banks, savings and loan shares, insurance policies, and pension rights. These are all claims against various financial institutions.

In order to increase the volume of financial claims against themselves, financial institutions must add commensurately to their assets, which consist predominantly of debt claims against the nonfinancial sectors of the economy. Looking at the relationship from one end, the flow of saving into these institutions provides much of the funds desired by borrowers. From

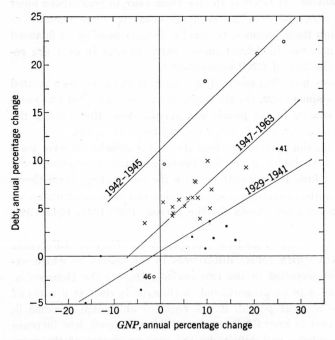

Figure 11-1. Year-to-year percentage changes in net public and private debt and in GNP expenditures, 1929–1963.

Source: Calculated from data in *Survey of Current Business, Economic Report of the President, U.S. Income and Output.*

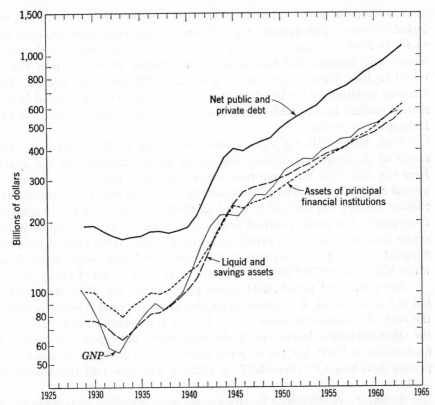

Figure 11-2. Debt, financial assets, and GNP, 1929–1963. Liquid and savings assets include money, time and savings deposits at commercial and savings banks, savings accounts with savings and loan associations and credit unions, United States savings bonds and postal savings deposits, and policy reserves of life insurance. Assets of major financial institutions include commercial and savings banks, savings and loan associations, credit unions, and life insurance companies.

Sources: Goldsmith, *A Study of Saving in the United States; Savings and Loan Fact Book; All-bank Statistics;* Friedman and Schwartz, *A Monetary History of the United States, 1867–1960; Flow of Funds Accounts, 1945–1962; Federal Reserve Bulletin; Supplement to Banking and Monetary Statistics: Banks and the Monetary System; Historical Statistics of the United States.*

the other end, the increase in debts by borrowers provides the earning assets which financial institutions hold, enabling those institutions to issue the specialized kinds of financial claims which the public particularly desires to hold.

In Figure 11-2, the close relationship is apparent among net public and private debt, GNP expenditures, liquid assets (including money), and the asset holdings of major financial institutions. In the liquid assets total, we include currency and demand deposits, commercial bank time deposits, deposits in mutual savings banks, savings deposits and shares with credit unions and savings and loan associations, United States savings bonds, postal savings deposits, and the cash value of life insurance policies. The financial institutions for which total assets are listed are commercial banks, mutual savings banks, savings and loan associations, credit unions, and life insurance companies.

Most striking is the close connection among GNP expenditures, the assets of financial institutions, and liquid assets—indeed, one can argue from the data that the three tend toward equality. The relation is one of mutual determination. The public evidently desires to hold liquid assets (including money) approximately equal to GNP. In the process of acquiring these assets, the public provides financial institutions with the funds to increase *their* asset holdings, chiefly by acquiring debt claims against the nonfinancial sectors. This latter operation finances the deficit spending activities which help to keep GNP moving up, starting another round of the cycle.

Net public and private debt moves parallel with the other magnitudes, but at a higher level. Here there seems also to be a normal relation in which the debt of nonfinancial sectors tends to bear a constant ratio to GNP and the other variables. Deviations in the ratio occur in response to short-run fluctuations in GNP, but the long-run constancy is striking. Net public and private debt was 1.83 times GNP in 1929; it was also 1.83 times GNP in 1962.

Again, the relationships involve mutual determination. Increase in GNP raises saving and investment, increasing both the supply of loan funds and the demand for them. The increases in debt help finance the deficit expenditures which keep GNP moving upward.

Increases in debt are thus intimately bound up with increases in those financial assets which we associate with prudence and thrift. Just how the connection operates for individual types of financial assets and institutions we shall explore further in this and the subsequent two chapters.

Debt and Real Wealth Additions to the nation's stock of real wealth play an important part in economic growth. Long-lived assets such as houses, factory buildings, and machinery tend to be costly relative to the incomes of prospective buyers. Consequently, purchases of such assets are financed to a considerable degree by borrowing. As a result, increases in debt are closely bound up with increases in real national wealth.

Some measures of the association between debt and real wealth are shown in Figure 11-3. There is a substantial parallel between debt and tangible national wealth, in current prices. To be sure, the increases in "deadweight" debt incurred by the Federal government during World War II distorted the relationship, but it was restored by 1950. The ratio of debt to wealth was about the same in 1939, 1950, and 1958—approximately 46 per cent. The similarity of movement in the two series is particularly evident in 1922–1939 and 1949–1958.

Much of the movement in the value of tangible wealth has arisen from price changes. When these are eliminated, as in the series for tangible national wealth in constant prices, variations are much smaller. The quantity of national wealth remained virtually unchanged between 1929 and 1945, but has grown at a fairly steady rate since then.

One source of stability in the figure for total tangible wealth is the inclusion of nonreproducible assets, chiefly land. Separate series are included for the quantity of reproducible wealth, at constant prices, and for its chief component, business real capital. The impact of the Depression of the 1930s is particularly impressive in the latter series, for business capital in 1945 was still below what it had been in 1929.

Debt and tangible wealth act upon each other. Increases in debt finance

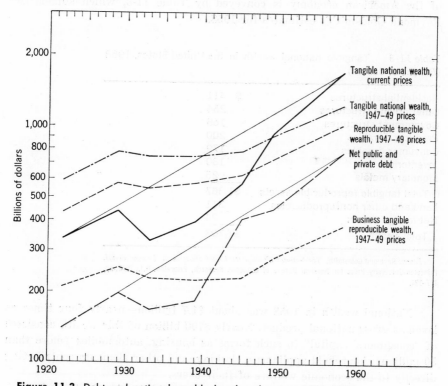

Figure 11-3. Debt and national wealth, benchmark years, 1922–1958.

Sources: Goldsmith, *The National Wealth of the United States in the Postwar Period; Survey of Current Business.*

the acquisition of currently produced real assets, adding to the quantity of tangible wealth. However, increases in debt may also finance transfers of existing wealth at rising prices, causing the value of wealth to rise more than its quantity. Looking at the process from the other side, real wealth is a highly acceptable basis for borrowing. The desire to acquire real wealth leads people to borrow, and the existence of real wealth as possible collateral security increases the willingness of the lenders to lend.

In the sections immediately following, we shall look more closely at tangible national wealth and particularly business capital, the manner in which real wealth is financed, and the role of financial institutions in the growth of wealth and productivity.

THE ACCUMULATION OF REAL WEALTH

Measurement   Some idea of the size and composition of the real wealth of the American economy is conveyed by Table 11-3, which summarizes Raymond Goldsmith's estimates for 1958.

Table 11-3   Tangible national wealth in the United States, 1958
(Billions of dollars)

Residential structures	$ 411
Other private structures	254
Government structures	168
Producer durables	200
Consumer durables	179
Inventories	130
Monetary metals	25
Total tangible reproducible assets	$1,367
Land and other nonreproducibles	311
Net foreign assets	24
Total wealth	$1,703

Source: Raymond Goldsmith, *The National Wealth of the United States in the Postwar Period*, Princeton University Press for National Bureau of Economic Research, Princeton, N.J., 1962, pp. 177–194.

National wealth in 1958 was about $1.7 trillion—nearly four times as large as gross national product. Nearly $700 billion of this wealth consisted of "consumers' capital" in such forms as housing, automobiles (more than 50 million), household appliances, clothing, and other elements contributing directly to the economic welfare of their users.

Business capital goods totaled about $600 billion in plant, equipment, and inventories, while government buildings added $170 billion to the total. According to C. Lowell Harriss, "In 1962 this country has 60 million dwelling units and 7,000 hospitals with 1.7 million beds. There are 220,000 miles of railroad main tracks, 1.7 million freight cars, and 5.1 million farm tractors. Pipelines for gas and oil exceed 700,000 miles. We have about 2.1 million miles of hard-surface highways and over 11 million trucks. There are nearly 300,000 factories." [1]

Capital Goods and Productivity The logic of directing current output into production of capital assets is that the total enjoyment yielded by resources may be greater if some of them are put into forms which yield their enjoyment only in the future. The durable assets held by consumers yield their enjoyment directly through use. Accumulation of business capital through investment helps to raise the nation's economic productivity.

The productivity of the labor force depends on the amount of capital goods and natural resources each worker has available to work with. Increased capital has vastly increased the amount of energy input available for production and distribution. Technically advanced capital equipment makes possible extremes of temperature, pressure, heat, and precision of operation which simply could not otherwise be achieved.

In an industrial economy, the need for current production of capital goods arises from three sources:

1. A substantial volume of gross investment is necessary merely to replace old capital assets wearing out. In recent years, about 8 per cent of our total output has been required for this purpose.

2. In the American economy, population and labor force have been growing steadily. Merely to keep each additional worker supplied with the same amount of capital goods requires a substantial addition to our total capital assets each year. In the early 1960s it required more than $15,000 to equip each additional worker. With our labor force growing at a rate of 1 million per year, at least $17 billion of annual investment is needed merely to keep pace and provide productive employment for the added workers.

3. In order to raise output per worker and per capita, it is desirable to increase the amount of capital investment per worker. This increase often means that different *kinds* of capital goods are used, more closely adapted to particular functions and capable of leading to economies of large-scale operation. In road building, for instance, more capital per worker means not more picks and shovels per man but more men equipped with bulldozers and other heavy mechanized equipment. Additional capital per man often comes into use indirectly through development of public utilities and transportation.

Capital Goods and Technology Even more important, capital formation is the chief medium through which technological progress operates to raise

[1] C. Lowell Harriss, *The American Economy*, 4th ed., Richard D. Irwin, Inc., Homewood, Ill., 1962, p. 53.

productivity. To an impressive degree, the important innovations in our economy have involved products or methods of production in which large capital investment was involved. Such products as the automobile, electricity and machines to use it, plastics, and synthetics are closely associated with high-capital industries. Likewise, large capital investment has been necessary for adoption of such methods of production as the assembly line, the continuous-strip rolling mill, and the automatic petroleum refinery. Most technological innovations must be embodied in capital goods to become effective. However, this embodiment can occur through replacement investment; it is the *gross* output of capital goods which is potentially significant.

Capital and Growth   We have already noted that Denison attributes about 20 per cent of the growth of total output to the increased size of the stock of capital for the period 1909–1957. Somewhere in the neighborhood of 15 per cent additional growth can be attributed to improved technology. If we isolate the contributions of elements tending to raise output *per person*, increased capital and improved technology show an even more important influence, on the order of one-half.

Since the rate of capital formation appears capable of being influenced by such government measures as taxation and monetary policy, there has been considerable academic interest in estimating how much we could increase our rate of economic growth by encouraging greater investment. Denison himself is not optimistic about the ease of stepping up growth by higher investment. He estimates that raising the annual growth rate by 1 per cent would require added net investment on the order of 10 to 15 per cent of national income, or 7 to 11 per cent if concentrated in business capital.

However, Robert Solow presents alternative estimates which incorporate an allowance for the more rapid introduction of technological improvement through the higher investment. These estimates indicate a much lower marginal investment requirement for added economic growth. Stepping up the growth rate from 3 to 4 per cent, according to Solow's estimates, would require only about 2 per cent more of GNP devoted to business capital formation. Denison, however, suggests that most important innovations will be embodied even at a lower rate of investment; consequently raising the investment level will not add proportionately to output.[2]

The causes of technological progress are difficult to get at; most estimates simply assume it will continue to be forthcoming. Its importance in the past is abundantly evident. Technological improvement has been sufficient to overcome the tendency toward diminishing returns as the size of

---

[2] Edward Denison, *The Sources of Economic Growth in the United States*, Committee for Economic Development, New York, 1962, p. 113, and "The Unimportance of the Embodied Question," *American Economic Review*, March, 1964; Robert Solow, "Technical Progress, Capital Formation, and Economic Growth," *ibid.*, May, 1962.

the capital stock has risen. Indeed, the capital-output ratio has tended to decline during the twentieth century, meaning that it takes less capital per unit of product than formerly. Technological progress has kept the marginal efficiency schedule shifting to the right, thus keeping incentives to new investment. Yet at the same time, the rate of return to investors has remained relatively constant per dollar invested; thus most of the actual benefit from the greater productivity of capital has gone to labor.[3]

Real Saving How does a nation acquire such a huge volume of real wealth? Some of it exists in nature, but most of it consists of accumulated products of past production. Ignoring international factors, we can note two conditions needed for such accumulation. First, the economy must have enjoyed a sufficiently high level of real income and productivity in the past for this stock of goods to be produced or acquired. Second, there must have been a willingness by the public to refrain from devoting all production to current consumption—that is, to save, in real terms.

What is the relation between this process of real saving and the financial system? Real saving can occur without financial saving. A substantial portion of the accumulation of capital goods by consumers and business firms is financed out of income. However, the financial process is brought into operation by two important factors. First, many people desire to save by accumulating financial assets rather than real goods. Second, other transactors desire to spend more than their incomes, usually to buy real capital assets. Many capital assets have large total costs and are beyond the reach of current income. Business firms are tempted to buy capital assets on credit because they are financially productive and can increase subsequent income by more than enough to repay their initial cost.

BUSINESS INVESTMENT AND FINANCING

General Data Business firms are the chief instrument through which productive capital formation occurs in our economy. Table 11-4 summarizes the behavior of business with respect to acquisitions of real capital and financial assets and to the manner of financing these assets.

Nonfinancial businesses and farms spent a total of $264 billion for capital goods in the five-year period 1959–1963. Of this sum, about three-fourths represented the replacement of old assets and one-fourth net increases in the stock of capital.

Business generated $230 billion of internal funds to finance the acquisi-

[3] John W. Kendrick, *Productivity Trends in the United States*, Princeton University Press for National Bureau of Economic Research, Princeton, N.J., 1961, pp. 111–130; John W. Kendrick and Ryuzo Sato, "Factor Prices, Productivity, and Economic Growth," *American Economic Review*, December, 1963, p. 975.

tion of real and financial assets. Firms drew a gross total of slightly more than $100 billion from outside financing, but returned about half this amount to the market for loan funds by acquiring financial assets.

The use of ownership capital to finance asset expansion came chiefly through reinvestment of corporate profits. Issues of corporate stock constituted a relatively small proportion of financing, and the owners of unin-

Table 11-4 Capital formation and its financing, nonfinancial business, 1959–1963 inclusive
(Billions of dollars)

	Corporations	Noncorporate and farms	Total
Gross capital formation	$176	$87	$264
(−) Depreciation	136	65	201
(=) Net investment	$ 40	$23	$ 63
(−) Reinvested profits or proprietor's income	38	−9	29
(=) Net external finance	$ 2	$32	$ 34
Gross external finance:			
Mortgage loans	16	21	37
Bank loans	15	6	20
Corporate bonds	19	—	19
Corporate stock	7	—	7
Trade credit and misc.	15	7	22
Total	$ 73	$33	$106
(−) Net increases in financial assets	54	*	55
(−) Statistical discrepancy	17	—	17
(=) Net external finance	2	32	34
% of external finance obtained through debt	90	100	93

* Less than $0.5 billion.
Source: Federal Reserve Bulletin, April, 1964, p. 511. Figures are rounded and may not add up to totals shown.

corporated businesses actually disinvested on balance. External finance was therefore dominated by sources involving the issue of debt claims. The business sector increased its indebtedness by just about $100 billion in the period covered.

Decisions on Financing The individual firm, whether incorporated or not, must make several decisions about obtaining external funds. It must decide whether to seek them, what to use them for, how much to obtain, what kinds of liabilities to issue, and from which sources to obtain the funds. These decisions will be conditioned by the expected profitability of the assets to be acquired, by the costs of funds (including underwriting costs, implicit obligations to pay dividends, etc.), by tax considerations, and by the implications of financing decisions for the control and management of the firm. The following list describes the major types of financing available, with a brief discussion of how these factors operate.

1. *Credit from suppliers.* Most firms buy on credit from their suppliers and thereby incur trade credit liabilities, often represented by book entries. Such credits are usually short-term and may be fairly costly, beyond the first few days, if substantial discounts for cash payment are forgone.

2. *Bank loans.* Commercial bank loans are the great general-purpose source of business credit. However, the traditional basis of bank lending has been for working-capital purposes—to finance inventories or accounts receivable. In recent years, banks have become increasingly willing to make "term loans" of more than one year in duration, but two-thirds of bank business loans are still for less than one year. Bank loans to business are generally low-cost.

3. *Mortgage loans.* A mortgage is a loan secured by real property, land and buildings; thus mortgage funds are available only to firms which own such assets. Such firms can usually obtain mortgage loans fairly easily and at relatively low cost.

4. *Bonds.* Bonds are long-term debt instruments issued by corporations. They may be claims against the general income and assets of the firm rather than against specific assets. A large and prosperous corporation can readily market bonds at low underwriting and interest costs, but most corporations find no public market for their bonds.

All four categories so far are debt claims which are legally binding obligations against the firm and (if unincorporated) its owners, with respect to both principal and interest. If these are not paid on time, creditors may sue the firm, and it may be reorganized or liquidated through bankruptcy proceedings.

Interest which a firm pays is deducted before determining profits subject to Federal profits tax. For a large firm, the Federal government in effect pays nearly half the costs of interest. However, interest received by creditors is fully taxable as income.

5. *Stocks.* The corporation can issue ownership shares against itself. The owners of a corporation (unlike those of a proprietorship or partnership) enjoy limited liability—their personal assets cannot be tapped to meet claims against the corporation. Corporation stocks can be transferred readily, and ownership claims can be subdivided into small fractions convenient for wide ownership.

Stockholders do, however, share in the risks and responsibilities of management. Owners of common stock usually have the right to vote on the choice of directors of the firm. The stockholder's claim against the income and assets of the firm has lowest priority. Neither the income nor principal of a stock constitutes a legally binding claim against the firm, but there is also no maximum limit on the amount the stockholder may receive if the firm is successful.

All corporations issue stock, for they are all owned by someone. However, out of more than 800,000 corporations, only about 5,000 are "publicly held" firms that enjoy a potential general market for stock issues. These firms manifest considerable separation of ownership from control, and stockholders participate chiefly as investors. Smaller corporations are usually owned by the same people who manage them, and stock ownership is often incidental to the management function. These firms have no real potential market for stock issues.

Even major corporations prefer incurring debt obligations to issuing new stock for external financing. (A large proportion of new stock is issued by public utility firms, which cannot readily reinvest profits.) Most firms prefer not to disturb existing patterns of stock prices, ownership, and voting strength. Tax considerations are also important. While interest costs are tax-deductible, dividends paid are not. Taxes must be paid on total profits, and dividends paid out of what is left. The result is that it may take twice as much earnings to pay a dollar of dividends as to pay a dollar of interest.

However, taxation works the other way at the investor level. Dividends enjoy a modest tax exemption; more important, capital gains resulting from selling an asset for more than its cost are taxed at a low rate. For wealthy persons, owning stock in a corporation which reinvests substantial profits is a convenient form of saving.

5a. Preferred stock. While technically an ownership claim, preferred stock shares some of the financial characteristics of debt. It is often nonvoting, enjoys higher priority of claim than common stock, and usually is issued with a fixed percentage rate of dividend (although no fixed maturity value or date).

Availability of Funds How much capital can a firm obtain? The amount and cost will depend on several factors. One is collateral. If the firm has salable assets to secure a loan, it can obtain funds on reasonable terms. Lenders will also check on the honesty and efficiency of management and on the profit prospects for the firm. They will be concerned about the amount of ownership capital already in the firm, to make sure the firm is not borrowing too much. Equity capital provides a cushion to protect creditors against declines in income or asset values. Lenders will also check on the liquidity of the firm. A high ratio of current assets (cash, liquid assets, receivables, and salable inventory) to current liabilities (accounts payable and other short-term liabilities) is a safeguard that the firm will meet its cash obligations when they fall due. Finally, the availability of credit to most firms will depend on the ease or tightness of national credit conditions.

Investment Appraisal   Almost any firm which obtains external funds subjects itself to expert scrutiny by the financial community as to its prospective profitability. Since these evaluations play a major role in determining the flow of capital available for various firms, it is important to consider whether their criteria are likely to accord with the public interest.

On the whole, it is in the public interest for funds to go where profitability will be high, for this is a sign of high productivity. Ideally, firms make profits because they are efficient, because they make products which rank high in public preference, and because they are in the forefront in developing new and improved methods and products. These are all qualities which financial institutions look for, and their evaluation efforts help direct capital into productive uses. Furthermore, firms seeking outside funds may be forced to take actions which promote their own efficiency—better record keeping, careful estimates of capital productivity, etc. Sometimes lenders can furnish useful advice to increase efficiency.

However, investment appraisal is also concerned with the safety of funds, and here the public interest is not always served. Many lenders tend to minimize risk on individual loans rather than seek to achieve actuarial soundness for an entire portfolio through interest rates proportional to risks. Safety considerations may lead lenders to stress low-productivity capital assets, such as distributors' inventories, to the detriment of higher-risk investment in complex machinery. Safety may lead to a preference for old, well-established firms and for larger firms rather than small, perhaps even a preference for firms enjoying a monopolistic position rather than those faced with intense competition. Yet some concern with safety is inevitable, especially under existing laws of limited liability and bankruptcy, through which the owner of a debt-ridden business can sometimes convert its resources to his personal benefit at the expense of creditors.

THE HOUSEHOLD SECTOR

General Data   Table 11-5 summarizes the important aspects of household financial behavior in the period 1959–1963 inclusive. Households increased their ownership of real assets (housing and durables, net of depreciation) by $87 billion and added slightly more than this ($99 billion) to their indebtedness. Acquisitions of financial assets were on a much larger scale, totaling $179 billion. Of this total, slightly more than $100 billion went into liquid assets—money and savings accounts of various types. An additional $61 billion went into public and private life insurance or pension saving (not including social security). In the aggregate, these categories accounted for acquisition by households of about $150 billion of claims against financial intermediaries.

Table 11-5   Household saving, borrowing, and investment, 1959–1963 inclusive
(Billions of dollars)

	Gross	Depreciation	Net	
Real assets acquired:				
Housing	$ 90	26	64	
Consumer durables	232	209	23	
Total	$322	$235	$ 87	$ 87
Financial assets acquired:				
Currency and demand deposits			13	
Savings deposits and shares			89	
Life insurance and pension saving			61	
Bonds and mortgages			25	
Corporate stocks			−1	
Proprietors' net investment in				
unincorporated business			−9	
Total financial assets			$179	179
Total assets acquired				$266
Borrowing:				
Mortgages		$ 68		
Consumer credit		25		
Other		6		
Total		$ 99	(−)99	(−)99
Net funds advanced to other sectors			81	
Increase in net worth (excluding capital gains)				$168

Note: Figures include small amounts for nonprofit organizations. Figures are rounded and may not add up to totals shown.
Source: Computed from data in *Federal Reserve Bulletin*, April, 1964, p. 512.

By contrast, households acquired only $25 billion of such primary debt securities as bonds and mortgages. And they actually reduced their holdings of ownership claims against corporations and unincorporated businesses. (These figures make no allowance for capital gains and thus are consistent with a large increase in the *value* of ownership claims by households against business.)

Purposes of Financial Saving   We can understand the pattern of asset acquisition by households better if we look at the motives for personal saving. Responses to surveys conducted in 1956 indicated that 66 per cent of the people interviewed saved in anticipation of some specific future expenditure need, with retirement, children's education, and purchasing a house as the leading objects. Since the respondents were allowed to list more than one motive, some of these were also among the 45 per cent who reported they saved as protection against emergencies. These motives lead people to acquire insurance and pension rights and financial assets possessing safety and liquidity, with little concern for income. By contrast, only 2 per cent reported they saved in order to bequeath wealth, and only 1 per cent saved in order to earn income from assets. These last motives, which lead people to choose assets on the basis of income, apply chiefly to the small proportion of the population having high incomes—people who account for a relatively large portion of personal saving.[4]

Saving and Income Distribution The volume and composition of household saving are influenced by the pattern of income and distribution. Both the proportion of income saved and the forms of saving vary greatly with income levels. Survey data for the late 1940s indicate that 75 per cent of net financial saving came from the 10 per cent of spending units with the highest incomes. Furthermore, the lowest 70 per cent of income receivers as a group went into debt as fast as their financial assets increased.[5]

A survey conducted in early 1963 reveals much information on the ownership of assets and, by implication, patterns of saving. Some of the results are summarized in Table 11-6.

Table 11-6   Income, net worth, and ownership of selected assets, 1962

| | | Per cent of income class owning assets | | | |
Income class	Per cent of families in income class	Liquid assets	Life insurance & pension rights	Stocks & other investment assets	Average net worth*
$0–4,999	48	63	40	17	$ 9,700
$5,000–$9,999	37	90	71	32	17,600
$10,000–$24,999	14	96	82	56	39,800
$25,000+	1	99	85	90	584,000
All	100	78	58	29	$ 22,600

* Net worth includes ownership of houses, automobiles, and unincorporated business as well as financial assets; debts are deducted.
Source: Calculated from data in *Federal Reserve Bulletin*, March, 1964, pp. 289–293.

Liquid assets and insurance and pension saving are widespread, but both increase substantially as income rises. Ownership of stocks and other investment assets is limited to 29 per cent of the population, with a sharp increase evident as income rises. The figures for average amounts held show even sharper increases as one moves up the income scale. Some idea of the rise is indicated by the average net worth (assets minus debts) of families in each income category.

[4] George Katona, "Attitudes toward Saving and Borrowing," *Consumer Instalment Credit*, part II, vol. I, Board of Governors, Federal Reserve System, 1957, p. 471.

[5] *Federal Reserve Bulletin*, September, 1951, p. 1063. Saving excludes currency and consumer durables.

Clearly, people with high incomes provide most of the net financial saving in the economy. They save large portions of their incomes, are interested in accumulating or preserving an estate, and derive substantial income from investments. Although they acquire large amounts of insurance and liquid assets, they put a relatively large proportion of their savings into business and investment assets which have substantial income or profit prospects but low liquidity. These people hold large amounts of financial wealth. A considerable part of it is in the form of personal trust funds, and much more of it is managed by professional investment counsel.

The bulk of the population does no appreciable net financial saving. They accumulate financial assets and debt at about the same rate. Their *real* wealth rises through increased ownership of housing and durable goods. For these persons, safety and fixity of principal, liquidity, and protection against risk are the chief objectives sought in financial assets. Thus their saving consists of acquiring liquid assets and life insurance. Most of them do not buy stocks, because they fear risks or merely because they are ignorant of opportunity and procedures. Many of these people prefer arrangements which force them to save—insurance premiums, installment payments, or similar contractual obligations.

Saving and Economic Welfare Aggregate saving may be evaluated in terms of its relation to the flow of spending and the volume of capital formation. In an economy plagued by deficient expenditure, a high level of financial saving may be harmfully deflationary; but the modern world tends more toward the dangers of inflation, under which circumstances financial saving furnishes a beneficial restraint. With the economy relatively near full employment, resources can be devoted to capital formation (ignoring government action) only if saving occurs, so that consumption is held below income.

What about the effect on the individual? Is saving good for him? Most of the motives for saving seem desirable—particularly, protecting against risks and providing funds for retirement and for children's education.

If anything, personal saving is likely to be too small. The psychological ability to save, particularly in financial assets, requires a long-range time horizon in which distant expenditure needs, known or unknown, are given emphasis. Most people find it difficult to keep these ends constantly in view; yet most of them also recognize their importance, in wiser moments. One consequence of this recognition is the popularity of arrangements whereby people force themselves to save by incurring binding commitments for insurance and pension programs, United States savings bonds, or Christmas club savings plans.

There may also be implications for economic welfare in the composition of personal saving. For instance, most personal saving flows through financial intermediaries rather than directly to the ultimate spenders. These intermediaries stress debt investments rather than equities and go heavily into low-risk assets. Their investments may tend to be concentrated rather arbitrarily in individual sectors of the economy (e.g., home mortgages) rather than spread where the needs are greatest. We shall examine this problem later.

Borrowing More than half of consumers' acquisition of financial assets in 1959–1963 was offset by borrowing. Most household borrowing is linked to acquisition of durable goods. About three-fourths of installment credit consists of IOUs originating in purchase of automobiles, other consumer durables, or household repair and modernization loans. In the late 1950s, credit furnished about three-fourths of the funds spent for new houses and about two-fifths of those spent for consumer durables.[6] Borrowing associated with the acquisition of durable goods does not reduce the household's net worth. It is also appropriate to note that consumers rely increasingly on credit to finance expenditures for medical care and higher education, both of which may represent not merely consumption but also "investment in human capital" of a sort which will ultimately yield higher incomes and higher productivity.

Borrowing by households is particularly large in the middle-income range. Poor people cannot obtain much credit, whether they want it or not. Rich people don't need it. Thus in the years around 1960 about 60 per cent of the spending units in the income range $5,000 to $10,000 owed install-ment debt, whereas the percentage was less than 50 at both higher and lower incomes.[7]

Mortgage loans are the largest items of household indebtedness. These loans often run for twenty years or more and are usually repaid in monthly installments. Home mortgages are well regarded by financial institutions, which made loan funds available at interest rates that averaged 6 to 7 per cent in the early 1960s.

The other principal household indebtedness consisted of consumer credit. This may come in the form of actual loans of cash or merely arrange-ments with a seller of goods to delay payment. Among the latter arrange-ments are charge accounts and service credit, which are short-term and bear no interest. These accounted for about 15 per cent of consumer credit outstanding in 1963. Other consumer credit commonly involves a charge for interest and may run for two or three years.

Borrowing and Consumer Welfare The use of credit may entail several disadvantages for the consumer:

1. Easy credit may lead people to spend too much altogether and to get excessively into debt. Some disturbing aggregate trends were evident in the

---

[6] Author's estimates, derived from data in *Federal Reserve Bulletin*, July, 1958, p. 77; *Consumer Instalment Credit*, vol. II, p. 193.

[7] Survey Research Center, University of Michigan, *Survey of Consumer Fi-nances*, 1960, p. 157; 1961, p. 45.

early 1960s. Home mortgage and consumer debt increased from about half of personal disposable income in 1958 to 62 per cent in 1963. An increasing number of home owners were obtaining mortgage loans on existing homes to finance other purchases. Mortgage lenders expressed concern over deteriorating loan quality, as indicated by such measures as the ratio of loan to value of property and the length of loan. The rate of foreclosure on mortgaged homes rose steadily from below 2 per thousand in the early 1950s to 4.4 per thousand in 1963. Personal bankruptcies, which numbered 34,000 in 1953, reached 139,000 in 1963. One sensationalized "exposé" commented on the apparent involvement of millions of Americans in the "on-the-cuff mania, the go-now, buy-now, live-now, pay-later craze," and solemnly observed that "the average American family is only three months away from financial failure." [8]

Such reporting greatly exaggerated the magnitude of the problem. The personal bankruptcies and mortgage foreclosures still represented only a tiny fraction of the millions of families relying on credit. Data on the proportion of consumer loans in default showed no upward trend and averaged less than 2 per cent. And survey data on the proportion of families with installment debt showed no increase over the period 1957–1961.[9]

2. Buying goods on credit may lead the buyer to pay too much for the product itself. Credit buyers may be more concerned with down payment and monthly payment requirements for an automobile or other durable good and pay little attention to the aggregate price.

3. Consumer credit is expensive in itself. Interest or "carrying" charges on personal loans may easily amount to the equivalent of an annual charge of 25 per cent or more. Calculating interest charges is complicated, and most installment borrowers probably do not bother.

As an example, a local loan company recently advertised that it would lend $500 repayable in 6 monthly installments of $90 each—a total of $540 to repay. This appears to represent a charge of 8 per cent—$40 interest on a $500 loan. Actually, the charge is much higher, since the average amount of money the borrower has to use is less than $500, and he has it less than a year. Since part of the principal is repaid each month, the actual average amount borrowed is only about $292; and since he has that for only 6 months, the annual equivalent is only about $146. Paying $40 interest for a loan of $146 represents a charge of about 27 per cent.

Such high rates may represent profiteering at the expense of gullible consumers, but many lending institutions find it necessary to charge such rates to cover the high costs and risks involved. Defenders of consumer

---

[8] Hillel Black, *Buy Now, Pay Later*, William Morrow and Company, Inc., New York, 1961, pp. 6–7. See also "Making Bankruptcy Pay," *Time*, Feb. 22, 1963; *Wall Street Journal*, Mar. 31, May 14, and June 17, 1964.

[9] *Survey of Consumer Finances*, 1960, p. 155; 1962, p. 71.

credit also point out that, while the nominal percentage rates may be high, the actual dollar costs frequently are not, and that consumers do obtain a service they desire. However, if consumers knew how high the interest rates are, they might be more willing either to save in advance or try to obtain bank loans, which are commonly much cheaper.[10]

In defense of consumer credit, however, there is no doubt that its availability has greatly helped to promote the acquisition of durable goods by consumers and to encourage their production by business. Whether or not consumers could finance such purchases by saving first and buying later, the fact is that many prefer not to do so. They find it easier to save when they have forced themselves to do so by assuming contractual repayment obligations. It is sound budgeting to pay for something as you use it, and this attitude is reinforced by the fact that so many families can look forward to rising incomes. For most people, access to credit is an advantage, not a detriment.

Reasons of this sort led the late Prof. Sumner Slichter to make this striking statement to a congressional committee in 1959:

> I am a great believer in people going into debt, particularly young people. Debt is a stabilizing influence. It is a very useful device for encouraging people to save regularly. The enormous debts that people have incurred in this country since the end of the Second World War on houses have certainly tended to make better citizens of them and help them get ahead faster in the world because they have had to begin paying off these mortgages right off. Going into debt has encouraged regular monthly, quarterly savings. . . .
>
> Every young man as soon as he can afford it should go into debt. He should be careful to acquire good assets when he goes into debt, but he will get ahead on his job faster, he will be a more valuable employee, and he will save regularly, and at the end of 5 years, or 10 years, he will own more property than he would have owned if he had never gone into debt in the first place.[11]

Serious problems remain in connection with the credit needs of low-income families. Some are led by unwise budgeting into credit expenditures

---

[10] Vance Packard reports, however, that many consumers are reluctant to borrow from banks. "The loan company's big advantage over the bank is its lower moral tone! The bank's big handicap . . . is its stern image as a symbol of unemotional morality. When we go to the banker for a loan . . . we are asking this personification of virtue to condescend to take a chance on us frail humans. In contrast, when we go to a loan company for a loan, it is we who are the virtuous ones and the loan company is the villain we are temporarily forced to consort with." *The Hidden Persuaders*, David McKay Company, Inc., New York, 1957, pp. 66–67.

[11] *Employment, Growth, and Price Levels, Hearings before the Joint Economic Committee*, U.S. Congress, 1959, p. 41.

they cannot manage. An even more serious tendency is that in times of financial emergency they often cannot or will not obtain credit through normal channels but turn to loan sharks and other illegal lenders. Paradoxically, past attempts to control "usury" often made it worse. Many states adopted maximum legal interest charges so low that respectable banks or other firms could not make personal loans on a paying basis. Consequently, illegal lending flourished. In recognition of this, many states subsequently adopted special small-loan legislation permitting higher interest charges on personal loans. Nevertheless, loan sharks still prey on poor and ignorant people in many areas of the country, frequently operating in league with criminal organizations and relying on intimidation and force to enforce their demands. Loan-shark extortion was revealed as a common manner in which organized crime preyed on the New York longshoremen. A recent study showed extensive loan-shark exploitation of Negroes and poor whites in Mississippi, where the legal maximum interest rate was 8 per cent.[12] More effective law enforcement would reduce the problem, but a more fundamental approach is to reduce the poverty and ignorance on which it feeds. The growth in the number of credit unions has increased opportunities for many to obtain credit where they work or through a union or fraternal organization.

GOVERNMENT

Government activities have contributed importantly to the growth of national wealth and productivity. Perhaps the greatest contribution has come through our vast system of public education, which accounted for more than $20 billion in annual outlay in the early 1960s and employed more government personnel than any other public activity except defense. Here, however, we shall limit our attention to government's proportion of tangible national wealth. Goldsmith estimates that government units held about $260 billion of tangible assets in 1958, of which $175 billion represented buildings and $40 billion land. Such government structures as highways, schools, water supply and sewage disposal facilities, and hospitals make a contribution to the productivity of our economy just as private capital assets do.

State and local government construction expenditures are financed in part by borrowing and are the chief purpose for borrowing by such gov-

[12] *The Wall Street Journal*, Dec. 26, 1957, quoted at length from a study of the Mississippi Economic Council. One typical case involved a loan of $10 for five weeks, for which total repayments under the original loan totaled $17.50. The council estimated that such loan sharks were cheating about $20 million a year from their victims with interest rates of 300 per cent and more, even though usurious loans could not be collected through legal processes.

ernment units. By contrast, Federal construction expenditures receive no special treatment financially. Federal borrowing is done to support general budgetary deficits, which have commonly occurred either because of high defense expenditures or because of depression fiscal policies. Table 11-7 summarizes government construction spending, borrowing, and acquisition of financial assets in the period 1959–1963 inclusive.

Table 11-7 Government construction and borrowing, 1959–1963 inclusive (Billions of dollars)

	Federal	State & local	Total
Construction spending (including land)	$19	$75	$94
Gross external finance:			
Borrowing	29	27	56
Increase in social insurance reserves	5	12	17
Total	$34	$39	$73
(—) Acquisition of financial assets	19	22	40
(=) Net external finance	$15	$17	$33
(+) Internal finance	4	58	62
Total finance	$19	$75	$94

Source: Federal Reserve Bulletin, April, 1964, p. 514. Details may not add up to totals because of rounding.

Who Finances Whom? Our examination of households, business, and government has indicated that each sector added substantially to its indebtedness and also to its holdings of financial assets during the period 1959–1963. The financial assets most commonly acquired represented claims against financial intermediaries, and people's willingness to hold such claims provided the opportunity for intermediaries to expand their assets. In doing so, intermediaries provided directly or indirectly most of the external financing demanded by the nonfinancial sectors of the economy. Table 11-8 indicates the role of principal types of financial intermediaries in financing various types of liabilities in the period 1959–1963.

Funds obtained externally by all sectors came to about $280 billion, while the acquisitions by financial intermediaries totaled about $214 billion, or about three-fourths of the total financing. The share of intermediaries was high for each type of liability except United States securities, for which intermediaries were net sellers. By coincidence, financial institutions bought just about as much corporate stock as was issued. Their purchases included issues already on the market, however, and the figures should not be interpreted to imply that all the new stocks issued were bought by financial institutions. The figure on consumer credit requires comment also. It includes the resale of consumers' IOUs to financial institutions by automobile dealers and other sellers of goods.

Table 11-8 also throws light on the relative importance of different types of financial intermediaries in the saving-borrowing relation. Commercial

Table 11-8   Financial intermediaries and external finance, 1959–1963 inclusive
(Billions of dollars)

Institution	U.S. securities	State & local govt. securities	Corporate & foreign bonds	Corporate stock	Mortgages	Consumer credit	Other loans*	Total	%
Funds supplied by purchase of specified assets									
Commercial banks	−3	13	†	—	17	11	33	71	33
Savings institutions‡	2	†	†	†	59	4	2	66	31
Life insurance	−1	1	11	2	13	—	3	29	13
Corporate pension funds	1	—	6	10	—	—	—	17	8
Other financial§	2	5	2	5	4	6	7	32	15
Total financial	−1	20	19	17	92	21	45	214	100
Funds raised by issuing specified liabilities									
Government	27	25	—	—	—	—	2	54	
Nonfinancial business	—	—	19	7	37	—	30	93	
Households	—	—	—	—	68	25	6	99	
Financial business	—	—	6	9	—	—	7	22	
Foreign	—	—	3	1	—	—	7	11	
Total	27	25	28	17	105	25	52	280	
Percentage from financial institutions	Neg.	79%	67%	99%	88%	83%	87%	76%	

* Excludes trade credit; thus total external finance by business differs from Table 11-4.
† Less than $0.5 billion.
‡ Savings and loan associations, mutual savings banks, credit unions.
§ Investment companies, nonlife insurance, brokers, etc.
Sources: Federal Reserve Bulletin, April 1964, and Board of Governors, Federal Reserve System, *Flow of Funds Accounts, 1945–1962,* Washington, 1963. Details may not add up to totals because of rounding.

banks played the largest role, accounting for about one-third of the institutional acquisition of specified assets. Savings institutions—chiefly savings and loan associations and mutual savings banks—accounted for nearly another third. Life insurance companies and corporate pension funds also contributed sizable amounts.

Table 11-8 shows only net changes in asset and liability positions by sectors of the country. This is the most significant single measure of financial activity, but it requires qualification in several ways. First, there is considerable open-market activity in most types of financial claims against nonfinancial business—government securities, mortgages, private stocks and bonds, and commercial paper. Through such activity, financial firms may acquire assets without furnishing funds for current spending. Thus some sectors bought and others sold United States securities. Such trading increases mobility of funds among various sectors of the economy.

Second, by using net sector accounts for the standard, we discount a large part of the financial flow going from the repayment of past borrowing into new lending. For instance, leaving out of account funds repaid in the same year by the borrower, we can estimate that household net borrowing of about $100 billion actually represented gross borrowing of about $380 billion offset by repayment of $280 billion.

Considerations of this sort remind us that financial intermediaries spend a good bit of effort rearranging the composition of their assets. In the process, they are continually redirecting a very large flow of funds coming through gross financial saving. It is through this process, for instance, that business depreciation funds find their way into investment—often by a different firm. This would be an important operation even if financial firms experienced no net increase in their assets from year to year.

SUMMARY AND GENERAL OBSERVATIONS

This chapter has provided a survey of the functions of financial institutions in relation to such magnitudes as debt, tangible wealth and capital goods, and financial assets. Historically the process of economic growth in the United States has been greatly aided by the accumulation of real wealth for both production and consumption and by the increased supply of money and liquid financial assets. Increases in net public and private debt have been involved in the process in three important ways. In the short run, changes in debt are associated with variations in the rate of increase of the expenditure flow. In the long run, increases in the debt of nonfinancial sectors have helped finance the growth in capital goods held by business and government as well as the increase in consumer assets such as houses and automobiles. Finally, increased debt of the nonfinancial sectors has furnished the earning assets held by financial institutions, which in turn issue the kinds of financial claims which the nonfinancial sectors prefer to hold.

Although debt is widely used, there remains a certain residual of Puritan distrust for it, a tendency to refer back longingly to the maxims of Polonius, Poor Richard, and Mr. Micawber. In evaluating debt, it is appropriate to treat it as one of many modern institutions which increase the freedom and opportunity available to people, but also their responsibilities.

No doubt it is conceivable that debt could become "too large" in some sense, relative to people's income and wealth. In assessing the likelihood that vast numbers will be led into distress, however, one should remember that the growth of debt depends on lenders as well as borrowers. Lender reluctance provides a built-in brake which is likely to operate on the side of prudence. The rising trend of private debt to income might cause trouble in another direction, however. It might make difficult the further increases in the total size of debt needed to fuel a rising trend of GNP expenditures. At the individual level, the morality of debt surely depends on what use people make of it. The opportunity to borrow enhances the opportunity to do foolish things, but also the chance to do wise ones. If anything, the safeguards and controls built into the borrowing process lead one to suspect that on balance people spend borrowed money more wisely than they do their own.

At the aggregative level, extensive debt is subject to one principal danger—the threat of deflation. If incomes and prices decline, the burden of debt in real terms increases, and obligations undertaken in good faith may become too onerous to fulfill. A debt crisis was an important welfare problem during the downswing of 1929–1933. Such a downswing is undesirable for many other reasons, however, and there seems relatively little likelihood of a repeat performance. Certainly the economic trends in the United States since World War II have not produced any indication of a debt crisis.

Financial institutions provide most of the funds borrowed by the non-financial sectors, with commercial banks, savings institutions, life insurance companies, and corporate pension funds dominating the totals. In turn these institutions provide the public with cash, liquid assets, and other specialized financial claims which provide safety and protection. Thus financial institutions reconcile the desire of the public to hold its assets in safe and liquid form with the fact that nonfinancial borrowers are generally unable or unwilling to issue such claims against themselves. Through the activity of financial institutions, the total volume of saving and investment is probably enhanced, and the welfare of savers is increased by furnishing the types of assets particularly suited to their needs.

In the two chapters following, we shall examine more closely the structure and functioning of major types of financial institutions and the role of government in their operations.

QUESTIONS FOR STUDY

1. "Most households are not net financial savers, but they are net *real* savers." Explain.

2. "By 1963 the American people, business, and government owed more than $1,000 billion in debts. Yet the total money supply was only about $150 billion. Clearly there is not enough money to pay all the debts. The country must be bankrupt." Comment.

3. A prospective automobile purchaser obtains a loan from his bank. He signs a note for $1,200 to be repaid in twelve monthly installments of $100 each. The bank charges him 6 per cent interest on the total (i.e., $72) and deducts it in advance, giving him $1,128 in cash. Estimate the actual annual interest rate involved.

4. It is frequently claimed that present tax laws and the inflationary tendency in the economy encourage businesses to issue bonds rather than stock and encourage investors to buy stock rather than bonds. Why is this? What consequences would you expect for stock and bond prices and yields?

5. "Contrary to the traditional view that debt is a burden, most people nowadays use debt as a way of becoming wealthier." Explain.

SUGGESTED READINGS

Board of Governors, Federal Reserve System: *Consumer Instalment Credit*, Washington, 1957.

————: *Flow of Funds Accounts, 1945–1962*, Washington, 1963.

Denison, Edward: *The Sources of Economic Growth in the United States*, Committee for Economic Development, New York, 1962.

Goldsmith, Raymond: *Financial Intermediaries in the American Economy since 1900*, Princeton University Press for National Bureau of Economic Research, Princeton, N.J., 1958.

————: *The National Wealth of the United States in the Postwar Period*, Princeton University Press for National Bureau of Economic Research, Princeton, N.J., 1962.

Kuznets, Simon: *Capital in the American Economy: Its Formation and Financing*, Princeton University Press for National Bureau of Economic Research, Princeton, N.J., 1961.

chapter twelve

THE COMMERCIAL
BANKING SYSTEM:
FUNCTIONS AND STRUCTURE

WHAT BANKS DO

Commercial banks have often been called "department stores of finance" because of the variety of functions which they perform. Among the principal functions may be listed the following:

1. Banks create and manage checking deposits; indeed, we identify commercial banks as those institutions which provide checking-deposit services.

2. Commercial banks also provide facilities for time and saving deposits, on which depositors receive interest.

3. Commercial banks extend credit to a great variety of borrowers through making loans and purchasing securities.

4. Banks provide their business customers with a variety of other services, including financial advice, credit information about customers, and assistance in collecting debts.

5. Banks provide a variety of trust services, which fall into three main categories. *Corporate trust services* arise in connection with issues of bonds. Bond issues ordinarily require the appointment of a trustee, who is responsible for ensuring that the obligations are fulfilled. Banks also hold

large amounts of *personal trust funds*, under which they manage property on behalf of individual beneficiaries, often in connection with the estates left by deceased persons. Third, banks are among the principal administrators of *corporate pension funds*, under which individual firms provide for retirement benefits to their employees. Trust assets are not included in the assets of the commercial banks themselves. Assets of bank-administered pension and personal trust funds were estimated at $144 billion at the end of 1963.[1]

The essence of commercial bank operations is the extension of credit through the creation of money. The ability to create spendable purchasing power in the form of checking deposits is the attribute by which we define commercial banks and one which gives them a unique quality among financial institutions. Because their liabilities are used as money, commercial banks have long been recognized as institutions "affected with a public interest" and therefore subject to special regulation and control.

Banks derive the bulk of their revenues from their operations as credit institutions—from their loans and securities. Commercial banks are the largest single source of credit, and the most diversified. Nevertheless, their credit function is similar in kind to the operations of other financial institutions.

The ability of the commercial banks to extend credit is determined by the willingness of the public to hold deposits with them. Willingness to hold checking deposits is determined in part by their apparent safety and security, but is also determined by the desire for the services which a checking account can provide. By using checks for payment in preference to currency, the depositor can reduce risks of loss or theft and can gain greatly in convenience, efficiency, and control and supervision of transactions, particularly those involved in business operations.

However, checking-account services are costly to administer. Nearly half of commercial bank employees and expenses are involved in processing checks and deposits. And while most banks assess service charges for checking accounts, these charges for the banking system as a whole cover at most about one-third of the total expenses of bank monetary operations.

Consequently, commercial bank credit activities are vitally important to the banks themselves as the source of revenue to pay expenses of deposit management. And they are of major importance to the economy as a whole as a part of the flow of loan funds to borrowers in all sectors. Nevertheless, banks' credit operations are in many respects conditioned, regulated, and

[1] Stanley Silverberg, "Bank Trust Investments: Their Size and Significance," *National Banking Review*, June, 1964, p. 585. Banks may exercise trust functions only when authorized individually by regulatory authorities. Only about one-third of commercial banks carry on trust operations. In addition, there are a few specialist trust companies which do not perform banking functions.

determined by their unique status as creators and managers of checkbook money. In this chapter, we shall deal with commercial banks as participants in the financial process, linking saving and investment. After an examination of their functions, we shall take up some current issues related to banking structure—matters relating to the numbers and sizes of banks and to their freedom and supervision.

BANK LOANS AND SECURITIES

The diversity of commercial bank activity is readily apparent in the composition of bank assets. Banks provide substantial amounts of credit to all major sectors of the economy; they acquire a wide variety of types of debt instruments, and their assets run the gamut of maturities from the shortest-dated Treasury bills to bonds with many years to run. Table 12-1 provides information on the composition of loans and securities at the end of 1962. All told, commercial banks held about $220 billion of debt claims against the nonfinancial sectors of the economy—consumers, business, and government. This represented about one-fourth of the total indebtedness of those sectors, a fraction which was approximated for most of the sectors individually as well. Commercial banks participate with many other lenders in the ownership of government securities and in home mortgage and consumer lending. However, commercial bank lending to business firms is sufficiently different from what other financial institutions do to warrant separate discussion.

Bank Lending to Business   Credit from commercial banks ranks with trade credit as one of the most widely used sources of funds for business. Extensive information on the distribution of bank credit is available from Federal Reserve loan surveys. Table 12-2 summarizes data for member banks from a survey of loans outstanding on October 16, 1957.

The number of loans is very large—about 1.3 million in 1957. To be sure, this total includes some duplications, since firms may borrow from more than one bank. However, these figures do not cover nonmember banks. After rough allowance for exclusion, we can estimate that the number of business borrowers is in the neighborhood of 1.5 million, which can be compared with a total business population of slightly over 4 million firms.

Large *numbers* of loans went to industry sectors where one finds large numbers of small firms. Retailing accounted for nearly 400,000 member bank loans, followed by services, construction, and wholesale trade, each exceeding 100,000.[2] However, these sectors received less impressive shares in the dollar

---

[2] The number of bank borrowers would be extended impressively if we extended the estimates to agriculture. Surveys for 1960 covering all banks indicated that farm borrowers numbered about 900,000. *Federal Reserve Bulletin,* December, 1962, p. 1574, and September, 1963, p. 1226.

Table 12-1   Commercial bank loans and securities, December 28, 1962
(Billions of dollars)

Type	Amount	U.S. gov't	State & local gov't	Con- sumers	Agri- culture	Financial business	Other business
Real estate loans:				$22	$2		$10
Residential mort- gages							
Insured	$ 9						
Conventional	14						
Nonresidential	11						
Business and related loans:							
Commercial & industrial	49						49
Farm	7				7		
Loans to banks	3					$ 3	
To other financial institutions	9					9	
To securities bro- kers & dealers	5					5	
Other securities loans	2			2			
Personal loans:				31			
Auto installment	11						
Other retail ins.	3						
Residential repair & modernization	3						
Other personal	14						
Other loans	4	(sector distribution not available)					
Securities	95	$69	$25				1
Total	$238	$69	$25	$55	$9	$17	$60

Sources: Federal Deposit Insurance Corporation, *Annual Report for 1962;* Board of Governors, Federal Reserve System, *Flow of Funds Accounts, 1945–1962.* Figures are rounded and may not add up to totals shown.

volume of lending. Manufacturing and mining, characterized by smaller numbers of large firms, received about 40 per cent of the loans, although accounting for only one-sixth of the firms.

Table 12-3 shows how the loans were distributed among borrowers of differing asset sizes.

By number, about three-fourths of all loans went to firms with assets of less than $250,000 each. However, because the loans were relatively small, these borrowers received only about one-sixth of the dollar volume of loans —less than the relatively small number of borrowers in the largest size category.

Table 12-2   Business loans of member banks, October 16, 1957

Industry	Number	Amount (billions)
Manufacturing and mining:		
Food, liquor, tobacco	30,000	$ 2.4
Textiles, apparel, leather	25,000	1.7
Metals, metal products	59,000	5.5
Petroleum, coal, chemicals, rubber	30,000	3.8
Other	68,000	2.8
Trade:		
Retail	396,000	4.6
Wholesale	101,000	3.0
Commodity dealers	10,000	0.8
Other:		
Sales finance companies	12,000	3.1
Transportation, communication, public utility	49,000	4.2
Construction	108,000	2.0
Real estate	82,000	3.0
Services	230,000	2.3
Other	83,000	1.6
Total	1,281,000	$40.6

Source: Board of Governors, Federal Reserve System, processed release, March 25, 1959. Number of loans is rounded to nearest thousand. The data do not cover mortgage loans.

Bank loans bulk larger relative to borrower assets for small and middle-sized firms than for large firms. Estimates for 1955 indicate that bank loans to firms with assets of less than $25 million averaged about 8 per cent of the assets of such firms, but constituted less than 3 per cent of the assets of

Table 12-3   Member bank loans and size of borrower, 1957

Assets of borrower	Number	Amount (billions)
0–$50,000	505,000	$ 1.5
$50,000–$250,000	494,000	5.3
$250,000–$1 million	158,000	6.3
$1–$5 million	48,000	6.8
$5–$25 million	13,000	5.9
$25–$100 million	5,000	4.9
$100 million+	7,000	8.8
Unknown	51,000	1.2
Total	1,281,000	$40.6

Source: Federal Reserve Bulletin, April, 1958, p. 396.

firms over $25 million. For the majority of firms using bank credit, such credit ranges from 6 to 12 per cent of total assets.[3]

Duration and Purpose of Loans Traditionally, the major function of bank loans has been to finance working capital in such forms as inventories and accounts receivable, and these uses still predominate.[4] In particular, firms in sectors subject to seasonal variations in activity rely on bank loans to carry them through peak periods. In the survey for 1957, about 62 per cent of the dollar volume of member bank business loans had original maturities of one year or less. Because they have a greater proportion of working capital to total assets, bank borrowers in wholesale and retail trade use substantially more bank credit relative to total assets than do borrowers in manufacturing industries.[5]

Despite the predominance of short-term financing, one should not ignore the substantial amount of longer-term bank credit to business and farming which tends to be more closely associated with financing of investment in durable capital assets. The 1957 survey indicated that about $15 billion of bank loans to business were "term loans" of more than one year original maturity, and half of this sum consisted of loans with more than five years original maturity. Term loans, which are usually amortized by installments, tend to be fairly large and go heavily into industries such as metals, petroleum, chemicals, rubber, transportation, and public utilities, where fixed capital is extensively used. They represent one of the few financial means available for financing fixed capital by small firms.

In addition to term loans, banks also make mortgage loans to business firms and farms which may run for long terms. In 1957 these added another $7 billion to the amount of relatively long-term loans held by banks.

Lending decisions by commercial banks can clearly have a substantial influence on the flow of investment funds. Bank lending affects the distribution of capital among industries and among firms within industries. Bank loan decisions may also influence the ability of firms to acquire one type of capital asset compared with another—plant and equipment versus working capital. It is in the public interest that capital flow where its productivity is highest, that freedom and opportunity to invest are available to all honest and competent firms, and that competition prevail in business markets generally.

The banks' credit decisions are made, however, on the basis of their own goals of solvency, liquidity, and profitability, within a framework of

[3] Paul B. Trescott, "Who Gets Bank Loans," *Bankers Magazine*, Spring, 1964, pp. 11–13.

[4] See Jacob Cohen, "What Do Bank Loans Really Finance?" in Deane Carson (ed.), *Banking and Monetary Studies*, Richard D. Irwin, Inc., Homewood, Ill., 1963.

[5] Trescott, *op. cit.*, p. 14.

regulation and supervision. Before we can analyze bank decisions regarding asset acquisitions, we must deal more fully with the framework of government controls under which they operate.

GOVERNMENT REGULATION OF BANKING

Objectives   Recognition that bank liabilities should be considered part of the money supply came early in American banking history. Such recognition brought continued efforts by Federal and state governments to control bank operations on the quality or quantity of the money supply. Quantitative aspects of the problem are now dealt with by the Federal Reserve System in the manner analyzed in Part Two. Safeguarding the quality of money created by banks can be discussed in terms of three overlapping objectives, as follows:

1. *Liquidity.* Individual banks must be able to pay out currency on demand to depositors and, in order that check payments can be widely used, must be able to meet drains of funds when checks are deposited with other banks.

2. *Solvency.* The outright failure of a bank obviously undermines the acceptability of its liabilities as part of the money supply. Furthermore, when bank failures are frequent, the general willingness of the public to hold bank deposits is reduced.

3. *Honesty and fair dealing.* The ability to create money can give rise to opportunities for unfair advantage or shady practice by insiders. This may merely mean that some borrowers gain an edge over others, but it may also inflict losses on depositors.

Because of the limit on deposit insurance coverage, large depositors must concern themselves with the solvency and liquidity of their banks. Thus bank management must treat these as elements in the competition for deposits.

Sound Money versus Easy Credit   It has long been recognized that one way to ensure that these goals will be achieved is to require that banks maintain cash reserves equal to their deposit liabilities. This would, of course, eliminate deposit creation as a source of loan funds.

This view still has its adherents, but it conflicts directly with another objective, that of easy credit. Cheapness and abundance of credit is a private goal among business firms and other borrowers; it is also a respectable social goal because easy credit can mean more investment and a more rapid rate of economic growth.

The desire for more credit led Americans to tolerate fractional reserve banking, despite the disadvantages it entailed for monetary soundness. Bank liquidity diminished as deposit liabilities increased in relation to cash reserves. Banking theory and policy struggled to reconcile the desire for easy credit with the desire for sound money.

Commercial-loan Theory An ancient but durable tradition is that fractional reserve banking can be reconciled with soundness in the quantity and quality of money if banks make only short-term business loans, particularly "self-liquidating" loans to finance the marketing of goods already produced. Such loans would be relatively liquid, for a bank in need of cash could rely on funds flowing in through loan repayment. Loans secured by goods in transit or in inventory would normally involve very little risk; thus bank solvency would be safeguarded.

For any single bank considered separately, these contentions were certainly valid. However, the commercial-loan principle would not actually provide liquidity if the banking system as a whole were confronted with a sudden demand for cash. As we noted in Chapter 3, bank loans will tend to be repaid chiefly in checks on demand deposits, rather than in currency. It may require a multiple contraction of loans and a massive reduction in the total money supply to induce any net flow of currency into the banks.

Furthermore, a large-scale reduction of bank loans, whatever it might do for bank liquidity, would be disastrous for the liquidity of the economy as a whole. The banks' efforts to contract would set off a paradoxical result: Reducing the quantity of money and the flow of spending would reduce the ability of debtors to pay off their loans and possibly undermine their solvency and that of their creditor banks. The dangerous fallacy of composition involved in "self-liquidating" loans was demonstrated periodically in American financial panics.

Defenders of the commercial-loan principle sometimes contended that it would provide an optimum basis for determining the quantity of money.[6] The volume of lending would be linked to the volume of goods produced. Thus increases in M could occur only (in the usage of the Fisher equation) in reflection of increases in O; consequently P would not be affected. Thus stated, the contention is obviously fallacious. Loans are made on the value of inventories, not their physical quantity. Indeed, adherence to the commercial-loan principle could be quite dangerous, for it would give justification to increases in the money supply whenever the price level was rising.

The commercial-loan theory of bank credit exerted a strong influence on the Federal Reserve Act of 1913 and on Federal Reserve policy during the first twenty years of the system. The results were disastrous. We shall describe them fully in Chapter 16.

Whatever its theoretical merits as a standard for individual banks, the commercial-loan principle has been honored more in the breach than in the

[6] For an ingenious early defense, see Adam Smith, *The Wealth of Nations* [1776], Modern Library, Inc., New York, 1937, p. 288.

observance in American banking history. The most urgent demands for credit—and thus the most profitable outlets for bank funds—arose in connection with investments in fixed capital. Consequently, banks were drawn into making long-term loans of a relatively risky nature, with consequent problems for their solvency and liquidity.

Requirements for Capital and Reserve   During the nineteenth century, regulatory policies attempted to meet these problems by imposing high requirements for bank capital relative to total liabilities. The larger a bank's capital account, the greater the amount by which its assets exceed its liabilities. If a bank maintains capital accounts equal to 20 per cent of its total assets, it can sustain a decline of 20 per cent in the value of those assets before depositors' claims are impaired.

High capital requirements were frequently imposed by state law in the nineteenth century. However, they did nothing for bank liquidity, and their contribution to bank solvency was often undermined by the willingness of banks to lend money to their stockholders with the stock as collateral—a practice now generally prohibited. High capital requirements were unpopular, moreover, because they conflicted with the community's desire for easier credit.

Currently, banks are not subject to a fixed minimum ratio of capital to total assets. Instead, they must usually maintain minimum absolute amounts of capital depending on the size of the community where they operate. In June, 1963, commercial bank capital accounts totaled about $25 billion, compared with total assets of $281 billion—a ratio of about 9 per cent. This amount did not represent a major protection for depositors.

Another approach to the same problem has been to prescribe minimum cash reserves which banks must maintain. Reserve requirements were adopted in the first national banking act (1863) chiefly as a protection for depositors. Again, the prevailing desire for abundant credit stood in the way of setting really high requirements. Furthermore, actual requirements tended to produce a strong contraction of loans whenever banks were pressed for cash payments. In any event, reserve requirements under the Federal Reserve System have long since ceased to serve chiefly as protection for depositors. They are now almost exclusively used as a technique for controlling the total volume of bank credit.

Modern Protection of Liquidity and Solvency   With the creation of the Federal Reserve System, American banking policy made a substantial shift in dealing with the problem of bank liquidity. Instead of trying to make the banks hold liquid assets, the new approach provided a source which was capable of creating additional liquidity—cash and reserve deposits—which commercial banks could obtain as needed. Today there is no danger that the banking system as a whole will suffer a liquidity crisis of the sort which periodically broke out prior to 1933. Of course, Federal Reserve credit is not available to individual banks without limit; thus each bank individually must avoid becoming unduly illiquid. But the penalty for a mistake is much less drastic than it was in the nineteenth century.

The years since 1914 have also witnessed an important shift in the style of bank lending for long-term purposes. This is the use of the installment loan, amortized by regular (usually monthly) payments. Such provisions are now commonly attached to mortgage loans, business term loans, and consumer loans. Regular amortization provides the banks with a regular inflow of funds and reduces risks.

The Depression of the 1930s brought a number of added developments which have reduced bank problems of solvency and liquidity. One is deposit insurance. Virtually all commercial banks are now members of the Federal Deposit Insurance Corporation, which insures each deposit up to $10,000. Insurance coverage has reduced the danger that the rank and file of depositors will be drawn into "a run on the bank" of the sort which often arose in the old-style panics. Another contribution is the development of Federal programs for insuring and guaranteeing loans, particularly home mortgage loans. Finally, the Depression led to very restrictive policies regarding the chartering of new banks, which helped to protect existing institutions from competitive pressure.

Regulation of Assets However important these developments have been, commercial banks remain subject to extensive and detailed regulation of their assets, designed to further the goals of solvency, liquidity, and honesty. Although details differ between national banks and state banks, the general principles are similar. Some of the major rules covering national banks are as follows:

1. A bank may not lend to any single borrower an amount exceeding 10 per cent of the bank's capital and surplus, except for certain types of loans. Since capital and surplus seldom exceed one-fifth of total assets, this restriction means that debts of one borrower are not likely to exceed more than 1 or 2 per cent of the bank's total assets.

2. Banks may not lend on their own stock as collateral.

3. A bank may not lend more than $2,500 to any of its officers.

4. A bank may not lend on mortgage more than an amount equal either to its capital and surplus or to 60 per cent of its time deposits, whichever is larger. No mortgage loans may exceed two-thirds of property value nor run for more than twenty years; however, these limits do not apply to mortgages with government insurance or guarantee.

5. A bank's ownership interest in, and loans to, subsidiaries or affiliates are limited to specified proportions of the bank's capital and surplus.

6. Loans for purchasing or carrying securities must conform to the margin requirements set by the Federal Reserve. At the end of 1964, margin

requirements for stock loans were 70 per cent; thus banks would be forbidden to lend more than 30 per cent of the market price of a stock at the time of its purchase.

7. Banks are forbidden to deal in stocks, real estate, and commodities except where such assets are acquired through foreclosure of a secured loan. However, banks are permitted to hold limited amounts of stock in their own subsidiaries and in special small-business investment corporations, of which we will speak later.

8. Banks are generally forbidden to engage in investment banking operations through which new security issues are marketed. However, the restriction does not apply to government securities, and commercial banks handle a large part of the marketing function for these.

9. Investments are limited by supervisory rulings to the highest-grade, low-risk items.

10. Supervisory practice limits loans (minus a few exceptions) to six times bank capital.[7]

Enforcing the Rules—Bank Examination   The authorities, national or state, from which a bank receives its charter generally require that each bank submit periodic reports of its condition and undergo detailed examination of its affairs on its own premises without advance notice at least once a year. Thus national banks are examined by the Comptroller of the Currency, and each state has its own banking commission or department. In addition, the Federal Reserve and the Federal Deposit Insurance Corporation maintain their own examination staffs. The various examining agencies cooperate and share examination reports, however, so that an individual bank is not ordinarily subject to examination by more than two authorities.

Bank examination is designed to check on compliance with the regulations concerning loans, reserves, and capital; to check on the accuracy of bank statements; to guard against possible dishonesty by bank employees; and to see that the bank is solvent and its assets sound. Bank examiners and regulatory authorities possess considerable discretion in evaluating the "soundness" of bank assets. Examiners concern themselves with the risk and maturity status of individual assets and of the bank's entire portfolio. The supervisory authorities may find fault with a bank's loan and investment policies and decisions, and with the adequacy of its capital. Such dissatisfaction may lead to informal suggestions for change of policy or to more formal demands backed by the authority's power to remove recalcitrant bank officers or close the bank. In practice, drastic measures are seldom necessary.

Although there is little dispute over the general principle of bank ex-

---

[7] See Thomas Gies, Thomas Mayer, and Edward Ettin, "Portfolio Regulations and Policies of Financial Intermediaries," Commission on Money and Credit, *Private Financial Institutions*, Prentice-Hall, Inc., Englewood Cliffs, N.J., 1963, pp. 163–169.

amination, questions have been raised about its application. Some critics find fault with the multiplicity of supervisory authorities with overlapping jurisdictions. A number of conflicts arose in the early 1960s among the Federal supervisory authorities as a result of some of the experiments and innovations attempted by Comptroller James Saxon.

Some critics also feel that bank examination tends unduly to enhance conservatism in bank asset holdings, to the detriment of risky loans. This is an aspect of a broader problem, which warrants separate attention.

Problem of Risky Loans For the protection of depositors, banking tradition and supervisory practice stress the avoidance of risk in bank loans and securities. There is a tendency, however, to try to minimize risk on individual items, rather than to consider each as an element in a diversified portfolio.

Conservative attitudes toward risk taking by bankers arise from factors other than a reluctance to defend their conduct to the bank examiners. First of all, bank capital accounts are thin in relation to total assets; thus a loan default which might appear small in relation to total assets could be large as a proportion of the capital accounts.

Furthermore, banks are subject to rather confining limits on the maximum interest rates they can charge. There are loopholes and special provisions, but for reasons of law and public opinion banks avoid charging high interest rates on business loans. This means they cannot adjust the interest charged on a loan to maintain proportionality with the risk. Instead, high-risk borrowers may be turned away.[8] One response to bank reluctance to make risky loans has been the development of "second-layer" intermediaries such as sales finance companies, who borrow from banks and relend to higher-risk borrowers at interest rates above bank levels.

One way of improving bank performance would be to relax regulations of bank assets. A study prepared for the Commission on Money and Credit made the following relevant observations:

> The state of portfolio regulation and policy today is largely the outcome of measures designed to prevent collapse in the face of economic distress. It

[8] "A questionnaire mailed to more than 15,000 commercial banks . . . in 1947 brought forth these significant findings: Of the nearly 8,000 banks which responded, half reported that they had refused to make some business loans which appeared to be sound credit risks. Several reasons were given, of which the most frequent were: the loan exceeded the bank's legal limit; the requested maturity was too long; the bank lacked experience with the requested type of loan, or the applicant was launching a new enterprise. Behind these reasons lay the restrictions on risk assumption imposed by banking laws and bank examining officers, and the need for liquidity imposed by the slender capital resources and the high ratio of demand deposits which characterize American banking." Raymond Saulnier, Harold Halcrow, and Neil Jacoby, *Federal Lending and Loan Insurance*, Princeton University Press for National Bureau of Economic Research, Inc., Princeton, N.J., 1958, p. 253.

is largely a defensive structure, and some of the measures appear needlessly restrictive in today's relatively stable and vigorous economy.

There has developed a fundamental conflict between a public policy framework best suited for promotion of economic expansion and a framework planned to assure survival during economic disaster. . . . The affirmative measures needed to assure adaptation of the capacities of banks to serve the expanding needs of a growing economy have received little attention.

The authors of this study recommend eliminating or relaxing the rules which limit the ratio of risk assets to capital, which limit the amount of real estate loans and their proportion to property value, which limit loans to one borrower to 10 per cent of bank capital and surplus, and which restrict investments to the lowest-risk grades. They urge a more favorable supervisory attitude toward risky loans, provided they are combined in a diversified portfolio, and suggest that relaxation of present maximum limits on loan interest charges may be needed so that allowance for higher risk can be made.[9]

"Portfolio Balance"—The Optimum Balance Sheet   In Part Two we noted that bank adjustments in assets and liabilities could be described as attempts to achieve some sort of equilibrium balance sheet best suited for the goals of liquidity, solvency, and long-run profitability (to which the other two are really subordinate). One element in achieving this optimum balance sheet has been the tendency to keep excess reserves close to the zero point. We can now make some observations about the adjustment within categories of earning assets. Clearly, the regulatory laws and the attitudes of bank examiners and supervisory agencies will be factors in the decision. Within the limits which these set, the following will be important elements in balance sheet adjustment:

1. The optimum combination of bank assets depends on the composition of bank liabilities among demand deposits, time deposits, and government deposits. Demand deposits are more volatile and thus entail greater need for liquidity in bank assets. Higher reserve requirements furnish some of this, but banks are likely to want more, in the form of deposits with other commercial banks and secondary reserve assets such as Treasury bills and commercial paper.

The lower turnover of time deposits entails a lower need for liquidity. Consequently, the larger the proportion of time deposits, the more banks tend to invest in longer-term, higher-yielding assets such as mortgages and state and local government securities. Furthermore, for national banks and many state banks, increased time deposits mean an increased amount which can legally be loaned on mortgage.

Aside from liquidity consideration, government deposits often carry

---

[9] Gies, Mayer, and Ettin, *op. cit.*, pp. 237, 255–257.

the provision that banks must hold government securities as security for the safety of those funds.

2. The optimum combination of bank assets depends on the size of bank capital accounts. Capital accounts figure prominently in the legal limitations on bank loans and security holdings. They limit credit which can be extended to any one borrower, as well as total bank mortgage lending and investment in bank subsidiaries.

Perhaps even more important, the size of bank capital accounts figures importantly in the attitudes of bank management and supervisory agencies toward risky loans and securities. The thinner the capital account relative to total assets, the less likely it is that the bank's funds will be directed into risky channels.

Neither of these first two considerations is beyond the control of a bank. It can influence the composition of its deposits by varying its service charges on demand deposits and the interest it pays on time deposits. However, individual banks have been inhibited by competitive pressures from doing much with service charges, while interest on time deposits is subject to maximum levels set by Federal Reserve and state banking authorities.

Banks can increase their capital accounts by selling additional stock and by plowing back current income. Since World War II, however, bank profits have not been high enough to permit much new capital to be raised through stock sales. Most capital increase has come through reinvestment of profits, which has absorbed more than half of bank profits in the postwar period. In each instance, capital growth is limited by current profit levels. Very probably, however, a higher proportional dividend payout would increase the attractiveness of new stock issues to investors.[10]

Commercial banks have been reluctant to rely much on the issue of formal debt securities as a source of funds. A few experiments with issue of medium-term interest-bearing debentures were under way in the early 1960s. Such security issues do not impose the liquidity burdens involved in deposit liabilities, and they offer a means of obtaining external funds more readily than through stock issue.

3. Banks must generally trade off liquidity and safety of earning assets against income. Competition among investors tends to keep yields low on safe and liquid earning assets, such as Treasury bills and commercial paper. To be sure, investment in long-term government bonds may provide higher income combined with certainty of income and capital value. However, bond investments sacrifice liquidity; a bank pressed for cash can indeed sell bonds but may sustain capital losses because their market prices have fallen.

[10] American Bankers Association, *The Commercial Banking Industry*, Prentice-Hall, Inc., Englewood Cliffs, N.J., 1962, pp. 326–327.

Because different assets have different advantages, the optimum portfolio is a diversified one. Some assets are selected because they are safe and liquid, others because their greater income yield compensates for the sacrifice of safety and liquidity. Diversity is also pursued in maturity and in number and types of borrowers.

4. The optimum combination of bank assets is heavily conditioned by the facts that banks can offer a variety of services to each individual customer and that many of these entail a continuing relationship over time.[11] This is especially true of bank lending to business. The business loan is ordinarily not a one-shot affair, but part of a continuing or repetitious process. Often a business firm enjoys a "line of credit" at its bank, giving the firm the privilege of borrowing up to some maximum amount at any time without special negotiation. Revenue to the bank comes from a credit relationship extending indefinitely into the future.

Furthermore, business firms are potential customers for other bank services. Banks lend to business firms in order to gain their deposit business, an objective often assured by requiring that each borrower keep on deposit a "compensating balance" equal to some proportion of his loan. Firms and their top management may also be potential customers for trust and other services.

Loans and investments which do not contribute to bank deposit or other business tend to appear less attractive to banks than their yield in isolation would suggest. Stress on deposit business arises because the individual bank's capacity to acquire assets is limited by its deposits. (In contrast, for the banking system as a whole it is the assets which determine the deposits.)

5. The optimum combination of assets is also conditioned by the fact that there may be efficiency gains through specialization. Different kinds of lending require different techniques of bank administration; each may require familiarity with a particular body of information concerning a particular industry. Individual banks may well choose to limit the scope of their operations in order to improve their efficiency and improve the service to the customers they do serve.

6. Many of the foregoing elements are analyzed by bank management and supervisory agencies in terms of certain balance sheet ratios. The ratio of loans to deposits is used as a measure of liquidity; the higher the ratio, the less liquid is the bank. Another is the ratio of risk assets (total assets less cash assets and United States government securities) to capital. Informal targets and limits on such ratios are more common than rigid and constant proportions.

[11] This point is effectively developed by Donald R. Hodgman in *Commercial Bank Loan and Investment Policy*, University of Illinois Bureau of Economic and Business Research, Urbana, Ill., 1963.

It is appropriate to conclude that bank balance sheet adjustment is a continuous process carried on under conditions of economic change, uncertainty, and risk. The actual results are likely to be "optimal" only in the qualified sense that things could have been a lot worse.

BANKING STRUCTURE AND COMPETITION

Categories of Banks The commercial banking system in the United States is unique in containing a large number of relatively small banks. Within this large number, significant distinctions exist between national and state banks, between banks which are members of the Federal Reserve System and those which are not, and between banks which are insured by the Federal Deposit Insurance Corporation and those which are not. All national banks must be members of the Federal Reserve System and must be insured. State banks may be members of the Federal Reserve System if they can meet the qualifications; if they become members, they must be insured. State banks may obtain FDIC deposit insurance coverage even if they are not member banks.

Figure 12-1 shows the composition of the commercial banking system with respect to these various classifications. The number of banks in each classification is measured horizontally along the base. The area for each classification represents the total assets in each classification. Some significant conclusions which can be drawn from the data are as follows:

1. National banks account for slightly more than half of commercial bank assets, although they constitute only about one-third of commercial banks by number.

2. Banks which are members of the Federal Reserve System hold about five-sixths of bank assets, although numbering slightly less than half of all commercial banks.

3. Virtually all banks and all bank assets are covered by Federal deposit insurance.

The division between national banks and state banks, reflecting the source of bank charters, has often been referred to as a "dual banking system." Nowadays, through Federal Reserve membership and FDIC coverage, virtually all commercial banks come under Federal authority in one manner or another. However, the existence of dual chartering authority has significance for the ease with which new banks can be formed and for their powers and competitive status.

Traditional Determinants The pattern of numerous, relatively small, relatively localized banks dates from the nineteenth century and reflects two important traditions.

One is the tradition of *unit banking*, of "one bank, one office." Prior to the twentieth century, both bankers and regulatory agencies strongly preferred unit banking. There were no particular advantages either in large-scale bank operations or in branching, and the state of transport and communication made branch management difficult. Unit banks were easier to supervise and examine, since all their records and documents were in one place.

Emphasis on unit banking was strengthened by the second tradition, an emphasis on *states' rights* in chartering and regulating banks. For many years it was believed that only state governments could constitutionally control ordinary commercial banks, and a bank created by one state was confined in its physical operations within the boundary of the state. Even when the Federal government began chartering commercial banks in 1863,

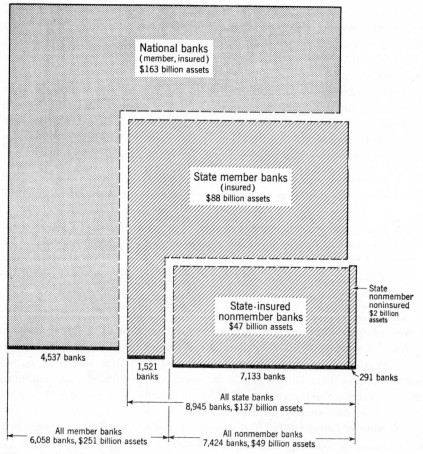

Figure 12-1. Composition of United States Commercial Banking System, June 29, 1963.

it chartered only unit banks. National banks were not and are not "national" —we have no banks operating nationwide branch systems. The states' rights tradition has remained evident in the fact that national banks are in several respects controlled by the laws of the states where they operate. This is particularly true of maximum interest charges on loans and of the authority to operate branches.

Correspondent Relations To enable a system of numerous local banks to deal with an integrated national economy, there has long existed a pattern of cooperation among banks in the form of a system of correspondent relationships. The smaller banks in smaller communities become allied with larger banks in larger communities, and those in turn may become correspondents of giant banks in New York or other major financial centers. Country banks tend to keep deposits with city banks, which often serve as clearing accounts. This is especially true for nonmember banks who do not have reserve accounts with the Federal Reserve banks; nonmember banks can ordinarily count such interbank deposits as legal reserves.

In exchange for the use of these deposited funds, the city correspondents perform various services for their country cousins. Besides clearing operations, many country banks receive assistance in buying, selling, and safe-keeping of securities, in credit and investment information and advice, and in foreign-exchange transactions. The correspondent relationship also allows for loan participation, in which several banks may join together to make a loan which would be too large for any one of them to handle alone.

Competition—Advantages and Limitations Competition is desirable in banking, as in any business, to stimulate efficiency in operations, to encourage innovations and high quality in services, and to provide fair opportunity for borrowers to obtain credit without discrimination. However, regulatory policy has reflected the view that restrictions of competition may be justified in order to protect the solvency of banks and particularly to minimize the danger of bank failure.

Economic analysis treats competition in two dimensions. On one hand, one can speak of competition in terms of a market structure which is identified by large numbers of small firms, each offering essentially the same product or service, and which is subject to entry by new firms. However, competition also refers to behavior patterns—to active efforts by each firm to win business away from rivals.

Some areas of bank operation are characterized by intense competition from nonbank financial institutions. The markets for government bonds involve an enormous number of buyers and sellers. Bank time deposits compete with United States savings bonds and with savings accounts in mutual savings banks, savings and loan associations, and credit unions. Savings institutions, plus insurance companies and mortgage companies, compete with commercial banks in the home mortgage field. And banks face competition in consumer loans from consumer finance companies and credit unions.

However, the most fundamental element of bank operation is the combination of business loans, demand deposits, and various trust and related services. This combination is unique to commercial banking. What is more, it is a combination of services which is offered in local or regional, rather than nationwide, markets. Geographic limits on market area also apply to home mortgage and consumer loans.

Bank Size and Concentration Commercial banks come in a wide variety of sizes. The giant Bank of America recorded some $14 billion of assets and more than 800 branches throughout California in 1963. There are still tiny banks in country towns with total assets less than $100,000. The majority of banks by number are of relatively modest Main Street size. Table 12-4 summarizes data on the size distribution of those insured banks which operated throughout the year 1962.

Table 12-4   Size distribution of insured commercial banks,
December 28, 1962

Deposits	Number of banks	Assets (billions)	Per cent of assets
0–$2 million	3,070	$ 4.4	1.5%
$2–$5 million	4,300	15.8	5.4
$5–$10 million	2,644	20.5	7.0
$10–$25 million	1,807	30.3	10.3
$25–$100 million	798	40.8	13.9
$100–$500 million	250	59.2	20.1
$500 million+	64	123.3	41.8
Total	12,933	$294.4	100.0%

Source: Federal Deposit Insurance Corporation, *Annual Report for 1962,* p. 134. Includes insured banks which operated entire year. Figures are rounded and may not add up to totals shown.

The importance of very large banks is readily apparent. The slightly more than 300 banks with assets exceeding $100 million held 62 per cent of bank assets. Still, on a nationwide basis, this is not a high degree of concentration compared with the standards of other types of business. In many industries—steel, automobiles, aluminum—a large proportion of industry assets can be found in the possession of a "big three" or some comparably small number.

However, the most relevant market for bank services is a local or regional one, and there the prevalent situation is one of fewness. A survey of 65 leading metropolitan areas in 1962 indicated that in 43 of them, the three leading banks accounted for more than 75 per cent of deposits. In small communities, fewness of banks is common. In 1962, more than 7,700 communities had only one banking office. To be sure, the majority of these were very small, with less than 1,000 population. But about 3,000 had populations of 1,000 to 5,000 and 240 had more than 5,000 people. And nearly 700 communities with populations over 5,000 had only two banking offices.[12]

None of these data prove lack of competition. Even if three metropolitan banks have most of a city's banking business, other smaller banks may be fighting hard for some of it. Even if a small town has only one bank, it may be a short drive to another community with a competing institution. But conceding the imperfect knowledge and imperfect mobility of bank customers, the concentration data suggest prevalent market situations of oligopoly, in which each bank avoids great emphasis on price competition, makes many of its decisions with an eye on the reactions of individual rivals, and puts much stress on nonprice forms of competition.

If concentration of banking is relatively high in many markets, it does not appear to be increasing nationwide. The FDIC reported that in a majority of areas, concentration declined between 1934 and 1958.[13]

Determinants of Concentration The existing degree of concentration of bank assets is largely the outcome of two forces—the expansion desires of individual banks, and regulatory laws and policies affecting the number and sizes of banks.

Individual banks seek larger size for a number of reasons. A larger bank can offer a greater variety of services, and a diversified bank can achieve greater operating efficiency as its size increases. Economies of large-scale operation are possible through greater specialization of personnel and through mechanization of routine operations. Small banks (with assets less than $5 million) appear to be at a substantial cost disadvantage. However, beyond that point no substantial economies of large-scale operation are evident until a bank achieves gigantic stature—about $500 million. Furthermore, large size achieved through large numbers of branches does not appear to result in cost savings—if anything, the contrary is true.[14]

However, there are other advantages in size. Because of the "10 per cent rule" governing loans to individual borrowers, the larger the bank, the larger the size of individual loans it can make. A larger bank can also expect to hold larger individual deposit accounts. Since it is just as cheap to process a large loan or large check as a small, there are cost savings in handling the business of large firms.

[12] Federal Deposit Insurance Corporation, *Annual Report for 1962*, pp. 56–60.

[13] *Ibid.*, pp. 47–61.

[14] Data on the relation of bank size to efficiency are reviewed by Paul Horvitz, "Economies of Scale in Banking," Commission on Money and Credit, *Private Financial Institutions*, Prentice-Hall, Inc., Englewood Cliffs, N.J., 1963. The conclusions cited in the text appear in pages 37–38. Horvitz interprets the data to imply that "four $15-million unit banks can be operated at a lower cost than a $60-million branch bank."

Finally, the larger a bank is, the more bargaining power it possesses in relation to its large customers. Important prices such as loan interest rates and service charges (explicit or implicit) on checking deposits are often set by negotiation with large customers, and bargaining power affects the outcome.

Regulatory policy affects banking structure at several points. It may permit or prohibit expansion through mergers or through the establishment of branches. It may help to maintain existing concentration by blocking the entry of new banks, or may encourage new banks and thus undermine the entrenched position of old ones. We shall elaborate some of these factors in subsequent paragraphs.

Competitive Behavior Competition among banks commonly displays the paradoxical features of oligopolistic structures—intense rivalry in some areas combined with a reluctance to compete in others. The major price terms involved in relations with business customers—interest rates and service charges—are often subject to a process of price matching and price leadership among major banks in a given regional market.[15] However, negotiation with individual customers provides the opportunity for a bank to experiment with secret price concessions. Banks are much more ready to engage in price competition in those areas where they face competition from nonbank institutions—time deposits, home mortgage loans, and consumer loans.

However, regulatory policies act as a rather pervasive damper on price competition in banking. This tendency is an outgrowth of the banking collapse of 1929–1933. Since that time, banks have been prohibited from paying interest on demand deposits (although they get around this to some extent by reducing service charges in proportion as deposit balances are larger). Maximum rates payable on time deposits are fixed by the Federal Reserve (and enforced upon nonmember insured banks by the FDIC). Interest rates on personal and some business loans are subject to statutory maximum limits set by individual states.

Given the prevalence of a climate of opinion not favoring price competition, those banks which choose to compete aggressively often do so through nonprice means. The chief form is through efforts to render better service—faster collections, better advice, less paper work and red tape, a more congenial atmosphere, more efficient handling of trust and agency operations, etc. Innovations may result in the kinds of business banks will handle, as well as in the manner of handling them.

Entry into Banking For about a century prior to 1933, it was relatively easy to start a bank in the United States. Not only were chartering au-

---

[15] For development of points relating to competitive behavior, see particularly Hodgman, *Commercial Bank Loan and Investment Policy*, pp. 97–144, 158–174; and Deane Carson and Paul Cootner, "The Structure of Competition in Commercial Banking in the United States," *Private Financial Institutions*.

thorities relatively lenient, but it was permissible to operate a "private" (unincorporated) bank without a charter at all.

Easy entry contributes to good performance in any industry in several ways. If monopoly or collusion develop, the high profits will attract newcomers who may restore competitive vigor. Entry of new firms may be a vehicle for new ideas and for new men, if existing institutions are unduly conservative and suffer from clogging of personnel channels. Such important innovations as extended trust operations and consumer lending were greatly promoted by easy entry into banking.

However, easy entry into an industry generally implies a high rate of turnover of firms, including numerous failures. This, unfortunately, was the consequence for the banking business, a consequence quite apparent in the 1920s. After the debacle of 1929–1933, regulatory policy became relatively hostile to new entry. Opportunities to operate without charters were virtually eliminated, and granting of charters was subjected to rather stringent conditions respecting not only the capital and apparent character and competence of the applicants, but also the apparent "need" for added bank facilities. One consequence was to give existing banks a vested interest in existing business and a first claim on expansion.

Since 1935, the number of new banks formed has been less than the number going out of existence through merger or liquidation. Consequently the number of commercial banks (which had already dropped sharply during the panic) declined steadily from about 15,500 in 1935 to about 13,400 in 1963. In the five years 1958–1962, 623 new banks were formed while about 800 went out of existence.[16]

Results of blocked entry are very evident in the age distribution of banks. Of the banks operating in 1959, only 12 per cent had been established within the preceding twenty years. Maine and Rhode Island had no banks that started since 1940, and Vermont only one. New York and Pennsylvania, with 1,100 banks between them, had only 23 which started since 1940.[17]

One of the controversial policies adopted by James Saxon when he became Comptroller of the Currency in 1961 was to increase the ease with which national charters could be obtained. This put pressure on state authorities to do the same. As a result, new bank formations jumped from an average of 111 per year in 1958–1961 to 179 in 1962 and 298 in 1963. The downtrend in total number of banks reversed. New York City and Boston wit-

[16] FDIC annual reports, 1958–1962. During the same period more than 3,500 new branches were established. Annual data on new bank and branch formations are conveniently summarized in Bernard Shull and Paul Horvitz, "Branch Banking and the Structure of Competition," *National Banking Review*, March, 1964.

[17] Author's tabulation of data for individual banks from *Rand McNally International Bankers Directory*, 1st 1960 ed., Rand McNally & Company, Chicago, 1960.

nessed their first new national-bank formations in decades. Within limits, easier entry into banking probably will tend to improve competition and opportunity without endangering solvency of existing banks. The "need" for additional facilities can be assessed as well by persons who are willing to stake their capital on their estimate, as by public officials subject to influence by the banks already in operation.

Branch Banking   While the number of banks has declined since 1935, the number of bank offices has been rising at a rapid rate. The vehicle has been the great increase in the operation of branch offices. Many existing banks have been absorbed as branches into larger systems, and a vast number of new branch offices have been opened. At the end of 1963, commercial banks were operating slightly over 13,000 branches—just about equal to the number of banks. However, only about 2,800 banks have branches; thus 80 per cent of commercial banks have adhered to the unit tradition.[18]

Establishment of a branch is always contingent on approval from supervisory authorities. In addition, many states have statutory limitations on branch operations (which are binding on national banks in the individual state as well). Tabulations by the FDIC indicate that states fall into three groups of relatively equal numbers. In one-third of the states the prevalent pattern is statewide branch banking; the most notable of these is California. In another third, the predominant arrangement is branch banking within limited areas, such as countywide. Leading industrial states, such as New York, Pennsylvania, Ohio, and Michigan, fall into this group. The final group of states is dominated by unit banking; this group includes eleven which prohibit branch operations almost entirely. Many Middle Western farm states are in this group, the most notable members of which are Texas and Illinois, with about 2,000 banks between them.[19]

On the whole, it has been the larger and more aggressive banks which have sought to undertake branch operations. Much branch activity has been stimulated by competition for consumer business—deposits, home mortgage loans, and consumer loans. This "retail banking" calls for proximity to customers. Branch development has also been one method of achieving some of the advantages of size which we noted above.

Much antagonism toward branch banking has arisen from smaller unit banks, particularly those confronted with prospective competition from large-branch operations. The smaller banks have protested that branch banking would lead to monopoly as well as absentee ownership and control. They contend that local unit banks have greater knowledge of and interest in local

[18] *Federal Reserve Bulletin*, April, 1964, pp. 518–519.

[19] Federal Deposit Insurance Corporation, *Annual Report for 1960*, p. 45; Gerald C. Fischer, "Changing Patterns in the Structure of Commercial Banking," *Bankers Magazine*, Winter, 1964, p. 20.

affairs, problems, and personalities. By contrast, branch banking has been defended as a method of increasing competition and as a method of providing banking offices in areas too small to support unit banks. Much depends, of course, on whether branches replace unit banks or are an addition to them, and on how many branch systems compete with each other in a given area.

Efforts to compare performance of branch versus unit banking produce rather mixed results. Substitution of branch operations does not appear to offer much probability of cost reduction. However, areas where branch banking predominates provide more banking offices per person. Concentration of banking facilities is generally higher in those states dominated by branch operations, but the difference is less significant when localities are considered.[20]

One very important variable is extremely difficult to evaluate—the quality of management. Many of the smaller, older unit banks are dominated by conservative, elderly bankers. Their organizations are not large enough to provide good training for younger men—or may not offer an attractive environment for them. Such banks often fail to capitalize on profit opportunities (such as those offered by consumer lending). A larger branch-bank system may find it attractive to buy out such a bank in order to capitalize on the unexploited potential business. And the old-style banker, faced with a problem of management succession, finds it simpler to sell out. This problem of management quality is acute because of the barriers to entry and the relatively protected position of the existing banks.

Another of Comptroller Saxon's controversial proposals has been to do away with the states' rights approach to branching, as far as national banks are concerned. He has suggested that Congress authorize branch operations by national banks regardless of the state where they operate. An even more extreme idea, advanced in some quarters, is that national banks be authorized to branch across state lines. Economically, the present limitations have no justification. Politically, however, the likelihood that branching would be permitted across state lines is minimal.

Bank Holding Companies   In many states where outright branch operations are prohibited or limited, some of the results of branching can be achieved through ownership of a controlling interest in the stock of individual banks. At the end of 1962, there were 49 bank holding companies,

---

[20] See the general evaluation of Shull and Horvitz, *op. cit.* The authors conclude that "neither in terms of number of competitors, nor concentration (measures of actual competition) nor in terms of the condition of entry (potential competition) have the structures of local banking markets been adversely affected by branch banking in the United States. The weight of evidence suggests that, to the contrary, market structures are adversely affected by restrictions on branch banking." (P. 341.)

controlling 442 banks with about $21 billion of deposits. Holding companies can extend across state lines, thus achieving something akin to extended branch banking. Under the Bank Holding Company Act of 1956, most of these groups are supervised and regulated by the Federal Reserve, which can veto additional acquisitions.

Bank Mergers   The absorption of banks through mergers has been proceeding steadily in recent years. In the 1950s, about 150 banks a year vanished by this route. Merger offers an attractive method by which a bank can achieve larger size, for reasons noted above. It is often a means of acquiring ready-made branches; indeed, it may be the only means open to a bank if supervisory authorities are stingy about granting authority for opening new branches in territories already served by existing banks. Mergers have provided a means for increasing diversification; it is not uncommon for a bank stressing "wholesale" operations involving business to merge with one stressing retail operations such as home mortgage and consumer lending. And, as we have noted, many mergers have involved a process whereby the more aggressive banks have gained access to business opportunities being neglected by relatively conservative small banks. Absorption through merger has also provided a relatively painless exit route for many banks too small to be efficient.

The effects of bank mergers on competition are ambiguous. Absorption of a lethargic bank by a dynamic one may greatly improve competitive vigor. Absorption by a large bank of small competitors in a metropolitan area may reduce it. Mergers always eliminate competition between the banks involved in the merger. In some cases this is inconsequential. Mergers may improve competition between the enlarged bank which emerges and its competitors.

The Clayton Act of 1914 contained several provisions dealing with banking concentration. It imposed limits on interlocking directorships in industry and in banking and gave the Federal Reserve Board authority to prevent one bank from acquiring stock in another where the effect might be substantially to lessen competition or to tend to create a monopoly. This provision was a counterpart to the power given to antitrust authorities over industrial stock acquisitions. In each case, the law was largely inoperative, since most mergers could be consummated by purchase of assets.

In 1950 Congress closed this loophole for industrial mergers by the Celler-Kefauver amendment to the Clayton Act; no one regarded it as applicable to banking. A separate Bank Merger Act was passed in 1960. It assigned authority to approve mergers to the respective Federal regulatory authorities: the Comptroller of the Currency for national banks, the Federal Reserve Board of Governors for state member banks, and the FDIC for insured nonmember banks. Each agency was instructed to consider the effects on competition, but also to weigh a variety of other traditional "banking" factors, such as the convenience and needs of the communities served and the character of the bank management. Each agency was also required to consider the advisory opinions of the other two and of the Justice Department.

Scarcely had the relatively mild merger controls of the 1960 act gone on the books than the banking industry was hit by a judicial bombshell. In June, 1963, the Supreme Court struck down a proposed merger between the Philadelphia National Bank and the Girard Trust–Corn Exchange Bank, the second and third largest banks in Philadelphia, ruling that the merger would violate the amended section 7 of the Clayton Act. This overturned a previous approval by the regulatory agencies and the Federal district court.

The "PNB" case established a number of far-reaching provisions. First, it applied the amended section 7 to banks. Second, it based the decision solely on competitive factors, not on the traditional "banking" factors prominent in regulatory approval. Third, it estimated the impact on competition within the local (Philadelphia) area, rejecting the banks' contention that they competed with other banks on a nationwide basis. Fourth, it concerned itself with competition within commercial banking, thus indicating that the services of nonbank institutions were not sufficiently close substitutes to figure competitively.

The decision would indicate more severe limits on the ability of dominant banks to combine with each other, and perhaps on their ability to expand through the merger route in general. How aggressively the Justice Department will pursue this policy remains to be seen.

Bank Failures During the relatively prosperous 1920s, bank failures occurred in the United States at an alarming rate. This undoubtedly reflected the existence of an excessive number (over 30,000 for a few years) of banks, most of them small, many poorly managed and inadequately diversified. During the crisis years 1930–1933, more than 8,000 banks failed. This mass failure was largely the result of the massive downswing in the general state of the economy.

Since 1933, bank failures have been relatively few. One reason is the absence of depressions. A second is the adoption of important new safeguards for bank liquidity and solvency, through the establishment of deposit insurance and through improvement in Federal Reserve policies. A third is the adoption of various regulatory policies restricting entry into banking, competition in the payment of interest, and risk taking in loan and investment policy. Of these three, the first two seem to have made the largest contribution.

In the five-year period 1958–1962, a net total of only 21 banks closed because of financial difficulties. Of these, 11 were insured banks and 10 were not.[21] All were banks of modest size. This is an impressive record. Whether it is still necessary for regulatory policy to work so hard at protecting bank solvency is questionable.

Bank Competition—An Appraisal   It is clear that the current state of competition in banking does not cause injury to the banks themselves. On the other hand, the banking industry does not appear to be making exorbitant profits or to be paying wages and salaries which are out of line with other industries—quite the contrary.[22]

It seems probable that if competitive forces were permitted to operate more fully, banking could improve the quality and variety of services, and quite possibly reduce costs, without the sacrifice of profits and employee incomes. There is an apparent redundancy in regulatory policy. Protection of bank solvency—which is an appropriate objective for public policy—would seem to be adequately pursued either by the careful examination of individual bank assets *or* by the restrictions on bank entry and interest-rate competition. To do both at once seems unnecessary.

If there is a monopoly problem in banking, it seems to exist mainly in the form of relatively sheltered small banks in unit-banking states. Virtually every economic investigation of branch banking has reached the conclusion that effective competition is impaired by state prohibitions on branch operations.[23] And there is abundant evidence that relatively well-managed unit banks of modest size can survive and prosper in the face of competition from larger branch systems.

At the same time, concentration of control in the hands of very large units poses a possible threat; the Court's decision in the PNB case is thus economically sound. The main danger in giant mergers lies in the diversion of funds away from small-business borrowers and toward larger firms. In general, however, the existing degree of large-bank concentration does no substantial economic harm. And it would be unfortunate if undue obstacles were imposed to impede the process whereby small, poorly managed banks can be painlessly transferred to strong hands through the merger process.

[21] Compiled from FDIC annual reports for 1958–1962. Total includes banks closed because of financial difficulties, including one bank absorbed by another with financial aid from FDIC. Suspended banks reopened have been deducted for a net total.

[22] Over the years 1947–1961 inclusive, annual profit rates for commercial banks averaged 8.2 per cent of capital accounts, compared with 10.7 per cent for electric utilities and 11.7 per cent for all manufacturing. See annual data in Donald Jacobs, "The Framework of Commercial Bank Regulation: An Appraisal," *National Banking Review*, March, 1964, p. 350.

[23] Note that the view, prevalent in many states, that it is better for branches to be confined to an area close to the head office is directly contrary to the competitive optimum. Effective competition would probably best be served by limiting the number of branches a bank might operate in a given locality, while permitting it to operate in as many localities as it might wish.

Competition in banking could be improved. However, in its present state it appears to be workable and does not compare unfavorably with competition in the economy in general.

SUMMARY AND GENERAL OBSERVATIONS

Commercial banking is the largest and most widely diversified element among American financial intermediaries. Commercial banking functions include management of checking deposits, time and savings deposits, and large amounts of trust and pension funds. Bank loans and securities holdings provide substantial financing to all major sectors of the economy. In particular, bank loans provide an important source of short- and medium-term credit for business firms and farmers, thereby serving an aggregate of borrowers which runs into the millions.

The asset-management policies of banks have an important impact on the allocation of loan funds to different sectors of the economy and on the access of individual borrowers to credit. Yet bank asset policies are dominated by the motive of protecting depositors—of assuring bank solvency and liquidity. This reflects the long-standing tendency for banks' operations as lenders to come into conflict with their role as creators and managers of money. Regulatory policies limit the kinds and amounts of earning assets which banks can hold. The management of a bank can be interpreted as an effort to achieve an optimum balance sheet consistent with management goals of liquidity and long-run profitability and with the rules and standards of regulatory policy.

The structure of the banking system reflects the traditions of unit banking, states' rights, and correspondent banking. However, formation of new banks has not been extensive since 1935. Branch operations have developed rapidly, until at present there are about 13,000 banks and a roughly equal number of branches. Entry into banking and permission to establish branches have been restricted by regulatory policy as additional means of protecting bank solvency.

Bank solvency and liquidity have been admirably protected since the Depression of the 1930s, and bank failures have ceased to be a problem of economic consequence. Part of the improvement is attributable to the prevalence of prosperity and part to the establishment of Federal deposit insurance and improved Federal Reserve operations.

However, it is possible that regulatory policy has gone too far in restricting bank competition. One consequence has been that banks have tended to avoid risky loans and investments to a degree which works adversely on the economy as a whole. This is partly the result of law and supervisory practice, partly the result of statutory or conventional limitations on interest charged, and partly the result of the artificial preservation, in some areas, of unduly conservative bank management. Policies intended to protect depositors have tended to become more concerned with protecting banks.

Proposals to liberalize bank regulation and improve the extent of competition have been widely advanced in recent years, particularly by the Commission on Money and Credit and its research staff. Among the desirable changes suggested are greater liberality in granting charters and authorizing branches and more flexibility for bank loan and investment policies. Adoption of such proposals can be consistent with supervisory safeguards and can thus improve the bank's credit functions while at the same time retaining good performance of its monetary responsibilities.

One aspect of regulatory policy that needs attention is the role of the Federal Reserve. For historical reasons, the Federal Reserve has been saddled with a number of supervisory and regulatory chores which have very little to do with central-banking responsibility for money and credit in the aggregate. There seems no good reason why the time and energy of the Board of Governors should be taken up with decisions concerning bank holding companies, bank mergers, the establishment of branches, and matters of this sort. It seems appropriate that such concerns be handled by the Comptroller of the Currency for national banks and by the FDIC for state banks.

QUESTIONS FOR STUDY

1. In his book entitled *Profitable Banking,* Clifford Hufsmith argues that banks make a serious mistake in failing to levy service charges which cover the full costs of handling demand-deposit transactions.[24] He argues that this failure violates the spirit of the law prohibiting interest payment on demand deposits. And he claims that higher service charges would bolster bank profits; would help attract more capital; and by enlarging capital accounts, would enable banks to make more risky loans and contribute to the better functioning of the economy. Would it be more economically efficient to levy fully compensatory service charges, instead of the present system under which interest on bank assets subsidizes deposit costs? If it would be advantageous to banks, why don't they do it?

2. Congressman Wright Patman recently suggested that there have been too *few* bank failures in recent years, from the standpoint of the welfare of the economy as a whole. What do you suppose he meant? Is it possible he was correct?

3. Explain the reasons for, and the economic merits and disadvantages of, each of the following bank regulations:

[24] The Bankers Publishing Company, Boston, 1959.

    a. No one can open a new bank without obtaining permission from state or Federal banking authorities.

    b. No bank may establish branch operations across state lines.

    c. No bank may lend to one borrower an amount exceeding 10 per cent of the bank's capital and surplus.

    d. No bank may make loans on security of its stock.

    e. Banks are not generally permitted to invest in stocks, real estate, or commodities.

    4. Contrast the efforts to protect bank liquidity by regulation of assets (including reserves) with the contribution to bank liquidity offered by access to Federal Reserve credit. Explain how the existence of Federal deposit insurance and a general stable and prosperous economic environment have reduced the problem of bank liquidity.

SUGGESTED READINGS

American Bankers Association: *The Commercial Banking Industry,* Prentice-Hall, Inc., Englewood Cliffs, N.J., 1962.

Carson, Deane (ed.): *Banking and Monetary Studies,* Richard D. Irwin, Inc., Homewood, Ill., 1963.

Commission on Money and Credit: *Private Financial Institutions,* Prentice-Hall, Inc., Englewood Cliffs, N.J., 1963.

Hodgman, Donald R.: *Commercial Bank Loan and Investment Policy,* University of Illinois Bureau of Economic and Business Research, Urbana, Ill., 1963.

Reed, Edward W.: *Commercial Bank Management,* Harper & Row, Publishers, Incorporated, New York, 1963.

Robinson, Roland I.: *The Management of Bank Funds,* 2d ed., New York: McGraw-Hill Book Company, 1962.

Trescott, Paul B.: *Financing American Enterprise: The Story of Commercial Banking,* Harper & Row, Publishers, Incorporated, New York, 1963.

chapter thirteen

OTHER
FINANCIAL
INSTITUTIONS

PRINCIPAL CATEGORIES

Besides commercial banks, a number of other types of financial institutions play important roles in the saving-investment process. We will divide them into four broad categories, as follows:

1. *Thrift institutions.* Here we include mutual savings banks, savings and loan associations, and credit unions. Thrift institutions receive a substantial proportion of personal saving in savings accounts of various types and use these funds to make loans.

2. *Insurance companies and pension funds.* A substantial flow of personal saving goes into life insurance and pension rights; these funds are used mainly for investment in long-term securities.

3. *Other institutional lenders,* chiefly sales finance companies, consumer finance companies, and mortgage companies, do not receive much of their funds directly from savers, but rely on funds borrowed from banks and other business sources to finance loans to consumers and business firms.

4. *Institutions concerned with the ownership and trading of corporate stock.* Investment companies, chiefly mutual funds, obtain funds by selling

their own stock to the public and use them to buy stock in other firms. Stock-brokers, investment bankers, and stock exchanges are involved in securities issue and trading.

In addition to these four categories of institutions, this chapter will include a discussion of Federal government programs of lending and loan guarantee.

MAJOR CHANNELS FOR PERSONAL SAVING

Composition of Savings Assets Commercial banks, thrift institutions, life insurance companies, and the government all offer the public types of savings assets which are liquid, are safe, and yield some income. Assets with these attributes meet the saving objectives of the majority of families and are consequently very widely held. Data on the kinds and amounts of savings assets and the institutions issuing them are shown in Table 13-1.

Table 13-1 Household savings assets, end of 1962
(Billions of dollars)

	Issued by							
Asset	Com-mercial banks	Mutual savings banks	Savings & loan assns.	Credit unions	Life ins. compa-nies	Pension funds	Gov't	Total
Currency and demand deposits*	($ 37)	—	—	—	—	—	($ 34)	$ 71
Savings accounts	82	$42	$80	$6	—	—	1	210
Savings bonds	—	—	—	—	—	—	47	47
Subtotal	120	42	80	6	—	—	81	328
Life insurance reserves	—	†	—		92	—	7	99
Pension reserves	—	—	—	—	22	42	41	104
Total	$120	$42	$80	$6	$114	$42	$128	$532

* Division between currency and demand deposits is rough estimate based on proportion of demand deposits imputed to households in *Federal Reserve Bulletin*, April, 1961, p. 406. Figures are rounded and may not add up to totals shown.
† Less than $0.5 billion.
Source: Board of Governors, Federal Reserve System, *Flow of Funds Accounts, 1945–1962.*

The table indicates that households held about $300 billion of cash and liquid assets, plus claims against life insurance and pension programs with a cash value of about $200 billion. The prominence of government as a financial institution is evident: it is represented in every line and accounts for the largest single share of the total. Commercial banks, life insurance companies, and thrift institutions combined provide roughly equal shares of the total.

Thrift Institutions Mutual savings banks, savings and loan associations, and credit unions accounted in combination for about $130 billion of household holdings of savings assets in 1962.

1. *Mutual savings banks.* Most of these institutions were established many years ago to encourage thrift among low-income groups by providing a safe outlet for their savings. There are only about 500 mutual savings banks, and more than 300 are in New York and Massachusetts, with the remainder concentrated in New England. More than 90 per cent of the institutions now operating were established prior to 1900. Most are large—their assets average nearly $100 million each. About two-thirds belong to FDIC, and these hold more than 85 per cent of industry assets. In Massachusetts, a state program fully insures mutual savings bank deposits.[1]

2. *Savings and loan associations.* These originated as cooperative groups through which savers could accumulate funds to purchase homes and borrowers could obtain home mortgage money. Although their numbers have been relatively stable at around 6,000 in the years since World War II, they have competed aggressively for savings by offering high interest rates, and their assets have increased rapidly. Savings and loan accounts may be insured up to $10,000 by the Federal Savings and Loan Insurance Corporation. About two-thirds of the associations are Federally insured, and they hold 95 per cent of industry assets. A state program covers associations in Massachusetts. The average association is about as large as the average country member bank—assets per association averaged about $17 million at the end of 1963.

After a wave of savings and loan failures in the 1930s, the Federal government established a program to promote and protect them and the mortgage market generally. This included provision for Federal charters, for insurance of accounts, and for establishment of the Federal Home Loan Bank System, which furnishes a source of short-term loans and a regulatory program somewhat resembling the Federal Reserve System.[2]

3. *Credit unions* arose as a means of dealing with the credit problems of

[1] See *Mutual Savings Banking: Basic Characteristics and Role in the National Economy*, Prentice-Hall, Inc., Englewood Cliffs, N.J., 1962, and "Facts and Figures: Mutual Savings Banks" (annual), both prepared by National Association of Mutual Savings Banks.

[2] See *The Savings and Loan Business*, Prentice-Hall, Inc., Englewood Cliffs, N.J., 1962, and "Savings and Loan Fact Book" (annual), both prepared by the United States Savings and Loan League.

low-income families, particularly industrial workers. The credit union movement has been promoted with philanthropic and humanitarian zeal: one of its founders told its story in a book entitled *Crusade: The Fight for Economic Democracy*.[3] A credit union is essentially a cooperative organized among a group of people who have some basis for social cohesion. They may be members of the same church or trade union, but 85 per cent of credit unions consist of employees working in a particular plant or government agency. The credit union accepts deposits and uses its funds to make personal loans to members at relatively low interest. The number of credit unions is large—over 21,000 in 1963—but their individual scale is very small. Assets averaged about $380,000 each in 1963. The percentage rate of growth in number and assets of credit unions has been more rapid than any other type of thrift institution since World War II.[4] Disgruntled competitors observed that this was often facilitated by free office space furnished by the employer and by the use of unpaid volunteer personnel.

Common Aspects   These thrift institutions have a number of elements in common, which can be summarized as follows:

1. They obtain virtually all their funds from savings in fixed-value interest-bearing forms, plus reinvested earnings.

2. They have relatively low operating costs; consequently 75 per cent or more of gross income is either paid to savers or reinvested.

3. They are predominantly "mutual" in form; that is, they have no separate group of stockholder owners as residual claimants. Saving and loan associations and credit unions are legally "owned" by their depositors, whose accounts are called "shares" and the income paid on them is termed "dividends." Economically, however, these shares and dividends are more nearly akin to deposits and interest. Mutual savings banks, however, are not "owned" by anyone; deposit accounts are debt claims.

Implications for control are mixed. Member participation is greatly encouraged by credit unions; it is technically possible but seldom significant for savings associations, which are run by relatively autonomous salaried management. Mutual savings banks are controlled by trustees, responsible to the state but often self-selecting.

4. Each type of thrift institution maintains a margin of assets in excess of savers' nominal claims. This margin, which averages 5 to 10 per cent of assets, arises chiefly from reinvested income. It is commonly termed a "reserve," but it is not to be confused with a type of asset. The margin acts as a cushion against losses similar to capital accounts of commercial banks.

[3] By Roy F. Bergengren, Exposition Press, New York, 1952.
[4] See Credit Union National Association, "Credit Union Yearbook" (annual); also John T. Croteau, *The Credit Union: An Economic Analysis*, Wayne State University Press, Detroit, 1964.

5. Each type of institution confines its asset holdings to a limited range of debt claims. Savings associations specialize in lending on home mortgages. Mortgages also dominate the portfolios of mutual savings banks, although they make a wider variety of mortgage loans than savings associations do, and they also hold some corporate bonds. Credit unions specialize in personal loans to members.

6. Thrift institutions reflect the same localized, unit-operation traditions which we observed in commercial banking. Actual physical operations of each institution are confined to offices within the boundaries of one state.

Chartering and Regulation   A dual system of chartering exists for credit unions and savings and loan associations. In each case, the Federal government undertook chartering authority during the 1930s to promote and regulate the type of institution in question. The consequences were to open up each state to the establishment of such institutions and to provide a basis for national uniformity in regulation.

Mutual savings banks are entirely state-created, however, and many states do not provide at all for their operation. Industry spokesmen have pressed for the Federal government to charter mutual savings banks as a means of permitting their establishment in states which now have none. It is not apparent that this would result in appreciable benefits for savers, except perhaps through opportunity to purchase the low-cost life insurance sold by MSBs in some states. However, the greater diversity of MSB assets might result in an improvement in the flow of funds to borrowers.

Regulation of savings associations and mutual savings banks is shared by state authorities, by the Federal Home Loan Bank Board (which grants Federal charters to savings associations) and by the two Federal deposit insurance organizations. Common regulations which seem fairly widely applicable include the following:

1. Requirement of a minimum holding of liquid assets in proportion to savings claims. This corresponds economically to reserve requirements for banks, but the terminology is different. Thrift institutions can satisfy liquidity requirements by holding demand deposits at commercial banks and even, in some cases, government securities.

2. Limitations on the types and specifications of earning assets. Savings and loan associations are limited chiefly to home and related mortgage loans originating within 50 miles of the head office. Mutual savings banks are permitted a somewhat wider range, but terms are carefully prescribed, and geographic limitations arise for them as well. Regulation is designed to protect the solvency of institutions.

3. These thrift institutions are required to maintain a minimum margin of assets over savers' claims in their so-called reserve accounts.

4. Restrictions are imposed on entry, on the formation of branches, and on interest which may be paid and charged. These are similar to, but not identical with, those imposed on commercial banks.

Regulation of credit unions is somewhat more flexible. Federal charters and supervision come from a Bureau of Federal Credit Unions in the Department of Health, Education, and Welfare. There is no program for Federal insurance of credit union accounts.

Appraisal and Problems The traditional problem facing thrift institutions was that of earning a modest income for savers while keeping risk to a minimum. Mutual savings banks and credit unions have enjoyed a high record of safety during most of their history, but savings and loan associations had a bad time of it during the 1930s, when about 1,700 of them failed. Since that time, the combination of improved supervision (particularly under Federal auspices), deposit insurance, and the superior condition of the economy generally has greatly reduced the risk problem for thrift institutions. Mutual savings bank failure is unheard of in our generation. Federally insured savings and loan associations have also shown impressive safety: in thirty years of operation, FSLIC has had to handle only about forty cases. Noninsured association failures have been somewhat more frequent, as indicated by the recent upheaval among Maryland associations. Credit union failures have been infrequent, especially under Federal charters.

One might question the tendency for thrift institutions to concentrate so heavily on mortgage lending, particularly since commercial banks have directed much of their time-deposit funds into mortgages as well. To be sure, the tendency would be self-correcting if carried very much to excess, because mortgage interest rates would fall. It appears, however, that the flood of mortgage money has tended to produce a deterioration of credit terms, reflected in longer repayment periods, lower down payment requirements, and perhaps more generous appraisals of property value. Much of this deterioration has been in government-underwritten mortgages, so that private lenders do not stand to lose by it and are thus not steered into other types of lending.

It is likely that some of the regulations to which thrift institutions are subject work adversely to economic efficiency. Mutual savings banks could certainly be entrusted with greater freedom in their lending, and there is no economic justification for restricting the maximum size of their deposit accounts as some states do. Geographic restrictions on loans and other functions are also undesirable. As with commercial banks, limitations on entry and the tradition of localized unit operations work adversely for the geographic mobility of funds. However, such devices as saving by mail and participation loans have helped overcome the obstacles somewhat.

INSURANCE

Nature of Insurance   Most financial intermediaries operate to reduce investment risks through pooling and diversification of assets, and many furnish low-risk financial assets suitable for individuals to hold as protection against financial emergencies. Insurance most of all deals with risks, primarily of two kinds: those relating to human mortality and those relating to property. On one hand, an individual's untimely death may inflict financial hardship on his dependents; on the other, he may outlive his capacity to support himself. Insurable property risks include fire, theft, and accidental damage. Occurrence of these adverse events, although unpredictable for an individual, is highly predictable for a large group. Consequently, a large number of persons subject to a given risk can form a mutual arrangement through which each assumes the burden of a small regular contribution in exchange for the right to be compensated if the insured event befalls him. Insurance enhances economic welfare directly if the gain to the people who collect outweighs the small loss borne by the luckier ones. Property insurance also enhances economic productivity by making individuals and firms more willing to own property and by enabling them to transfer certain risks to a specialized agency and concentrate their own energies on management.

Nonlife Insurance   Property and casualty insurance—that is, fire insurance, automobile insurance, health insurance, and insurance against theft, loss, damage, or liability—is sold essentially on a current basis. Premiums are the sum of the mathematical expectation of loss for each policyholder plus his share of operating costs and profits. However, a small proportion of premiums is used to build up a backlog of earning assets to protect companies against heavy claims. At the end of 1962, nonlife insurance companies held $37 billion of financial assets. Because of favorable tax provisions and investment regulations, some stockholder-owned insurance companies are able to use their investment operations as a source of considerable profit to owners. Nearly one-third of their investments were in the form of common stock.

Life Insurance—Types of Policies   It would be possible for life insurance companies to operate on a current basis also. They could sell policies running for one year, two years, etc., for which the premiums would reflect the current probability of death. Indeed, such insurance is available under the name of "term insurance." Companies dealing only in term policies would pay out most of their premiums in benefits and operating costs, as the nonlife companies do.

Since World War II, the term-insurance principle has been extensively used in the form of *credit life insurance*. Nowadays it is customary for firms extending consumer credit to insist that the borrower obtain sufficient added life insurance to cover the loan; indeed, many lenders act as salesmen for such insurance. Credit life insurance protects both the borrower and lender and has been a factor in the relatively high quality of consumer loans. Many homeowners purchase so-called mortgage-protection policies, which provide an amount of term-insurance coverage that diminishes over time as the mortgage is repaid.

Should an individual rely entirely on personal term insurance, however, he would find his premiums rising over time as advancing age increased the probability of death. However, group insurance policies, frequently written to cover all the employees of a firm, provide a way around this. Premiums are based on the age distribution and life expectancy of the group as a whole, which may be relatively constant. A person in the group may be insured for a long period without encountering the sort of premium increases he would face under a personal term-insurance policy.

Group and credit life insurance have grown rapidly. From the end of 1952 to the end of 1962, coverage under group and credit life insurance policies increased by 256 per cent, compared with only 107 per cent for other forms of life insurance. By the end of 1962, group and credit coverage was 37 per cent of all life insurance in force.[5]

Most life insurance sold to individuals is, however, written on a level-premium basis, which creates a different financial pattern. In the simplest case, that of straight life, the insured pays the same annual premium throughout his lifetime. In the insured's early years, the premium exceeds the mathematical expectation of death. The additional sum is held as a reserve and invested. The principal and interest of this reserve make it possible for the premium to remain constant in later years when the mathematical expectation of death rises above it.

Thus the level-premium policy introduces a large element of saving which is not inherent in the insurance principle itself. The policy accumulates a reserve of cash value which belongs to the policyholder in the sense that he can borrow on it or even withdraw part of it on canceling the policy. The element of saving is largest in limited-payment or endowment policies, which build cash reserves rapidly.

Policies sold to individuals are generally classified as *ordinary* life and *industrial* insurance. Industrial insurance is the misleading name given to small ordinary life policies sold widely to low-income families. The policies are sold in small amounts (the average policy in 1962 was only $420), and premiums are usually collected weekly in small sums by the agent. Although the number of industrial policies has been declining since 1953, such policies

[5] Statistics on life insurance are generally from "Life Insurance Fact Book" (annual), published by the Institute of Life Insurance. See Life Insurance Association of America, *Life Insurance Companies as Financial Institutions*, Prentice-Hall, Inc., Englewood Cliffs, N.J., 1962.

still accounted for about one-third of all policies by number in 1962. About 20 per cent of ordinary and industrial coverage is in term policies. The remaining 80 per cent consists of higher-saving policies. Table 13-2 summarizes the major types of coverage in force at the end of 1962.

Table 13-2   Life insurance coverage in force, end of 1962

Type of policy	Amount (billions)	Number (millions)
Ordinary	$389	99
Industrial	40	95
Group	209	48
Credit	38	48
Total	$676	290

Source: Institute of Life Insurance, "Life Insurance Fact Book," New York, 1963.

Life Insurance and Saving   About two-thirds of all Americans—men, women, and children—have their lives insured. The proportion rises to nearly 90 per cent for men between the ages of 25 and 65. Since these are commonly the family breadwinners, it is most important that their dependents be protected.

As we noted in Chapter 11, life insurance is, next to the accumulation of liquid savings assets, the most popular form of saving. The combinations of accumulation and protection available through insurance contribute highly to the most prevalent savings objectives. In particular, individuals recognize a need to force themselves to save, through regular contractual payment obligations.

However, criticisms are periodically directed at life insurance practices, particularly those of zealous agents eager for commissions. Younger families with small children have a large need for insurance protection but relatively limited means. A portion of their needs can appropriately be met by term insurance. Yet for a long time it was difficult for individuals to obtain term coverage. Instead, claim the critics, insurance agents tended to oversell the high-saving policies, such as endowment and limited payment, particularly to relatively low-income families. These provide less protection per dollar of premium.

Doubts are even cast on the virtues of straight life as a savings medium. One critic claims the goals of protection and accumulation are in conflict and repeats a common suggestion: Buy term insurance for protection and "invest the difference"—that is, use the savings on premiums as a fund for buying stocks or high-income savings assets.[6] Insurance agents are properly skeptical of this advice. It takes a lot more will power to invest the difference without being prodded, and a good bit more judgment is needed in the choice of assets to make it worthwhile. Insurance policies do yield an implicit interest return on the policy reserve. It tends to be somewhat lower than the yields on savings accounts, but is not subject to current income taxation. For most people, straight life insurance represents a satisfactory savings medium.

Since 1950 policies based on the term-insurance principle have grown much faster than the more traditional high-saving types of policy. People continued to devote about the same proportion of their incomes to life insurance premiums, but because the term-type policies provide more protection per dollar of premiums, the ratio of insurance coverage to disposable income rose substantially, from about 115 per cent in 1952 to 175 per cent in 1962. With total life insurance protection still amounting to less than two years' income, the American public was certainly not overinsured.

Investment Practices of Life Insurance Companies Through their sales of policies and annuities involving large amounts of saving, life insurance companies have become one of the most important types of financial intermediary. Their assets totaled $141 billion by the end of 1963 and were increasing at a rate of more than $7 billion annually. Table 13-3 summarizes

Table 13-3   Life insurance company assets, December 31, 1963
(Billions of dollars)

Government securities:	
United States	$ 6
Other	7
Corporate securities:	
Bonds	54
Stocks	6
Mortgages:	
1–4-family houses	28
Other	22
Policy loans	7
Real estate	4
Other assets	8
Total assets	$141

Source: Federal Reserve Bulletin, May, 1964. Figures have been rounded.

the composition of life insurance company assets at the end of 1963. Nearly 90 per cent of life insurance funds was invested in long-term fixed-value

[6] See Ralph Hendershot, *The Grim Truth about Life Insurance,* G. P. Putnam's Sons, New York, 1957.

financial claims. Mortgages and corporate bonds together accounted for about 75 per cent of total assets. At the end of 1963, life insurance companies owned half of all corporate and foreign bonds held in the United States. The stress in life insurance investments has been on safety of principal and stability of income. Life insurance companies do not need to hold substantial amounts of liquid assets; their needs for cash are relatively predictable and can generally be met from inflowing premiums and investment income and repayment. In their policy contracts, however, they have in effect guaranteed their policyholders a certain rate of return. Consequently they concentrate on long-term investments in which the income risk is low.

Life insurance investment practices are regulated by state authorities, who usually prescribe acceptable types of assets. Some states permit companies to invest limited amounts in stocks and real estate. Such assets totaled about $10 billion in 1963, but were a small fraction of total assets. Among their real estate investments, life insurance companies own and manage large housing projects and other properties.

The quest for safety has been quite successful. The life insurance industry as a whole weathered the financial crisis of the 1930s far better than commercial banks or savings and loan associations did. Now the question is whether this emphasis on caution has not been pushed too far for the best interests of policyholders or the economy. Are not life insurance funds unduly concentrated in debt securities, particularly those of large well-established firms, to the possible detriment of new firms or small firms? The sheer magnitude of funds flowing through the large insurance companies drives them to seek large outlets—although some companies make a special effort to seek small-business securities.

PENSION FUNDS

Closely allied to life insurance are the financial operations related to pensions and annuities. Life insurance protects against the financial adversities which result from dying too soon; pension and annuity rights protect against adverse financial consequences of living too long. With the increase in the proportion of the United States population aged sixty-five and over, financial problems of older people have gained greater attention.

Provision for the financial needs of old age has long been an important savings motive. Home ownership, both for occupancy and rental, has been a traditional outlet. In addition, many persons have purchased life insurance policies and annuities with terms explicitly arranged to provide incomes after retirement. Furthermore, most Americans are now covered by the retirement provisions of the social security program.

Recently, however, the most dramatic developments in financing retirement have come in connection with the rapid growth of private pension funds. These are funds set up on behalf of individual employers to finance pensions to their employees on retirement. In earlier times, companies which promised pension benefits sometimes simply undertook to pay them out of current income. But at present most pension plans are funded—that is, funds are set aside during the working lifetimes of covered workers to finance the firm's commitments to them after they retire. The bulk of funds is nominally contributed by employers (an arrangement with tax advantages), although some firms require the employees to contribute also.

Many funded plans are purchased from life insurance companies as group annuities. Costs, benefits, and the investment of funds are carried on according to insurance principles. "Insured" pension plans covered about six million persons in 1963; the assets of such programs are included among the total life insurance assets listed above.

Much more rapid growth has occurred in the "noninsured" pension programs. Some of these are simply managed directly by the employer, perhaps with joint participation by labor union representatives. Most of them are, however, managed partly or entirely by commercial bank trust departments. Indeed, it appears that the bulk of pension-fund assets is concentrated in a small number of state-chartered banks in New York City.

By 1963, some twenty million workers were covered by noninsured pension programs. Such pension funds held about $45 billion in assets and were expanding at an impressive rate of $4 billion a year. Pension funds are one of the few major types of financial institutions that invest heavily in corporate stocks, which constituted about half their assets in 1963.

Because the rapid expansion of pension funds has come since World War II, the funds have much more experience in collecting money than in paying it out. Only about 2½ million retired persons were receiving pensions from insured and noninsured funds in 1963. Consequently, numerous uncertainties remain in the appraisal of pension-fund operations. Among the principal problems, the following can be enumerated:

1. Just what effective right does the individual worker have to his pension? Traditionally, the answer was "Not much," and this is still true of nonfunded plans, as members of the United Mine Workers have discovered to their regret. Even with funded plans, many provide for loss of benefit rights if the worker leaves the company prior to retirement. However, the trend has been toward "vesting" the employee with rights to a lump sum if he leaves the employer, or with partial pension on attaining a specified age. Nevertheless, half the covered workers probably still do not enjoy this protection.

2. Will the noninsured funds be able to meet their obligations? Many of the benefit provisions are of a sort which cannot easily be anticipated—

for instance, a common provision bases a worker's pension on the number of years worked for the company and on the wage received in the years just preceding retirement. Since employer contributions dominate, some companies may skimp unduly on contributions and build up an inadequate backlog of assets.

3. Can pensioners be protected against inflation? Most funds provide for flat-rate benefit payments. A few companies have voluntarily liberalized benefits to existing pensioners when their programs were liberalized for employees. And there are some programs which provide for variable benefits based on the income from stock benefits, or which provide automatic cost-of-living adjustments.

4. Is there danger that stock purchases by pension funds may create undue concentration of power and control? There is probably no direct danger, since there are a lot of individual funds, and the banks which manage most of them try to avoid getting involved in management decisions of the firms whose stock they own. Even so, if a large portion of a firm's stock comes to be institutionally owned, this situation may give incumbent management an unnecessary cushion against discontent among individual stockholders or may open the way for a small block of noninstitutional stock to exercise undue control. Most concern is directed toward the future, since pension-fund stock ownership is expected to continue growing rapidly.[7]

5. What sort of regulations should be applied to pension funds? Without more information on how well they perform, one cannot provide an answer to this. Actual regulation occurs primarily at the state level; insured programs are covered by insurance regulation, and bank-administered funds come under the regulations of trust operations generally. Noninsured funds have considerable freedom in their investment policies. In 1958, following exposure of abuse in some union-management controlled funds, Congress voted to require that funds submit financial statements to the Department of Labor. No directives have been laid down regarding pension-fund management, and the Federal government has made little use of the information so received.

OTHER LENDING INSTITUTIONS

A number of types of financial institutions carry on important lending functions, but do not receive important savings flows direct from the public. Major categories are briefly described in the following paragraphs.

[7] This problem is analyzed by Paul P. Harbrecht, *Pension Funds and Economic Power*, Twentieth Century Fund, New York, 1959, and Robert Tilove, *Pension Funds and Economic Freedom*, Fund for the Republic, New York, 1959. On financial aspects, see also Eugene Miller, "Trends in Private Pension Funds," *Journal of Finance*, May, 1961.

1. Consumer finance, or "small-loan companies," are credit retailers who provide personal loans through a large number of local offices (12,000 in 1960). They operate under the relatively strict state small-loan laws, which require a license for each office and limit the size of loan and the interest charge permitted. Funds come chiefly from stockholder capital, reinvested earnings, and the issue of long-term debt securities. However, companies do obtain substantial loans from commercial banks and in some cases solicit savings accounts. In 1963 they held about $5 billion of consumer credit.[8]

2. Sales finance companies are credit wholesalers who purchase customers' IOUs from the originators of loans. Their major activity is the purchase of consumer automobile installment loans from retailers and commercial banks. However, they also purchase some business IOUs arising out of installment sales of capital goods. In 1963 sales finance companies held about $14 billion of loan assets, including $8 billion of auto installment loans.

Sales finance companies overlap with factors, who extend credit by purchasing accounts receivable (IOUs of business customers), and commercial finance companies, who lend on security of accounts receivable.

3. Mortgage companies handle a substantial business in originating mortgage loans, which they generally resell to other institutions such as insurance companies. Often they continue to service the mortgages for a fee.[9]

CORPORATE STOCK

Corporate stock is in a class by itself financially. Whereas most business debt financing comes through financial intermediaries, most stock is sold to individuals. New stock issues furnished only about 10 per cent of corporate external funds in 1959–1963. However, funds which corporations reinvest out of current profits are also technically the property of the stockholders and tend to raise the value of existing stock. In this section we shall consider stock issue, trading and speculation, and the operations of stock-buying intermediaries.

Stock Issue and Trading New issues of corporate stock (like most bond issues) are often marketed through investment bankers. Investment banking is not banking in the usual sense; indeed, commercial banks are forbidden to engage in it. The investment bankers may "underwrite" a new issue, in which case they buy it from the issuing firm and resell it at their own risk in the expectation of a margin of profit, or they may sell it on com-

[8] *Federal Reserve Bulletin*, April, 1964, pp. 492–493; National Consumer Finance Association, *The Consumer Finance Industry*, Prentice-Hall, Inc., Englewood Cliffs, N.J., 1962.

[9] Miles Colean, *Mortgage Companies*, Prentice-Hall, Inc., Englewood Cliffs, N.J., 1962.

mission with the issuing firm taking the risk. New stock is often issued by giving the existing stockholders of the issuing firm rights to buy the new shares. Such distributions may be handled through brokerage firms, although investment bankers may still underwrite the issue.

In terms of money volume, the issue of new stock is small in relation to trading in existing shares. It is in the latter activity that organized stock exchanges and brokerage firms play their major roles.

Most stock trading passes through the hands of brokerage firms. Generally, the broker merely buys from and sells to others on behalf of his clients and collects a commission as his own compensation. However, brokers do serve as financial intermediaries in furnishing loans to customers, generally with funds from bank loans.

Trading in stocks may be carried on through organized markets or "over the counter." About 85 per cent of stock exchange trading occurs on the New York Stock Exchange. Stock exchange listing is highly selective. Of more than 1 million corporations in existence in 1963, about 2,400 were traded on exchanges, slightly more than half of them on the NYSE. However, stocks of listed companies accounted for nearly 75 per cent of the value of all stock.[10] A stock exchange is simply a public marketplace where stock trading takes place through competitive bidding in which all prices must be shouted aloud and all transactions concluded publicly. Prices can fluctuate from minute to minute as supply and demand vary.

A large volume of stocks is also traded over the counter. Such trading generally takes place by telephone arrangements among brokers and dealers, with no central meeting place. The number of firms whose stock is so traded averaged about 40,000 to 50,000 in the late 1950s, but less than 5,000 were actively traded. Such trading covers stocks of important financial firms and some major industrial firms who do not wish listing on exchanges. Most bond trading is also carried on over the counter.

Speculation Stock prices fluctuate substantially. In part this is because corporate profits and dividends fluctuate, in part because expectations of future profits and dividends change, and in part because people buy and sell on the basis of what they expect stock prices themselves to do. As a result, stocks are a prime object of speculation.

Much speculation is conducted on credit by means which can enhance the potential gains (and losses). The "bull" who expects stock prices to rise can buy "on margin" by borrowing a part of the purchase price of the stock from his broker (at interest). The amount of margin he must put up (his down payment, in other words) depends on current Federal Reserve regulations and on the standards of his broker or bank. In early 1965, margin requirements were at 70 per cent, so that not more than 30 per cent could be

[10] *29th Annual Report of the Securities and Exchange Commission,* 1963, pp. 39–40.

borrowed. Earlier, requirements went as low as 50 per cent. Suppose a specu-lator purchased $10,000 worth of stock on 50 per cent margin by putting up $5,000 of his own money. If the stock rose 10 per cent in price, he could sell it for a profit of $1,000, a gain of 20 per cent on his own capital. The larger the amount of credit used, the bigger the percentage gain which can be ob-tained if the price rises. But this works both ways—if the price falls, the loss may be greater.

Short selling is a mysterious device whereby the "bear" who expects the market to fall can profit by the fall. To sell short, the bear borrows *stock* from his broker and sells it, with the promise to return it later.[11] If the price falls, he can buy back the stock cheaply and return it. Of course, if the price should rise, he might be obliged later to buy the stock for more than he had sold it and could lose heavily. Regulations prohibit short sales which force the price below its existing level.

Stock Trading and Welfare The facilities for securities trading perform two basic functions. One is to increase the ease with which stocks can be transferred and the knowledge of the terms on which transfer can be made. Knowledge and ease of transfer probably increase the willingness of inves-tors to hold stocks. This helps to increase the volume of saving and invest-ment and to shore up the important equity-capital side of business finance.

The second function of the securities-market institutions is to influence the flow of new capital into investment. Although new issues of stocks are not marketed through the exchanges, the prices in effect there determine the prices at which new issues can be sold. This function places a respon-sibility on the securities institutions to help create a price structure which will direct funds into firms which can make best use of them.

Does this direction of funds actually occur? Certain tendencies help to promote it. In recent years, investment counsel has stressed stocks of com-panies which are efficient and progressive, which are producing products for which demand is likely to rise, and which are leading innovators in cutting costs and providing new or improved products. It is in the public interest that such firms should have easy access to capital, and the high prices for stocks of this type have promoted such access. However, this process works chiefly for the larger, well-known companies with a public market for their stock.

What about speculation? Does it promote useful objectives? Sometimes it does, and sometimes it doesn't. To be desirable, speculation ought to help stabilize security prices (to enhance stock liquidity in the true sense) and to lead to values on individual stocks proportional to the social utility of added investment in their companies.

---

[11] Where does the borrowed stock come from? From the people who buy on margin. They must agree to allow the broker to lend it as a condition of getting loans.

Some observers have argued that profitable speculation is usually stabilizing. The speculator has an incentive, they claim, to buy when prices are low and sell when they are high. By doing this, he tends to raise the low prices and lower the high. Critics point out that speculators are concerned with the direction of stock-price movements, not their level. Rational speculators are likely to buy when prices are rising, because they expect the rise to continue, and to sell in a falling market. Such trading clearly helps aggravate the unstable movements in either direction.

Statistics on the value of stock market credit outstanding and on the volume of short-sales contracts show that such speculation tends to affect the market in an unstabilizing manner. Thus, at the time of the 1929 market peak, margin buying was at an all-time high, whereas short selling had dwindled away to nothing. As stock prices subsequently declined, margin buying fell and short selling rose. During the substantial drop in stock prices in 1957–1958, margin buying again fell and short selling rose, while both tendencies reversed when stock prices began to rise in 1958. Such behavior does not help to stabilize prices. In mitigation, it may be noted that outstanding margin and short accounts together account for only about 2 per cent of the value of listed stocks. But speculative trading accounts for a much larger proportion of current transactions—15 to 27 per cent in sample studies.[12]

Speculation also does not necessarily produce stock values proportional to the potential utility of new investment in particular firms. To a speculator, the present value of a stock depends on what its price is likely to be in the near future, which depends more on what other people think of it than on inherent characteristics of the firm.[13]

Much opposition to speculation arises from a feeling that it is merely a form of gambling and therefore immoral. Granted that the motivation is often the same, speculation differs from gambling in several important ways.

[12] *Factors Affecting the Stock Market,* Senate Committee on Banking and Currency, 1955, p. 109; *The Security Markets,* Twentieth Century Fund, New York, 1935, pp. 63–96, 271–396.

[13] According to Keynes, "professional investment may be likened to those newspaper competitions in which the competitors have to pick out the six prettiest faces from a hundred photographs, the prize being awarded to the competitor whose choice most nearly corresponds to the average preferences of the competitors as a whole; so that each competitor has to pick, not those faces which he himself finds prettiest, but those which he thinks likeliest to catch the fancy of the other competitors, all of whom are looking at the problem from the same point of view. It is not a case of choosing those which, to the best of one's judgement, are really the prettiest, nor even those which average opinion thinks the prettiest. We have reached the third degree where we devote our intelligence to anticipating what average opinion expects the average opinion to be." John Maynard Keynes, *General Theory of Employment, Interest, and Money,* Harcourt, Brace and Company, Inc., New York, 1936, p. 156.

First, the odds are favorable. Since stocks tend to rise in the long run, a well-diversified and patient bull speculator has a good chance to make profits. Second, speculation may lead to analysis which helps direct funds into beneficial uses. Third, since prudent speculation calls for buying, speculation probably creates some additional saving and investment. However, a strong case cannot be made for stock speculation. On the other hand, drastic measures to curb it (beyond the margin requirement) might interfere with beneficial investment and with the useful activities of market specialists.

Institutional Investors in Stocks Most major financial institutions—commercial banks, savings institutions, life insurance companies—buy little or no corporate stock. Federal Reserve estimates indicate that at the end of 1963 nearly 90 per cent of corporate stock was held by individuals (including trust funds). Among financial institutions, the leading holders were pension funds, nonlife insurance companies, and investment companies.

Investment companies (chiefly open-end "mutual funds") obtain funds by selling stock in themselves and invest them in securities of other firms. They offer the investor advantages of diversification and expert management. Under the impetus of vigorous selling efforts and a buoyant stock market, they have grown rapidly and were handling something over $1 billion a year of investment inflow in the early 1960s. Industry data listed 165 open-end companies with $25 billion of assets and 6 million shareholders in 1963. Closed-end companies held an additional $7 billion of assets.[14]

A large volume of stocks is also held by personal trust funds administered by commercial banks. Trust funds are often established by wealthy individuals to provide income and property management for their survivors; they provide certain advantages in reducing estate tax liabilities. Estimates placed the assets of bank-administered personal trust funds on the order of $100 billion in 1963, including about $60 billion in stock. Ownership of such funds is highly concentrated. National banks, which held about $50 billion in personal trust assets, reported about 300,000 accounts, with an average size of $160,000.[15]

The number of persons owning stock in the United States has increased substantially in recent years. Estimates by the NYSE indicate that the number of stockholders rose from about 6.5 million in 1952 to 17 million in 1962. Although stocks are not well suited for saving objectives requiring liquidity and fixity of capital value, they fit in well with long-run accumulation programs for such goals as retirement and children's education, since they

[14] Sources, prepared by Investment Company Institute, are "Mutual Funds, A Statistical Summary, 1940–1963," and *Management Investment Companies*, Prentice-Hall, Inc., Englewood Cliffs, N.J., 1962. An open-end company is one which stands ready to issue new shares or to redeem existing ones at values determined by the current market value of the company's assets.

[15] Stanley Silverberg, "Bank Trust Investments: Their Size and Significance," *National Banking Review*, June, 1964.

provide the particular charm of a hedge against inflation. However, the bulk of stock by value is still held by a very small proportion of the population.[16]

Government Regulation of Securities Markets and Institutions The great wave of public indignation which followed the stock market crash led during the 1930s to passage of numerous regulatory laws covering many aspects of the securities business. The Securities and Exchange Commission was established and given the chief regulatory jurisdiction. Its regulations are aimed primarily to assure the general public access to complete and accurate information about securities and to protect them from certain dishonest, careless, or otherwise harmful practices. In brief, these requirements include:

1. Each corporation issuing new securities must file registration statements with the SEC and publish a prospectus available to investors. In this material it must set forth extensive data on the condition of the firm, proposed use of security proceeds, costs of issuing, etc. However, issues under $300,000 and all private placements are exempt.

2. Officers of corporations must provide information on their ownership of stock, so that taking unfair advantage of inside information can be controlled.

3. Both law and exchange rules prohibit or limit manipulation of the stock market. In the past, collusive "pools" with large funds could exercise monopolistic influence on prices, driving them up and down artificially and often, with the aid of false information, drawing outsiders in to be bilked.

4. Most persons connected with securities trading, including brokers, dealers, investment bankers, and investment advisers, are prohibited from disseminating false or misleading information about securities. Many such establishments are required to register with the SEC and to file financial information about their own personnel and operations.

5. Investment companies are required to register with the SEC and to provide it with information about their operations. The Commission can block practices which appear unfair, and the investment companies are limited in the amount they can invest in an individual firm.

6. The Federal Reserve has authority to prescribe minimum margins for stock market credit.

7. Commercial banks are forbidden to operate as investment bankers or investment companies.

These controls and others enforced by government or by interested private organizations have not completely eliminated fraud and abuse, but

---

[16] The top 1 per cent of wealth holders has held about two-thirds of stock outstanding. See estimates for various dates in Robert J. Lampman, *The Share of Top Wealth-holders in National Wealth, 1922–1956*, Princeton University Press for National Bureau of Economic Research, Princeton, N.J., 1962, pp. 208–209.

they have vastly improved the general degree of honesty and integrity in this important area of the economy.

FEDERAL LENDING AND GUARANTEE PROGRAMS

In addition to its roles as issuer of financial assets and regulator of private financial institutions, the Federal government exercises an important influence in the world of finance as a lender, as an agency guaranteeing private loans, and as a source of deposit insurance.

In the middle of 1963, the total amount of loans extended by or guaranteed by the Federal government was roughly $100 billion, of which four-fifths consisted of guarantee. Loan and guarantee provisions have been popular for pursuing a bewildering variety of objectives; they have extended to such esoteric activities as making loans to radio stations in Uruguay during World War II and lending cattle to Indians. A survey for the Commission on Money and Credit identified 51 distinct programs.[17] A listing of major elements is presented in Table 13-4.

Federal Lending Agencies In June, 1963, Federal lending agencies had about $21 billion of loans receivable; they were expanding at a rate of about $1 billion a year in the early 1960s. Two major goals of policy are evident. The first is to stimulate and promote certain sectors or activities, notably agriculture, housing, education, and exports. The second is to fill "credit gaps" by making credit available to borrowers who cannot obtain it through private sources.

In the agricultural sector, the Federal government sponsored the formation of several types of specialized lending institutions under the Farm Credit Administration. Three provide long- and intermediate-term credit to farmers and cooperatives; the fourth lends to the other three. FCA institutions have provided about 20 per cent of all farm credit in recent years. They operate with relatively conservative standards, easily pay their way, and have been "mutualized" through a process of gradual sale to their customers. Here the Federal government has acted to sponsor innovation and then withdraw as Federal support becomes unnecessary.

By contrast, three major agencies lend Treasury funds to farmers. The Farmers Home Administration makes loans to farmers unable to obtain it through private channels. The Rural Electrification Administration lends at

---

[17] See Stewart Johnson, "Statistics on Federal Lending and Loan Insurance Programs in the United States, 1929–1958," and Warren A. Law, "The Aggregate Impact of Federal Credit Programs on the Economy" (p. 248), Commission on Money and Credit, *Federal Credit Programs*, Prentice-Hall, Inc., Englewood Cliffs, N.J., 1962. Additional material is in the other papers in this volume and its companion, entitled *Federal Credit Agencies*.

Table 13-4   Loans outstanding or guaranteed, major Federal agencies, June, 1963
(Billions of dollars)

Agency	Loans	Guarantees
Agriculture:		
Commodity Credit Corporation	$ 1.8	$ 0.8
Farmers Home Administration	1.6	0.5
Rural Electrification Administration	3.7	—
Housing:		
Federal National Mortgage Association	4.9	—
Veterans Administration	1.6	30.0
Federal Housing Administration	0.6	42.4
Community Facilities Administration	1.7	—
Urban Renewal Administration	0.1	1.0
Public Housing Administration	0.1	4.4
Business:		
Export-Import Bank	3.3	1.3
Small Business Administration	0.8	0.1
Other (Defense, Maritime, ICC)	0.3	0.7
Other:		
Office of Education	0.3	—
Life insurance policy loans (VA et al.)	0.6	—
Total	$21.4	$81.5

Agencies sponsored by Federal government but relying on private funds

Farm Credit Administration:		
Federal land banks	$ 3.2	
Intermediate credit banks	2.3*	
Production credit associations	2.3	
Banks for cooperatives	0.7	
Net total FCA	$ 6.3	
Federal Home Loan banks	3.3	
Total Federally sponsored	$ 9.6	

* Virtually all consisted of loans to other FCA institutions. Excluded from total.

Source: Budget of the United States Government, Fiscal Year 1965, pp. 371–382. Foreign-aid loans by Treasury and State Department have been omitted. Figures are rounded and may not add up to totals shown.

low interest rates to special power-distribution or telephone cooperatives. The Commodity Credit Corporation, while technically a lender, is primarily the instrument through which farm prices are supported by Federal purchase.

In the home-finance field, the Federal National Mortgage Association ("Fannie May") buys insured mortgages in the open market to make more funds available for new loans. It draws substantially on private funds through the sale of debentures. The Veterans Administration makes direct housing loans to veterans unable to obtain private credit. The Home Loan banks (also now mutualized) provide short-term loans to savings and loan associations, much as the Federal Reserve lends to commercial banks. The Urban Renewal and Public Housing administrations lend to or guarantee loans for local governments and special local public housing authorities. The Community Facilities Administration provides low-cost loans for college housing and specified public works by state and local governments. Education is also promoted by the student-loan program of the Office of Education.

The Small Business Administration provides direct loans to small businesses which cannot obtain credit on reasonable terms from private sources. In addition, it sponsors the formation of small-business investment companies (SBICs) designed to provide equity capital or long-term loans to small firms. The SBA is authorized to invest in or lend to SBICs, of which about 700 were in operation in mid-1964, with total assets of about $700 million.

Loan Guarantee In the 1930s it was discovered that frequently government guarantee or insurance of loans was as effective as government lending in achieving desired results. Peacetime use of loan guarantee has occurred chiefly in home mortgage credit, under the auspices of the Federal Housing Administration and the Veterans Administration. To be eligible for FHA insurance, the property must be appraised by FHA examiners, and the mortgage must conform to standards relating to down payment and interest rate. A fee for the insurance is added to the interest charged the borrower. The VA will guarantee or insure mortgages for veterans if they meet standards of appraisal, down payment, and interest rates. Maximum interest rates have usually been below those set by the FHA, and since 1955 the VA has been willing to insure mortgages involving no down payment. No fees are charged for VA insurance; thus the program operates at a loss. By contrast, the FHA program is financially self-supporting. At the end of 1963, about $65 billion in mortgages on one- to four-family housing was covered by these government programs, compared with $117 billion of such mortgages not covered. FHA also provides insurance for apartment-house and for home-repair loans.

Deposit Insurance Federal deposit insurance is available for commercial and mutual savings banks through the Federal Deposit Insurance Corporation and for savings and loan associations through the Federal Savings and Loan Insurance Corporation. Individual accounts in insured institutions are covered up to $10,000.

Virtually all commercial banks are Federally insured. Thus practically every depositor enjoys a measure of insurance coverage. Since most demand-deposit accounts contain less than $10,000, most depositors are fully insured. However, a large proportion of demand-deposit funds are in the small number of large accounts with more than $10,000, predominantly business accounts. In consequence, only about 40 per cent of demand-deposit funds are actually covered by insurance.

About two-thirds of savings banks and associations are Federally insured. However, these hold about 90 per cent of funds in such institutions. Additional insurance coverage is provided by state government programs in Massachusetts, Ohio, and Maryland. The proportion of savings in large accounts is small, a situation which holds true for commercial bank savings deposits also. Consequently deposit insurance fully covers more than 80 per cent of the dollar volume of savings in these three types of institutions.

The insurance agencies operate not merely to indemnify depositors, but to reduce the probability of insolvency through regulation and inspection of insured institutions. The preventive approach has kept to a minimum the need for actual disbursement of insurance funds. Only 57 insured commercial banks failed in the twenty years 1944–1963, while 28 noninsured banks failed in the same period. During the same period, FSLIC had 9 savings and loan failures.

Prior to 1955, FDIC relied extensively on the technique of "deposit assumption," whereby an insured bank in financial difficulties would be taken over by a sound bank, with FDIC funds being used to compensate the latter for any deficiency in assets. This technique protected all depositors against loss. Since 1955, however, FDIC has generally used deposit payoff. Holders of large deposits are assured of the first $10,000, but are likely to recover only a fraction of their claim beyond that. Even the smaller depositors may find their claims settled by offset, as debts owed to the failing bank by depositors are deducted from their deposit claims.

Despite these minor slippages, depositors have fared well in FDIC settlements. More than 99 per cent of the value of deposits in failed insured banks has been restored to depositors, of which less than 2 per cent went by way of offsets. FSLIC, by relying on deposit assumption, has been able since the 1930s to avoid inflicting any losses on savers in Federally insured institutions.[18]

Appraisal Without attempting to deal with all individual programs, it is possible to make some general evaluations of the virtues and defects of Federal programs of lending, loan guarantee, and deposit insurance. Observations relating to the mortgage market and small business will be taken up in a subsequent section.

[18] Data in this paragraph are chiefly from Federal Deposit Insurance Corporation, *Annual Report for 1963*, and *Insurance of Deposits and Share Accounts, Hearings before the Committee on Banking and Currency*, House of Representatives, 1963.

1. These Federal programs have helped to make our economy depression-proof. Loan and deposit protection programs do not merely insure against given risks; by supervisory controls they reduce the risks themselves. Home Loan banks and intermediate credit banks protect the liquidity of lending institutions.

2. Federal lending and loan guarantee programs have helped to bring about beneficial innovations, such as the monthly-payment home mortgage, term lending to business, loans to savings institutions and farm cooperatives, SBICs. By competition and example, private lending operations have been improved to meet needs better, especially for farm and home mortgage lending.

3. The contribution of these Federal programs to short-run economic stabilization is mixed. Federal lending has shown a relatively random relation to the business cycle. However, FHA and VA mortgage guarantee programs have made an inadvertent contribution to economic stability. Because of the relatively rigid interest-rate ceiling on mortgages, they tend to become very unattractive to lenders during periods of tight money, sufficiently so as to cause the total volume of mortgage lending to decline. However, much more could be done to make lending and loan guarantee programs operate as economic stabilizers.

4. These Federal programs do not generally operate for the benefit of the poor and downtrodden. The proportion of low-income persons is much lower among borrowers receiving government-underwritten mortgage loans than among borrowers whose mortgages are not so protected. Farm Credit Administration borrowers tend to be larger farmers than those obtaining credit through other channels. The Farmers Home Administration is probably the only lending agency which reaches low-income persons systematically.

5. Quite possibly Federal lending programs have increased the total volume of spending for real assets (including housing). One cannot establish this effect for certain, since it is impossible to identify the ultimate source of loan funds which come from the Treasury. It appears likely, however, that loan programs during the 1930s and again during the slack period 1958–1963 were financed by borrowing by the government, that such borrowing helped increase either the money supply or its velocity, that the increased spending raised output and employment, and that the added output went partly into durable assets.

6. Federal credit programs have probably altered the allocation of resources among various uses. The case of agriculture is a particularly interesting one. One can argue that government programs have directed more capital into farming and in the process have aggravated the overallocation of resources which has chronically affected the farm sector since the 1920s. On the other hand, the expansion of farm credit facilities in general and

rural electrification in particular have contributed greatly to the rapid advance in farm productivity since the 1930s. Despite price-support programs, this higher productivity has benefited primarily consumers, through lower farm prices. Indeed, on balance it is doubtful whether farm credit programs have helped farmers, except for the contribution which rural electrification has made toward a more comfortable home life. The chief misallocation in farming involves labor, not capital. The consuming public has probably gotten good value for its money in expanding farm credit facilities.

7. It is unfortunate that Federal programs aimed at making credit available to borrowers who cannot obtain it from private sources (principally the Farmers Home Administration and Small Business Administration) also tend to lend at abnormally low interest rates. This creates the problem of the flies and the honey—that is, the cheap credit attracts sharp operators or outright cheats. If the program is strictly policed to keep these out, it may also eliminate many deserving beneficiaries. If liberally administered, much of the money may go to persons who don't need it and were not intended to benefit. If the lending agency is under pressure to show a good record on loan repayments, it may be tempted to be unduly lenient toward relatively larger borrowers. On the other hand, if the agency has a lax attitude toward repayments, firms with small ownership equities may be tempted into improper actions, such as running down the firm's assets through excessive salaries or improper payments.

8. Nevertheless, the principle of lending to marginal borrowers is probably sound. It operates as a competitive influence to encourage private lenders to accommodate them. Particularly wholesome is the use of the cooperative approach involving, say, the SBA and a commercial bank. Ideally, temporary assistance by SBA might well result in a creditworthy borrower and initiate a self-sustaining banking connection. If marginal-borrower programs were operated with more realistic interest charges (comparable to commercial bank business loan rates to small borrowers) the problem of freeloaders would be reduced.

9. Federal programs have increased the mobility of credit. Government-underwritten mortgages are much more suitable for transfer, and many are bought by insurance companies and savings banks far from their point of origin. Federal insurance of savings and loan accounts aids associations to solicit such accounts by mail from distant savers. Federally sponsored intermediaries such as Home Loan banks and intermediate credit banks help to channel funds to those local lending institutions facing strong demands for credit.

10. It is doubtful that there exist major credit gaps not served in some degree by existing programs.

THE WORLD OF FINANCE—SOME GENERAL OBSERVATIONS

Intermediation and Mobility of Funds   Table 13-5 summarizes the pattern of financial asset ownership by major American financial institutions. These data cover the principal forms of financial claims against the nonfinancial sectors of the economy, with the exception of trade debt, which is largely internal to the business sector. Financial institutions held about half of all the loans and investment assets listed. Their proportion was about half for government securities. It ranged upward to a very impressive

Table 13-5   Loans and investments of financial institutions, December, 1962
(Billions of dollars)

Institution	U.S. gov't sec.	State & local gov't sec.	Corpo- rate & foreign bonds	Mort- gages	Con- sumer credit	Other loans	Corpo- rate stock	Total
Federal Reserve banks	$ 31	—	—	—	—	*	—	$ 31
Commercial banks	69	$25	$ 1	$ 34	$24	$ 88	—	241
Mutual savings banks	7	1	4	32	—	—	$ 1	44
Savings & loan, credit unions	6	—	—	79	7	—	—	92
Life insurance companies	6	4	53	47	—	7	7	124
Other insurance companies	7	11	3	1	—	—	11	33
Noninsured pension funds	3	—	17	2	—	—	20	41
Other financial institutions	5	1	1	3†	17‡	16§	19¶	62
Total	$133	$40	$ 80	$198	$47	$111	$ 58	$ 668
Nonfinancial holders	123	41	21	53	16	29	448	730
Total	$256	$81	$101	$251	$64	$140	$505	$1,398
Percentage financial	53%	49%	79%	79%	74%	79%	11%	48%

* Less than $0.5 billion.
† Chiefly held by mortgage companies.
‡ Chiefly held by finance companies.
§ Includes security loans by brokers, business loans of finance companies.
¶ Chiefly held by investment companies.

Source: Board of Governors, Federal Reserve System, *Flow of Funds Accounts, 1945–1962*, 1963. Figures are rounded and may not add up to totals. Corporate stock excludes holdings of nonfinancial corporations, holding companies, and closed-end investment companies. Federal debt excludes intragovernment holdings. Other loans excludes trade debt.

three-quarters for corporate bonds, mortgages, consumer credit, and other loans, and dipped to a modest tenth of corporate stock.

These data also indicate that the nonfinancial sectors of the economy, and principally individuals, hold a large proportion of the ownership claims against business but a relatively small proportion of the direct debt claims against nonfinancial business, government, and persons. Instead, individuals hold vast claims against financial intermediaries, because of their advantages of safety, liquidity, and financial services.

Horizontally, commercial banks stand far in front, with about one-third of the institutional loans and investments. Life insurance companies come in a distant second. These two are also the most widely diversified; between them they hold a sizable position in each asset category except corporate stock. Vertically, mortgages show the most areas of major holdings, although every sector made some showing in United States securities. No single vertical column was the exclusive or near-exclusive domain of one institutional type.

How well does this very extensive intermediation system allocate funds into the areas where the economic demand for them is strongest? Generally, the lure of profit provides the impetus in this direction, effective for both institutions and individuals. However, we have noted that portfolio regulations may prevent financial institutions from acquiring certain types of assets, or limit the amounts of their holdings, in ways which impede the economical allocation of funds. It would be desirable if most institutions had the benefit of the kinds of "leeway clauses" sometimes available for life insurance investment. These permit a certain modest fraction of a firm's assets to be invested in any manner it chooses. Mobility of funds has also been burdened by the tradition of local unit operation which still dominates banking and savings institutions. Limits on the geographic area for lending worsen the impediments.

On the other hand, mobility of funds is promoted by many elements of our financial system. It is promoted by the existence of individual diversified institutions, such as commercial banks and life insurance companies, who can shift funds from one asset to another. Mobility can take place among several intermediaries in areas where their holdings overlap. For instance, a strong increase in demand for consumer credit at the expense of mortgage loans could be met by commercial banks, who might sell mortgages to savings institutions if the latter held abundant loanable funds. Mobility is enhanced by increasing the layers of intermediation: for instance, through bank creation of SBICs, through bank loans to finance and mortgage companies, through savings banks' investment in a mutual fund which they have sponsored for this purpose. And we have already noted how Federal lending and loan guarantee programs have contributed to the mobility of funds. Finally, the relatively "free-lance" financial institutions, such as pension funds, nonlife insurance companies, and sales finance companies, operating under relatively liberal regulation, seem to be alert to ferret out profitable opportunities and plug gaps which may be left by the more conservative savings-type institutions.

Virtues and Defects In general, the performance of the American financial system in relation to saving and borrowing has been good, particularly since the Depression of the 1930s. It has provided facilities for mass savings which offer a respectable income (4 per cent or more) while retaining maximum liquidity and safety. Life insurance and pension institutions have developed a wide variety of programs for personal financial security. On the lending side, the system has always been relatively "democratic," providing wide opportunities for fair access to credit. At present, American facilities for loans to individuals—home mortgage loans and consumer credit—far surpass such facilities in other countries. And the local unit tradition in banking and savings institutions, for all its shortcomings, did produce institutions accessible to the small borrower, institutions with a stake in the development of local enterprise and the local community.

There are, of course, many refinements of detail which could improve the performance of the system. Portfolio regulation is too much dominated by a "defensive" outlook and could be improved by measures designed to encourage constructive risk taking, particularly by commercial banks. Two areas of credit policy are worthy of more detailed appraisal. One relates to the problems of small business, the other to housing.

Credit Problems of Small Business There are many reasons why it is desirable that small business firms have adequate access to financing. Such access helps promote social goals of fairness and equal opportunity. The small firm can still contribute to innovation (the Polaroid camera) and provide a useful source of competitive vigor.

It is also true that the small firm faces certain obstacles in obtaining funds. Investors may avoid it because it is costly to obtain information about the small firm, because funds invested in a small business may be relatively illiquid (by contrast with stock in a large corporation), and because tax treatment of such investment is not particularly favorable.

It is useful to remember that most small firms, by number, are in retailing, services, and construction. If some of these face credit obstacles, the results may be regrettable from a moral standpoint, but it is doubtful that any detriment results to the economy as a whole. Certainly these sectors of the economy do not lack for credit opportunities. It is also fairly clear that credit problems as such are not the most pressing difficulties facing small firms. Quality of management stands out as a much more common reason for small-business failures.

There are many elements in the private financial system which work favorably for small business. Most of our commercial banks are small and must of necessity limit their lending to small borrowers, who constitute the vast majority of all bank borrowers by number. The small firm can usually rely on trade credit from suppliers. Mortgage loans serve extensively to finance small firms and farms owning real estate. And the individual starting up in business may also benefit from the relatively abundant facilities for personal loans.

The real problem seems to involve a relatively small, but not therefore unimportant, number of firms, particularly in manufacturing, whose initial success has caused them to outgrow the funds available from these sources, but who are not large enough to "go public" by selling stock or bonds through investment channels. Owners of such firms may be reluctant to dilute their managerial autonomy sufficiently to obtain outside ownership capital.

Widespread efforts have been made to improve the financial facilities available to the small firms. Among the most promising is the establishment of the SBIC program; others include the older SBA loan program and special small-business credit programs of major life insurance companies and state development corporations. To date, the number of firms aided through such financial channels has not been very large. Quite possibly the problem was never a serious one; in any case, it is not clear that much more can be done about it without lowering credit standards in a manner inviting to the sharp operators and freeloaders.

Housing If the small-business situation is relatively better than it looks, the reverse is probably true of housing. On the surface, the contribution of the financial system, strongly influenced by government programs, appears excellent. The quantity and quality of American housing have been substantially increased since World War II. Government lending and insurance programs have helped to promote this result. Evaluations of these programs indicate, however, that they have not actually reduced home mortgage interest rates appreciably, but rather have tended to bring about "easier" credit terms—that is, longer maturities and higher ratios of debt to property value. One study estimates that, in consequence, residential construction attracted about $18 billion more than it otherwise would during the decade of the 1950s. Part of this flow merely went to bid up house prices and construction costs, but the total housing stock rose by 1.5 million units more than it would have without Federal influence.[19] Since this was a period of relatively full employment, a corresponding reduction in output must have occurred somewhere else, but cannot be identified. However, it is not self-evident that the shift in resource use toward housing improved consumer welfare on balance, particularly in view of the relatively small benefit going to low-income families from Federal housing credit programs.

[19] See James Gillies, "Federal Credit Programs in the Housing Sector of the Economy: An Aggregate Analysis," *Federal Credit Programs*, p. 427.

However, one's attitude may be somewhat more favorable if economic conditions are predominantly slack, as in the 1930s and to a lesser degree in 1958–1963. More spending on housing can then mean more total output and employment.

On balance, the Federal housing credit program has a very one-sided quality. It has tended greatly to stress the construction of one-family owner-occupied homes, the vast majority of which have been built in suburban developments. The proportion of homeowners among the American population has consequently risen above 60 per cent, which is without precedent here or anywhere else.

Now home ownership has many virtues, and it is good that people have the opportunity to become homeowners. But it is a monumental paradox that home ownership, financed by debts of increasingly long maturity, has gone so far at the same time that the geographic mobility of Americans has been going up. In fact, home ownership is poorly adapted to the needs of many Americans. But the easy credit terms promoted by Federal policy, plus the favorable income tax treatment of home ownership, often lead people to buy a house on credit when they should be renting. The result has been to make many mobile Americans into real estate speculators.

Federal housing programs have neglected the needs of renters and particularly of city dwellers wanting rental accommodations. To be sure, tax discrimination and other elements worsen the picture. In theory these deficiencies are somewhat remedied by urban renewal and public housing. Unfortunately, the evidence suggests that such programs may well be worse than nothing. A brilliant and provocative study by Jane Jacobs reaches most pessimistic conclusions concerning such programs. Moreover, Mrs. Jacobs is highly critical of the role of private lenders in relation to urban problems. Too often, she argues, an urban area becomes designated as "blighted" and is then blacklisted by lenders. In consequence, grass-roots efforts by residents to upgrade their properties fail, and many sell out and move out. Properties are transferred to less scrupulous landlords, who rent each room separately, ignore sanitary violations, and maximize short-run gains. Ultimately "cataclysmic money" from a government program is used to destroy existing buildings and erect the standard high-rise public or private housing which has proved singularly ill-suited to city life.[20]

The Jacobs case goes far beyond credit programs, for the major deficiencies seem to lie in city planners' attitudes toward housing and urban vitality in general. All this is not intended to deny that many people have benefited from the housing credit programs. Unfortunately, these programs

[20] Jane Jacobs, *The Death and Life of Great American Cities*, Vintage Books, Random House, Inc., New York, 1963, especially Chap. 16, "Gradual Money and Cataclysmic Money."

have tended to turn into a sacred cow. They have also developed a large and very influential clientele among real estate and construction firms, whose primary concern is not with the general welfare of the public. However, there is no reason to believe that housing markets would work optimally if restored to more nearly free-market conditions. At best, one can hope that a reexamination of housing policies might reduce their tendencies to contribute to suburban sprawl and urban blight. Establishment in 1964 of a program stressing loans for rehabilitation of existing structures was probably a step in the right direction.

SUMMARY

Financial intermediaries play a very large part in the processes of saving and borrowing. Much of the saving of the public flows into such intermediary claims as deposits with banks and thrift institutions, life insurance policies, and pension rights. Consequently financial institutions provide a large part of the loanable funds and hold the major share of the indebtedness of the nonfinancial sectors of the economy. However, their freedom to acquire assets is limited by regulatory practices designed to ensure the safety and liquidity of the public's savings. Such practices may inhibit the flow of funds into the areas of highest priority, particularly into risky ventures. Government lending and loan guarantee programs have helped to reduce the magnitude of credit gaps, with particular success in farm credit. Financial problems of small business remain, but are being handled about as well as one can expect. However, the public and private policies with respect to housing could benefit from a more skeptical appraisal than they have been getting.

Financial intermediaries hold only a small proportion of corporate stock, although personal trust funds account for a substantial additional amount. Investment banking firms and brokers handle new issues and transfers of existing shares.

QUESTIONS FOR STUDY

1. Terminological ambiguities provide many pitfalls for the uninitiated in the world of finance. Here are a few to watch out for:

   a. What is the difference between a commercial bank, a mutual savings bank, and an investment banking firm?

   b. What is the difference between the "reserves" which the Federal Reserve requires its members to hold, and the "reserves" held by mutual thrift institutions?

 c. How does "term insurance" differ from ordinary life insurance? Why are credit life and group life insurance regarded as similar to term insurance?

 d. Distinguish between the two major types of "finance companies" dealing in consumer credit.

 2. Suppose you expect stock prices to rise 10 per cent in the near future and have $1,000 to invest. How much profit could you make buying on margin if the margin were 50 per cent? 90 per cent? 10 per cent? Suppose prices fell 10 per cent instead and you decided to sell, fearing further declines. How much would you lose in each case?

 3. A prospective automobile purchaser obtains a loan from his bank. He signs a note for $1,200 to be repaid in 12 monthly installments of $100 each. The bank charges him 6 per cent interest on the total (i.e., $72) and deducts it in advance, giving him $1,128 in cash. Estimate the actual annual interest rate involved.

 4. An insurance company recently announced that it was prepared to sell insurance against breaking one's spectacles. Why is this not a very good application of the principles of insurance?

 5. According to a life insurance mortality table adopted in 1958, out of a normal group of 100,000 people of age twenty, about 179 would die within a year and about 930 within five years. What would be the approximate annual premium per $1,000 to buy "pure insurance" on a one-year or five-year term basis at that age? To buy ordinary life policy at age twenty would cost you $15 to $20 per $1,000 per year. Why?

 6. The kinds of assets which commercial banks, savings institutions, and life insurance companies may acquire are determined in large degree by the nature of their liabilities to the public. Describe and evaluate the relationship.

SUGGESTED READINGS

The following volumes were all sponsored by the Commission on Money and Credit and published by Prentice-Hall, Inc. (Englewood Cliffs, N.J.), in 1962 and 1963:

 The Consumer Finance Industry
 Life Insurance Companies as Financial Institutions
 Management Investment Companies
 Mortgage Companies: Their Place in the Financial Structure
 Mutual Savings Banking: Basic Characteristics and Role in the National Economy
 The Savings and Loan Business
 Federal Credit Agencies

Federal Credit Programs
Private Financial Institutions
Federal Reserve System: *Financing Small Business,* Report to the Committees on Banking and Currency and the Select Committees on Small Business, U.S. Congress, 1958.

Goldsmith, Raymond: *Financial Intermediaries in the American Economy since 1900,* Princeton University Press for National Bureau of Economic Research, Inc., Princeton, N.J., 1958.

part five

INTERNATIONAL FINANCIAL RELATIONS

chapter fourteen

INTERNATIONAL ASPECTS
OF MONEY AND FINANCE:
THEORY

So far our analysis has been directed primarily to monetary relationships within one country. In this chapter we shall concentrate on the interplay between international finance and domestic income levels, interest rates, monetary and fiscal policies, and economic welfare.

WHY TREAT INTERNATIONAL FINANCE SEPARATELY?

International Specialization International transactions do not differ much economically from those which occur within one national economy. Goods and services are exchanged internationally in reflection of the potential benefits of specialization on productivity. Some of these benefits arise from the unequal distribution of natural resources about the earth. Beneficial specialization may also arise from differences among countries in the *relative* supply of various resources. Thus a country with an abundance of capital in relation to labor and land is likely to specialize in products in which capital-intensive methods are efficient (petroleum refining, steel). Countries with much land relative to labor and capital may find it more advantageous to specialize in the products of extensive agriculture (wheat, cattle). Each country can obtain a greater amount of the things it wants by concentrating its resources in those products for which they are relatively well suited and trading some of these products for the things its people desire. International trade, like all trade, takes place because the parties to the exchange find it mutually advantageous. Compared to self-sufficiency, specialization and exchange among nations will usually result in a higher value and volume of world output, since it encourages the use of resources where their productivity is high.

Besides the important commerce in goods and services, there are important international transactions involving the movement of securities, claims, and other intangibles—so-called capital transactions. A large part of this movement consists of media of exchange moving opposite to the flow of goods and services, but part of it represents a flow of financial saving from some countries into financial investment in others. Ideally, the international flow of capital funds should be in accordance with desirable patterns of productivity and resource use. If capital funds flow from areas where the marginal efficiency of investment is low to areas where it is high, investors benefit from higher incomes, while the recipient country can enjoy the benefits which investment can confer on employment and productivity.

Significance of National Boundaries   International economic relations differ from intranational activities in several respects. Productive resources do not move as easily across national boundaries as they do inside them. International transactions are complicated by the fact that each nation may have its own monetary units. Thus traders may find it necessary not only to exchange goods and services for money but also to exchange one type of money for another. Problems arise when national monetary units fluctuate in relative value and when deliberate government restrictions on monetary exchanges replace free convertibility.

Politically the "nation" is a basic policy-making unit, and its policies will generally give more attention to the welfare of residents than to outsiders. There has generally been a bias in favor of self-sufficiency and an attitude that international transactions are suspect and inferior. While international transactions are usually mutually beneficial to the trading countries, they are often *not* beneficial to all parties within those countries. Freedom to import may reduce income and employment in some import-competing industries, even though incomes and employment expand in export industries and consumers benefit from lower prices. Military or strategic considerations may dictate interference with free transactions, and in some circumstances freedom of international transactions may be incompatible with domestic economic welfare. National policies to prevent depression and maintain full employment have led to extensive restrictions on international transactions, sometimes with ample justification.

TYPES OF INTERNATIONAL TRANSACTIONS AND PAYMENTS

The Balance of International Payments   The central concept for the analysis of the financial or money-flow aspects of international transactions is the balance of international payments. This is simply an orderly listing of all types of international transactions which a country engages in during a given year. Table 14-1 shows the United States balance of international payments account for 1963.

For analytical purposes, it is convenient to subdivide international transactions into three broad categories. The first consists of *current-account* items, chiefly imports and exports of currently produced goods and services. Most important is trade in goods, which involved $22 billion of private exports and $17 billion of imports in 1963. Here also we include income payments on investment abroad, payments arising from military programs, and international transfer payments and grants such as those involved in United States foreign-aid programs. Finally, the current account includes payments for services—transportation, insurance, and particularly tourist expenditures abroad.

The current-account items in the balance of payments are direct parts of the main money circuits of the trading countries. Exports from a country represent an outlet for current production, and receipts from their sale and from investment income are a part of current income.

The second category of international transactions consists of *investment* transactions, involving the acquisition of assets abroad. *Direct* investment reflects acquisition by American business of productive real assets in foreign countries—factories, oil refineries, and the like. *Portfolio* investment consists of acquisition of financial assets. United States government loans to foreign countries are also included in the investment account.

The data indicate that in 1963 the United States showed a surplus of receipts on its current account, but a substantially larger deficit—excess of payments—from investment transactions. The combined net position of current and investment accounts provides a measure of the surplus or deficit position of the country's international accounts as a whole. In 1963, the United States incurred a deficit of $3.3 billion by this measure.

The third general category of international transactions consists of what we will term *monetary and reserve* transactions. Here are involved net transfers of gold, cash, and liquid assets of two general types. Some of these consist of ordinary means of payment—currency, bank deposits—used in international transactions. Others involve assets used as international financial reserves by private and public financial institutions, of which the most important is gold.

The gross flow of monetary and reserve assets is of course very large;

Table 14-1   United States balance of international payments, 1963
(Billions of dollars)

	Receipts	Payments
Current account		
1. Merchandise imports and exports	$22.0	$17.0
2. Military sales and purchases	0.7	2.9
3. Investment income	4.5	1.2
4. Other services transactions	4.9	5.2
5. Transfer payments and grants	net	2.7
Total current	$32.0	$29.1
Investment transactions		
6. Direct private investment	net	1.9
7. Other long-term private investment	0.3	1.7
8. Private short-term capital	*	0.7
9. U.S. gov't	0.7	2.6
Total investment	$ 1.1	$ 6.9
10. Errors and omissions		0.3
Total, lines 1–10	$33.1	$36.3
Deficit	3.3	
Monetary and reserve transactions		
11. Advance repayment of U.S. gov't loans	0.3	net
12. Advances on U.S. military exports	0.3	net
13. Sales of special Treasury securities abroad	0.7	—
14. Increase in foreign holdings of short-term dollar liabilities	1.6	net
15. Change in U.S. monetary and foreign-exchange reserves:		
Gold exports	0.5	net
Convertible currencies	net	0.1
Total, lines 11–15	$ 3.4	$ 0.1
Total, lines 1–15	$36.4	$36.4
Memo: U.S. government totals in lines 1–9	$ 1.9	$ 7.4

* Less than $50 million.
Source: Federal Reserve Bulletin, January, 1965, p. 204. Figures are rounded and may not add up to totals shown.

however, for statistical purposes totals are generally shown net. Net international transfers of monetary and reserve assets represent a balancing item; they represent the means by which the net surplus or deficit on current plus investment account is financed.

In 1963, the United States incurred a deficit of $3.3 billion. Lines 11 to 15 show the means by which this deficit was financed. First, the United States Treasury resorted to special borrowing and encouraged advanced repayment from debtor countries (lines 11 to 13). Second, foreign business firms and central banks added substantially to their holdings of dollar assets in such forms as deposits in American banks and ordinary United States

Treasury bills. Third, the Treasury sold about half a billion dollars worth of gold to foreign countries.

Statistical Balance When the three types of transactions are combined, the two sides of the balance-of-payments account must balance, because of the definition of terms. Every transaction gives rise to an equal entry on both sides. This can be illustrated by a few sample transactions, as follows:

An American importer buys $5,000 of British goods, and the seller accepts a check on an American bank in payment. If we use the terms from Table 14-1, this would be entered on the American balance-of-payments account in this way:

14. Increase, foreign holdings of dollar assets	$5,000	1. Merchandise imports	$5,000

Britons send $5,000 worth of goods to the United States as gifts:

5. Transfer payments received	$5,000	1. Merchandise imports	$5,000

A British firm borrows $5,000 from an American bank and uses the funds to buy American goods for sale in Britain:

1. Merchandise exports	$5,000	8. Private, (probably) short-term investment	$5,000

Thus in theory, the account must always balance. In practice, the statisticians never have full information on all transactions; therefore they must make an allowance for errors and omissions.

Surpluses and Deficits Generally speaking, a country experiences a surplus internationally when its receipts for current and investment transactions exceed its payments for such transactions. Such a surplus brings with it increased holdings of gold and other international reserve assets, or a decrease in certain types of short-term monetary liabilities to foreigners.

A country experiences an international deficit when its payments for current and investment transactions exceed its receipts for such transactions. A deficit is associated with a decrease in the country's holdings of gold and other international reserve assets, or an increase in its monetary liabilities to foreigners.

The United States has experienced deficits in its international accounts fairly consistently since 1950. Much public attention has been directed to this fact. What factors have caused the deficit? Is it good or bad? If it is bad, what can be done about it? These questions, which have received wide attention, will be dealt with in this chapter and the next. Before we can deal with them adequately, we must do a lot of describing and analyzing. However, it may be useful to clarify some terminological ambiguities before going further.

First, a deficit in a country's balance of payments does not necessarily mean that it is importing more goods (and services) than it is exporting. The United States has maintained export surpluses consistently since World War II.

Second, an international deficit does not necessarily entail a loss of gold. Most of the United States deficit since 1950 has been financed by increased foreign holdings of monetary and near-monetary claims against the United States.

Third, an international deficit does not necessarily make a country financially "worse off." Although United States deficits have caused a decrease in our monetary gold stock and an increase in our liabilities to foreigners, we have added large sums to our holdings of foreign assets, both direct and portfolio. Our international net worth has been increasing, not decreasing.

Fourth, it is useful to remember that one country's deficit is another's surplus. For all countries combined, (assuming transactions are consistently valued) surpluses and deficits cancel out.

THE INTERNATIONAL ROLE OF MONEY

The Price System   Internationally, the functions of money are essentially those it serves within each national economy. Money prices serve internationally as a guide to specialization and exchange. They help to determine what products will be produced and what resources and techniques will be used in making them. Prices play a major role in determining which commodities a nation will produce for export and where they will go and what things it will import and from what sources. In so doing, the international price system exerts a strong influence on the domestic production, resource, and income patterns of individual countries.

The international influence of prices is complicated by the fact that individual consumers and business firms make their decisions chiefly in terms of their own monetary unit. But each monetary unit is linked to others through foreign-exchange rates, which become an additional variable in international price comparisons. Thus an American exporter must estimate the price in foreign currency at which he can sell his products and multiply this by the exchange rate to obtain an estimate of dollar revenues.

At any given set of exchange rates, buying and selling decisions of consumers and business firms will take account of foreign as well as domestic alternatives. Buyers will choose imports rather than domestic products when the imports yield more utility or productivity per dollar. Sellers will supply export markets when they yield more revenue than domestic markets.

This interplay of decisions will tend toward a definite pattern. In each country, the prices of individual resources will tend to reflect their relative scarcity or abundance. If land is abundant relative to labor and capital, for instance, land prices and rents will be low relative to interest rates and wages. Where land is cheap, extensive agricultural production can be carried on at low cost. Products such as grain and meat can then be produced cheaply enough to keep out imports and to be sold successfully in export markets. At the same time, the scarcity of labor and capital will give those resources higher prices and cause domestic products using chiefly those resources to be more expensive than imports. Thus the country will tend to import those items which are not so well suited to its peculiar pattern of resource availability. Each country tends to specialize in products for which it has a *comparative advantage*—for which its resources are relatively well suited.

A change in rates of foreign exchange will alter the prices on which import and export decisions are based. If foreign currencies become more costly in dollars, imports into the United States will become correspondingly more costly—assuming their prices remain unchanged in the country of origin. The same shift will raise the prospective sale value in dollars of American exports. However, if foreign currencies fall in value relative to the dollar, imports will become cheaper in dollars, and the prospective sales proceeds of American exports in dollars will fall. Thus the volume of imports and exports may be dependent on foreign-exchange rates.

International Medium of Exchange Money also serves its function as medium of payment and exchange internationally. Since goods and services can be sold for money, which can in turn be spent for other goods and services, exchanges of a multilateral nature can easily be conducted. Further, the use of money permits these exchanges to be spread out over time.

Freedom for multilateral exchanges is of vital importance among nations. If country A can sell exports to B, C, and D and use the proceeds to buy from E, F, and G, it is free to specialize along the lines of comparative advantage and be relatively indifferent to the specific destination of exports or the origin of imports. In recent years, European countries have relied on export surpluses to South America and other less industrialized countries to finance import surpluses from the United States.

Without such freedom, trading tends to degenerate into bilateral exchange. National specialization is restricted by the problem of "double coincidence of wants"—each country must consider what the trading partner wants and what it has to offer in exchange. Tendencies toward bilateralism may arise from exchange controls which restrict the use of regional payments surpluses to meet needs in other areas.

Media of International Payment The international functioning of money as a medium of payment is complicated by the fact that individual national monetary units are not generally acceptable in payments in other countries. Generally, prospective import buyers start out with a supply of their domestic money, whereas prospective sellers ultimately want to receive payment in *their* type of money. In practice, one or the other will take the initiative in making an exchange of money units. The prospective importer may "buy" some of the money of the exporter's country and pay him with it; or the exporter may accept payment in the importer's national money and "sell" it to obtain the desired units in exchange. For most traders, the normal foreign-exchange transaction is simply the exchange of one type of bank deposit for another. These exchanges are made through banks and other foreign-exchange institutions, who settle balances among themselves chiefly with near-money foreign-exchange assets such as gold or short-term credit instruments.

In the nineteenth century, the pound sterling was the primary medium of international payment. Foreigners held large deposits with British banks, which they used to make payments not only to British exporters or investors but also to residents of other countries. However, the American dollar has become an important medium in recent years. American importers and tourists can spend dollars almost anywhere. Foreign sellers are willing to accept them and take the responsibility of converting them into their own currency units. A substantial volume of checking deposits in American banks is held by foreigners—over $7 billion at the end of 1963.[1]

Store of Value Types of money which are widely used internationally are likely to be held to some extent as a store of value in order to meet expected or unexpected future international payment needs. Individuals may hold the money of a foreign country as a store of value because they regard their own money as inferior. Holding of domestic balances may be encumbered with exchange restrictions, or the holder may risk taxation or confiscation. Or individuals may hold foreign money as a speculation, because they expect the foreign-exchange value of their domestic money to decline. Attempts to acquire foreign money for these purposes are often called "capital flight."

However, money as an international store of value competes with other types of assets. Unless there is some pressing desire for liquidity (as in transactions balances), foreigners often prefer to hold interest-bearing short-term debt claims, such as time deposits and government securities. Foreign holdings of dollar assets of this type amounted to $16 billion at the end of 1963.

In recent years, most foreign holdings of American money or near-money have represented foreign-exchange reserves for central banks and other financial institutions. These reserves provide a medium through which net settlements of international positions can be made among these institu-

[1] *Federal Reserve Bulletin*, June, 1964, p. 792.

tions. Of the $26 billion foreign holdings of dollar demand deposits and near-money assets in December, 1963, about $23 billion was held by banks or other financial institutions.[2]

This function of international foreign-exchange reserves is shared by gold. By the end of 1963, the monetary gold stock of the free world totaled about $42 billion, of which $15.5 billion was held by the United States Treasury. West Germany, France, and Great Britain accounted for another $10 billion. Much of the free world's gold is kept physically in the United States. "Earmarked" gold, belonging to foreign countries but stored in Federal Reserve banks, amounted to about $13 billion at the end of 1963.[3]

Money as the Unit of Debt International trade and investment give rise to a large volume of debts and other claims expressed in money units of individual countries. According to estimates of the Department of Commerce, the total value of American claims against foreigners at the end of 1963 was about $88 billion. About half of this consisted of debt claims and other securities. Foreign claims against this country totaled about $52 billion.[4]

Variations in foreign-exchange rates can also alter the international values of assets and liabilities. For example, when the British devalued the pound from $4.03 to $2.80 in 1949, an American who owed £1,000 to a Briton would have found the dollar burden of the debt reduced from $4,030 to $2,800. An unfortunate Briton who owed $5,000 to an American would have found the burden of his debt increased from about £1,240 to about £1,785.

MECHANICS OF FOREIGN EXCHANGE

Kinds of Foreign-exchange Transactions The continuous swapping of different national moneys among traders provides the basis for the foreign-exchange market. This is not a central physical location like a stock exchange but consists of a number of banks and other firms in financial centers. When an individual wishes to exchange one national money for another, he may deal directly with one of these firms or indirectly through his own bank.

The transaction may take several technical forms. At one extreme, the buyer of foreign exchange may exchange "cash for cash." He may pay in currency or check and receive foreign currency or some sort of demand claim against a foreign bank. This may be a cable draft, through which very rapid transfer of funds can be made to the payee in the foreign country;

[2] *Ibid.;* total includes $3 billion of special Treasury obligations held by International Monetary Fund.

[3] *Ibid.*, pp. 786, 797.

[4] U.S. Department of Commerce, *Survey of Current Business*, August, 1964, p. 24.

or he may receive a sight draft, which is similar to a cashier's check on a foreign bank. This can be mailed to the payee in the foreign country. Tourists often buy travelers' checks payable abroad.

Basis for Foreign-exchange Transactions Foreign-exchange transactions involve people who have one kind of money and want another kind. Before proceeding to more complex aspects, let us take a look at a prototype situation which helps to relate the foreign-exchange market to other economic activities.

Figure 14-1 illustrates a very simple foreign-exchange situation. Suppose all imports from Great Britain came through American importing firms who paid for them with pounds sterling. And suppose that all export sales to Great Britain were handled through American exporting firms which received payment in sterling. This would provide the basis for the foreign-exchange situation shown in the diagram.

The export firms receive pounds in payment, but they need dollars in order to buy more American goods for export and to pay their employees. Consequently they enter the foreign-exchange market to sell pounds for dollars. On the other hand, the importing firms receive dollars for the imported goods they sell to Americans, but need sterling to pay for more imports. They enter the foreign-exchange market to buy pounds for dollars. The foreign-exchange flows would, in this oversimplified case, be closely related to the flow of imports and exports. American exports would provide Americans with the foreign exchange needed to purchase imports.

The illustration is useful, but too simple. In the real world both pounds and dollars are used to finance Anglo-American trade, so British importers and exporters will be involved in a counterpart operation on their side.

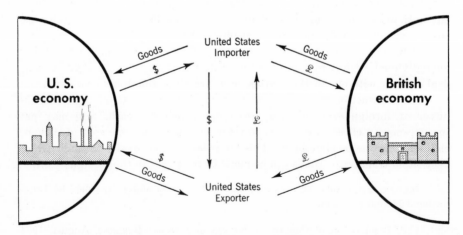

Figure 14-1. Foreign-exchange transactions: a simplified view.

Furthermore, pounds and dollars will be involved in transactions with other countries. Consequently, Americans can obtain pounds indirectly by selling to other countries as well as directly by selling to England. Investment transactions are involved, as well as trade. Finally, foreign-exchange transactions very commonly contain elements of credit as well as mere money changing. Generally the exporter wishes to receive money immediately, while the importer prefers to delay payment until he has had time to resell the goods to final buyers. Credit may reconcile the difference at either end of the transactions. We turn to some common types of credit involved in foreign-exchange dealings.

Bills, Drafts, and Acceptances One of the commonest traditional forms of credit in international transactions has been the bill of exchange, which is now used chiefly in the form of a banker's acceptance. Suppose an exporter ships $10,000 worth of goods to an importer. The exporter might send along with the shipment a draft ordering the importer to pay the $10,000 to the exporter or someone else designated by him. This might be payable on demand or after some specified time. The importer, as a condition of receiving the shipment, might be required to "accept" the draft— to endorse it so as to promise to fulfill its conditions. This converts the draft into a promissory note, reflecting the importer's debt to the exporter. The importer can in turn have his bank "accept" the note—in effect, to endorse it (for a fee) as a sort of cosigner to guarantee payment. Such a banker's acceptance enjoys high credit standing and can be used by the exporter as collateral for a loan on favorable terms. The exporter could sell the acceptance to his bank (at a discount from face value representing interest), which would in turn collect the proceeds from the importer (through *his* bank) when the time period of the draft expired. Transactions of this sort involve both foreign exchange and credit. In effect, the exporter receives payment in his own currency immediately, while the importer makes payment in *his* currency later on.

There are many forms of credit and payment documents connected with international finance. However, we shall confine our attention to acceptances and sight drafts, which illustrate all the important principles.

How Intermediaries Can Sell Drafts From the standpoint of the individual trader, the foreign-exchange transaction is simple enough. But what about the banks and other firms which serve as intermediaries? How do they arrange to make the transactions come out even?

Very commonly foreign-exchange transactions are arranged by a pair of correspondent banks in two countries. (Sometimes a single bank may have branches in several countries.) Each of the banks might set up a deposit credit (or overdraft privilege) in favor of the other, on which the latter could sell drafts. Suppose bank A (American) and bank B (British) make such an arrangement, so that bank A has a deposit credit of £1,000 with bank B and bank B has a credit of $2,800 with bank A. Since £1,000 equals $2,800, this will balance on their balance sheets, as follows:

Assets		Liabilities	
	Bank A		
Due from B	$2,800	Due to B	$2,800
	Bank B		
Due from A	£1,000	Due to A	£1,000

Now bank A is in a position to sell sterling drafts to Americans who may want to make payments in England. Suppose it sells a draft for £500 to an importer who pays $1,400 (plus commission, which we ignore) by check on his account with bank A. This action reduces bank A's domestic demand-deposit liabilities and also cuts down its deposit credit with B. Its account would be as follows:

	Bank A		
Due from B	$2,800 / −1,400	Due to B	$2,800
		Demand deposits	−1,400

The American importer will in turn send the draft to England. Let us assume that the recipient exporter deposits it in his checking account with bank B. Bank B's account will then look like this:

	Bank B		
Due from A	£1,000	Due to A	£1,000 / −500
		Demand deposits	+500

This transaction increases the money supply in Britain and reduces it in the United States.

Bank B can operate in similar fashion. Britishers wishing to make payments in the United States would be purchasing dollar drafts from B and paying with checks on their sterling accounts. If B sells a $1,400 draft for £500 paid by check on bank B and if the draft is deposited in bank A, the final balance sheets would show:

	Bank A		
Due from B	$2,800 / −1,400	Due to B	$2,800 / −1,400
		Demand deposits	−1,400 (as above) / +1,400

	Bank B		
Due from A	£1,000 / −500	Due to A	£1,000 / −500
		Demand deposits	+500 (as above) / −500

The purchase of dollars has pulled bank B's deposit liabilities back down to their original value, and the deposit of the dollar draft pushed bank A's deposits back to where they started from. Thus the money supplies return to their starting positions in both countries. The reciprocal credits of the banks are reduced, but there is no reason why they should not agree to raise them back to the original level.

Intermediaries Deal in Acceptances The banks can achieve automatic replenishment of their foreign balances by purchasing acceptances or other credit instruments payable in the foreign country and then collecting the proceeds when they fall due. American exporters may receive bills or acceptances drawn on their British customers and payable in sterling. Bank A may buy these for dollars and send them to Britain for collection through bank B. When collected, the proceeds will be credited to bank A's account. The initial purchase of a sterling acceptance by bank A would affect its account as follows (before maturity):

	Bank A	
Loans +$1,000	Demand deposits	+$1,000

So far, the transaction is similar to an ordinary loan. (Creation of deposits can occur only if bank A has excess reserves.) On maturity, the loan asset would disappear. When the loan is repaid by the British importer with a check drawn on bank B, the latter's demand-deposit liabilities would decline, and bank A would acquire a sterling credit with bank B as follows:

	Bank A	
Due from B +$1,000	Demand deposits	$1,000
	Bank B	
	Due to A	+£357 (= $1,000)
	Demand deposits	−357

If bank B purchases dollar acceptances, analogous effects will operate in the opposite direction. Bank B will create sterling deposits in favor of the sellers of acceptances, and dollar deposit liabilities will be canceled in the United States when the loans are collected. Thus if the purchases of acceptances by the two banks are roughly equal, there will again be no net change in the money supply in either country. However, there would be a tendency for the reciprocal deposits of the banks to mount up—a tendency which could be used to offset the depletion from the sale of drafts. Since acceptances are traded in the open market, individual institutions can vary the volume of their purchases to achieve a desired balancing of accounts.

Origin and Clearing of Payments There is a close similarity between the purchase of sterling drafts by American importers and the sale of dollar acceptances by British exporters. Both transactions tend to decrease the money supply in the United States and increase it in Britain. Both arise chiefly from the shipment of goods from Britain to the United States and represent an offer of dollars for pounds. Likewise, there is a similarity between the purchase of dollar drafts by British importers and the sale of sterling acceptances by American exporters.

Looking at the process as a whole, one can say that, in effect, each nation's export sales provide funds to pay for its imports. The foreign-exchange market transfers dollar deposits from American importers, who exchange them for pounds, to American exporters, who receive them in exchange for pounds.

When the payments pattern is in balance, so that the offer of dollars just equals the demand for them, the foreign-exchange intermediaries in each country find their international accounts in a clearing equilibrium. Inflows are balanced by outflows, with no net change in the national position as a whole. In our example, we simplified this by assuming that the domestic check transactions all involved deposit liabilities of banks A and B. If this does not occur, the banks may face domestic clearing imbalances. Internationally, however, our simplification does not misrepresent the degree of balance.

Settling Imbalances Suppose the banks find themselves with an international imbalance—perhaps bank A's deposit in Britain is rising, while bank B's deposit in the United States is declining. This indicates that the offer of pounds for dollars exceeds the offer of dollars for pounds. For a time bank A may extend credit to B, perhaps charging interest. This in itself will put pressure on bank B to take steps to end the disequilibrium. Bank B will have an added incentive if bank A refuses further credit.

Bank B can attempt to remedy the disequilibrium by sending assets such as securities or gold to the United States for sale. Such actions will replenish its dollar credit. It might also be more aggressive in buying dollar acceptances payable in the United States. It will probably raise the price it charges for dollars and thus change the exchange rate and discourage transactions involving imports from the United States. Bank A may meet the imbalance by reducing its purchase of sterling acceptances or cutting the rate at which it will sell pounds for dollars. Since some of these actions involve creating demand deposits, they can occur only if the banks have excess reserves.

Thus payments imbalance is likely to set off movements of interbank credit or foreign-exchange assets between the financial intermediaries, with resulting changes in exchange rates and interest rates in the respective countries. We turn now to a more detailed investigation of how exchange rates are determined.

DETERMINATION OF EXCHANGE RATES

Supply and Demand The determination of rates of exchange between national moneys can be analyzed in terms of supply and demand. The balance-of-payments table furnishes a convenient framework for supply and demand analysis, since it lists all the transactions which represent the demand for, say, dollars and all the transactions which make dollars available to the rest of the world.

We can think of each balance-of-payments item as reflecting a separate supply and demand schedule. If we assume for the moment that the domestic prices of goods and services are given, the quantities which will be offered and taken internationally will depend on exchange rates. If a country's currency is low in foreign-exchange value, its residents will find imports expensive and export sales remunerative. When the pound was reduced in value from $4.03 to $2.80, the pound price of a $2,000 American auto was raised from £484 to £714. The quantity of a country's imports will tend to vary directly and the quantity of its exports inversely with the foreign-exchange value of its currency.

However, the demand and supply schedules relating to foreign exchange depend on the *value* of transactions rather than the quantity. If the elasticities of demand and supply are not extremely low, value and quantity will move in the same direction, and the supply and demand schedules will appear as shown in Figure 14-2.

When the pound is cheap internationally, Americans will want a larger quantity of pounds because they will spend more on British goods. But the supply of pounds will be smaller when the pound is cheap, because Britons will be spending less on costly American goods. Note that the demand for pounds is the supply of dollars, and vice versa.

The rate of exchange will tend to settle where demand and supply are equal. If the supply of pounds arising from British import purchases exceeds the demand for pounds to buy British exports, foreign-exchange firms

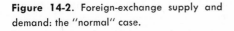

Figure 14-2. Foreign-exchange supply and demand: the "normal" case.

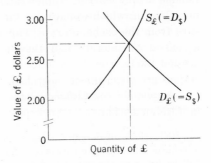

will find pounds piling up and other currencies becoming scarce. They will therefore tend to cut the price of pounds relative to other kinds of money. Only if supply and demand are equal will there be no tendency for the rate to change.

However, if elasticities of demand are low, the value of goods traded may not move in the same direction as the quantity.[5] If the pound declines in value, Britons may reduce slightly the quantity of American goods they buy but still spend more because each item purchased carries a higher price in pounds. Thus the supply of pounds might be larger when the pound is cheap! The demand for pounds will still show the normal downward slope, but if American demand for British goods is inelastic, Americans will want only slightly more pounds when they are cheap. Such a situation may produce the pattern shown in Figure 14-3.

When the supply curve is sloped backward in this manner, the market may be unstable. At the point of intersection (£1 = $2.80), there would be no tendency for the rate to change, but deviations from this point would not tend to correct themselves. If the rate were £1 = $2.50, the supply of pounds would exceed the demand, which would drive the price of pounds down still further. If the pound were selling for $3, the demand for pounds would exceed the supply and force the price up further. There are limits to this divergence of supply and demand, but considerable instability of rates might result if left uncontrolled.

Capital Movements and Exchange Rates International movements of capital, particularly short-term capital, may affect the determination of exchange rates. We have already seen one instance of this. When demand for one currency exceeds supply, there is a strong tendency for banks and foreign-exchange firms in the deficit country to borrow from their counterparts abroad. Such transactions may reduce rate fluctuations.

Traditionally, monetary policy has attempted to influence the international flow of short-term capital through interest-rate variations. If the supply of pounds exceeded the demand for them, the Bank of England might raise its discount rate, and short-term lending rates would tend to rise in the London money market. Higher rates might stimulate a flow of loanable funds into Britain, which would raise the demand for pounds and remove the pressure from the exchange rate. This use of discount-rate policy has long been a central consideration of the Bank of England. Such capital movements are not likely if exchange-rate risks are high or if foreign-exchange transactions are government-controlled.

Speculation and Exchange Rates Foreign-exchange dealers may speculate in foreign exchange in anticipation of changes in rates. Such speculative

---

[5] Elasticity of demand is the ratio between the percentage change in quantity purchased and the percentage change in price. If demand is inelastic, less money will be spent on the product at a lower price.

transactions will influence the supply and demand schedules. In some cases, speculation will tend to increase demand and supply elasticities, which will facilitate reaching equilibrium and reduce rate fluctuations. This will be the case if the speculators have expectations of "normality." If the value of the pound declines and if speculators believe it is below "normal" and will tend to rise again, they will buy pounds and thereby slow the decline.

If speculators interpret current movements as heralding larger movements in the same direction, the results will be different. A decline in the pound may then set up a flight from it, for fear it will decline further. Speculators will sell it for other currencies, and its value *will* tend to fall further unless some other force intervenes.

If exchange rates are expected to change, persons having international payments to make may alter their timing for speculative purposes. If the pound is expected to decline, persons having payments to make into Britain will tend to delay them, while outpayments from Britain will tend to be accelerated. This will add to the downward pressure on the value of sterling. Speculation of this nature was a major factor in the periodic foreign-exchange crises experienced by Britain, France, and other countries in the 1950s.

Although foreign-exchange rates might be allowed to fluctuate freely without government influence, our analysis of elasticities and speculation has indicated that under certain circumstances the result might be extreme instability of rates. Rate instability would undermine the willingness of firms to trade and invest internationally and would weaken the price system as a guide to import and export decisions. Consequently, most governments have adopted policies designed to keep exchange rates fairly stable. We shall examine some of these in the next few sections.

Exchange Rates under a Gold Standard In the late nineteenth and early twentieth centuries, the normal exchange-rate policies centered on the gold standard. Each country defined its monetary unit in terms of a certain physical weight of gold. Gold coins circulated as full-bodied money, and currency

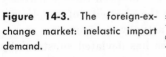

Figure 14-3. The foreign-exchange market: inelastic import demand.

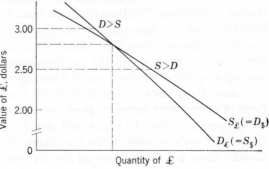

and checking deposits were freely convertible into gold on demand. Under these conditions, national currency units tended to exchange for one another in the same ratio as their respective gold equivalents.

This tendency can be illustrated by the pound-dollar relationship prior to 1931. The gold content of the dollar was 23.22 grains, giving a price for gold of $20.67 an ounce (= 480 grains). The pound sterling had a gold content of 113 grains, giving a price for gold of £4 4s. 11d., or about £4¼ per ounce. From either of these ratios, one can determine the mint par between the dollar and pound, which was about £1 = $4.87. Thus at any time during this period gold worth £1,000 in Britain would have been worth $4,870 in the United States.

The exchange rate would stay close to the ratio of gold values. Should the pound rise in value relative to the dollar, persons wishing to buy pounds might soon find it advantageous to buy gold for dollars, send it to England, and sell it for pounds. However, because such shipment would entail costs for freight, insurance, interest, etc., it would be worthwhile to ship gold only when the exchange rate diverged enough from par to cover these costs. Suppose costs of gold movement were 1 per cent of the value. It would be possible to buy 1,000 ounces of gold in the United States for $20,670, ship it to England for $207, and sell it for about £4,250. Pounds obtained in this manner would cost about $4.92 each (= $20,877/£4,250). This would be the top limit to the value of the pound, since no one would pay more for it.

A similar limit would exist on the other side. Britons could obtain dollars at a ratio of about £1 = $4.82 by shipping gold to the United States. Consequently, they would never accept less than $4.82 to the pound, and the pound would never sell for less.

The pound's value would therefore remain within the range between $4.82 and $4.92. These limiting values are called the "gold points." For England £1 = $4.92 would be the gold-import point and £1 = $4.82 the gold-export point. The actual spread of the points would depend on shipping and other costs. There would be no demand for pounds above the gold-import value, and no supply of them in the market below the gold-export value.

Gold-standard conditions tended to create a stabilizing pattern of exchange speculation. The further a rate went from mint par, the greater the likelihood that the movement would reverse itself. Thus speculators would tend to buy pounds when they went below mint par and sell them when they went above it. Such speculation would increase the elasticity of supply and demand and reduce the necessity for gold flows actually to occur.

Since 1931, the use of gold in world finance has deviated substantially from this simplified example. Most countries do not have gold coins circulating, nor do commercial banks hold gold as reserves. National gold supplies are usually concentrated in the possession of central banks and treasuries. Usually there are restrictions on the freedom of private individuals to acquire gold. The United States Treasury will sell gold only for approved use in manufacturing or for export sale to foreign central banks or similar agencies. Most gold settlements are carried on among official bodies, not by private arbitragers.

Furthermore, the "movements" of gold may be nominal. Since the 1930s a large part of the free world's gold stock has been deposited for safekeeping in the custody of the Federal Reserve Bank of New York. A "shipment" of gold from Britain to France might occur by having a Federal Reserve employee shift a couple of gold bricks from one pile to another!

Exchange Stabilization without a Gold Standard A country can stabilize its exchange rates without relying on a formal gold standard. The government may instead buy and sell foreign exchange as needed to keep rates stable. After Britain left the gold standard in 1931, the British government instituted an exchange stabilization program of this sort which is still in operation. Such a program means that the British authorities are prepared to buy pounds and sell foreign exchange when the demand for foreign exchange is high—else the pound will depreciate. To do this, they must have a supply of foreign exchange. This will impose on the authorities responsibility for settling imbalances through the shipment of gold, through international credits, or through other settlement transactions. Otherwise they may run out of foreign exchange during deficit periods or accumulate more than they want during surpluses.

FOREIGN–EXCHANGE CONTROL

Purposes of Exchange Control In the 1930s and 1940s, many countries imposed detailed restrictions on foreign-exchange transactions. Many of them prohibited free international transfers of funds and required that individual transactions be made only with government approval. Firms acquiring foreign exchange through exports or other receipts were usually obliged to sell it to the government, while prospective purchasers were required to buy exchange from the government, which was under no compulsion to sell.

Widespread use of exchange controls came initially as individual countries sought to protect themselves against the Depression of the 1930s. Exchange controls provided a means of preventing outflows of gold and foreign-exchange reserves which threatened deflationary monetary consequences. Later in the Depression, exchange controls were used to assist programs for expanding export sales and domestic incomes. World War II brought a widening of the use of exchange control, as countries endeavored to control the composition of imports and exports in order to promote national objectives.

At all times, one of the attractions of exchange control has been to prevent capital flight—movement of funds out of a country to escape onerous political conditions, inflation, or high taxes, or merely to speculate against the domestic currency. In some cases, countries resorted to exchange control to prevent their currencies from depreciating in foreign-exchange value in face of international payments deficits. Such depreciation would have brought adverse shifts in the terms of international trade—that is, made imports more costly per unit of exports—and in the burden of international indebtedness.

At the end of World War II, most of the countries of the world were imposing exchange controls, with the leading exception of the United States. The conditions of disorder and disequilibrium which characterized the postwar years provided countries with good reasons not to relinquish controls. However, the economic recovery of Western Europe, the readjustment of exchange rates, and pressure from the United States all contributed to change this attitude. In a series of moves in the 1950s the major currencies were liberated from administrative controls and were made "convertible"— meaning that holders could exchange them without limit for other currencies at official rates of exchange.

However, use of exchange control remains common in less developed countries, where balance-of-payments deficits have been a constant problem. Such controls have been managed in an effort to promote national development goals. A common pattern in Latin America has been a combination of multiple exchange rates, officially controlled, plus a "free" rate. The authorities sell foreign exchange cheaply for "essential" imports. They pay a liberal price in the home currency for foreign exchange received from sale of favored export products and perhaps also for inflows of foreign capital. However, persons wanting to buy foreign exchange to purchase "nonessential" imports or to transfer profits or capital funds out of the country may have to buy at the free rate, at which foreign exchange is likely to be very expensive indeed.

Problems of Exchange Control The use of administrative control of foreign-exchange transactions is likely to contribute to economic inefficiency; moreover, it may aggravate the very problem it was meant to solve. When controls are used, individuals are not free to import, export, and invest the amounts they desire to at existing prices. Thus the price system is not permitted to guide production and trade decisions. Multilateral transactions are impaired when money received from one country cannot be used to buy from another.

The combination of exchange control plus an overvalued currency tends to create or perpetuate an excess of demand for foreign exchange over supply. Incentives to import are artificially stimulated because foreign currency appears cheap. Consequently the authorities must ration foreign exchange among the claimants. Scarcity may create opportunities for corruption; favored importers may reap windfall gains.

No control system can eliminate opportunities for evasion. Travelers may carry currency out of the country; importers and exporters may use false invoices. Ownership of bank deposits can be transferred on the books of the banks, perhaps through the use of false identification. If evasion is extensive, the control system may aggravate the country's problems.

With the coming of relative economic stability, the industrialized nations have generally preferred the efficiency offered by the price system, convertible currencies, and stable exchange rates. Underdeveloped countries, by contrast, feel that development goals may warrant a certain degree of inflation and considerable interference with free-market forces. Controls are likely to remain in use in such countries for considerable time.

EQUILIBRIUM IN THE BALANCE OF PAYMENTS

Meaning of Equilibrium A country's balance-of-payments account always balances statistically, because of the definition of terms; but it is not always in equilibrium. The manner in which the equilibrium adjustments in international payments interact with domestic national incomes, prices, money and credit conditions, etc., is an important matter of economic concern.

For our purposes, we shall identify equilibrium in the balance of payments as a situation which contains no inherent tendencies toward change. If things are there, they will tend to stay there; and if they are not there, they will tend to move toward the equilibrium position. Since conditions are usually out of equilibrium, it is the direction and speed of change rather than the destination which is of chief interest.

Let us assume that a country's international account consists of only three types of transactions—imports and exports of goods and services; imports and exports of long-term securities, which depend solely on relative interest or profit rates in various countries; and movements of gold, money, or foreign-exchange assets, which are balancing items required to make the entire account come out even statistically. With these assumptions, the balance of payments will be in equilibrium when there are no net movements of gold, money, or similar assets. If the country has an export surplus, it will be exporting long-term capital (by importing securities) in equal amounts. If it has an import surplus, it will be importing long-term capital.

Such a situation contains no inherent forces tending to move the balance of payments from its position, although of course it may be moved by forces originating autonomously in the trading countries. However, if the equilibrium conditions are not met, forces originating within the pattern of international transactions itself will tend to cause changes in the economies of the trading countries which will in turn react on their international transactions.

Equilibrium in the balance of payments will correspond to a state of balance in the foreign-exchange market. The demand for foreign exchange to buy imports and invest abroad will be matched by the supply from exports and securities sales. No traders or foreign-exchange firms will find themselves stuck with unwanted balances of foreign money, and no international movements of foreign-exchange assets between financial institutions need occur.

Nature and Causes of Disequilibrium In a disequilibrium situation, a country may have a deficit or surplus in its international balance. A deficit means that a country is buying more goods, services, and investment assets than it is selling and that it is losing gold, money, or other foreign-exchange media in payment. A surplus means the opposite. For the world as a whole, if some countries have deficits, others must have surpluses of equal amount.

Let us examine some of the ways in which disequilibrium may come about and the ways the trading countries may adjust to it. We shall concentrate on the deficit country. For simplicity, let us assume that country A is in equilibrium and that it has no long-term capital movements, so that current imports and exports are equal. Country A may experience a deficit in two ways—its imports may increase, or its exports may fall. The chief reason for the former is likely to be higher demand in country A; for the latter, lower demand in other countries. For most countries, short-run variations in imports arise chiefly from changes in the level of GNP expenditures. One can speak of a "propensity to import," since imports tend to rise or fall with GNP in a manner similar to saving and tax revenues.

Country A's deficit may reflect cyclical movements in incomes at home or abroad. If country A is experiencing rising GNP, its imports will tend to rise. If other countries' incomes are falling, they may buy less from country A. These tendencies can be reinforced by price changes accompanying GNP movements. However, the disequilibrium may also arise from changes in consumer tastes or technology in country A or abroad.

Country A's deficit can set off numerous repercussions on levels of GNP, prices, exchange rates, money, and credit conditions in the trading countries. These repercussions can operate to push country A back toward a position of international balance. Let us examine some of them individually.

Equilibrium Adjustment through Income Effects Country A's deficit can have important effects on GNP in that country and in the rest of the world. If GNP is increasing in A to begin with, the rise in imports will operate to check that increase. The funds spent for imports are withdrawn from A's main money circuit. Imports combine with domestic taxes and saving to slow the rise of GNP, which in turn reduces the tendency for imports to rise still further. If A is already near full employment, so that rising GNP is likely to cause price inflation, the check imposed by imports may be a beneficial one, helping to restrain inflation. But if A is emerging from a depression and has considerable unemployment, the restraint imposed by rising imports may be most unwelcome. It is easy to see why countries which were in this position in the 1930s imposed restrictions on imports.

If country A's deficit arises because a change in taste or technology leads its residents to buy more imports and less home products, GNP will actually be reduced. Domestic producers will find their sales reduced and will cut back on their payments of income. The multiplier effect will go to work in a downward direction, and the resulting decline in GNP will curtail country A's imports.

Similarly, country A's GNP will decline if foreign countries reduce their purchases of A's exports. This time it will be export producers who initiate the decline, but reduced incomes will tend to spread the decline as consumers cut their purchases of domestic products in turn.

When GNP declines, it is likely that economic welfare in country A will be adversely affected by falling production and employment. Country A may thus be the innocent victim of economic depression which is taking place in some other country. In the 1930s, declining GNP in major countries like the United States tended to pull the rest of the world down as well. International trade can be an important transmission line for instability. In such circumstances, again, one could understand why country A might impose import restrictions to insulate itself against depression.

However, the decline in economic welfare in country A may be somewhat counteracted by what happens in the rest of the world. If country A initiates the disequilibrium by increasing its imports, other countries will find themselves with increased export sales. This condition will raise their incomes and GNP and will probably result in higher imports by them and higher exports by A.

Whether this process is beneficial or not will again depend on the state of production and employment. If other countries are at full employment, A's higher imports may produce inflation and will be unwelcome. However, if resources are unemployed, the other countries will welcome the rise in sales to A.

Of course, if other countries suffering declining GNP have initiated A's deficit by their reduced purchases, they may succeed merely in pulling A down with them. Although their reduced imports from A will slow their decline in GNP, A's probable cut in imports from *them* will add to their troubles.

The income reactions discussed here are really a type of multiplier effect. Rising incomes in one country tend to transmit themselves abroad. Country A buys more imports, the exporting countries' incomes rise, they buy more from A, therefore A's income rises, etc. Imports and exports may chase each other up and may not settle at any level so long as the expansionary forces are at work in individual countries.

Likewise the international multiplier can work downward. The country initiating the decline cuts its import purchases; exporting countries experience declining sales, incomes, and expenditures and consequently reduce their imports, which may push the first country down still further. Both imports and exports may fall and can only stabilize when internal forces making for depression have been counteracted.

We can conclude that, when forces making for disequilibrium originate in country A, its balance-of-payments adjustments will tend to counteract them. Thus an initial increase in imports by A will tend to set off forces cutting imports back. But if A's deficit results from depression in other countries, the response is not really stabilizing. Although A's imports will tend to be pulled down to match the declining exports, this cutback will pull foreign incomes down still further, which may reduce A's exports again.

Equilibrium situations in GNP and international payments are thus mutually dependent. The balance of payments cannot be stable if GNP in the trading countries is changing, since that will lead to import-export changes. Conversely, if a country's international account is not in equilibrium, its GNP will tend to be affected.

Equilibrium Adjustment through Exchange Rates   A country experiencing a deficit in its international account will find that the supply of its currency on the foreign-exchange market tends to exceed the demand for it at the existing rate. Thus the international value of the deficit currency will tend to fall. However, under a gold standard or equivalent system, only a slight decline can occur. To maintain the exchange rate, the deficit country will be obliged to obtain enough foreign currencies to purchase its own. Some short-run assistance may come through stabilizing speculation, but this will not survive an indication that the deficit country cannot maintain the "peg" under its currency.

Why not let the exchange rate fluctuate? In face of a deficit, let the rate decline. This would make foreign currencies more costly, and deter imports, while the cheapening of the deficit currency should stimulate exports. This could help restore equilibrium without unpleasant domestic consequences to the deficit country.

This solution has appeared attractive to some economists—Milton Friedman, for instance, has been a strong advocate of flexible exchange rates. As we have seen, however, the usefulness of exchange-rate variations depends on the price elasticity of balance-of-payments items. A country with relatively inelastic demand schedules for imports and exports may find that international depreciation of its currency actually worsens imbalance. Capital flows may also be price inelastic, or worse, depreciation may lead to capital flight. Finally, speculation in a currency with no par value might tend to instability. Taking these factors into account, the standard argument against flexible exchange rates is that they would fluctuate so widely as to cause undue risks for persons engaged in international transactions and would consequently interfere with efficiency and international specialization along the lines of comparative advantage.

However, the superiority of fixed rates has not been proved conclusively, nor is it certain that flexible rates need to work badly. The theorists argue that exchange risks could be kept within tolerable limits through the functioning of the market for "forward exchange." This is a futures market, where sales and purchases of foreign currency can be made for some future date.

Another possibility is that a country may maintain a "managed" flexible rate. The monetary authorities may buy and sell in the foreign-exchange market to offset "disorderly movements" of a short-run speculative sort, but may allow the rate to rise or fall in response to the long-run tendencies of the balance of payments. Canada maintained such a flexible rate system from 1950 until 1962. It was abandoned in the face of heavy downward pressures on the rate, both speculative and otherwise, which the authorities chose to terminate by fixing a par value and by obtaining large international loans to assure that the par value would be maintained.

The experience in Canada, and those in Great Britain in 1919–1925 and 1931–1939, suggest that flexible but managed exchange rates can be workable. What would happen in a world where most rates were of this sort cannot be anticipated.

Most of the free-world countries are signatories to the Articles of Agreement of the International Monetary Fund, and each undertakes to establish and maintain a fixed exchange rate (within narrow limits) between its currency and either gold or the American dollar. Procedures are available whereby a country may alter its exchange rate to cope with disequilibrium in its balance of payments, but such change is envisioned as a move from one relatively fixed rate to another—a "movable peg." However, exchange-rate adjustment under such conditions is not a very satisfactory method for meeting disequilibrium. It is almost impossible to avoid speculative anticipations, which may themselves worsen the disequilibrium, and it is very difficult to hit at one stroke the new exchange rate appropriate for equilibrium. In practice, therefore, the IMF arrangement has tended to stress the fixity, rather than the adjustability, of exchange rates.

Equilibrium Adjustment through Monetary and Credit Conditions Disequilibrium in the balance of international payments is likely to set off several repercussions in the area of money and credit. The payments deficit in country A is likely to reduce the money supply there. Private demand deposits are destroyed as importers buy foreign exchange or gold from the banking system. Correspondingly, the surplus countries experience an increase in private demand deposits as their banking systems buy gold or acceptances. (See pages 379–381.)

In addition, commercial bank reserves may be decreased in A if the banks buy gold or other foreign-exchange assets from the treasury or central bank and export them. Correspondingly, bank reserves will tend to increase in the surplus countries receiving such assets.

Partly in consequence, interest rates may rise and credit tighten in country A. In addition to the influence of reduced money and bank reserves, A's central bank may follow the traditional pattern of the Bank of England and raise its discount rate. Correspondingly, interest rates may fall and credit ease in the surplus countries. Tighter credit and higher interest rates may push GNP down in country A or slow its increase by curbing spending on credit. Likewise, easing of credit should tend to raise GNP or slow its decline in the surplus countries. These GNP movements should tend to reduce A's imports and increase its exports. If there are capital movements, they may produce an additional equilibrating force. Higher interest rates in A may attract an inflow of foreign loanable funds, whereas the lower rates in other countries may repel them.

If country A's international deficit is the result of domestic inflation, the tightening of credit may be salutary; but if A is pulled into a deficit by declining foreign demand, this sort of monetary policy may impose tight credit on top of existing tendencies toward depression. Thus international equilibrium might be put ahead of domestic stability.

Equilibrium Adjustment through Price Changes　The various forces we have noted may set off changes in the price levels of the trading countries. If country A sustains a decline in GNP, its products may fall in price, a change inducing foreign buyers to purchase more of them. The surplus countries may experience price increases if their GNP levels increase, thereby encouraging them to import more and reducing A's desire to buy their products.

Traditionally, it was expected that price adjustments would play a major role in correcting disequilibrium. If country A could correct its deficit by price reductions, it might avoid painful reductions in production and employment. However, there are several serious impediments to achieving this result, as follows:

1. Elasticities of demand for imports and exports may be low. If demand for A's exports is inelastic, a reduction in their price will reduce the money value of sales. Likewise, country A may spend more money to buy more expensive imports. Thus price shifts may aggravate disequilibrium. This problem is of particular contemporary concern to countries exporting large quantities of "primary products" such as coffee, sugar, and rubber, for which demands are often inelastic.

2. Price flexibility downward may be difficult to obtain in industrial countries because of wage inflexibility, government price supports, business oligopoly, etc. If prices do not fall when GNP declines, the burden of the decrease is thrown on production and employment.

3. Countries with payments surpluses may wish to restrict price increases to prevent inflation. If they do, such action may increase the adjustment burden in the deficit country.

Capital Movements and International Equilibrium So far most of our discussion of equilibrium adjustment has been based on the assumption that country A's international transactions were confined to imports and exports of goods and services. However, movements of long-term and short-term capital must also be taken into account for two reasons. First, capital movements can be a source of disequilibrium and set off repercussions on other international transactions. Second, capital movements will be influenced in part by the rest of the foreign balance and may react to help restore equilibrium.

Suppose country A is in equilibrium, with imports equal to exports and long-term capital inflows and outflows just equal. Then some current saving is diverted from the domestic loanable-funds market into foreign investment. This change can set off many of the adjustments noted above. The reduction in loanable funds in A may tighten credit, reduce GNP somewhat, and hence cut A's imports. Exchange rates will turn against A. More important, the flow of investment funds into country B will have a stimulating effect on GNP there and will raise B's currency in foreign-exchange value. These effects will encourage more imports and less exports by B. If country A is lucky, the buoyancy in country B may be strong enough to counteract any tendencies toward depression in A. The normal tendency, in any case, would be for the country exporting capital (by importing securities) to develop an export surplus on current account, and for the country importing capital to develop an import surplus. GNP levels, exchange rates, prices, and credit conditions may all contribute to this result.

Capital movements can also help a country adapt to a disequilibrium on current account. The deficit country may attract a flow of capital from abroad by permitting interest rates to rise. In addition, the excess imports will frequently be purchased on credit, so that temporarily at least they create their own financing. Further, the decline in country A's currency on the exchange may lead speculators to hold it and sell others. However, these factors will ward off the consequences of disequilibrium only temporarily. International balance based on large net movements of short-term capital is not really equilibrium.

Capital movements also may aggravate disequilibrium. If country A is incurring an international deficit, foreign investors may fear that its economy is headed for depression and become less willing to invest there, or they may fear that A's currency will decline further in foreign-exchange value. The problem may be aggravated if country A is likely to adopt domestic counterdepression policies which offend sensitive investors—taxes on high incomes and wealth, deficit spending—or if exchange controls are likely. Capital flight originating in such fears can exacerbate the problems which created it; it may lead to a monetary panic which worsens deflationary tendencies and to a rapid depreciation in the international value of A's currency, which makes exchange control seem necessary.

Adjustment through Direct Controls of Trade and Exchange In the last thirty years, countries have frequently rejected the kinds of automatic market adjustments to disequilibrium which we have been describing. In large part, this rejection arose from the disturbances attending depression or war. During the Depression, countries were "innocently" subjected to disequilibrium by depressions elsewhere which cut their export markets and created incentives toward capital flight. During the war and postwar reconstruction periods, it was generally felt that monetary conditions were unavoidably inflationary and that capital flight or exchange depreciation would result if international transactions were left uncontrolled.

In consequence, many countries reacted to payments deficits by imposing or increasing direct controls over trade and foreign exchange. Exchange controls were particularly popular because they could restrict current imports as effectively as tariffs or quotas and could also provide protection against capital flight, which might otherwise drain off scarce foreign exchange and undermine a nation's financial structure.

One of the most drastic and distinctive programs of exchange and trade control was developed by Germany. Early in the Depression, the Germans obtained "standstill agreements" which enabled them to pay their heavy short-term debts with "blocked" accounts in German banks. These could be spent in Germany, but not elsewhere. After Hitler came to power in 1933, emphasis shifted to a policy which deliberately rigged exchange rates and sales to expand German exports and also extend German influence in Eastern Europe. When full employment in Germany was reached, emphasis shifted to the manipulation of controls to obtain imports cheaply. The latter policy is well described in the following passage:

> Germany . . . exploited this bilateral clearing system to borrow, in effect, from the poorer countries of southeastern Europe. Germany bought raw materials and foodstuffs from Yugoslavia, Rumania, Bulgaria, Hungary, etc., with an open hand, paying high prices in terms of dinars, lei, leva, and pengoes. The exporting interests, powerful in these countries, succeeded in getting the central bank to finance their export surpluses. Large claims on Germany were accumulated, but these could be used only as Germany reluctantly made goods available from its rearmament program, at prices dictated by Germany. This is the explanation of the fact that countries of southeastern

Europe were flooded with aspirin and harmonicas, which were among those goods made most readily available by Germany to its creditors.[6]

Adjustment by Surplus Countries It takes two to make an international payments disequilibrium. If some countries have deficits, others have surpluses. We have stressed the adjustment by the deficit country because it is difficult to maintain a deficit position indefinitely. A country with chronic international deficits is likely to run out of foreign exchange and suffer an involuntary devaluation, with attendant reduction in its ability to import. A surplus country, on the other hand, is not faced with corresponding urgency. However, if the surplus country is willing to make adjustments, the problem of the deficit country may be eased.

Many of the automatic tendencies we have discussed operate for surpluses as well as deficits. A surplus on current account tends to raise GNP directly. It may bring an inflow of capital and monetary assets, easing credit and lowering interest rates, which raises GNP indirectly. Prices may rise. The surplus country's currency tends to appreciate internationally. All these can make the surplus country increase its imports and its foreign lending.

However, many of these tendencies can be annulled by government action. A country already at full employment may adopt counterinflation policies which prevent GNP from rising and interest rates from falling. Fortunately, in such a situation some measures of improvement may be in the self-interest of the surplus country. One is a reduction in restrictions on imports. Another is a deliberate appreciation of the foreign-exchange value of the currency, such as that carried through by West Germany in 1961. Such measures tend to lower prices in the surplus country, while at the same time encouraging more imports.

A surplus country may well choose to extend financial assistance to a deficit country rather than see the latter adopt restrictive policies. Willingness of European countries to provide various forms of credit to the United States in the early 1960s arose in part from their recognition that they were benefiting from the prosperity diffused by American deficits.

INTERNATIONAL EQUILIBRIUM AND ECONOMIC WELFARE

The Traditional View Our analysis illustrates clearly the possibility that a serious conflict may arise between the requirements of international equilibrium (without direct controls of trade or foreign exchange) and domestic full employment. A country experiencing a deficit in its international payments may be forced into a domestic deflation to restore equilib-

[6] Charles P. Kindleberger, *International Economics*, 3d ed., Richard D. Irwin, Inc., Homewood, Ill., 1963, p. 293.

rium. This has led many economists to conclude that maintenance of domestic stability is incompatible with free international trade.

The traditional view has been that this conflict is not substantial. It stressed the potential benefits to productivity arising from free international exchange directed by the price system—benefits which could be expected only if exchange rates were relatively stable and currencies freely convertible into each other. Second, this view argued that adjustments required to eliminate international disequilibrium could be made in relatively painless fashion through changes in prices, exchange rates, and interest rates. Conditions required for such painless adjustment would include the following:

1. Prices (and costs) must be flexible upward and downward.
2. Elasticities of demand for imports and exports should not be unduly small.
3. Capital movements must be sensitive to interest-rate changes.
4. Foreign-exchange speculation must be generally stabilizing.
5. Countries experiencing an international surplus should be willing to increase imports to ease the adjustment burden on the deficit countries.

Finally, the traditional view argued that the discipline of the international gold standard, working automatically, was a better basis for monetary policy than domestic management by individual governments, which might lead to chronic inflation and irresponsible increases in government expenditures.

Impact of the Depression The catastrophic Depression of the 1930s eclipsed this traditional faith in the beneficial workings of free trade and payments. Instead, international transactions became a means of transmitting disaster from one area to another. Deflation and depression came through reduced exports, reduced foreign investment, and capital flight. Once into the Depression, free international transactions appeared as an impediment to national policies for recovery. The coming of war provided additional excuses for direct controls of trade and payments.

But the experience of the 1930s may have been interpreted to prove too much. For one thing, although international trade and payments served to transmit deflation and depression, they clearly did not cause them. The underlying forces for depression came from domestic economic conditions and were aggravated by inappropriate government monetary and fiscal policies in major countries, notably the United States, Germany, and Great Britain.

Second, the experience of the 1930s probably led to an unduly pessimistic estimate of the degree to which the five technical conditions which the traditional argument premised were fulfilled. Elasticities of demand were unduly depressed by protectionism and domestic surpluses and deflation. Inappropriate capital movements and speculation were aggravated by depression itself and by the deterioration of the world political climate. Furthermore, the depressed 1930s appeared to contemporaries to be a period of surpluses, in which problems of efficiency in resource allocation were eclipsed by the problem of putting existing resources to some use.

Toward a Reconciliation?   Experience of the world economy in the last fifteen years has increased appreciation of the virtues of the traditional attitude. Full employment, scarcities, and pressures for higher real incomes have revived concern over the efficient use of resources and the benefits from international specialization and exchange. Willingness by the major trading countries to follow appropriate domestic policies to maintain full employment has made repetition of the international financial debacle of the 1930s unlikely.

Recent experience has been a reminder that a country experiencing an international deficit is not always the innocent victim of external pressure but may itself be to blame because its domestic policies are unduly inflationary. Postwar payments deficits in Western Europe have usually resulted from domestic inflation, and this influence has been even more true for other areas. The disciplines and checks which international balance imposes may be quite appropriate and desirable to curb such tendencies.

The revived recognition of the virtues of relatively free international trade and payments has not, however, involved a rejection of the goals of full employment and domestic stability. The postwar period has seen effective steps taken by the industrial nations of the free world to seek reconciliation of these goals through a combination of domestic commitments to countercyclical finance by individual countries and a cooperative effort toward eliminating barriers to trade and payments. Each nation's adjustment problem is eased if the others avoid depressions. Further, the mutual relaxation of trade restrictions avoids the danger that one country acting alone to reduce import barriers might sustain a disastrous payments deficit.

This movement toward reconciliation of economic objectives had made impressive strides by the end of 1958. Most European nations had generally eliminated exchange controls for nonresidents and relaxed those imposed on residents. The process of restoring freedom of trade and payments was greatly aided by the operations of such international organizations as the European Payments Union, the International Monetary Fund, and the General Agreement on Tariffs and Trade.

However, the chronic deficit in the United States balance of payments, dramatized by a steady gold outflow from 1958 on, prevented undue complacency. The problems involved can best be examined in a historical context, which will be provided in the next chapter. It is appropriate to close this section with what appear to be the general issues.

1. How important is international equilibrium as a goal of economic policy? What harm is there in a balance-of-payments deficit?

Ultimately, international economic conditions, like those at home, can be evaluated in terms of their effects on economic welfare. Such economic institutions as convertible currencies and fixed exchange rates are useful in promoting efficiency in production and exchange, but if this is achieved at the cost of depression and unemployment the net effect may not be advantageous.

An international payments deficit is not intrinsically good or bad. It is, however, a symptom of disequilibrium. A deficit country may be enjoying more goods and asset acquisitions than it is entitled to, in a sense. Existence of a deficit is a warning that it cannot expect to continue at the present rate. Perhaps delaying adjustment will make it more painful. But it may not. In any event, the desirability of taking drastic action to eliminate an international deficit involves weighing the disadvantages to economic welfare of removing the deficit versus those of letting it continue.

2. How are situations of international disequilibrium to be rectified if all the economic mechanisms for equilibration are immobilized? Countries now appear unwilling to permit their domestic levels of GNP, employment, prices, and interest rates to serve as equilibrating media for international accounts, if the result is adverse to domestic economic welfare. Yet they have generally committed themselves to a regime of convertible currencies and fixed exchange rates and to reduction of barriers to trade.

One possibility is that relatively automatic forces may still operate to restore equilibrium, if only they are given enough time. A recession in the United States may pull other countries toward international deficits, but this tendency should be only temporary. A raw material exporter may suffer a deficit because of crop failure, but can hope for better things next year. A longer period may be required when resources must be reallocated to reduce an international deficit—perhaps by enlarging export production, perhaps by greater output of items formerly imported. A supply of international financial reserves, in gold or in high-grade foreign currencies, provides a country with the opportunity to await such developments.

Another possibility is that complex policy measures will be used to split off international from domestic finance. Thus the United States has authorized the payment of higher interest rates on time deposits when held by foreigners and has imposed a discriminatory tax on foreign securities held in the United States. Still another possibility is that international political negotiations will be the means of settlement. These may produce reductions in trade barriers by surplus countries, or a willingness to shoulder a greater burden of aid to underdeveloped countries. Finally, by political means, the world may approach a situation in which disequilibrium is made perpetual. Through special loans and exchanges of currency, a country can sustain a deficit as long as the surplus countries are willing.

One thing is certain. One cannot interpret balance-of-payments problems in the 1960s merely in terms of private commercial motives and transactions. Political objectives and techniques have come to exercise a major role. We shall explore this further in the next chapter.

SUMMARY—THE THEORY OF INTERNATIONAL FINANCIAL RELATIONS

International financial relations promote economic welfare through international specialization and exchange of goods and services along the lines of comparative advantage. If individual countries specialize in production of things for which their resources are best suited instead of being self-sufficient, the total world output of goods and services can be increased and general welfare enhanced.

International financial relations are complicated by the fact that countries have different monetary units, which must be exchanged for one another. The level of foreign-exchange rates becomes an important factor in the influence of the price system on international specialization. Currency and checking deposits are generally used in making international payments, but short-term credit instruments such as acceptances are also employed. The purchases and sales of foreign exchange by dealers represent a large clearing operation within each country, a transaction in which foreign funds are transferred from export sellers to import buyers. However, when the transactions do not clear, financial institutions may have to settle their international accounts by sending gold or other assets abroad.

Foreign-exchange rates are determined by the supply of and demand for currencies in terms of each other. The foreign demand for dollars arises from the demand for the things dollars can buy—American goods, services, or investments. American demand for foreign funds reflects demand for foreign products or assets. Ordinarily, the value of a currency will vary directly with the demand for it and inversely with the supply, but exchange rates are seldom allowed to fluctuate freely. The gold standard provided one institutional mechanism for keeping exchange rates fairly stable. In the modern world, some countries practice exchange stabilization by open-market dealings in foreign exchange, while others impose direct controls on foreign-exchange dealings and rates.

A country's international transactions can be shown in an orderly fashion by means of the balance of international payments. Statistically, this transactions record always balances, but it is not always in equilibrium. Equilibrium exists when the value of "things" (goods, services, securities, etc.) which people are willing and able to import equals the value of things they are willing and able to export. At equilibrium there are no "induced" movements of gold or money to other countries.

If the balance of payments is out of equilibrium, it may be pushed back toward it by a number of forces. In the deficit country, these may include reductions in GNP, rising interest rates and tighter credit, falling prices, and lower exchange rate. All these can induce reduced imports, more exports, and a smaller capital outflow and a larger inflow. The surplus country will experience opposite forces with opposite effects. However, the equilibrating process may impose painful adjustments on individual countries, who may suffer depression or inflation. To avoid this, many countries imposed direct controls over trade and payments in the 1930s and 1940s, but this policy entailed sacrifices of economic efficiency.

The central problem of current international finance is how to reconcile the traditional advantages of price-directed specialization under stable, convertible currencies with the goals of full employment and economic development. Experience since World War II indicates that a fairly good reconciliation of these has been made.

QUESTIONS FOR STUDY

1. Explain each of the following:

    a. Economic stability in the United States is a matter of vital concern to the other countries of the world.

    b. A country which is undergoing domestic inflation is likely to generate a deficit in its balance of payments.

    c. Substantial movements of gold and monetary assets from one country are a symptom of a deficit in its international accounts.

    d. Disequilibrium in the balance of payments is associated with disequilibrium in the foreign-exchange market.

    e. An increase in interest rates in a country tends to raise the value of its currency on the foreign-exchange markets.

2. Between 1955 and 1958, United States imports of automobiles increased from about $60 million to about $500 million. Assuming this represented a shift of equal amount away from home-produced autos, trace the effects of this on GNP in the United States and abroad, on exchange rates, and on American imports and exports of other products.

3. According to the "purchasing-power-parity" theory of foreign-exchange rates, two countries' currencies should exchange for each other in proportion to the price levels of the countries. Explain why this is superficially plausible; then try to think of some factors which might cause exchange rates to depart from the expected relation to prices.

(*Hint:* How might foreign investment and the price of haircuts figure in the analysis?)

4. The following fantasy is quoted from *Mathematics and the Imagination* by Edward Kasner and James Newman (Simon and Schuster, Inc., New York, 1940, p. 162):

The International Beer-drinking Puzzle

In a certain town lying on the border between Mexico and the United States a peculiar currency situation exists. In Mexico a U.S. dollar is worth only ninety cents of their money, while in the United States the value of the Mexican dollar is only ninety cents of our money. One day a cowhand strolls into a Mexican cantina and orders a ten-cent beer. He pays for it with a Mexican dollar, receiving for change an American dollar, worth just ninety cents there. After drinking his beer, he strolls over the border to an American saloon and orders another. This he pays for with an American dollar receiving a Mexican bill in change. He takes this back across the border and repeats the process, drinking beer merrily all day, and ends up as rich as he started, with a dollar.

The question: Who paid for the beer?

The moral: Visit sunny Mexico on your vacation.

Comment on the foreign-exchange aspects of this situation.

SUGGESTED READINGS

Holmes, Alan R.: *The New York Foreign Exchange Market,* Federal Reserve Bank of New York, 1959.

The following essays are published in pamphlet form by the International Finance Section, Princeton University:

Haberler, Gottfried: "A Survey of International Trade Theory," 1955.

Schott, Francis H.: "The Evolution of Latin American Exchange Rate Policies since World War II," 1959.

Stein, Jerome L.: "The Nature and Efficiency of the Foreign Exchange Market," 1962.

Kindleberger, Charles P.: *International Economics,* 3d ed. Richard D. Irwin, Inc., Homewood, Ill., 1963.

chapter fifteen

THE EVOLVING PATTERNS
AND PROBLEMS OF
INTERNATIONAL FINANCE

INTRODUCTORY

Modern ideas, policies, and institutions of international finance represent the accumulated developments of history. In particular, they reflect the interplay of the "orthodox" theories of trade and finance developed in the nineteenth century with the newer ideas which have emerged from the successive crises attending two world wars, the Great Depression of the 1930s, and the friction between the United States and Russia. This chapter is designed to provide a historical setting to illustrate some of the principles set forth in the previous chapter and to give fuller meaning to current problems and policies of international finance.

International trade and finance have passed through three important stages. The first comprised the period of the gold standard, during which trade was conducted for private profit and subject to very little government control under monetary arrangements which secured convertibility of currencies and stable exchange rates. In the second stage, the unity and freedom of the gold-standard period were shattered by two world wars and the Depression of the 1930s. In the third stage, since 1945, the countries of the free world have sought some new basis for unity and freedom which would avoid some of the shortcomings of the pre-1914 pattern.

THE AGE OF GOLD, 1815–1914

Origins Western Europe underwent an accelerating process of economic development from the time of the Renaissance. Central to this process was a rapid expansion in trade and commerce, sometimes termed the "commercial revolution." Facilitated by technical improvements in ships and navigation, it was associated with the extension of European culture into far-flung colonies and with the evolution of capitalist economic organization based on specialization and exchange and the use of money.

The years between 1776 and 1815 witnessed the early phase of the Industrial Revolution as well as important political revolutions in France and the United States. Conditions attending the Napoleonic Wars provided a forcing ground for industrial development in Great Britain, highlighted by technical developments in spinning and weaving, in development of steam power, and in metallurgy. Output expanded at a rapid pace.

Great Britain emerged from Waterloo as the dominant economic power of the world. The British economy surpassed all others in its technical proficiency and degree of industrialization. Britain soon became the world's leading exporter of goods and of capital, and the center of international finance.

As industrial capitalism spread during the nineteenth century, production increased enormously, particularly in such basic items as food and clothing. The expanded output consisted chiefly of standardized bulk commodities produced by numerous small enterprises. Prices were flexible and were not dominated by monopoly influences. Government restraints on trade and on domestic economic activity were relaxed in many countries. Capitalistic morality with respect to debts, contracts, and related matters came to prevail among nations as among merchants. Despite frequent minor wars, the century after Waterloo was a relatively peaceful one. And it was an era in which European culture came to dominate the world. Nonwhite underdeveloped regions were economically unprogressive and politically inert, and backward cultures were pushed aside or subjugated.

The Gold Standard On these foundations, there emerged a world economic and financial order based on the gold standard. Great Britain initiated the movement by establishing the pound sterling on a gold basis after Napoleon's defeat. As sterling was the leading medium of international transactions, this act in itself put much of the world on gold.

Many countries retained silver currencies or bimetallic systems until the second half of the century. However, in the 1870s, the high production of silver and its drop in value led most of these to adopt gold. Germany went to gold in 1871, France in 1876, and the United States returned from inconvertible paper to a *de facto* gold standard in 1879.

The gold standard rested fundamentally not on mutual agreements among nations but on voluntary individual adherence to a fairly well understood set of "rules of the game." Each country's monetary unit was established as a given weight of gold, and coinage policies were adjusted accordingly. Changes in these values were not made lightly. Other types of money were kept convertible into gold, and monetary and fiscal policies were adjusted to help maintain convertibility. Loss of gold dictated tight credit and possibly reduction of the money supply to maintain gold parity. Large-scale deficit spending which might inflate the money supply and endanger convertibility was to be avoided.

Gold and International Balance   We have seen that the gold standard performs important functions with respect to exchange rates and the balancing of international payments. Under a gold standard, exchange rates will not vary except within a narrow range determined by the costs of shipping gold, and the gold standard actually required very little gold movement to settle international accounts. Short-term capital movements induced by exchange-rate speculation or interest differentials did most of the work.

The gold standard provided a close link between a country's international balance and its domestic money and credit situation. An international deficit would tend to reduce the money supply of the deficit country and possibly cause a loss of gold from bank reserves. Of course, the surplus country would receive an increase in its money supply and gold reserves. Contemporary economists expected that such movements of money and gold would reduce prices in the deficit country and raise them in the surplus country and that this would restore equilibrium.

As a matter of fact, the prices of most internationally traded goods were flexible and did respond to international imbalance. However, these changes were not chiefly attributable to reductions in the money supply but rather to declining demand resulting from lowered incomes.

For countries exporting chiefly agricultural products, international price movements were often not a stabilizing force. Total demand for such products was generally inelastic. Supplies fluctuated at random with weather conditions but were inelastic with respect to price. Fortunately, climatic variations in various exporting areas often canceled each other out, so that actual price variations were not extreme. This had a definite stabilizing influence on the position of the importing countries, such as Great Britain. In nonagricultural commodities, where random supply variations were less likely, the size and integration of the world market were influences making for stability.

Capital Movements and Credit Policy One of the most important lubricating mechanisms for trade and payments in the age of gold was the international movement of short-term capital. Import and export trade involved extensive reliance on acceptances and similar short-term credit instruments. Both borrowers and lenders were sensitive to differences in interest rates among the international financial centers—London, Paris, New York, Vienna, etc.

European central banks influenced this flow of credit as a means of protecting their gold reserves. If England was threatened with a loss of gold, the Bank of England would tighten credit and raise its discount rate. This would drive borrowers away and attract lenders into the London money market. As a result, the demand for pounds would be strengthened, the demand for foreign money reduced, and pressure toward gold export possibly eliminated.

Such credit movements, as well as others set off by foreign-exchange speculation, made it possible for operation of the gold standard to minimize actual gold movements. Contemporary observers were always amazed and often shocked by the tiny amount of gold actually held by the Bank of England as reserve for the nation's monetary and credit structure.

Britain's financial system was the nerve center of the world trading community under the gold standard. Sterling bills and deposits served as the principal medium of payment, and the great bulk of trading credit to finance imports and exports was obtained in Britain. Within Britain, there developed an extensive community of specialized, competitive firms dealing with various aspects of foreign trade and finance. At the center of this network was the Bank of England.

During the eighteenth and nineteenth centuries, the Bank of England was essentially a private corporation, but it gradually acquired a sense of public responsibility. During the nineteenth century the Bank came, more through practice than through pronouncement, to serve two functions. First, it was the custodian of the nation's gold reserve. Other commercial banks came increasingly to keep their cash reserves with the Bank. Thus if the demand for gold rose, it would ultimately be drawn from the Bank of England. This custodial relationship was formally recognized in the terms of recharter of the Bank in 1844, under which variations in the Bank's note issue could occur only in response to equal variations in its gold reserves. As we have seen, the Bank played its role as custodian by tightening credit in periods of loss of gold.

The Bank also served as a lender of last resort in periods of crisis. This meant that while it could (and presumably should) raise its discount rate during crises, it should not restrict its willingness to make loans at that rate. Borrowers might be inconvenienced by having to pay high rates, but they would always be able to obtain funds at some price if pressed for liquidity. In the United States, both of these functions were exercised by the Federal Reserve System after 1913.

The Gold Standard and Economic Welfare The pattern of world economic organization which developed under the aura of the gold standard contained many desirable features. The stability and security of exchange rates, together with relative freedom of trade, vastly enlarged international specialization and exchange. England, which carried this freedom to its extreme degree, also exemplified extreme specialization. The nation became primarily an international middleman, dependent on imported food and raw materials financed by exporting the products of her skill, capital, and ingenuity. British trade volume reflected this specialization: "By 1913 British exports were ten times what they had been in 1840 and more than 30 times greater than in 1770." [1]

Gold-standard conditions also promoted a *multilateral* arrangement of trade and payments. The United States could sell cotton to England and use the proceeds to buy sugar from the West Indies or to pay interest on public securities owned in Switzerland.

Gold-standard conditions were also favorable to a bountiful flow of international capital. By 1913, British investments abroad amounted to over £4 billion, and the nation derived about 10 per cent of its national income from interest and profits on these investments.[2] The rapid industrial growth of the United States was greatly aided by this inflow of foreign capital, particularly into railroads and subsequently into steel and other heavy manufacturing. By 1914, the United States was a net international debtor to the extent of about $4 billion.

However, the impact of foreign investment and economic development in the nonwhite colonial areas was much less beneficial. Investment in such areas often did not develop productive skills and experience among the indigenous population or produce an intelligent and eager entrepreneurial and managerial class. The imposition of marginal capitalist operations on static, traditional peasant cultures proved socially disastrous in areas such as India. Population growth and urbanization created seriously unbalanced economies which could not generate increasing economic welfare for their own population.

Gold and Instability The age of gold was notable also as an age of economic instability, insecurity, and social tension. Most of this was, to be sure, not the result of the monetary system itself but arose from rapid increases in population, the movement into cities, and the substitution of factory discipline for agriculture or cottage industry.

---

[1] J. B. Condliffe, *The Commerce of Nations*, W. W. Norton & Company, Inc., New York, 1950, p. 287.

[2] *Ibid.*, pp. 336–337.

One shortcoming of the gold standard was revealed in the latter part of the nineteenth century, when gold production was relatively low. This low production level held to a slow pace the expansion of the money supply in the major industrial countries at a time when output was increasing rapidly. The consequence was a prolonged and painful period of price deflation which worked considerable hardship and set off extensive political repercussions in the United States.

Europe and America passed through several major economic depressions —one just after Waterloo, another in the 1840s, and a third in the 1870s. Major causes were wartime dislocations and unstable patterns of private capital investment. Much investment was highly risky and sensitive to variations in psychological expectations as well as objective circumstances.

The gold standard tended to transmit and augment these unstable movements both internationally and within individual countries. Domestically, boom periods often gave way to panic when distrust of banks led to increased demand for gold for hoarding. Internationally, recession in one major country would tend to spread by inflicting payments deficits on its trading partners. The process was particularly burdensome for countries such as the United States whose exports were agricultural staples and who were heavy capital importers. Every major depression through which the United States passed in the nineteenth century involved both reduced export sales and declining inflow of foreign capital (which reduced domestic investment spending).

However, with flexible prices (and wage rates) the effects of instability on production and employment were less serious than they were to become in the twentieth century. And it is a remarkable fact that while the period from 1815 to 1914 was one of considerable fluctuation in world prices, the long-run trend of prices was very stable. In the end, it was the apparent tendency for the gold standard to sacrifice domestic economic stability to the maintenance of gold parity and convertibility which brought its downfall; but this abandonment came only after the extraordinary crises associated with war and economic upheaval after 1914.

By 1914 the principles that dominated the age of gold were put on the defensive. Nations newly risen to international prominence, such as Germany and the United States, were committed to tariff protection rather than to free trade. The relative tranquillity of international relations had been disrupted by the colonial expansion and military posturing of imperial Germany. The era of British supremacy was over. There were strong pressures within the major countries to replace laissez-faire government with more active intervention in economic life. The degree of price flexibility was reduced by the growth of giant firms, collusive cartels, and labor unions. These influences were not sufficient to overthrow the world unity of the gold standard before 1914, but they provided strong barriers against its successful reconstruction after 1918.

WORLD WAR I AND RECONSTRUCTION EFFORTS, 1914–1929

The War   World War I and its aftermath completely shattered the economic unity of the prewar world, just as it destroyed the political basis of European society. In both the economic and political spheres, events in the years since 1914 have been shaped by a groping for some new basis of international order.

World War I was for Europe the first modern "total war." Its enormity was not faintly foreseen when it began, but ultimately it became, in terms of injury, loss of life, and human suffering, the costliest war of any in history. Belligerent countries expended vast quantities of valuable resources and had even more valuable ones destroyed. Loss of manpower from the most vigorous and creative age and social groups proved a long-standing affliction to Britain, France, Germany, and Russia.

Throughout the world, production and employment were expanded greatly. Nonbelligerents enlarged their capacity to produce industrial and agricultural products, either to sell profitably abroad or to replace goods formerly imported from the belligerent nations. These enlargements permanently altered the pattern of world production. Financial relations among nations were also greatly altered to purchase needed goods. The European countries sold foreign assets and borrowed abroad—including $10 billion of war loans from the United States government. By 1918, the United States emerged from its long-standing debtor status to that of a major international creditor.

The internal finances of the belligerent countries were greatly strained. Without exception they resorted to heavy deficit financing, based on credit expansion by central and commercial banks. Gold convertibility was suspended. Supplies of currency and deposits expanded greatly, and price levels rose substantially.

Finally, the war created an atmosphere of international animosity and hatred throughout Europe. Public opinion in each belligerent nation was whipped up by propaganda to a fever pitch of emotion. More than any other factor, these hostile attitudes among national groups shaped the postwar period in a manner which made peace impossible.

Postwar Period: Eastern Europe in Chaos   Although the war on the Western front ended in November, 1918, the years after 1918 were a period of continued violent upheaval in Eastern Europe, erupting in national reorganizations, social revolutions, and continued outright warfare. The great imperial powers which had ruled Germany, Austria-Hungary, and Russia were all overthrown. Two powerful forces operated in the space they left—social revolution and nationalist revolution. The first involved efforts to substitute democratic and relatively socialistic political and economic policies and institutions for the old feudal-aristocratic pattern. The second entailed breaking up the old empires into smaller states dominated by formerly submerged national groups. These forces kept the entire area in chaos. The newly created states in Eastern Europe were politically weak and divided by boundaries which bore no relation to existing patterns of production and exchange. Economic and ethnic nationalism soon erupted in local wars, boundary disputes, tariffs, and trade restrictions.

The wreck of national economies east of the Rhine was reflected in one searing experience shared by most of the area—hyperinflation. We have already described how the German price level skyrocketed a trillionfold by 1923. Similar experiences were suffered in Russia, Poland, Austria, and Hungary. Details differed, but all had in common vast government expenditures for reparations, reconstruction, or continued hostilities, administrative breakdown of tax systems, and political weakness of government. Currency and bank deposits expanded astronomically. Money and prices ceased to function as adequate guides to economic life. Production and distribution were thoroughly disrupted.

Allied Policies The Allied powers contributed to the postwar calamity in two ways—through their policies toward the defeated areas and through management of their own imports and monetary and foreign-exchange systems.

The dominant attitude of the Allies toward Germany was one of revenge, and the instrument of vengeance was reparations. Germany was compelled to relinquish real capital goods, raw materials, and border territories. More important, a crushing burden of monetary reparations, totaling about $32 billion payable in gold, was imposed.

Germany, not a gold producer, could obtain gold only by international purchase, which ultimately required either an export surplus or foreign loans. Import restrictions by the Allies, particularly the United States, made the first alternative difficult, and the deteriorating condition of the mark militated against the second. Lacking foreign exchange from exports or credit, Germany resorted to government deficits financed by bank credit to buy gold. This process inflated the money supply and raised prices—including the price of gold. Collapse of the mark followed the French invasion of the Ruhr in 1923.

Faced with economic ruin, the German government finally braced itself to halt the catastrophe. A new currency was created; the government deficits and credit expansion were brought to a halt. French troops were withdrawn. In 1924, under the Dawes Plan, the annual burden of reparations was scaled down, and Germany secured loans abroad. Domestically and internationally the German economy was restored to stability, if not tranquillity. However, the Versailles treaty and the inflation had aroused social tension and discontent in Germany which would simmer down only if prosperity and stability were maintained for a long time. And Germany's international balance after 1925 rested precariously on a flow of private loan funds from the United States. These loans provided the foreign exchange for reparations payments to Britain and France, who used the proceeds in turn to make payments on their war debts to the United States. Prosperity and stability hinged on the continuation of this flow.

American Policies By the end of the war, its creditor status and productivity placed the United States in a position of prominence in the international economy to which it was unaccustomed. Unfortunately the responsibilities which this economic power brought with it were not well executed.

Poor monetary and fiscal policies contributed to a rapid speculative inflation in 1919 and 1920, followed by a sharp depression in 1921 and 1922. The consequent reduction in imports and foreign lending unbalanced European payments at a critical time. A major consequence of this depression was the worldwide collapse of agricultural prices. Domestically, the farm depression created the chronic demand for "parity" and undermined the solvency of a large portion of the banking system. Other agricultural countries were also injured, with drastic results for living conditions and political stability.

The United States reacted to the recession by passing the highly protective Fordney-McCumber Tariff in 1922. This act increased the export problems faced by Germany and other nations in trying to meet their debt and reparations obligations. The government did, to its credit, waive claim to direct German reparations but insisted on strict fulfillment of the war debts from the Allied and succession states. This insistence led the Allies in turn to keep pressure on Germany for reparations.

International Cooperation The 1920s witnessed some promising experiments in international financial cooperation. The newly formed League of Nations provided useful aid in stabilizing the currencies of nations suffering from inflation. Central banks, particularly the Bank of England, provided stabilization credits to aid the monetary reconstruction of Eastern Europe. In 1924 an international committee of financial experts produced the Dawes Plan for German reparations. In subsequent years, cooperation among central banks (including the Federal Reserve) provided a ray of hope that a pattern of international financial order might be restored.

Back to Gold In revulsion against the inflation and financial disorder of the decade following 1914, leaders of most countries sought eagerly for a return to the gold standard. Gold had always evoked a somewhat irrational attachment; now it appeared almost a magic touchstone which would restore the good old days. An almost religious devotion to gold arose among many who equated it not merely to prosperity but to morality. Unfortunately, there was little understanding of the very exacting conditions required for a successful gold standard or of the alarming degree to which those conditions had been destroyed.

One by one the European nations straggled back to gold, each making its own decision about the proper value for its currency. In Britain, Winston Churchill, as Chancellor of the Exchequer, led the restoration of the pound to its prewar gold value. The objective was to maintain Britain's traditional position as an international financial center. Unfortunately, British prices had risen so much that the restoration of traditional sterling parity made British goods expensive to foreign buyers and imports cheap for Britons. Furthermore, the money supply was much larger relative to the gold reserve than before the war, even though the British had withdrawn gold coins from circulation and would merely buy and sell gold bullion at the mint par.

The overvaluation of sterling had a depressing effect on the British trade position, which in turn led to large-scale unemployment and depression in British industry. The government was deterred from expansionary financial policies, such as easy credit, by fear of losing gold from the already skimpy reserves. When employers in the coal industry tried to force wages down to improve their competitive position internationally, class conflict was aggravated, culminating in the General Strike of 1926.

By contrast, the French, after a decade of inflation, restored the franc to gold at a valuation only one-fifth as great as before 1914—a valuation which attracted gold.

The Gold-exchange Standard Most other countries, like Great Britain, felt pressed to economize on gold. Most of them ceased to issue gold coins. In addition, many of them came to use for their central-bank reserves not gold itself but foreign-exchange assets convertible into gold—chiefly deposits in New York and London banks. The authorities of each gold-exchange country undertook to maintain their currency at par with gold by means of purchases and sales of foreign-exchange drafts. They could meet international deficits by drawing on their balance in, say, London to pay creditors. This gold-exchange arrangement tended to pyramid heavy liabilities on a limited gold reserve. Great Britain's position as international banker was rendered extremely vulnerable by the fact that a large portion of its liabilities to foreigners were of this sort and were heaped on a thin gold reserve. When creditors demanded gold to hoard instead of deposits to spend, the system was doomed.

At the same time, many of the devices by which international payments had been settled without gold no longer functioned as well as before 1914. Stabilizing movements of short-term capital responding to exchange-rate or interest-rate variations had pretty well vanished as a result of the chaotic state of exchange rates prior to 1926. Speculation tends to be stabilizing when there is confidence that a "normal" value will be restored; a fall in a

currency then tempts speculators to buy it. Such confidence had been replaced by a kind of pessimism; consequently, evidence that a currency was
under selling pressure might set off a flight from it.

Notwithstanding these conditions, the return to gold did restore orderly
exchange rates. Stable currency values in dollars came into existence for
Germany in 1924, for Britain in 1925, and for France in 1926.

Prosperity, 1925–1929   As conservative financial leaders had predicted,
the period of gold restoration was one of general prosperity in Europe and
the United States (though not in Britain). Capital investment needs after
a long period of war and disorder were sufficient to support high incomes
and employment levels, even at relatively high interest rates. Capital formation, technological development, and the return to the market economy
stimulated high output. The volume of world trade returned to high levels.

Nevertheless, the period was characterized by situations of structural
imbalance involving failure to adjust production of individual products to
demand. This was particularly true in agricultural products. In many areas,
apparent overproduction led to public or private schemes to buy up "surpluses" of such products as coffee, tin, and rubber in order to prevent price
declines. Such "valorization" programs were financed in part by borrowing
in the United States.

Structural imbalance persisted in a more pervasive sense as well. The
European countries which had lost colonies and foreign investments needed
to devote more resources to exports if their imports were to be maintained,
while the new creditor nations, such as the United States, needed to import more if their exports were to stay high. Both the latter necessities
were put off by the large flow of private loans from the United States. From
1920 through 1931, Americans invested about $12 billion abroad, chiefly
through portfolio investments in European securities.[3]

THE COLLAPSE OF THE INTERNATIONAL ECONOMY, 1929–1939

Initial Downswing, 1928–1931   The stock market boom which gripped the
United States in the late 1920s eventually brought a slackening in the flow of
American private lending abroad. American investors preferred to speculate
in stocks rather than buy imported bonds. Foreign funds began to flow
into the United States. The reduction in American foreign lending in 1928
spread the virus of deflation in two directions. First, it pulled an important
prop out from under the credit-financed price-supporting programs for various raw materials. For this and other reasons, supplies of commodities were

[3] Condliffe, *The Commerce of Nations*, pp. 446–447.

dumped on the market. Prices of agricultural and other raw products dropped precipitously in 1929 and 1930. Countries dependent on exports of primary products found themselves faced with an international financial crisis. By the end of 1929 Argentina, Brazil, and Hungary had been forced off gold, and bearish sentiment prevailed as foreign-exchange experts wondered who would be next.

The decline in American foreign lending also spread rapid deflation in Europe, and especially Germany. Germany was dependent on American loans to finance her large international obligations; in addition, investment spending in Germany had been supported by capital inflow. By 1930 Germany was rapidly slipping into depression at home and financial difficulties internationally.

The American stock market crash in October, 1929, worsened the problem of international capital flows. Pressure of financial liquidation spread to bonds and other credit as banks and other financial institutions struggled for liquidity.

These capital-account problems were soon eclipsed by greater difficulties in the current account. Even before the stock market break, incomes and expenditures in the United States had begun to decline. As a result, American imports also fell, a process aggravated by the passage in 1930 of the highly protectionist Smoot-Hawley Tariff. This process meant lower export sales for other countries, and through an international multiplier process, brought lower incomes and expenditures, lower imports and exports, all over the trading world. The impact on Germany was particularly drastic, for one-third of German industrial output was exported. By 1930, when most of the world was still in mild recession, the German economy was seriously depressed, with more than 10 per cent of the labor force unemployed. As a consequence, electoral support for Nazi and Communist political candidates increased alarmingly.

Throughout Europe governments of every political coloration vigorously pursued the orthodox policies dictated by the gold-standard dogma. In Britain a Labor government eager to prove its soundness and reliability was prepared to cut unemployment benefits in order to reduce the government deficit and hold the pound on gold. In fascist Italy, Mussolini's government also pursued deflationary policies which threw the supposedly regulated economy of the corporate state into serious depression and unemployment. In Germany, the conservative government of Brüning pursued deflation with a vengeance. The Germans had a pathological fear that a deterioration of the international value of the mark would herald a repetition of the inflation nightmare of the early 1920s. In addition, the government hoped (with some justification) that lower prices and costs in Germany would help sustain exports; but deflation aggravated social tension and encouraged political extremism.

Financial Panic, 1930–1931 The financial structure of the gold-exchange standard was too weak to survive the disequilibrium pressures. Experience with hyperinflation and exchange instability had weakened confidence in the value and convertibility of currencies just when the pyramiding of liabilities on a thin gold reserve rendered such confidence indispensable.

However, for a time it appeared that international financial cooperation might stave off panic. Under the Young Plan for German reparations, a Bank for International Settlements (BIS) was established at Basel, Switzerland, in 1930. It was designed as a "central-bankers' central bank," holding deposits for individual central banks and making international transfers for them. During the panic, it assumed an important role in bringing financial aid to distressed central banks.

In May, 1931, serious financial panic burst forth in Vienna when the Credit-Anstalt, a prominent bank, suspended cash payments. To stem the panic, the Austrian government assumed some of its liabilities and received loans from the Bank of England and the BIS. But the panic spread through Europe as individuals and financial institutions tried frantically to collect their short-term claims. In June, President Hoover granted a moratorium on war-debt payments, and a corresponding stay was extended for German reparations payments. Germany was losing gold rapidly and, despite emergency loans from foreign central banks and BIS, discarded convertibility of the mark by imposing exchange controls in July.

Next the pressure spread to England, as Continental financial institutions scrambled to withdraw their funds for self-defense. The Bank of England received emergency foreign loans, but in September, 1931, gold payments were stopped and the pound went off gold. Soon after, the British imposed a protective tariff after nearly a century of free trade.

After similar financial crises, nearly all countries in Eastern Europe suspended gold payments, and many adopted exchange controls. The United States was subjected to large withdrawals, exceeding half a billion dollars in October, 1931. Although this depleted the gold stock by only one-fifth, it led to an increase in the Federal Reserve discount rate which many critics felt was unfortunate.

Going off the gold standard was for most countries not a catastrophe but a relief. In Britain (and in the United States after 1933), going off gold heralded a more expansionary monetary and fiscal policy aimed at domestic recovery.

Down to the Depths, 1932–1933 The real crisis of the world economy lay in the steady decline of production, employment, incomes, and price levels after 1929. Consumer incomes fell, dragging down consumer spending. Business investment declined as markets shrank, thereby reducing incomes more and shrinking markets further. In particular, the continued contraction of income and expenditure in the United States, arising in part from the banking crisis, monetary contraction, and credit stringency, spread downward pressure to the rest of the world. The fall of industrial production raised unemployment in the United States to one-fourth and in Germany to one-third of the labor force. Agricultural prices collapsed as declining incomes and trade restrictions reduced demand in face of relatively constant supply. Price and income deflation brought debt crises, defaults, foreclosures for producers, and insolvency for financial institutions. Lower incomes, lower prices, and trade barriers reduced the value of world trade from $37 billion in 1929 to $14 billion in 1932.[4]

Social tensions and unrest provoked by the Depression produced violent political and diplomatic upheavals. The most notable of these brought Adolf Hitler to power in Germany in 1933. Dictatorships were established or strengthened in Austria, Hungary, Poland, Bulgaria, Rumania, and Greece. In Japan, political power shifted from moderates to militarists. For Germany, Japan, and too many other countries, rabid nationalism provided a generally acceptable basis for the kind of expansionary government financial policies needed to promote recovery, and offered something to divert the public's attention from economic hardships. Considerations of this sort led Mussolini to invade Ethiopia and the Japanese to invade Manchuria.

Further Devaluations   In the United States, the Republicans were swept from office by the landslide victory of Franklin Roosevelt. The country was being wracked by a renewed monetary panic, as the public withdrew gold and currency from the tottering banks. Immediately upon his inauguration in March, 1933, Mr. Roosevelt closed the banks and suspended gold convertibility of the dollar. Gradually the banks reopened, and in 1934 a new gold-bullion standard was established. The price of gold was raised from $20.67 to $35 an ounce, in the vain hope that it would cause commodity prices to rise. This made the dollar much cheaper internationally and foreign currencies relatively more expensive—for instance, the pound went above $5. This devaluation tended to weaken the European balance of payments. As one consequence, France devalued the franc in 1936.

The unilateral devaluation of the dollar had the appearance of a "beggar-my-neighbor" action designed to improve American conditions at the expense of the rest of the world. Fortunately, the American attitude changed soon afterward. Under the Reciprocal Trade Agreements Program initiated in 1934, the United States assumed leadership in a movement for the reduction of trade restrictions. After the French devaluation in 1936, the United States and Britain joined her in the Tripartite Declaration, agreeing to refrain from further competitive devaluations. These moves were important as a sign of changed attitude, but the new attitude itself made little impact on economic conditions until after 1945.

[4] *Ibid.*, p. 450.

Exchange Controls and Trade Restrictions   Many countries imposed high tariffs, import quotas, or exchange controls either for defensive purposes, to stem deflation, or as an attempt to exert a positive influence toward recovery. In Germany, exchange controls were initiated in 1931 to halt capital flight, control settlement of short-term foreign debts, and protect the mark against foreign-exchange depreciation. By 1933 the controls came to be used as a technique of export subsidy, whereby various categories of "blocked" marks sold internationally at a discount. Later, exchange controls and bilateral trade and payments agreements became a technique for buying imports on credit and practicing monopolistic price discrimination in exports.

When Great Britain went off gold in 1931, she did not establish foreign-exchange control. The pound remained directly convertible into other currencies, and the British government maintained rate stability by use of an exchange stabilization fund, by means of which foreign currencies were bought and sold in the open market. Net balances were settled by the authorities and might involve gold shipments as well as credit. However, the basis for the sterling-area trade group was established by the British tariff, which provided preferential rates for other Commonwealth countries, and by a series of bilateral trading agreements with other countries.

Although world production and employment improved after 1933, the world economy was increasingly poisoned by deterioration in the political and diplomatic atmosphere. Japan and China were already at war. In 1935 the Italians invaded Ethiopia, and the following year civil war broke out in Spain. Germany's trade penetrations into Eastern Europe were succeeded by the actual territorial annexations of Austria and Czechoslovakia and by the invasion of Poland, which set off World War II.

In consequence of heightened animosity and tightened trade controls, the volume of international economic transactions dwindled. By 1938 the proportion of national output exported by Britain, France, and Germany was about half of what it had been ten years earlier.[5] The character of trade had shifted from the pursuit of long-run comparative advantage in the allocation of resources to the short-run pursuit of full employment and military and diplomatic power.

International capital transactions also dwindled and deteriorated. Long-term capital outflow from the United States, so large in the 1920s, fell below the inflow of repayments in the 1930s. International debt relations were complicated by outright defaults and repudiation and by exchange controls and standstill agreements. Germany ceased to pay reparations, and the major European nations stopped payments on their war debts to the United States.

Thus the pattern of trade and payments in the 1930s had a distorted and artificial character. In international payments, considerable freedom

[5] Stephen Enke and Virgil Salera, *International Economics*, 3d ed., Prentice-Hall, Inc., Englewood Cliffs, N.J., 1957, p. 338.

remained because the United States and Great Britain did not impose exchange controls. However, most other major trading countries restricted the freedom of their residents to use and transfer these and other foreign-exchange media. Most countries maintained relatively stable exchange rates in the late 1930s, but these were partly imaginary "official" rates or were sustained by administrative restrictions rather than on a free-market balance of demand and supply. The United States was, indeed, still on a gold standard, although domestic gold hoarding was not permitted. Under the combined impact of the increased price of gold and the social and political upheavals in Europe, gold flowed in a steady stream into the United States from 1934 on. In the period 1934–1940, gold imports totaled about $16 billion, as compared with world production of about $8 billion. The one-way journey of this costly treasure into the ground symbolized its decay as an active instrument of international exchanges.[6]

THE SECOND WORLD WAR AND RECONSTRUCTION, 1939–1949

Impact of War Although World War II was a far-reaching influence in the control and demoralization of economic patterns, it came after a long experience with both control and demoralization. The war brought many of the same consequences as its predecessor—destruction of productive resources, shifts in the pattern of world production and specialization, inflation, and the release of nationalistic and revolutionary forces. In addition, it accelerated the shift in world power away from Western Europe toward the United States and Russia.

For many nations, such as the United States, the war brought final complete recovery from the Depression. As a result, world production increased vastly. International transactions increased in volume but were determined by military and strategic considerations. Controls over private trading and payments were extended.

As during the first World War, important European economic problems centered around the loss or deterioration of resources; the disorganization of economic life; the loss of external assets, both financial and territorial; and monetary inflation. As much as 20 per cent of Europe's capital goods were worn out or destroyed between 1939 and 1945. Labor forces declined in quantity and quality. Economic relations were disrupted by internal controls and by shifts in political sovereignty. Heavy liquidation of foreign

[6] A good indication of the changed status of gold in United States policy is found in the attitudes toward Federal Reserve gold-reserve requirements. After World War I, decline in the gold ratio led to a policy of credit restraint and deflation. In 1945 when the ratio again fell close to the legal minimum, Congress merely lowered the minimum!

assets reduced future income from such investments. As an extreme example, Britain's net international-asset position declined by about $16 billion from 1939 to 1945.[7]

Inflation   The problem of monetary inflation was pervasive. All belligerent countries relied heavily on the traditional techniques of war finance—large-scale government deficits financed in part by bank credit. By the end of the war the public held large amounts of cash and government securities. Some countries, notably Britain and Germany, imposed such tight controls over wages, prices, and foreign-exchange dealings that the inflationary pressures were not allowed to raise the price level. However, this required extensive programs of rationing to deal with the excess demand for goods at the fixed prices. In other countries, price levels soared to the verge of hyperinflation. In France, prices by 1947 were ten times as high as in 1938. In Italy they had risen more than 40-fold, and in Greece almost 200-fold.[8]

Both rapid price increases and direct controls interfered with the price system. Inflation also created pressure toward international payments deficits and capital flight. Consequently, a number of countries undertook drastic programs of monetary reform in 1944–1945 to mop up excess liquidity and prevent its further accumulation. Old currency forms were withdrawn and replaced by new ones, perhaps after a scaling down of amounts. Bank deposits were frozen, to be released gradually for use—if at all. By such means, cash holdings were reduced.

For Western Europe, these reform measures did not eliminate the problem of inflation. Some countries (Britain, Sweden) did not undertake them at all; while in others, such as Belgium and France, continued government deficits restored the inflationary pressure. In Germany, controls and excess liquidity kept the economy prostrate until subsequent reform, which we shall discuss below. Outside Europe, a hyperinflation of classic proportions raged in China and added to the chaos in which the Communists successfully gained power.[9]

Planning for Reconstruction   Before the war ended, Allied leaders had given much thought to the economic and social problems to come. In this thinking they were guided constructively by the lessons of the past and were able to avoid many of the mistakes of the 1920s. This was notably true with respect to the generosity of American aid, the attitude toward the defeated countries, and the effectiveness of European cooperation. During

[7] Charles P. Kindleberger, *International Economics*, 1st ed., Richard D. Irwin, Inc., Homewood, Ill., 1953, pp. 474–477.

[8] Robert Triffin, *Europe and the Money Muddle*, Yale University Press, New Haven, Conn., 1957, pp. 53–70.

[9] On the European situation, see John G. Gurley, "Excess Liquidity and European Monetary Reforms, 1944–1952," *American Economic Review*, March, 1953, pp. 76–100. On China, see Chang Kia-Ngau, *The Inflationary Spiral: The Experience in China, 1939–1950*, John Wiley & Sons, Inc., New York, 1958.

the war, the United States furnished nearly $40 billion (net) of lend-lease aid that entailed very slight repayment obligations for her allies. When the war ended, additional reconstruction aid was extended. About $5 billion of this came through continued lend-lease and contributions to the United Nations Relief and Rehabilitation Agency. Another $5 billion was extended on long-term loan to Britain and France in 1946. These and other acts of assistance were reflected in the United States export surplus of $15 billion in 1946–1947.

Wartime reconstruction planning also stressed the need for improved mechanisms for international cooperation. To meet this necessity, the United Nations Organization came into formal existence in 1945. Beside its primary purpose of maintaining collective security against future wars, the United Nations took over or created agencies for international cooperation and technical assistance in such areas as health and agriculture. Economically, reconstruction planning stressed the need for a system of international trade and payments capable of achieving high world productivity but consistent with the maintenance of domestic full employment and economic stability. At an international financial conference at Bretton Woods, New Hampshire, in 1944, representatives of forty-four governments drew up plans for two institutions designed to meet this need—the International Monetary Fund and the International Bank for Reconstruction and Development.

The International Monetary Fund The International Monetary Fund (IMF) agreement and organization were designed to avoid repetition of the international financial chaos of the 1930s. By making available short-term loans of foreign exchange to countries experiencing international payments deficits, the Fund was expected to enable such countries to resist depressions originating outside their borders without resorting to exchange control or devaluation. In addition, the Fund agreement sought reduction of existing exchange controls and an orderly method for the adjustment of exchange rates to deal with disequilibrium. The Fund agreement was ratified from the start by the United States, Britain, and other major trading countries; since then it has admitted Germany and Japan, and by 1964 it embraced more than one hundred countries. The major nonmembers consisted of the Communist countries.

Technically, the loan operations of the Fund consist of selling foreign currencies. Each member must contribute to the capital of the Fund a sum reflecting its size and economic importance. While a portion of this must be in gold, the bulk is in its home currency, commonly in the form of bank deposits. The United States provided 34 per cent and Great Britain 16 per cent of the initial capital. In compensation, voting power in Fund decisions is roughly proportional to size of national quota.

Sales of foreign currencies ("drawings") from this pool may be made to any member nation suffering a payments deficit, provided it deposits an equal par value of its own currency plus a small premium. Each country's right to draw is ordinarily limited to its quota of the Fund's capital. Drawings are to be repaid within 3 to 5 years. Finally, the Fund may make access to its funds contingent on compliance by the applicant with recommendations concerning exchange-rate or domestic financial policies.

The responsibilities of member countries with respect to exchange rates were threefold:

1. Countries established initial par values for their currencies, most of which were put into effect for Fund operations in 1946. Many critics thought this a hasty action.

2. Countries were bound by the Fund agreement to make no devaluation of more than 10 per cent from the initial par values without consent of the Fund. Such devaluation would be permitted only to meet a "fundamental disequilibrium" in the petitioner's international balance. Though fundamental disequilibrium was not defined in detail, the implication was that it did not mean cyclical or other temporary maladjustment.

3. Each member country was obliged to maintain exchange-rate stability between its currency and gold or the dollar, either through appropriate gold points or through exchange stabilization activities by the monetary authorities. Rates were not to diverge by more than 1 per cent from par.

In regard to exchange controls, the member countries agreed in principle to maintain convertibility of their currencies. However, members were entitled to retain exchange restrictions during the "transition" period immediately following the war and were permitted (almost encouraged) to impose exchange restrictions on capital transactions.

During its first decade, the Fund's operations were of limited scale and significance. The European countries were slow to remove exchange restrictions, and the Fund's influence was not great even on such relaxations as did occur. The need for Fund lending was also kept down by American foreign assistance. Furthermore, postwar payments problems experienced by industrialized countries were not those for which the Fund was designed. International deficits originated more often from inflationary pressure in the deficit countries than from depression elsewhere.

By 1960, however, the international environment had evolved into one in which the Fund could play an important role. We shall examine that environment and the place of the Fund in a subsequent section.

The International Bank   While the emphasis of the IMF was on stability and freedom in international payments, the International Bank for Reconstruction and Development (commonly called the World Bank) was established to promote long-term international investment. Like the IMF, it commenced with a capital subscribed by its members, totaling about the same as that of the Fund—about $8 billion. However, only one-fifth of this was called for in cash, and only 2 per cent had to be paid in gold or dollars (except for the United States, of course). The 18 per cent paid in local currency could be used only with the consent of the country involved, and the 80 per cent remainder was simply a guarantee fund. With this backing, the Bank was authorized to issue bonds, and these in practice have been its chief source of loan funds. In addition, it is authorized to guarantee loans from private sources. In practice, it has also acted in an advisory capacity to aid borrowers to become eligible for private credit.

Lending operations by the Bank are hedged by several restrictions. The Bank may make or guarantee loans only if funds are not available from private sources at reasonable terms. The loans are designated for specific projects, such as a dam or a highway. The Bank expects loans to be repaid, and is entitled to consider the likelihood of repayment when reviewing an application. The government of the borrowing country must guarantee the loan. And the Bank itself must secure the consent of any country in which it raises funds.

The Bank made its first loans in 1947. About half a billion dollars were lent to European countries for reconstruction purposes. Since 1948 its loans have gone chiefly for development projects in countries outside Western Europe. We shall review its recent operations subsequently.

Crisis of 1947 and the Marshall Plan   Despite the attention devoted to postwar reconstruction, it proved more difficult than anticipated. United States wartime assistance was cut off rapidly, and the Bretton Woods agencies could not fill the gap. The United States extended a large loan to Great Britain, but its benefits were largely dissipated in a premature attempt to restore sterling convertibility (at the insistence of the United States).

On the European continent, postwar recovery was unexpectedly complicated by the aggressive and intransigent policy of Russia. At the war's end, Russian troops moved rapidly into the entire area of Central Europe, overrunning East Germany and Austria as well as prewar Poland, Rumania, Hungary, and Bulgaria. In 1948 internal subversion and external pressure brought Czechoslovakia behind the Iron Curtain. It was then apparent that the spread of communism was a threat to Western Europe. Low living standards and political unrest went hand in hand. In France and Italy, particularly, Communist party voting strength reached alarming levels. Production and consumption were well below prewar levels in such areas as Germany, Austria, Greece, Italy, and France, and efforts to obtain more consumer and capital goods by import threw the European payments balance seriously out of line. Exports were one-third below 1938, and invisible earnings from foreign investment had fallen sharply from prewar levels. Despite American aid and although the volume of imports was below the prewar level, Europe incurred an enormous deficit with the rest of the world, reflected in an alarming decline of gold and dollar holdings.

To meet the economic and political crisis, the United States undertook a massive new program of aid through the Marshall Plan—formally the European Recovery Program (ERP). This program provided $12 billion of economic aid over a four-year period. In addition, ERP furnished a stimulus for significant steps toward European cooperation. Recipients of aid formed the Organization for European Economic Cooperation (OEEC), which soon took charge of allocating aid among countries and helping to determine its use. OEEC has served as a source and clearinghouse for information on productivity, technology, and economic development. One of the most important developments under OEEC was the European Payments Union, which we shall describe later.

Restoration of Germany   The German economy was in a chaotic condition in 1945–1947. Productivity had been greatly impaired by destruction, depletion, and disorganization. Although Germany did not suffer spiraling hyperinflation of prices, since controls of wages and prices were rigidly maintained, the volume of money so greatly exceeded the supply of goods available at legal prices that the incentive to earn money income was weakened by inability to spend the money. Speculation and nonmarket production flourished. Reform of these conditions was impeded by the split between Russia and the Western occupying powers.

In 1948, however, the Western powers decided to go ahead without Russian cooperation. A drastic reform of the monetary system was instituted, under which a new Deutsche mark currency was issued for the old reichsmarks. The exchange was not made at par but was operated like a progressive tax—the more marks a person exchanged, the smaller the ratio of new marks received for them. In addition, some of the new marks were in blocked accounts, which could not be spent until later and which in some cases were canceled. At the same time, most direct controls were removed. These policies, combined with Marshall Plan aid, worked a remarkable transformation on the German economy. Inventories of goods which merchants had been holding back were now offered for sale. Incentives to undertake productive activity in line with price considerations were restored. Given the existence of a relatively abundant and skilled labor force and a highly competent and vigorous entrepreneurial group, the essential conditions for the successful operation of a free-market economy were fulfilled. By 1955, German production had approximately doubled its 1948 level.

Exchange-rate Adjustments   When the International Monetary Fund commenced its operations in 1946, it succeeded in obtaining from most of its member nations nominal par values for their respective currencies. Most of these were based on the relatively arbitrary patterns of the war. Most currencies were overvalued in relation to gold and the dollar. In markets where free currency exchanges could take place, they sold at discounts ranging from 10 to 60 per cent in 1947. In 1948 the French franc was devalued by nearly one-half.

The major readjustment in this pattern of par values occurred in September, 1949, when Britain decided to reduce the value of the pound from $4.03 to $2.80. This reduction had several notable aspects. First, it was contrary to the spirit of the IMF requirements of prior notice and approval for rate changes. The British simply handed an ultimatum to the Fund on a take-it-or-leave-it basis. The Fund acquiesced hurriedly. Second, a large number of other countries, chiefly members of the sterling area, made similar devaluations at the same time. Third, the devaluation was probably excessive from the standpoint of Britain's welfare. The chief constructive purpose was to expand markets for British exports by making them more attractive in price. (Since imports were held in check by controls, no significant effects were being sought there.) However, the devaluation tended to worsen Britain's "terms of trade"; that is, the prices of her exports fell by more than imports, so that more exports were needed to obtain a given quantity of imports. One consequence was to push British prices up another notch. Continued demand pull at home prevented an easy solution to British payments difficulties.

A DECADE OF TRANSITION, 1950–1959

Shocks and Disturbances   The process of European recovery was still woefully incomplete when the Korean crisis erupted in 1950. Military expenditures by the United States, Britain, and free-world allies increased sharply. One consequence was to step up inflationary pressures, particularly for raw material prices. Inflation was also a problem in Latin America and Asia, where it resulted partly from development programs.

The early 1950s continued to be a period of "dollar shortage." Foreign countries seemed determined to buy more from the United States than they could sell. Initially arising from reconstruction needs, the excess demand came increasingly to be a reflection of inflation—although alarmist hypotheses about inability to compete with the Americans were sometimes offered.

Just as the reverberations of the Korean episode were dying out, the international economy received another shock from the Suez crisis of 1956.

These surface dislocations directed attention away from the fact that the United States had shifted to a deficit position internationally from 1950 on. Since American foreign-aid payments exceeded the deficit, this trend did not automatically mean the end of dollar shortage. It did mean that European countries had progressed sufficiently that they could now afford to build up their sadly depleted holdings of gold and dollars instead of spending all they could for American goods. Behind this lay the impressive rise in European production of goods and services. And with the backing of more production and greater international liquidity, the major countries became willing to move toward currency convertibility.

The Growth of Output   The impact of World War II on production and the impressive pattern of postwar recovery can be observed in Table 15-1, which presents index numbers of industrial production for major (non-Communist) countries and areas.

Table 15-1   Index numbers of industrial production, selected areas (1938 = 100)

Country or area	1938	1948	1953	1959
Europe*	100	96	139	196
Common Market countries	100	78	135	208
France	100	106	137	202
West Germany	100	53	129	212
Italy	100	102	163	258
United Kingdom	100	110	133	156
Japan	100	39	105	217

* Total for Europe excludes Communist nations.
Source: United Nations, *Statistical Yearbook*, New York, 1962. Original index numbers are on a 1958 base.

Looking at total industrial output, Western Europe had just about restored prewar production levels by 1948, although the defeated powers, Germany and Japan, still lagged far behind. This lag was soon made up, however, as those countries registered spectacular output growth in the subsequent decade. By 1959 European industrial output was about double the prewar level, and of the major countries only Great Britain fell substantially below that mark.

Increased output was facilitated by capital financed by United States foreign aid and by increases in population and labor force. Increases also stemmed from high rates of domestic saving and investment and from introduction of technically more efficient production methods.

Another important development which became increasingly visible as the decade of the 1950s progressed was the slackening in the rate at which prices were increasing. By the late 1950s, the major industrial countries, with the notable exception of France, were holding annual consumer price increases to less than 2 per cent.

Toward Convertibility—Background   The great increase in productivity and the dwindling of demand-pull inflationary forces led to great improvement in the European balance-of-payments situation. Europe's ability to export was greatly increased, both in physical capacity and in cost competitiveness. As a result, the physical volume of exports by Western European countries increased from an index of 80 in 1948 to 224 in 1959 (using 1938 as 100).[10]

Higher productivity also reduced Europe's dependence on American products. All in all, the rest of the world found itself able during the 1950s to add very substantially to its holdings of gold and dollars. In Western Europe (including Britain) holdings of such reserve assets increased from $21 billion in 1949 to $46 billion in 1959.

These developments enabled the major nations to reexamine their prevailing patterns of foreign-exchange controls. It was becoming increasingly evident that such restrictions interfered with efficiency in the conduct of economic affairs; moreover, their continuation was in contrast to the trend toward the dismantling of direct controls proceeding domestically in several countries. The major transitions to convertibility took place through two important regional economic groupings—the sterling area and the European Payments Union. We shall look at each in turn.

Toward Convertibility—The Sterling Area   The economic basis for the sterling area was established by British tariff and trade agreement policies in the 1930s, bringing together the members of the British Commonwealth and a number of other countries outside Europe. During World War II this group became the basis for a unified system of exchange control. Payments within the sterling group were relatively free from control. But payments going outside the area could only be made with official approval, and most sterling balances received by nonresidents could not be converted into other currencies without official sanction. A single exchange rate applied to all transactions. Because of the diversity of countries included, the system provided considerable scope for market-directed specialization and exchange.

When the war ended, controls were retained for several urgent reasons. By sales to Britain during the war, other countries had acquired balances equivalent to about $15 billion. Much of this money would have been withdrawn if controls were relinquished. In addition, Britain's current account tended toward a deficit under pressure of domestic inflation resulting from reconstruction and welfare expenditures. Further, the Labor government was content to operate the economy through the strings of direct controls.

But there remained, as in the 1920s, a strong desire to restore the pound to convertibility and bulwark Britain's position as banker for the world. The electoral victory of the Conservatives in 1951 brought a shift of emphasis away from direct economic controls generally and toward the use of monetary and fiscal policy to control inflation and prevent pressure toward international deficits. In 1954 and 1955 a series of measures increased the ease with which foreigners acquiring sterling in payments could convert it

[10] United Nations, *Statistical Yearbook, 1962,* New York, p. 453.

into dollars at values close to par. Finally in 1958 nonresident sterling balances arising out of current-account transactions were made fully convertible, and convertibility was extended to resident transactions soon after. Capital transfers remained nominally under control, but the administrative regulations were greatly relaxed.

Toward Convertibility—The European Payments Union The countries of Western Europe had in 1945 no vehicle for regional multilateralism comparable to the sterling area. In consequence, early postwar moves toward expanded trade chiefly took the form of bilateral trade and payments agreements. It soon became apparent, however, that this approach to payments and credit was unsatisfactory. Individual countries found themselves accumulating large surpluses with some partners and large debts with others, but with no ready means to offset one against the other.

The establishment of the European Recovery Program provided the basis for achieving such offsetting through a regional payments system, the European Payments Union, which began operations in 1950. Its goals were to promote freer trade and multilateralism within Europe, to provide individual countries with standby credit facilities to tide them over small-scale disequilibrium, and to encourage needed domestic adaptations to more basic maladjustments.

The Union extended to seventeen countries and through the membership of Great Britain overlapped with the sterling area. It provided for a regional clearinghouse, operated through the Bank for International Settlements. Initially, foreign-exchange dealings in each member country were monopolized by the central bank or other monetary authority. Exporters sold foreign currencies to the central bank, which forwarded them to EPU for credit. Importers bought foreign currencies from the central bank, which in turn was charged for them in the EPU account. Monthly settlements were made by individual countries against each other (at par values of individual currencies) in the traditional clearinghouse manner, in which each country emerged with a single debit or credit vis-à-vis the EPU. Because of this pooling, exports to one EPU country were as good as to another, and imports from one no more burdensome than another. Thus incentives for discrimination in favor of individual trading partners were largely removed.

Deficit countries were permitted to remain in debt to the EPU up to a certain fraction of their trade, thus providing them with automatic credit against payments deficits. Beyond that point, partial or complete settlement of deficits in gold or dollars was required. Creditor countries in turn agreed to accept credit on the books of the EPU for a certain percentage of their surpluses. These credits could, of course, be applied against subsequent deficits, and their possession encouraged surplus countries to expand their imports. Beyond a certain point, however, the creditor countries were entitled to draw part of their surplus in gold or dollars. The terms were such that both deficit and surplus countries had incentives to remove the disequilibrium.

The EPU was established under the auspices of the OEEC and received its initial capital from Marshall Plan aid funds. This organization framework became an effective medium for negotiating the relaxation of restrictions on trade and payments among the members. It was able to stress reciprocal concessions and also to link trade liberalization with the payments positions of individual countries, so that import restrictions were eased when this could be most easily tolerated. The percentage of intra-European trade free from quotas or exchange prohibitions rose from 30 per cent in 1949 to 80 per cent in 1957. However, the EPU countries also made great improvements in the freedom of external trade, particularly after 1953.[11]

The Union came into operation just as the Korean crisis was upsetting the international economy. Resulting deficits and surpluses were so large that some countries (e.g., France) exhausted the credit facilities of EPU. After 1953, with the improvement of the economic environment, EPU began to evolve toward a free-market system. Member countries began to permit private trading and arbitrage in foreign exchange, ending the monopoly position of central banks. As a result, most of the clearing of international payments did not get to EPU. Dealers would buy foreign currencies from exporters and sell them to importers. Most central banks remained in the foreign-exchange market through open-market dealings for currency stabilization, but they could settle their net deficits or surpluses without going through EPU. Restoration of exchange markets made the automatic-credit provision of EPU less necessary, and in 1955 the Union required that 75 per cent of net balances be settled in gold.

With increasing freedom for foreign-exchange trading, the facilities of EPU became less important. At the end of 1958 twelve European countries, accounting for the bulk of production and trade, made their currencies convertible for nonresidents. A month later, West Germany extended virtually full convertibility to its own residents as well. At the same time France adjusted the external value of the franc to gain a closer alignment between prices in France and elsewhere.

With these major movements toward exchange freedom, EPU was terminated. In its place was adopted the European Monetary Agreement of 1958. Each member agreed to fix a price in its own currency at which it would buy and a price at which it would sell dollars. These dollar points were to be fairly close together and would provide limits to exchange-rate movements among member countries. In addition, the agreement established a European Fund of $600 million to be made available for short-term loans to aid members in payments difficulties. Further, the agreement provided

[11] Triffin, *Europe and the Money Muddle*, p. 267.

that each member would make available to the others short-term loan facilities.

Toward European Unification By the end of the 1950s, the most dramatic development concerning European economic affairs was the movement toward unification. The Treaty of Rome of 1957 established a European Economic Community, better known as the Common Market, to consist of France, West Germany, Italy, Belgium, Luxembourg, and the Netherlands. Rapid steps were taken in the early 1960s to remove the obstacles to the mobility of people and goods within the member countries and to erect a uniform external tariff. In 1961 Greece became associated with the Common Market, but hopes to include Great Britain were dashed by French veto in 1963. Instead, Britain became the leading member of the European Free Trade Association, covering Austria, Portugal, Switzerland, and three Scandinavian countries.

The Common Market program includes several financial features. It established a European Investment Bank, patterned after the World Bank, to make development loans in Europe. An Overseas Development Fund was established as a vehicle for assistance to underdeveloped countries. The Common Market nations have also discussed proposals for monetary integration—that is, the establishment of a single currency unit and unified monetary policy—but no firm commitment has been made. Instead, coordination of monetary policies of individual members occurs through a Monetary Committee. In the absence of monetary integration, members are still vulnerable to balance-of-payments difficulties. The Treaty of Rome explicitly obliges each state to pursue domestic policies consistent with international equilibrium, but does permit a member with payments difficulties to impose special restrictions on imports.

THE INTERNATIONAL ECONOMIC ENVIRONMENT OF THE 1960s

Survey By the 1960s, the major trading countries of the world had restored an international regime of convertible currencies with stable exchange rates. Convertibility initially introduced for nonresidents was extended to residents as well by most European countries in 1959 and 1960. The Canadian dollar was pegged in 1962 after a long experiment with a floating exchange rate. The chief remaining spheres of exchange control were underdeveloped areas such as Latin America, particularly where inflation continued.

The trend toward convertibility did much to restore money and the price system to their traditional international roles, particularly in view of the attendant liberalization of tariffs and other trade restrictions. Individuals have become relatively free to trade and invest on the basis of price-profit considerations, with resulting gains for international efficiency. The results were particularly favorable for countries such as Japan and Germany, whose domestic growth rates were aided by aggressive expansion of exports.

Restoration of a "liberal" environment for international finance had other consequences as well. One was the emergence of a relatively mobile supply of short-term capital, sensitive to interest-rate differentials among different countries. This added a new dimension to monetary policy—or rather brought back into play the style of central banking which the Bank of England had developed a century before.

The new situation also provided an opportunity for rapid, massive movements of "hot money," moving to speculate on the possibility of currency revaluation or related change.

Role of the IMF The trend toward convertibility gave scope for a much greater role for the International Monetary Fund. Beginning with the Suez crisis in 1956, the IMF became a sort of international financial fire brigade, lending foreign exchange to countries faced with heavy drains internationally. Without such assistance, speculative runs might drain a deficit country of foreign exchange and oblige it to impose controls or allow its currency to depreciate.

In 1961, Great Britain sustained a serious international financial drain, originating in a trade deficit and aggravated by speculation against the pound. The crisis was halted by massive aid from the Fund—a direct drawing of $1.5 billion and additional standby commitment of $0.5 billion. This aid provided breathing space for the British to attack the trade deficit by domestic monetary and fiscal restrictions. Similarly, the Fund lent heavily to Canada to aid in establishing a fixed rate for the Canadian dollar in 1962.

The Fund was also frequently involved in trying to straighten out the financial affairs of less developed countries. Typically, it would be called in to assist a country in which inflation, perhaps arising from an ambitious development program, was causing foreign-exchange difficulties. In such situations, the Fund was usually willing to advance funds to stabilize the currency, provided the country took steps domestically to halt the inflation (balance the budget, tighten credit) and also simplified its foreign-exchange controls. These elements were present in the assistance to Egypt in 1962, for example.

The potential scale of Fund operations was substantially increased by a series of actions. In 1959 member countries agreed to substantial increases in quotas, bringing the total Fund capital up to $15 billion. However, much of this would invariably consist of currencies already in excess supply. Consequently, in 1962 the Fund arranged with ten leading countries a series of standby credits. Under the arrangement with West Germany, for instance, the Fund could obtain up to $1 billion in marks to deal with a situation in which the mark was in excess demand internationally.

These extensions in Fund size came at a time when the potential demands on it were growing. In particular, the United States had become for the first time a potential customer. This is an appropriate point to examine the American international position more closely.

The Great American Deficit The United States balance of payments had shifted to deficit status in 1950, but this shift attracted little attention. Beginning in 1958, however, conditions changed radically. First, the deficits became much larger. Second, it was necessary to finance part of the deficit by exporting gold. The United States monetary gold stock, which had been relatively constant, suddenly began to decline. From $22.8 billion at the end of 1957, it was reduced to $15.6 billion at the end of 1963. The outflow was temporarily halted in 1964, but resumed in 1965.

What caused the deficit? Superficially, the statistical evidence is clear. It is summarized for 1958–1962 in Table 15-2. The United States enjoyed

Table 15-2 United States balance of payments, 1958–1962 inclusive (Billions of dollars)

Current account	Receipts	Payments	Net
Merchandise trade	$ 93	$ 74	+$19
Military purchases and sales	2	15	−13
Investment income	17	4	+13
Other services	20	22	−2
Private transfers—net		4	−4
Government grants and capital	5	18	−13
Private capital	3	17	−14
Unrecorded		2	−2
Totals	$140	$155	−$16

Source: Economic Report of the President, 1964, p. 297. Figures are rounded and may not add up to totals shown.

large net inflows of funds from merchandise trade and from income on investments. Large net outflows were sustained for military transactions, government grants and capital, and private investment. For the five years, the total deficit was $16 billion. Gold outflows financed about $6 billion of this; increased foreign holdings of dollar deposits and other claims accounted for the rest.

Prima facie, therefore, the deficit arose from American investment abroad and from foreign-aid and military expenditures of the United States government. However, identifying deficit items statistically is not the same as explaining the deficit. The size of our receipts was influenced in many ways by the payments. In particular, much of the expenditure for military and economic aid induced export sales, partly because of deliberate "tying" of aid. American investment abroad stimulated exports of capital goods of which the United States is a leading producer. And obviously our inflow of funds from income on investments reflected to some extent the outflow of capital funds.

Put another way, the deficit would probably have been smaller had government programs and private investment been cut, but the reduction in the deficit would not have been nearly as large as the reduction in the named programs. Indeed, without the dollar flow engendered by such payments, our export surplus itself might not have occurred. Some authorities went so far as to attribute much of the deficit to the American export position. They noted that prices of American exports had risen relative to those of other countries in the 1950s and that the United States had consequently lost ground in world markets. Our shift from exporter to importer of steel was a clear case of this sort.

Was the deficit a bad thing? Not directly—indeed, one can argue that it made Americans better off. We relinquished a useless asset (gold) in exchange for useful assets in the form of overseas investments. In addition, the effective size of the national debt was reduced to the extent that the Federal Reserve bought securities to offset the reduction in bank reserves arising from the gold loss. However, more rapid expansion of export sales would have raised output and employment at home.

Of course, the trouble with such a deficit is that it cannot go on forever. Sooner or later the gold would be all gone, and then what? Well, even then it is not clear that the economic welfare of Americans would be harmed. Should the gold stock run out, the dollar would decline in foreign-exchange value. This would be inflationary, primarily through the fact that we should have to pay more for our imports. Considering the small ratio of imports to national production, however, the effect would be slight. Even if the external value of the dollar were cut by half and the prices of imports were doubled, the effect would be to raise American price levels by about 4 per cent. Some additional increase might come through prices of export commodities.

Nevertheless, the deficit did have an adverse effect on the economic welfare of Americans, although it cannot be measured. The effect resulted because the monetary policy of the Federal Reserve was undoubtedly somewhat more restrictive in 1958–1963 than it would have been without the deficit. Consequently production and employment were not as large as they might have been. But considering the anti-inflation bias of the Reserve authorities, their policy would not have been substantially easier without the international complications.

Concern for the balance of payments was not confined to the Federal Reserve, but was widespread in the top levels of the government. To understand why, we must look at the status of the dollar as an international reserve currency.

The Gold-exchange Standard Again   The economic environment of the early 1960s was marked by a return to a gold-exchange standard somewhat like that of the 1920s. That is, most countries held a substantial portion of their monetary reserves not in gold itself, but in dollar assets convertible (through official channels) into gold.

One consequence of the United States deficit was a corresponding increase in the holdings of gold and dollars by the rest of the world—of "international liquidity," as it was often termed. For the most part, this expansion in liquidity was helpful in providing countries with the financial reserve they needed to manage convertible currencies. Indeed, with world gold production averaging only about $1 billion a year, partly offset by industrial uses, United States deficits were the chief source of liquidity for the rest of the world.

Paradoxically, however, the deficits which increased the *quantity* of world liquidity also threatened to undermine the *quality* of the dollar as the prime form of liquidity. The United States was in the position of a banker expanding credit. Its deposit liabilities were increasing, while at the same time its reserves—gold—were decreasing. If the reserves became too small relative to the liabilities, foreigners would lose confidence in the banker's ability to pay and might instigate a run on the bank.

Defense of the dollar and its reserve status through curtailment of the gold outflow and reduction of the international deficit became objectives of United States policy primarily to sustain the trend toward convertible currencies, stable exchange rates, and relative freedom of international transactions. The system was promoted not so much for the economic welfare of Americans but as a means to the economic growth, strength, and security of the free world. The ultimate goal of policy was not economic, but political and military. A weakening of the dollar might mean the necessity for devaluation or for exchange control, either of which would breach the system. So, however, would short-sighted efforts to strengthen the dollar by raising import barriers or reducing foreign-aid expenditures.

Viewed in this light, "defense of the dollar" internationally could be considered as part of United States diplomatic and military policy generally, a policy which accepts some economic costs as necessary for peace and freedom. At the same time, stress on defending the dollar has manifested several disturbing characteristics. The policy has been discussed largely in emotive terminology. Little specification has been given to the costs of present policy, or to the harm to be expected if it were changed, say, by a sudden United States decision to terminate gold convertibility of the dollar. In particular, critics of recent policy have stressed that the security of the free world depends more on the productivity and prosperity of the American economy than on any purely financial arrangements relating to gold and foreign exchange. Such critics have cautioned against the use of restrictive monetary and fiscal policies as means of reducing the United States deficit internationally.

United States Policies The avowed policy of the United States government was to reduce the deficit itself or halt the gold outflow without imposing deflationary burdens on the domestic economy. Federal Reserve actions raised short-term interest rates relative to long-terms and authorized member banks to pay higher rates of interest on foreign time deposits. In 1963 the administration proposed an "interest-equalization tax" on foreign securities issued in the United States. The proposal was retroactive, and it reduced foreign borrowing even before the tax was actually enacted in 1964. Foreign-aid expenditures were tied more tightly to American exports. Foreign governments were pressed to prepay debts to the United States government. Business taxes were reduced to keep more capital at home.

Policies to protect the gold stock involved substantial innovations. The Treasury and the Federal Reserve began to carry on open-market operations in foreign-exchange markets. The Treasury acquired stocks of foreign currency by selling special securities denominated in foreign currencies to foreign central banks. The Federal Reserve opened a set of standby "swap" arrangements with other central banks, whereby it could obtain foreign currencies if needed. Thus the monetary authorities were in a position to buy dollars back without giving up gold in exchange. Federal Reserve authorities drew on these foreign-exchange resources to meet heavy temporary sales of dollars following President Kennedy's assassination in November, 1963.

These were only a part of a wider array of matters in which central-bank cooperation was helpful. Central banks came to the aid of Britain in 1961, and they were commonly involved in the kind of fire-fighting operations to which the IMF was likely to be summoned. Of particular interest was the formation in 1962 of a "gold pool" among the central banks of six continental European countries, the Federal Reserve, and the Bank of England. Operating through the latter, the pool's chief function has been to buy and sell gold in the London gold market in order to keep the market price from varying much from the United States par of $35 an ounce. Transactions have been prorated among the countries. Favorable supply and demand conditions enabled the pool to buy gold on balance after late 1962.[12]

Gold reserves of leading central banks could also be said to have been pooled in a broader sense by the arrangements for foreign-exchange swaps and loans. These arrangements substituted credit for gold as the principal means of settling imbalances within the group.

[12] Charles Coombs, "Treasury and Federal Reserve Foreign Exchange Operations, and the Gold Pool," *Federal Reserve Bulletin*, March, 1964.

In addition to participation in these arrangements, the United States made formal use of the resources of the IMF; its first drawing of $125 million came in February, 1964. The move was undertaken to "break the ice" at a time when no emergency was involved.

Unsettled Problems Even assuming that the United States deficit and gold outflow would be brought under control, the environment of the 1960s contained some unsolved problems.

1. *Conflict between international equilibrium and domestic economic goals such as full employment and rapid growth.* In the modern world, countries may have only two major methods for coping with persistent international deficits—restraint of aggregate demand at home, or exchange-rate devaluation. The tendency under the IMF has been to discourage exchange-rate adjustment. In particular, the United States and Britain have found themselves blocked from the use of devaluations by their position as providers of "key currencies" held by other countries. Since World War II Britain has undergone a series of international financial crises, particularly in 1956, 1961, and 1964. In each case, restrictive monetary and fiscal policies were imposed. Critics have argued that the result was an undue restraint on investment, to the detriment of the rate of economic growth.

In assessing the seriousness of the conflict, several things need to be noted. First, individual countries now possess much more determination and ability to avoid domestic instability; this in turn stabilizes the external environment for all countries. Second, the worst tragedies of the past arose when men made an irrational fetish out of the gold standard. That tendency is now much less in evidence, although it is still unsettling to hear the issue discussed so much in terms of the "integrity" and "soundness" of the dollar, as if a purely moral issue were involved.

So long as the adjustment process operates chiefly through variations in the domestic money flow, the possibility exists that domestic objectives may be sacrificed to adjustment. Since there tends to be more pressure on the deficit countries to adjust by restrictive financial policies, the system may contain a deflationary bias.

2. *Adequacy of the gold-exchange and reserve-currency system.* Is it sound to rely on a system which does impose economic burdens on the reserve-currency country, or which makes the supply of international liquidity depend on deficits by that country? Central-bank cooperation and pooling of resources represent a method of transcending this problem, but many others have been proposed. One of the most striking is Triffin's proposal for the creation of an international central bank. Its deposit liabilities could serve as a medium for settling international accounts, and it could increase the supply of liquidity by expanding its loans. Although such an extreme proposal seems unlikely of adoption, the world payments system has been

under intense scrutiny by major countries, and further modifications appear likely.

3. *Problems of underdeveloped areas.* Plagued by high birth rates, political instability, declining raw material prices, and shortage of capital, many less developed countries failed to share very much in the prosperity of the early 1960s. A number of efforts were made to provide more capital through international channels. The capital of the World Bank was enlarged in 1959. In the fiscal years 1958–1962 combined, the World Bank extended about $3.6 billion in development loans. The Bank does not finance "social overhead capital" in forms which do not yield revenue. Much of its lending has gone for transport and electric power facilities. Its importance has been greater than the volume of its lending would indicate, for it has provided valuable technical assistance to project planning and has also aided borrowers to achieve sufficient credit standing to obtain private funds.

The World Bank's relatively conservative operations were supplemented by creation of two flexible affiliates. The International Finance Corporation, established in 1956, is designed to provide funds to private firms in underdeveloped countries without government guarantee. Its individual investments have been on a relatively small scale, hopefully designed to provide a catalytic influence. The International Development Association (1960) was designed to provide long-term loans for projects which could not meet the relatively strict terms of the parent Bank. For instance, it is authorized to lend for such social investments as housing or sanitary systems. Unlike the other two, IDA charges no interest. Operations of IFC have been modest—it extended about $100 million in credits in 1956–1963. However, IDA provided $800 million by mid-1964.

Regional lending institutions have also been formed. We have already noted those related to the Common Market. In 1960 the Inter-American Development Bank was formed by the twenty members of the Organization of American States; it furnished $271 million in its first two years.[13]

Of course, much American foreign aid took the form of loans through the Agency for International Development and the Export-Import Bank. However, the appropriations for American foreign aid were cut back substantially in 1963–1964. Private investment filled some important gaps, but was frequently repelled by the instability so often encountered. In consequence, the total flow of government aid and private investment from leading industrial nations to underdeveloped countries fell from about $8.7 billion in 1961 to $8.2 billion in 1963.[14]

[13] A convenient review of these agencies is in "Lending for International Development," *Monthly Business Review*, Federal Reserve Bank of Cleveland, February, 1963.

[14] *New York Times*, July 25, 1964.

SUMMARY

International financial history has passed through three important stages in the last century. The first was the emergence, spontaneous and unplanned, of the nineteenth-century gold standard. The stable exchange rates and full convertibility which this standard provided were well designed to permit the price system to operate internationally. Further, the system tended to encourage stabilizing movements of short-term credit which helped ease equilibrium adjustments. Under the gold standard, however, international disturbances did contribute to domestic instability in the trading countries—first in areas of prices, money, and credit; later to an increasing degree in incomes, output, and employment.

The second phase was the long period of financial disorder which began with World War I. In this period, the unity and order of the gold standard were lost. The chief disrupting force was the nationalistic hatred which poisoned international relations throughout the period. During this time the world economy passed through the inflations of the early 1920s. Next, most countries returned to shaky gold-bullion or gold-exchange standards that were based on a thin gold reserve and lacked public confidence in exchange rates and convertibility. The coming of depression after 1929 turned loose a financial panic which drove most of the world off gold. To ward off deflation or promote domestic recovery, many countries resorted to currency depreciation and exchange controls. Direct controls were extended still further during World War II.

The third stage, which began at the end of World War II, witnessed a gradual return to a relatively liberal pattern of international economic affairs. Exchange controls were gradually relaxed and then, in the late 1950s, virtually eliminated by major industrial nations. Other trade barriers were reduced. This process was greatly facilitated by the expansion of European production and by the buildup of gold and dollar holdings. United States leadership was deeply involved in the process, underwriting output growth with Marshall Plan aid and exerting pressure toward a return to free markets.

By 1960, the third stage was completed, and the free-world countries had entered a new environment. Major currencies were linked together by stable exchange rates and convertibility. The new system offered its problems; it represented a resurrection of a gold-exchange standard resting heavily on the dollar as a reserve currency. Large deficits in American payments in 1958–1963 added greatly to foreign gold and dollar holdings, but reduced the attractiveness of the dollar as an international asset. Eliminating the deficits would create another problem, however, since the supply of world liquidity would then cease to expand. Cooperation among central banks offered one tentative way out of the problem, but more radical solutions were being proposed.

Notwithstanding these problems, the performance of the free-world economy after 1945 was impressive. The developed countries scored very large gains in output and avoided serious depression. Price inflation was slowed down to manageable proportions. And the tone of international relations among the Western nations was far superior to that between the world wars. However, less optimistic elements were the continued frictions with the Communist bloc and the economic difficulties of the underdeveloped countries.

QUESTIONS FOR STUDY

1. What were the advantages and disadvantages of the United States international deficit (*a*) for Americans and (*b*) for the rest of the world, in 1958–1962?

2. Comment on the following statement made by Robert Roosa, Under Secretary of the Treasury for Monetary Affairs, in 1962:

> We are now thankfully, and at last, living in a highly competitive world. Together with the other free, democratic, capitalist countries, the United States has begun over the past few years to experience some of the shocks of actually living in economic conditions which resemble rather closely many of the ideals which we have for generations been endorsing.

3. In March, 1961, West Germany increased the external value of the mark by 5 per cent in face of a large balance-of-payments surplus and threat of domestic inflation. An analysis of the action commented as follows: "Savings banks, life insurance companies, and retail enterprises generally welcomed the action as a move to help stabilize the price level. However, leaders of industries with sizable export interests understandably were somewhat apprehensive about the appreciation." [15] Comment on the effect of a currency appreciation on the balance of payments, the price level, and the export industries.

4. Monetary policy aimed at protecting a country's gold reserve may require tightening of credit during recession. Why?

5. "For a country with large foreign trade and few import restrictions, trying to get out of a depression by expansionary monetary and fiscal measures may be like trying to heat a house in winter with all the doors and windows open." Explain.

6. Compare the role of gold in international economic affairs prior to 1914, during the 1920s, and since 1958.

[15] *Monthly Review*, Federal Reserve Bank of New York, April, 1961, p. 63.

7. Some economists have argued that the United States international deficit in the early 1960s reflected an overvaluation of the dollar internationally. In what ways might a devaluation have improved the American financial position? What would have been its domestic effects? Since devaluation would require an act of Congress, what international repercussions would you expect to occur while such a measure was being considered?

SUGGESTED READINGS

Condliffe, J. B.: *The Commerce of Nations,* W. W. Norton & Company, Inc., New York, 1950.

Harris, Seymour (ed.): *The Dollar in Crisis,* Harcourt, Brace & World, Inc., New York, 1961.

The following are publications of the International Finance Section, Princeton University:

Aliber, Robert Z.: "The Management of the Dollar in International Finance," 1964.

Machlup, Fritz: "Plans for Reform of the International Monetary System," rev. ed., 1964.

Triffin, Robert: "The Evolution of the International Monetary System: Historical Reappraisal and Future Perspectives," 1964.

Lewis, W. Arthur: *Economic Survey, 1919–1939,* George Allen & Unwin, Ltd., London, 1949.

Triffin, Robert: *Europe and the Money Muddle,* Yale University Press, New Haven, Conn., 1957.

———: *Gold and the Dollar Crisis,* rev. ed., Yale University Press, New Haven, Conn., 1961.

Young, John Parke: *The International Economy,* 4th ed., The Ronald Press Company, New York, 1963.

part six

HISTORY OF MONEY AND MONETARY POLICY IN THE UNITED STATES SINCE 1914

chapter sixteen

MONETARY AND BANKING DEVELOPMENTS IN THE UNITED STATES, 1914–1940

BACKGROUND

The Economy By 1914 the United States had completed a half century of rapid industrial development. The nation's output had risen nearly eightfold since 1860. The spectacular developments appeared in the expansion of the steel industry, the construction of a nationwide rail network, the commercial application of electricity, and the introduction of the automobile and the airplane. Yet the United States was still predominantly a nation of small towns and farms. In 1910, 30 per cent of the work force was still in farming, and more than half the population lived in rural areas.

Rapid economic growth had brought increased real incomes for millions, but the process aroused social tensions as well. Some of these came from the inevitable social disorganization attending the influx of millions of immigrants. However, financial conditions contributed their share. A long period of price deflation from 1865 to 1896 brought hardship to many farmers. And periodic bouts of depression, particularly in the 1870s and

1890s, produced industrial unemployment, business bankruptcies, and added woes for farmers.

The Banking System   The nation's financial system was well designed to promote economic growth, but also aggravated instability. Commercial banks were the dominant form of financial institution. Although their clientele was limited to business firms and farms, their operations extended into the investment banking business. Thus banks handled a large part of financing business capital, either through conventional loans and investments or through their role in marketing new securities issues to investors. Flexibility and innovation in banking were promoted by relatively easy entry into banking and by relatively lenient regulation, particularly for nonnational banks.

However, easy entry led to a proliferation in the number of banks, which exceeded 26,000 by 1914. While a few city giants were beginning to emerge, the vast majority were small banks in small towns. About 7,000 of them were national banks; these held about half the assets of the banking system. The great majority of banks preferred state charters or operated as unchartered private banks.

National banks were authorized to issue paper currency in the form of national-bank notes, but the issuing bank had to pledge an equal amount of government securities as backing. National banks were required to hold reserves equal to a fixed proportion of deposits. The reserves could be in vault cash, but banks outside the "central reserve cities" of New York, Chicago, and St. Louis could carry part of their reserves on deposit with city banks.

Regulations of national-bank currency and reserves created the widely discussed problem of an "inelastic" currency—perhaps better identified as a problem of bank liquidity. The system provided no way for the supply of currency to expand in response to economic growth or seasonal increases in the demand for it. And it furnished no source from which the banking system as a whole could obtain additional cash to meet depositors' claims during the periodic banking panics which punctuated the post-Civil War years. The reserve system tended to transmit panic demands for cash from one bank to another, and from the banks to the stock market (where big-city banks loaned heavily). Such a process caused the banking system as a whole to reduce loans and the money supply, thus tending to aggravate cyclical contractions. The nonnational banks were more likely to meet a panic situation simply by temporarily refusing to pay out currency, a solution which enraged depositors but avoided squeezing bank debtors.

The Money Supply   The long controversy over the nation's monetary standard had ended with the defeat of William Jennings Bryan in the election of 1896. In 1900 Congress officially declared gold to be the standard money of the United States, at the value of $20.67 an ounce. Gold coins and fully backed gold certificates circulated as money, and all other forms of money were convertible into gold.

Adherence to the gold standard was not merely a financial convenience; it was a moral commitment. Money based on gold was "sound"; it was "honest." This attitude dovetailed with the widespread faith in laissez-faire economic policy and with a distrust of government intervention. In particular, the notion that the government should deliberately control the quantity of money was generally rejected in favor of having the quantity determined through the interplay of private commercial decisions.

Paradoxically, after the nation had weathered thirty years of price deflation with, first, an inconvertible paper system and, second, a limited form of gold and silver bimetallism, the adoption of the gold standard was accompanied by a steady rise in prices. The cause was the vast increase in gold production, chiefly from South Africa. The result was to diffuse a rosy aura of prosperity, not calculated to undermine faith in the virtues of the gold standard.

The Panic of 1907 Notwithstanding the elevated status of gold, three-fourths of the money supply consisted of bank checking deposits. In 1907 the country was again wracked by a banking panic, in which many banks temporarily refused to pay out currency. This brought to a head public dissatisfaction with the monetary performance of the banks. Congress in 1908 adopted the Aldrich-Vreeland Act, which authorized national banks acting in groups in an emergency to issue currency on security of assets other than government bonds. The act also established a National Monetary Commission, which conducted an extensive investigation of the banking system. Its report in 1912 led to the adoption of the Federal Reserve Act in 1913.

This chapter is concerned largely with the fortunes of the Federal Reserve System through a stormy quarter century. It started operations during the turbulence of World War I. A period of relative success and stability in the 1920s ended in the stock market crash and the Depression of the 1930s. Inability of the Federal Reserve to prevent the worst financial panic in American history led to extensive changes in its structure and in the financial system generally. Since the changes of the 1930s largely created our modern financial system, it is important to see why they occurred as they did.

THE FEDERAL RESERVE ACT

Objectives The Federal Reserve Act of 1913 compromised on many points of dispute and was deliberately ambiguous on others. The act was the work of the Democrats, and leaders of finance generally opposed it. The American Bankers Association characterized it as "hard to accept . . . for those who do not believe in socialism." However, the System soon won the support of the financial community.

The preamble to the act announced its purpose: ". . . to furnish an elastic currency, to afford means of rediscounting commercial paper, to establish a more effective supervision of banking, and for other purposes. . . ." This statement described largely the functions of the System rather than the end results hoped for. It said nothing explicit about stabilizing the economy, preventing panics and depressions, promoting economic growth, or similar objectives. A further directive appeared in the substance of the law, which directed that discount rates be set "with a view of accommodating commerce and business. . . ." This was vague and implied, if anything, a commitment to easy money.

Structure and Organization   A large part of the law was concerned with technicalities of organization. The law envisioned a federation of regional Federal Reserve banks, each serving member banks in its district. The Reserve banks would be financially interdependent and would maintain clearing accounts and rediscount facilities for each other. Each was to be controlled by a nine-man board of directors, six of whom were to be chosen by member banks and three by the Board in Washington. These directors would select the actual executives.

The regional banks would be supervised and coordinated by the Federal Reserve Board in Washington. The seven Board members included the Secretary of the Treasury, the Comptroller of the Currency, and five other presidential appointees. The Board was authorized to suspend reserve requirements in an emergency. It was also given the power of "review and determination" over discount rates—a vague provision which led to frequent conflicts of opinion between the Board and individual Reserve banks. The general intent of the law was to leave most operating responsibility with individual Reserve banks, so that the System was to be a federation with regional autonomy.

The lines of organization laid down by the original act subsequently revealed many defects. The law left undetermined the location of power, responsibility, and initiative within each Reserve bank, among the banks as a group, within the Board, and between banks and Board. The emphasis on group executive power, particularly at the Board level, created an administrative atmosphere which was deadening to initiative and provided too many opportunities for delay and inaction. This muddled structure was consistent with the notion that the System's operation would be largely automatic and passive, so that initiative and leadership were unnecessary.

Each member bank was required to buy stock in its regional Federal Reserve bank. It was obliged to clear checks at par, to conform to reserve requirements, and to submit to Federal bank examination. In exchange, it received voting rights for directors and access to Federal Reserve discount facilities.

Fundamentally, membership in the System was voluntary. To be sure, national banks were required to join, but a reluctant bank could always shift to a state charter, as a few did.

The law relaxed some regulations for national banks in hopes of making national charters more attractive. And state-chartered banks were invited to join the system. At first few came in, but after further liberalizations of requirements in 1917, the System rapidly recruited more than a thousand. However, most decided to remain outside, preferring to avoid the requirements for capital, reserves, or par clearance.

Federal Reserve Notes and Rediscount Facilities   The law created new paper currency to be issued by Reserve banks. Federal Reserve notes were declared to be obligations of the government and were convertible into gold or other currency on demand. Reserve banks were allowed to issue notes only on condition that they put up 100 per cent collateral in the form of rediscounted commercial paper, plus a reserve of 40 per cent in gold. The collateral provision was designed to link note issue with rediscount.

Each Reserve bank was authorized to discount commercial paper for the member banks, provided that the paper was "eligible." The IOUs must arise "out of actual commercial transactions" and have not more than 90 days to run until maturity (six months for agricultural paper). The expectation was that rediscounting would be the means for the member banks to obtain additional currency and that variations in the volume of commercial loans would provide an automatic guide for the proper volume of notes. For instance, during the crop-moving season, the member banks would tend to enlarge their short-term agricultural credits and could rediscount some of these to obtain the added currency traditionally needed.

Thus the Federal Reserve Act enacted the commercial-loan theory of credit. There was certainly a paradox in this, for one of the basic premises of that theory was that commercial loans were by their nature liquid. The fact that a central bank was needed to rediscount these IOUs proved that this liquidity was a fictitious property for the banking system as a whole. If liquidity had to be conferred by rediscount, it could with equal facility be conferred on any asset on which the Federal Reserve was prepared to lend, including the bank building itself.

Devotees of the commercial-loan theory tended, however, to stress the fact that it provided a desirable directive for the kind of credit created and for its total volume. They wanted bank loans to be "productive" instead of "speculative" and believed that the volume of commercial paper gave an indication of the "needs of trade" for money, the supply of which should vary with the demand.

The theory was naïve in assuming that the type of IOU involved would also correspond to the actual use of the funds. A merchant could buy inventories with his own money and then borrow on them to raise funds for speculation. Nor would the volume of commercial paper be an ideal guide to the appropriate quantity of money, particularly over cyclical variations. During a period of inflation, for instance, a given quantity of goods could give rise to an increasing amount of commercial loans and thus expand the money supply. Contrariwise, a recession would tend to reduce loans and the money supply.

Applying this theory to the Federal Reserve's rediscount operation magnified the fallacy, for it ignored the possibility that the proceeds of rediscounting would go not into currency but into bank reserves, each dollar of which could support several dollars of deposits. Thus an increase in rediscounting could make it possible for the money supply to expand by more than the "needs of trade." The commercial-loan principle created a tendency for Federal Reserve credit to fluctuate perversely over the business cycle.

The rigid requirements of the original law did not remain in force long. In 1916 the Reserve banks were authorized to lend to member banks on collateral of government securities, and such loans thereafter always constituted a substantial fraction of Reserve bank lending. In 1917 the collateral requirement for notes was revised to require merely the 40 per cent gold reserve plus 60 per cent of additional gold or commercial paper. These changes meant that Reserve note issues could vary with gold, government securities, and commercial paper. Although the commercial-loan principle was thus weakened, its tendencies toward cyclical perversity remained operative.

Member Bank Reserves   Reserve requirements for national banks were already in force. The new law reduced their level while retaining the principle of imposing the highest requirement on central reserve city banks, a lower requirement on reserve city banks, and the lowest for the others ("country banks"). Classification of cities and banks was based on the structure of interbank deposits. For the first time, a separate, lower reserve requirement was set for time deposits.

Reserve provisions of the 1913 law proved temporary and transitional. In 1917, the principle was established that all member bank reserves be kept on deposit with the Federal Reserve banks. However, to make this requirement less unpalatable, requirements for demand deposits were set at relatively low levels of 13, 10, and 7 per cent for the three classes of banks. The time-deposit rate became 3 per cent. No discretion was given to change the requirements, but the Board was authorized to suspend them temporarily.

The Federal Reserve itself was subjected to reserve requirements of 40 per cent in gold for notes and 35 per cent in gold or currency for deposit liabilities. Thus proper respects were paid to the gold standard, as well as to the commercial-loan principle. The gold reserve was certainly expected to limit credit expansion by the Federal Reserve, but whether increased gold required expansion of Federal Reserve credit is not clear.

The common attitude toward member bank reserves was that they had been pooled in a sort of warehouse. The idea that the Federal Reserve banks could create or destroy reserves through credit variations was not recognized. Furthermore, member bank reserve requirements were generally regarded simply as a protection of liquidity, with little recognition of their function as a limit on the ability of the banks to create money.

The Reserve banks were explicitly authorized to conduct open-market purchases and sales of securities. Two reasons were given for including this provision. First, it was perceived as a technique of credit control, but in a rather roundabout way. Open-market sales were expected to raise interest rates and thus "make the discount rate effective" in times when banks were not borrowing from the Federal Reserve. Emphasis was on the withdrawal of loan funds rather than on reduction of bank reserves. Second, Reserve banks might carry on open-market purchases "as a method of profitably employing their funds in times of easy money, when member banks are making few calls on them for rediscount." [1] This attitude clearly reveals ignorance of the effect on bank reserves. A period of low discounts and easy credit might be a poor time for Federal Reserve purchases, if the policy objective were economic stabilization. It was nearly a decade before open-market operations developed into a rational instrument for influencing bank reserves through the initiative of the Federal Reserve.

Other Provisions The law provided for a nationwide check-clearing system operated by the Federal Reserve and open to all banks willing to pay for checks at par. Member bank reserve accounts became the medium for settling balances, supplemented by a gold settlement fund for balances between one Reserve bank and another. The law also authorized member banks to deal in bankers' acceptances and in this manner helped create a national market for commercial paper. These provisions greatly helped to create a nationwide checking system and to enhance the geographic mobility of credit.

The Federal Reserve authorities undertook a vigorous campaign against nonpar clearance, whereby some banks deducted an "exchange charge" from the face value of checks drawn on them. However, many small banks stuck with the practice as an important source of revenue. With this limitation, the clearing system helped enhance the monetary status of checks. Unfortunately, a provision to establish Federal deposit insurance, included in the Senate version of the act, was ultimately stricken out, and that

[1] Edwin W. Kemmerer, *The ABC of the Federal Reserve System*, Princeton University Press, Princeton, N.J., 1919, pp. 42–43.

experiment was delayed another twenty years. The Treasury was authorized to use the Reserve banks to manage its funds, a provision which has greatly facilitated Treasury operations over the long run.

The Federal Reserve Act, despite its novelties, reflected the search for a structural panacea. It created a mechanism which was expected to function automatically in the public interest to prevent panics and adjust the supply of money and credit to the demand. It provided no great area of discretionary action, nor did it provide any standards for the exercise of such discretion.

A DECADE OF TRIAL AND ERROR, 1914–1923

The War Years, 1914–1918   The modern Federal Reserve is vastly different from the institution created in 1913, and one of the reasons for this is that the world in which the Reserve operates has become vastly different from the one in which it originated. The great change began in 1914, when war commenced in Europe.

The outbreak of war set off a sharp monetary panic in the United States, which was met in part by the issue of Aldrich-Vreeland notes. Conditions soon improved; purchases by European countries renewed the rapid upward trend that American output and prices had been on for nearly twenty years. Gold poured into the country. The banks had large excess reserves and expanded loans readily. The Federal Reserve banks had no way of checking credit expansion, for no one was rediscounting and they had no securities to sell. Indeed, Reserve banks bought some securities and acceptances to acquire earning assets and ignored the inflationary consequences of their action.

The period 1915–1917 was one of the most severe peacetime inflations in American experience; wholesale prices rose by 60 per cent through March, 1917. Inflation put the nation's economy at full output and employment but left little slack for protection against worse inflation when the country joined the war in April, 1917.

Although the United States was an active belligerent for only a year and a half, during that period government finance unleashed an inflation of serious proportions. Federal expenditures, which averaged less than $1 billion annually before the war, totaled over $30 billion in the two years ending June, 1919. Although substantial increases in the newly developed income and profits taxes were enacted, taxes covered only about 30 per cent of expenditures.

The resulting large deficits were financed by a large further expansion of credit, to which the Federal Reserve lent its support. Reserve banks did not buy large amounts of government securities directly but encouraged commercial banks to buy them or to lend to nonbank buyers. Reserve banks rediscounted at low rates notes secured by the government issues. Nearly $2 billion of Federal Reserve credit was created in this way, but a substantial part of this went to provide increased currency for circulation.

The banks had plenty of excess reserves, however, and were able to buy directly about $4 billion of the $22 billion of securities issued by the Treasury during the war. They also expanded their loans by nearly $6 billion, of which some $3 billion financed nonbank purchases of securities. Treasury policy was to encourage large nonbank purchases, to the extent of encouraging people to "borrow and buy" securities. Sales to banks, when necessary, should be short-term. It was hoped that the credit expansion resulting would be temporary, as the nonbank buyers would pay off their debts and the government would redeem bank holdings out of taxation.

Table 16-1   Money, velocity, output, and prices in the United States, 1914–1920 (Dollar figures in billions)

Year	M	V_g	Output (1914 dollars)	Prices (1914 = 100)	GNP (current prices)
1914	$12	3.2	$39	100	$39
1917	17	3.6	42	146	61
1918	20	3.8	46	167	77
1919	23	3.8	46	184	85
1920	24	3.8	44	210	92

Note: Money supply includes Treasury cash and deposits and is figure for June 30.

Sources: Banking and Monetary Statistics; U.S. Income and Output. Conversion to 1914 prices and computation of velocity are by the author.

The behavior of money, output, and prices is summarized in Table 16-1. Since output and velocity both rose only slightly, prices were left to absorb the impact of the big increase in the money supply. The two maintained almost exact proportionality, giving a striking illustration of the quantity theory.

The resulting inflation was very substantial, though clearly not severe enough to cause any great rise in velocity. Inflation was ineffective in raising output. Its only function was to substitute for taxation as a way of reducing private consumption to permit the government to take a larger share of the relatively fixed output. Easy credit conditions enabled the Treasury to finance its deficits with only a slight rise in interest rates (from about $3\frac{1}{2}$ per cent in 1917 to about $4\frac{1}{2}$ per cent in 1919). This financing was achieved at the cost of substantial injustice to many income receivers (including bondholders) and set the stage for the severe postwar recession.

Mechanically, war finance was administered very smoothly, and the

Federal Reserve earned many plaudits for its handling of Treasury funds and the public debt. For the first time during a major war, the gold standard was maintained. Although an embargo was placed on gold exports and informal pressure was applied to discourage domestic gold withdrawals, the country's money remained convertible. The Reserve, which had worked hard to draw much of the gold stock into its vaults, was given credit for this achievement.

It is paradoxical that an institution established to promote monetary stability should win its first public acclaim for its skill in making it possible to have a severe inflation with a minimum of administrative difficulty. However, the basic defects in war finance were the weak tax policy and the Treasury's eagerness for low interest rates. Federal Reserve officials worked to promote bond sales to nonbank investors and to persuade banks to limit credit expansion. Indeed, they conducted an informal but successful program of regulating margins for stock market lending, which was unfortunately discontinued when the war ended. Still, Reserve activity was scarcely a major influence against inflation.

Postwar Boom and Bust, 1919–1921   After a slight recession at the close of hostilities in 1918, the economy resumed its inflationary upsurge, as shown clearly by Table 16-1. Federal deficit spending continued into 1919, and private investment, much of it of speculative nature, rose. By 1920 consumer prices were over 30 per cent above 1918 levels. Continued expansion of bank credit contributed to the inflation, and Federal Reserve credit also expanded. From an average of $2.4 billion in November, 1918, it rose to $3.5 billion two years later—the increase coming in the discount category. While most of this went into currency, bank reserves rose $300 million as well.[2]

Federal Reserve officials were greatly disturbed by this continuing credit inflation; but the influence of the Treasury, which was still involved in borrowing and refunding existing debt, kept them from taking any real restraining action until the end of 1919. By then the embargo on gold had been withdrawn, and gold was moving out of the country. Loss of gold reserves spurred quick Reserve action. Starting in November, 1919, discount rates were raised in several stages until they topped 5 per cent in New York in June, 1920. Both bank credit and rediscount volume, however, continued upward for several months.

Nevertheless, the bubble had burst. Beginning in May, 1920, prices and GNP expenditures began a sharp decline. Federal government finance,

[2] These statistical data, and many which follow, are from Board of Governors, Federal Reserve System, *Banking and Monetary Statistics*, 1943, and U.S. Bureau of the Census, *Historical Statistics of the United States: Colonial Times to 1957*, 1960.

which shifted to a surplus, exerted a deflationary influence; but the chief downward pressure probably came from a drop in business inventory spending. This decrease was induced by changing expectations of prices and sales, and once the decline commenced, the downward acceleration effect came into play. Tightening of short-term credit added downward pressure in 1920.

GNP expenditures fell from $92 billion in 1920 to $70 billion in 1921—a drop of almost 25 per cent. Much of this decline was reflected in a great drop in prices, so that output fell only about 10 per cent, which was still enough to create extensive unemployment. Fortunately, fixed-capital expenditures did not decline seriously, and additional support came from exports and government spending. Inventory expenditures consequently soon bounced back, and the economy was substantially recovered by 1922, when output surpassed its previous peak.

Federal Reserve policy did little to ease the recession. High discount rates were kept in effect until May, 1921. These high rates did not cause any appreciable decline in rediscounting volume, which began to fall only when the demand for loans declined in 1921. But high discount rates and high member bank indebtedness kept bank credit tight during the deflation period in late 1920. Credit eased in 1921 only when the demand for it declined. Reserve bank credit followed the curve of business conditions, and bank reserves declined $200 million from June, 1920, to the following June. The money supply, which had risen during the inflation, turned down in April, 1920, and declined sharply over the following year.

There was no monetary panic, however, and the rise in interest rates was not severe. The Federal Reserve had followed the traditional policy of the Bank of England: when gold flows out and a crisis develops, raise the rate but lend freely. The higher rate was supposed to attract foreign capital and shut off the gold flow; in addition, it would apply pressure to dealers' inventories which would push prices down. Federal Reserve action in 1920–1921 achieved these results very effectively. Many observers felt that continuing tight credit was necessary to reduce excessive inventories and get the price level back where it belonged. They had confidence that a decline in spending would operate mainly to reduce prices and that no serious or long-lasting harm would result to output and employment. On the whole, experience tended to confirm their views, which were, unfortunately, not so appropriate in the next crisis.

Although industry recovered quickly, this depression left a permanent mark in the farm sector. Wartime boom demands for food had encouraged great increases in farm debt, and the price collapse brought another of the familiar crises. Much criticism was directed at the Federal Reserve for its role in the deflation, but a congressional investigation of farm prices exonerated it from blame. High output and loss of export markets (when Europe revived) kept farm prices at low levels during the 1920s. The farm depression originated the chronic demands for "parity" which came to fruition in the 1930s.

The immediate effect of the farm crisis was to undermine the solvency of a large number of small rural banks. By 1921 the number of commercial banks had grown to about 30,000. In the previous decade, an average of about 100 banks a year had been obliged to suspend operations, 90 of these on the average being nonnational. In the years 1921–1928 inclusive, more than 600 banks suspended each year, of which about 100 were Reserve member banks. This performance indicated the shaky condition of nonmember banks but was hardly reassuring about member banks. Federal and state supervisory authorities were accused of "competition in laxity." Clearly the holder of a bank deposit still ran a risk, for the government had not succeeded in giving deposits the protection it had given paper currency.

New Concepts of Monetary Management In 1922 and 1923, important changes appeared in the attitude of Reserve officials toward their responsibilities and techniques. This change was most pronounced in the case of Benjamin Strong, head of the New York Reserve bank. Disappointed at the performance of the economy since 1914, Strong argued that Federal Reserve policy could not function adequately if it followed mechanical guides such as its gold reserve or the commercial-loan theory. Strong came to hold the view that the proper goal of monetary policy was the stabilization of economic activity and that a quantitative rather than qualitative approach was needed.[3]

The members of the Board did not go so far in their views. In their annual report for 1923, they conceded that variations in credit should not always follow variation in gold reserves and came out reservedly for a countercyclical policy. But they pledged their faith to the qualitative standard by reiterating: "The Federal reserve system is a system of productive credit. It is not a system of credit for either investment or speculative purposes." They concluded "there will be little danger that the credit created and contributed by the Federal reserve banks will be in excessive volume if restricted to productive uses."[4] Recognizing that paper rediscounted was not a guide to the use of funds, they still argued that Reserve banks could and should determine and control the uses made of Reserve credit.

This period also saw the development of open-market operations as a full-scale technique of monetary control. The great increase in the Federal debt resulting from the war had enlarged the scope for such operations. In

[3] Lester V. Chandler, *Benjamin Strong, Central Banker*, The Brookings Institution, Washington, 1958, pp. 194–204.

[4] Board of Governors, Federal Reserve System, *Annual Report for 1923*, pp. 32–35. The idea that discount rates should be varied to exert a countercyclical influence was clearly stated on p. 10 of the report.

1922, when discounting business was slack, several Reserve banks bought securities purely for income. They discovered that these purchases were promptly reflected in a further decline in member bank rediscounting. It became clear that open-market operations affected member bank reserves. In consequence, the Board in April, 1923, resolved that open-market operations be conducted "with primary regard to the accommodation of commerce and business, and to the effect . . . on the general credit situation." The Board established an Open-Market Investment Committee of five Reserve bank presidents to participate in policy formulation but left little doubt that the last word remained with the Board itself.

Thus Federal Reserve thinking shifted from a role of passive accommodation to one of active participation in the state of the economy. The shift in objective was matched by the shift in understanding and use of techniques.

TRIUMPH AND TRAGEDY, 1923–1932

"New Era" Prosperity   It was an ironic paradox that the greatest failure of Federal Reserve policy came after its objectives, theories, and powers had been developed to a high degree of sophistication and after their exercise had won extensive public confidence. In retrospect, it is clear that the Federal Reserve and the financial system still contained serious deficiencies which rendered them very vulnerable.

Beginning with the recovery of 1922, the American economy entered a period of sustained prosperity and growth. From 1923 to 1929, output expanded by about one-fourth. Despite mild recessions, average annual unemployment never exceeded 5 per cent of the labor force. Consumer prices remained stable during this prosperity and actually declined slightly after 1926.

Prosperity was sparked by high levels of investment and a rapid rate of technical progress. Industrial productivity increased rapidly and raised real incomes and leisure as well as profits. Mass production and distribution of automobiles, and the attendant stimulus to highway building and such industries as steel, glass, rubber, and petroleum, were dominant factors in stimulating investment.

Federal Reserve Policy, 1923–1927   Federal Reserve actions in the mid-1920s were chiefly directed at offsetting fluctuations in the domestic economy. In prosperous 1923, Reserve banks sold almost $300 million of securities and raised discount rates from 4 to 4½ per cent. In 1924, in the face of a mild recession, discount rates were cut to 3 per cent and $400 million of securities purchased. Gradual tightening was imposed in 1925–1926 again, to be modified in 1927 when another mild recession developed. The New

York discount rate temporarily went from 4 to 3½ per cent, and about $300 million of securities were purchased. These actions did not eliminate the tendency (caused by rediscount volume) for Reserve bank credit to rise in booms and decline in recessions. But bank interest rates did follow the Reserve rediscount rates, so that the cost of credit on the whole was a countercyclical influence, whatever its importance.

During this period, Reserve officials, particularly Benjamin Strong, were concerned with aiding in restoration of the international gold standard. They recognized that low interest rates in the United States would help Great Britain and other countries to return to gold. Long-term capital would be encouraged to flow out of the United States, and short-term international balances would not tend to flow in. These considerations contributed to the easy-money policies adopted in 1924 and 1927. In retrospect, they were criticized for adding fuel to the speculative fire which was developing, and some Reserve officials conceded that they might have gone too far in 1927; but these policies were neither extreme nor irreversible.

The Big Bull Market By contrast to the placid condition of the productive economy, stock market speculation reached a state of turbulence in the late 1920s. From a low point in 1921, stock prices moved upward with only slight interruptions and by 1926 had doubled their 1921 values. By 1925 some Reserve officials expressed concern over speculation, but their attention was focused on the use of bank credit rather than on speculation itself.

At first stock prices paralleled rising profits, but as time passed, the price rise became increasingly speculative. Margin requirements, subject to no legal restrictions, were often as low as 20 per cent, and credit buying grew rapidly. The volume of brokers' loans rose from $2 billion in 1924 to $4 billion in 1927 and reached a peak above $8 billion in 1929. By the end of 1928, member bank loans on securities amounted to almost $10 billion and constituted 40 per cent of their total loans! This growth was made possible by a rapid rise of time deposits; indeed, some corporations engaged in arbitrage by issuing stock and using the proceeds to acquire time deposits or make loans to brokers. While neither the money supply nor GNP velocity rose appreciably in the late 1920s, transactions velocity, as measured by the turnover of demand deposits, shot up from 38 in 1926 to 54 in 1929.

From mid-1927 to mid-1929 stock prices approximately doubled, as did the volume of stock market credit. Rising prices enabled speculators to pyramid their holdings, since they could borrow more on a given stock when its price went up. The ease of floating new stocks led to a proliferation of holding companies, particularly in public utilities. Investment companies, which had not amounted to much in American finance previously, also multiplied—Galbraith estimates that by 1929 new ones were being spawned "at the rate of approximately one each business day." Some of these were downright fraudulent, and many more were simply carelessly thrown together and incompetently managed, with little accurate public disclosure of their affairs. The bull market encouraged misrepresentation, manipulation, and slipshod conduct among many other financial and nonfinancial firms as well.[5]

By the beginning of 1929 the market contained the seeds of its own destruction. Dividend yields on stocks had fallen below the interest on bonds, and credit costs were rising on margin loans. There was little point in holding stocks unless their prices continued to rise, and there was increasing likelihood that prices could not continue to rise. When the market stopped going up, it would start going down—and rapidly.

Federal Reserve Policy, 1928–1929   Federal Reserve officials were caught between the desire to reduce the flow of credit into speculation and the desire not to interfere with the credit needs of nonfinancial business. Members of the Board, faithful to the qualitative tradition, believed speculation could be curbed by pressure on member banks not to lend on securities. The New York Reserve bank officials believed that no such separation of purpose was possible—if loans of any kind were made, funds would find their way to areas where returns were high, which meant stock market lending. Indeed, many nonfinancial businesses that appeared entitled to "productive" credit were actually lending large sums into stock market credit. The New York officials believed the only approach was to tighten credit for all comers but feared this might reduce real investment, cause a recession, and contribute to international financial imbalance.

Actual policy vacillated between these points of view. Once the 1927 recession was clearly over, the previous ease of credit was ended early in 1928. Discount rates moved up from 3½ to 5 per cent, and Reserve banks sold $400 million of securities—two-thirds of their holdings. The member banks merely increased their rediscounts, and in the autumn the Reserve banks unwisely purchased acceptances in the open market to aid in financing the harvest—a triumph for the qualitative approach. By the end of 1928 the volume of Reserve bank credit was $300 million higher than a year before; but rising demand for loans did pull interest rates up.

The rise of market interest rates convinced Reserve bank officials that discount-rate increases were imperative, but repeated petitions for increases were turned down by the Board. Instead, the Board issued an ambiguous directive to the Reserve banks indicating that they should curtail discounts for banks lending for speculation. Some curtailments were made, and interest rates rose further. Stock prices faltered, then resumed their dizzy rise. In August the New York discount rate (only) was raised, but purchases of acceptances were increased and the net effect was to ease, not tighten, credit. Reserve officials remained afraid of the effects tight money would have on

[5] John Kenneth Galbraith, *The Great Crash*, Houghton Mifflin Company, Boston, 1955, p. 54.

the domestic and international economic situation and never undertook a strict curtailment.

Stock prices reached their pinnacle in October, then broke dramatically. The crash was undoubtedly brought on in part by evidence that a recession was beginning in the productive economy. Once the decline began, the inherent weaknesses of the market became apparent. Speculators' margins were wiped out, and when they could not put up additional funds, their stocks were sold on the falling market. Jerry-built investment companies collapsed, and many financial irregularities which could be concealed as long as prices rose were brought to light. In about a month stock prices fell off one-third from their peak values.

The Federal Reserve officials never directly attacked stock prices or speculation itself, nor did they operate effectively to curtail the flow of credit into speculation. In their defense, it must be admitted that their reluctance to undertake general credit stringency was reasonable and that the tightening of credit which occurred in 1929 did impair real investment and upset the flow of international capital.

Perhaps there was more Reserve officials could have done. They could have asked for authority to impose margin controls like those informally administered during the war. Such authority would have been bitterly opposed by the financiers and quite likely would not have been supported by a complacent Congress and administration. Professor Galbraith argues that in early 1929 "a robust denunciation of speculators and speculation by someone in high authority and a warning that the market was too high would almost certainly have broken the spell" and reversed the upsurge. But he feels that "the Federal Reserve was less interested in checking speculation than in detaching itself from responsibility for the speculation that was going on." [6]

Undoubtedly the Board, loaded as it was with mediocrities appointed by Harding and Coolidge, did not distinguish itself. Had it succeeded in breaking the speculation by some heroic move, however, it is easy to imagine a repetition of the inquisition of the early 1920s. If there is to be blame for complacency, it belongs with Congress and the President.

Much of the discussion of the stock market crash is biased by the assumption that it rendered inevitable the full sequence of deplorable events which sent the economy into deep depression; that is, given 1929, 1933 was inevitable. This is a great exaggeration. The stock panic of October, 1929, soon halted. In December, stocks began rising again and continued to rise until April, 1930, at which time prices had regained the levels of late 1928. The interim was certainly a serious dip but hardly enough to wreck the economy for three years afterward. The real drop in stock prices began in May, 1930, from which point they fell by 80 per cent to the low of 1933.

[6] *Ibid.*, pp. 37, 40.

This drop was a symptom of the decline in profits and dividends and was quite separate from the panic itself. It took a great many more blunders than those of 1929 to bring the economy to its wretched state of 1933.

DOWN INTO DEPRESSION, 1929–1933

The Boom Ends The sequence of events attending the economic turning point of 1929 contains three significant events. First, as we noted in Chapter 15, American foreign lending fell off in 1928, setting off economic troubles in various raw material price-support schemes and also initiating an economic downswing in Germany.

Second, in July, 1929, several months before the stock crash, production and employment in the United States began to decline. Two major causes can be identified. First, the stock of capital goods (including housing) had been built up very substantially in the 1920s. Because of slackening in the rate of growth of demand for such products as automobiles, and in the rate of population growth and family formation, the desired stock of capital did not rise as much. Second, a substantial tightening of credit occurred in 1928–1929, partly through Federal Reserve actions, partly because of the strong demand for credit. In combination, these factors turned investment downward.

The third element was the stock market crash itself. Although it would be improper to consider this *the* cause of the Depression, it probably contributed. It is possible that speculators who suffered capital losses reduced their consumption, although it would be hard to find statistical evidence of this. Most probably, the collapse of stock prices helped to worsen business attitudes toward the future, thus reducing the marginal efficiency schedule. However, with the pressure of demand on capacity already weakening, investment in fixed capital would probably have declined anyway.

Identifying the elements which initiated the downswing still does not explain why the Depression went so deep and lasted so long. After all, recovery had been rapid from the 1920–1921 dip. The Depression which followed 1929 was so serious in part because of the destruction of incentive to invest in fixed capital, and partly because of the collapse of the banking system.

Cumulative Downswing Once the expenditure flow began to decline, the multiplier and accelerator operated strongly to continue the decline. As GNP fell, induced investment, particularly in inventories, dropped. Businesses with excess capacity had no incentive to replace worn-out capital. As investment dropped, it pulled down consumer incomes and consumer spending, which in turn made the investment outlook worse. In 1920–1921, business firms were short of fixed capital and therefore never lost the incentive to expand. In 1929 they had too much capital, and as demand fell further, the excess became worse. By 1933 GNP expenditures had fallen by almost half from 1929—from $104 billion to $56 billion. Table 16-2 shows how the various spending components contributed to this decline.

Consumer spending was the biggest contributor to the decline—it fell by $33 billion. This decline is most accurately attributed to the fall in disposable incomes, however, for actually the percentage of income consumed rose, until at the lowest level of the downswing consumers as a group were spending more than their incomes. The drop in consumption was induced; it was not an independent cause of the decline.

Table 16-2   GNP expenditures, 1929-1933
(Billions of dollars)

| Year | GNP | Consumption | C/PDI, per cent | Domestic investment | | |
				Fixed	Inventory	Total
1929	$104.4	$79.0	94.9	$14.6	$1.7	$16.2
1930	91.1	71.0	95.4	10.6	−0.4	10.3
1931	76.3	61.3	96.1	6.8	−1.3	5.5
1932	58.5	49.3	101.2	3.5	−2.6	0.9
1933	56.0	46.4	101.3	3.0	−1.6	1.4

| | | | Government purchases | |
Year	Exports	Imports	Federal	State and local
1929	$7.0	$6.3	$1.3	$7.2
1930	5.4	4.8	1.4	7.8
1931	3.6	3.4	1.5	7.7
1932	2.5	2.3	1.5	6.6
1933	2.4	2.3	2.0	6.0

Source: U.S. Income and Output. Figures are rounded and may not add up.

Domestic investment was the chief villain. By 1933, it had fallen 90 per cent below 1929. Certainly the initial decline in fixed investment was largely an autonomous development, but in subsequent years a large part was induced. Inventory reduction was clearly an induced response to falling sales. Fixed-capital investment fell below the $7 billion annual rate of depreciation—something which would not have happened if the customers had not vanished. The decline in investment was aggravated by declining business income and bankruptcies—corporations as a group registered losses of about $2 billion a year in 1932 and 1933. Housing construction fell off, partly because of lower consumer incomes. To all these depressants was added the credit problem, to which we shall return.

The decline in export sales was also very large in percentage terms and reduced domestic income by nearly $5 billion by 1933. The drop in exports was largely induced by the decline in American foreign lending which began in 1928 and by the subsequent declines in foreign incomes resulting from lower American imports. The United States aggravated the latter decline by the Smoot-Hawley Tariff in 1930, and many other countries retaliated by increasing import restrictions. As we noted in Chapter 15, the European economy was in shaky condition financially when the downswing began in 1929 and was thus very vulnerable to the shock from America. The European collapse reacted upon the United States through reduced export sales and gold withdrawals.

Of all the components of GNP, government purchases remained most stable. Federal purchases rose as the Hoover administration enlarged public-works programs, but the amount was comparatively tiny and failed to offset declines in state and local government spending which resulted when tax revenues fell. Furthermore, the benefits of Federal spending were seriously undermined by the great increase in tax rates which was adopted in 1932 to reduce the budget deficit.

Financial Collapse   The downswing was aggravated by the almost continuous banking crisis which finally terminated in the drastic measures of 1933. As business income fell, bank loans went into default, undermining bank solvency. Public alarm about bank safety led to increased withdrawals of currency, which reduced reserves and forced the banks to curtail lending —a tendency accentuated by pessimism. Credit curtailment forced business spending down, which in turn reduced the ability of many other firms to pay their debts. Thousands of banks were forced to close, and depositors were deprived of spending power just when it was needed most.

What was the Federal Reserve doing during the worst financial panic in American history? Once the downturn was apparent in 1929, the Reserve banks wasted no time in relaxing credit tension. Rediscount rates were cut repeatedly until they were down to 2 per cent at the end of 1930. Reserve banks bought $500 million of securities, which was enough to keep member bank reserves from declining, although Federal Reserve credit did go down in face of declining discount volume. In the twelve months after the stock collapse, interest rates generally declined and credit eased. In late 1930, however, conditions deteriorated. Banks were unloading bonds in an effort to bolster their liquidity, and prices of the lower grades of bonds began to rise. The market for new issues largely dried up. The availability of credit to higher-risk borrowers was reduced. All told, bank loans declined by $4 billion in 1930. And the rate of bank failures took a sharp jump at the end of the year with the closing of a large New York City bank.

Nevertheless, some important economic indicators showed signs of recovery in early 1931, and Friedman and Schwartz argue that "perhaps if those tentative stirrings of revival had been reinforced by a vigorous expansion in the stock of money, they could have been converted into sustained recovery. But that was not to be." [7]

Instead, Federal Reserve credit declined in early 1931 in face of a spreading liquidity crisis. Financial conditions turned sharply for the worse in the middle of the year as the United States felt the backwash of the European panic. In six weeks, beginning in September, the gold stock was depleted by $700 million, and over $400 million of currency was withdrawn from the banks. Faced with a crisis, the Federal Reserve authorities blundered seriously. They raised rediscount rates from 1½ to 3½ per cent—a traditional technique for "protecting" the gold reserve. Member bank borrowing increased nonetheless, but reserves were dangerously depleted. The gold drain halted, but the rate of bank failures increased sharply. In all, some 2,300 banks, holding deposits of $1.7 billion, closed in 1931.

Why were Federal Reserve authorities, who could have ended the panic if they had undertaken massive open-market purchases, so paralyzed? Friedman and Schwartz indicate that a principal cause was their failure to see the connection between bank failures and bank solvency, on one hand, and bank liquidity on the other. The authorities tended to treat insolvency as a reflection of mismanagement and sin on the part of individual banks—particularly since failures were heaviest among nonmember banks. They failed to see that the scramble for liquidity was itself a cause of bank failures.[8] This was evident in the bond market, where sales by desperate banks caused lower prices which in turn reduced the value of bond holdings of other banks. The result could be a vicious circle: "The examiner finding that a bank's assets at current market prices were not equal to its liabilities would cause the bank to be declared insolvent. Bank suspensions by administrative action contributed to difficulties by tying up funds, causing the dumping of assets, and spreading alarm." [9] Retrospectively, it is clear that many of the suspended banks could have weathered the storm if given the benefit of the doubt; their assets would have been sound once recovery began. Federal Reserve purchases, by raising bond prices, would have strengthened bank solvency.

Even as a source of liquidity, the Federal Reserve was a failure. As

[7] Milton Friedman and Anna Jacobson Schwartz, *A Monetary History of the United States, 1867–1960*, Princeton University Press for National Bureau of Economic Research, Princeton, N.J., 1963, p. 313. This book provides a fascinating detailed account of the monetary features of the downswing.

[8] *Ibid.*, pp. 353–359.

[9] E. A. Goldenweiser, *American Monetary Policy*, McGraw-Hill Book Company, New York, 1951, pp. 170–171.

business declined, banks' holdings of eligible paper fell also. And because of the tradition against discounting, those banks which did borrow struggled all the harder to reduce their loans.

The reluctance of Reserve authorities to make extensive open-market purchases may also have reflected the restrictive provision that required Reserve banks to hold eligible paper as collateral for Federal Reserve notes. That requirement was abolished by the Glass-Steagall Act in February, 1932. This measure authorized the Reserve banks to lend to member banks on any collateral they wished to accept and permitted Reserve bank holdings of government securities to serve as collateral for note issues. With this, the restrictions of the commercial-loan theory were abandoned, but not until they had done much harm.

The Reserve banks thereupon embarked on an aggressive campaign to ease credit. Beginning in March, they purchased over $1 billion of securities in the remainder of 1932. Discount rates were reduced. By the end of the year, member banks had $500 million of excess reserves, and most interest rates had declined.

At the same time the government took another important step to aid the banks. In January, 1932, Congress created the Reconstruction Finance Corporation to make emergency loans to banks and other businesses. During 1932 the RFC extended about $1.5 billion of loans, of which banks received about $850 million.

As a result of these measures, the rate of bank failure in 1932 was reduced, although it was hard to be complacent when nearly 1,500 banks closed with $700 million of deposits. Late in 1932 a new wave of panic began to rise. Many banks had become seriously insolvent through loan defaults, and their continued closings led to panic withdrawals from others. The problem was aggravated by a requirement that the RFC publish the names of banks to which it lent. In October, 1932, the governor of Nevada declared a statewide "bank holiday," and the device spread to other states. This innovation intensified the panic where banks were still open. Through it all, the Federal Reserve sat tight; its holdings of government securities remained virtually unchanged from July, 1932, until May, 1933.

In February, 1933, nearly $1 billion in currency was withdrawn from the banks, and more than twenty states sponsored bank closings. On March 4, the day of his inauguration, President Roosevelt persuaded the governors of the other states to close their banks as well, and the move was backed by Federal authority two days later. The government also suspended gold payments, although there had been no serious depletion of the gold stock, and the Federal Reserve banks closed. "The central banking system, set up primarily to render impossible the restriction of payments by commercial banks, itself joined the commercial banks in a more widespread, complete, and economically disturbing restriction of payments than had ever been experienced in the history of the country." [10]

Perhaps only such drastic action could halt the panic, but it was a harsh remedy. The banks remained closed for a week, which severely hampered the functioning of the economy. Desperate for currency to pay wages and support consumer purchases, many business firms or local governments resorted to issues of "scrip." Banks were permitted to reopen only when licensed as to their soundness; this bolstered confidence in those which reopened immediately, but more than 5,000 did not reopen promptly, and 2,000 of these remained closed.

Nevertheless, the panic was over. The new President's words and his willingness to take forthright action restored a measure of public confidence. By March 15, banks accounting for 90 per cent of the preholiday deposits were back in operation. Currency flowed back. But what frightful damage had been done! Some 9,000 banks had been obliged to close, involving deposits of nearly $7 billion. Bank loans outstanding had fallen from $36 billion in 1929 to a mere $16 billion in 1933. Credit had dried up and money became desperately scarce just when easier credit and more money were most urgently needed.

Money and Economic Welfare The real adversities of the Depression were generated by declining incomes and output, by unemployment, bankruptcies, and increased debt burdens. The behavior of money and its relation to prices, output, and employment is shown by Table 16-3.

Table 16-3   Money and the economy, 1929–1933
(Dollar figures in billions)

Year	M	V_g	GNP	Output (1929 prices)	Prices (1929 = 100)	Unemployment, per cent
1929	$27	3.9	$104	$104	100	3
1930	26	3.6	91	95	96	9
1931	24	3.2	76	89	86	16
1932	21	2.8	59	75	78	24
1933	20	2.8	56	73	77	25

Sources: Banking and Monetary Statistics; U.S. Income and Output. Conversion of price and output data to 1929 base and calculation of velocity are by the author.

The money supply declined by $7 billion from 1929 to 1933. Behind this decline lay the tremendous pressure on bank reserves exerted by currency withdrawals—by early 1933 the public's currency holdings were nearly 50 per cent higher than in 1929. In the face of the Federal Reserve's failure to

[10] Friedman and Schwartz, *op. cit.*, pp. 327–328.

add sufficiently to reserves, the banks were obliged to curtail their earning assets. Loan renewals were refused, and interest rates on all types of private debt claims shot upward. To be sure, the currency withdrawals were a response to the economic downswing already under way, as defaults on loans and securities produced bank failures. But once started, the monetary deflation developed a life of its own and undoubtedly worsened the economic collapse.

Total GNP expenditures fell by over 40 per cent, which in turn reduced output and prices. The reduction of output by one-fourth created unemployment of a similar proportion of the labor force. This meant severe hardship for the unemployed, for there was no program of government unemployment compensation, and the amount of local relief or private charity was pitifully small. But President Hoover resolutely blocked efforts to extend Federal assistance to relief programs.

The crushing burden of deflation also fell severely on debtors—business firms, farmers, and home buyers. As their sales revenues declined, many businesses went bankrupt and thereby added to the disorder and demoralization by forced liquidations. Mortgaged farms and homes were subjected to extensive foreclosure, often by creditors such as banks who were themselves desperate to raise funds to pay *their* debts. Such confiscations of property met violent resistance in many areas; often whole communities united to see that foreclosed properties were "sold" for a nominal price at sheriff's sale to the original owner. Many states adopted laws providing for a moratorium on debts that made them temporarily uncollectible—which increased the problems of the banks.[11]

STAGNATION AND REFORM, 1933–1940

Financial Reforms New Deal spokesmen liked to think that their program contained three elements—relief, recovery, and reform. Monetary and financial measures were included in all three categories, but chiefly in the third. Once the panic ended in 1933, government investigators did a thorough job of exposing the shortcomings of the financial structure and policies of the previous years. New legislation produced the most pervasive overhauling of the nation's financial system ever undertaken. In general, the financial reforms did not do much to restore prosperity, but they vastly reduced the danger of another crisis like that of 1929–1933. Rather than deal with individual enactments in sequence, we shall simply summarize the most important end results.

[11] Broadus Mitchell, *Depression Decade*, Holt, Rinehart and Winston, Inc., New York, 1947, p. 186.

1. *Gold.* In 1933–1934 the United States abolished the gold-coin standard and raised the price of gold from $20.67 (where it had been for 100 years) to $35 an ounce. Gold coins and certificates ceased to circulate as money. Instead, the country went on a modified gold-bullion standard, with the Treasury standing ready to sell bullion for export or manufacture. Private ownership and trading of gold were severely restricted. Gold was still the ultimate reserve of the monetary system, but its influence on monetary policy was greatly reduced.

2. *Silver.* The United States resumed a silver-purchase program similar to that of 1878–1893. In 1934 Congress directed the Treasury to buy silver at prices above the market, but below the monetary, value. At first considerable discretion was allowed, but in 1939 the Treasury was required to take all domestic production offered to it at 71 cents an ounce. The program did enlarge the money supply slightly, but its chief objective was to subsidize producers.

3. *Federal Reserve structure.* In 1935 the Federal Reserve Board was abolished, and in its place was established a new Board of Governors, to which (with two exceptions) new men were appointed. To increase the Board's independence, the ex officio memberships of the Secretary of the Treasury and the Comptroller of the Currency were revoked. Terms of office of Board members were lengthened, and they were protected against removal except for specified cause. The Federal Open-Market Committee was given statutory authorization and was to consist of the seven Board members plus five Reserve bank presidents. While the general intent of these and other changes was to increase the power of the Board over the Reserve banks, the Open-Market Committee formalized the role of Reserve bank presidents in System policy.

4. *Federal Reserve powers.* The Board was given authority to alter reserve requirements for member banks up to levels double those set in 1917. The Board was also authorized to set minimum margin requirements for securities loans. This measure, which was so badly needed in 1929, was significant in that it set no limits to Board discretion and gave the Board authority over *all* lenders, not merely banks. The Board was authorized to set maximum interest rates on member bank time deposits, while member banks were forbidden to pay interest on demand deposits. The power of the Board to dictate rediscount rates to individual Reserve banks was made explicit.

5. *Deposit insurance.* The Federal Deposit Insurance Corporation was established with authority to insure individual deposits of commercial banks up to $5,000 (later raised to $10,000). A proposal to make insurance contingent on joining the Federal Reserve System was rejected, and membership in FDIC became available to all commercial banks. Most of them joined.

FDIC was given authority to examine banks under its jurisdiction, which meant a great extension of Federal bank supervision to state-chartered banks. In this program, the government finally recognized the monetary status of deposits as deserving of the type of guarantee extended to bank notes in 1863. Under a separate organization, deposit insurance was also extended to savings and loan associations.

6. *Financial regulation.* Extensive regulations and structural changes were imposed on banks, other financial institutions, and on corporate financial practices generally. The government established the Securities and Exchange Commission, with authority to require corporations issuing securities to make full and truthful disclosure of their circumstances. Securities exchanges were also brought under regulation to regularize trading and prevent fraud and manipulation. In 1940 activities of investment companies were brought under SEC regulation, requiring chiefly full disclosure of activities. Commercial banks were required to divorce themselves from previous affiliations with investment banking and investment companies. Such connections had been an important channel for getting bank credit into speculation and had served to weaken the banks when these security operations began to turn sour.

7. *Government credit agencies.* An extensive program of government loans and guarantees was undertaken. The RFC continued to play an active role—first, in bailing out firms in difficulty; later, in furnishing funds to small businesses. New financial institutions were particularly significant in relation to agriculture and housing. Prominent among many new farm credit agencies were the Rural Electrification Administration, which carried on extensive lending for the extension of power facilities in rural areas, and the Commodity Credit Corporation, established to make crop loans to farmers as an adjunct to the price-support programs which began at that time.

In the field of housing, the government created in 1933 the Home Owners Loan Corporation (HOLC), designed to refinance existing mortgages to avert foreclosures. The following year the Federal Housing Administration was established, with the authority to insure home mortgages. In 1938 the Federal National Mortgage Association was set up to provide a secondary market for mortgages similar to that provided by the Federal Reserve for commercial paper and government securities.

Some of these agencies and activities, such as RFC and HOLC, were chiefly defensive in purpose. They were designed to provide financial relief for firms and individuals whose long-run solvency appeared certain but whose immediate situation was desperate. Most of the agencies also had the objective of promoting lending and spending to get out of the Depression. Some agencies loaned government funds directly or provided them to private financial institutions. Others guaranteed or insured the assets or liabilities of financial institutions. While they probably made some immediate contribution to recovery, their long-run effects in changing the character of the country's financial structure were much greater.

8. *Other effects.* Besides these governmentally imposed changes, one should not ignore the direct effects which the Depression had on financial institutions and practices. One effect was to wipe out a great number of weak banks. The number of commercial banks dropped from 25,000 in 1928 to 14,000 in 1933. In addition, the traditional policy of easy entry into banking was reversed. Charters became difficult to obtain, and the opportunities for private banks to operate without charters were drastically curtailed.

The Recovery Program President Roosevelt and his advisers were strongly influenced by the conviction that depression was at root a problem of prices. If prices could be restored to their earlier high levels, they felt, producers would have the incentive to expand production, and unemployment would disappear. This outlook, while superficially plausible, proved unfortunate as a basis for policy. For the real trouble was that spending on goods and services was too low; low prices were merely a symptom of inadequate spending. Measures to raise spending would have taken care of prices as well as output and employment. Unfortunately, not all measures to raise prices would necessarily raise output and employment. To a disappointing degree, the New Deal relied on measures which tended to raise prices by curtailing supply or competition and which did not stimulate higher GNP expenditures.

One of the first attacks on the price problem came through the revaluation of gold in 1934. The administration seems to have been persuaded that reducing the "value" of the dollar must inevitably mean raising the price level. The chief effect was to reduce the foreign-exchange value of the dollar. This raised the prices of certain products exported in large amounts (as well as imports), but contributed to the unsettled state of foreign-exchange markets generally.

Revaluation and the withdrawal of gold from domestic circulation raised the value of the monetary gold stock to about $8 billion in 1934. Subsequently, gold flowed in at an increasing rate from Europe—chiefly in capital flight—and by the end of 1940 about $14 billion worth had been imported. This inflow greatly increased bank reserves and contributed to rapid expansion of the money supply.

The major weight of New Deal recovery policy was concentrated on nonfinancial measures. In 1933 major emphasis was on the agricultural adjustment program (AAA), designed to raise farm prices by curtailing supply, and on the National Recovery Administration (NRA), designed to raise industrial prices by curbing competition and to raise wages by encouraging unionization and collective bargaining. Both of these measures were held unconstitutional in 1935–1936, but some of their principles were reenacted in other legislation. Their basic restrictionist approach was unsound, and they made no appreciable contribution to general recovery. Their principal effect was to impair free competition in several sectors of the economy, in some cases permanently.

Much sounder were those programs which increased government expenditures and thus raised GNP. The government undertook for the first time a program of general relief to the needy and unemployed, and public-works expenditures were greatly enlarged under such programs as TVA. These benefits were undermined by reliance on an unfortunate tax program. Contrary to popular mythology, President Roosevelt sought to avoid deficit spending, and consequently taxes were steadily increased in 1933–1937. Many of the taxes were severely burdensome on low-income groups—notably the processing tax on farm products under the first AAA, the increased excises on tobacco and alcohol, and the social security wage tax. Other taxes on high individual and corporate incomes were adopted in a spirit of hostility to business which helped create an atmosphere adverse to investment. On the average, the increases in Federal spending over 1932–1933 levels were matched by increases in tax revenues. New Deal deficits were no larger, on the average, than those of the last two years of the Hoover administration, and as a percentage of expenditures, they were much smaller. The tax increases reduced disposable incomes and slowed the rise in consumption. Thus the New Deal can hardly be taken as a case study in countercyclical fiscal policy.

The State of the Economy, 1933–1940 The period of the New Deal was one of great activity in government. Its acts created many controversies, enlisted a vast number of devoted partisans, and incurred bitter animosities. The emotional tensions aroused have not died down yet. Some of the reform measures, particularly in finance, were highly desirable and strengthened our modern economy. Some of the other policies, designed to shield politically powerful pressure groups against competition and change, were deplorable. One general conclusion about the New Deal stands out—it failed to get the country out of the Depression.

In 1933 one-fourth of the labor force was unemployed. In subsequent years, conditions improved, but unemployment never went below 14 per cent in the years through 1940 and averaged 17 per cent. Output did reach the 1929 level again (temporarily) in 1937, but the population and labor force had increased substantially by then. Real personal disposable income per capita matched its 1929 level only in 1940. Table 16-4 traces the behavior of GNP expenditures in the New Deal era.

The largest contributor to increasing GNP between 1933 and 1940 was consumption, but its increase was induced by higher incomes—indeed, spending rose less than incomes. The chief autonomous forces making for recovery were investment and government purchases. The shift from negative to positive inventory investment helped, but fixed-capital investment remained anemic throughout the decade. In 1936–1940, it exceeded capital-consumption allowances by only about $1 billion a year. This weakness of investment contributed to the slow growth of consumer incomes and expenditures. It is possible that the climate of political opinion contributed to the stagnation of investment; many businessmen were upset by taxation, labor policy, and the termination of the gold standard. But a more vigorous growth of consumer demand would certainly have encouraged greater investment.

Table 16-4　　GNP expenditures, 1929–1940
(Billions of dollars)

Year	GNP	Consumption	C/PDI, per cent	Domestic investment		Government purchases	Net exports
				Fixed	Inventory		
1929	$104.4	$79.0	95.0	$14.6	$1.7	$ 8.5	$0.8
1933	56.0	46.4	101.3	3.0	−1.6	8.0	0.2
1936	82.7	62.6	94.6	7.4	1.0	11.8	−0.1
1937	90.8	67.3	94.7	9.5	2.2	11.7	0.1
1938	85.2	64.6	98.4	7.6	−0.9	12.8	1.1
1939	91.1	67.6	95.9	8.9	0.4	13.3	0.9
1940	100.6	71.9	94.5	11.0	2.2	14.1	1.5

Source: U.S. Income and Output.

Government fiscal policy provided a means to break this vicious circle. The increased government purchases after 1933 contributed almost as much as rising investment to the growth of GNP. Had tax rates been left at their pre-1933 levels, however, fiscal policy would have exerted much more stimulus to consumption, which would in turn have encouraged more investment.

Money and Recovery　Once the panic ceased in 1933, the Federal Reserve receded into the background. After substantial open-market purchases brought Reserve holdings of government securities to $2.4 billion, that level was maintained until 1937. Rediscount rates, which had been raised a full point during the panic, were cut to 1½ per cent in early 1934. The gold inflow furnished member banks with plenty of reserves, and the volume of rediscounting fell to almost nothing after 1934. Table 16-5 shows the relationship between the money supply and the behavior of GNP expenditures during the New Deal. By 1936 the money supply was substantially above its 1929 level.

The large increase in the money supply was associated with increases in two major assets of the monetary system. The monetary gold stock increased from $4 billion in 1933 to $22 billion in 1940, partly through revaluation, partly through imports. Much of the inflow from abroad represented capital flight and led to increased time deposits or idle cash. The other asset increase was in commercial bank holdings of Treasury securities. Federal deficits of the 1930s drew substantially on newly created money and put it directly into the main money circuit.

Bank *loans* increased hardly at all; they were $16.5 billion in mid-1933 and $17.4 billion in mid-1940. In part, this condition resulted from a slack demand for credit, but chiefly it reflected a pessimistic attitude toward risk

Table 16-5   Money, velocity, output, and prices, 1929–1940
(Dollar figures in billions)

Year	M	V_g	GNP	Output (1929 dollars)	Prices (1929 = 100)
1929	$27	3.9	$104	$104	100
1933	20	2.8	56	73	77
1936	34	2.5	83	100	83
1937	35	2.6	91	107	88
1938	33	2.6	85	102	83
1939	37	2.5	91	110	83
1940	42	2.4	101	120	84

Note: Money-supply figure is for June and includes Treasury deposits.
Sources: Friedman and Schwartz, *A Monetary History of the United States, 1867–1960; U.S. Income and Output.* Velocity calculation and conversions to 1929 are by the author.

by the banks. This attitude was clearly reflected in interest rates. Short-term United States securities consistently sold at rates below 1 per cent in the 1930s, as banks eagerly snapped them up—indeed, in 1938–1939 their rates averaged less than 0.1 per cent per year! By contrast, interest rates on medium-risk corporate bonds (Baa classification), which had risen in 1929–1933, fell only slightly and remained as high as in the earlier 1920s. Bank interest rates were low, but the banks were not eager to accommodate high-risk borrowers. Thus easy credit made it very cheap for the government and other low-risk borrowers to obtain funds but did not penetrate into all categories of borrowers. One response to this problem, already noted, was the extension of government lending and guarantee operations, which did help break the barrier between high- and low-risk credit markets. By 1940 the FHA was insuring about $1 billion of new mortgages annually, and this certainly aided the recovery of residential construction somewhat.

Table 16-5 reminds us of an important principle—that increases in the expenditure flow, when unemployment is high, tend to raise output and to have very little effect on prices. Between 1933 and 1940, output rose by about two-thirds, while prices increased only about 10 per cent. Seldom have the welfare consequences of increased expenditures been more clear-cut.

Recession of 1937–1938   The gradual improvement in economic conditions received an unpleasant setback in 1937, when a short but painful recession intervened. The chief cause was Federal fiscal policy. President Roosevelt, eager to balance the budget, reduced Federal spending just at the time the unfortunate social security wage tax was going into effect. The combination shifted the government from a cash deficit of $3 billion in fiscal 1937 to a position of virtual balance the next year.

Government monetary policy also took some blame. In late 1936, Federal Reserve officials, alarmed at the huge volume of bank excess reserves and noting some upward movements in wholesale prices, for the first time used their power to raise reserve requirements. Although this increase was designed merely to limit further expansion, it was followed by a sharp drop in security prices and soon after by the downturn in the economy.[12]

The recession convinced President Roosevelt that there was some relation between Federal fiscal policy and the state of the economy. From that time, deficit spending was practiced deliberately as a way of raising GNP; but the deficits were no larger than in the earlier 1930s.

SUMMARY AND GENERAL OBSERVATIONS

The first twenty-five years of the Federal Reserve could hardly be described as happy and successful. The difficulties stemmed in part from the original conception that the System would be a relatively passive agency helping to adjust the currency supply to the "needs of trade" by rediscounting and serving as lender of last resort in panics. The Reserve was given a weak administrative structure, and its powers over note issue and rediscount were hedged about by collateral and eligibility requirements.

Soon after its formation, the Federal Reserve was turned into an engine of inflation to help finance World War I. In this it had little choice, and the real blame certainly lay with the Treasury and Congress for their undue willingness to use credit rather than taxation to finance the war. Less defensibly, the Reserve failed to slow the rate of monetary expansion after the war, despite a continued serious and speculative inflation. Only a loss of gold induced it to apply the brakes, and it maintained high discount rates during the painful recession of 1920–1921. However, it continued to lend freely, and there was no monetary panic.

[12] Friedman and Schwartz attribute a major deflationary impact to the Federal Reserve's action—*A Monetary History of the United States, 1867–1960*, pp. 511–534. For a dissenting opinion, see George Horwich, "Effective Reserves, Credit, and Causality in the Banking System of the Thirties," in Deane Carson (ed.), *Banking and Monetary Studies*, Richard D. Irwin, Inc., Homewood, Ill., 1963.

These experiences helped bring about an enlarged sense of the powers and responsibilities of the Reserve. Open-market policy was discovered, and the automatic guides to monetary policy furnished by the commercial-loan theory and the gold reserve were largely replaced by the concept of the Reserve banks as a continuous stabilizing force for business. The Reserve banks pursued this role with apparent success in 1922–1927, though the success was probably a reflection of the absence of serious tendencies toward instability.

The Federal Reserve proved incapable of halting the flood of credit into stock speculation, partly because its officials were (rightly) reluctant to tighten credit for the economy as a whole. However, the stock market crash did not make inevitable the great decline of the economy after 1929. A more important factor was the failure of the System to prevent the collapse of the monetary and banking system which developed as the economy moved into depression in 1930–1933. Lack of understanding of the relationship of bank failures to bank liquidity kept Reserve officials from undertaking the massive open-market operations which might have reversed the downswing much sooner. Instead, bank failures and credit contraction aggravated the existing problems of excess capacity and weak investment incentives.

The Depression brought a vast program of financial reforms, beginning in 1932. These changes centralized control of the Federal Reserve, gave the Board power over reserve requirements and stock market margins, and liberated note issue and rediscount from the restraints of the commercial-loan theory. Thus the structural approach was largely rejected, and the way opened for a free exercise of discretionary power.

In other areas, the government discarded the gold-coin standard and raised the price of gold; it resumed purchases of silver; it established a wide range of government lending and guarantee agencies, including insurance of bank deposits; and it extended regulation to many areas of securities and finance where weaknesses had been revealed in the 1920s.

For all its activity, the New Deal failed to get the country out of the Depression. Too many of its recovery measures were restrictionist, designed to raise prices but not to stimulate spending. The government did increase its expenditures but vitiated much of the benefit by raising taxes *pari passu*.

The money supply increased and interest rates fell as gold inflows enlarged bank reserves. The money supply increased rapidly during the 1930s, with the notable exception of the period in 1936–1937 when the Federal Reserve unfortunately doubled reserve requirements. Much of the new money was channeled into the spending stream by Federal deficits. Bank loans did not increase, however, and despite very low interest rates on Treasury securities, interest rates on many private obligations did not fall to low levels during the Depression.

As the experience of 1928–1933 discredited the automatic basis for monetary policy, so the experience of the 1930s led to a downgrading of the apparent importance of monetary policy and the quantity of money. Theoretical emphasis shifted to the Keynesian analysis of income and expenditures, with emphasis on the marginal efficiency of capital and the propensity to consume. Policy emphasis shifted to fiscal policy—manipulation of tax rates and government expenditures.

The Influence of Money Emergence of the new quantity theory of money has reopened the question of monetary influence on the economy prior to 1940. Figure 16-1 shows the general contours of the period, in terms of money, expenditures, prices, and output. The general similarity of shape is readily apparent.

Figure 16-2 presents a comparison between the rate of change of money and of industrial production for the years 1919–1940. In some periods, the rate of monetary change clearly leads or coincides with fluctuations in output. However, one must be circumspect in interpreting such cases. During

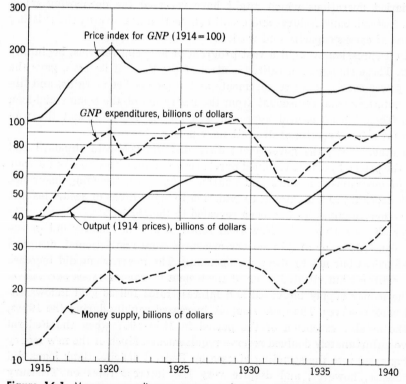

Figure 16-1. Money, expenditures, output, and prices, 1914–1940.

Sources: Banking and Monetary Statistics; All-bank Statistics; U.S. Income and Output.

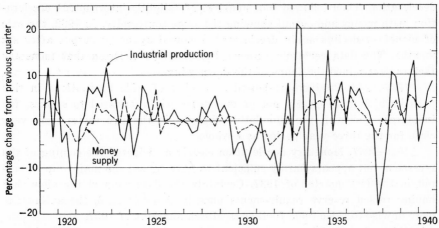

Figure 16-2. Quarter-to-quarter percentage changes in money and industrial production, 1919–1940.

Sources: Friedman and Schwartz, *A Monetary History of the United States, 1867–1960;* *Federal Reserve Bulletin,* December, 1959.

much of the period, the supply of money was allowed to adapt in a relatively passive manner to changes in the demand for credit. Such adaptation can produce correlation without proving causation. This was the case in the earlier 1920s, because of the operation of the commercial-loan principle. And it was true to some degree after 1933, when the commercial banks held large excess reserves. Some comments on subperiods may be useful.

1919–1926. In general, changes in money and in output show a close correspondence. The data certainly support a monetary interpretation of the depression of 1920–1921. However, the monetary series does not lead in the recovery phase. From 1922 on the monetary series anticipates remarkably well many of the swings in output. But this may reflect the passive adaptation of money to variations in the underlying propensity to spend.

1926–1929. During this important period, the diagram shows little correspondence between changes in money and in output. The money supply grew hardly at all; instead, this was a period of rapid growth of bank credit, time deposits, and velocity. Perhaps it was inevitable that such monetary starvation would produce a downswing, but the rate of monetary change does not forecast one. The shape of output change through mid-1930 does not appear to occur in response to prior monetary change.

1930–1933. Here the parallel between monetary and output change is striking. The downswing clearly structures itself into succeeding periods of accelerated and decelerated decline. Four quarters of monetary deceleration in 1930 were followed. after a six-month lag, by four quarters of output deceleration. Then followed four quarters of (slightly interrupted) acceleration, with money and output showing the same conformity. In 1932, the rate of monetary decline again decelerated, followed again by output after six months. The data certainly support Friedman's conviction that monetary factors determined the shape of the downswing.

1933–1936. Production showed a number of wide fluctuations in this period which were clearly not of monetary origin (related to strikes, for instance). However, the cumulative changes in the two series were very close for the three-year period as a whole.

1936–1937. Monetary deceleration clearly anticipated the coming of the recession, but appears hardly sufficient to have caused the major dip of output in the last quarter of 1937. Certainly the data support the view that having raised reserve requirements once in August, 1936, the authorities were unwise to raise them further in March and May of 1937.

1938–1940. Swings in monetary and output change show a high conformity. However, this may again reflect merely the existence of a high elasticity of credit supply, so that the money supply was pulled about by the variations in the propensity to spend.

On the whole, the evidence from this period is equivocal in relation to the new quantity theory. Conformity in the two series is sufficient to suggest the possibility of significant monetary causation at some points. The case cannot be convincing, however, when so much of the period was characterized by high monetary elasticity. Furthermore, there are obviously important economic developments not explained by monetary change.

Monetary misbehavior certainly stands convicted of a substantial contribution to the length and seriousness of the downswing in 1930–1933. However, the role of money in bringing on the downswing and in the recovery process is not so easy to establish.

The period of the New Deal was a watershed in the history of finance. It occasioned rejection of old concepts and dogmas and created a new institutional structure for money, banking, and finance. It very largely created the monetary system as we know it today. However, the period of the 1930s was so abnormal that it furnished little evidence of how the innovations would work or what the objectives of their manipulation should be.

QUESTIONS FOR STUDY

1. How was the commercial-loan theory of bank credit embodied in the original Federal Reserve Act? What were its consequences?

2. What was the relationship between bank solvency and bank liquidity during the banking panic of 1930–1933? How could Federal Reserve action to support liquidity have helped solvency as well?

3. A doctrine which influenced the antidepression efforts of both President Hoover and President Roosevelt was the "purchasing-power theory" of wages. According to this view, increases in wage rates, either through voluntary business action or through government influence (support to trade unions, minimum-wage legislation, etc.), are an appropriate means to fight depression and unemployment. Analyze the merits of this view.

4. Analyze the probable effects and evaluate the desirability of each of the following government policies used to deal with depression in the 1930s:

    a. Increased tariff rates

    b. Federal Reserve open-market purchases of government securities

    c. Resumption of silver purchases

    d. Direct Federal payments for relief of needy and unemployed

    e. Increased tax rates

    f. Suspension of antitrust laws (under NRA, 1933–1934)

    g. Destruction of farm commodities

    h. Increase in the dollar price of gold

    i. Establishment and promotion of United States savings bonds (1935)

SUGGESTED READINGS

Chandler, Lester V.: *Benjamin Strong, Central Banker,* The Brookings Institution, Washington, 1958.

Eccles, Marriner: *Beckoning Frontiers,* Alfred A. Knopf, Inc., New York, 1951.

Friedman, Milton, and Anna Jacobson Schwartz: *A Monetary History of the United States, 1867–1960,* Princeton University Press for National Bureau of Economic Research, Princeton, N.J., 1963.

Galbraith, John Kenneth: *The Great Crash,* Houghton Mifflin Company, Boston, 1955.

Goldenweiser, E. A.: *American Monetary Policy,* McGraw-Hill Book Company, New York, 1951.

Gordon, Robert A.: *Business Fluctuations,* 2d ed., Harper & Row, Publishers, Incorporated, New York, 1961.

Studenski, Paul, and Herman E. Krooss: *Financial History of the United States,* 2d ed., McGraw-Hill Book Company, New York, 1963.

chapter seventeen

MONETARY AND BANKING DEVELOPMENTS IN THE UNITED STATES, 1941-1964

SURVEY

The American economy has passed through two broad phases since 1941. The first was a decade of "high pressure," in which very strong money demand for production restored full employment and caused a substantial degree of inflation. This pressure began with the government's expenditures for World War II; it was carried further by the release of pent-up private expenditures in the immediate postwar years and was given a third impetus from renewed public and private spending set off by the Korean conflict. During this entire period, monetary policy was devoted to maintaining low interest rates in order to facilitate Treasury finance.

After the early 1950s, however, the pressure of demand against productive capacity was less intense. Prices continued to rise, but at a slower rate. Despite periodic recessions, the predominant direction of the economy was toward expansion. Beginning in 1958, unemployment consistently exceeded the 4 per cent target generally regarded as "full employment." Large gold outflows signaled the appearance of a problem in the nation's balance of international payments. Monetary policy, liberated in 1951 from subordination to Treasury finance, produced slower monetary growth and higher interest rates during the 1950s, but took a more expansionary course after 1960. Having been denounced for failure to curb inflation in the 1940s, the monetary authorities were now denounced for failure to take more aggressive action against unemployment.

WORLD WAR II

Fiscal and Debt Policies The American economy felt the economic impact of World War II even before the Japanese attacked Pearl Harbor in December, 1941. Rising defense orders from abroad and increased defense spending at home raised GNP one-fourth in 1941 and cut unemployment sharply. Once the war commenced, Federal expenditures expanded at a rapid rate, until near the end of the war in 1945 they were running at an annual rate of about $100 billion a year. An unprecedented portion of national output was devoted to war purposes—about 40 per cent for the war period as a whole.

During the period from July, 1941, through June, 1945, the Federal government spent an average of $76 billion a year. While it managed to finance nearly half of this expenditure by taxes—a record far superior to that of previous major wars—a large amount remained to be financed by borrowing. The national debt was enlarged by over $200 billion. Federal Reserve policy was utilized to enable these securities to be sold without subjecting the Treasury to heavy interest burdens. Indeed, interest rates were maintained at the extremely low levels to which they had fallen during the depressed 1930s. The interest cost of war issues averaged only about 2 per cent.

Federal Reserve assistance came in three forms. Reserve banks themselves purchased over $20 billion of securities. This action created additional reserves which helped the commercial banks purchase over $70 billion. The Federal Reserve also committed itself to supporting the prices of securities, so that nonbank investors had no reason to fear price declines below par and thus, presumably, were willing to buy more.

The Treasury sought aggressively to sell bonds to nonbank investors. Instead of encouraging sales by offering higher interest rates, the Treasury emphasis was on "fitting the security to the needs of the investor"—creating a variety of securities with special features to make them attractive to particular buyers at low interest.[1] The most important development was the wide use of United States savings bonds, which had first been introduced

---

[1] Henry Murphy, *The National Debt in War and Transition*, McGraw-Hill Book Company, New York, 1950.

during the 1930s. These were (and are) nonmarketable securities issued in small denominations and redeemable on demand (after sixty days) at predetermined values. Those issued during the war had maturities of ten years and an interest rate of 2.9 per cent compounded to maturity, but much less if redeemed earlier. Business firms were not permitted to buy them, and individual purchases were limited to $5,000 a year. The bonds were well designed as savings assets, and ownership was very widespread. The Treasury also issued short-term securities designed for use by corporations to accumulate funds for tax payments.

The Treasury did issue a considerable volume of conventional marketable securities ranging from three-month bills to long-term bonds maturing after twenty years or more. A striking feature of the marketable issues was the pronounced "rate pattern" under which short-term bills carried a rate equivalent to only 0.375 per cent a year, while the bonds of longest maturity were issued at 2.5 per cent. Federal Reserve support ensured that each issue, whatever its maturity, would be highly liquid and that its price would not decline below par. Commercial banks were forbidden to buy bonds with more than ten years remaining until maturity, and thus bank purchases were diverted into the shorter maturities. Other investors had little incentive to hold the low-yield short-term issues, since longer-term ones were just as liquid and paid much better. The Treasury insisted on issuing three-month bills, with the inevitable result that most of them gravitated into the Federal Reserve. By the end of 1945, $13 billion of the outstanding $17 billion of three-month bills was held by Reserve banks.

The general tendency of wartime debt management was to make all United States securities highly liquid, chiefly through the support of the Federal Reserve. Treasury officials reasoned that the assurance of liquidity would do more to promote bond sales than would higher interest rates; and they could not offer both incentives, since higher rates on new issues would have reduced prices of the older marketable issues. The increase in the national debt, expressed in billions of dollars, is shown by the following table:

End of year	Total debt	Federal Reserve	Commercial banks	Portion owned by — Others — Saving bonds	Others
1940	$ 39	$ 2	$17	$ 3	$17
1945	256	24	91	43	98
Increase	$217	$22	$74	$40	$81

Source: Federal Reserve Bulletin, June, 1948. Total debt excludes holdings of Federal agencies and trust funds.

Certainly the campaign to sell securities to nonbank buyers met considerable success. Savings-bond drives were conducted with all the resources of modern advertising, and it was estimated that about one hundred million Americans bought savings bonds at one time or another during the war. But the sales to nonbank buyers were large in part because of the large sales of securities to banks! These sales created a great amount of money, part of which the Treasury was then able to borrow back. By the end of the war the public had increased its money supply by $60 billion and had added $120 billion of highly liquid government securities to its holdings.

Money and Monetary Policy The Federal Reserve was torn between the objectives of aiding Treasury finance through easy credit and trying to curb inflationary pressure. In addition to buying $22 billion of securities, it maintained low discount rates, although the volume of rediscounting remained low during most of the war. Reserve requirements were held at the maximum levels outside the central reserve city group, which was subjected to only 20 per cent instead of the maximum 26 per cent. Margin requirements on stock market loans were kept at 50 per cent until 1945, as the market was relatively quiescent.

The chief innovation in Reserve policy was the imposition of direct control over consumer credit, beginning with Regulation W in 1941 under authority of an Executive order of the President. Under this credit control program the Board established minimum down payments and maximum maturities for various types of purchases. As in margin control, this regulation placed the Federal Reserve in direct authority over nonbank firms, both financial and nonfinancial. Consumer-credit control probably exerted some counterinflationary influence, but the shortages of durable goods were a more important reason for the substantial reduction in installment debt which occurred during the war.

The Federal Reserve also used whatever powers of persuasion it could muster to encourage banks to limit their private lending activities, particularly to curtail "nonproductive" loans (for example, those for accumulating large inventories). Such influence may have helped produce the relative stability shown by commercial bank loans in 1941–1944. However, reduced needs for such loans were more important. Firms producing for war got their credit from the government, while others soon had ample funds from rising incomes.

The effects of war finance on the money supply were strikingly simple. Commercial bank and Federal Reserve holdings of United States securities increased about $100 billion, while other monetary assets showed little change. Nonmonetary liabilities and capital rose about $40 billion, leaving a $60 billion increase in the money supply. By 1945 the public's money supply was 2½ times that of 1940.

The commercial banks entered the war with enormous excess reserves

—over $6 billion—which provided most of the lending power they needed during the war. However, the demand for coin and currency rose by an abnormally large amount—$17 billion—which would have stripped the banks of reserves had it not been for the large Federal Reserve purchases of securities.

GNP Expenditures   Table 17-1 shows the relation between the money supply, fiscal policy, and GNP expenditures during the war. The increase in

Table 17-1   Money, velocity, and GNP expenditures, 1941–1945
(Dollar figures in billions)

| | | | | Con- | | Domestic | Government purchases | | Net |
| | | | | sump- | C/PDI, | invest- | | State | ex- |
Year	M*	V_g	GNP	tion	per cent	ment	Federal	and local	ports
1941	$ 47	2.66	$126	$ 82	88	$18	$17	$8	$1
1942	57	2.82	159	90	76	10	52	8	†
1943	84	2.29	193	101	75	6	81	7	−2
1944	102	2.08	211	110	75	7	89	8	−2
1945	118	1.82	214	122	81	10	75	8	−1

* Money supply for 1941 is for June; others are annual averages. All include Treasury deposits.
† Less than $0.5 billion.
Sources: Federal Reserve Bulletin; U.S. Income and Output. Money and velocity are computed by the author.

the money supply was greater than the increase in GNP; hence velocity fell substantially. This drop was a reflection of the increased holdings of idle cash in the face of low interest rates, shortages, and rationing of goods.

The great rise of GNP during the war can be explained entirely in terms of fiscal policy. Although consumer spending increased by $40 billion, the rise was an induced response to higher incomes. Actually, consumption rose much less than its normal ratio to income would have indicated. Domestic and foreign investment declined, while state and local government expenditures remained constant. The rise in Federal expenditures was directly responsible for more than half the rise of GNP spending and created the higher incomes which raised consumption. Easy credit and the swollen money supply had no apparent expansionary influence in their own right, in view of the behavior of investment and the propensity to consume.

Output and Prices   Table 17-2 relates these increases in GNP expenditure to the behavior of output and prices during the war.

The large extent of unemployment at the beginning of the war made it possible for output to increase greatly in response to rising GNP expenditures. This performance was in contrast to that of World War I and provided an impressive demonstration of the capacity of fiscal policy to raise output and employment. By 1943, however, full employment had been reached, and output did not rise much thereafter.

As GNP expenditures rose rapidly and unemployment declined, prices began to move upward. Consumer prices rose about 20 per cent in 1941–1942, which restored them to their 1929 level. To check the inflation, the government sharply increased taxes, so that its deficits actually grew smaller after 1943. Also, an extensive program of direct economic controls was established.

Table 17-2   GNP, output, and prices, 1941-1945
(Dollar figures in billions)

Year	GNP	Output (1941 prices)	Prices (1941 = 100)	Unemployment, per cent
1941	$126	$126	100	9.9
1942	159	140	114	4.7
1943	193	158	122	1.9
1944	211	170	125	1.2
1945	214	168	128	1.9

Source: *Economic Report of the President*, July, 1951 (prices) and January, 1964 (GNP). Output and prices converted from 1939 base by author.

Direct controls were imposed on prices in 1942, and their scope and administration were extended as the war progressed. Wage rates were brought under regulation, and allocation of some critical materials was subjected to administrative decree. As a result, an effective lid was imposed on the cumulative upsurge of prices and costs, and between early 1943 and early 1946, consumer prices rose only about 10 per cent. However, the decline in the value of money was more severe than the price statistics indicate. Some products became totally unavailable (automobiles and many appliances were not produced at all). Other items deteriorated in quality or were available in quantities less than purchasers desired at existing prices. Thus the official price figures understate the degree of inflation, since a free market was not functioning.

However, direct controls undoubtedly worked to keep private spending from rising even more. Individuals and firms were restrained from indulging in scare buying or speculative hoarding. Scarce resources were shifted into government uses by direct pressure and without undue increases in procurement costs. Direct controls helped to sustain the "money illusion," so that people responded to monetary incentives to produce even though the money they received could not be spent immediately.

Thus war finance greatly increased incomes and the money supply, while direct controls prevented the increased spending which normally would have followed. The inevitable consequence was that cash and liquid assets accumulated in people's hands to an unprecedented degree and set the stage for postwar inflation. On the whole, direct controls were successful, with the help of a public opinion influenced by experience with deflation rather than inflation and by wartime patriotism. Nevertheless, controls merely postponed inflation rather than eliminating its underlying causes.

Appraisal of War Finance   In view of the fact that consumer prices rose about one-fourth during the war and by an additional one-third in the three years afterward, were wartime financial policies unduly inflationary?

Since the root of inflation was Federal deficit spending, higher taxes would presumably have meant less inflation. However, at some point higher taxes would have had adverse effects on work incentives. Possibly a Federal sales tax could have been imposed without such effects, but public opinion generally did not support it. On the whole, wartime tax policy does not merit severe criticism.

What about monetary and public-debt policies? It is clear that monetary policy as such had no independent existence during the war. The Federal Reserve had no choice but to subordinate its powers to the financial decisions made by the administration and Congress.

If there was a defective element in financial policy, it must have been public-debt management. In retrospect, the decision to maintain during the war a pattern of interest rates appropriate to deep depression seems very unwise. Higher interest rates would not have led to reduced private spending but would probably have led the public to hold more securities and less cash, thus reducing the increase in the money supply which resulted from bank purchases and keeping excess liquidity from growing so much. However, the Treasury was to some degree trapped. There was no good reason to pay high rates early in the war; but once they issued low-interest securities, Treasury officials were reluctant to let rates rise because the earlier issues would fall in price. If investors began to expect rate increases (and falling bond prices), they might become less, not more, willing to buy. The problem was how to achieve the advantages of high rates without the disadvantages of rising rates! These objectives could have been reconciled to some degree by paying higher rates on short-term issues than were offered and by raising the rate on savings bonds.

But what was the point of going through the motions of borrowing, anyway? In particular, why should the government have paid so much interest to the banks for creating money, when the Treasury could do that for itself? Even borrowing from the nonbank public was done to a large degree by giving them securities virtually as liquid as cash—savings bonds might almost be considered interest-bearing money. Why not just issue greenbacks and save the interest costs?

There was certainly an element of naïveté in Treasury borrowing. However, some unconventional justifications can be made for it. First, interest paid to the banks helped compensate them for the work involved in managing the country's money supply at a time when income from private lending was low. Second, the public did not, in fact, regard savings bonds as interest-bearing money but held on to them. There was no mad rush to cash them in after the war. Besides reducing the public's liquidity, issuing interest-bearing assets instead of more cash might be defended as a slight compensation for the loss in real value of fixed-dollar assets resulting from price inflation.

No doubt wartime financial policies could have been improved. Whether the results would have been worth the costs and possible interference with productive incentives, no one knows. The war was successfully prosecuted, and the injustices resulting from financial policy were small relative to the tragedies which war itself brings. The postwar inflation, while unpleasant in some ways, did help achieve reconversion without depression.

INFLATION AND COLD WAR, 1945–1951

The Employment Act of 1946 Many people in and out of government were impressed by the rapidity with which the economy was restored to full employment by wartime finance, but they feared that prosperity would not automatically sustain itself when the economy returned to peace. This view drew support from past experience and also from the predictions of economic forecasters. Using data on the prewar behavior of consumption and investment, many forecasters drew the gloomy conclusion that investment could not absorb all the saving people would try to do at full-employment income levels, so that renewed stagnation might result. However, the spread of Keynesian ideas and the wartime experience with fiscal policy appeared to furnish an answer.

As the end of the war approached, strong pressure was brought on Congress to commit the government to a policy of maintaining full employment through fiscal policy. After a lengthy tussle, a compromise was enacted in the Employment Act of 1946, a landmark in the attitude of government toward the economy. The law was chiefly a declaration of good intentions; it pledged the government "to use all practicable means consistent with its needs and obligations . . . to promote maximum employment, production, and purchasing power." But the law did not involve any specific policy directives, and the objectives were stated in very vague terms. What was meant by *"maximum* employment, production, and purchasing power"? Some detected an inflationary bias in its terms, but in practice the law has been interpreted as providing a mandate for avoiding both depression and inflation.

The Employment Act of 1946 required the President to submit to Congress each January a report on the conditions and prospects of the economy, with recommendations for policy actions. The law established a three-man Council of Economic Advisers to assist in preparing this report, and it set up a joint committee of both houses of Congress to receive the report and make further economic investigations and recommendations— what is now the Joint Economic Committee.

The Postwar Inflation, 1945–1948   The alarm about postwar depression proved unwarranted. With the end of the war in 1945, private spending began to increase. Most wartime controls were removed by 1946, and consumer prices, which had held fairly stable, now rose rapidly. By 1948 they were about one-third above 1945 and 70 per cent above 1940. The behavior of GNP expenditures and their relation to output and prices are shown by Table 17-3.

Table 17-3   Spending, output, and prices, 1945–1948
(Dollar figures in billions)

Year	GNP	Con- sump- tion	C/PDI, per cent	In- vest- ment	Government purchases Fed- eral	Government purchases State and local	Net ex- ports	Output (1947 prices)	Prices (1947 = 100)
1945	$214	$122	80.9	$10	$75	$ 8	$—1	$261	82
1946	211	147	91.6	28	21	10	5	234	90
1947	234	165	97.2	32	16	13	9	234	100
1948	259	178	94.2	43	19	15	4	243	107

Source: U.S. Income and Output. Conversion to 1947 base is by the author.

Federal fiscal policy shifted from being an inflationary to a counter-inflationary force. Federal purchases dropped a cool $50 billion in 1946, and the government shifted from a cash deficit of $37 billion in 1945 to a balanced position in 1946. Taxes were reduced somewhat, but revenues stayed high, and Federal cash surpluses totaled nearly $14 billion in 1947–1948 combined.

The decline in Federal purchases was large enough to reduce total GNP spending in 1946, but private spending rose rapidly and soon reversed this decline. The biggest contributor to the rise was consumption spending. Some of the higher consumption was induced by rising incomes, but most of it reflected a return of the propensity to consume to more normal levels (and above, in 1947). Consumer credit expanded over $8 billion in 1946–1948.

Business investment, which had been abnormally low ever since 1929, rose to record levels. The war had depleted productive capacity, while the demand for most products now appeared insatiable. State and local government purchases, virtually unchanged for fifteen years, now rose rapidly. Net exports were also abnormally high in response to large loans to foreigners for relief and reconstruction.

The great rise in spending coming at a time when resources were fully employed could not elicit much more output—indeed, the data show that production in 1946–1948 was below the 1945 peak. The index of industrial production, which stood at 123 in 1945, ranged between 86 and 104 for 1946–1948. Actually, the economy had been at "hyperfull" employment during the war. Since some people who had been in the labor force or military service preferred to return to housework or school when the war ended, the total labor force (including military) dropped by 4 million in 1946. Average weekly hours worked declined from 45 in 1944 to 40 in 1946.

Although total output and input declined, at least the economy was now turning out products people wanted. Real consumption per capita in 1946–1948 was about 40 per cent above 1929 levels. And despite the demobilization of 8 million servicemen in 1945–1946, unemployment never exceeded 4 per cent of the labor force.

The increase in GNP spending which occurred in 1947 and 1948 served almost entirely to raise prices. Granting the desirability of high output and employment, it might have been possible to curb the inflation without reducing appreciably the level of economic welfare achieved.

Monetary Policy, 1946–1948 Despite the inflationary upsurge of prices, the Federal Reserve remained chained to the support of bond prices—or, as they repeatedly phrased it, to "maintaining orderly conditions" in the bond market. Aggressive initiative for this objective came from the administration, and particularly the Treasury. The administration wanted stable bond prices and low interest rates to keep down the costs of the national debt, which exceeded $250 billion and included about $100 billion of securities either maturing or redeemable in the near future. Although the Treasury was not a net borrower, it wanted to avoid higher rates on refunding issues. Furthermore, Treasury spokesmen argued, falling bond prices might impair the solvency of financial institutions which held large amounts, would be unfair to other investors who bought in expectation of stable prices, and would impair "confidence" and undermine the government's "credit."

There was a more sophisticated economic defense of low interest levels: they would promote a high level of investment which would help fill the deficiencies of productive capacity left by depression and war. Furthermore, despite the inflation, there was the lingering fear that serious depression would loom soon and that credit restriction might bring it on.

The Federal Reserve Board sympathized with these objectives. Marriner Eccles, the Chairman of the Board, expressed the conviction that restoration of an uncontrolled bond market would confront the Treasury with "an impossible debt-management problem." He argued that "it could not tell from day to day on what terms it could do its refunding or sell new securities. It would be entirely at the mercy of uncontrolled factors in the market, if, indeed, conditions did not become so confused and chaotic as to demoralize completely its refunding operations." The Board felt responsible for ensuring that individual Treasury refunding operations would not fail.[2]

Reserve officials objected bitterly to the terms which the Treasury insisted on, particularly the rates on short-term securities. By a gradual process and against much Treasury opposition, they managed to reassert their point of view. In 1946, the preferential rate of 0.5 per cent for discounts on collateral of United States securities was discontinued. In 1947, support was withdrawn from short-term securities, and rates rose from the artificial wartime levels to slightly over 1 per cent.

Nevertheless, the basic principle was maintained; that is, long-term securities should not fall below par, nor rates rise above 2½ per cent. In January, 1948, President Truman's economic report reasserted this rule as a matter of faith.[3]

What were the actual effects of the support program? Federal Reserve holdings of government securities did not rise above their 1945 peak and actually diminished during much of 1947, though a sharp rise followed. Interest rates on the long-term bonds remained below the 2½ per cent support level during 1946–1947. Yet credit expanded rapidly in 1946–1948. Commercial bank loans rose from $26 billion at the end of 1945 to $43 billion at the end of 1948.

Three factors enabled the banks to carry out this great expansion. First, the banks emerged from the war with over $1 billion of excess reserves. Second, the gold stock increased by $4 billion in 1946–1948. Third, Treasury debt retirement provided the banks with the funds to expand loans. As we noted, the Treasury in 1947–1948 took in over $13 billion in surplus revenue which it used for debt retirement. Furthermore, at the end of the war the Treasury bank account was swollen to over $25 billion with the proceeds of the last loan drive. Much of this was used for subsequent debt retirement.

In its retirement policy, the Treasury followed the economists' rule that retiring Reserve-held debt is the best policy to combat inflation. Some $10 billion worth of Reserve-held securities were retired; but as fast as these retirements drew reserves out of commercial banks, the banks merely sold more securities to the Federal Reserve. Thus the funds withdrawn

[2] Marriner Eccles, *Beckoning Frontiers*, Alfred A. Knopf, Inc., New York, 1951, pp. 420–421, 480.

[3] *Economic Report of the President, 1948*, pp. 85–86.

through tax surpluses returned to active circulation through bank loans. The bond-support policy greatly reduced the counterinflationary influence of the tax surpluses.

In recognition of the weakness imposed by the support program, Reserve officials sought methods by which private credit could be restrained without raising interest rates on government securities. They retained consumer-credit controls until November, 1947, when a congressional resolution forced discontinuance. Margin requirements on stock market lending were held at 100 per cent during 1946 and at 75 per cent from February, 1947, until 1949. These qualitative controls may have reduced the flow of specific kinds of credit, but this simply made more available for other uses.

Reserve officials also urged Congress to extend provisions for reserve requirements to nonmember banks and to add a required reserve of government securities to the existing requirements. Congress went so far in 1948 as to authorize a temporary increase in reserve requirements above the levels in existing law, and this authority was promptly put to use. Federal Reserve officials also took advantage of temporary authority to reimpose Regulation W in August, 1948. The increase in reserve requirements brought heavy sales of securities by banks to the Federal Reserve. The long-term interest rate rose to the 2½ per cent ceiling, but no further.

An appraisal of postwar monetary policy can better be made by inspecting the behavior of the rates of change of important financial variables, as shown in Figure 17-1. Price level changes, the focal point of attention, were closely associated with the rate of change of GNP expenditures, sometimes after a slight lag. Expenditure growth entered a decelerating phase after the first quarter of 1948, and price changes conformed closely. The movement from decelerating expansion into actual contraction follows a smooth curve on the chart.

Changes in the privately held money supply and in the monetary base are also shown. (The measure of the monetary base used here is somewhat broader than we have used before; it includes all factors influencing the sum of member bank reserves plus currency in circulation. As usual, it is adjusted for changes in reserve requirements.) The money supply increased a great deal in 1946 as funds were shifted from Treasury to private deposits. By 1947, however, both the monetary base and the money supply were undergoing a definite slowdown. The maintenance of the support program for long-term government bonds clearly did not prevent a substantial application of the brakes by the monetary authorities. In combination, the withdrawal of support from the short-term end of the market, and the increases in reserve requirements in 1948, permitted the Federal Reserve to carry out a substantial contraction of the effective monetary base in late 1947 and early 1948.

The inflationary movement of spending and prices continued until the

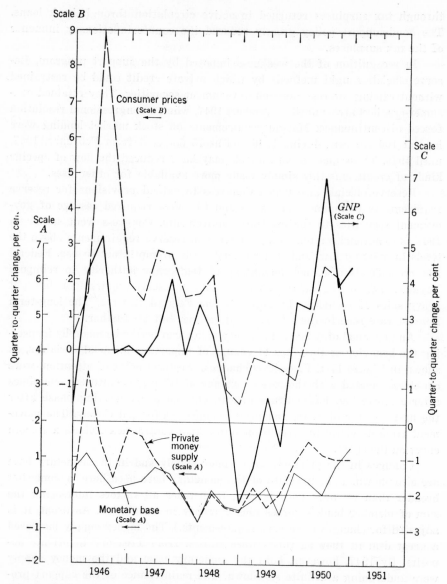

Figure 17-1. Quarter-to-quarter percentage changes in money, spending, and prices, 1946–1950.

Sources: Monthly Labor Review, U.S. Income and Output; Supplements to Banking and Monetary Statistics. Money supply here excludes Treasury cash and deposits.

latter part of 1948, but by then the money supply was actually declining. The abundant liquidity already in the hands of the public permitted spending to be maintained for a time, on the basis of a rise of velocity. But the sequence of events certainly suggests that halting monetary expansion did eventually bring the inflationary sequence to an end. However, an even more restrictive policy in 1946 and 1947 might have been appropriate.

The Recession of 1949 By the end of 1948, the rise of prices had stopped, and the economy had entered a mild recession. Industrial production and employment fell off toward the end of the year.

The chief Federal action to deal with the recession was inadvertent. President Truman, to his great credit, staunchly resisted congressional desires to cut taxes during the postwar inflation and vetoed two tax-cut bills in 1947. In April, 1948, Congress succeeded in passing a reduction over his veto. At the time, the President's action was completely correct, for he feared possible inflationary consequences; but Congress later turned out to be right —for the wrong reasons. The tax reduction went into effect just in time to provide a cushion against declining private disposable incomes.

Between the fourth quarter of 1948 and the second quarter of 1949, GNP expenditures fell by about $10 billion. The biggest factor was a large shift in inventory investment from +$4 billion to −$5 billion. Declines in fixed-capital spending were offset by increased government purchases and higher export sales. Because of lower taxes and higher transfer payments, the drop in personal disposable income was only $4 billion. Best of all, consumer spending did not decline at all, but rose very slightly. The increase was encouraged by price reductions in food and clothing and by easing of credit as Regulation W lapsed.

Federal Reserve authorities relaxed other restraints. Reserve requirements on demand deposits were cut 4 per cent for all member banks. This move caused the effective monetary base to expand after early 1949. Interest rates fell, and private spending was on its way back up by the end of the year. Still, the Reserve authorities could not resist the temptation to lighten their holdings of government securities when bond prices tended to rise above par in the summer of 1949. This move, which reversed the expansion of the monetary base, was hardly well advised even if it did no serious damage.

The Korean Inflation In June, 1950, North Korean troops invaded South Korea, and President Truman dispatched American forces in a "police action" to halt the aggression. The news brought visions of a return to wartime economic conditions. Consumers, fearing rationing and shortages, rushed to buy. Business firms hurried to accumulate inventories. Although Federal defense spending increased slowly, a rapid expansion in defense contracts encouraged a rise in business investment. As a result, GNP expenditures rose rapidly. Their behavior and composition are shown in Table 17-4.

Table 17-4   GNP expenditures, prices, and output, 1949–1952
(Dollar figures in billions)

Year	GNP	Con- sump- tion	C/PDI, per cent	Domestic invest- ment	Gov't purchases	Net ex- ports	Output (1954 prices)	Prices (1954 = 100)
1949	$258	$181	95.5	$33	$40	$4	$293	88
1950								
1st ½	270	188	94.1	43	37	2	307	88
2d ½	299	202	94.9	56	41	*	329	91
1951								
1st ½	322	209	94.1	59	54	1	337	96
2d ½	336	211	90.9	54	67	4	347	97
1952	347	220	92.1	50	76	1	354	98

* Less than $0.5 billion.
Sources: U.S. Income and Output; Economic Report of the President, 1953. Data for 1950 and 1951 are seasonally adjusted annual rates.

The great upsurge in spending was concentrated in the twelve-month period following the outbreak of hostilities. During the rest of 1950, private spending provided the force, while in the first half of 1951 government spending predominated. Scare buying shows clearly in the rise in the propensity to consume in late 1950, followed by its drop. Business investment shot up in late 1950 but increased very little subsequently.

The rise in spending raised both output and prices. Between 1949 and 1952, prices went up slightly over 10 per cent, while output increased by 20 per cent. The rise of output helped support a big rise in defense spending without the need for substantial reduction in private use of goods and services. Nevertheless, the economy sustained another unpleasant inflation, though it was short in duration.

The chief reason inflation was not more serious was Federal fiscal policy. As soon as increased expenditures were in prospect, President Truman recommended and Congress enacted substantial tax increases. As a result, the government had slight cash surpluses in 1950 and 1951 and a deficit of only $1.6 billion in 1952. In 1952 and 1953 combined, Federal defense spending took over 13 per cent of GNP, almost as much as during World War I, without appreciable further inflation. This amazing record has not received the commendation it deserves.

Fiscal policy was assisted by the reimposition of direct economic controls. Under the Defense Production Act of September, 1950, a system of allocating scarce materials was set up, and in January, 1951, price controls were imposed. Some observers felt the government could have moved faster to put controls into effect and criticized the fact that controls were not as stringent as those of World War II. Consumer rationing was not used.

The great weak spot during the inflationary upsurge of 1950 was monetary policy. Private scare buying raised the demand for private credit and brought extensive sales of government securities by lenders. The Federal Reserve was obliged to purchase on a large scale to maintain the support program; its holdings increased by $3 billion between the end of May and the end of the year. In the same period commercial bank loans increased from $44 billion to $52 billion, while their holdings of United States securities dropped $4 billion. The public's money supply in December, 1950, was $6 billion higher than in the previous December.

Reserve officials did not regard these moves with equanimity but took what steps they could without abandoning support. Reserve requirements and discount rates were raised. Under the authority of the Defense Production Act, controls were again imposed on consumer credit and, for the first time, on housing credit. These regulations took the familiar form of specifying minimum down payments and maximum maturities. Margin requirements were raised to 75 per cent.

These measures, plus the rapid rise in demand for loans, did produce some tendency toward higher interest rates, but not enough to curb the inflationary surge appreciably. Reserve officials manifested increasing dissatisfaction with their obligations under the support program. They allowed some short-term securities to fall below par. Although they did not want a radical change, they tried to induce the Treasury to agree to somewhat higher interest rates. But the administration announced that the existing rate pattern would be maintained and claimed that Reserve officials had agreed to support it. When the Reserve officials denied this, the controversy was brought into the open. Having failed to achieve the moderate compromise they sought, Reserve leaders now demanded more freedom of action. In the famous "accord" of March, 1951, they got it.

Under this agreement, Reserve officials renounced any rigid commitment to support bond prices at par, although they would continue to maintain "orderly conditions" by preventing large fluctuations. The Treasury agreed to give attention in its debt-management operations to the views of the Reserve Board, and also agreed to issue a 2¾ per cent bond. In return, Reserve officials agreed to hold discount rates at their existing level of 1¾ per cent for another year.

The abandonment of the support program was overdue. Whatever defense could be made for it in the period 1946–1948, it was indefensible in 1950. Although a Reserve refusal to expand bank reserves would have been offset in part by rising velocity, there is little doubt that the inflation would have been less drastic had effective credit restraint been imposed.

MONETARY POLICY, 1951–1958

The Setting   The performance of the economy immediately after the accord was generally good. The rise in prices slowed to insignificance, while output expanded and employment was high. Cessation of hostilities in 1953 reduced defense spending, and the cut set off a mild economic recession. Strong recovery began in 1954. The economy remained prosperous until mid-1957, when another mild recession began; this slight downturn ended in 1958. The general contours of the period are shown in Figure 17-2.

The chart indicates the less than ideal behavior of prices and unemployment. The price deflator crept upward during the entire period, but its rise during 1956–1957 was on the order of 3 per cent a year. Unemployment, which had gone below 3 per cent in the early 1950s, never went below 4 per cent during the boom period of 1956–1957, and its level during the recession of 1957–1958 was substantially higher than it had been in the previous recession.

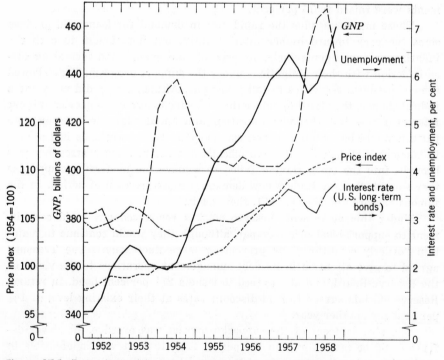

Figure 17-2. Economic conditions in the United States, 1952–1958.

Sources: U.S. Income and Output; Joint Economic Committee, Staff Report on Employment, Growth, and Price Levels; Federal Reserve Bulletin.

Politically, the period was notable for the first Republican administration since the Depression and since the passage of the Employment Act. General Eisenhower came to the Presidency pledged to a more vigorous attack on inflation and a more flexible use of debt-management and monetary policies toward that objective. He had also pledged to end the conflict in Korea. With the termination of hostilities, military spending was cut back substantially. This was the initiating cause of the economic recession of 1953–1954. Fortunately, certain temporary wartime tax increases were due to expire. By allowing these to die, Federal tax rates were effectively lowered. In combination with easing of credit, these measures turned the economy upward. Lingering doubts about the administration acceptance of the principles of the Employment Act were pretty well dissipated.

Use of Monetary Instruments The accord of 1951 marked the beginning of the first real trial of Federal Reserve policy under the augmented powers of the 1930s and the objectives reflected in the Employment Act. Judged by interest rates, the influence of Federal Reserve policy was countercyclical in the 1950s. Figure 17-2 indicates that interest rates moved downward during business cycle recessions and early recovery, and upward during the later phases. However, judged by the behavior of the money supply and the monetary base, performance was not so consistent. We will look at the timing and magnitude of operations after an examination of the use of individual policy techniques.

The chief effect of the accord was to liberate open-market policy, which took on major status as a flexible device. In addition, the discount rate once again became significant as member banks could no longer count on being able to sell their government securities at par. Reliance on these instruments enabled Reserve authorities to ease up on reserve requirements, which were lowered as an additional antirecession measure. Some selective controls were discarded.

1. *Open-market operations.* In 1953 Federal Reserve authorities officially adopted a "bills-only" policy, under which they committed themselves to deal only in short-term government securities. These have the largest floating supply and the highest elasticities of demand and supply; thus the direct influence of Reserve operations on price would be small. The authorities wished to avoid dealing in the long-term markets, where their activities might have more influence on price and also set off private speculative activities of an unstabilizing sort. They were probably also eager to disclaim responsibility for the bond market, lest political pressures build up for a return to the price-support policy.

Economists criticized "bills-only," feeling that Reserve operations in long-term securities would be economically desirable to produce direct effects on long-term interest rates, which were presumably most influential on spending decisions. Reserve officials defended the policy on grounds that open-market operations exerted their influence chiefly through bank reserves, which would be affected the same way whatever the securities traded. Further, they expressed confidence that arbitrage would cause long-term rates to move in the same direction as short-terms.

After small-scale purchases during the recession of 1953–1954, Federal Reserve holdings of securities were gradually reduced as a means of tightening credit during the subsequent upswing. On a seasonally adjusted basis, they moved from a peak of slightly over $25 billion in early 1954 to a low of $23 billion in late 1957. Then policy shifted to purchases to combat the recession and also to compensate for reserves lost because of the gold outflow. By the end of 1958, holdings were back to $25 billion again.

2. *Rediscount policy.* During the years 1934–1950, the volume of rediscounting was insignificant. When banks needed reserves, they sold securities. Federal Reserve support prevented the prices from falling, and if banks generally were selling, more reserves would be created. Removal of support changed this condition. Sales by banks were at times allowed to depress prices in the hope that prospective capital losses would deter further sales. If sales were made, they did not bring forth additional reserves unless Federal Reserve officials decided that conditions warranted the increase. In consequence, member banks again turned to rediscounting as a major method of adjusting reserve positions.

The increase in discount volume came with the accord, and by the end of 1952 discounts had gone above $1.5 billion. Discount-rate policy was still passive: the New York rate had been 1½ per cent in the depressed months early in 1950; it remained at 1¾ per cent during the inflationary surge of 1950–1951 and went only to 2 per cent in 1953. Subsequently, however, discount-rate changes became more frequent and vigorous. This increased activity was apparent in 1955–1957, when rates were steadily moved up until they reached 3½ per cent in 1957, the highest level since the 1920s. Substantial reductions were made during the recession of 1957–1958, but rates moved up again in late 1958 when recovery was apparent.

Despite the vigorous countercyclical movement of discount *rates,* the movement of discount *volume* was procyclical. Thus discounting was very low in 1954, when the rate was 1½ per cent, but hovered around $1 billion in 1955–1957 at rates of 2½ to 3½ per cent. These variations in borrowing reflected the fact that the discount rate was not raised and lowered sufficiently to counter changes in market interest rates.

Increased borrowing by banks came in part as a response to the pressure on their reserves which resulted from Federal Reserve sales of securities. Reserve officials believed that such a shift from "owned" reserves to borrowed reserves would make member banks less willing to expand credit.

3. *Reserve requirements.* Prior to 1951, when open-market policy was hampered by the support program and discount policy was moribund, the Federal Reserve made much use of reserve requirement changes. Revival of the first two instruments of Reserve policy was accompanied by a change in the use of the third. From the high levels attained in 1951–1953, reserve requirements were reduced during each recession, but at no time were they increased. This behavior is easy to understand. Reducing the requirements in recession permitted all the member banks to expand more or less proportionally, and thus such action seemed fair. As a means of tightening credit, increasing the requirement seemed too crude and massive a technique. Furthermore, there were good reasons for the Federal Reserve Board to prefer permanently lower requirements. In general, reducing reserve requirements appeased the member banks, and in particular it reduced their competitive disadvantage relative to nonmember banks.

4. *Selective controls.* Restoration of the vigor of general credit controls was accompanied by decreased emphasis on selective controls. The controls on consumer and housing credit imposed during the Korean conflict were removed in 1952 and were not subsequently reauthorized. Margin controls were vigorously used, however, in the face of active movements in stock prices and credit. Margins were cut from 70 to 50 per cent in 1953, and they remained at this level until 1955 despite a substantial rise in both stock prices and credit in 1954. They were raised to 70 per cent again during 1955–1957, and both prices and credit tapered off. A reduction to 50 per cent in 1958 was short-lived, as market revival soon called forth successive increases to 90 per cent late in 1958. Nevertheless, prices and credit kept expanding.

Federal Reserve Policy: Timing and Magnitude   To facilitate quantitative analysis of the period 1951–1958, Figure 17-3 compares the percentage rates of change from quarter to quarter of GNP expenditures, the money supply, and the monetary base. (Treasury deposits are here included in the money supply; their inclusion smooths short-run swings without changing broader movements.)

It is apparent that Federal Reserve policy remained somewhat passive even after the accord. The reserve base and the money supply were permitted to expand at a fairly rapid rate. Reserve growth came chiefly through expanded member bank borrowing. The Federal Reserve kept the rediscount rate stable in 1951 and 1952 in face of rising interest rates in the financial markets; thus the incentive to borrow increased steadily. When the rediscount rate was raised in January, 1953, the volume of member bank borrowing began to decline, and the expansion of money and reserves halted. In view of the slowdown in GNP growth already under way, the shift toward monetary restraint appears inappropriate.

Once actual recession was evident in 1953, the Federal Reserve reversed its course rapidly. Member bank reserve requirements were reduced in July sufficiently to add about $1 billion to excess reserves. The change is reflected in high levels for reserve and monetary increase in the third quarter. However, much of the increase in reserves was withdrawn in the fourth quarter.

Since both monetary and reserve expansion occurred at a lower rate during the recession than during the preceding expansion, one may question whether Federal Reserve policy was really expansionary. In defense, one may note that interest rates did fall and that some credit-sensitive expenditures such as housing were stimulated. However, the remarkable similarity in shape between the three curves during the recession period suggests that GNP expansion could well have been restored sooner had the reserve base been more vigorously expanded.

In the summer of 1954, with the recession at its bottom, reserve re-

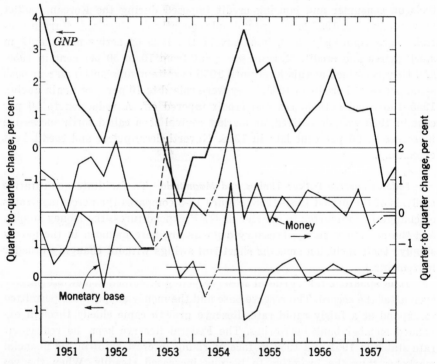

Figure 17-3. Quarter-to-quarter percentage changes in money, the monetary base, and spending, 1951–1958.

Sources: Federal Reserve Bulletin; Survey of Current Business. Data are seasonally adjusted; money supply here includes Treasury cash and deposits. Horizontal lines show average values of monetary series during business cycle phases.

quirements were reduced again, producing another big increase in the expansion of reserves and money. Monetary ease and tax reduction helped produce an accelerated rise in GNP expenditures. By the end of 1954, however, reserve-base expansion was slowed considerably, and the slowdown was soon reflected in the behavior of the money supply as well.

During the upswing in 1955–1957, both the amount of bank reserves and the reserve requirements were virtually frozen. The result was that growth in the money supply was almost totally halted. From the second quarter of 1955 to the same quarter in 1957, monetary growth was slightly under $2 billion. Coming at a time when the expansion of the economy was driving up the demand for cash and for loans, this monetary "freeze" sent interest rates soaring. Repeated increases in the discount rate were used to hold member bank borrowing in check.

Why was the monetary policy so restrictive? The chief reason was to combat the rise in the price level, which accelerated to a rate of 3 per cent a year in 1956 and 1957.

Since the quantity of money was not permitted to rise, the scramble for funds to finance economic expansion caused velocity to increase substantially. From a recession low of 2.67 in the third quarter of 1954, GNP velocity rose to 3.17 three years later.

Banks contributed to this process by selling securities in order to expand loans. In 1955 and 1956, banks' holdings of securities were cut by $13 billion, and loans grew by $20 billion. Selling securities reduced their prices and raised their yields. The higher yields drew funds out of idle balances, and the bank loans put them into active circulation. Banks also raised interest rates on time deposits, which grew by $10 billion in 1955–1956. As depositors shifted funds from demand to time deposits, bank lending power increased because of the lower reserve requirement.

In view of this rise in velocity, did monetary policy exert an effective restraining influence on aggregate spending? The evidence is in the affirmative. The most striking restraining effect was on housing expenditures, which declined from $18.7 billion in 1955 to $17.7 in 1956 and $17.0 in 1957, despite rising consumer incomes. Maisel estimates that higher interest rates reduced housing starts by an annual rate of 200,000 units between early 1955 and early 1958. For all categories of expenditure, Brownlee and Conrad estimate that a reduction of $5.7 billion would accompany a one-percentage-point rise in rates as of 1957; the actual rise in interest rates from 1954 to 1957 was on that order or a little more.[4] To estimate the total effect

---

[4] Sherman J. Maisel, "A Theory of Fluctuations in Residential Construction Starts," *American Economic Review*, June, 1963, p. 375; Oswald Brownlee and Alfred Conrad, "Effects upon the Distribution of Income of a Tight Money Policy," Commission on Money and Credit, *Stabilization Policies*, Prentice-Hall, Inc., Englewood Cliffs, N.J., 1963, p. 509.

of monetary restraint, one would have to add an estimate of the multiplier effect, doubling or tripling the initial impact.

One should remember that higher interest rates cause measured velocity to increase not by inducing people to spend more (which would be a nonsense result), but by leading them to hold less idle cash in relation to their expenditures. The expansionary force in 1955–1957 came chiefly from the propensity to consume and the marginal efficiency of investment. Measured velocity rose because the money supply was not allowed to expand. Had interest rates been held down by monetary expansion, velocity would have risen less, but GNP expenditures would have gone up more.

The Tight-money Controversy The extreme degree of monetary restraint in 1956 and 1957 evoked much criticism. Three major contentions are worth examination.

1. Some critics argued that it was improper to restrain credit and aggregate expenditures when the unemployment level was as high as it was in 1956 and 1957—4 per cent or more, compared with 3 per cent or less during previous boom periods. Considering how difficult it has been to get the unemployment rate even as low as 4 per cent since 1957, this criticism may appear less forceful than it did at the time. Generally speaking, critics taking this position argued that monetary restraint was acting chiefly to reduce production and employment and was not holding down price increases, which they felt to be largely a manifestation of cost push or "sellers' inflation."

However, subsequent studies have made it clear that demand pull exerted an important influence on the price increases of 1956–1957. The effect was direct for the prices of farm products, medical services, and machinery. It also worked indirectly by causing high business profits and a strong demand for labor, thus contributing to large wage increases which formed an important part of the alleged cost push.

Considering the historical patterns we described in Chapter 7, it is likely that prices would have risen more had demand been allowed to expand more. But it is also likely that production would have been greater and unemployment less. Monetary policy confronted a conflict of objectives, and it is not easy to determine whether economic welfare would have been augmented by a more expansionary policy. However, the year 1957 is a special case, discussed below.

2. Tight money "caused" the recession of 1957–1958, according to a few rather extreme critics. This view probably should be rejected, although the whole concept of causation in economics is too slippery for reliable analysis. The principal "cause" of the recession was that the concentrated auto boom of 1955 and the capital-goods boom of 1956–1957 were too intense to be maintained. That is, in both cases the actual stock of capital caught up

rapidly with the desired stock, causing the demand for additional durable goods to weaken. Monetary policy contributed to the economic downswing, however, insofar as lagging responses to tight credit depressed housing and other expenditures into the recession period.[5] However, valid elements in this criticism and the previous one can better be expressed in a third form, to wit:

3. Monetary restraint was maintained too long. Industrial production (a series compiled by the Federal Reserve itself) reached a (seasonally adjusted) peak in December, 1956. It remained virtually unchanged until September, 1957, then started definitely down. Unemployment reached a seasonally adjusted low of 3.9 per cent in March, 1957, and then began to rise steadily.

Despite these warning signs, monetary restraint was increased, not relaxed, during most of 1957. On a seasonally adjusted basis, Reserve bank holdings of government securities were steadily reduced during 1957, reaching a low of $24.8 billion in the fourth quarter. And in August, discount rates were increased from 3 to 3½ per cent. In consequence, interest rates rose until late in the year; yields on government securities did not reach a peak until October. After seasonal adjustment, the monetary base failed to rise, and the money supply actually declined in the last half of 1957.

Still, was not credit restraint justified in 1957 to hold down the rate of price increase? Not if we make certain assumptions about time lags. First, it appears that some industrial price increases in 1957 reflected "pattern" wage bargains made largely in response to profit and employment conditions of 1955 and 1956. Though demand-induced, the price increases lagged behind the demand conditions which had induced them. Second, we know that the effect of monetary restraint operates only after a lag, so that at best perhaps half the effect is exerted by the end of six months. Given these conditions, it is possible that the Federal Reserve was taking actions which would be restrictive in 1958 against price increases which had been caused by demand pressures in 1956!

Viewing with the advantages of hindsight, it seems clear that Federal Reserve policy was unduly restrictive during 1957. Perhaps also the undue bunching of auto and capital-goods expenditures might have been alleviated had restraint been imposed a little sooner. Federal Reserve officials evidently thought so.

MONETARY POLICY, 1958–1964

Survey Important aspects of the behavior of the economy are shown in Figure 17-4. The behavior of GNP expenditures displays two noteworthy

[5] Thus Maisel's estimates show that the decline in housing starts attributable to credit restraint was not reached until the second quarter of 1958.

features. First, it shows an impressive expansion. From the cyclical low in the first quarter of 1958, it rose by 40 per cent in six years. Prices rose at a remarkably stable rate of about 1.5 per cent per year. Consequently the nation's output in early 1964 was about 30 per cent above early 1958.

However, the behavior of GNP expenditures was markedly different in 1957–1960 and in 1961–1964. The first was a period of stop-and-go, with three definite, if brief, recession periods clearly visible. The second was a period of steady expansion of a sort almost unprecedented in American economic history.

However, the period was notable for the tendency for unemployment to remain at uncomfortably high levels. During recessions it went above 6 per cent, and even during the period of prosperity and expansion 1961–1963, it seemed incapable of dipping below 5.5 per cent. Two factors on the supply side contributed to the problem. First, the measured labor force grew faster, as the products of the "baby boom" of the late 1940s came of working age. Between 1955 and 1959 the labor force grew 5 per cent; between 1959 and 1963 it grew 7 per cent. Second, labor productivity increased at a more rapid rate, reflecting a high rate of technical advance. Output per man-hour rose by 10 per cent in 1955–1959 and by 13 per cent in 1959–1963. These advances

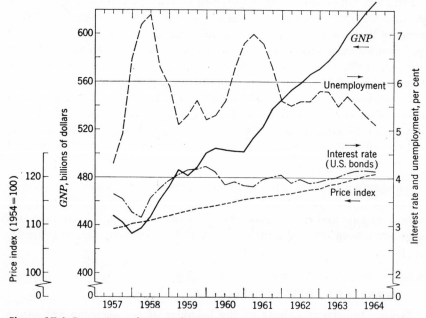

Figure 17-4. Economic conditions in the United States, 1957–1964.

Sources: Survey of Current Business; Federal Reserve Bulletin; Bureau of Labor Statistics processed release on unemployment.

facilitated the growth of output, but raised the rate of expenditure growth needed to restore full employment.

The period was also notable for the emergence of a large and sustained deficit in the balance of international payments of the United States, discussed in Chapter 15. Monetary policy was strongly influenced by this international factor. First, the gold outflow, which aggregated about $6 billion in 1958–1962 combined, tended to reduce bank reserves and the money supply. Federal Reserve open-market purchases were used to offset this unwanted restrictive effect. Second, because of the sensitivity of international short-term capital to interest rates, Federal Reserve policy was aimed at raising short-term rates relative to long-terms. Third, it is probable that interest rates in general were kept at somewhat higher levels in 1960–1963 than would have been the case without the international factor, although this cannot be proved.

Stop-and-Go, 1957–1960   We have noted that Federal Reserve policy was somewhat tardy in meeting the recession which began in 1957. However, once policy shifted, it shifted vigorously. Beginning in November, 1957, discount rates were cut repeatedly, from the peak rate of 3.5 per cent to a low of 1.75 per cent in the spring of 1958. Three rounds of cuts in reserve requirements came in February, March, and April. The stimulus to growth in reserves and money is evident in Figure 17-5. Interest rates fell substantially and easy credit stimulated a rise in expenditures. Housing expenditures rose by $1 billion in 1957–1958 and by $4 billion more the following year. Recovery was also promoted by increased government transfer payments, particularly for unemployment compensation, which contributed to avoiding a fall in PDI and consumption.

Once the economy had started upward, however, Federal Reserve policy shifted to the restrictive side in a hurry. This is apparent in Figure 17-4, which shows the sharp rise in interest rates paralleling the rise of GNP. Since prices were not rising very fast, and unemployment was high, the chief explanation for Federal Reserve restraint is that it was an effort to prevent a repetition of the distortions of 1955–1957. And indeed, neither the unsound bunching of durable-goods purchases nor the acceleration of price increases took place. Instead, the pace of economic expansion, knocked off stride by the steel strike in 1959, ran out of gas in early 1960 at a point definitely short of full employment. The slowdown in housing expenditure alone would have been enough to cause trouble; while total GNP was going down $5 billion from the second quarter of 1959 to the first quarter of 1960, housing outlay alone fell by $2 billion, chiefly in response to tight credit in the preceding months.

Judged by the growth of money and the reserve base, monetary policy in 1959 was viciously restrictive. The reserve base actually declined in the last quarter of 1959, and the money supply responded with decreases in three successive quarters. Even the partial inclusion of vault cash in member bank reserves, initiated in December, 1959, was not sufficient to produce a net expansion of the reserve base.

However, once recession was clearly identified, in mid-1960, Federal Reserve policy undertook a variety of expansionary steps. Discount rates, raised all the way to 4 per cent in September, 1959, were cut in June and again in August. The remainder of the vault cash provision was made effective in September and November. As a result, the expansion of the reserve base in the last half of 1960 was substantial.

Federal Reserve policy during the recession was influenced by a desire not to cause a large drop in short-term interest rates, which would probably have accelerated the outflow of short-term funds and aggravated the gold and international payments problems. Open-market purchases were made, but the bills-only policy was put aside and some purchases were made in

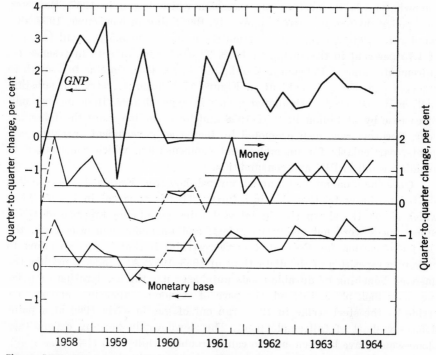

Figure 17-5. Quarter-to-quarter percentage changes in money, the monetary base, and spending, 1958–1964.

Sources: Federal Reserve Bulletin, Survey of Current Business. Data are seasonally adjusted; money supply here includes Treasury cash and deposits. Horizontal lines show average values of monetary series during business cycle phases.

longer-term issues. Furthermore, reductions in discount rates were not nearly as deep as in previous recessions.

The results were generally successful. The combination of open-market purchases and the vault cash provision raised member bank reserves by more than $1 billion between December, 1959, and December, 1961. Long-term interest rates were effectively reduced, while Treasury bill rates did not dip nearly as far as in previous periods of recession and credit easing. In 1954 and 1958 they had fallen below 1 per cent; in 1960–1961 they did not go below 2.2 per cent.

The recession of 1960–1961 was relatively shallow. Failure to fall as deeply as the one in 1957–1958 may be attributed to the absence of over-investment and to the more rapid easing of credit. In addition, government expenditures and higher exports provided expansionary force.

However, the recession coincided with the election campaign, and the Democrats directed plenty of criticism at the tight-money policy. "As the first step in speeding economic growth," said their platform, "a Democratic President will put an end to the present high-interest tight-money policy."

Sustained Expansion, 1960–1964 Partly by luck, partly by design, the change of administration did coincide with resumption of economic expansion. Recovery brought the unemployment rate down from nearly 7 per cent to 5.5 per cent in a year's time, but there it stuck. In 1962 and 1963 the nation witnessed a paradoxical situation of a fairly high sustained rate of increase of expenditures and production, while unemployment remained between 5.5 and 6 per cent.

Conflicting explanations and policy proposals were offered. One view attributed the recalcitrant unemployment to structural factors, reflecting the mismatch between supply and demand in labor and product markets. This view suggested that remedies, if any, should be sought through upgrading labor skills and improving mobility. In contrast, the administration took the view that higher unemployment reflected a deficiency of aggregate demand. Our conclusion in Chapter 7 was that the structural problem was not significantly greater than in earlier years, and that higher expenditures would have reduced the rate of unemployment. However, this would also have entailed somewhat more increase in prices.

Perhaps the Federal Reserve, like the Supreme Court, follows the election returns. At any rate, after 1960 there was no repetition of the violent stop-and-go policies of 1956–1959. Interest rates drifted upward slightly during 1961, sank slightly in 1962, rose slightly again in 1963. The rates of expansion of the monetary base and the money supply were maintained at much higher levels than had prevailed in 1954–1959. Maximum interest rates on time and savings deposits were raised in January, 1962, and again in July, 1963, while the reserve requirement on such deposits was cut from

5 to 4 per cent in the last quarter of 1962. As a result, much of the expansion of bank credit was matched by growth of time deposits, accounting for the paradoxical slowdown in growth of the money supply during 1963 while the reserve base continued to grow rapidly.

International financial considerations produced numerous policy innovations in this period. The Treasury and Federal Reserve undertook direct operations in foreign-exchange markets. Agreements for currency "swaps" were concluded with major foreign central banks. Under special legislation enacted in 1962, interest-rate ceilings for foreign-held time deposits were eliminated for a three-year period. Concern for the high level of unemployment also brought efforts to make fiscal policy more expansionary. Federal expenditures were increased in 1961, partly for defense needs. Tax rates on business were revised to provide more generous depreciation allowances and credit for capital expenditures. Finally, in his Economic Report of January, 1963, President Kennedy urged a general reduction of tax rates. The proposal was strongly supported by President Johnson when he succeeded Mr. Kennedy, and it ultimately passed Congress in 1964.

The tax reduction was a landmark in American economic policy. It was adopted for purely economic reasons, at a time when the government was already running a deficit. Its adoption came not during a period of slump, but after a long sustained rise in GNP. It was adopted as a deliberate expansionary measure to accelerate economic growth and reduce unemployment. Initial indications were that it would be successful and that, if anything, a bigger reduction would have been beneficial.

SUMMARY

During World War II (1941–1945), Federal Reserve policy was subordinated to the Treasury objective of financing the wartime deficits at the low interest rates of the 1930s. High taxes and direct controls reduced the inflationary force of wartime finance, but the public was left with tremendously increased holdings of cash and liquid assets at the war's end. In consequence, there was a rapid rise of GNP expenditures after the war that aided greatly in reconversion without depression but sent the price level up further.

After the war, the Federal Reserve continued to hold up long-term bond prices, but this obligation did not prevent a substantial monetary retardation in 1947 and 1948. The inflation came to a halt, and a mild recession ensued. However, a new burst of inflation resulted from the outbreak of the Korean conflict in the summer of 1950. The upsurge of private spending was financed in part by selling securities to the Federal Reserve at the support prices. This poor showing led the monetary authorities to break away from the bond-support program in the accord of March, 1951.

Since the accord, the Federal Reserve has been free to utilize open-market operations flexibly. They have been extensively used not merely for countercyclical actions but to make seasonal adjustments and also to offset the loss of money and bank reserves through the export of gold. Termination of the bond-support program led to increased use of the Federal Reserve discount facilities by member banks and to more flexible use of the discount rate. Reduction in reserve requirements served as an important method for adding to bank lending capacity during recession periods. With the revival of general credit controls, the selective controls over consumer and housing credit which had previously been employed on a temporary basis were discarded.

Judged by the behavior of interest rates, Federal Reserve policies were countercyclical in effect. However, if we look at the rate of expansion of the monetary base, this tendency is not very pronounced. In fifty-one post-accord quarters through 1963, GNP actually declined in ten. During these ten quarters, the rate of reserve-base expansion was a very skimpy 0.4 per cent per quarter. This was a little higher than the 0.3 per cent during the expansion periods between 1954 and 1960, but well below the rate maintained in 1951–1953 and 1961–1964.

A defense of actual antirecession policy could, however, simply point to the results as justification for what was done. The recessions were in fact not very serious, and recovery did come very quickly in each case. Perhaps more serious criticism should be directed at the tendency for the Federal Reserve to put on the brakes during late phases of expansion. Pronounced slowdowns in the expansion of reserves and money were evident in 1952, 1957, and 1959 and contributed, according to the new quantity theory, to the advent of recessions soon after. In particular, restraint was too vigorous and prolonged during 1955–1957. Fortunately, Federal Reserve policy from 1960 on was much more lenient. Still, with the unemployment rate reluctant to fall below 5 per cent, an even more liberal policy might have been beneficial. At any rate, Congress took over some of the burden of expansionary finance by reducing tax rates in 1964.

Federal Reserve policy from 1957 on was plagued with the problem of conflicting objectives. On the one hand, curbing price increases and reducing the gold outflow appeared to call for restrictive measures. On the other hand, unemployment was unpleasantly high. More nearly full employment, higher output, and more rapid growth seemed to dictate easier credit.

Some reconciliation took place through ad hoc measures—the increase in maximum interest permitted on time deposits held by foreigners, the effort to raise short-term interest rates relative to long-terms. the interest-equalization tax on foreign securities issues, and cooperation with foreign central banks to prevent gold outflow. In addition, tax reduction offered a plausible method for raising domestic expenditures while at the same time keeping interest rates up.

As an exercise in economic stabilization, it would be hard to beat the performance of the American economy from 1960. Unfortunately, unemployment was stabilized at too high a level. The prevailing sentiment among economists in 1964 was that the growth of expenditures could beneficially be stepped up even further.

In the perspective of the long run, however, the performance of the American economy after World War II was impressive. In particular, the nation avoided any kind of serious depression. Performance of the "liberated" Federal Reserve after 1951 probably could have been better, but it also could have been a great deal worse.

QUESTIONS FOR STUDY

1. "Federal Reserve experience during the 1940s indicates that monetary policy can peg the rate of interest only by relinquishing control over the quantity of money." Discuss.

2. During World War II, Treasury finance might have been aided by *high* interest rates but injured by *rising* interest rates. Why the distinction?

3. Although the accord of March, 1951, directly concerned Federal Reserve open-market operations, it ultimately changed the status of their other policy instruments as well. Describe and explain the changes.

4. How do you suppose an advocate of the new quantity theory of money would feel about each of the following?

   a. The desirability of selective controls over consumer credit and other specialized types of lending.

   b. The desirability of having the Federal Reserve conduct open-market operations in all maturities of securities versus a policy of "bills only."

   c. The tendency to assume that declining interest rates during a business recession indicate that the Federal Reserve is following an expansionary policy.

SUGGESTED READINGS

Chandler, Lester V.: *Inflation in the United States, 1940–1948,* Harper & Row, Publishers, Incorporated, New York, 1951.

Culbertson, John M.: *Full Employment or Stagnation?* McGraw-Hill Book Company, New York, 1964.

Friedman, Milton, and Anna Jacobson Schwartz: *A Monetary History of the United States, 1867–1960,* Princeton University Press for National Bureau of Economic Research, Inc., Princeton, N.J., 1963.

U.S. Congress, Joint Economic Committee: *Staff Report on Employment, Growth, and Price Levels,* 1959.

part seven

CURRENT PROBLEMS
OF MONETARY POLICY

chapter eighteen
MONETARY POLICY:
OBJECTIVES AND CHANNELS

INTRODUCTORY

One of the main reasons for studying money is to get a better idea of what should be done about it. Description, theoretical analysis, and historical review are all valuable because they provide guides to wise public policies in the future. In any discussion of policies, one must start with a clear notion of the ultimate objectives to be sought. These goals involve basic social values, which may differ among persons, places, and times. Given the goals of policy, one can examine the techniques of policy and the channels through which they influence the goals. Our attention in this chapter will be concentrated on policy goals and how well monetary policy can achieve them. In the next chapter, we shall consider specific instruments of policy and the organization of the policy-making process.

Broadly speaking, the goals of monetary policy are involved with the flow of GNP expenditures. Policy should aim to prevent GNP expenditures from being so low as to cause unemployment and loss of output, and from being so high as to cause undue increases in the price level. It is useful to classify methods for dealing with the money flow as *structural* and *discretionary*.

Structural changes involve basic rearrangements in the institutions of the economy. An extreme example of structural change would be the nationalization of industry. The improvement of economic stability was in fact one of the reasons advanced by the British Labor Government for its nationalization program in 1945–1950. In the United States, structural changes aimed at stabilization have chiefly been concerned with the financial system. The careful supervision of banks and other financial institutions, the existence of reserve requirements, deposit insurance, government-underwritten mortgages, and margin requirements, all have helped to reduce the vulnerability of the economy to instability, particularly to depressions.

The existence of "automatic stabilizers" in government finance may be mentioned as another structural element. Progressive tax rates on incomes and profits, benefit payments for unemployment compensation, and other fiscal elements tend to adjust automatically to fluctuations in a manner which helps to reduce their magnitude.

By contrast with structural changes, the monetary policy measures of the Federal Reserve are classed as discretionary changes. So would variations in credit conditions arising from Treasury public-debt management or government lending programs. Aside from monetary policy, the most important discretionary policies are those involving government revenues and expenditures—fiscal policy. We shall examine the operation of these policies in the next chapter.

OBJECTIVES OF MONETARY POLICY

Federal Reserve Goals   The official statements of the Federal Reserve System state the economic goals of the organization in ambitious terms. In 1963 its objectives were given as follows:

> . . . to help counteract inflationary and deflationary movements, and to share in creating conditions favorable to a sustained, high level of employment, a stable dollar, growth of the country, and a rising level of consumption.
> . . . Today it is generally understood that the primary purpose of the System is to foster growth at high levels of employment, with a stable dollar in the domestic economy and with over-all balance in our international payments.[1]

We have noted numerous times that these objectives may not all be mutually consistent. We should also stress that monetary policy is not the only way in which government can pursue these objectives.

The Federal Reserve's statement gives us a list of "target variables" which it desires to either maximize or minimize. Monetary policy influences these targets through a rather complex sequence of relationships. Principally, Federal Reserve actions operate on the reserve position of the commercial banks, which in turn affects the supply of loanable funds, which

---

[1] Board of Governors, Federal Reserve System, *The Federal Reserve System: Purposes and Functions*, 5th ed., Washington, 1963, pp. 1–2.

influences interest rates and credit conditions, which help to determine the level of GNP expenditures, which produce the ultimate effects on the welfare targets. This relationship is diagrammed in Figure 18-1.

The transmission sequence involves some time lag—particularly the adjustment of spending to interest-rate changes. And at each of the "transmission points" marked by arrows, other influences enter to affect the result. Commercial bank reserves are being continually influenced by gold and currency transactions, the composition of deposits, etc. GNP expenditures and interest rates are affected by the propensities to spend and save of the various components of the economy. Output, prices, and unemployment are influenced by changes in the size of the work force, changes in productivity, and market imperfections relating to monopoly or mobility. The balance of payments depends on what other countries are doing.

It is a sobering thought that the policy makers must somehow or other make allowance for all these forces. Fortunately, many of them are not subject to large, unpredictable changes. It is also useful to remember that other government policies can be used to exert influence at various points in this transmission sequence. In particular, fiscal policy provides a powerful alternative method for influencing the flow of GNP expenditures. For this reason, the management of monetary policy can be looked at as part of a larger problem, which is to choose the appropriate "mix" of policies which will provide the best results.

Our method of analysis is to start on the right-hand side of Figure 18-1 and work to the left. Thus we shall examine the welfare targets and their determinants and gradually work our way back to the specific techniques available to the monetary authorities.

Quantifying Objectives   Most of the major objectives for which monetary policy is useful are quantitatively represented. We have statistical measures of the price level, unemployment, the balance of payments, the level and growth rate of output. For simplicity, we shall limit our analysis initially to the domestic variables, postponing discussion of the balance of payments. Attention will be focused at first on the goals involving prices, unemployment, and output, and on the flow of GNP expenditures as their chief determinant. Later, additional elements will be brought into the picture.

As a first approximation, the problem facing the monetary authorities can be expressed as the achievement of an optimum level of GNP expenditures—or better, an optimum change in GNP from the present level. To illustrate, we will deal with the specific problem of estimating an optimum percentage rate for GNP expenditures to change in the year following the date of observation.

To determine such an optimum requires two kinds of information. The first consists of technical data on the manner in which a given change in GNP expenditures will affect each of the welfare targets. The second con-

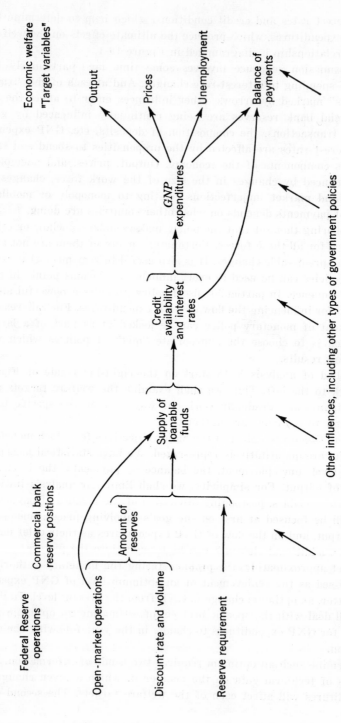

Figure 18-1. Federal Reserve operations and economic welfare objectives.

sists of the community's evaluation of the "goodness" or "badness" of a given amount of price increase, output increase, or level of unemployment.

The technical data can be estimated; indeed, we devoted much of Chapter 7 to observing historical patterns of response to GNP change. For illustration, Table 18-1 presents a hypothetical set of estimates relating GNP change to measured change in three welfare variables. The relations are derived from those in Chapter 7 and thus have some rough resemblance to reality, but are not intended as a literal forecast of how the economy will behave in the 1960s. For the sake of precise exposition, it is assumed that unemployment at the date of observation is 5.5 per cent and the population is growing at a rate of 1 per cent per year. Since decreases in GNP normally decrease welfare, the table deals only with increases.

Table 18-1 Hypothetical estimates of the impact of one-year change in GNP on prices, output, and unemployment

Increase in GNP expenditures	Increase in prices	Increase in output	Increase in output per capita	Unemployment rate	
				Average for year	End of year
0	−0.4%	0.4%	−0.6%	6.3%	7.2%
1%	0	1.0	0	6.2	6.9
2	0.4	1.6	0.5	6.0	6.6
3	0.9	2.1	1.1	5.9	6.3
4	1.3	2.7	1.7	5.7	6.0
5	1.7	3.2	2.2	5.6	5.7
6	2.2	3.8	2.7	5.4	5.4
7	2.6	4.3	3.3	5.3	5.1
8	3.0	4.8	3.8	5.1	4.8
9	3.5	5.3	4.3	5.0	4.5
10	4.0	5.8	4.7	4.9	4.3
11	4.6	6.1	5.0	4.8	4.1
12	5.3	6.4	5.3	4.7	3.9

Some comment is in order on the shape of these technical response coefficients. We have assumed that the higher the increase in GNP from "this" year to "next" year, the higher will be the rise in prices and output and the greater the reduction in the unemployment rate. Further, we have kept the estimates linear up to a projected 10 per cent GNP rise. The historical data show a linear pattern ex post, but it is a bit dangerous to rely on this assumption for ex ante analysis. Conceptually, as the rise in GNP expenditures goes up, we would expect the price increase to become larger at an increasing rate. In a sort of diminishing-returns pattern, less and less of the marginal GNP rise would go into output. In Table 18-1 the last two lines of figures have been arbitrarily shifted to show such a pattern. Had we assumed less unemployment initially, the departure from linearity would come sooner. All that is involved is the commonsense assumption that the closer the economy is working to capacity, the harder it is to increase output and the smaller the increment of output which can be achieved by a given expansion of expenditures.

The actual size of the response coefficients depends on many factors operating on the supply side. Of particular importance will be the rate of increase in the labor force and the rise of productivity. Table 18-1 implicitly reflects the patterns of these variables as they operated over the forty-year period 1923–1962. However, in recent years both labor force and productivity have grown somewhat faster. Any effort to forecast the response coefficients accurately should allow for this. More rapid growth in supply factors would probably raise the amount of output increase associated with a given rise of GNP and reduce the degree of price increase. However, it would also entail higher unemployment at each prospective rate of GNP increase.

Although the balance of international payments is not included in the table, its tendency would be to behave something like the price level—which is in fact a cause of its behavior. Higher GNP would raise imports and thus enlarge the international deficit. The greater the price increase, the greater the probable deficit. However, direct investment abroad by business firms may not follow this pattern. If the rise of GNP at home improves the profit outlook in the domestic economy, the result may be lower direct investment abroad, thus offsetting to some extent the tendency for the current-account deficit to vary directly with the size of the GNP increase.

"Valuing" the Objectives   Table 18-1 displays in quantitative form the fact that our goals are in conflict; this conflict would be accentuated had we included an estimate for the balance of international payments. Because of the conflict, the community is confronted with a problem of choice. It can obtain "more" welfare from one variable only by accepting less from another. Specifically, the greater the year-to-year rise in GNP, the more welfare will result from higher output and reduced unemployment, but the greater will be the extent of price inflation (and presumably the balance-of-payments deficit).

The only manner in which one can determine an optimum combination of these variables is to attach some sort of welfare coefficient to each of them. This is not an objective process; *it involves purely a value judgment.* In a democratic society, value judgments of this sort should arise ultimately from public opinion. But often the policy makers have only the roughest idea of how much importance the public attaches to individual welfare components.

Purely for illustration, one particular set of "weights" is offered below.

Note that these determine the relative importance of each welfare target and also the importance of incremental change in each target. The value assumptions and weights are as follows:

1. *Prices.* It is assumed that relatively small changes in the measured price deflator have no statistical significance, because of changes in types and quality of products. The greater the price increase, the more likelihood that it is real, and the greater its proportional adverse effect on welfare. To produce this shape, the welfare index for price change is the negative of the square of the percentage rise in prices. This makes the adverse welfare effect rise sharply with higher price increases.

2. *Output.* The welfare benefits are assumed to be in direct proportion to the rise in output per capita. An arbitrary coefficient of three is attached.

3. *Unemployment.* It is assumed that no adverse welfare effect attaches to unemployment of 3 per cent or less. The welfare index for unemployment is obtained by multiplying the excess of unemployment over 3 per cent by an arbitrary coefficient of 3.

By combining the welfare weights given above with the technical response coefficients predicted in Table 18-1, we obtain an index of the "welfare" associated with each projected rise of GNP. The result is shown in Figure 18-2.

The shapes of the components of Figure 18-2 reflect both the technical coefficients and the value indexes. The welfare gain associated with rising

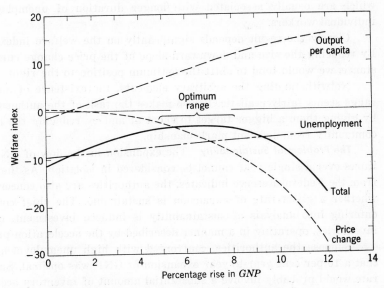

Figure 18-2. Welfare indexes of GNP change (hypothetical).

output and decreased unemployment rises in linear fashion most of the way, since both the technical coefficients and welfare indexes are linear. Ultimately both tend to flatten out because of technical reasons; the flattening would become more pronounced if we extended the range under consideration. The adverse welfare effect of rising prices increases rapidly after a slow start. In a small degree, this reflects the shape of the technical coefficient; but mainly it reflects our choice of an exponential welfare index.

The total welfare index for each possible GNP increase is shown separately. (It is negative throughout, reflecting the fact that our analysis involves two "bad things" and only one "good thing." Of course, the absolute numbers have no significance.) The total index improves along a curving path and reaches a relatively flat plateau covering the values between a 5 and 8 per cent GNP rise. In this range the welfare index is approximately constant. The community gains by higher output and lower unemployment, but loses in higher prices. Presumably the welfare of the community is essentially the same anywhere in this range.

Beyond 8 per cent the welfare index drops at an increasing rate. The gains from output and lower unemployment slow down slightly for technical reasons, and the loss from price inflation becomes rapidly greater.

Guessing the shape of the community's welfare evaluations is a game anyone can play. The reader should try his own hand at it. Perhaps the welfare gains from higher output per capita should be evaluated at an exponential rate, causing that line to curve upward. Perhaps we should also give an exponential weight to the adverse effect of high rates of unemployment, which are usually associated with longer duration of unemployment for individual workers.

Clearly the result depends significantly on the welfare indexes chosen. By reducing the size and downward slope of the price change curve, for instance, we would tend to shift the optimum position to the right.

Notwithstanding the arbitrary elements, the existence of an optimum range seems fairly realistic. It also makes the task of the authorities easier by giving them a bigger target to shoot at and by reducing the loss to the community from deficient marksmanship.

The Problem of Sustainability   The expansion in the flow of GNP expenditures over a single year cannot be considered in isolation. As the quotation from the Federal Reserve indicates, the authorities are also concerned about whether a given rate of expansion is sustainable. The chief complication entering into analysis of sustainability is induced investment, chiefly for inventories, operating in a manner described by the acceleration principle.

Suppose the authorities, confronted with high unemployment, decided that a 10 per cent year-to-year expansion of GNP was optimal. Such a high rate would probably involve a substantial amount of inventory accumulation and also perhaps a stimulus to high investment in fixed capital. If these came soon enough, they could help achieve the projected rate of expansion. But the economy could not continue indefinitely to turn in optimal performance at this rate of growth of total spending. If sustainability were ignored, the authorities might find it necessary to aim only for a 5 per cent expansion rate in the second year. Such a slowdown might lead to a collapse of investment incentives, to the extent that instead of a 5 per cent expansion, the economy might experience a recession.

A concern for sustainability is thus an allowance for next year's problems while dealing with this year's. Such a concern would presumably lead the authorities to try to work off high unemployment somewhat less rapidly than they otherwise might.

In terms of Figure 18-2, concern for sustainability might impose a boundary on the right side of the diagram—an absolute limit on how much expansion the authorities would accept. This might also lead them to aim at the lower (leftward) edge of the optimum range rather than at its middle.

The problem of sustainability can also be viewed in terms of the composition of expenditures. In general, the larger the proportion of expenditure growth made up of inventory expansion, the more worried the authorities are likely to be about sustaining the expansion. The absence of rapid inventory buildup during the long expansion beginning in 1961 was one reason the Federal Reserve authorities were willing to refrain from applying the brakes more vigorously. Another area which receives attention is the volume of consumer durable-goods purchases financed on credit; there are limits to the rate at which consumer debt can expand in sustained fashion.

But while a concern for sustainability may be appropriate, it can also be overdone. Critics argue that the Federal Reserve authorities have fallen back on a concern for sustainability to buttress an anti-expansion bias.[2]

What about Growth? Our analysis of the optimum rate of expenditure growth takes account of the existing degree of unemployment and also the prospective rise in labor force and productivity. Thus it tailors demand to supply. But could not monetary policy also assist directly in the growth of supply? In particular, cannot monetary policy raise the level of investment and capital formation?

If monetary policy is successful in producing an economic environment in which violent instability is infrequent and in which expenditures grow at a reasonable pace, this should certainly be a favorable environment

[2] "This 'sustained' talk has been used constantly by the Fed to choke off an expansion on the ground of 'we had better put on the brakes here because if this economy gets going too good, we won't be able to sustain it,' and this I think has been very harmful in 1957 and 1960 and at other times." Congressman Henry Reuss in *The Federal Reserve System after Fifty Years, Hearings before the Sub-Committee on Domestic Finance*, Committee on Banking and Currency, House of Representatives, 1964, p. 1217.

for investment. However, it is hard to see how monetary policy by itself can do more to stimulate investment without setting off undue inflationary tendencies.

However, the problem can more fruitfully be explored in terms of the policy "mix" through which a given GNP expansion can be pursued. Suppose a given rise in GNP expenditures can be achieved either by a high-interest, tight-credit policy combined with large government deficits, or by a low-interest, easy-credit policy combined with "tight" budgets and a government surplus. A desire to promote growth might lead to a preference for the latter. Assuming that aggregate demand and output are the same in the short run in either case, however, such a decision involves reducing current consumption to increase investment. Presumably such a policy decision should be made only if public opinion in fact supports a higher rate of "saving."

Whatever the merits of trying to rig the policy mix for this objective, the effort runs head-on into the problem of the balance of payments. Higher GNP *may* cause the nation's international deficit to increase, but lower interest rates at any given level of GNP most certainly lead to an increase in the deficit. One can attack the international problem by relying on fiscal policy for expansionary stimulus and keeping interest rates high. This may appear to leave the growth objective stranded. However, there are many other things the government can do to promote growth. It can direct a greater proportion of its expenditures into capital formation directly or into lending programs which promote private investment. And it can increase support for education and for technical research and innovation.

Other Objectives   Several other policy goals have influenced monetary policy at times. Historically, one of the most important has been the goal of assisting Treasury financing, and particularly keeping down the interest cost of the public debt. This dominated Federal Reserve policy in the 1940s and clearly conflicted with the objective of price level stability.

Federal Reserve policy has also traditionally been concerned over various aspects of the "quality" of credit. The original Federal Reserve Act was intended to promote some kinds of credit ("productive" lending through short-term, self-liquidating loans to business and agriculture) and discourage others (chiefly "speculation"). Because of problems of sustainability, one can make an economic case for preventing speculation from getting out of hand. But much of the qualitative approach to credit policy rested on dubious economic analysis, such as that embodied in the commercial-loan theory of credit. Moreover, it always contained and still does contain a large element of misplaced moralizing, which keeps cropping up in official discussions of member bank borrowing.

Another consideration in policy objectives came up in connection with the tight-money experience of 1957 and 1959. This is the possibility that extremely restrictive monetary policy may fall with an undue weight upon small-business borrowers. The most extensive analysis of the problem concluded that no substantial discrimination existed, but this conclusion was not universally accepted by other economists.[3]

Does the Federal Reserve Do All This?   The quantitative exposition of how output, prices, and unemployment respond to GNP change, and how much "welfare" is involved in various responses, is intended to bring out into the open matters which are generally only implicit in Federal Reserve policy positions. In public pronouncements, Federal Reserve authorities and staff generally avoid committing themselves to quantitative predictions relating to such variables as output, prices, and unemployment. This can be defended on grounds that history records considerable dispersion around the average behavior patterns and that there are always additional variables which need to be considered *ad hoc*. It is even more understandable that policy makers do not attach explicit welfare indexes to possible movements of prices, output, and unemployment. Yet it must be stressed that some assumptions about the importance and behavior of these targets are implicit in whatever policy actions are followed. The annual reports prepared by the Council of Economic Advisers go much further toward treating these matters explicitly.

The looser approach characteristic of Federal Reserve statements has definite dangers. Failure to specify the technical analysis underlying policy may open the way for analytical nonsense. As an illustration, Chairman Martin of the Board of Governors has repeatedly insisted that measures to curb price increases will *ipso facto* promote economic growth—a position supported by neither logic nor experience.[4]

Only a loose approach to technical and value judgments could support the kind of restrictive policy followed in 1959. The Board's view in March, 1959, was that "the state of economic activity appeared to be one of budding inflationary boom," despite the admitted existence of 6 per cent unemployment, and recurrent concern was expressed about the likelihood of undue "speculative or otherwise unsustainable elements in the further expansion

---

[3] G. L. Bach and C. J. Huizenga, "The Differential Effects of Tight Money," *American Economic Review*, March, 1961, and comments by Deane Carson and by A. Dale Tussing, *ibid.*, December, 1961, and September, 1963; Donald R. Hodgman, *Commercial Bank Loan and Investment Policy*, Bureau of Economic and Business Research, University of Illinois, Urbana, Ill., 1963, pp. 154–158. One point on which the evidence is clear is that interest charges to small borrowers rose less than those to large borrowers.

[4] See citations and analysis in John M. Culbertson, *Full Employment or Stagnation?* McGraw-Hill Book Company, New York, 1964, esp. pp. 157–158. Here is another interesting Martin view (1962—cited on p. 156): "I think one of the reasons we have had as much unemployment as we have had, and you may think this is silly, is because we have had too easy money." It is silly.

of activity." [5] More precise exposition might have made it clearer that the likelihood of price increases and the economic dangers from speculation were questionable on technical grounds. More precise identification of welfare premises would have shown the large amount of welfare significance ascribed by the authorities to curbing price increases and the international deficit, relative to the goals of raising output and reducing unemployment.

One can sympathize with the Federal Reserve authorities, who must in any event struggle to anticipate the uncertain effects of their own actions, as well as the balance of autonomous forces affecting the economy. Their judgments and actions, however expressed, are subject to criticism and analysis after the results are in. But anyone who reads much Federal Reserve literature and testimony can also sympathize with Senator William Proxmire's remarks to Chairman Martin:

> I have the greatest respect for your ability, and I think you are an outstanding and competent person, and everybody agrees with that, but the fact is, when you try to come down and discuss this [Federal Reserve policy goals] in meaningful specific terms, it is like nailing a custard pie to the wall.
>
> And frankly, Mr. Martin, without specific goals, criteria, guidelines, it is impossible to exercise any congressional oversight over you, and I think you know it. [6]

BANK RESERVES, MONEY, AND GNP EXPENDITURES

The Problem   Assuming that the monetary authorities have some sort of target for the flow of GNP expenditures (implicitly or explicitly), the next problem is how to achieve it. Since the behavior of GNP will respond to many forces which are autonomous from the viewpoint of the policy makers, they must begin by making some sort of guess or forecast about the direction in which things are heading. The task of monetary policy can then be viewed as one of applying either stimulation or restraint to these forces. Of course, the problem is complicated by the uncertainty of forecasting the autonomous forces, by the lack of precision in measuring the impact of monetary policy on them, and by the time lag involved before monetary policy changes take effect. [7]

[5] Board of Governors, Federal Reserve System, *Annual Report for 1959*, pp. 33, 38.

[6] *State of the Economy and Policies for Full Employment, Hearings before the Joint Economic Committee*, 1962, pp. 612–613, cited in Culbertson, *op. cit.*, pp. 154–155.

[7] However, Karl Brunner and Allan Meltzer conclude from a study of Federal Reserve statements and actions that the authorities have assumed there is no significant time lag at all in their actions. *The Federal Reserve's Attachment to the Free Reserve Concept*, A Staff Analysis, Subcommittee on Domestic Finance, Committee on Banking and Currency, House of Representatives, 1964, pp. 46–47. Evidence on the time lag is reviewed in the following chapter.

To state the problem this way implies that it is possible to calculate what changes will occur if the monetary authorities do nothing. But just what does it mean for them to do nothing? Judging from Board policy statements, it means maintaining the existing degree of ease or restraint on credit expansion. This is an ambiguous notion, but the authorities appear to judge it in terms of the level and change of interest rates and the reserve positions of member banks.

Conceptually, the sort of forecasting involved here can be expressed in terms of the concepts we used in Chapters 8, 9, and particularly 10. The authorities would have to judge the strength of business investment incentives (marginal efficiency), the propensity to consume, and the fiscal policy of Federal, state, and local governments. These propensities to spend give some idea of the probable path of GNP expenditures, starting from a given level of incomes and interest rates. The authorities would also have to evaluate the impact of these sector decisions on saving and borrowing and thus on the loanable funds market and the rate of interest. An upswing in expenditures will commonly bring a rise in interest rates through increased demand for credit, unless the monetary authorities permit some commensurate expansion of bank credit.

The flow-of-funds accounts, developed in large part by the staff of the Board of Governors, provide a tidy statistical framework for analyzing sector activity in the main circuit and in the financial circulation. Some staff members have experimented with a full-fledged forecasting model based on these accounts; however, it does not appear that policy decisions so far are based on any very precise estimates of the "normal" or "probable" behavior of the flow-of-funds categories in the upcoming time period. In particular, Federal Reserve policy analysis appears to lack a quantitative treatment of the determination of interest rates and of their impact on the expenditure flow.

The Money Supply   In the terms of our analysis in Chapter 10, the attention of monetary authorities could simply be focused on the money supply. We can visualize their decision as a choice of the appropriate change in M in the near future from its present level. In extreme cases, the choice might extend to a decrease in M, or to keeping it constant. More commonly, one would suppose, the real issue would be over an appropriate rate for it to expand.

Such an outlook would certainly be appropriate if the money supply itself were the principal determinant of target variables, such as prices, output, and employment. However, it is more in harmony with the evidence to regard GNP expenditures as their chief determinant and to analyze the impact of monetary change on GNP. This requires estimating the degree to which a given increase in M will lower interest rates and ease credit, the extent to which investment and other expenditures will be stimulated by easier credit, and the strength of the multiplier and other induced reactions resulting.

If the authorities had complete estimates covering the marginal efficiency of capital, the propensity to consume, government fiscal policy, and the demand schedule for cash balances, they could presumably calculate the response of GNP expenditures to any given change in the money supply. The analytical process involved is essentially that of Table 10-1 (page 246). In discussing the impact of monetary expansion, we stressed the importance of the division of new money between increased expenditures and idle balances. This depends on the relative sensitivity to interest rates and credit conditions of expenditures (chiefly investment) on one hand, and desired cash balances on the other. If investment spending has a high credit sensitivity, and desired cash balances are relatively insensitive to interest rates, then GNP will be highly responsive to variations in M. If spending is insensitive but cash balances are highly sensitive to interest rates and credit conditions, the response of GNP to M will be much smaller.

According to the calculations shown in Table 10-1, an increase of $10 billion in the money supply raised the equilibrium level of GNP by about $16 billion, of which slightly less than $10 billion occurred within one year. Since the equations underlying that table have some empirical realism, it is tempting to suggest that the response coefficient $\Delta GNP/\Delta M$ is roughly unity for a one-year time span. This is relatively low, when we remember that the average velocity of the total money supply (GNP/M) was nearly 4 in the early 1960s.

Actually, a forecast value of unity for $\Delta GNP/\Delta M$ probably represents a rock-bottom estimate. It would reflect a monetary injection coming entirely through open-market purchase of existing securities, with no induced expansion of bank loans. We have observed that the greater the rise of bank loans rather than securities, the greater the expansionary influence of money creation tends to be. By making an estimate of the composition of added bank assets, the authorities could improve their forecast of the impact of monetary change on the economy.

In the view of the new quantity theory, efforts to quantify all the stages of transmission between monetary policy and the expenditure flow may be misleading and unnecessary. Instead, it might be possible on the basis of the historical evidence to determine a correspondence between the rate of monetary expansion and the rate at which GNP expenditures are increasing. Perhaps an examination of the recent past would suffice: if the expansion of GNP was too low "last year," the implication is that the rate of monetary expansion which preceded it by three to six months was also too low.

There are some difficulties in carrying out a policy aimed at the rate of expansion of money. One is the definition of the money supply. Should it include time deposits, or not? Analysis utilizing a more inclusive definition produced a very different appraisal of events in 1961–1964 from that based on the more conventional definition. Should Treasury deposits be included? Should the rate of growth be estimated by comparing this month's figure with last month's, or with the same month a year ago? These represent differing points of view among advocates of the new quantity theory.

It is only proper to note, however, that many defenders of the new quantity theory feel that the time lags and quantitative imprecision in the relation between monetary growth and expenditures growth make it unwise to base monetary policy on short-run cyclical conditions. Milton Friedman, at the extreme, urges adoption of a fixed monetary rule calling for growth in the money supply at a constant rate based on the growth needs of the economy. Many others, while not desiring a literally fixed and frozen rate of expansion, urge that the monetary authorities keep the rate of growth of money fairly stable, rather than engaging in abrupt sequences of stop-and-go.

Bank Credit An alternative approach, which can be defended by the historical evidence, might be to stress the rate of expansion not of the money supply, but of bank credit—loans and securities. Historically, the rate of change of bank credit has followed a path very similar to the rate of change of the money supply (as shown in Figure 10-7). Further, at some points the credit series shows significant turning points even earlier than the money series.

Interest Rates Since variations in interest rates and credit conditions provide an important channel for the influence of money on expenditures, it is not surprising that the Federal Reserve authorities have relied on interest rates as an intermediate target of policy and have also inferred from interest-rate behavior what the effects of recent policy actions have been. It seems eminently logical to equate declining interest rates with easing of credit and rising rates with credit tightening.

Yet this use of interest rates as a criterion of credit tightness or ease is full of pitfalls as a guide to policy. The reason is that interest rates are sensitive to variations in the demand for loanable funds, which tends to vary strongly with the rate at which GNP is rising. Suppose a recession commences. Marginal efficiency slumps, causing a reduction of investment. As GNP falls, the demand for cash balances declines. Even if the monetary authorities take no action, interest rates fall. Has there been countercyclical monetary policy? If the authorities merely watch the interest rate, they may feel that there has been. Indeed, if the demand for loan funds falls sufficiently, declining interest rates may ensue even if the monetary authorities permit a slowdown in the rate at which money is being created, as they have at times done. Critics argue that a truly countercyclical monetary policy should involve at least a maintenance of the same monetary expansion characteristic of expansion periods. Indeed, part of the argument for steady monetary expansion over the business cycle is that it would provide a better countercyclical influence than has been achieved by (allegedly misguided) discretionary authority.

Use of interest rates as a criterion of policy would be appropriate if the authorities had some quantitative notions of the impact of interest-rate changes on spending. Such quantitative estimates would provide a method for judging whether (for instance) the decline in interest rates already achieved would be sufficient to reverse a recession. It is significant that in fifty years the vast research facilities of the Federal Reserve System have apparently scrupulously avoided this problem.

Commercial Bank Reserves It is very possible that the monetary policy makers could avoid a lot of dilemmas and ambiguities if instead of concerning themselves with the money supply itself or the flow of bank credit, they directed their attention to commercial bank reserve positions. After all, the state of bank reserves is a prime determinant of the expansion of both money and credit.

Of course, changes in bank reserve positions (and potential expansion) are the outcome of many factors. The amount of their reserves depends on such sources as the monetary gold stock, Federal Reserve credit, and Treasury currency, as well as on competing uses such as currency in circulation and Treasury and miscellaneous accounts with Federal Reserve banks. The level of required reserves depends on reserve requirements set chiefly by the Federal Reserve authorities and on the existing amounts of deposit liabilities. The relative amounts of currency in circulation, demand deposits, and time deposits depend on the public's asset preference pattern. These are the factors we analyzed in Chapter 5.

However, some of these determinants of commercial bank reserve positions are small, or remain stable, or change only in relatively predictable ways. Important changes in reserve positions arise chiefly from a very limited number of influences, chiefly the monetary gold stock, Federal Reserve credit, and reserve requirements, with Treasury and other accounts with Federal Reserve banks possibly meriting inclusion. These relatively important factors produce the changes in the monetary or reserve base we have referred to at many points. In particular, Figure 10-7 points out that the year-to-year rate of change of a simple measure of the monetary base, consisting merely of the gold stock plus Federal Reserve credit, adjusted for variations in reserve requirements, shows a very high time-series correspondence to the changes in the money supply and in bank credit. Each of these three variables—rates of change of the monetary base, the money supply, and bank credit—leads or coincides with the movements in GNP expansion and thus may claim a causal influence. One can well argue, therefore, that the policy makers should concentrate on the monetary base, which is well within their control and which seems to have such a strong and regular causal influence.

To be sure, not all the determinants of bank reserve positions are under the authorities' direct control. However, the uncontrolled items can generally be compensated sufficiently to produce the desired ultimate result. An undesired reduction in bank reserves from gold outflow can be compensated by open-market purchases; an undesired reserve increase from currency inflow can be offset by open-market sales, and so on.

Much effort is devoted in the Federal Reserve System to forecasting the impact of the relatively autonomous forces on commercial bank reserve positions and trying to prevent undesired effects from them. Suppose autonomous forces such as gold and currency flows are expected to reduce bank reserves by $100 million in the next month. If the authorities desire such a change, all they have to do is sit still. But suppose they feel that the appropriate change is an *increase* of $100 million. They must extend their expansionary activities in order to produce the desired end result.

Federal Reserve analysis has distinguished between "defensive" and "dynamic" responsibilities. The defensive aspect consists of offsetting undesired changes, such as the gold outflow of 1958–1963 or the seasonal outflow of currency at the end of the year. The dynamic aspect consists of the positive modification needed to produce a desired final change in reserve positions.[8] Some critics have argued that the authorities work too hard at trying to iron out very short-run money-market disturbances to the neglect of the more important longer-run factors.[9]

Free Reserves In addition to total reserves and excess reserves, the Federal Reserve leadership has devoted much attention to the "free" reserves of member banks. Free reserves are defined as excess reserves minus borrowings from the Federal Reserve. Borrowing from the Federal Reserve generally imposes an obligation on the borrowing bank to reduce its earning assets. Consequently, the authorities have assumed that a given amount of excess reserves would be less expansionary if a large proportion of it were borrowed than if all of it were "owned" by the commercial banks.

The concept of free reserves is useful in dealing with situations where there is some degree of offsetting between open-market operations and member bank borrowing. Suppose the Federal Reserve buys $1 billion of securities in the open market, but member banks use the funds to repay borrowings from Federal Reserve banks. Total and excess reserves have

[8] Analysis in these terms is developed by Robert V. Roosa, *Federal Reserve Operations in the Money and Government Securities Markets*, Federal Reserve Bank of New York, 1956.

[9] See comments of G. L. Bach in *The Federal Reserve System after Fifty Years, Hearings before the Subcommittee on Domestic Finance*, p. 1390.

not increased, but presumably the banks will be more inclined to expand credit than before. The figure for free reserves would show an increase and possibly anticipate this.

However, statistical studies have indicated that the level of free reserves is not a very reliable determinant of monetary behavior or a good indicator of monetary ease or tightness. The adjustment of bank credit and reserves does not appear to be affected significantly by whether the reserves are owned or owed. And the rate of expansion of bank credit and money is not uniquely determined by the level of free reserves.[10]

Recently, Professors Brunner and Meltzer have taken the Federal Reserve severely to task for relying unduly on free reserves as an appropriate indicator of existing credit conditions and an appropriate target for policy. In their view, "guidance based on the free reserve doctrine frequently leads the Federal Reserve authorities into a position where they believe that a countercyclical monetary policy is underway, while for many months almost no relevant action is taken." [11]

It should be noted that the need for a concept such as free reserves arises from member bank borrowing. If this were reduced to a nominal level by adoption of the penalty-rate proposal discussed in the next chapter, the precision and effectiveness of Federal Reserve action would probably be increased.

Other Channels   Although the principal channel for the influence of Federal Reserve policy is commercial bank reserve positions, there are others. Open-market operations place the Federal Reserve banks directly in the loanable funds market. Buying securities from nonbank investors directly injects added funds into the market. Further, open-market operations directly affect security prices and yields. There is also some direct influence from the Federal Reserve rediscount rate on private interest rates. A higher rediscount rate tends to mean a higher Treasury bill rate; banks avoid borrowing and sell bills instead to meet reserve deficiencies. And interest charges on bank loans are sometimes adjusted to follow changes in the rediscount rate.

There are in addition Federal Reserve policy measures which do not operate on bank reserve positions at all. Selective controls over the permissible terms of credit are an example. Setting margin requirements for stock market credit affects the amount of such credit which can be created at a given level of stock market values. But it does not limit the supply of

---

[10] See A. James Meigs, *Free Reserves and the Money Supply*, The University of Chicago Press, Chicago, 1962. Meigs notes that there is a very high correlation between "the monthly per cent change in total reserves adjusted for changes in reserve requirements and the monthly per cent change in total member-bank deposits subject to reserve requirements. . . ." p. 27.

[11] *The Federal Reserve's Attachment to the Free Reserve Concept*, p. 43.

credit in general. Setting maximum limits on interest paid on banks' time deposits does not affect their reserve positions directly. However, the interest rates influence the public's willingness to hold time deposits relative to money, which does affect potential credit expansion.

Finally, there is the possibility that overt Federal Reserve actions will influence the economy through their effects on people's expectations. Unfortunately, there is no telling how this may occur. In a recession, indications of a vigorous expansionist monetary policy may spread optimistic views that recovery will soon occur. However, people may also react just the other way; they may interpret the Federal Reserve's actions as a sign that things are really in bad shape.

Policy Instruments and the Achievement of Goals One advantage of concentrating attention on the behavior of some measure of the monetary base is that it reduces the chief effects of various policy instruments to a common denominator. Each can (and probably should) be evaluated in terms of its influence on the monetary base and thus on potential bank reserves. Such quantification is easiest for open-market operations. It is also fairly simple for changes in reserve requirements, since in a realistic study one can ignore the marginal changes in expansion coefficients associated with reserve requirement changes. Variations in the discount rate are the most difficult policy measure to quantify. This difficulty arises because the volume of member bank borrowing is strongly influenced by movements in the Treasury bill and other market interest rates.

Greater precision in policy would be gained if the discount rate were kept at all times sufficiently high to limit member bank borrowing to low levels reflecting genuine emergency needs. Such a policy would also eliminate the need to rely on such an unreliable guide as free reserves. Indeed, a policy which stressed the behavior of the monetary base could well be built almost entirely around open-market operations. In the next chapter, we shall look more carefully at individual instruments of monetary policy.

In their dreams, advocates of the new quantity theory probably visualize a situation in which the authorities direct their immediate concern toward the rate at which open-market purchases are made. By varying this rate they produce a relatively stable growth in the monetary base and in bank reserves. This in turn leads to similar behavior by the money supply and total bank credit. As a result, GNP itself expands at a fairly stable rate. To be sure, variations in propensities to spend push it above or below its trend. But the monetary environment consistently acts to cushion these disturbances, chiefly through variations in interest rates. While the authorities do not maintain a literally stable rate of monetary expansion, they do not deviate very much from a constant trend. Consequently there are no periods of violent monetary expansion and thus no need for a subsequent excessive slamming on of brakes.

It is easy to be skeptical about this resurgent faith in the ability of monetary policy to reduce economic instability below the levels experienced since World War II. Certainly the quantity theorists cannot guarantee an absence of disturbances arising from nonmonetary causes. On the other hand, there is not much reason to anticipate harmful results from following their prescriptions, and there is some reason to believe the outcome might be an improvement over the policies of the past.

SUMMARY

The chief goals for which monetary policy is used are price stability, rising output, and low unemployment, modified by concern for sustainability and the balance of international payments. These target variables respond principally to variations in the flow of GNP expenditures. By quantifying the expected response of output, prices, and unemployment to various rates of GNP expansion, and by attaching welfare indexes to each goal, it is conceptually possible to derive an optimum target for GNP for the upcoming time period. However, it is not apparent that Federal Reserve authorities make any precise quantification of such matters.

Monetary policy operates on the expenditure flow through its effects on the monetary base and the reserve position of the commercial banks. Changes in bank reserve positions in turn influence the expansion of the money supply and the supply of loanable funds. From these arise changes in interest rates and credit conditions, which in turn cause increases or decreases in credit-sensitive expenditures such as housing. These effects are then augmented by multiplier and accelerator repercussions.

Economists do not agree on how much impact monetary change can be expected to have on the expenditure flow. Some feel that, in view of the relatively small influence attributed to interest rates in statistical studies of investment, monetary change will operate only with a substantial amount of slippage. Advocates of the new quantity theory, on the other hand, point to the impressive time-series correspondence between changes in money and expenditures to defend their conviction that control of money is a powerful method for influencing the expenditure flow.

QUESTIONS FOR STUDY

1. "Public opinion will not tolerate inaction during a depression. If the government does not do the right things to promote recovery, it is likely to do things which cause more harm than good." What are "the right things"? What evidence can you find in the record of the 1930s of the danger that depression will furnish a pretext for harmful policies?

2. Why are rising prices and unemployment regarded as bad things? Assuming it is necessary to have more of one in order to reduce the other, how would you assign relative importance between them?

3. What reason is there for the monetary authorities to modify policy because of the balance of international payments? Why not concentrate on domestic economic welfare?

4. "The central task of monetary policy is to achieve an optimum level (or change) in GNP expenditures." Discuss. Using the latest data you can obtain, and making explicit assumptions about welfare indexes, identify the optimum change in GNP for the upcoming twelve months.

SUGGESTED READINGS

The following are publications of the Commission on Money and Credit, published by Prentice-Hall, Inc., Englewood Cliffs, N.J.:

The Federal Reserve and the Treasury: Answers to Questions from the Commission on Money and Credit, 1963.

Inflation, Growth, and Employment, 1963.

Money and Credit: Their Influence on Jobs, Prices, and Growth, 1961.

Committee on Banking and Currency, House of Representatives, 1964:

Some General Features of the Federal Reserve's Approach to Policy.

The Federal Reserve's Attachment to the Free Reserve Concept.

The Federal Reserve System after Fifty Years, Hearings before the Subcommittee on Domestic Finance.

Culbertson, John M.: *Full Employment or Stagnation?* McGraw-Hill Book Company, New York, 1964.

Meigs, A. James: *Free Reserves and the Money Supply,* The University of Chicago Press, Chicago, 1962.

chapter nineteen

MONETARY POLICY:
TECHNIQUES AND
SUPPLEMENTS

Having examined the objectives of monetary policy and the channels through which it operates, we now take a closer look at the individual techniques of Federal Reserve policy. Following this, we shall deal with other policies available for achieving the same goals, chiefly fiscal policy.

Major Federal Reserve policy techniques all have their principal direct effects on the reserve positions of the commercial banks. Open-market operations directly inject or remove reserve funds. Variations in the discount rate affect the volume of reserves borrowed by member banks. Changes in reserve requirements affect the extent to which existing reserves are tied up by existing deposits. However, there may be side effects which go beyond commercial bank reserve positions—open-market operations directly affect the prices and yields of securities, for instance. And there are Federal Reserve policies, such as fixing margin requirements and setting maximum interest rates on time deposits, which do not have direct effects on bank reserve positions. Nevertheless, the main channel for Federal Reserve influence is through commercial bank reserve positions.

534

TECHNIQUES OF FEDERAL RESERVE POLICY

Open-market Operations In its open-market operations, the Federal Reserve buys or sells marketable United States securities. Since it holds a large volume of short-term securities, some of which mature every week, its chief operation is buying. When it wishes to reduce its holdings, it can merely let them mature, thereby putting the burden of finding buyers on the Treasury. Such refunding has the same effects as a Reserve sale.

Open-market operations are managed by the Federal Reserve Bank of New York on the basis of directives from the Open-Market Committee. The "trading desk" of the New York bank deals with established government-securities dealers who stand ready to buy or sell at quoted prices and who transmit Reserve influence throughout the market for United States and other securities. Reserve transactions may occur almost every business day, since they bear the brunt of adjusting bank reserves to meet seasonal and other short-run variations.

The most important effect of open-market operations is on commercial bank reserves. Federal Reserve purchases are paid for by checks drawn on the New York Reserve bank. When these are deposited, bank reserves increase. Federal Reserve sales (or their equivalent in Treasury refunding) remove bank reserves when the purchasers pay for the securities. Since commercial bank deposit liabilities are never changed more than reserves, excess reserves are always increased or decreased almost as much as total reserves.

Open-market transactions may have a number of other effects. Purchases from nonbank investors increase the money supply by creating demand deposits, while sales to such investors take deposits out of existence. Reserve transactions can directly affect interest rates. Purchases may raise security prices and reduce market yields; sales may lower prices and increase yields.

The virtues of open-market operations are impressive and include the following:

1. *Initiative.* The Federal Reserve decides the timing and magnitude of operations. It can produce desired effects on bank reserves whether the banks cooperate or not, since it can always find someone who will deal at a price.

2. *Flexibility.* Open-market operations can be conducted at any quantitative magnitude desired and can be concluded at whatever time desired, down to the day and hour.

3. *Power.* The ability to achieve desired effects on reserves is now clearly well within the Federal Reserve's power. Its holdings of securities are large enough to extinguish all existing member bank reserves through sales. Reserve and collateral requirements do not pose barriers to Reserve purchases.

4. *Ability to reach around the banks.* Open-market operations are the only general credit instrument through which the Federal Reserve can directly change the money supply and market rates of interest.

In view of these advantages, it is very probable that the Federal Reserve could manage monetary policy quite satisfactorily were it to rely only on open-market operations.

Open-market operations also provide a method whereby the Federal Reserve can influence the structure of interest rates. For instance, by selling short-term securities and buying long-terms, they could nudge short-term interest rates higher and long rates lower. However, for roughly a decade after the accord of 1951, the authorities resolutely refrained from such action. Instead, they adhered to a bills-only policy which confined operations to the short end of the market. However, the emergence of the problems of international deficits and gold outflow led to modification in the early 1960s. The composition of the Federal Reserve portfolio was then varied as a method of keeping short-term rates high in relation to long-term rates. Certainly it is desirable for the authorities to feel free to operate in long-term markets as well as short, particularly if long-term interest rates have, as some economists believe, greater influence on investment decisions.

Reserve Requirements Since the 1930s the Board of Governors has had authority to vary reserve requirements for member banks within limits set by law. When open-market policy was immobilized by supporting bond prices, reserve requirements received considerable emphasis. Since 1951, reduction in reserve requirements has been used as an important method of easing credit during recessions, but requirements have not been raised at any time.

Federal Reserve officials regard reserve requirement changes as a "clumsy and blunt instrument" for flexible credit control. Such changes are disruptive to bank management. As actually utilized, they have commonly involved at least half a percentage point, equivalent to about a $500 million change in excess reserves in the early 1960s. However, there is no legal or economic obstacle to using much smaller changes if desired.

Variations in reserve requirements have two effects: They alter the amount of reserves needed for existing deposits, and they alter expansion coefficients. However, if one allows for currency drains, the net changes in expansion coefficients are relatively insignificant.

Reserve requirement changes provide a means to reach every member bank individually. When credit easing is desired, this may provide a more rapid method than open-market purchases, which have their impact initially in New York and other money-market centers. As a means for tightening credit, however, this uniformity is a disadvantage. An increase in reserve requirements is likely to force many banks into reserve deficiency and produce somewhat unpleasant and disorderly adjustments. The power to impose high reserve requirements probably has its chief utility for situations such as World War II, when the government is incurring large deficits. High reserve requirements can help curb expansion of bank credit while enabling interest costs to be kept down for the Treasury.

In recent years, much attention has been given to the structure of reserve requirements. Economists have been increasingly critical of several features, particularly differences between member and nonmember banks, differences between city and country member banks, and the reserve requirement for time deposits.

Reserve requirements for member banks are not in general higher than those for nonmembers, but the latter have much greater latitude in what they may include as legal reserves. In particular, nonmember banks can count deposits with other commercial banks. The differences in reserve requirement provisions have been a major reason for banks to stay out of the Federal Reserve System. However, member bank discontent has been allayed somewhat by the lowering of requirements since 1951 and by the inclusion of vault cash as reserves since 1959.

Higher requirements on demand deposits are imposed on reserve city banks than on country member banks. This practice dates back a century and reflects the concentration of interbank deposit liabilities in the city banks. The differential arose when reserve requirements were intended to protect liquidity. Now that the emphasis has shifted to credit control, it seems unnecessary.

Member banks are subject to reserve requirements on time and savings deposits which are lower than those on demand deposits but higher than those imposed on mutual savings banks and savings and loan associations (chiefly because the latter can count deposits with commercial banks or government securities as liquidity reserves). If depositors showed a high propensity to shift funds from one kind of commercial bank deposit to the other in a cyclically unstabilizing manner, there would be a case for the present requirement, or even a higher one, on time deposits. Depositors do not appear to do this, however. Lowering the rate on member bank time deposits would improve the equity of treatment between them and their savings competitors without any apparent harm to the effectiveness of monetary policy.

A simple and defensible reform would be to impose equal reserve requirements on demand deposits of all commercial banks. This could be approached by making the reserve requirement standard a condition for obtaining deposit insurance. Likewise, a uniform rate for time deposits could be set on a level comparable with those applying to savings institutions.[1]

The Discount Window Originally, the rediscount process was at the heart of Federal Reserve policy, the source of "elasticity" in the currency supply. However, it failed dismally to live up to expectations during 1929–1933. Abundant excess reserves in the 1930s and the Federal Reserve bond-support program in the 1940s kept the volume of member bank borrowing at microscopic levels. Since the accord in 1951, use of the "discount window" has revived. However, it commonly involves borrowing on collateral of government securities rather than customers' IOUs.

Federal Reserve authorities do not control the actual dollar volume of member bank borrowing. They can influence it by raising and lowering the discount rate—the interest charged borrowers. However, discount volume is also affected by market rates of interest, particularly the rate on Treasury bills.[2] Banks borrow to escape from a deficiency of reserves. However, if the Treasury bill rate is lower than the discount rate, they will reduce their bill holdings in preference to borrowing. Another escape route available for large banks is to borrow reserves from another bank through the Federal funds market.

Member bank borrowing is also affected by the tradition of banker dislike for operating on borrowed funds. The majority of member banks borrow from the Federal Reserve infrequently or not at all.[3] This reluctance is reinforced by the authorities, who regard member bank borrowing as a

---

[1] The Commission on Money and Credit recommended (in effect) that uniform reserve requirements for demand deposits be imposed on all insured commercial banks and that requirements for time deposits be eliminated or reduced. *Money and Credit: Their Influence on Jobs, Prices, and Growth*, Prentice-Hall, Inc., Englewood Cliffs, N.J., 1961, pp. 69, 77. For detailed analysis in support of a similar position, see Warren L. Smith, "Reserve Requirements in the American Monetary System," Commission on Money and Credit, *Monetary Management*, Prentice-Hall, Inc., Englewood Cliffs, N.J., 1963.

[2] According to Arthur Okun, the volume of member bank borrowing in 1946–1959 can be reasonably well expressed by the equation $B = 0.188 + 0.487b - 0.306d$, where b is the Treasury bill rate and d is the discount rate. "Monetary Policy, Debt Management and Interest Rates: A Quantitative Appraisal," Commission on Money and Credit, *Stabilization Policies*, Prentice-Hall, Inc., Englewood Cliffs, N.J., 1963, p. 359.

[3] Out of slightly more than 6,000 member banks, the total number borrowing in each recent year was as follows:

1960	1,920
1961	1,285
1962	1,117
1963	1,232

The Federal Reserve System after Fifty Years, Hearings before the Subcommittee on Domestic Finance, Committee on Banking and Currency, House of Representatives, 1964, p. 310.

privilege and not a right, and scrutinize each loan request. Their attitude is well expressed by the revised text of Regulation A issued by the Board of Governors in 1955, which stated:

> Federal Reserve credit is generally extended on a short-term basis to a member bank in order to enable it to adjust its asset position when necessary because of developments such as a sudden withdrawal of deposits or seasonal requirements for credit. . . . [It] is also available for longer periods when necessary in order to assist member banks in meeting unusual situations, such as may result from national, regional, or local difficulties or from exceptional circumstances involving only particular member banks. Under ordinary circumstances, the continuous use of Federal Reserve credit by a member bank over a considerable period of time is not regarded as appropriate.
>
> In considering a request for credit accommodation, each Federal Reserve Bank gives due regard to the purpose of the credit and to its probable effects upon the maintenance of sound credit conditions, both to the individual institution and the economy generally. It keeps informed of and takes into account the general character and amount of the loans and investments of the member bank. It considers whether the bank is borrowing principally for the purpose of obtaining a tax advantage or profiting from rate differentials and whether the bank is extending an undue amount of credit for the speculative carrying of or trading in securities, real estate, or commodities, or otherwise.[4]

Reserve bank authorities keep an eye on the behavior of borrowing banks to maintain the standards quoted. If a borrower's reserve deficiency is not eliminated by a flowback of deposits, it is ordinarily expected to take steps to reduce earning assets. "Abuse" of the discount privilege may be grounds for an admonitory word to the offender. But member banks know the ground rules pretty well, and the authorities apparently seldom find it necessary to issue warnings, much less to refuse credit to an applicant.[5] By law, the maximum a bank can borrow from all sources combined is limited in relation to its capital accounts.

Looking at the array of Federal Reserve techniques, discount policy stands out as an anomaly. The authorities have clearly been reluctant to rely entirely on the cost of borrowed funds to limit member bank borrowing. Instead, Regulation A and its administration contain an abundant dose of the kind of moralizing which was so common when the Federal Reserve Act was originally passed. The authorities appear in the role of a finger-shaking Mrs. Grundy, tut-tutting against "speculation" and "profiting from rate differentials."

[4] Board of Governors, Federal Reserve System, *Annual Report for 1957*, pp. 9–10.

[5] A good description of discount administration is George W. McKinney, *The Federal Reserve Discount Window*, Rutgers University Press, New Brunswick, N.J., 1960.

Indeed, the whole rediscounting process is anomalous. Its survival is rationalized as providing for a "lender of last resort," a source of ultimate liquidity for the banks. But the liquidity of the commercial banking *system* is adequately protected by Federal Reserve open-market powers. Borrowing from the Federal Reserve is not necessary to bolster the liquidity of individual banks. So long as the system as a whole has sufficient liquidity, individual banks can borrow from each other, through Federal funds transactions or correspondent relationships.

In truth, individual banks do not borrow from the Federal Reserve literally to obtain funds to meet cash or clearing drains. They borrow to avoid falling below legal reserve requirements, which are themselves a contrivance of policy. The entire borrowing process could readily be eliminated if greater use were made of the provision that member banks falling below the reserve requirement pay a financial penalty on their deficiency.

Federal Reserve authorities have not been acting simply as a "lender of the last resort" for the banking system as a whole. Instead, in the 1950s they kept the discount rate low enough so that borrowing was usually profitable for those banks which were willing to push their opportunities, but they have relied on nonprice means to discourage banks from maximizing profits through borrowing.

The result has hardly been an improvement in the administration of monetary policy. Variations in the discount rate have been inconsistent in terms of the Treasury bill rate. The volume of member bank borrowing itself becomes a relatively erratic influence on reserves which has to be estimated in formulating optimum open-market policy. The signals given by changes in discount rates may work undesired effects on expectations. Induced changes in member bank borrowing make it more difficult to estimate the effects of other policy actions.

To improve the precision and efficiency of monetary policy, critics have suggested various improvements in discount policy. One extreme possibility would be to abolish it entirely. A more feasible change would be to make the discount rate a "penalty" rate, which would always be higher than the bill rate. Indeed, the authorities might adopt a practice followed in some other countries of simply setting the rediscount rate a certain number of points above the Treasury bill rate and letting it fluctuate as market conditions change. The necessity of nonprice credit rationing would be eliminated. Banks would resort to other channels to obtain funds unless they were in real trouble. Borrowing would be infrequent and limited to those cases where central-bank aid would really be advantageous.[6] The discount rate would cease to operate as an element in general monetary policy, where

[6] For analysis of the discount function along these lines, see Joseph Aschheim, *Techniques of Monetary Control,* The Johns Hopkins Press, Baltimore, 1961, pp. 83–98.

its role has varied from redundancy to inconsistency. Access to Federal Reserve credit would be reduced to a real emergency resource, as it was originally intended.

Selective Controls   Since 1935 the Federal Reserve Board has exercised authority over margins for stock market loans. Margin requirements have been raised or lowered chiefly on the basis of the rate of growth of stock market credit. Although the authorities disclaim any direct responsibility for stock prices, margin requirements have exercised a stabilizing influence over them. By keeping requirements fairly high (never lower than 50 per cent) at all times, and by raising them when the market is rising rapidly, the Federal Reserve has helped to prevent speculative runaways through pyramiding—that is, using the rise in stock values as a basis for borrowing and buying more stock. High margins have also insulated the market against the downside vulnerability which could result from selling out thinly margined accounts. Insofar as stock market instability threatens the stability of the productive economy (not a great threat, ordinarily), margin controls contribute to the objectives of general monetary policy.

At various times during 1941 the Federal Reserve also controlled consumer credit and, during the Korean conflict, housing credit. It was authorized to specify minimum down payments and maximum repayment periods. The attraction of such controls was that they helped reduce credit expansion along some lines without conflicting with the bond-support program. Since the accord, however, Federal Reserve officials have repeatedly disclaimed a desire to operate through such controls. Their attitude has been that monetary policy should determine the aggregate supply of credit and allow market forces to allocate it among specific uses.

This is a commendable attitude in many ways. However, some economists have noted that selective controls offer perhaps the only feasible method for slimming down undue bulges in particular sectors of credit use. Most especially they feel consumer-credit control could have curbed the excessive level of auto sales and consumer-credit expansion in 1955.

On the other hand, consumer-credit controls have involved considerable difficulty in administration and have been a political "hot potato" because of their concentrated impact on specific industries such as automobiles. And of course, selective controls do not limit the expansion of bank reserves and the money supply. If one accepts the view of the new quantity theory that it is these aggregate magnitudes which are critical, then the potential contribution of selective controls is not large.

Federal Reserve Strategy   In this chapter, we have treated Federal Reserve policy actions as efforts to achieve some optimum rate of expansion of GNP expenditures chiefly through influence on commercial bank reserves. Because the effects of policy have to be transmitted through several links, it is not easy to estimate the quantitative effect of a given policy change on

GNP and on the target variables of output, prices, and unemployment. Precision is further impaired by the time lag between policy action and result, and by the need to forecast the uncertain behavior of autonomous forces which also affect GNP and the target variables.

However, the problem may not be so serious if the target itself is a big one. Such is the case in the illustration contained in Table 18-1, and probably in the real world. This is a consolation prize for attempting to pursue several inconsistent goals. At the margin, a better performance in one dimension is just about offset by a worse performance in another.

Things would be different if the economy seemed to function along a right-angled supply schedule, so that increases in GNP expenditures would increase output until full employment was reached and then would raise prices. In such a case, the corner point on the angle is clearly a welfare optimum and may present a fairly minute target for policy. However, if the target is as wide as a range between a 5 and 8 per cent rise in GNP, the authorities have more latitude.

Since the accord in 1951, Federal Reserve authorities have shifted emphasis around among policy techniques. They have relied substantially on reductions in reserve requirements (including implementation of the vault cash provision) to bring about expansion during slack periods. Open-market purchases have been used to offset the gold outflow and to provide for seasonal variations in the demand for currency and loans. And the composition of the Federal Reserve portfolio has been varied to raise short-term interest rates relative to long-terms. Provision for growth in the money supply has come almost entirely through the lower reserve requirements. Total member bank reserves at the end of 1963 were lower than at the end of 1952.

Discount-rate strategy has varied also. In the period 1945–1959, movements in the rate were fairly frequent and covered a wide range. This was especially evident in 1955–1959. The rate was raised to apply restraint and lowered to promote ease. However, its relation to the Treasury bill rate was erratic; sometimes it was above, sometimes below. Discount volume was also somewhat erratic, but in general it rose in boom periods to quite high levels. Reserve officials did not regard this as a loophole in restrictive policy, feeling certain that borrowing banks would limit their further expansion.

During the recession of 1960, the discount rate was not lowered very much. Keeping it up helped keep the Treasury bill rate from falling very much, as part of the strategy for dealing with the balance of payments. As things turned out, the discount rate was substantially above the bill rate from late 1960 through 1963; consequently member bank borrowing, which had been relatively high in 1951–1960, fell to very low levels in the next three years.

After 1951, Federal Reserve policy underwent a process of streamlining. Objectives were simplified by casting off concern for government bond prices. Techniques were simplified by dispensing with selective controls, reducing the emphasis on reserve requirements, and limiting open-market operations to short-term securities.

However, complexity increased with the addition of the balance-of-payments problem to Federal Reserve objectives. Open-market policy then became concerned with the structure of interest rates as well as the level of bank reserves. However, simplicity was gained in discount policy by use of a more consistent penalty rate.

A renewed streamlining might well be beneficial. It could well involve a continued downplaying of reserve requirement changes and of rediscounting, shifting nearly all the burden of flexible policy onto open-market operations. A car may run better on four wheels than on two, but proliferation of steering wheels is not an advantage. The present multiplicity of techniques is more like an abundance of steering wheels.

Streamlining could also be advanced by removing from the Federal Reserve some of the purely banking responsibilities we noted in Chapter 12. Federal Reserve officials have more important things to do than passing on bank mergers, holding-company activities, and the like.

As the use of individual policy instruments has varied, so has the total influence of monetary policy on the rate of expansion of money and the monetary base. In the period between the accord of 1951 and the end of 1962, the money supply and monetary base tended to expand most rapidly during the early phases of cyclical upswings (1954, 1958, 1960). As the expansion phase of GNP change continued, however, the creation of money tended to be slowed and even halted or reversed (1952–1953, 1956–1957, 1959). The slackening of monetary expansion in these cases was sufficient to support charges that tight money brought GNP expansion to a halt. During recessions, monetary expansion was stepped up to a rate higher than that of late expansion, but not so high as early expansion. All these patterns can be observed in Figures 17-3 and 17-5.

This pattern, fairly consistently maintained for a decade after the accord, was sufficient to produce conformity between interest-rate changes and the business cycle. Whether it was really a stabilizing policy is not so evident. Critics argued that the Federal Reserve authorities were too frequently diverted by concern with free reserves and will-o'-the-wisps in the money market and did not have a sufficient appreciation of the critical importance of the monetary base. One consequence, in the eyes of the critics, was to make monetary policy appear less powerful than it really is. Not a lack of power but a lack of proper guidance was the real problem, in their view.

In any event, the pattern of expansion of money and reserves made a pronounced shift from 1961 on. A more nearly steady and sustained expansion of the monetary base was maintained. This did not prevent a decline in the expansion of the money supply in 1963, caused by a shift to time deposits, but was certainly conducive to continued expansion of the expenditure flow. The change of policy was widely approved by economists, whether devotees of the new quantity theory or not.

EFFECTIVENESS OF FEDERAL RESERVE ACTIONS

Magnitude of Effects   In recent years, two very different methods of investigation have been applied to the vital problem of measuring the effects of Federal Reserve policies. The first has been to make econometric studies of the response patterns at the various links in the chain of causation. Simply stated, these studies try to measure the extent to which given actions of the authorities affect interest rates and the extent to which individual categories of expenditures are affected by interest-rate variations. Many studies of the latter problem were reviewed in Chapter 10. In the following paragraphs, we show how they might be fitted together.

A study by Arthur Okun produced estimates of the impact on interest rates of various policy measures, assuming economic conditions as of late 1959. Some of the findings are summarized in Table 19-1.

Table 19-1   Estimated effects of hypothetical policy actions, 1959 (Percentage-point change)

Action	Treasury bill rate	Long-term bond rate
Sale of $1 billion short-terms	+0.19 to +0.41	+0.06 to +0.08
Sale of $1 billion 20-year bonds	+0.17 to +0.39	+0.07 to +0.09
Increase of 1 point in reserve requirements	+0.42 to +0.44	+0.09 to +0.13
Decrease of 1 point in reserve requirements	−0.48 to −0.50	−0.09 to −0.14
Increase of 1 percentage point in rediscount rate	+0.04 to +0.14	+0.01 to +0.03

Source: Arthur Okun, "Monetary Policy, Debt Management and Interest Rates: A Quantitative Appraisal," Commission on Money and Credit, *Stabilization Policies*, Prentice-Hall, Inc., Englewood Cliffs, N.J., 1963, p. 361.

Suppose the Federal Reserve buys $1 billion of securities under recession conditions so that the only results occur through the lowering of interest rates. Averaging Okun's estimates indicates that the bill rate would be lowered about 0.3 point. Applying this to Maisel's equation for housing starts, we obtain a stimulus of approximately $0.4 billion.[7]

The Federal Reserve's purchase would lower the long-term government bond rate by about 0.08 point and would reduce private interest rates slightly more, according to Okun's estimates—say 0.1 point. If we link this with the interest-elasticity estimates of Brownlee and Conrad for expenditures other than housing, we obtain an estimate of about $0.5 billion of stimulus.[8]

Combining these two suggests that the open-market purchase will directly stimulate increased spending by an amount at most equal to the amount of the purchase itself. Of course multiplier effects would then augment the result.

Whatever the precise results, the general tendency of such econometric studies has been to suggest a relatively low impact of monetary policy on the expenditure flow. However, there are a number of reasons to believe this technique produces estimates which are too low. First, it tends to concentrate on the effects which operate through changes in interest rates and thus does not give sufficient weight to variations in the availability of credit.

Conceptually, the econometric method, which relies on statistical correlation techniques, may be ill suited to measuring influence of any causal force when that influence is effective only after a substantial time lag of inconstant length. For this reason, partisans of the new quantity theory have relied on data of a different sort to support their contention that expenditures are more sensitive to monetary conditions. Time-series data on the rate of change of the monetary base, the money supply, and the expenditure flow certainly suggest a line of causation running in the order listed. Figure 10-7 presented typical evidence of this sort.[9]

Whether one accepts the high degree of monetary causality inferred by the new quantity theory, there can be no doubt that it provides useful concepts for policy determination and evaluation. The sort of monetary policy favored by new quantity theorists would probably have been an improvement over actual policy in 1954–1960, even if money did not turn out to have the

[7] Sherman J. Maisel, "A Theory of Fluctuations in Residential Construction Starts," *American Economic Review*, June, 1963. We have assumed that the Federal Reserve operation lowers the bill rate by 0.3 point for an entire nine-month period and have converted housing starts to expenditures at a rate of $17,000 each.

[8] Oswald Brownlee and Alfred Conrad, "Effects upon the Distribution of Income of a Tight Money Policy," *Stabilization Policies*, p. 509.

[9] One study using conventional econometric analysis is Milton Friedman and David Meiselman, "The Relative Stability of Monetary Velocity and the Investment Multiplier in the United States, 1897–1958," in *Stabilization Policies*. The authors attempt to show that consumption can better be explained by the behavior of money than by the behavior of "autonomous" expenditures.

degree of causal importance they ascribe to it. Such a policy would have involved a somewhat higher rate of monetary expansion throughout the period. The tendency toward slowdown in late expansion would have been eliminated, as would the tendency to undue acceleration in early booms.

Policy Lags and Forecasting Various lags can be identified in the operation of monetary policy. To the extent that monetary policy is directed at existing conditions, it is subject to a *recognition* lag. That is, it takes time before statistical measures are available in which changing conditions are shown. Data on sensitive indicators such as industrial production, unemployment, prices, average workweek, and others may lag as much as a month. Even when the data are available, the authorities may want to wait to make sure that conditions have changed. One month's decline in industrial production may be due to random factors; they may want to see three or four back to back before being convinced that action is necessary. One estimate places the recognition lag at about three months.[10]

Once action is taken to alter the degree of credit ease or restraint, additional lags enter the picture. It takes time for an open-market purchase to produce an expansion of bank credit and an increase in borrowing. However, Okun's study concludes that credit conditions respond to substantial Federal Reserve actions within three months or less.

The most substantial lag occurs in the actual alteration of expenditures on the basis of changed credit conditions. Maisel indicates that housing starts are affected by the interest rates of the previous two to four quarters, and of course, total housing expenditure lags somewhat more. In the case of business investment in equipment, the lag is also substantial. There is a delay in the reaction of investment *decisions* and orders, and a further delay until the change in orders is reflected in production. A study estimating both these lags implies that about 20 per cent of the response to change in interest rates would take place within six months of the change and another 20 per cent in the next six months.[11]

It is possible that more rapid responses to changed credit conditions come about when the stringency of bank credit rationing is altered, whatever kind of expenditures may be involved.

The kind of lag involved here is a distributed lag—that is, some of the reaction of expenditures will come fairly soon and the rest after delays of

---

[10] Albert Ando, E. Cary Brown, Robert M. Solow, and John Kareken, "Lags in Fiscal and Monetary Policy," *Stabilization Policies*, p. 4. However, Karl Brunner and Allan Meltzer argue that the Federal Reserve authorities have recognized the need for policy change with virtually no lag at all; the appearance of lag arises because they have taken the wrong actions. *The Federal Reserve's Attachment to the Free Reserve Concept*, Subcommittee on Domestic Finance, Committee on Banking and Currency, House of Representatives, 1964, pp. 44–47.

[11] Ando, Brown, Solow, and Kareken, *op. cit.*, pp. 6, 30, 38. This study estimated the interest elasticity of equipment investment at approximately 0.4.

various periods. In addition, the effect on aggregate GNP expenditures operates after a still further lag involved in the multiplier process.

Let us put some of these considerations together into a conjectural but not totally improbable pattern. Assume a recession begins. At the end of three months ($Q1$) the monetary authorities have recognized it and have stepped up the rate of monetary expansion. Suppose further that their action lowers interest rates sufficiently to stimulate expenditure increases of $6 billion, on the basis of equilibrium elasticities. However, only about $1 billion of this increase occurs in the quarter following the easing of credit ($Q2$).

In the next quarter ($Q3$), another $1.5 billion of expenditures is stimulated by the easier credit; in addition, GNP increases by about $0.7 billion in multiplier response to the rise of the preceding period. In $Q4$, expenditures rise by another $1.5 billion in direct response to easier credit, plus $1.2 billion of multiplier responses to the increases in $Q2$. We are assuming that the multiplier coefficient has an equilibrium level of 3 and that effects are lagging by one quarter.

In tabular form, the pattern would look like this:

Quarter	Expenditures induced by monetary expansion and lower interest rates	Multiplier effects	Total
1	0	0	0
2	+$1 billion	0	+$1 billion
3	+ 1.5	+$0.7 billion	+ 2.2
4	+ 1.5	+ 1.2	+ 2.7
Total after one year	$3.5 billion	$2.9 billion	$6.4 billion

The total cumulative impact on GNP after one year would be somewhat more than $6 billion, most of which would come six months or more after the recession began. There would of course be considerable momentum left: multiplier effects alone in $Q5$ would be $1.8 billion.

No doubt monetary policy would be more effective if the lag were shorter. But the disadvantage of the lag appears much less significant if the economy is faced with serious disequilibrium situations. The more persistent a recession or inflation proves to be, the more influence from monetary policy can be brought to bear. The actual behavior of housing investment indicates that the monetary measures have been felt soon enough to provide a stabilizing influence.

One problem raised by the existence of time lags is that policy may be out of phase. The authorities may take action to deal with inflation, only to have it become effective just in time to worsen a recession. Something of this sort probably resulted from the monetary restraint exercised in 1957 and 1959.

Conceptually, of course, one way out of the lag problem is for the authorities to base policy not on the existing situation, but on what the situation is forecast to be at the time when policy actions taken now would become effective. However, the monetary authorities have tended to avoid prognostication. The problem is well described by two former members of the Federal Reserve staff, as follows:

> There exists in the Federal Reserve System an unwritten rule against explicit forecasting of business conditions; even modest attempts at prognosis are blue-penciled if written and ignored if expressed verbally. Members of the FOMC [Federal Open-Market Committee, policy-making focal point for the system] often remark that "we are making policy only for the next 3 weeks," the implication being that inaction or wrong action can be reviewed or corrected at the next meeting. Now it is manifestly impossible to frame an intelligent monetary policy without at least implicit forecasting. . . . Fortunately, many FOMC members have their own unstated projections. But the emphasis on the short term, the avoidance of a solid, common forecast, and the frequency of FOMC meetings all lead to erratic action, lagged responses, and policy more often than not based on correction of past errors rather than on anticipation of future events.[12]

THE PRINCIPAL ALTERNATIVE—FISCAL POLICY

Theory Many critics of monetary policy argue that its shortcomings can be avoided by relying on fiscal policy as the major instrument of stabilization. Fiscal policy has the great advantage of acting directly upon incomes and GNP expenditures. If GNP spending is too low, thereby resulting in unemployment and unused capacity, fiscal policy can raise it. The government's own purchases of current output can be stepped up in order to raise GNP directly and also increase private disposable incomes and expenditures. Tax rates can be reduced and transfer payments increased to raise private spending. If GNP spending threatens to rise too much and cause inflation, contrary actions can be taken. Higher tax rates and reduced government expenditures will help contain the rise in private incomes and expenditures.

There can be no doubt about the power of fiscal policy to raise or lower the flow of GNP expenditures. The experience of World War II is the most

---

[12] Delbert C. Hastings and Ross M. Robertson, "The Mysterious World of the Fed," *Business Horizons*, Spring, 1962, reprinted in *The Federal Reserve System after Fifty Years*, p. 1523.

dramatic illustration of its expansionary power and its consequences in achieving high output and low unemployment. And the recessions of 1937–1938 and 1953–1954 can serve as evidence of the manner in which reduced Federal expenditures can cause GNP to decline. However, using fiscal policy to influence GNP expenditures does not eliminate the problem of conflict of objectives. We may have to pay just as much of an inflationary penalty for full employment and maximum output achieved through fiscal policy as through monetary policy. But there is the possibility that using an appropriate combination of monetary and fiscal measures may reduce the conflict between balance-of-payments considerations and domestic economic welfare.

Unfortunately, fiscal policy is still encumbered by dogma and prejudice. There is widespread conviction that it is immoral for the government to engage in deficit spending and that deficits are inflationary. Certainly the morality of government actions is best determined by their consequences. If depression deficits succeed in raising output and employment, this hardly seems reprehensible. When there are unemployed resources, deficits tend to raise output rather than prices. Outside of wartime periods, Federal deficits have not been associated with rising prices. For instance, between 1931 and 1940 the Federal government incurred a deficit every year; yet the price level was lower at the end of the period than at the beginning. Overemphasis on deficits also tends to direct attention away from the danger that rising expenditures, even if tax-financed, can be inflationary during a boom.

A more justifiable concern is that deficit spending may be a vehicle for wasteful expenditures or for undesirable extensions in the scope of government activity in the direction of "creeping socialism." It may be desirable to stress tax changes and transfer payments to minimize this danger.

There is also opposition to increases in the national debt. However, as we noted in Chapter 11, if GNP expenditures are to expand, *somebody's* debt must increase. If we rely on government deficits to furnish expansionary push, it may be less necessary for business firms, consumers, and state and local governments to increase their indebtedness.

Problems of Fiscal Policy The real difficulties involved in fiscal policy come in practice, not in theory. Fiscal policy is really a composite of innumerable separate policies involved in taxation and individual expenditure programs. The policy-making process tends to play up these detailed crosscurrents. Therefore it is rather optimistic to speak of fiscal "policy" at all, for the pattern of total government revenues and expenditures during any given year is never determined deliberately by a conscious and rational decision among government officials. Prospective changes in tax rates or expenditure programs must pass through the heart of the political process, through the competing claims of powerful interest groups. The outcome of such a process may bear little resemblance to the objectives of economists.

Such fiscal policy making is not geared to the needs of flexibility in timing and in magnitude of operations. In particular, the successive actions of budget preparation, appropriation, and expenditure constitute a slow and uncoordinated process in which time lags between initiation and execution may reach two or three years. Because of problems in timing tax and expenditure changes, there is a serious danger that fiscal policy may be out of phase. A recession may lead to tax cuts or spending increases which go into effect just in time to aggravate subsequent inflation. Actions to curb inflation may make ensuing recession worse.

Fortunately, the situation is not hopeless. One of the virtues of fiscal policy is that tax revenues and transfer payments tend to fluctuate in a countercyclical manner without the need for legislation or administrative discretion. Income and profits taxes in particular show rising revenues during booms and falling revenues during recessions even if rates are unchanged, and expenditures such as unemployment compensation tend to do the opposite. Such automatic flexibility has helped during recessions; unfortunately during booms there is a tendency for other government expenditures to be increased to eat up revenue surpluses which develop. Beyond the automatic stabilizers, there is some administrative discretionary power over the timing of expenditures, particularly in housing and public-works programs; but this has not been of major importance.

The record of the postwar years makes it quite clear that fiscal policy has serious limitations as a continuous sensitive instrument of economic stabilization. In fact, variations in Federal expenditures have been themselves a source of substantial instability. To be sure, national security considerations have been the chief reason for this, but other expenditures have not been ideally managed either. Tax policy has been better. Tax-rate increases were promptly imposed at the outset of the Korean hostilities and helped bring the inflationary upsurge to a halt. Tax reductions were used appropriately and effectively to stimulate the economy in 1954 and 1964.

The proper role for fiscal policy may be something like this: make the most of the automatic stabilizers, reserve deliberate legislative changes for clear-cut situations of serious depression or inflation, and concentrate the rest of the time on trying to avoid turning fiscal policy into a substantial engine of instability in its own right.

Relation of Monetary to Fiscal Policy   Monetary and fiscal policy are highly complementary—each is strong where the other is weak. Monetary policy enjoys a high degree of flexibility and precision in timing and operations. Further, it is directed almost exclusively at the objective of economic stabilization, thus minimizing the crosscurrents of competing political claims. On the other hand, it does not operate directly on incomes, and its influence on the expenditure flow is uncertain. Fiscal policy has the power to deal with major disequilibrium situations which may overwhelm monetary policy; it can also provide a direct and sensitive stabilizing influence on incomes through the automatic variations in revenue and expenditures. Beyond these advantages, fiscal policy suffers from a serious lack of flexibility. Because of conflicting objectives, decisions may not come out right.

It should be possible to improve the performance of fiscal policy either through changes in the policy-making process or through better presidential understanding and influence. Presidents Kennedy and Johnson have looked for methods of enlarging the area of administrative discretion in fiscal policy. One proposal which has been widely endorsed among economists is that Congress give the President standby powers to alter personal income tax rates, within limits, in order to deal with changing economic circumstances.[13] Legislation could prescribe the conditions for such action—for example, tax reduction might be contingent on three consecutive declines in industrial production and increases in unemployment. Administrative action on such a basis is termed "formula flexibility."

A suitable strategy for avoiding extreme movements in GNP certainly calls for use of both monetary and fiscal measures. Monetary policy and the automatic fiscal stabilizers are the first line of continuous sensitive adjustment. Ideally, such adjustments might prevent the development of serious disequilibrium, particularly if private expectations are not sensitive to short-run aberrations in the GNP flow. Major fiscal changes (of a sort requiring legislation) can be reserved to deal with serious departures from the optimum in the GNP flow.

However, many different combinations of monetary and fiscal influence can be used to exert a given pressure on the GNP flow. Variations in the "mix" between policy instruments may improve the achievement of individual objectives. A combination of tight budgets and easy credit might be well suited for a high rate of investment and growth of productive capacity. However, the opposite combination, relying on budget deficits for expansionary push while interest rates are kept relatively high, has emerged in an effort to improve the country's international position without sacrificing domestic economic goals.

Other Policies Besides the general categories of monetary and fiscal policies, it is useful to look particularly at specific policies which fall somewhere in between them, chiefly management of the public debt and the administration of government lending and loan guarantee programs. These are both areas in which administrative officials possess enough discretion to carry through policy changes without legislation.

The chief problem of public-debt management involves the choice of new securities to issue, either to finance current deficits or to refund maturing issues. By its selection, the Treasury will influence the total supplies

---

[13] See proposals in Commission on Money and Credit, *Money and Credit: Their Influence on Jobs, Prices, and Growth*, pp. 129–130; *Economic Report of the President, 1962*, pp. 18–19.

of securities in individual maturity categories, and through them the structure of interest rates. Some economists have argued that debt management can contribute to stabilization policy. They suggest that during a period of slack, the Treasury should stress the issue of short-terms and if possible reduce the outstanding supply of longs. Such a measure would increase the total liquidity in the economy and perhaps stimulate higher spending. Higher short-term rates might reduce the desired level of cash balances, while lower long-term rates might stimulate higher investment.

Public-debt management would also be suitable for the sort of rate-structure manipulation employed to reduce the outflow of short-term capital. Oddly enough, in 1960–1962 the Treasury stressed the issue of long-term securities in its refunding, an operation which tended to conflict with both the need for a more expansionary policy at home and the desirability of raising short-term rates relative to longs for international reasons.

Government lending and loan guarantee programs (as described in Chapter 13) contain considerable potential for use as instruments of administrative discretion in dealing with economic stabilization. Such programs as mortgage buying by "Fannie May" and advances to savings and loan associations by the Home Loan banks could certainly be phased into a general countercyclical policy. However, their record since World War II shows relatively random behavior with respect to the business cycle. A main reason is conflict of objectives. Most of these programs are set up to serve a particular clientele, and neither the agency nor its customers nor their friends in Congress are eager to see cutbacks made.

Federal programs for guarantee of home mortgage loans have been used in a somewhat countercyclical direction. The FHA and the Veterans Administration have authority to vary the minimum down payment and maximum maturity for government-underwritten mortgages. These terms have been managed somewhat to produce "easier" credit in recessions and to reduce ease in boom periods. Like other clientele programs, however, the tendencies toward ease have predominated. An important, though inadvertent, stabilizing influence also operates through the ceiling interest rate on government-underwritten mortgages. In periods of tight credit, lenders find these mortgages very unattractive, so the flow of funds into them drops sharply, without a corresponding rise in other mortgage lending.

SUMMARY

The chief discretionary instruments of Federal Reserve monetary policy are open-market policy, variations in reserve requirements, and rediscounting. Open-market operations are the most powerful and precise of policy instruments and could probably provide a sufficient stabilizing influence by themselves. Reserve requirement changes are a clumsy instrument, but have been suitable for providing all banks simultaneously with added reserves. Rediscounting is the least satisfactory of Reserve policies. Failure to maintain a constant relation between the rediscount rate and the Treasury bill rate has caused the incentive for member bank borrowing to fluctuate in a manner doubly disadvantageous. Such borrowing has tended to reduce the precision with which the effects of other policies can be estimated and to move contrary to the goals of countercyclical policy.

The chief effects of these three policy instruments are on the reserve positions of the commercial banks. Federal Reserve actions can largely determine the rate of change of the monetary base, which in turn determines within narrow limits the rate of growth of the money supply. According to the new quantity theory, variations in the rate of monetary growth are then transmitted to the rate of GNP change. But econometric studies directed at measuring the effects of monetary policy on expenditures have generally found a relatively low impact.

Fiscal policy, which operates directly on incomes, is much stronger than monetary policy and probably acts more quickly once a policy has been taken. However, conflicting objectives and a slow policy-making process pose obstacles to fiscal actions requiring legislation. Fortunately the built-in stabilizing action of tax revenues and some expenditures can be relied on to supplement monetary policy.

QUESTIONS FOR STUDY

1. A recent cartoon in the *Wall Street Journal* showed two counterfeiters at work. One says, "I like to think that we're doing our bit to ease the tight money situation." Is counterfeiting equally harmful to the public in all phases of the business cycle? Discuss.

2. The Federal Reserve Board reduced member bank reserve requirements during the recessions of 1953–1954 and 1957–1958. Some members of Congress felt that the Board should have relied more on open-market purchases of securities instead. This would have helped reduce Treasury financing costs, without compromising objectives of credit policy. In fact, in 1959 Congress very nearly passed a resolution urging that open-market purchases be used whenever practicable. Discuss the merits of the actual policy and of the suggested alternative.

3. Consider the following utopian proposal: "To establish effective monetary policy, we should subject the commercial banks to 100 per cent reserve requirements, not on their total deposits, but on any addition to their total demand-deposit liabilities. Increases in the money supply would then be completely in the power of the central bank. It would meet the country's needs for an expanding money supply by purchasing government securities. Thus the public debt would be reduced and money effectively controlled." What disadvantages might this entail?

4. Many economists feel that the precision and simplicity of monetary policy would be greatly improved if the Federal Reserve discount rate were consistently kept at a "penalty" level in relation to the Treasury bill rate. Discuss the merits of this view.

5. "Although it is customary to speak of the instruments of monetary control, there is really only one—the extension and absorption of central bank credit." Discuss this statement by Hastings and Robertson.[14]

SUGGESTED READINGS

Aschheim, Joseph: *Techniques of Monetary Control,* The Johns Hopkins Press, Baltimore, 1961.

The following are publications of the Commission on Money and Credit, published by Prentice-Hall, Inc., Englewood Cliffs, N.J.:

> *The Federal Reserve and the Treasury: Answers to Questions from the Commission on Money and Credit,* 1963.
>
> *Monetary Management,* 1963.
>
> *Money and Credit: Their Influence on Jobs, Prices, and Growth,* 1961.

Committee on Banking and Currency, House of Representatives, 1964:

> *Some General Features of the Federal Reserve's Approach to Policy.*
>
> *The Federal Reserve's Attachment to the Free Reserve Concept.*
>
> *The Federal Reserve System after Fifty Years, Hearings before the Subcommittee on Domestic Finance.*

Culbertson, John M.: *Full Employment or Stagnation?* McGraw-Hill Book Company, New York, 1964.

Friedman, Milton: *A Program for Monetary Stability,* Fordham University Press, New York, 1959.

McKinney, George W.: *The Federal Reserve Discount Window,* Rutgers University Press, New Brunswick, N.J., 1960.

Smith, Warren L.: "The Instruments of General Monetary Control," *National Banking Review,* September, 1963.

Yeager, Leland B. (ed.): *In Search of a Monetary Constitution,* Harvard University Press, Cambridge, Mass., 1962.

[14] Quoted in *The Federal Reserve System after Fifty Years,* p. 1522.

chapter twenty

ORGANIZATION
OF MONETARY POLICY

INTERNAL STRUCTURE OF THE FEDERAL RESERVE

Structure and Functions The organization of monetary policy must be considered in relation to the content of that policy. The initial structure of the Federal Reserve was definitely appropriate to the sort of policy it was expected to carry out. Since it was not obliged to mediate conflicting claims of competing groups, it could be placed well outside the sphere of active politics. Since its operations were expected to be largely passive administration of automatic rules of discount and currency issue, there was no need for a focal point of leadership or policy responsibility. The Federal Reserve was expected to be very much like what the Farm Credit Administration has turned out to be.

The upheavals of the 1930s shifted power toward the Board of Governors but retained a formal role for the individual Reserve banks. The status of the Board Chairman was somewhat elevated, but the group executive concept was also retained.

In the period 1940–1951, this organization was plagued with conflicting responsibilities of a political nature. The hardest decision was whether to support the bond market or fight inflation, but the administration of selective controls also imposed the need to deal with contending private interests. Since 1952, both these difficulties have been resolved. There is good reason to believe that limiting the variety of Reserve functions, both technically and politically, is in harmony with the organizational logic of the System. We shall elaborate on this hypothesis subsequently.

Key roles in Federal Reserve decision making are played by the members of the Board and by the presidents of the individual Reserve banks. The seven members of the Board are government officials. Each is appointed by the President, subject to Senate approval, for a term of fourteen years. Terms of office are staggered, and Board members cannot be removed from office except for personal delinquencies. The Chairman's tenure on the Board is the same, but he is selected as Chairman by the President for a four-year term. These terms expire in the last year of the Presidential term, but it has been customary for Board chairmen to offer to resign to permit a newly elected President to choose his own Chairman.

Each Reserve bank president is chosen by the board of directors of the Reserve bank, but his selection is subject to the approval of the Board of Governors. Indeed, the influence of the Board of Governors and its Chairman appears to dominate the nomination process. The Reserve bank president is not a government employee but is responsible directly to his own board of directors. They fix his salary, which in most districts is well above that for a member of the Board of Governors. The Reserve bank board itself plays a policy role in voting on discount-rate changes. In practice, however, Reserve bank presidents, like corporation executives, have held operating power, with their directors likely to follow the president's leadership. Membership of directors changes regularly, while presidents tend to hold office for a long time.

Each Reserve bank board consists of nine directors. Three (class A) are chosen by member banks from among district bankers, and three more (class B) are chosen by the banks from among nonbank businessmen or farmers. The other three (class C) are picked by the Board in Washington to represent the public. Terms are for three years and rotate so that there will tend to be three new directors each year. One of the class C directors, a man of "tested banking experience," is chosen as chairman.

A final element in System organization is the Federal Advisory Council, which consists of one commercial banker chosen by the directors of each Federal Reserve bank. The FAC meets quarterly with the Board in a purely advisory capacity.

Responsibility for Policy Actions   Responsibility for the most important Reserve action, viz., open-market operations, rests by law with the Federal Open-Market Committee. This consists of the seven Board members and five Reserve bank presidents. The New York president is a permanent member, while the others rotate. In practice, all Reserve bank presidents attend meetings of the Committee, and its discussions cover the entire range of monetary policy.

The Open-Market Committee meets about once every three weeks. At each meeting it prepares (or retains) a broadly worded directive laying down the general guidelines for policy. These directives go to the manager of the System Open-Market Account, who is an official of the New York Reserve bank. It is his job to translate the general terms of the directive into a pattern of daily and hourly trading.

For example, the directive issued May 29, 1962, stated:

> In view of the modest nature of recent advances in the pace of economic activity, the continued underutilization of resources, and the uncertainties created by the disturbed conditions in some financial markets, it remains the current policy of the Federal Open-Market Committee to promote further expansion of bank credit and the money supply, while giving recognition to the country's adverse balance of payments.
>
> To implement this policy, operations for the System Open-Market Account during the next 3 weeks shall be conducted with a view to maintaining a supply of reserves adequate for further credit and monetary expansion, taking account of the desirability of avoiding sustained downward pressures on short-term interest rates.

At the next meeting, on June 19, the directive was amended to state:

> It is the current policy of the Federal Open-Market Committee to permit the supply of bank credit and money to increase further, but at the same time to avoid redundant bank reserves that would encourage capital outflows internationally. . . .
>
> To implement this policy, operations for the System Open-Market Account during the next 3 weeks shall . . . be conducted with a view to providing a somewhat smaller rate of reserve expansion in the banking system than in recent months and to fostering a moderately firm tone in money markets.[1]

Technically, responsibility for discount-rate policy is divided between the Board and the Reserve banks. The individual banks have the initiative in changing discount rates, but no change can become effective without approval of the Board of Governors. In practice, changes may originate in meetings of the Open-Market Committee or simply by direct suggestion from the Chairman to one or more reserve-bank presidents.

Responsibility for changing reserve requirements and margin requirements rests with the Board alone. Since these measures are treated as part of general monetary policy, however, they are likely to be dealt with in meetings of the Open-Market Committee.

Open-Market Committee Meetings Some important features of procedure at Committee meetings are noted in the following description by former Federal Reserve staff members:

[1] Board of Governors, Federal Reserve System, *Annual Report for 1962*, pp. 78, 81.

In the conduct of FOMC meetings, a formality is observed that requires each Governor and President in attendance, whether currently a member of the Committee or not, to give a brief economic analysis and state his policy recommendations. By custom each member, together with the Board secretary, the senior advisers and the Manager of the Open-Market Account, occupies a fixed position around the great oval table in the Committee room. After a brief business and financial analysis by the senior staff members, the Account Manager reports on his activities since the last meeting. Next, the Governors and Presidents take turns in order of their seating at the table. . . . The Chairman speaks last, customarily framing his closing remarks in the form of a consensus of the preceding recommendations. Often, however, there is less than complete agreement among Committee members; less often, but not infrequently, the Chairman may wish to give stronger than usual direction to current policy. In such circumstances, the "Martin consensus" has emerged, this consensus being largely the view of the Chairman himself, whether or not it coincides with that of the majority. Rarely—if then—are policy recommendations put into a motion and voted upon.

The Account Manager listens to the discussion and at its conclusion is asked by the Chairman if he comprehends the wishes of the Committee. He almost always answers in the affirmative. But though the Account Manager listens with great care, even tabulating the recommendations of each speaker, FOMC members frequently complain that they cannot communicate precisely with the Manager. The problem has several dimensions. First, each Committee member, being a rugged individualist, would probably be satisfied with little less than complete direction of current policy. Second, because the FOMC does not make a precise statement of its wishes, the Account Manager must consider 19 sets of recommendations, some of them rambling discourses on the state of the Union. Third, the 3-week interval between meetings is long enough to require adaptations on the part of the Manager, and these cannot possibly coincide with all 19 Committee opinions. Fourth, policy recommendations of FOMC members are stated in terms that are at best ambiguous. . . . It is little wonder then that communication between the FOMC and the trading desk is poor. Nor is it any wonder that Chairman Martin, for better or worse, must determine a consensus that would lead only to endless argument if it were brought to a vote.[2]

The Power Structure In this sprawling administrative tangle, who really makes the decisions? According to Hastings and Robertson, the major power centers (in descending order) take the following pattern:

1. *The Chairman of the Board of Governors.* His position as guiding spirit in the relatively large meetings of the Open-Market Committee provides an opportunity for a man of strong and agreeable personality to

[2] Delbert C. Hastings and Ross M. Robertson, "The Mysterious World of the Fed," *Business Horizons*, Spring, 1962, reprinted in *The Federal Reserve System after Fifty Years, Hearings before the Subcommittee on Domestic Finance,* Committee on Banking and Currency, House of Representatives, 1964, p. 1523.

provide structure and leadership. This tendency is strengthened by the Chairman's strong influence on personnel appointments and by his role as system spokesman and liaison man with Congress, other government agencies, and the public.

2. *The other Governors,* depending on their personal qualities.

3. *The staff of the Board.*

4. *The Open-Market Committee as a group.*

5. *The trading desk* of the New York Federal Reserve Bank, and especially the System Account Manager, who has the responsibility for translating often ambiguous directives into policy actions and for interpolating policy during the intervals between meetings of the Open-Market Committee.

6. *The president of the New York Federal Reserve.* In earlier times, this position vied for preeminence with the chairmanship, but its importance has waned, particularly since the retirement of Allan Sproul in 1956.

7. *Other Reserve bank presidents.*

Criticisms of Policy-making Structure and Process Two possible dangers may be noted in the existing Federal Reserve structure. The first is that diffusion of authority and responsibility among so many participants in decision making will lead to a lack of vigor and leadership. Modern administrative theory tends to regard boards as "long, narrow, and wooden" and to stress the advantages of concentrating power and responsibility in the hands of a single administrator. This problem has been evident in past Federal Reserve policy, particularly in the 1920s. It has been less evident since World War II, when the principal chairmen, Marriner Eccles and William McChesney Martin, have exerted forceful leadership. However, it is not entirely wholesome to structure an administrative agency so that it can function well only when led by a man of unusual gifts.

The shortcomings of an unwieldy group executive are somewhat diminished when the number of variables involved is small. Efforts to utilize a multiplicity of techniques and to mediate among a number of conflicting objectives seem to fit in very poorly with the kind of decision-making process described above by Hastings and Robertson. If the authorities were to focus their attention more narrowly on the rate of expansion of money and reserves, and concentrate on open-market policy as the means of achieving their goals, the problems of policy-making organization might be significantly reduced.

A second criticism of the existing structure is that it gives too much influence to commercial bankers, either in fact or appearance. Commercial bankers predominate on the boards of directors of individual Reserve banks, of which they are formally the stockholders. Technically, these boards are the masters of the Reserve bank presidents, who participate in the policy-making operations of the Open-Market Committee. Finally, bankers constitute the membership of the Federal Advisory Board.

Impartial investigations have repeatedly dismissed the charge that the System is subject to any undue clientele interest, in the narrow sense, from commercial bankers. In particular, the presidents of the Federal Reserve banks, although not technically government officials, have consistently maintained an attitude of responsibility to the public interest, rather than to a narrow sector group. Still, critics have suggested that a lessening of the appearance of banker participation might increase the "legitimacy" of Federal Reserve actions, giving them more public acceptability, particularly in the eyes of organized labor.[3]

There may be a more substantial disadvantage in the prominent role played by Reserve bank presidents. This arises from the fact that their "world view" tends to be that of the financial community. Their dedication to the public interest may be unfailing, but the values which they esteem and the means by which they believe goals ought to be pursued may still suffer from serious bias. Overemphasis on money-market conditions, exchange rates, and the value of money, and a tendency to give relatively little concern to output and unemployment, are among the viewpoints which have been ascribed to men dominated by a background of financial experience.

These shortcomings would be remedied by some of the changes in Federal Reserve policy making recommended by the Commission on Money and Credit,[4] as follows:

1. Policy-making authority for open-market operations, rediscount rates, and reserve requirements should be vested in the Board of Governors. The Board should consult with the Reserve bank presidents in taking policy actions.

2. The Board should consist of only five members, serving overlapping ten-year terms.

3. The Federal Advisory Council should include representatives of "all aspects of the American economy," not merely commercial bankers.

4. The present capital stock of Federal Reserve banks should be retired, perhaps to be replaced by a "nonearning certificate" of membership with a nominal value.

Such proposals would have the effect of placing final responsibility for action in the hands of politically responsible officials and would reduce the role of Reserve bank presidents and commercial bankers in the policy-making structure. However, retiring Reserve bank stock would reduce incentives to System membership, since the stock bears an attractive rate of return.

[3] Michael Reagan, "The Internal Structure of the Federal Reserve: A Political Analysis," Commission on Money and Credit, *Monetary Management*, Prentice-Hall, Inc., Englewood Cliffs, N.J., 1963.

[4] Commission on Money and Credit, *Money and Credit: Their Influence on Jobs, Prices, and Growth*, Prentice-Hall, Inc., Englewood Cliffs, N.J., 1961, pp. 87–91.

Whatever improvements might be designed for Federal Reserve internal structure, it is not likely to be changed unless some emergency occurs. The immediate problem is therefore to gear Federal Reserve functions to the existing structure. Streamlining policy by minimizing its variables is one way of doing this. Another is to minimize the burdens on the Board for purely banking tasks—regulation of mergers, holding companies, branches, and even bank examination itself.

External Relations and Responsibilities Since the Federal Reserve exercises a public responsibility, it must be held accountable for its actions. In particular, there must be channels through which public opinion can influence the choice of policy goals and the relative importance assigned to each, even if this can be done only by criticizing mistakes. Public officials may properly exercise discretion in the choice of *means* to achieve the goals set for them by public opinion, provided their actions can be evaluated after the fact.

Modern political theory stresses that top decision-making officials in government should be elected and that appointive officials should be clearly held responsible to elected ones. Elected officials should concern themselves with the broad objectives of policy; they should give administrators a general mandate of ends desired but should not necessarily specify the details of technique. American monetary policy has generally done just the opposite. Legislation has lavished great attention on mechanism but has not provided clear statements of general policy goals.

The major congressional pronouncement on the goals of economic policy is in the Employment Act of 1946. The statement is worth quoting:

> It is the continuing policy and responsibility of the Federal Government to use all practicable means consistent with its needs and obligations and other essential considerations of national policy, . . . to coordinate and utilize all its plans, functions, and resources for the purpose of creating and maintaining, in a manner calculated to foster and promote free competitive enterprise and the general welfare, conditions under which there will be afforded useful employment opportunities, including self-employment, for those able, willing, and seeking to work, and to promote maximum employment, production, and purchasing power.

For all its circumlocutions and provisos, this statement clearly stresses the objectives of high output and low unemployment. It does not say anything about price stabilization or balance-of-payments equilibrium. Efforts to amend the Employment Act to include a specific mandate for price stability have been unsuccessful.

Federal Reserve authorities have repeatedly declared themselves to be pledged to the objectives of the Employment Act. However, they have reinterpreted it to incorporate a concern (sometimes overriding) for price stability, on the rather tenuous ground that price increases constitute a threat to full employment.

Nevertheless, Federal Reserve authorities do not select their objectives in a vacuum. A more vigorous stand against inflation was made after the election of 1952 indicated an apparent public dissatisfaction with recent inflationary experience. A reverse shift toward more concern for unemployment followed evidence of public concern in the election of 1960. Introduction of balance-of-payments considerations into Federal Reserve objectives clearly followed evidence that prevailing sentiment in Congress and the White House favored such considerations.

Federal Reserve Independence The Federal Reserve is held accountable to Congress and to the President. Congress possesses the ultimate authority of legislation. The legislature created the System, and it can change its structure or technical features (as it has done numerous times) or abolish it entirely. Congress can impeach an individual member of the Board or, as it did in 1935, create a new Board (with a slightly different name) and thereby vote all the incumbents out of office. The Senate may refuse to approve nominations to the Board.

For all this, Congress lacks one important influence over the Federal Reserve—the power of the purse. Expenses of the System are paid out of the income from Reserve bank loans and securities. Surplus revenues, after being used to provide the 6 per cent dividend to the member banks, are mostly paid back into the Treasury. Reserve officials, unlike most administrators, need not come hat-in-hand to an appropriations subcommittee which chastises their past misdeeds and authorizes their future funds only after assurance of mended ways. Reserve officials may of course be called to testify in defense of their policies, and such proceedings may provide a forum for critical congressmen. Still, the financial status of the System contributes to substantial short-run independence.

Although the Federal Reserve is subject to presidential influence, chiefly through the appointive power, the long and staggered terms of Board members mean that the composition of the Board cannot be greatly altered during any one presidential term. Nor can the President freely remove Board members as he can Cabinet members. However, he has the important power to designate the Chairman, a power enhanced by the unwritten rule that the incumbent Chairman offers to resign when a new President enters office. Perhaps, as Bach suggests, this rule should be enacted into law.

The financial freedom of the System liberates it from an important executive control. Ordinary agencies must clear their annual requests for funds with the Bureau of the Budget, which takes that opportunity to ride herd on their activities. Such agencies must clear recommendations for legislative change through the Bureau to ensure that they are in harmony with "the program of the President." The Federal Reserve is not subject to these controls.

Federal Reserve independence has acquired a considerable aura of sanctity, as a good thing in itself. Ideologically, such tendencies may be unwholesome. In particular, there is little defense for the attitude that economic policies should be "above politics," that they should be delegated to some august body of "philosopher-kings" whose decisions must be accepted uncritically.

The Patman investigation in 1964 revealed widespread discontent with Federal Reserve independence among professional economists. A striking statement of the critical position, by Prof. Harry Johnson, is worth quoting at length:

[The case for central-bank independence] assumes that, if free of control by the Executive and Legislature, the monetary authority will govern monetary policy in the light of the longrun best interests of the economy, and will conduct its policy [with] flexibility and efficiency in the short run. This assumption is not consistent with the historical evidence of the behavior of monetary authorities; the evidence is rather that central banks have done little if anything to restrain inflationary policies in wartime—and war and its aftermath have been the almost exclusive source of serious inflation in the major countries in the 20th century—while in peacetime they have displayed a pronounced tendency to allow deflationary policies on the average. Moreover . . . in the short-run conduct of policy they have tended to overreact to changes in the economy and to reverse their policy with a substantial delay, thereby contributing to the economic instability that their policies are intended to combat.

These defects are in my judgment inherent in the conception, constitution, and operating responsibilities and methods of an independent monetary authority, and are unlikely to be modified greatly by gradual improvement of the techniques of central banking on the basis of accumulated experience and research. For one thing, freedom of a central bank from direct political control does not suffice to render it insensitive to contemporary political opinion. On the contrary, its position as the one agency of economic policy formation outside the normal political structure both exposes it to subtle and sustained political pressures and forces it to become a political animal on its own behalf, devoting considerable effort either to justifying its policies by reference to popularly-esteemed objectives or to denying responsibility for economic conditions and passing the buck on to the Executive or the Legislature, the result being to obfuscate the policy choices that have to be made. Secondly, the position of the central bank as controller of the money supply inevitably must bias the monetary authority—except in times of national emergency such as war—toward emphasizing the pursuit of objectives connected with the value of money—resistance to domestic inflation, and preservation of the international value of the currency—to the underemphasis or neglect of other objectives such as high employment and economic growth. Thirdly, the methods of monetary management, which involve the central bank concentrating its attention on money market conditions and interest rates, and on member bank reserve positions and lending, rather than on the performance of the economy in general, are extremely conducive to the behavior pattern of overreaction and delayed correction of error already mentioned.

Because it concentrates on money market and banking phenomena, rather than the effects of its policies on the quantity of money and economic activity, and because the effect of monetary policy on the economy operates with a substantial lag, the central bank is extremely likely to push its policy too far and too fast before it realizes that the policy has taken effect and begins to consider moderating it; and because the realization of effectiveness comes late, it is likely to reverse its policy too sharply. In addition, the fact that the central bank stands in a special relation to its Government and domestic economy fosters the existence of an international fellow club member relationship among central banks, a relationship congenial to the formation and propagation of policy fads in central banking. It is only on the basis of fads in central banking opinion, I believe, that one can understand the emergence of the fear of runaway inflation as a dominant motif in central bank policy statements in 1957–58. . . .

I believe that monetary policy should be brought under the control of the Executive and legislature in the same way as other aspects of economic policy, with the administration bearing the ultimate responsibility for monetary policy as part of economic policy in general. In making this recommendation, I must admit that there is a danger of monetary mismanagement in the pursuit of political objectives; but I consider it preferable for such mismanagement to be a clear responsibility of the administration, and accountable to the electorate.[5]

On the other hand, the defense of the independence of public officials is that it enables their policies to be judged by the results, with some attention to the long run. Federal Reserve independence raises the threshold above which dissatisfaction must rise before its actions can be overruled. This gives it more freedom in the short run. If it does fail, however, the threshold is low enough to permit effective reform. Such reform will be obliged to come through formal public action, which will entail debate on the broad aspects of monetary policy, rather than through informal channels which will permit the big issues to escape adequate consideration. Streamlining Federal Reserve objectives and techniques helps focus debate on major issues and keeps political questions in Congress, where they belong. At the same time, insulating detailed Reserve operations from Congress protects the individual congressman from undue pressure to turn monetary policy to the benefit of narrow economic groups and makes it easier for him to keep sight of the general public interest.

[5] *The Federal Reserve System after Fifty Years*, pp. 970–973.

There are certainly measures which could be taken to increase the formal political responsibility of the Federal Reserve without throwing it completely into the political arena. For instance, Congressman Patman proposed in 1964 that the President be instructed to include in his annual economic report a set of guidelines for monetary policy, and particularly for the growth of the money supply. The Federal Reserve authorities would be expected to follow these, but could deviate from them if prepared to publish a statement of reasons for the divergence. And the Commission on Money and Credit recommended that the President be authorized to designate the Chairman and Vice-chairman of the Board of Governors, to serve four-year terms conterminous with his own. Selection would still be made from Board members.

Federal Reserve Jurisdiction and Powers   The Federal Reserve has jurisdiction only over such banks as choose to be members of the System. Of course, all national banks must join, but no bank is obliged to operate under a national charter. Slightly more than half the nation's banks remain outside the System, but they account for only 15 per cent of deposits. It is not likely that their operations will seriously undermine Federal Reserve policy. The real problem is that member banks can drop out of the System if they feel themselves abused, and this option may render the Federal Reserve unduly reluctant to take needed actions. As Goldenweiser put it, "To command with proper discipline an army which sanctions desertion as an inalienable right of every soldier would impose a superhuman task on any general, yet this is in effect what the Federal Reserve Board is required to do." [6]

Because of the importance of access to Federal Reserve clearing facilities, there is not much danger that big banks will drop out of the system. Such access is useful to the bank directly and also enables it to compete for correspondent-bank deposits. For smaller banks, however, membership has less attraction. It does offer direct access to the discount window as well as certain other Federal Reserve services, but most of these can be obtained from correspondent banks. The smaller bank may feel that Federal Reserve membership helps it to attract deposits, but since the coming of deposit insurance, depositors pay less attention to membership. The small bank is likely to be aware that membership has costs. Reserve requirements imposed by the Federal Reserve are generally more onerous than those imposed by state law, not so much in level, but because many states permit banks to include deposits with correspondent banks and sometimes government securities as legal reserves. Many small banks oppose par clearance and utilize exchange charges.

For these reasons, probability of Federal Reserve membership varies directly with size of bank. Of small banks with less than $1 million deposits

[6] E. A. Goldenweiser, *American Monetary Policy*, McGraw-Hill Book Company, New York, 1951, p. 287.

each, 88 per cent were nonmembers in 1959. By contrast, only one bank with deposits over $500 million was not a member.[7] The danger that small member banks may drop out if membership becomes more onerous may act as a restraint against high reserve requirements, and perhaps against a high rediscount rate as well.

Still, we are entitled to ask, Are member banks necessary? The answer is probably in the negative. We have seen that the Federal Reserve can probably operate effectively even if it places sole reliance on open-market operations. And membership in the System has little to do with the effectiveness of open-market operations (assuming that large banks would continue to hold deposits at the Federal Reserve). By the same token, however, there is no particular reason to do away with membership. Effective use of open-market operations is not likely to drive banks out of the System, and even if a few are nudged out by other changes (such as consistent use of the rediscount rate as a penalty rate), no harm results.

The need for member banks has largely been eliminated by the spread of Federal deposit insurance. Virtually all banks are subject to Federal examination and to *some* requirement to hold reserves.

A case can be made for doing away with System membership as a method of removing burdensome "banking" chores and permitting Federal Reserve authorities to concentrate on their "monetary" responsibilities. Bank examination duties could easily be shifted to FDIC. Reserve authorities would probably oppose such change, however, partly because they desire the direct flow of information and opinion which comes through bank examination contacts and partly because they want to retain a grass-roots clientele.

RULES VERSUS AUTHORITIES

Shortcomings of Discretionary Authority   History records abundant examples of the abuse by governments of the power to create money. In particular, the temptation to finance government expenditures by means of the printing press has given rise to inflation in countries with weak standards of political responsibility. Use of monetary expansion to finance wars, and the inflations resulting, turned public opinion in the nineteenth century against discretionary control over the money supply. Much of American monetary history prior to the 1930s involves a search for a "structural panacea," an automatic monetary mechanism.

Criticism of discretionary authority generally has followed two principal lines. One is that the authorities *won't* behave properly; the other

[7] Clark Warburton, "Nonmember Banks and the Effectiveness of Monetary Policy," *Monetary Management*, p. 336.

is that they *can't.* The first of these focuses on the problem of political responsibility. In this view, the government cannot be trusted to manage money, since it will abuse its power. At root, this is a criticism of democracy itself. American history furnishes very little support for the view that government will deliberately pervert monetary control.

The second criticism has more bite. It is that the authorities may mean well, but for technical reasons are incapable of taking the proper actions. Perhaps their understanding of technical monetary analysis is deficient, as it clearly was in 1929–1933. Or perhaps the problems of lags and forecasting put them in a position where efforts to make things better tend to make things worse. Certainly American financial history furnishes abundant evidence of mistakes in monetary management.

The Role of Gold In the nineteenth century, "right-thinking" people assumed that a proper monetary system would be founded on the precious metals, particularly gold. The money supply might contain other elements, such as bank deposits and currency, but the total would rise and fall with variations in the gold stock. Sometimes this was defended as economically beneficial, providing for international financial order with stable exchange rates, convertible currencies, and automatic elimination of balance-of-payments disequilibrium. More often, it was simply an element in the "old-time religion" which upheld sound money and balanced budgets and regarded bankruptcy and unemployment as forms of Sin.[8]

In an industrial economy, the international "discipline" of the gold standard imposed a heavy cost on output and employment. And ultimately the irrational dedication to the gold standard contributed to the economic disasters of 1929–1933. A valiant remnant of Old Believers still urge a return to the true faith, but neither public opinion nor economic analysis supports such a course.

Under present arrangements, gold is the ultimate "reserve" of our monetary system. As of 1965, the law requires that Federal Reserve notes have a 25 per cent reserve in gold certificates representing Treasury gold. At the end of 1964, the monetary gold stock was slightly over $15 billion and the public's money supply somewhat over $160 billion, giving a ratio of more than 10 to 1.

Domestically, however, the gold "reserve" is meaningless. Federal Reserve policy does not respond automatically to changes in the gold stock.

---

[8] "By common consent of the nations, gold and silver are the only true measures of value. . . . I have myself no more doubt that these metals were prepared by the Almighty for this very purpose, than I have that iron and coal were prepared for the purposes for which they are being used." So spake Hugh McCulloch, first Comptroller of the Currency and twice Secretary of the Treasury, in *Men and Measures of Half a Century,* Charles Scribner's Sons, New York, 1888, p. 201. A few years later, William McKinley solemnly cautioned that "we cannot gamble with anything so sacred as money."

Of course, a gold flow tends to change the money supply and bank reserves unless offset by Federal Reserve actions, but such offsetting has been consistent. Domestic money is not convertible into gold; the Treasury sells gold only to foreign monetary authorities or for manufacturing and artistic use.

The chief role of gold in the modern world is as a means of settling international balances and as a basis for foreign-exchange rates. The gold-reserve requirement for Federal Reserve obligations serves no useful purpose domestically and may cast doubt on the ability of the United States to maintain gold convertibility of the dollar internationally. Thus many authorities have advocated its repeal.[9]

The "Automatic Pilot" Growth Proposal   Recently another approach to automatic monetary policy has gained prominence through notable statements by Profs. Milton Friedman and Edward S. Shaw. The proposal stems from a dissatisfaction with discretionary policy as exercised—indeed, Professor Friedman argues that time lags make it probable that discretionary actions will move in the wrong direction much of the time.

The proposed solution is to stop trying to use monetary policy as a countercyclical device, since such attempts will fail. Instead, in Shaw's terms, the monetary system should be put on an "automatic pilot" by increasing the money supply each year by a constant percentage, calculated in terms of the long-run growth needs of the economy—probably about 3 to 4 per cent per year. The money supply would rise enough to take care of normal growth needs but not enough to permit serious inflation.[10]

Quite possibly such expansion could be produced by an equally constant percentage rate of injection of bank reserves through open-market purchases. Reliance on such an automatic pilot would not do away with countercyclical variations in credit conditions. Weakening demand for loans during recessions would cause interest rates to fall, perhaps even more than in actual recent recessions. During booms, demand for loans might cause interest rates to rise, though not so much as in the 1950s.

The proposal has not won wide support from economists. There is no agreement on a single ideal rate of expansion for the money supply, and since the appeal of the proposal is that, once set, it requires no tinkering, the first choice has to be a good one. Friedman's pessimism concerning lags in

[9] For instance, the Commission on Money and Credit in *Money and Credit: Their Influence on Jobs, Prices, and Growth*, p. 234.

[10] Milton Friedman, "The Supply of Money and Changes in Prices and Output," in *The Relationship of Prices to Economic Stability and Growth*, papers submitted by panelists to the Joint Economic Committee, U.S. Congress, 1958, especially pp. 254–256; Edward S. Shaw, "Money Supply and Stable Economic Growth," in Neil Jacoby (ed.), *United States Monetary Policy*, rev. ed., Frederick A. Praeger, Inc., for the American Assembly, New York, 1964, pp. 73–93.

policy is not generally shared, and other economists have more optimism about the ability of the authorities to perform without serious blunders.

A modified version of the proposal is to establish a monetary rule whereby the authorities would increase the money supply each year by an amount corresponding to the estimated growth in the nation's productive capacity. An even more flexible arrangement, which commands much broader support, is that the authorities should use the long-run monetary growth needs of the economy as a starting point for monetary policy, while permitting some discretionary variations around this norm.

Strengthening Discretionary Authority A commitment to discretionary monetary policy is general among economists and public officials. The real issue, then, is how to improve it. Much attention has been given to the possibility that new techniques or wider direct authority would improve its effectiveness. We encounter proposals to extend Federal Reserve reserve requirements to nonmember banks or even to nonbank financial institutions. More extensive use of selective controls has been urged.

A more promising approach is to try to improve the use of the techniques already available. Federal Reserve policy could benefit from a more explicit and careful treatment of objectives and from improvements in the technical foundations of policy. In particular, the policy makers should be able to do a better job of judging the effects of their actions on the expenditure flow and on target variables such as output, prices, and unemployment. Economics may not be an exact science yet, but quantitative knowledge has advanced a great deal in recent years. Much of the analysis and comment presented by economists to the Patman Subcommittee in 1964 indicated areas where improvement in practice could be achieved without change in structure.[11] Fortunately, the performance of the Federal Reserve since 1961 showed substantial improvement over that of the 1950s.

SUMMARY AND CONCLUSIONS

The formal organization of Federal Reserve policy making is an administrative monstrosity, with important power being shared by seven members of the Board of Governors and twelve Reserve bank presidents. These nineteen men participate in the work of the Open-Market Committee, in which basic directives for policy are formulated. Internally, this is an unwieldy structure, although strong leadership from recent Chairmen has

[11] See *The Federal Reserve System after Fifty Years*, vol. 2; also staff reports entitled *Some General Features of the Federal Reserve's Approach to Policy* and *The Federal Reserve's Attachment to the Free Reserve Concept*, Subcommittee on Domestic Finance, Committee on Banking and Currency, House of Representatives, 1964.

kept it fairly cohesive. However, the formal policy-making role of Reserve bank presidents may give undue power to men who are not public officials and who reflect unduly the values and attitudes of a financial background.

Externally, the Federal Reserve enjoys relative independence within the Federal government structure because of its financial status and the tenure of its members. This has the advantage of permitting monetary policy to be judged by long-run standards, but also may permit the goals of the monetary authorities to diverge substantially from general public opinion.

Monetary policy might be handled by an automatic monetary system, with its structure set by legislation and no discretionary elements left to administrators. But the traditional gold standard did not do well as a stabilizer, and recent proposals for expanding the money supply at a constant rate have not won wide support. Many economists have urged, however, that discretionary monetary policy might adhere a bit more closely to a normal pattern of monetary expansion appropriate to long-run growth.

The Federal Reserve authorities would be aided in concentrating on their primary responsibility for money and bank reserves if they could be liberated from the clutter of trivial and extraneous matters which have tended to accumulate over half a century. The discount window could be closed, except for real emergencies, and variations in reserve requirements likewise reserved for extreme situations. Extensive responsibilities for purely "banking" matters could be transferred elsewhere; indeed, effective monetary policy has no real need for "member" banks at all. Ultimately, all that might remain is responsibility for varying the expansion of Federal Reserve credit through open-market operations—a responsibility involving as much power and importance as any other economic policy of the government.

PROSPECT AND CHALLENGE

The renewed emphasis on the money supply which has attended the development of the new quantity theory has brought with it a renewed optimism about the possibilities for relatively stable, rapid economic expansion. Quantity theorists now argue that many of the unpleasant fluctuations in the economy in the past resulted, not from wide and erratic variations in marginal efficiency, fiscal policy, or the propensity to consume, but from inappropriate monetary policies. The first item on their monetary agenda, therefore, is a demand that the monetary authorities stop making mistakes. And some clearly feel that if extremes of stop-and-go in the rate of monetary expansion are avoided, it may prove possible for the economy to eliminate periods when the expenditure flow actually declines.

If monetary policy is so powerful, how did attention get diverted from it? Partly, say the critics, by the monetary authorities themselves, who have in the past gotten their monetary responsibilities all confused with problems of banking and credit. It is not true, claim the critics, that we have had well-managed policy which has not been powerful enough to avoid unpleasant disturbances; instead, we have had a powerful policy which was mismanaged and authorities who have taken refuge from criticism by disclaiming that their actions really can do much to affect the economy.

These judgments may be unduly harsh, but our analysis of the behavior of bank reserves and the money supply certainly has revealed episodes which might be considered mismanagement. The real point at issue, however, is the degree to which the expenditure flow is not merely influenced by, but dominated by, variations in money.

The Keynesian viewpoint has tended to create the impression that variations in the money flow are normally initiated by variations in someone's propensity to spend, and particularly by shifts in the marginal efficiency of capital. Money and interest rates appear on the periphery of important items. Monetary policy can act as a buffer against the inherently unstable patterns of expenditures, but not much more.

Some quantity theorists have argued, in effect, that variations in the propensities to spend are much less frequently the real source of economic disturbance. They do not deny that wars have set off major autonomous disturbances to the expenditure flow; but they feel that, for the most part, it is not instability in marginal efficiency or fiscal policy but instability in the growth of the money supply which is the common cause of economic instability. Such a view certainly implies a much more ambitious target and standard for monetary policy.

So far the evidence is ambiguous. However, the behavior of the economy in the 1960s may well furnish a valuable test of the new quantity theory. Maintenance of monetary expansion by the Federal Reserve has been associated with one of the longest continued periods of economic expansion on record. One might hope that the authorities will not panic, but will have courage enough to sustain expansion. One would then be able to test whether the economy remains buoyant or whether nonmonetary forces are still sufficiently unstable to cause repetitions of the business cycle experiences of the past. It should be interesting to watch.

QUESTIONS FOR STUDY

1. In addition to recommendations noted in the text above, Congressman Patman also recommended the following changes in Federal Reserve structure and powers in 1964. Evaluate the probable importance and effects of each:

   a. Provide for the retirement of the Federal Reserve stock.
   b. Vest all power to conduct open-market operations in the Federal Reserve Board.
   c. Reduce to five the number of Governors of the Federal Reserve Board.
   d. Reduce to five years the terms of office of the Governors and allow for reappointment.
   e. Make the term of the Chairman of the Board of Governors conterminous with that of the President.
   f. Require the Federal Reserve to pay into the Treasury all its income and receive funds for expenditures through regular appropriations by Congress.
   g. Transfer to other agencies the present bank supervisory responsibilities lodged with the Federal Reserve.

   2. Are member banks necessary? Discuss.

   3. Some economists have argued that the man who really determines Federal Reserve policy is the manager of the System Open-Market Account, who heads the trading desk in the New York Reserve Bank. What is his role in policy determination? What opportunities does he have for independence of action?

SUGGESTED READINGS

Commission on Money and Credit: *Money and Credit: Their Influence on Jobs, Prices, and Growth,* Prentice-Hall, Inc., Englewood Cliffs, N.J., 1961.

————: *Monetary Management,* Prentice-Hall, Inc., Englewood Cliffs, N.J., 1963.

The Federal Reserve System after Fifty Years, Hearings before the Subcommittee on Domestic Finance, Committee on Banking and Currency, House of Representatives, 1964.

Jacoby, Neil H. (ed.): *United States Monetary Policy,* rev. ed., Frederick A. Praeger, Inc., for the American Assembly, New York, 1964.

Yeager, Leland B. (ed.): *In Search of a Monetary Constitution,* Harvard University Press, Cambridge, Mass., 1962.

INDEX

Abstract money, 27–28
Acceleration principle, 195–197, 459–460
Acceptances, 76–77, 379–382
"Accord" of 1951, Federal Reserve and Treasury, 493–494
Administered prices, 155, 160–162
Aggregate demand (see Gross national product)
Agricultural Adjustment Act (AAA), 157, 469
Aldrich-Vreeland Act, 445, 450
Ando, Albert, 198n., 546n.
Annuities, 344–345
Arbitrage, 142
Arnold, Arthur Z., 17n.
Aschheim, Joseph, 540n.
Asset balances, 213–218
Asset preference, 70–72, 110–113
Assets, commercial banks, 61–62, 75–77, 306–319, 359–360
    relation to velocity, 254–255, 260–263, 499
    Federal Reserve banks, 82

Assets, liquid, 278–282
    monetary system, 104–115
    nonbank financial institutions, 338, 343–346, 359–360
    U.S. Treasury, 92
Assignats, 37
Automatic monetary mechanisms, 566–569
Automatic stabilizers, 514, 550
Availability of credit, 194–195, 199–200
    in 1930s, 461, 471

Bach, George Leland, 523n., 529n., 562
Bagehot, Walter, 21
Balance of international payments, 371–374, 389–401
    and interest rates, 100–101
    and policy goals, 514, 522–524
    U.S., since 1950, 371–373, 432–436
Balance-sheet data, commercial banks, 62